HOLT
Health

Jerrold Greenberg, Ed.D.
University of Maryland
College Park, MD

Robert Gold, Ph.D.
University of Maryland
College Park, MD

HOLT, RINEHART AND WINSTON
Harcourt Brace & Company

Austin • New York • Orlando • Atlanta • San Francisco
Boston • Dallas • Toronto • London

Acknowledgments

Staff Credits

Executive Editor
Ellen Standafer

Project Editors
Jean Armstrong
Janis Gadsden
Christopher Hess
Meredith Phillips
Tracy Schagen

Managing Editor
William Wahlgren

Copyediting
Steve Oelenberger, *Copyediting Supervisor*
Amy Daniewicz
Denise Haney

Editorial Permissions
Janet Harrington

Book Design
Christine Schueler, *Design Manager*
José Garza

Image Services
Greg Geisler, *Art Director*
Elaine Tate
Michelle Rumpf

Photo Research
Peggy Cooper, *Photo Research Manager*
Caroline Robbins

Prepress
Beth Prevelige, *Senior Production Manager*
Simira Davis
Rosa Mayo Degollado
Sergio Durante
Beth Sample

Media
Kim Anderson, *Production Manager*
Susan Mussey

Manufacturing
Michael Roche

Electronic Publishing
Carol Martin, *Electronic Publishing Manager*
Barbara Hudgens, *Electronic Publishing Supervisor*
Heather Jernt, *Project Coordinator*
JoAnn Brown
Mercedes Newman
Rina Ouellette
Michele Ruschaupt
Charlie Taliaferro
Ethan Thompson

Photo Studio
Sam Dudgeon, *Senior Staff Photographer*
Victoria Smith

Media Design
Joe Melomo, *Design Manager*

Cover Design
Nantucket Design

Copyright © 1999 by Holt, Rinehart and Winston

All rights reserved. No part of this publication may be reproduced or transmitted in any form or by any means, electronic or mechanical, including photocopy, recording, or any information storage and retrieval system, without permission in writing from the publisher.

Requests for permission to make copies of any part of the work should be mailed to the following address: Permissions Department, Holt, Rinehart and Winston, 1120 South Capital of Texas Highway, Austin, Texas 78746-6487.

Portions of this work were published in previous editions.

Acknowledgments: See page 709, which is an extension of the copyright page.

Printed in the United States of America

ISBN 0-03-051123-2   7 8   048   02

Contributing Authors

Clint Bruess, Ph.D.
Dean, School of Education
University of Alabama
Birmingham, AL

George B. Dintiman, Ph.D.
Professor
Virginia Commonwealth University
Richmond, VA

Susan J. Laing
Associate Chief of Staff for Education
Birmingham Veteran's Affairs Medical
Center
Birmingham, AL

Teacher Reviewers

Beth Barry, M.P.H., C.H.E.S.
Health Education Consultant
Richland County School District One
Columbia, SC

Alan D. Blakely
Newfound Regional High School
Bristol, NH

Janice E. Burke, M.A.
Reed High School
Sparks, NV

Cathleen Chavez
Chinle High School
Chinle, AZ

Burney Drake
Shelby High School
Shelby, NC

John A. Garcia
Castro Valley High School
Castro Valley, CA

Geri Grocki, M.S.
Weston Public Schools
Weston, CT

Debra C. Harris, Ph.D.
West Linn High School
West Linn, OR

**Virginia "Ginger" Lawless, M.Ed.,
C.H.E.S.**
Fort Bend Independent School District
Sugarland, TX

Bonna Marie Lesko, M.A., C.H.E.S.
Health Education Department Chair
Hopewell Area School District
Aliquippa, PA

Loretta McHan
Crockett High School
Austin, TX

Shirlee Nelson
Greenacres Elementary
Pocatello, ID

Michael J. Palazzo
West Torrance High School
West Torrance, CA

Becky Reeder
Jacksonville Middle School
Jacksonville, TX

Ann C. Slater, Ed.D., C.H.E.S.
Irmo Middle School
Columbia, SC
and
Adjunct Assistant Professor
University of South Carolina
Columbia, SC

Denise Swan
Naugatuck High School
Naugatuck, CT

Linda S. Tucker
Silver Creek High School
Sellersburg, IN

Pamela Cates White
San Marcos High School
San Marcos, TX

Content Reviewers

Timothy Aldrich, Ph.D.
Director
Central Cancer Registry
Raleigh, NC

Linda A. Berne, Ed.D., C.H.E.S.
Professor
University of North Carolina
Charlotte, NC

Robert W. Boyce, Ph.D., F.A.C.S.M.
Owner
Robert Boyce Health Promotion
Charlotte, NC

Diane Brinkman, M.D.
Physician
Austin Regional Clinic
Austin, TX

Ileana Corbelle, LMSW-ACP
Clinical Director
Austin Rape Crisis Center
Austin, TX

Doris Dedmon, R.N.
Nurse
Shelby, NC

Deborah A. Fortune, Ph.D., C.H.E.S.
Director, HIV/AIDS Project
American Association for Health
Education
Reston, VA

B. Don Franks, Ph.D.
Professor and Chair
Department of Kinesiology
Louisiana State University
Baton Rouge, LA

Bob Frye
Health Consultant
Raleigh, NC

Steve Furney, Ed.D., M.P.H., C.H.E.S.
Professor and Director
Health Education Division
Southwest Texas State University
San Marcos, TX

Judy Harris, R.N., C.H.E.S.
Director
Institute for Health Professionals
Portland Community College
Portland, OR

James Heffley, Ph.D.
Nutrition Counseling Service
Austin, TX

Carol Higy, Ed.D
Title III Program Coordinator
University of North Carolina
Pembroke, NC

Donna J. Jones, M.Ed., A.T.C., L.A.T.
Athletic Trainer
Texas A&M University
College Station, TX

Gary Klukken, Ph.D.
Director
Student Counseling Services Center
University of Tennessee
Knoxville, TN

Nancy J. Lipinski, R.N.
Licensed School Nurse
Annandale District 876 Public Schools
Annandale, MN

**Arlene Marks Montgomery,
LMSW-ACP**
Lecturer
University of Texas
Austin, TX

Emily Ousley, C.N.M.
Certified Nurse Midwife
Lawndale, NC

Barbara L. Potts, R.D., L.D.
Cooper Clinic
Dallas, TX

Robert Wandberg, Ph.D.
John F. Kennedy Senior High School
Bloomington, MN

Royal E. Wohl, Ph.D., C.H.E.S.
Lecturer
Washburn University
Topeka, KS

Kenneth A. Zeno, C.H.H.D.
Director
Center for Health & Human
Development
West Peabody, MA

Table of Contents

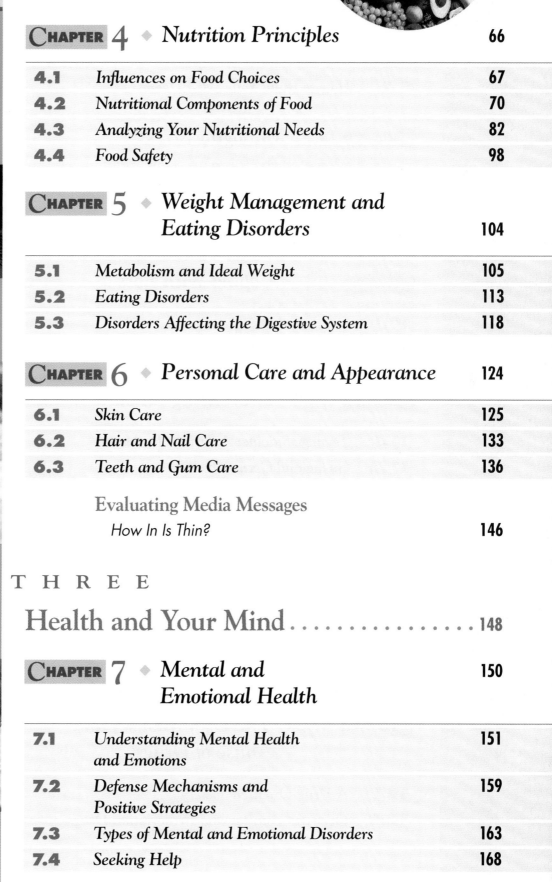

UNIT FOUR

Protecting Your Health in a Drug Society......... 242

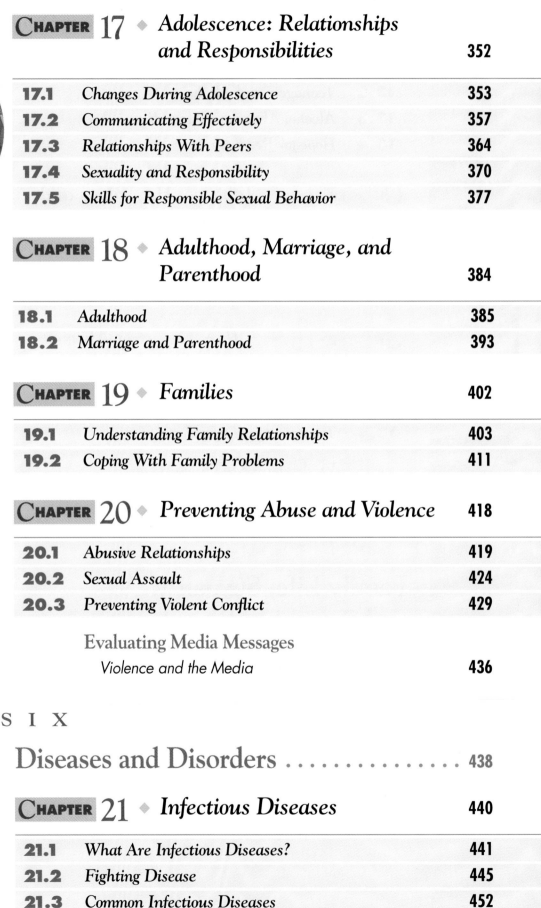

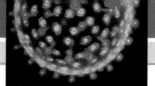

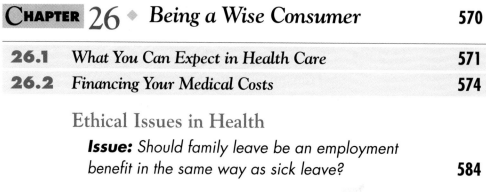

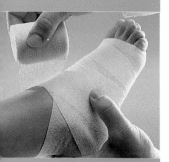

$\mathscr{L}$ife SKILLS:

$\mathbf{W}$hat Would You Do ❖ | Making Responsible Decisions

INTRODUCTION TO HEALTH AND WELLNESS

CHAPTER 1

HEALTH AND WELLNESS:
A QUALITY OF LIFE

CHAPTER 2

MAKING RESPONSIBLE DECISIONS

CHAPTER 1

Health and Wellness: A Quality of Life

◆ ◆ ◆ ◆

Section 1.1 Health and You

Section 1.2 Health Concerns in the United States

Lifestyle plays an important role in managing your overall health. Forming satisfying relationships and engaging in physical activity help make you healthy.

INTRODUCTION TO HEALTH AND WELLNESS

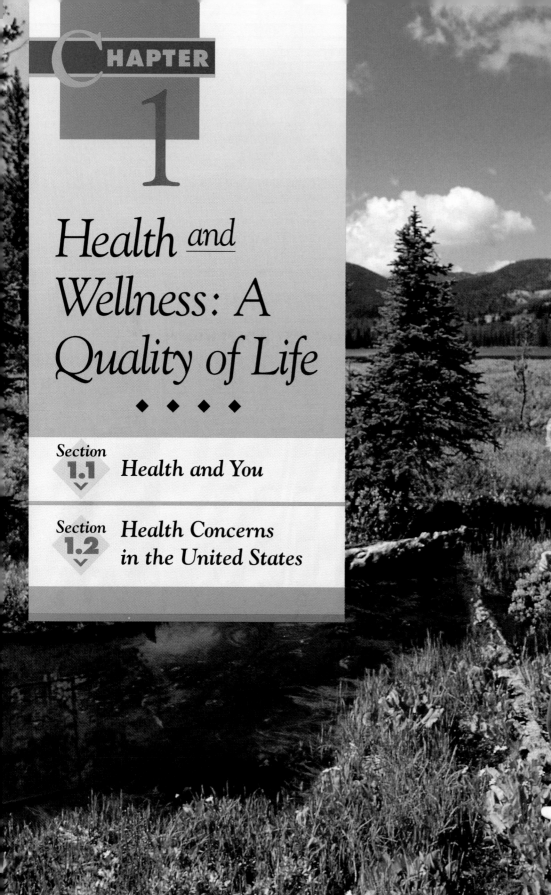

Health and Wellness: A Quality of Life

◆ ◆ ◆ ◆

Section 1.1 Health and You

Section 1.2 Health Concerns in the United States

Lifestyle plays an important role in managing your overall health. Forming satisfying relationships and engaging in physical activity help make you healthy.

Tara looked at her schedule. Fourth-period health was coming up next. Now that was the last class she felt like taking. Health class in grade school had been boring. Memorizing parts of the body and reading about diseases was not something she looked forward to doing again.

Right now all she could think about were the problems at home. Her mother's drinking was getting worse. Everything seemed to fall apart during the divorce. Her parents continued to argue all the time and Tara really felt caught in the middle. Her younger sister was talking about running away. Tara felt helpless in dealing with it all. Who could she turn to?

Section 1.1

Health and You

Objectives

- *Explain how the five components of health provide a picture of overall health.*

- *Describe the difference between wellness and health.*

- *Plot your current state of health on the health-illness continuum.*
  - **LIFE SKILLS: Assessing Your Health**

- *Describe the ways in which self-esteem, social support, health, and wellness are related.*

- *Describe the health benefits of physical fitness.*

You are at one of the most exciting yet challenging times of your life. You are no longer a child who requires constant care and the closeness of family. Your adult identity is in the early stages of formation. Your body is changing as you make this transition from child to adult. Your relationships with your friends and family are changing too. You want to spend more time with your friends and less with your family. Your family may be adjusting well to your need for independence or you may feel that you are still being treated like a child. The teen years are a time of adjustment to many new freedoms and responsibilities. It can also be a time of tremendous conflict in your relationships with your family and friends. During this time, you will establish habits and views that you will carry with you throughout your life.

You are faced with many choices that can have a major effect on your future. You know it is unhealthy to smoke, or to use alcohol. In fact, if you are under 21 it is illegal to use alcohol. However, an occasion may arise where you are offered tobacco, alcohol, or other drugs. Virtually every American teen has to make decisions concerning these issues.

You may now be experiencing problems in your life that have a profound effect on your health both now and in the future. The story about Tara in the introduction to this chapter is an example. Tara's family is not functioning properly. Everyone is under a lot of stress. Tara's mother has an alcohol abuse problem. Tara and her family need help. One goal of this course is to give you the knowledge you need to work through problems like these, should you be going through them now or sometime in the future. Throughout the text, you will be encouraged to seek help when you can't resolve a problem on your own. You will find out where in your community you can get help for yourself or others close to you. This course will put you in an active role in managing your health.

Describing Health

How do you generally respond when someone asks "How are you?" If you respond that you are "fine," take a moment to write down what you think it means to feel fine. If you respond in some other way, write down what your response really means. If you are not fine, are you sick? Now look at your description. How you feel is really part of describing your health.

Cultural DIVERSITY

Being Healthy— What Does It Mean?

Health means different things to different cultures. In the United States, slender people are viewed as healthy and attractive. But in some less prosperous cultures, thin people are viewed as unhealthy and less attractive. A fuller figure is a sign of having enough money to eat well and is considered desirable and healthy. These examples show how physical health can be defined by one's cultural beliefs.

Mental health can also be defined culturally. In the United States, a retired older relative who desires to meditate and prepare for death would probably be considered strange or even mentally ill, whereas in India, this decision would be understood as the fulfillment of one of the stages of a religious Hindu's life. A bank clerk in Milwaukee makes an appointment with a mental health therapist when he starts hearing voices, but an Inuit shaman expects to hear voices because he relies on advice from the invisible world. Again, how behavior is viewed depends on the culture of the person viewing it.

Remedies for treating illnesses can also be linked to culture. In some Jewish households, chicken soup is a medicine for various illnesses. A vitamin pill might be chosen to boost an Arizona accountant's energy level, but ginseng root might be the remedy in China. A housewife in Virginia could choose either of these, but chooses the ginseng because her mother and grandmother prepared the roots using an old family recipe.

Health was once thought to be the absence of disease. Health is now described in much broader terms, because we know so much more about what it takes to be healthy. There are five major components of health—physical health, social health, mental health, emotional health, and spiritual health. All five components must be in balance for you to be truly healthy.

Physical Health   **Physical health** covers those aspects of health related directly to the body. Your weight, strength, and the way your body functions are physical characteristics that are part of your physical health.

The absence of disease is part of physical health. Being physically healthy means you can get through your day at school and still have the energy to do your homework, engage in outside activities, and socialize with friends. Developing your physical fitness improves your physical health.

Audra is on the track and volleyball teams. She gets a lot of exercise and picks foods that keep her performance level high. Her boyfriend, Josh, has been smoking for two years. Because he smokes, Josh often skips meals and snacks throughout the day instead. He had five colds last winter alone. Audra is obviously doing a better job than Josh in attending to her physical health.

physical health:

your physical characteristics and the way your body functions.

One culture's practices may be slowly adopted by others. Once condemned as superstition, the ancient Chinese healing art of acupuncture is now being used in the West to relieve pain. Many western physicians and scientists believed acupuncture was nothing more than mind over matter until first-hand observation of the results changed their opinions. Now several kinds of treatment for pain relief apply the ideas of acupuncture for pain relief. This and other forms of traditional medicine from Eastern cultures are gaining a new degree of acceptance and scientific respect in the Western world.

There is one word, however, that is central to the definition of health in many cultures. That word is *balance,* or *harmony.* Good health is achieved by balancing mind, body, and spirit so that

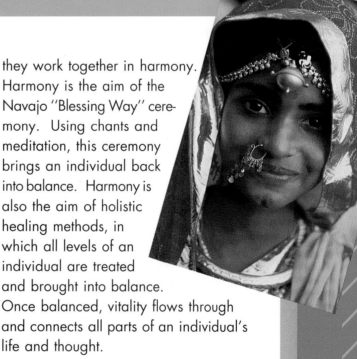

they work together in harmony. Harmony is the aim of the Navajo "Blessing Way" ceremony. Using chants and meditation, this ceremony brings an individual back into balance. Harmony is also the aim of holistic healing methods, in which all levels of an individual are treated and brought into balance. Once balanced, vitality flows through and connects all parts of an individual's life and thought.

Regardless of how your culture defines health and beauty, remaining open to new and different ideas not only will enrich your appreciation of culture diversity but also may expand your own view of health.

social health:

interactions with people to build satisfying relationships.

spiritual health:

maintaining harmonious relationships with other living things and having spiritual direction and purpose.

health:

state of well-being that comes from a good balance of the five aspects of health.

wellness:

optimal health in each of the five aspects of health.

mental health:

the ability to recognize reality and cope with the demands of daily life.

emotional health:

expressing feelings in an appropriate way.

Social Health Your **social health** involves interacting with people and your environment. Having satisfying relationships is a major part of your social health. Your social health development started when you were an infant and began interacting with parents and others in your family. Your social skills will continue to develop more fully now that you are a teen interacting with your peers. Your social health is influenced by your social networks and the support that you get from the people that you care about and love. Your social connections actually help to determine your state of physical and emotional health. During times of crisis and ill health, your network of family and friends becomes an especially important source of support. Your family, close friends, and the formal and informal groups to which you belong form your social networks. Healthy connections with these groups give you a sense of belonging and help you feel good about yourself. Being considerate of others, sharing your true feelings, serving your community, and asking for help when you need it are part of being socially healthy.

Mental Health The state of mind that enables you to cope with the emotional demands of your everyday life is described as **mental health**. Being mentally healthy means you can accept new ideas and recognize the reality of a situation. You have a sense of self-worth and tolerate things that are different. You can cope with stressful situations because you know that stress is a part of life that you can manage. You work to develop your individual strengths and accept your weaknesses.

Emotional Health Your ability to express feelings in appropriate ways defines your **emotional health**. While everyone experiences unpleasant or negative feelings

at one time or another, emotionally healthy people can overcome the difficulties. An emotionally healthy person enjoys life and views hardships or difficulties as challenges. An emotionally healthy person can express anger without violence and sadness without serious depression.

Spiritual Health **Spiritual health** involves your relationship to other living things and the role of spiritual direction in your life. This description means different things to different people. For some people, spiritual health is defined by a religion. For others, it involves understanding your individual purpose in life. Being spiritually healthy means you are working to achieve your spiritual potential and to find harmony in living. You are at peace with yourself and those around you.

Health and Wellness

These five aspects of health contribute to your overall health. It should be obvious that if you are physically fit, but you cannot get along with your teachers and parents, then you are not completely healthy. If you are very active in your church, synagogue, and community, but feel depressed and anxious most of the time, you are not completely healthy. **Health** can now be formally defined as the state of well-being that comes from realizing your potential in each of the five aspects of health. Optimal health is described by the term **wellness**. A state of wellness is experienced by looking at your overall health as a range of possibilities.

Health-Illness Continuum Your overall health can be illustrated by a plot on the health-illness continuum shown in Figure 1-1. Plotting your health position on the continuum involves looking at your health status in each of the five aspects of health. The right side of the continuum represents optimum health or wellness, an ideal state.

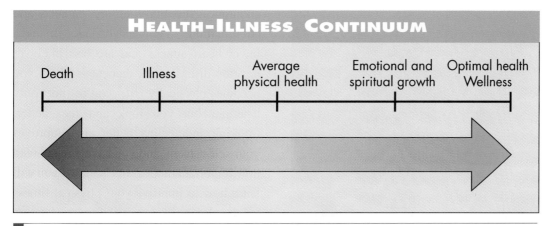

HEALTH-ILLNESS CONTINUUM

Death   Illness   Average physical health   Emotional and spiritual growth   Optimal health Wellness

(FIGURE 1-1) **Your health status on the continuum depends on how well you attend to each of the five areas that make up your total health picture.**

Achieving wellness involves making choices and behaving in ways that benefit your health. Making life-threatening choices like abusing alcohol or extreme dieting puts you on the left side of the continuum, which is the path to illness or an early death.

Self-Esteem and Wellness In order to achieve wellness, you have to feel good about yourself. Feeling good about yourself is called having positive **self-esteem**. You can be free of disease, you can get good grades in school, you can have nice friends, and be physically fit, but if you don't feel good about yourself you have not reached a state of wellness. In fact, when you get to Chapter 9, Managing Stress, you will discover that low self-esteem can actually make you physically ill. The stress you feel from not feeling good about yourself reduces your ability to fight off disease. So how you feel about yourself is related not only to your mental and emotional health, but is also related to your physical health.

Self-esteem is such an important component of health and wellness that it is a theme of this book. Chapter 8 focuses on self-esteem and what you can do to improve your self-esteem if you need to. Throughout this book you will see surveys that help

you learn more about yourself. Sometimes your strengths will show up. At other times, you'll see areas where you might want to change what you know, what you believe, what you say, or what you do. Everyone will find areas that can be improved. After all, no one is perfect.

Wellness Involves Social Support It is quite clear to people in the health profession that people need people. In fact, there is a name given to the benefits one gets from

self-esteem:

feeling good about yourself and your abilities.

(FIGURE 1-2) **Building relationships and receiving support from others is essential to your overall health and wellness.**

(FIGURE 1-3) **Physical activity can improve your physical health as well as provide for your social health.**

endurance, flexibility, agility, balance, and coordination. People who are fit have fewer heart attacks and are less likely to develop diseases like diabetes. When you become physically fit, you're not only healthier but you look and feel better. Looking and feeling better also improves your self-esteem, and you have already read how important that is. In Chapter 3 you will learn how to improve your physical fitness by developing a personal fitness program and then working to stick to it.

There is much you can do if you make up your mind to do it. Your potential is unlimited. Bob Weiland realized this when he decided to compete in the Marine Corps Marathon. It took him 79 hours and 57 minutes to complete the 26.2 miles. Despite having lost his legs in Vietnam and having to propel himself with his hands and no wheelchair, Bob finished the course.

social support:

deriving positive feelings from sharing life situations with others.

talking to others about joys, sorrows, problems, and stressors. It's called **social support**. It is now well known that a lot of stress in your life can make you physically sick. However, if you have social support, it is more likely you'll be able to manage stressors without becoming ill. Hasn't there been a time when you felt better about a bad situation after discussing it with a friend or relative? Throughout this course you will be encouraged to seek the help or advice of someone you can trust when you are having a problem. The purpose of this course is to give you a set of skills that will enable you to live a healthy lifestyle. Employing these skills when needed throughout your life keeps you on the path to wellness.

physical fitness:

a state in which your body can meet daily life demands.

Wellness and Physical Fitness **Physical fitness** is a state in which your body can meet the daily demands of living. It means you have a healthy heart, blood vessels, and lungs (cardiorespiratory endurance), and that you have sufficient muscular strength,

Review

1. How might a physical health problem, such as a disease, affect the other components of your health?

2. Why is self-esteem so important to overall health?

3. How can being physically fit improve your self-esteem?

4. List the people you use for social support.

5. **Critical Thinking** List two things you could do to improve your position on the health-illness continuum.

Health Concerns in the United States

Objectives

■ *Compare the leading causes of death at the turn of the 20th century with the leading causes of death today.*

■ *Relate lifestyle factors that contribute to disease and to the leading causes of death in the United States.*

■ *Identify your current lifestyle behaviors that reduce your health risks.*

   LIFE SKILLS: Assessing Your Health

In the early 1900s, the major health issue facing teens was early death due to diseases caused by microorganisms that spread from person to person. Today the **communicable diseases** that caused deaths in the early 1900s have either been controlled or wiped out, but lifestyle factors have taken their place as the major threat to teen health. Your choices and your behaviors, including how, when, and where you socialize or resolve problems, are part of your lifestyle. Figure 1-4 shows how unhealthy lifestyle behaviors relate to overall causes of death.

Teen Health Issues

One in five teens in the United States has at least one serious health problem. Figure 1-5 gives some teen health statistics. Did you know that each year 3 million teens are infected with a sexually transmitted disease? This statistic is especially alarming when you realize that one of those diseases

is HIV infection, which leads to AIDS and ends in death.

Teens and Risk

Taking risks is a natural part of living. For teens, it's part of growing up. Everything you do has some risk involved. Each action you take has a consequence. Most of your daily actions pose little risk; the results of those actions don't seriously threaten your life or your health. Other actions carry great risk; their consequences may actually threaten your life. This course will help you recognize the risks that exist for you as a teen. If you are like most other teens, you think that no harm will come to you. Because of that belief, you may be willing to take risks that can have serious consequences. Assessing risks and considering the possible consequences of your actions is a part of moving through adolescence into

communicable disease:

a disease that is passed from person to person by an organism.

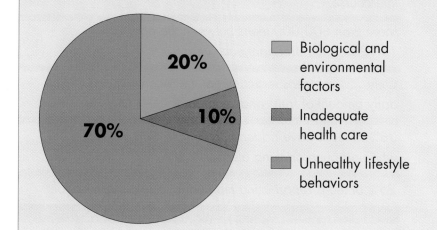

OVERALL CAUSES OF DEATH

20%

10%

70%

Biological and environmental factors

Inadequate health care

Unhealthy lifestyle behaviors

(FIGURE 1-4) **Most early deaths in the United States are related to lifestyle factors.**

adulthood. Taking responsibility for your actions is a sign of maturity and well-being.

National Health Risks

Pneumonia, tuberculosis, and influenza (flu) were the leading causes of death in the United States in the early part of this century. These three diseases fall into the category of communicable diseases, which means a person can get the disease from someone else. The government responded to this health problem by enacting laws on quarantine (isolation of disease victims), sewage disposal, and food and water sanitation. These actions caused a significant reduction in the number of people that got communicable diseases.

Figure 1-6 shows the 10 leading causes of death in the United States today and the factors that contribute to those causes. Contributing factors can actually be controlled by the choices made and the actions taken. In other words, most of the premature deaths and disabilities in the United States could be prevented. If people would exercise regularly, eat properly, have periodic medical exams, avoid the use of tobacco, and manage stress, more premature deaths could be avoided.

Developing Life Skills

Health professionals and medical professionals now stress prevention as their guiding principle to achieving wellness. Community health specialists have taken a more active role in educating the public concerning healthy living practices and disease prevention. Many hospitals and clinics now sponsor health education programs for the public that focus on diet, exercise, stress reduction, and emotional well being. It is believed that these programs will help reduce health care costs by getting people to accept more responsibility for their health.

In keeping with the prevention philosophy, Life Skills pages throughout this text help you apply what you learn in this class. The first Life Skills, on page 14, helps you identify your potential health risks.

Stopping to assess your behavior or feelings about a subject or issue may be a difficult task, but it is something that you will be frequently asked to do in this course. A journal will be a handy place to record this information. You may not want to admit that you are having trouble coping

Teen Health Statistics

38% of high school students reported they had been in a fight within the last year.

20% of high school students reported that they have carried a weapon.

24% of teens have considered suicide. Almost 9% of teens have attempted suicide.

34% of teens smoke cigarettes, and more than half of these teens buy their own cigarettes even though this is illegal for most teens.

Over 53% of high school students report having had intercourse.

More than 800,000 teens between the ages of 15-19 become pregnant each year.

Only 15% of teens regularly eat the recommended daily amount of fruits and vegetables.

38% of teens have ridden in a vehicle with a driver who had been drinking alcohol.

25% of teens report using marijuana; 51% used alcohol.

(FIGURE 1-5) **Teen health problems are widespread and varied. All these statistics involve health-related decisions that you can control in managing your own health.**

CAUSES OF DEATH IN THE UNITED STATES TODAY

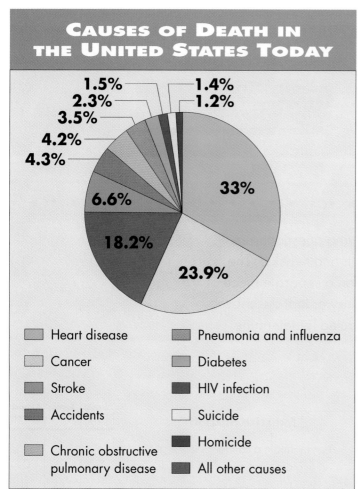

- 1.5%
- 2.3%
- 3.5%
- 4.2%
- 4.3%
- 6.6%
- 18.2%
- 1.4%
- 1.2%
- 33%
- 23.9%

- ☐ Heart disease
- ☐ Cancer
- ☐ Stroke
- ☐ Accidents
- ☐ Chronic obstructive pulmonary disease
- ☐ Pneumonia and influenza
- ☐ Diabetes
- ☐ HIV infection
- ☐ Suicide
- ☐ Homicide
- ☐ All other causes

UNDERLYING CAUSES OF DEATH IN THE UNITED STATES IN ONE YEAR

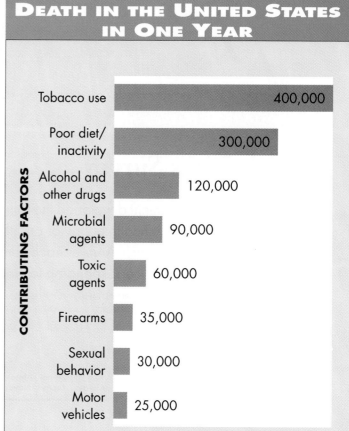

CONTRIBUTING FACTORS

- Tobacco use — 400,000
- Poor diet/inactivity — 300,000
- Alcohol and other drugs — 120,000
- Microbial agents — 90,000
- Toxic agents — 60,000
- Firearms — 35,000
- Sexual behavior — 30,000
- Motor vehicles — 25,000

NUMBER OF DEATHS

■ (FIGURE 1-6) **Today most leading causes of death could be prevented by changes in lifestyle.**

with a situation at home or that you are under too much pressure from friends or family. You may be much more comfortable expressing these feelings in the journal.

Keep a copy of your answers to this first Life Skills survey in your journal. Complete the survey again at the end of the course to find out if you have reduced your health risks. Other Life Skills pages will cover the following areas.

- Solving Problems
- Coping
- Setting Goals
- Resisting Pressure
- Assessing Your Health
- Using Community Resources Effectively
- Communicating Effectively
- Being A Wise Consumer

- Making Responsible Decisions
- Practicing Self-Care
- Intervention Strategies

Review

1. List three health-related decisions that you might make in the next year.

2. In what ways do your health risks differ from those of your grandparents when they were teens?

3. How might the Life Skills listed on this page assist you in reducing your health risks?

Health Risks Survey . . . .

The United States government developed the following questionnaire to help people assess their health behavior and their health risks. The questionnaire has six sections. Answer each item on a separate piece of paper by listing the number corresponding to the answer that describes your behavior. Then add the numbers you have circled to determine your score for that section.

Eating Habits

	Almost Always	Some-times	Almost Never
1. I eat a variety of foods each day, such as fruits and vegetables, whole grain breads and cereals, lean meats, dairy products, dry peas and beans, and nuts and seeds.	4	2	0
2. I limit the amount of fat, saturated fat, and cholesterol I eat (including fats in meats, eggs, butter, cream, shortenings, and organ meats such as liver).	2	1	0
3. I limit the amount of salt I eat by not adding salt at the table, avoiding salty snacks, and having my meals cooked with only small amounts of salt.	2	1	0
4. I avoid eating too much sugar (especially frequent snacks of sticky candy or soft drinks).	2	1	0

Your Eating Habits Score: _____

Exercise and Fitness

	Almost Always	Some-times	Almost Never
1. I maintain a comfortable weight, avoiding overweight and underweight.	3	2	0
2. I exercise vigorously for 15 to 30 minutes at least three times a week (examples include running, swimming, brisk walking).	3	2	0
3. I do exercises that enhance my muscle tone for 15 to 30 minutes at least three times a week (examples include yoga and calisthenics).	2	1	0
4. I use part of my leisure time to participate in individual, family, or team activities that increase my level of fitness (such as gardening, bowling, golf, or baseball).	2	1	0

Your Exercise and Fitness Score: _____

Stress Control

	Almost Always	Some-times	Almost Never
1. I enjoy school or other work I do.	2	1	0
2. I find it easy to relax and express my feelings freely.	2	1	0
3. I recognize early, and prepare for, events or situations likely to be stressful for me.	2	1	0
4. I have close friends, relatives, or others whom I can talk to about personal matters and call on for help when needed.	2	1	0
5. I participate in group activities (such as church/synagogue or community organizations) or hobbies that I enjoy.	2	1	0

Your Stress Control Score: _____

Safety

	Almost Always	Some-times	Almost Never
1. I wear a seat belt while riding in a car.	2	1	0
2. I avoid driving, or getting in a car with someone else who is driving, while under the influence of alcohol and other drugs.	2	1	0
3. I obey the traffic rules and observe the speed limit when driving or ask others to do so when driving in a car with them.	2	1	0
4. I am careful when using potentially harmful products or substances (such as household cleaners, poisons, and electrical devices).	2	1	0
5. I avoid smoking in bed.	2	1	0

Your Health Score: _____

Alcohol and Other Drug Use

	Almost Always	Some-times	Never
1. I avoid drinking alcoholic beverages.	4	2	0
2. I avoid using alcohol or other drugs (especially illegal drugs) as a way of handling stressful situations or the problems of my life.	3	1	0
3. I read and follow the label directions when using prescription and over-the-counter drugs.	3	1	0

Your Alcohol and Drugs Score: _____

Tobacco Use

	Almost Always	Some-times	Almost Never
1. I avoid smoking cigarettes.	4	1	0
2. I do not use chewing tobacco, smoke a pipe, or smoke cigars.	3	1	0
3. I avoid areas where others are smoking.	3	1	0

Your Tobacco Use Score: _____

Your Health Score

Make sure you have figured your score for each of the six sections.
Use the scale that follows for assessing each section.

Tabacco Use	Alcohol and Drug Use	Eating Habits	Exercise and Fitness	Stress Control	Safety
10	10	10	10	10	10
9	9	9	9	9	9
8	8	8	8	8	8
7	7	7	7	7	7
6	6	6	6	6	6
5	5	5	5	5	5
4	4	4	4	4	4
3	3	3	3	3	3
2	2	2	2	2	2
1	1	1	1	1	1

Interpreting Your Scores

Scores of **9 or 10** are excellent! You are putting your knowledge to
work for you by practicing good health habits.

Scores of **6 - 8** indicate your health practices in this area are good,
but there is room for improvement. Look again at the items you
answered with a "Sometimes" or an "Almost Never." What changes
can you make to improve your score?

Scores of **3 - 5** mean you have behaviors that put your health at risk.

Scores of **0 - 2** mean you may be taking serious, unnecessary risks
with your health. This course will make you aware of the risks and
what to do about them.

Fill out this survey again at the end of your health course. Our goal is
to give you the information you need to improve your scores.

Highlights

Summary

- Health is more than the absence of disease; it is the state of mental, physical, and social well-being.

- The concept of health requires a balance of five components: physical health, social health, mental health, emotional health, and spiritual health.

- A state of wellness is achieved by looking at your total health picture from a positive perspective.

- Making choices and behaving in a way that maximizes your health are the strongest positive influences on your level of wellness.

- To achieve wellness, you have to feel good about yourself.

- If you have social support, it is more likely you'll be able to manage stressors without becoming ill.

- Most of the health issues affecting teens are related to lifestyle.

- The major health dangers for teenagers today include accidents, suicide, homicide, unwanted pregnancy, and sexually transmitted diseases.

Vocabulary

physical health your physical characteristics and the way your body functions.

social health interactions with people to build satisfying relationships.

mental health the ability to recognize reality and cope with the demands of daily life.

emotional health expressing feelings in an appropriate way.

spiritual health maintaining harmonious relationships with other living things and having spiritual direction and purpose.

health state of well-being that comes from a good balance of the five aspects of health.

wellness optimal health in each of the five aspects of health.

self-esteem feeling good about yourself and what you can do.

social support deriving positive feelings from sharing life situations with others.

physical fitness a state whereby your body can meet daily life demands.

communicable disease a disease that is passed from person to person by an organism.

Chapter Review

Concept Review

1. The well-being of your body, your mind, and your relationships with other people is called _____.

2. _____ refers to the care of your body and the way your body functions.

3. The way people get along with one another and make and keep friends is called _____.

4. _____ means maintaining harmonious relationships with other living things and having spiritual direction and purpose.

5. A special scale that shows your total health has many levels is called a _____.

6. Feeling good about yourself is called having positive _____.

7. The benefit one gets from talking about joys, sorrows, problems, and stressors is called _____.

8. _____ is the foundation of wellness.

9. Communicable diseases have been replaced by _____ _____ as the leading causes of death in the United States.

10. The _____ you make about how you live have a direct impact on your overall health.

Expressing Your Views

1. Benton is 15 years old. He has started to exercise regularly, has lowered his fat intake, and doesn't drink alcohol. Where would you place him on the Wellness Continuum?

2. What are some of the indications that Americans are becoming more fitness oriented?

3. Most of the health issues facing teens today are determined by lifestyle. In your opinion, what are the two risk behaviors that will most influence a teen's health?

4. Demetra just received her driver's license. What are some of the risks involved in driving a car? What do you think Demetra could do to reduce the risks?

Life Skills Check . . . .

1. Assessing Your Health

You are content with your current state of wellness, but you would like to make sure you are healthy in the years to come. What are some things you could do now to ensure your future well-being?

2. Assessing Your Health

Lately you have not been getting along with your friends or family. The stress in your life is sometimes almost overwhelming. Often you just want to be alone. Who could you talk to? Explain your choice.

3. Assessing Your Health

Keep a list of all the choices you make for one day. How many of them are related to health? Explain how they are related.

Projects . . . .

1. Interview a person over age 50 and a person over age 70 to find out what health problems were most common during their teenage years. Prepare a brief report to the class comparing what you learned in the two interviews with what you learned in this chapter about health problems facing teens today.

2. Collect newspaper or magazine pictures that depict healthful behaviors and harmful behaviors. Glue these pictures on a poster board. Show your poster to the class and discuss how advertisements can influence your health choices both positively and negatively.

Plan for Action . . . .

Identify one healthful behavior from the Health Risks Survey that isn't now included in your daily life and that could positively affect your health. Make a month-long plan to adopt that behavior, and do weekly check-ups to track your progress.

Making Responsible Decisions

◆ ◆ ◆ ◆

When you are a teenager, making responsible decisions is often difficult. But if you learn a method of making choices that takes into account your values, you will be able to live with your decisions.

Richard can't decide what to do. His friend Nicole asked him if he wants to go to a party with her and her friend Selena this Saturday night. Richard has always wanted to ask Selena out but has been afraid she would turn him down. Going to this party would be the perfect way to get to know her without putting his pride on the line. But Richard has a big problem. He figures that a few people may be drinking alcohol at this party, and he decided last year that he didn't want to drink. First of all, he knows it's illegal for teenagers to drink alcohol. In addition, his brother was arrested twice for drunken driving and finally went into an alcoholism treatment program. Even though his brother is doing better now, Richard doesn't want to go through what his brother did. So far he's been able to stick to his decision. He's worried, though, that at this party someone may offer him a drink, and that he'll feel pressured to take it. What should he do? What would you do?

Why Does Health Involve So Many Decisions?

Objectives

- Name the top three causes of death of people ages 15–24.

- Explain how decisions made today can affect how long you live.

- Name the top three causes of death of people ages 55–64.

- Explain how decisions made today can affect your quality of life when you are older.

This is not the first time that Richard has had to make a difficult choice. Each day *everyone* faces decisions. Some choices are pretty easy to make—like deciding which shoes to wear, or which shoe to put on first. But other decisions have important consequences for your health, and these are often the difficult ones to make. In this chapter you'll learn a method for making responsible decisions that you can use for the rest of your life.

Responsible decision making is an important part of health; the choices you make give you a great deal of control over your own health.

The decisions you make could be more important to your health than any other factor. Your lifestyle—your way of living—could affect your health more than the traits you inherited from your parents, more than your environment, and more than the kind of health care you get.

Sometimes the choices you make affect your health immediately. Other times, the consequences are not seen until many years later. The choice that Richard has to make about the party is one that can have both short-term and long-term consequences for his health.

Short-Term Consequences of Health Decisions

Many decisions will affect your life today and in the coming weeks. Getting enough sleep, eating properly, managing your time, and staying active may help you fight off viruses and bacteria that could cause a cold, the flu, or a sore throat. In a similar way, your skin is affected by your activity habits, your diet, your use of alcohol and other drugs, and sun exposure. Think of other ways in which your decisions affect your appearance or your physical health.

Your emotions can also be affected by decisions you made last night or on the weekend. When you're tired, you may be-come emotional and upset at things that wouldn't usually bother you. When you're rested, you can better handle new situations or stressful events. In what other ways might your decisions and health habits affect your emotions today or later this week? How might these emotions affect your health?

While you're young, you believe your whole life is ahead of you; however, the consequences of some health decisions can be dramatic, immediate, and anything but short-term. Figure 2-1 shows the top six causes of death among young people 15 to 24 years old. These causes of death are often directly related to the choices a person makes. **Unintentional injuries** are the leading cause of death for teens. These injuries are not the result of purposeful acts. They include deaths involving motor vehicles. Unintentional injuries are no longer considered accidents, because at least 85% of them could have been prevented.

unintentional injuries:

injuries that are not the result of purposeful acts.

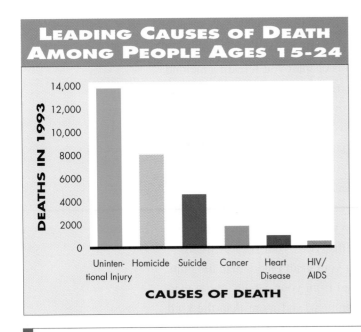

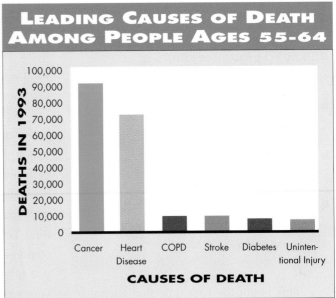

(FIGURE 2-1) **These charts show the leading causes of death for young people (left) and for older people (right). The decisions you make now can affect your health immediately *and* later in your life. (Source: United States Department of Health and Human Services.)**

(FIGURE 2-2) **Health decisions can have immediate consequences. A decision to wear a helmet while bicycling can save your life.**

Long-Term Consequences of Health Decisions

Some decisions might not have immediate consequences for your health, but they can determine what your life will be like when you are older. Look again at Figure 2-1. The top three causes of death among people between the ages of 55 and 64 are:

1. cancer
2. heart disease
3. chronic obstructive pulmonary disease

Each of these causes of death is often the result of choices made early in life. People who choose to smoke, for instance, are much more likely to get lung cancer than those who don't. Smoking begun in the teenage years and continued over long periods of time is the cause of most deaths due to lung cancer.

Suppose a man succeeded in living all the years of his life expectancy. But during the last 20 of those years he was always sick and in pain. He had emphysema, a lung disease, as a result of smoking cigarettes since the age of 16. Even though he lived a *long* life, his **quality of life** was poor. Quality of life is the degree to which a person lives life to its fullest capacity with enjoyment and reward.

If Richard's brother hadn't taken steps to recover from his alcoholism, he could have developed any number of ailments that would have severely damaged his quality of life. You are not likely to have a good quality of life if you smoke for 40 years and get emphysema. Similarly, you probably won't have a good quality of life if you develop heart disease as a result of poor diet and inadequate exercise.

You may not be able to do all the things you would like to do in your later years unless you make healthy choices now. The decisions you make today will influence not only how long you live, but also how you *feel* years from now.

quality of life:

the degree to which a person lives life to its fullest capacity with enjoyment and reward.

Review

1. Name the top three causes of death of people ages 15–24.

2. Explain how decisions made today can affect how long you live.

3. Name the top three causes of death of people ages 55–64.

4. Explain how decisions made today can affect your quality of life when you are older.

5. **Critical Thinking** If Richard's brother hadn't decided to quit drinking, how do you think his quality of life would be affected if he lived into his fifties?

How to Make a Responsible Decision

decision-making model:

a series of steps that helps a person make a responsible decision.

• • • • •

Objectives

■ *Name the steps of the decision-making model presented in this chapter.*

■ *Discuss the importance of values to responsible decision making.*

■ *Demonstrate the ability to use a decision-making model to make a responsible decision.*

■■ **LIFE SKILLS: Making Responsible Decisions**

Why is it necessary to teach people how to make decisions? Don't people just naturally learn how? No, it doesn't always work that way. Many people—perhaps most of us—

have great difficulty making decisions, and then worry about it long after the choice has been made. "Did I do the right thing?" they wonder. "What if I had made the other decision?" A lot of people need specific instructions before they know how to make responsible decisions.

A Decision-Making Model

In this section you'll see how Richard uses a **decision-making model** to make his choice. A decision-making model is a series of steps that helps a person make a responsible decision.

The decision-making model used in this textbook is shown in Figure 2-4. Follow along as you see Richard go through the steps to make his decision.

(FIGURE 2-3) **When making a difficult decision, it often helps to talk with someone you trust, such as a parent, teacher, counselor, or friend.**

• • • • •

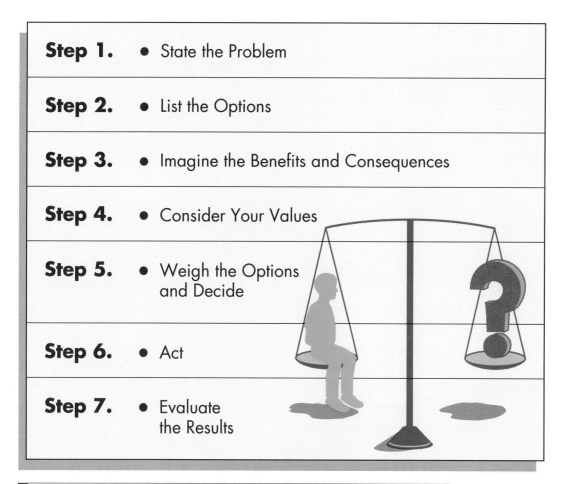

Step 1.	•	State the Problem
Step 2.	•	List the Options
Step 3.	•	Imagine the Benefits and Consequences
Step 4.	•	Consider Your Values
Step 5.	•	Weigh the Options and Decide
Step 6.	•	Act
Step 7.	•	Evaluate the Results

(FIGURE 2-4) **A decision-making model is a series of steps that helps a person make a responsible decision. Richard used the steps shown above to make his decision about the party.**

Step 1. State the Problem The first step in making a decision is to state the problem clearly. This is how Richard states his problem: "Should I go to the party even though I don't want to drink?"

Step 2. List the Options Before deciding what to do, Richard needs to list all the options. As he sees it, these are his options:

1. Go to the party and refuse a drink if it is offered.
2. Stay home and watch reruns of "Who's the Boss?"

Not very appealing options. Surely there are other alternatives. Well, Richard thinks, he could tell Nicole and Selena ahead of time that he isn't going to drink.

That way they might not try to pressure him into drinking. So now he has a third option:

3. Go to the party, and tell Nicole and Selena ahead of time that he is not going to drink.

Richard can't think of any more options. It seems that he will have to choose among these three. But that's not necessarily true. A person in the middle of trying to solve a problem may not be able to *recognize* all the options.

If Richard discusses his problem with other people, however, they may be able to think of other options or at least provide additional information. In this case, Richard talks to his good friend Carlos about his dilemma. Carlos tells him he has heard that

Selena doesn't drink either. Richard hadn't even considered that possibility. "What about going to a movie?" Carlos suggests. "That way you can see Selena but not have to worry about drinking." So now he has a fourth option:

4. Persuade Nicole and Selena to go to a movie instead of the party.

If Selena doesn't drink, Richard thinks, he might have a pretty good chance of getting the girls to change their plans.

Having someone to talk to whose opinions you trust is a valuable asset. It's important to remember, though, that you don't want to be persuaded to do something that isn't good for you.

Step 3. Imagine the Benefits and Consequences of Each Option

Many people have the hardest time with this step because they don't want to think about all the painful things that could happen as a result of choosing some of their options. But that's why this step is so important. In the long run, it's less painful to just imagine the consequences of a bad decision than to actually *experience* the consequences.

Take some time and carefully think through the benefits and negative consequences of each of your options. Make separate lists of the short-term consequences and the long-term consequences. A solution that solves the immediate problem might have terrible consequences later. And a solution that has uncomfortable consequences at first can be the best one in the long run.

Figure 2-5 shows the possible benefits and negative consequences that Richard imagined during his decision-making process. Remember that this is how *Richard* saw his situation. If you had Richard's problem, your lists of benefits and consequences might be entirely different.

Step 4. Consider Your Values

The next step in making a responsible decision is to think about how each option fits with your **values.** There are many definitions of the word "values," but when you see the word in this book it means a person's strong beliefs and ideals.

Your values allow you to choose between good and bad, and between right and wrong. Your values show the kind of person you are and what you care most about.

A person's values develop over time and are influenced by the teachings of family, culture, and religious and spiritual leaders. It's important to realize that not everyone will share your values. Each person develops his or her own value system, based on individual life experiences. However, there are some values that seem to be important to people from many backgrounds and cultures. These values, which are sometimes called "universal values," are:

- honesty
- trustworthiness
- responsibility to oneself and others
- self-control
- social justice

Richard feels that the value most relevant to his problem is responsibility to himself and others. It is very important to Richard to protect himself from harm. It is also important to him to avoid needlessly hurting his family. If he developed a drinking problem like his brother's, it would cause his family a lot of pain.

He also recognizes that his problem involves self-control. He had vowed to himself that he would not drink, and he doesn't want to break his promise to himself by losing control.

When Richard looks over his list of options, he sees that Option 2 and Option 4 fit his values. If he chooses either of these options, he will be certain not to drink.

Richard's Options

(FIGURE 2-5)

Options	Possible Benefits	Possible Short-Term Negative Consequences	Possible Long-Term Negative Consequences
1. Go to the party and hope that I am not tempted to drink.	I will be sure to spend the evening with the girls.	I may drink and feel guilty about it. I may drink and lose the chance to go out with Selena, since she doesn't drink. I may drink and end up in a dangerous situation, such as driving while drunk.	If I drink after I've decided not to drink, I could become a problem drinker like my brother. The negative consequences of being a problem drinker would take all day to list. Some of them are increased risk of injuries, physical illness, emotional depression, and damaged relationships with people I care about.
2. Stay at home and watch reruns.	I will not have to deal with the pressures to drink alcohol. I will keep my promise to myself about not drinking.	I will not get to spend the evening with the girls.	The girls might think I'm no fun.
3. Go to the party but tell Nicole and Selena ahead of time that I am not going to drink.	I will have a better chance of keeping my promise to myself about not drinking than if I choose Option 1.	I might drink anyway and have the same possible short-term consequences of Option 1.	If I drink, I have the same possible long-term consequences of Option 1. In addition, I might lose the respect of Nicole and Selena if I drink after I said I would not.
4. Persuade Nicole and Selena to go to a movie instead of the party.	I will get to spend the evening with the girls. I will know that Nicole and Selena would rather spend time with me than go to the party. I will keep my promise to myself about not drinking. I may improve my chances with Selena, since she doesn't drink.	Nicole and Selena might insist on going to the party, with or without me. If I do convince them to go to the movie instead, they may still feel a little upset about not going to the party.	If they don't want to go to the movie, the girls might think I'm no fun.

Step 5. Weigh the Options and Decide

The next step is to weigh your options and make the decision. Carefully examine the possible benefits and negative consequences of each option. Which option has the most benefits and the fewest negative consequences? Pay special attention to the long-term consequences of the options.

Most important, remember what you learned in Step 4—how the options fit your values. If you have trouble deciding between two options that seem equally desirable, choose the one that better reflects your strong beliefs and ideals. There is a very practical reason to act in accordance with one's values: When people go against their values, they are likely to feel bad about themselves. Always ask yourself, "How will I feel about myself later if I choose this option?"

Richard knows that Options 1 and 3 are not compatible with his values because they might lead to drinking. Option 2, to stay home, *is* compatible with his values. But it doesn't have as many benefits as Option 4, to persuade the girls to go to a movie instead of the party.

Option 4 has more benefits than any of the other options, does not have many negative consequences, and is consistent with his values. It has now become clear to Richard that Option 4 is the best option for him.

He has made a responsible decision.

Step 6. Act

It may seem that things should be smooth sailing after you finally make a decision. You just *do* it, right? In reality, it takes some thought and planning

> **❝***I don't want to drink, but it's hard when some people at a party may be drinking.***❞**
>
> **Richard**

to ensure that you will act on your decision. Richard made the following list of actions he would take to implement his decision:

1. I will find out ahead of time which movies will be showing the night of the party and make a note of several that sound good.
2. I will make sure I can get the car that night so I can drive everyone to the theater.
3. I will tell Nicole and Selena about all the good movies showing in town and ask them if they would like to go to one of them instead of going to the party.
4. I will be prepared to tell them the truth if they ask me why I don't want to go to the party.

Step 7. Evaluate the Results Once the decision is made and you have acted on the decision, you should evaluate the results.

Ask yourself the following questions. How well did the decision work out? How well did you identify the potential benefits and negative consequences of the option you chose? How can you improve the way you make decisions in the future?

As it turned out, Nicole and Selena went along with his idea to go to the movie. Nicole was a little reluctant because she had been looking forward to the party, but Selena was happy to avoid the pressure to drink. No one quizzed Richard about why he didn't want to go to the party. All three had a good time at the movie, and Richard got to know Selena better. When Richard evaluated the results, he felt he had made the best decision possible.

But what if the situation had turned out differently? What if the girls had refused to go with him and had made fun of him? It wouldn't mean that he had made the wrong decision. It would mean that no matter how good his decision was, he couldn't control other people's behavior. All Richard could

control was his *own* behavior. A good decision is not necessarily one that works out well, but one that is made responsibly.

What Would You Do ?

Making Responsible Decisions

A Friend Needs Your Help

You've seen Richard use the decision-making steps to work through his problem and make a responsible choice. Now practice using those same steps by making a decision about what you would do if faced with the following dilemma.

You know your friend Juliette has been depressed lately, but every time you ask her what's wrong, she changes the subject. Then one day you notice a bruise on her face that she's tried to cover with makeup. At first she tells you that she got hit in the face with a softball, but then, leaning against her locker and crying, she admits that her stepfather beat her up. "He knocks me around every time he has a bad day at work," Juliette says. "Mom doesn't even know about it because she gets home from work after he does."

"Why don't you tell your mother about it?" you ask. But Juliette shakes her head. "I don't want to break up Mom's marriage. She's happier now than she's been in a long time."

That night you keep thinking about Juliette. You want to help your friend, but you don't want to make her situation worse. What would you do?

Remember to use the decision-making steps:

1. State the Problem
2. List the Options
3. Imagine the Benefits and Consequences
4. Consider Your Values
5. Weigh the Options and Decide
6. Act
7. Evaluate the Results

(FIGURE 2-6) **What if you're riding around in a car with friends and you have to make a quick decision about whether to go to a party? When under this kind of pressure, consider your values first.**

What Happens When You Have to Make a Quick Decision? Because Richard had plenty of time before the night of the party, he was able to systematically follow the decision-making steps. He was lucky that time. But let's say Richard was riding around in a car with some friends who wanted to go to a beer party right then. He wouldn't be able to whip out his notebook and pencil and make lists of the options, benefits, and consequences. He would have to respond immediately.

When under pressure, it is best to consider your values first. It also helps if you have practiced the decision-making steps many times before. Then the process would come almost naturally. The "What Would You Do?" activity on the previous page will give you an opportunity to sharpen your decision-making skills in preparation for the times when you have to make quick decisions.

Review

1. *Name the steps of the decision-making model presented in this chapter.*

2. *Why are values important in making responsible decisions?*

3. **LIFE SKILLS: Making Responsible Decisions** *Here is your dilemma: You are very attracted to someone in your school named Kris, but a friend recently told you that Kris smokes. Decide whether you should pursue your interest in Kris, using the steps of the decision-making model.*

4. *Critical Thinking Name three values that are very important to you.*

Highlights

Summary

- People who are able to make responsible decisions have a great deal of control over their own lives.

- The top three causes of death among Americans between the ages of 15 and 24 are accidental injury, homicide, and suicide. Each of these can directly result from the choices a person makes.

- The top three causes of death for Americans between the ages of 55 and 64 are cancer, heart disease, and chronic obstructive pulmonary disease. Each of these can result from choices made early in life, such as smoking.

- A person who has a high quality of life leads a life that is full of enrichment and reward.

- There is a series of steps you can learn that will help you make responsible decisions.

- Talking to someone whose opinions you trust can help you make a decision. Be sure, though, that you are not persuaded to make a decision to do something that is bad for you.

- A person's values, or strong beliefs and ideals, can be influenced by family, culture, and religious and spiritual leaders.

- Whenever you are under pressure to make a quick decision, make sure you consider your own values first.

- The most important values include honesty, trustworthiness, responsibility to oneself and others, self-control, and social justice.

Vocabulary

unintentional injuries injuries that are not the result of purposeful acts.

quality of life the degree to which a person lives life to its fullest capacity with enjoyment and reward.

decision-making model a series of steps that helps a person make a responsible decision.

values a person's strong beliefs and ideals.

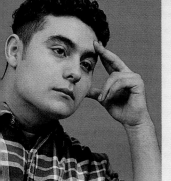

Chapter Review

Concept Review

1. The top three causes of death of people ages 15–24 are _____, _____, and _____.

2. The top three causes of death of people ages 55–64 are _____, _____, and _____.

3. It has been shown that the use of _____ and other _____ greatly increases the chances that a person will experience serious injury, be involved in violence, or commit suicide.

4. Health decisions you make today will have a profound effect on your future _____.

5. If you choose to smoke, you are more likely to get lung cancer or _____, a lung disease.

6. The degree to which a person lives life to its fullest capacity with enjoyment and reward is known as _____.

7. The first step in making a decision is to _____.

8. Your _____ allow you to choose between right and wrong and show the kind of person you are.

9. If you have trouble deciding between two options that seem equally desirable, choose the one that better reflects your strong _____ and _____.

10. Once a decision is made and you have acted on the decision, the next step in the decision-making process is to _____.

Expressing Your Views

1. What are some changes you could make in your lifestyle to improve your quality of life in later years?

2. You have a friend who smokes cigarettes and is reluctant to quit. He says smoking has never made him feel sick, and that it's not going to harm him.
   What would you tell him?

3. Your best friend was drinking at the party Saturday. You think she may be drinking often, but you're not sure whether you should say something to her about it. What do you think you should do? What are some long- and short-term consequences for her health?

Life Skills Check

1. Making Responsible Decisions
Terry is someone you've always wanted to be friends with, so you're pretty happy the two of you have started to do stuff together. Unfortunately, one thing Terry really likes to do most is skip class and go to the park. You haven't done it yet, but Terry wants the two of you to cut math class Friday. You don't want to miss the class; you have a quiz the next week, and you'd feel really funny about cutting a class anyway. But you also don't want to lose Terry's friendship. What would you do?

2. Making Responsible Decisions
Some close friends of yours have started using alcohol and other drugs on a regular basis. Using the steps of the decision-making model, decide whether you want to continue associating with this group of friends.

Projects

1. Design a bulletin board that displays the leading causes of death for Americans between the ages of 15 and 24, and for those between the ages of 55 and 64. Suggest ways to reduce the number of deaths from these causes.

2. Work with a group of students to come up with a list of problems for which the decision-making model might be useful. What issues would not be suitable for the model?

3. Write a short essay about how a person's values are important in a friendship. Include how your own values may have changed over the years.

4. Work with a partner to find magazine pictures that show people attempting to improve their quality of life. Create a collage on a poster board using the pictures you have found. Next to the collage, list the ways the people in the pictures are striving for a more satisfying life.

Plan for Action

Make a list of four situations that require a spur of the moment decision that could negatively affect your health. Select one situation and use the decision-making model to make a decision about what to do.

What Is a Media Message?

Mike needs some new athletic shoes. Like many of his friends, Mike wants a popular name brand endorsed by famous athletes. He loves to think that wearing those particular shoes will impress his friends and make him more popular at school. Unfortunately, the shoes cost three times as much money as Mike has to spend. When Mike asks his father if he will help with the purchase, his father says no.

"Come on, Dad," Mike says. "All the NBA stars are wearing these shoes. They're the best!"

"That may be, Mike," his father replies, "but they are not the best choice for you. They're just too expensive. Before you make a decision based only on the influence of a media message, why don't you do a little research on several kinds of shoes."

"Okay, Dad," Mike agrees. "But what's a media message, anyway?"

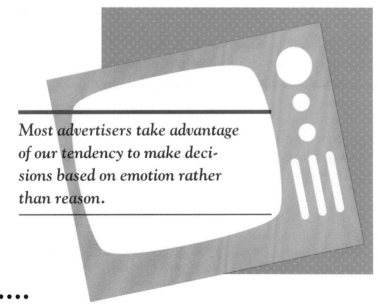

Most advertisers take advantage of our tendency to make decisions based on emotion rather than reason.

As Mike's father explained, media messages are the information conveyed by television, radio, magazines, newspapers, and other types of mass media (forms of communication that reach large numbers of people). They are found primarily in advertisements, television programs, and movies, but are also found in news stories, art, literature, and even rock music lyrics.

Media messages not only contain information but also express social values and persuade people to make judgments and to take certain actions. Because such messages reach so many people, they greatly affect people's opinions of what is normal, attractive, successful, and even healthy. Often, the forms of persuasion used in media messages encourage people to make decisions based on emotion rather than reason. Consequently, the purpose, source, and nature of any media message should be carefully evaluated before making a decision based on the message.

The ads that make Mike feel he must have a certain type of athletic shoes are examples of media messages designed to persuade. Some of the ads mention comfort, foot support, durability, and endorsements by medical experts, which are all logical reasons for buying a particular shoe. But many ads rely on visual images of athletes wearing that brand of athletic shoes. The athletes project an image of attractiveness and success that is emotionally appealing. By association, whatever the athlete is wearing, eating, or doing may be perceived as contributing to the athlete's attractiveness and success. This is why Mike feels that if he wears the same athletic shoes, he too will be attractive and successful.

All of us have a tendency to make decisions based on emotion rather than reason. Most advertisers take advantage of this tendency. When evaluating media messages like athletic-shoe ads, it is important to remember the purpose of the ads—to sell shoes and make money for the shoe companies. The athletes also make money by doing the ads. Such interests may conflict with the best interests of buyers.

Once Mike understood how and why he came to desire the expensive athletic shoes, he realized that he would rather base his decision on his own best interests. After making a list of several types of athletic shoes and their features, Mike talked to some of the coaches at school about how the different brands compare in terms of performance and durability. By applying the decision-making model he learned in health class, Mike finally chose a style that is more comfortable, lasts longer, and costs a lot less money than the brand he wanted originally.

It also provides good foot support and looks great. Even though Mike's choice still costs more money than he has, it is clearly his best choice overall. And his father agreed to help with the purchase after all.

Critical Thinking

1. Find several ads for a common item such as a type of clothing, a toy, a kids' cereal, a type of sporting equipment, or an automobile. Analyze the ads for the media messages they convey.

   - What information is given upfront?
   - What information is unspoken or in the background?
   - What type of media—print, radio, or television— does each ad use? Which do you think is the most effective?
   - Does the ad appeal to your emotions or your sense of reason?
   - Choose what you think is the best ad upon which to base a decision to buy.

2. For each ad you analyzed for item 1, ask yourself the following questions.

   - How will I benefit if I buy what the ad is trying to sell?
   - How will the advertiser benefit if I buy what the ad is trying to sell?

HEALTH AND YOUR BODY

CHAPTER

3

Physical Fitness

◆ ◆ ◆ ◆

The healthiest physical fitness programs will include plenty of aerobic exercise.

Christine can't seem to stay awake anymore. She has to drag herself out of bed every morning, and at school she sits bleary-eyed in class, counting seconds until the bell rings. After staring into space at her after-school job, she barely begins her homework before nodding off, at around 8 P.M. Her friends, family, and teachers have noticed that she's been acting strange lately, and Christine herself is concerned about her lack of energy.

She's also worried about the layer of fat that she has recently noticed on her waist and the back of her arms. Christine knows that having some body fat is perfectly normal, but she also realizes that she has been eating too many sweets between meals. She wonders whether her busy, stressful life has something to do with her constant exhaustion and huge appetite. Then one day it dawns on her that she can't remember the last time she got any exercise.

Section 3.1 — Why Exercise?

Objectives

- *Name three physical benefits of exercise.*

- *Name two mental benefits of exercise.*

- *Name the four categories of physical fitness.*

You've probably heard all about how good exercise is for you. You know that it can help you develop muscles and lose weight. What you may not realize is that regular exercise helps you cope better with the stress and anxiety you probably face every day, and that it greatly increases your energy level. It can even help you avoid some serious diseases later on in life.

Some people like to exercise more than others. If you're the wide receiver on your school football team, you will have an easier time figuring out how to be physically active than if you hate the thought of lacing up a pair of sneakers. But exercising regularly does not have to mean competing against the best athletes in your class or taking a swimming lesson when it's freezing outside. Walking for half an hour before supper, or biking to school instead of taking the bus, is often enough to give your body the **exercise** it needs.

exercise:

physical activity that consists of a regular series of activities to train and strengthen the body.

The Benefits of Exercise

Christine bought an exercise tape and started working out four times a week. It surprised her how quickly she started feeling better. Her energy level bounced back to normal, and she found it hard to believe that at one time she could barely stay conscious until early evening. By combining physical workouts with a new diet of nutritious, low-fat foods, she began to lose the extra weight.

In addition, Christine forgot that her days were once filled with depression and anxiety. Her dark moods lifted, and she no longer woke up in the morning with a sense of dread in the pit of her stomach. Her exercise routine became a part of her day-to-day life, so she no longer had to force herself to do the activities that improved her physical and mental well-being so dramatically.

Not everyone will get the same benefits from exercise as Christine. It could be that your body will not respond as easily or as quickly to physical activity. In addition, many teenagers are depressed or anxious—not because they haven't exercised, but because something is happening at school or at home that may be troubling them. If you are feeling sad or stressed out, and you don't think it has anything to do with the amount of exercise you've been getting, you may want to talk to someone, like a teacher, a coach, or a counselor. See Chapter 7, Mental and Emotional Health, for more information on this.

Physical Benefits All body systems benefit from regular physical activity, including exercise. When you perform a regular series of activities to train and strengthen your body, you are exercising. But there are occasions when you just need to walk to the store, climb a flight of stairs, mow the lawn, or wash the car. Although that's not formally exercise, it is physical activity, and it, too, benefits your physical health.

Many teens are concerned about weight gain. Christine herself was worried about the fat on her body. Exercise can help her achieve a **body composition** with the appropriate fat percentage to be healthy. Christine's exercise tape keeps her moving continuously for about 20 minutes. In doing so, she uses energy. At some point in time and with changes in her diet, Christine can reach a healthy weight. A healthy weight is one that is suited to her body build and the size of her bones. She'll be able to maintain her weight if she continues her physical activity, because physical activity is the key to long-term weight maintenance.

When Christine saw people exercising who looked trim, she wondered why they even needed to exercise. Exercise is not just for people who have fat to lose. Thin people have as much reason to exercise as not-so-thin people. While exercising, Christine is keeping her heart rate and breathing rate up which strengthens her heart, the muscles of her lungs, and her blood vessels. Not only do these tissues get stronger, but they also remain elastic, relaxing and contracting steadily as needed. This, in turn, reduces her risk for heart attack, stroke, and high blood pressure, which is often a result of the build-up of plaque in the blood vessels. Plaque forms within arteries in the heart, the brain, and throughout the body. These deposits can clog arteries in the heart and lead to a heart attack, or they can clog arteries in the brain and lead to a stroke. Plaque formation can begin in infancy, but regular exercise can slow down the build-up by raising the levels of chemicals in the blood that help to remove the fatty deposits.

Christine's tape also has an exercise segment to strengthen abdominal muscles. Stronger muscles in her abdomen help support her lower back. Given that back problems are often caused by weak muscles,

body composition:

the division of total body weight into fat weight and fat-free weight which includes bone and muscle.

For more information on where to seek help for anxiety and depression, see Chapter 7.

Christine is working to prevent lower back problems. Each time these and other strengthening exercises place a strain on her bones, her bones get stronger and more dense. Increased bone density will help Christine later in life when osteoporosis could otherwise result in brittle and easily broken bones. And because she is active, Christine is reducing her chances of getting diabetes as she moves into her forties.

In the short term, the moderate pace of her exercise tape will boost Christine's immune system. A strong immune system is necessary to prevent disease. Christine might find that she has fewer colds and sore throats during the coming winter. Other systems like her digestive and excretory systems are strengthened by regular exercise and adopting a more nutritious diet. Because she is now sweating regularly, Christine's skin is working more efficiently to remove wastes from her body. Research suggests she may also be reducing her risk of cancer with exercise.

Myths and Facts About Exercise

MYTH	FACT
No pain, no gain.	Exercise does not have to hurt in order to be effective. Jogging, walking, or cycling at a pace that allows you to carry on a normal conversation, for example, will improve your aerobic fitness without pain.
Drinking water right before exercising can cause stomach cramps.	Drinking water does not cause stomach cramps; dehydration does and drinking water before and during exercise prevents dehydration.
When you stop working out, your muscle will turn to fat.	It is impossible for muscle to turn into fat because muscle and fat are two different kinds of tissue.
There is no such thing as exercising too much.	Too much exercise can be unhealthy. Make sure that exercise is part of your life, but don't let it dominate every thought. Believe it or not, people have become addicted to exercise.
You can't be too thin.	Being underweight is possible, and can be very dangerous. If you do think you need to lose weight, set limits for yourself. Remember that you're dieting and exercising for your health. Overdoing either one can defeat this purpose.

(FIGURE 3-1)
Not everything you hear about exercise is true. Here are some examples of some popular but untrue statements.

Mental Benefits Studies have shown that aerobic exercise helps people with emotional problems control their mood swings. So it makes some sense that doing physical activity can help everyone cope with everyday anxiety and occasional, mild forms of depression. Exercise is good for your mental well-being for several reasons. First of all, knowing that you are doing something healthy for your body is very satisfying. Second, studies show that exercise improves your mood. According to research, certain types of physical activity may cause your brain to manufacture hormones called **endorphins**, which are natural substances that make you feel good. Vigorous physical activity helps your body produce greater amounts of endorphins, which may be part of the reason why people who get exercise on a regular basis are often more emotionally stable and more confident than those who don't.

People who are physically fit also tend to be less nervous and less stressed. Exercise relaxes your muscles and eases anxiety, which not only helps you cope with tensions during the day but also lets you put them aside at night, when you're trying to sleep. This is one reason why people who exercise regularly sleep better than those who don't. Another is that they are more tired. Physical activity may give you more energy during the day, but it makes you more tired at the right time—at night. You'll learn more about sleep later on in this chapter.

What's Physical Fitness?

Ask a few experts what "**physical fitness**" means, and you may very well get a few different answers. Most experts do agree that people who are physically fit (1) perform their day-to-day tasks with energy and vigor and (2) can participate in a variety of physical activities. They can do these while staying relatively clear of diseases related to a

lack of exercise. Physical fitness can be divided into four categories:

- aerobic fitness
- muscular strength and endurance
- flexibility
- body composition

Aerobic Fitness Aerobic fitness refers to your body's ability to endure 10 minutes or more of continuous exercise. These activities increase the heart rate and use large muscles in a steady and continuous motion. They range from activities such as swimming, walking, or jogging to team sports such as basketball and soccer.

Muscular Strength and Endurance Muscular strength refers to the amount of force you generate using your muscles. Muscular endurance is the amount of force you can generate repeatedly using your muscles for an extended period. Attempting to lift a 300-pound sofa alone requires tremendous muscular strength. Unloading one hundred, 50-pound bags of potatoes takes a great deal of muscular endurance. To develop muscular strength and endurance you need to do exercises that force the muscles to move against a force heavier than normal.

Flexibility Flexibility refers to your body's ability to use its major joints fully. Peak flexibility is achieved in the teen years, but as one ages, joints become stiff and lose their range of motion if they are not stretched regularly. Flexibility can improve performance, reduce the risk of injury, and make your daily activities easier and more enjoyable.

Body Composition Body composition refers to the proportion of fat and fat-free tissue, such as muscle and bone, in your body. This proportion changes as your eating and activity habits change. Aerobic activity can reduce body fat. Resistance training increases muscle mass and bone density.

endorphin:

a substance produced inside the brain that has pain-killing effects.

physical fitness:

the ability to perform daily tasks vigorously and to perform physical activities while avoiding diseases related to a lack of activity.

Another way to think of physical fitness is to consider it in terms of your own needs and goals. If you are in good physical condition, you should be able to perform your everyday tasks without getting too tired to function. If you find that, like Christine, you're yawning at your desk a lot, you have trouble relaxing, and even low levels of exertion exhaust you, your physical fitness level may be lower than it should be. What about mood swings? Do you get depressed or anxious easily? These may also be symptoms of a lack of physical fitness, and they can disappear quickly if treated with a program of regular exercise.

Physical Fitness and Physical Disabilities

Have you ever tried pushing yourself in a wheelchair for 26 miles? Or sprinting for 100 meters with one real leg? How about pitching to major-league hitters when you have only one hand? Chances are you haven't. But think for a moment of how difficult these activities are, and then ask yourself: Can having a physical disability prevent a person from being physically fit?

Sharon Hedrick, Dennis Oehler, and Jim Abbott know the answer to that question. Hedrick, a paraplegic, used tremendous arm and shoulder strength to push her wheelchair to victory in an exhibition marathon race at the 1988 Olympics in Seoul, South Korea. Oehler, who lost his right leg in an automobile accident, wears a prosthesis, or an artificial leg. His time of 12.01 seconds in the 100-meter dash is a world record for athletes with disabilities, and is only 2 seconds slower than that of two-time Olympic champion Carl Lewis, who has two legs. Being born without a right hand did not stop Abbott, who is able both to throw and catch with his left hand, from winning 18 games for the California Angels in 1991.

(FIGURE 3-2) **Jim Abbott (left), who is missing a right hand, is a major-league pitcher. Paraplegic Sharon Hedrick (right) is a champion wheelchair marathoner.**

Of course, you don't have to perform athletic miracles in order to be in good physical condition. Most people who are physically fit could not win 18 games in the Major Leagues, but they do know how to keep themselves healthy. And just as physical disabilities do not stop world-class athletes from achieving greatness, they do not block people who want to be in good physical condition from doing so. Most important, the state of wellness—of being physically, emotionally, and spiritually healthy—is a realistic, reachable goal every person is capable of achieving. People with physical disabilities have as much chance as anyone does of leading long, full, healthy, and happy lives.

Review

1. *Name two physical benefits and two mental benefits of exercise.*

2. *What are the four categories of physical fitness?*

3. *Critical Thinking* *Why is it important to be physically fit?*

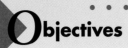

How Physically Fit Are You?

Objectives

- *Know the ways to test physical fitness.*
  - **LIFE SKILLS: Assessing Your Health**

Before you plan an exercise program or a program to increase your physical activity, assess your current fitness level. The following are some simple tests you can do to determine your current level of fitness.

Aerobic Fitness Level

aerobic fitness:

the ability to endure at least 10 minutes of moderate activity.

Before you begin you will need to know how to take your pulse. Place the middle and index fingers of your right hand on your left wrist, just below the base of your thumb.

Can you feel your pulse? Using a second hand on a watch, count the beats for 10 seconds. Now you are ready to begin the test. Time yourself running or walking a mile as quickly as you can. As soon as you finish the mile, check your pulse for 10 seconds. Now multiply that number by six to determine your beats per minute. A rate between 100 and 140 means you are reasonably fit. Then check your time against Figure 3-3 to see where it falls.

Muscular Strength and Endurance Level

Lie on your back with your knees bent and your feet flat on the floor as shown in Figure 3-5. Cross your arms over your chest and rest your hands on your shoulders. Exhale as you tuck your chin toward your chest, curling your torso until your shoulder blades leave the floor. Inhale as you return

	Aerobic Fitness Standards: One-Mile Walk or Run	
The times below define a low level of fitness. If your time is slower for the mile, use the time shown as your first goal when you begin your program.		
Age	**Minimum Standards for Boys**	**Minimum Standards for Girls**
12	10 minutes	11 minutes, 35 seconds
13	8 minutes, 35 seconds	11 minutes
14–16	8 minutes, 10 seconds	12 minutes
17–19	8 minutes, 30 seconds	11 minutes, 30 seconds

(FIGURE 3-3) **If your times are faster than the ones shown in the table by a minute or more, your fitness level is moderate to high.**

(FIGURE 3-4) **In order to test your muscular strength and endurance, see how many curl-ups you can complete in one minute.**

your shoulder blades to the floor, completing one curl-up in about 3 seconds. To be fit, girls should complete 33 to 35 curl-ups, boys between 40 and 44, in one minute.

To test your upper body, perform a pull-up test, using a horizontal bar that is high enough so that your feet don't touch the floor once you're up. Keep your arms and legs straight, and grasp the bar, palms facing away from you. Using your arms, raise your body until your chin is above the bar. Girls should be able to do one pull-up, and boys three to five, without stopping.

Flexibility Level

To test lower back and hamstring **flexibility,** sit on the floor as shown in Figure 3-5. Bend forward from your hips, and reach your arms forward without straining. Do this slowly several times, until you feel stretched. Repeat the reach and measure your distance. If you're flexible, you'll be able to reach between 1 and 4 inches past your feet.

Body Composition

Grasp a fold of skin from your abdomen with your thumb and forefinger. Now grasp the flesh on the back of your upper

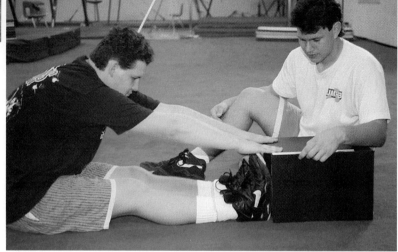

(FIGURE 3-5) **The more flexible you are, the farther you can reach your arms beyond your feet in this "box test."**

arm, your thigh, and the back of your lower leg. If you can pinch more than an inch in any of these areas, consider changing your diet and increasing your physical activity.

Review

1. **LIFE SKILLS: Assessing Your Health** What are four ways to test physical fitness?

2. What areas of fitness do you need to improve?

3. **Critical Thinking** Why is it a good idea to test your level of physical fitness before you begin an exercise program?

flexibility:
the ability to move muscles and joints through their full range of motion.

Section
3.3 *About Exercise*

Objectives

- *Know the difference between aerobic and anaerobic exercise.*

- *Name three examples of aerobic exercise.*

- *Name three effects of steroid abuse.*

- *Know what to do to avoid basic injuries.*

- *Know the range of your target heart rate.*
  - **LIFE SKILLS: Assessing Your Health**

You have just found out that physical fitness is divided into four categories. You should also know that exercise has different subsets as well:

- aerobic exercises are physical activities that continue for more than 10 minutes.
- anaerobic exercises are intense, all-out actions that last from a few seconds to a few minutes.

Aerobic Exercises

Aerobic exercises are the most important, most healthy things you can do for your body. Every time you run, walk, bike, or do any kind of aerobic activity for an extended amount of time, you breathe rapidly and your heartbeat temporarily increases. When this happens your lungs transfer more oxygen to your bloodstream. But most important, aerobic activity lowers your heart rate and helps your respiratory and cir-culatory systems stay healthy. For these reasons, you should make sure you include at least one of the following aerobic exercises in your exercise schedule, no matter what your ultimate physical fitness goal is.

Walking Walking can be aerobic when it is brisk and raises your heart rate into your training zone. Slower-paced walking can also be aerobic if you carry three- or four-pound hand weights or a five-pound pack, or if you walk hills or stairs. Aerobic walking causes you to breathe harder and sweat, and it can stimulate endorphins and raise

(FIGURE 3-6) **Walking for an hour or so is a good way to exercise your muscles and relax your mind.**

aerobic exercise:

physical activity that increases the supply of oxygen to the muscles, and that can be continued for a period of time without resting.

46 CHAPTER 3 PHYSICAL FITNESS

your mood. Because its impact on the bones and joints is low, walking is a great way to begin a fitness program if you are trying to lose weight. Walking alone or with a friend can also give you a chance to catch up on your day, unwind, and relax.

Running Running is harder to do than walking, but you may find that the things it can do for you make the extra effort worthwhile. Studies show that running causes your brain to produce endorphins, and it burns calories at a faster pace than walking does. In addition, running causes you to breathe more rapidly, which, as you learned earlier, allows more oxygen into your system. This extra effort eventually increases your lung capacity. If you find that you're breathing very heavily after you've run a mile today, try running the same distance three times a week for a month. At that point you may very well laugh when you think about how tired and breathless it once made you.

Swimming and Biking Swimming and biking can give you the same benefits as running, but they may not be as convenient, because they require equipment that can be expensive. If you have a bike, you may find that you prefer cycling to running, or that it provides a good change of pace. Swimming is an excellent aerobic activity because it exercises not only your legs but also your arms and torso. If your school doesn't have a pool, try calling your neighborhood YMCA. These organizations often have good pools (as well as other exercise programs at a fair price).

Aerobic Exercise to Music Aerobic exercise to music can be an enjoyable way to increase your physical activity. In an aerobic class you use your entire body, which provides the same aerobic benefits as swimming or basketball. There are some important questions to consider before join-

(FIGURE 3-7) **Aerobic exercise to music is a great workout for just about every muscle in the body. If you want to do this type of exercise, make sure you find a class that is on the right level for you.**

ing a class. What kind of class is best suited to my fitness level? Should I select a class that is high, mixed, or low impact? What are the qualifications of the instructor? Is it someone who is well educated about aerobic exercise? Is the facility set up to accommodate aerobics classes? Answers to these questions can help you select the aerobics class that is best for you.

You can also get a good aerobics workout to music using a videotape at home. If you decide to purchase an aerobics exercise tape, be sure to do some research on the tapes available. Tapes made by celebrities may not provide the best kind of instruction or workout. Fitness magazines will often provide ratings of aerobics tapes that you can use to select the tape that is best for you.

Team Sports Team sports such as basketball, hockey, and soccer can give you many of the same benefits as other aerobic exercise, and they can become great social events, because they are activities you can do with friends. If you like playing team sports more than any of your friends do, find out if your neighborhood has pickup games

(FIGURE 3-8) **Anaerobic exercises develop speed and muscular strength.**

you can join. You may also want to call the YMCA in your neighborhood, which may be able to set you up with a team that matches your skills and ability.

Anaerobic Exercises

Because **anaerobic exercises** take so much immediate energy and effort, they make you breathe even more rapidly than aerobic activities. This type of exercise does not necessarily help the body's respiratory and circulatory systems, and it does not burn calories as effectively as aerobic exercises do. Anaerobic exercise will improve your speed and muscular strength. Sprinting, weight lifting, and gymnastics are three examples of anaerobic activities.

Some Basic Rules

When you like an activity, it is automatically enjoyable. But you can make almost

any activity enjoyable if you know some basic rules of fitness training.

Make Sure You Exercise Often Enough, Long Enough, and at the Right Intensity When you start a fitness program, you'll want to start slowly. Avoid doing too much, too soon. Once you're on your way, you'll need to progress gradually, doing more only as you become stronger and more fit.

Aerobic fitness requires intense activity at least three times per week. **Intensity** is the term used to describe how hard you're working. What is the intensity that is suited to you? The Life Skills feature on page 49 will help you answer that question as it relates to your aerobic training. You can monitor your heart rate as an estimate of intensity. When your heart rate falls within your target heart rate range, you are exercising at the proper intensity. If your heart rate is too low, you'll need to change something about your workout. Taking bigger steps, adding jumps, lifting your knees higher, moving your arms more, or increasing your speed will raise your heart rate. If your heart rate is too high, you'll need to lower the intensity. Shorten your stride, stop using your arms, slow down—all will lower intensity. When the intensity of your program is correct, you'll be perspiring slightly but you'll also be able to carry on a conversation. If you cannot pass this "can you talk" guideline, your intensity is too high. Likewise, if you're tired for more than an hour after your workout, your activity was too intense.

How long is long enough? A minimum of 20–30 minutes per day is recommended. You can do all of your aerobic work at once or split it into segments that are each 10 minutes or longer.

anaerobic exercise:

physical activity that increases speed and muscular strength, and that cannot be continued for a few minutes without stopping.

Determining Your Target Heart Rate Range . . . . .

In order to find out your target heart rate range, you must know your maximum heart rate (MHR), which is the fastest your heart can possibly beat. If you happened to take your pulse the last time physical activity left you so worn-out that your heart pounded and you were completely breathless, you may know what your MHR is. If you didn't, you can find out your MHR by subtracting your age from 220.

Your target heart rate, or the pace you want your heart to beat when you exercise, should be between 60 percent and 80 percent of your maximum heart rate. In order to find your target heart rate range, multiply your MHR first by .6 to determine the lower end of the range, and then by .8 to determine the upper end of the range.

You can find your MHR and your target heart rate range by checking this chart:

Age	Maximum Heart Rate	Target Heart Rate Range
13	207	124-166
14	206	123-165
15	205	123-164
16	204	122-163
17	203	122-162
18	202	121-162

A good way to remember all this information is to think of the word FIT:

- F stands for frequency, which should be three to four times per week.
- I stands for intensity, which should be at or slightly above your target heart rate.
- T stands for time, which should be at least 30 minutes of continuous exercise.

Warm Up and Cool Down Every athlete talks about how important it is to warm up before doing any strenuous physical activity. It is a good rule of thumb to spend a few minutes walking or jogging, and then do some mild stretching to warm up your muscles and raise your body temperature before you begin exercising.

It's also important to cool down *after* you finish exercising. If you don't, you may get dizzy or feel nauseated, and your muscles can become sore and cramped. Don't stop moving immediately after a strenuous exercise. Slow down, but continue walking or moving for another five minutes or so, to cool down your muscles in the same way that you warmed them up.

Start Slowly No matter how impatient you are to get your body into top physical shape, don't begin your exercise program by doing too much too soon. If your goal is to run 5 miles without stopping, but you haven't run in a while, pushing yourself beyond your current limitations can hurt you both physically and mentally. You may find yourself nursing cramped muscles, struggling for breath, and figuring that you would rather do just about anything rather than set foot on a track again.

Here's another example. Let's say you're in a weight-training program, and your goal is to lift a certain amount of weight that seems impossibly heavy right now. The best way to reach your goal is to choose a program that forces you to lift

slightly more weight each workout. This is called using the progressive resistance principle, and it can and should be used in any type of exercise program you choose.

Vary Your Workout Just as you can get sick of hearing your favorite song too often, doing one exercise all the time can become boring. It can also injure your muscular and skeletal systems. Try to include a variety of aerobic exercises—called cross training—in your schedule. If you run one day, cycle another, and play tennis a third, you can both cut down on your chances of injury and keep yourself interested in each activity. This will help you receive the full benefit from each workout.

In addition, place some limits on the amount of exercise you do each week. Don't exercise intensely more than three or four times a week, and try to arrange your schedule so that you have a day to rest between each workout.

Avoiding Injuries

Even if you follow every exercise rule perfectly, you still run a small risk of injury when you exercise. The more physically fit you are, the lower this risk will be. But to be on the safe side, even if you are in terrific physical condition (and especially if you're not), read the following suggestions carefully and follow basic safety rules so you can keep your chances of getting hurt at a minimum.

Listen to Your Body Signals Make sure you pay close attention to the way your body is feeling. Minor aches and breathlessness are a normal part of exercise, but anything more serious than that—a sharp pain, for instance—probably means something is wrong and should not be ignored.

Even when everything seems fine, take time after each workout to let your body analyze things for you. Are you sweating?

If you're not, the workout was probably too light. If you're out of breath, are you still that way after 10 minutes of rest? If so, you may have exercised too hard. Of course it's normal to feel tired after exercising, but exhaustion that lasts for more than 24 hours is definitely a signal of some sort. Do you feel nauseated or dizzy? Next time you exercise, wait two minutes after the end of your workout, and then check your heart rate. If your pulse is more than five beats quicker than the upper limit of your target heartbeat range—and especially if you are experiencing these other symptoms as well—you must lighten your workouts.

When you're feeling ill, don't make things worse by exercising. It won't make you feel any less sick, and you'll be much better off if you rest instead. When you're completely well again, work out lightly for a few days before returning to your full exercise schedule, just to be on the safe side.

Dress for the Weather Don't let the fact that exercise increases your body temperature fool you into thinking that it's perfectly fine to exercise outdoors on extremely cold days without dressing properly. The best thing you can do when it's freezing outside is to exercise indoors. If you do insist on being outside, make sure you're dressed for it. Put on two or three layers of clothing instead of one heavy outfit. Wear a hat to keep your head warm, and make sure your ears, fingers, nose, and toes are covered properly. Keep your clothing as dry as possible, and take extra time warming up before you begin your workout.

Be even more careful on hot, humid days. Again, you're best off staying in a cool gymnasium when the weather's hitting 90 degrees, but if you do go out, wear light-colored, lightweight clothing. Never wear rubberized suits or try to lose weight by sweating. This could seriously overheat your body. Most important, drink lots of water before, during, and after your workouts. The water will keep you from becoming dehydrated, and it will help you sweat so you can stay cooler.

(FIGURE 3-9) **When you exercise in the cold, layer your garments. For the first layer, use a garment that draws (wicks) moisture from your skin. For the second layer, use a garment that absorbs the moisture. Add other layers as needed.**

Don't Be Just a Weekend Exerciser
It's always easier to find time to exercise on a Saturday or Sunday than it is during the week, especially during the school year. Unfortunately, exercising only on the weekends can be risky. People who rely on weekend activity to improve their aerobic fitness can overdo it, and they often find themselves nursing sprained ankles and sore knees after they have burned up the tennis court or running track. In addition, exercising only once a week will do little for your overall fitness level.

If you can exercise only on weekends, make sure that you warm up thoroughly before each activity and that you take frequent breaks. If at all possible, try to find time for a short workout at least once during the week. By following these suggestions, you will make your weekend sports routine less hazardous to your health.

anabolic steroid:

an artificially made, complex substance that can temporarily increase muscle size.

How to Treat Basic Injuries

No matter how careful you are, accidents and injuries can happen. In case one happens to you, keep in mind the five simple actions—known as PRICE—involved in the emergency treatment of injuries:

- P (physician): decide whether you need to see a doctor immediately, or whether it's safe to wait a few days.
- R (rest): stop exercising immediately, and stay off the body part you've injured. If you've hurt a leg, ankle, or foot, use crutches if you have them.
- I (ice): to keep swelling to a minimum, put ice on your injury as soon as possible.
- C (compression): wrapping a towel or bandage firmly around the ice also helps limit swelling.
- E (elevation): keep your injured limb raised above your heart level. This will drain extra fluid from the injury.

If you decide that you're not hurt badly enough to see a doctor—and make this decision very carefully—begin treating your injury as soon as you can. Apply ice, in periods of 15 to 20 minutes, until the swelling goes down. At that point, remove the ice and use moist-heat compresses instead. Once swelling has disappeared, pain is gone, and your range of motion is restored, you can usually start exercising again in four or five days. Be very careful when you do this—take extra care to follow the basic safety rules. You don't want to reinjure yourself and start the treatment process all over again.

Anabolic Steroids

Even if you're not a big sports fan, you may remember Canadian runner Ben Johnson, who was stripped of his gold medal after breaking the Olympic and World records in the 100-meter dash at the 1988 Olympics. Johnson, it turned out, had taken **anabolic steroids**, an illegal drug some athletes use to make them stronger and faster.

Steroids, which are made from a hormone called testosterone, do have some medical value. Doctors prescribe them to treat people with a blood condition called anemia, to help patients recovering from

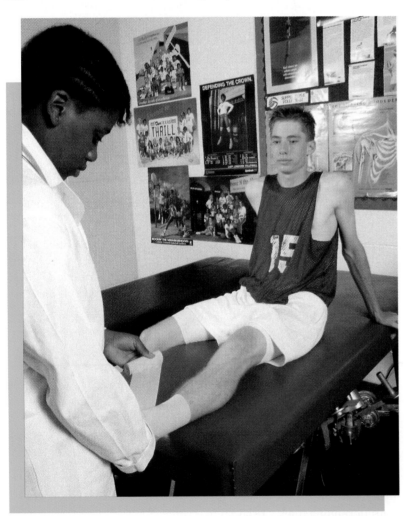

(FIGURE 3-10) **If you think you've seriously injured yourself exercising, seek medical attention immediately.**

surgery, and also to replace a missing hormone in people who have not grown properly. But steroids have also become very popular illegal drugs, because they can increase muscle size and body weight. Famous athletes are not the only ones known to use steroids—thousands of high school students have taken them as well.

Not only are steroids illegal, but they're also very dangerous. They can cause high blood pressure, liver damage, cancer, damage to the reproductive system, and facial deformities, as well as violent behavior and other psychiatric problems.

It's not always easy to know if someone is taking steroids, but some common symptoms of this type of drug abuse include the following:

- noticeable change in muscle mass
- dramatic increase in ability to lift heavy weights
- aggressive behavior
- dramatic amounts of acne

It may seem as though steroids have their advantages. After all, they can make you stronger and faster without your having to work too hard. Even so, they're not worth the risk. A lot of the damage they cause may be permanent. Why ruin your life over some extra muscle? And anyway, depending on steroids to make you look good robs you of the pleasure of achievement. It doesn't count for much if you're strong just because you took a drug. Finally, you don't need steroids to make you stronger and faster. By combining weight training with a healthy diet and a program of regular aerobic exercise, you can help your body produce natural hormones to make your muscles grow. For additional information on gaining body weight, read the Gaining Weight Safely section in Chapter 5. For more information on steroid abuse, see Chapter 15.

(FIGURE 3-11) **Ben Johnson (right) was stripped of his gold medal at the 1988 Olympic games when traces of anabolic steroids were found in his blood.**

Review

1. *Describe the difference between aerobic and anaerobic exercise.*

2. *Name two examples of aerobic exercises, and two examples of anaerobic exercise.*

3. **LIFE SKILLS: Assessing Your Health** *Your workouts are making you tired, and you wonder whether they may be too intense for you. What's a good way to find this out?*

4. *Critical Thinking Which is more important to overall physical fitness: aerobic exercise, or anaerobic exercise? Why?*

For more information on how to gain weight safely, see Chapter 5.

Anabolic Steroids are also discussed in Chapter 15.

Section 3.4 — Getting Started

Objectives

- *Set your exercise goals.*
- *Design your own exercise schedule.*

Your exercise schedule should reflect your personal goals, and may for that reason be very different from those of your close friends. That's why it's so important that you take plenty of time to design your own program.

Now that you've read through all the rules and regulations of physical activity, not to mention the benefits of being physically fit, it's time to sit down and figure out what your exercise goals are. Then you can design a program that can help you meet them. Remember that your main ambition does not have to be to play basketball like Michael Jordan or tennis like Jennifer Capriati. It could be that you're looking to lose weight, or that you want to have more energy, or that you just want to stay healthy.

Your Goals and How to Achieve Them

By now you most likely have some idea of what you want from your exercise program. In case you don't, here's a list and brief description of goals you may want to strive for. When you've decided what's best for you, look at Figure 3-13 to find out what type of exercises you should do.

Aerobic Fitness Earlier in this chapter you learned that when you are aerobically

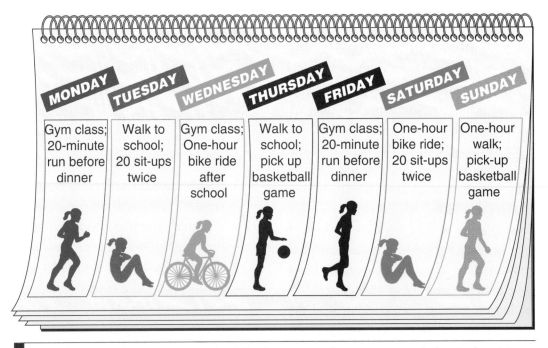

■ (FIGURE 3-12) **Good exercise schedules leave time for some sort of physical activity every day of the week.**

Your Exercise Goals and How to Achieve Them

Goal	Type of Exercise	What to Do
Weight Loss	Aerobics	Four or more times a week, within your zone, 45–60 minutes
Better Health	Aerobics	Every other day, at 70–85% of your heart rate maximum, 30 minutes
Muscular Endurance and Good Body Composition	Resistance Training	Two or more times a week, 70–85% of the heaviest weight you can lift, 30 minutes maximum
Muscular Strength	Resistance Training	Three or more times a week, at 90% of the heaviest weight you can lift, enough to do 10 exercises and multiple sets eventually
Flexibility	Stretching	Each time you workout, 10 exercises, 3 reps each, hold each position 20 seconds or longer

(FIGURE 3-13) **Remember when you design your exercise program to keep your goals simple. Too much exercise too soon can do more harm than good.**

fit, not only is your body able to undergo 10 minutes or more of continuous exercise, but your circulatory system and respiratory system are working more efficiently. These health benefits are the most important part of physical fitness. Aerobic exercise is an important part of a total fitness program. Remember that if you start taking care of your circulatory and respiratory systems now, you can reduce your risk for disease.

Strength and Muscle Development
Muscles grow stronger and may increase in size through resistance training. Resistance training involves overcoming the resistance caused by the weight of another object or a force. Resistance can come from free weights, weight or hydraulic machines, rubberized resistance, or your body weight.

Your muscles will adapt to working with greater and greater resistance over time if you vary the following in your workout.

- load—the weight or force being overcome or moved
- repetitions—the number of times you repeatedly overcome the resistance without resting
- sets—groups of repetitions, separated by a rest period of 30 seconds to 3 minutes

Various Aerobic Activities and the Calories They Burn

Activity	Approximate Calories Burned (per minute)
Walking (3.75 miles per hour)	5
Badminton	6.6
Cycling (9.4 miles per hour)	6.8
Tennis (singles)	7.5
Swimming	8.3
Field Hockey	9.1
Basketball	9.4
Skiing	13
Handball	14.4
Ice Hockey	15.5
Walking Up Stairs	18
Running:	
5.8 miles per hour	9.5
8.0 miles per hour	12.5
10.0 miles per hour	15
11.4 miles per hour	21.5
13.2 miles per hour	39

(FIGURE 3-14) **You have a wide range of choices in selecting aerobic activities that match your preferences and your schedule.**

Resistance training can increase strength, endurance, or both depending on how you change the three variables. Building strength requires that you use heavier loads (90% or more of your maximum) with fewer repetitions (1–5). Building endurance requires lighter loads (70–85% of your maximum) and higher repetitions (12–15). Building both strength and endurance requires 10–15 repetitions. A personal trainer or a physical educator can work with you to develop a program that will help you achieve your personal goals.

One set of muscles that deserves special attention is your abdominal muscles. (Actually there are four sets of abdominal muscles.) Strong abdominal muscles will protect your lower back from injury and support your internal organs. Figure 3-15 shows several beginning exercises for building abdominal strength and endurance.

Weight Control Exercise is a vital part of every weight-loss program. Consider the following facts.

- Exercise can decrease your appetite.
- Exercise burns calories.
- Exercise helps you lose fat without losing muscle.

You learned earlier that physical activity is the key to long-term weight management. Aerobic activities burn fat. Resistance exercises, which build stronger muscle and greater muscle mass, also play a part in weight control. When you increase your muscle mass with resistance exercises, you burn more calories during your workouts, and you'll also burn more calories when you're not active. As you lose fat, you can tighten and tone your muscles by regular, moderate resistance training. Just remember, though, that more is not always better. While exercise is healthful and a crucial part of reaching and maintaining a healthy weight, over-exercising can be dangerous.

Reverse Curls

Lie on the floor with your arms by your sides. Knees are bent. Contract your lower abs to curl hips off the ground about 3 to 5 inches bringing knees towards chest. Slowly return to the floor. Do not ''whip'' your legs. Let the abs do the work. Remember to press your lower back into floor throughout the exercise.

Lower abdominal kips

Lie on the floor with your legs extended straight up toward the ceiling. Place your arms on the floor by your sides or extend them overhead. Inhale. Exhale as you push your heels toward the ceiling, tilting your pelvis upward while keeping your buttocks relaxed. Inhale as you lower your legs.

Bent knee curl-ups

Lie on the floor with your knees bent and your feet flat on the floor about one foot from your hips. Fold your arms across your chest or leave them by your sides. Exhale as you tuck the chin and curl the shoulder blades lifting them from the floor, toward your thighs. Inhale as you return to the floor.

Lying side bends

Lie on your side with your knees flexed and your thighs slightly forward. Fold the arm resting on the floor, across your chest. Extend your other arm along your side. Inhale. Exhale as you raise your shoulders off the floor and reach your extended arm toward your feet. Inhale as you return to the floor.

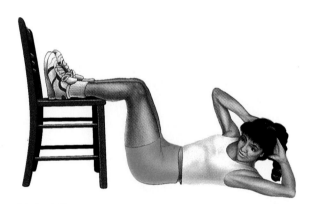

Feet high oblique curl

Lie on the floor with your legs supported on the seat of a chair or a high aerobic bench. Keep your thighs perpendicular to the floor. Place your hands so that your head rests on your fingertips. Inhale. Exhale, as you lift your right shoulder toward your left knee, while leaving the other shoulder on the floor. Inhale as you return to the floor and repeat the movement on the opposite side.

Feet high curl-ups

Lie on the floor with your legs supported on the seat of a chair or a high aerobic bench. Keep your thighs perpendicular to the floor. Fold your arms across your chest and inhale to begin. Exhale as you tuck the chin and curl the shoulder blades lifting them off the floor, toward the thighs. Inhale as you return to the floor.

(FIGURE 3-15) **These exercises can strengthen your abdominal muscles, but they can also cause injury if they are not done correctly. Check with your health or physical education teachers to be sure you are doing them correctly.**

Shoulder stretch
Hold onto an object about shoulder height. With hands on the support, relax and keep arms straight and chest moving downward, feet under hips, and knees slightly bent.

Hamstring (a)
While sitting down with knees slighty bent, reach foward from the hips until you feel a stretch in the back of your legs.

Hamstrings (b)
Keep only a slight bend in the front leg, with the other foot next to the inside of the leg. Bend forward at the hips until you feel slight pressure.

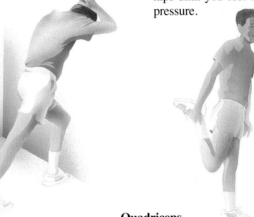

Hip
Lying on your back, relax and straighten both legs. Pull the left foot toward the chest. Repeat using the right foot.

Calf
Stand slightly away from a wall and lean forward with the lead leg bent and the rear leg extended. Move the hips forward with the heel of the straight leg on the ground until you feel a stretch in the calf.

Quadriceps
Stand on your left leg. Now bend your right leg at the knee, hold your ankle behind you, and pull upward slowly and gently until you feel a slight stretch in your thigh. Switch legs and repeat.

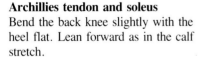

Archillies tendon and soleus
Bend the back knee slightly with the heel flat. Lean forward as in the calf stretch.

Groin (a)
With soles of the feet together, place hands around the feet and pull yourself forward.

Groin (b)
Move one leg forward until the knee is directly over the ankle. The back knee rests on the floor. Lean forward and hold.

(FIGURE 3-16) **Stretching exercises not only increase flexibility, but also decrease your chances of injury. Take time to stretch before doing any vigorous physical activity.**

(FIGURE 3-17) **Having good flexibility is an important requirement for dancers and gymnasts.**

Increasing Flexibility Even if you are not a gymnast or a dancer, flexibility can still be a goal for you. Doing stretching exercises results in the kind of flexibility shown in Figure 3-17. Warming up and cooling down should be part of your regular exercise routine. Keep in mind that good flexibility helps prevent injuries. A good time to stretch the muscles you will be working is after your cardiovascular warm-up. Again after your aerobic segment, while your muscles are very warm and full of blood, stretch each in turn for 10–20 seconds.

Changing Body Composition

The most effective program for achieving healthy body composition includes adequate aerobic exercise and resistance training coupled with a balanced diet. Starving yourself or using steroids may give results in the short-term, but the long-term consequences are not worth the risks to your health. Regular physical activity and sensible eating habits make a long term plan for enhancing your health.

Review

1. *What are your exercise goals?*

2. *Write out a realistic exercise plan to achieve your goals.*

3. *Critical Thinking You and your friend want to work out together, but you have different exercise goals. How might this difference affect your plan and results?*

Section 3.5 Sleep

Objectives

- *Know the two different categories of sleep.*
- *Describe what happens during each phase of the sleep cycle.*
- *Name two ways to cope with insomnia.*
- *Know how much sleep you need each night.*
  - **LIFE SKILLS: Solving Problems**

brain waves:

electrical patterns produced by the brain that fluctuate greatly during the sleep cycle.

There is another aspect to physical fitness. No matter how strong, flexible, lean, and aerobically healthy you are, you're not going to feel or function well if you don't get enough sleep. Most high school students need about eight or nine hours of sleep, but you may find that you do fine with seven, or that you can't stay alert unless you've gotten ten. Whatever your personal requirements are, try to stick to them, because it is while you are asleep that your body recovers from the activities of the day that has just ended, and prepares itself for the new day ahead.

What Happens When You Sleep?

It may seem as though your body shuts off completely while you're asleep. This is not totally off the track, because your breathing and heart rate do slow down, and your blood pressure and body temperature drop slightly. But at the same time, your brain continues to recognize outside information, so it remains about as active, in a different way, as it is when you're awake. It exhibits this activity in the form of **brain waves**, or electrical changes that take place in the brain. By studying these brain waves, scientists have been able to recognize the different stages of sleep, and what goes on in the brain during each phase.

The Sleep Cycle

Sleep can be divided into two categories. The first of these, called nonrapid eye movement sleep, or **NREM**, has four stages of its own. If you're like most teenagers, you spend only a short amount of time in stage I, which ends as soon as you have fallen asleep. When this happens, you enter stage II, in which your brain waves slow down. Those brain waves are at their slowest in stages III and IV, the phases of deepest sleep. Evidence indicates that the more you exercise, the more time you spend in stages

(FIGURE 3-18) **Your brain remains active and continues to process information when you are asleep.**

60 CHAPTER 3 PHYSICAL FITNESS

III and IV. These stages are believed to be the phases at which the body does most of its resting and restoring. Even so, most people enter these stages only during the first half of the night.

As brain wave activity increases again, you pass back through the sleep stages. When you return to Stage I, you enter the second category of sleep—rapid eye movement, or **REM.** Your brain waves become similar to those of the waking state, and your eyes move back and forth rapidly. Most dreams occur during this time. Although you might not remember your dreams, researchers think that everyone dreams during REM sleep. During the course of your night's sleep, you will experience four or five sleep cycles. About a fourth of your total sleeping time will be REM sleep.

The function of sleep is poorly understood. What is known is that adequate sleep is essential to good health. Also, people who suffer from chronic lack of sleep are more prone to accidents.

Insomnia

Everyone has **insomnia**, or trouble sleeping, from time to time. You may find it hard to get to sleep when you've got a big exam the next day, for instance, or when you've eaten too much at dinner. Maybe it's hot outside, and you find your room stuffy even with the windows open. In general, these are temporary situations. When they disappear, your insomnia should too. But if you have had trouble sleeping over the course of a few months, it could be more serious.

Long-term insomnia can cause moodiness and concentration lapses. It can also wear down your immune system, making you more vulnerable to illness. If you have had trouble sleeping for a long period of time, it could be that you're not getting enough exercise. You know now that exer-

cise helps the sleeping process because it makes you more tired at the right time. If you are exercising regularly and still have trouble sleeping, you may want to see a doctor.

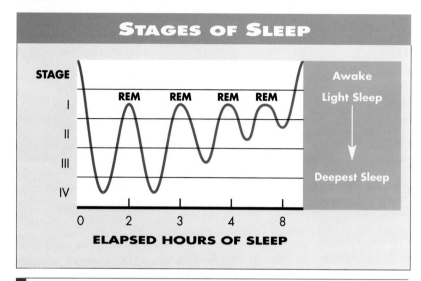

(FIGURE 3-19) **During a typical night you may pass through each stage of sleep four or five times.**

Tips for Sound Sleeping

If not everyone needs the same amount of sleep, how can you tell whether you're getting enough? You're the only one who can answer that question, so be honest about it. Recognize that you may need more sleep if you're feeling irritable, having trouble concentrating, or if you're just plain tired. It doesn't prove anything to stay up until 11:30 when you secretly felt like going to sleep at 10:00.

If you decide that you do need to get more sleep, or if you're suffering from insomnia, here are some ways to get back on track:

1. Keep a regular sleep schedule. Try to set a regular bedtime, so that you're "programmed" to get tired when it's time to turn in.
2. Go to bed when you're tired. It's pointless to stay up when you can't. If it's a little earlier than usual, enjoy the extra sleep you'll be getting.

REM:

(rapid eye movement) the dreaming part of the sleep cycle, in which the eyes move back and forth rapidly under the eyelids.

insomnia:

temporary or continuing loss of sleep.

(FIGURE 3-20) **If at all possible, eat dinner early in the evening. A too-full stomach can keep you awake at night.**

3. Finish your exercise program at least three hours before bedtime. It's not a great idea to do anything too physically trying right before going to sleep. Instead, do some reading, listen to music, or watch a little television, to get your mind off your day.

4. Keep your room dark and quiet. You may love to listen to the radio, but if you're having trouble getting to sleep, it may be keeping you up. Try doing without it.

5. Don't lie in bed if you can't sleep. In general, tossing and turning won't help you fall asleep. Get out of bed and try reading. A warm bath or shower sometimes helps too.

6. Don't use alcohol or tobacco. Alcohol may cause drowsiness, but it does not help insomnia. Besides being addictive and dangerous, tobacco contains ingredients that stimulate your mind and body, and is therefore the worst thing to take late at night.

7. Don't drink caffeine, which is also a stimulant, after about 6 P.M. If you do drink soda at night, be sure that it's decaffeinated.

8. Don't eat too late. Indigestion or a too-full stomach can cost you precious hours of sleep. If at all possible, eat dinner before 6 P.M., and avoid snacking right before going to bed.

9. Don't rely on over-the-counter sleep medications. They may help you sleep for a night, but they often leave you groggy in the morning. And if they do work once, you may start to depend on them to get to sleep.

If you find that none of these help you get the sleep you need, see a doctor. Long-term insomnia can be caused by a number of things, from mental depression to poor eating habits. A health professional can determine what the problem is, and can often help you sleep well again in no time. Getting the sleep you need is probably the easiest part of any physical fitness program, and is well worth the time you put into it.

Review

1. *Name the two categories of sleep.*

2. *Describe what happens during each phase of the sleep cycle.*

3. *Name two things you can do to help yourself sleep better.*

4. **LIFE SKILLS: Solving Problems** *You have a big test in the morning, and you know you haven't finished studying for it. But it's late, and you're getting really tired. What should you do?*

5. *Critical Thinking How does studying brain waves help scientists figure out what happens while we sleep?*

Summary

- Exercise offers benefits in four broad areas: aerobic fitness, muscle strength and endurance, body composition, and flexibility.

- Aerobic exercises such as walking, running, biking, and swimming can help your circulatory and respiratory systems stay healthy.

- Anaerobic exercises such as sprinting and weight lifting increase your muscle strength and muscle endurance.

- You can avoid many exercise injuries if you warm up correctly before your workout, and if you exercise regularly without pushing yourself.

- The sleep cycle consists of four stages of NREM sleep and a period of REM sleep.

Vocabulary

exercise physical activity that consists of a regular series of activities to train and strengthen the body.

endorphin a substance produced inside the brain that has pain-relieving properties.

flexibility the ability to move muscles and joints through their full range of motion.

body composition the division of total body weight into fat weight, and fat-free weight which includes muscle and bone.

aerobic exercise physical activity that increases the heart rate and supplies enough oxygen to the muscles so that the activity can be continued for a long period of time without resting.

anaerobic exercise physical activity that requires continuous effort over a short period of time, and that cannot be continued without resting.

anabolic steroid a drug that can temporarily increase muscle size.

brain waves electrical patterns produced by the brain that fluctuate greatly during the sleep cycle.

REM (rapid eye movement) the dreaming part of the sleep cycle, in which the eyes move back and forth rapidly under the eyelids.

insomnia temporary or continuing loss of sleep.

Concept Review . . . .

1. What are some physical changes resulting from regular, moderate exercise that you can't see?

2. What effect do endorphins have on your body?

3. How does rapid breathing during aerobic activity differ from that which results from anaerobic activity?

4. What are the three basic rules to know before you begin an exercise program?

5. What are three ways to avoid injuries when exercising?

6. If an accident or injury happens, what are the five simple actions involved in emergency treatment?

7. Name three effects of steroid abuse.

8. Describe what happens to your body while you sleep.

9. How do you know if you are getting enough sleep?

Expressing Your Views . . . .

1. Do you think Americans are more physically fit today than a century ago? Why or why not?

2. You've noticed that the football team begins every practice session with stretching exercises and ends every session jogging around the track. Why do you think the coach has the players do this?

3. Tim is 15 years old and wants big muscles. What type of exercise would be helpful for him? Sophia is 14 years old and wants to help her heart and lungs stay healthy. She doesn't enjoy exercising alone. What type of exercise would be suitable for her?

4. Why is it important to set goals when you start an exercise program? How can knowing your current fitness level help you to set goals?

Life Skills Check . . . . . .

1. Testing Physical Fitness

You would like to start an exercise program but you are not sure at what level you need to begin. What can you do to test your physical fitness?

2. Sleeping Well

Your friend has been having trouble sleeping at night. Often he is late to school or cancels weekend plans in order to catch up on sleep. What advice could you give your friend?

3. Determining Your Heart Rate

Work with a partner to identify each other's target pulse rates. One at a time, run in place for two or three minutes and take your pulse to find your MHR. Then determine your target pulse rate by using the directions on p. 47. What is your target pulse rate? Do you think this rate changes according to how fit you are?

Projects . . . .

1. Work with a group of students to find out what exercise, health, or sports facilities are available in or near your community. Are there swimming pools, tennis courts, jogging or biking trails, aerobics classes, basketball courts, or volleyball sand pits? If you live in a large city, each group might investigate one recreational area.

2. Design a survey to find out why people exercise. Think of four questions to ask, then work in a small group to collect and combine responses. Analyze the results to determine whether physical or psychological benefits were more motivating.

3. Write to the President's Council on Physical Fitness and request suitable programs or fitness norms for your age group. The address is
202 Pennsylvania Avenue NW
Suite 250
Washington DC 20004

Plan for Action . . . .

Plan a balanced weekly exercise program to fit your own personal needs.

CHAPTER 4

Nutrition Principles

◆ ◆ ◆ ◆

Section 4.1 Influences on Food Choices

Section 4.2 Nutritional Components of Food

Section 4.3 Analyzing Your Nutritional Needs

Section 4.4 Food Safety

Making sound choices about food involves reading labels and applying principles about nutrition.

Mary Anne is really hungry and tired. She's got two more classes and then band practice. A snack would be great right about now. Standing in front of the vending machine, she wonders what to pick—chips, candy, gum, pretzels, or cookies. The candy bar looks really good, especially since Mary Anne feels she needs energy to stay awake through her next two classes and get through the band workout. A half-hour after eating the candy bar, she feels terrible. Could Mary Anne have made a better snack choice from the machine to satisfy her hunger and give her a boost of energy?

4.1 Influences on Food Choices

Objectives

- Describe the difference between hunger and appetite.

- Describe how different factors affect your food choices.
  LIFE SKILLS: Assessing Your Health

- List the short-term consequences of making poor nutritional choices.

Picture yourself in this scene. Your best friend says she is hungry and wants a snack. You are not really hungry, but you decide to join her and eat anyway.

Hunger Selecting snacks and eating when you are not hungry are two situations that may be common in making choices about what and when you eat. To understand some important issues regarding food, you need to think about why you eat. There are two important terms that are related to

eating: hunger and appetite. **Hunger** is the body's physical response to the need for fuel. Your body uses food as the fuel to power the many chemical reactions that keep you alive and functioning. Hunger is a feeling you are born with. Symptoms of hunger include hunger pangs, weakness, dizziness, nausea, and a loss of concentration. Symptoms of hunger are relieved by eating. So how much should you eat? That is a question you will explore in detail in this chapter and the next one. For now, it is enough to say that you should eat until you feel full. The feeling of fullness you feel after eating is called *satiety*.

Appetite Hunger differs from appetite. **Appetite** describes your desire to eat based on the pleasure you get from eating certain foods. When you are dealing with appetite, you might ask, What do I want to eat? There are a number of factors that influence your appetite, such as the taste, texture, or aroma of certain foods. Your physical health can affect your appetite. If you are

hunger:

the body's physical response to the need for food.

appetite:

the desire to eat based on the pleasure derived from eating.

Check Up

Charting Your Appetite

Answer the following questions related to hunger and appetite on a separate sheet of paper.

1. When is your desire to eat strongest?

2. When is your desire to eat weakest?

3. What moods cause an increase in your appetite?

4. What moods reduce your appetite?

5. What people affect your appetite?

6. What places cause an increase in your appetite?

7. What times of day do you notice an increase in your appetite?

8. At what times of day or in what situations do you eat, even if you aren't hungry? Why?

Now look at your responses. Do you have food habits that can lead to overeating? What changes can you make to have better control over your appetite?

(FIGURE 4-1) Eating can be a highly social activity, causing you to eat even when you are not hungry.

sick, you generally don't feel like eating. If you become very active, your appetite can change. The weather can affect your appetite. Some people lose their appetites when it is very hot outside, or they will only eat cold foods. Your culture and religion can have a major effect on your appetite. You may derive a lot of pleasure from eating certain foods that you grew up eating. You may also lose your appetite when presented with foods from another culture that appear unappealing to you.

Appetite refers to a desire for food. Hunger is your body telling you to eat. When hunger and appetite work together, you have a nice balance. But if you let appetite drive your eating behavior, you eat even when you are not hungry. When some people are depressed, they eat because they think they will feel better. Other people refuse to eat when they are depressed. Some people eat out of habit. They eat dinner at 5 P.M. whether they are hungry or not. All these reasons for eating help explain why so many people have trouble managing their weight. To strike the right balance between hunger and appetite, you need to understand when and why you eat.

What you should learn from this chapter is to make your food selections based on sound nutritional practices. Selecting foods in this way will help maintain your physical and emotional well-being. Figure 4-2 lists major health problems related to poor nutrition. For young people, there is another special issue related to diet. Young people who are overweight are more likely to become obese adults.

Environmental Factors There are several factors that influence your choice of foods and how much of them you eat. Perhaps most important among these factors are the social influences. The kinds of food you select are often determined by such

Some Health Problems Related to Diet

Short Term Conditions

Fatigue
Bad moods
Depression

Long Term Conditions

Obesity
Heart disease
Stroke
Adult-onset diabetes
High blood pressure
Cirrhosis of the liver
Tooth decay
Cancer (some types)
Birth of low birth weight babies
    with poor mental and physical
    development
Dietary deficiency diseases
    (such as scurvy)

(FIGURE 4-2)

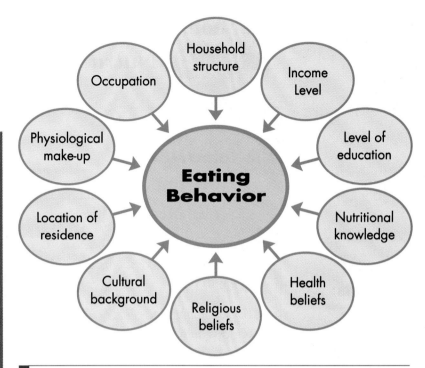

(FIGURE 4-3) **What you eat and when you eat is influenced by many factors. Describe how each of these factors affects your own food selections.**

things as your own family experiences, cultural heritage, cost, and other factors shown in Figure 4-3. For example, if you have grown up in the southwestern United States, you probably have eaten a lot of Mexican food even if it was not part of your ethnic background. Growing up on the East Coast, you might have eaten more seafood than someone who grew up in the Midwest Farm Belt. Your personality can also influence your food selections. Some people are very adventuresome about food and like to try new things. Other people feel very uncomfortable when faced with the thought of trying something new.

Review

1. How does hunger differ from appetite? Should you eat to satisfy hunger or to satisfy your appetite?

2. ▦ *LIFE SKILLS: Assessing Your Health* List two ways in which your ethnic background may affect the types of food you eat.

3. Describe two consequences of poor nutrition that could affect you as an adult.

4. *Critical Thinking* How do you know when you are hungry? How do you know when your appetite is at work?

• • • • •

Objectives

- Describe the roles and functions of the six classes of dietary nutrients.

- Identify problems that can occur from inadequate amounts of certain nutrients.

- List recommended dietary levels for various nutrients.

- Describe the differences among the various types of fats.

essential nutrients:

six categories of substances from food that nourish the body: carbohydrates, fats, proteins, vitamins, minerals, water.

calorie:

a unit of measurement for energy. 1 nutrition calorie = 1 kilocalorie.

carbohydrates:

a class of nutrients containing starches, simple sugars, glycogen, and dietary fiber.

Nutrition refers to the study of the way in which the substances in food affect our health. Over the last 100 years, the American diet has changed drastically. It was not uncommon for a person's diet 100 years ago to reflect a heavy dependence on grains, fruits, and vegetables. While there is far more attention paid today to health and nutrition, the typical American diet is not as nutritionally balanced as that of our grandparents. Analyzing your eating patterns is very important because diet is related to six of the ten leading causes of death in the United States. Diet also plays a role in infant death, tooth decay, and being overweight, as shown in Figure 4-3.

In a national survey of 10th-graders, most students knew that too much fat, sugar, or salt is unhealthy. They knew these substances increase the risk of getting diseases such as heart disease and cancer. However, most students didn't know which foods are high in fat, sugar, salt, and fiber. It is clear that their eating patterns frequently included fried foods, nutrient-poor snack foods, and beverages high in sugar.

Basic Principles of Nutrition

Foods contain substances needed for growth and development. The substances are classified into six groups called **essential nutrients,** which are necessary for the maintenance of health. There are six categories of essential nutrients: *carbohydrates, fats, proteins, vitamins, minerals, and water.* Of these six groups, carbohydrates, fats, and protein provide energy for the body in the form of **calories** *. The remaining three nutrients—vitamins, minerals, and water—are essential for the body to use these other nutrients properly.

Carbohydrates The term *carbohydrate* comes from the names of the three chemical elements in carbohydrates: carbon, oxygen, and hydrogen. In fact, the oxygen and hydrogen in carbohydrates are in the same proportions as found in water. Therefore, we get the name carbo (carbon) and hydrate (water).

Carbohydrates are our main source of food energy. One gram of carbohydrate provides 4 calories of available energy.

Carbohydrates can be divided into three classes based on their size: simple sugars, short-chain sugars, and long-chain sugars. Simple sugars are also called monosaccharides. The most important simple sugar is glucose because it is the major energy source for cells in your body. Carbohy-

---

*The nutrition calorie is actually a kilocalorie of energy (abbreviated kcal). There are 1000 calories in a nutrition calorie (sometimes spelled with a capital C).

(FIGURE 4-4) **Complex carbohydrates have the added value of providing dietary fiber.**

drates must be converted to glucose before they can be used as energy.

The carbohydrates in food except milk sugar (lactose) and glycogen are formed in plants. Simple sugars naturally occur in fruits, vegetables, honey, and molasses. The sugar you get from the sugar bowl is sucrose, a short-chain sugar. Sucrose is a disaccharide meaning that it is made from two monosaccharides.

Common long-chain sugars are starch, glycogen, and dietary fiber. These consist of long chains of simple sugars. Starches and fiber come from vegetables, potatoes, grains (such as rice, corn, wheat, and oats), and beans. Breads, cereals, and pasta are also made from grains. Almost all these sources of **complex carbohydrates** are low in fat and rich in vitamins, minerals, and fiber. Glycogen is "animal starch," a form of stored carbohydrate in the liver and muscles of animals.

Dietary fiber is a complex carbohydrate, but it does not provide energy (calories). Dietary fiber that does not dissolve in water is commonly called roughage because it provides bulk in the large intestine. Roughage helps to move undigested food through the digestive tract, preventing constipation and reducing the risk of certain diseases, such as colon cancer. Whole-grain wheat bran, corn, rice, corn bran, and rice bran are good sources of roughage. Some dietary fiber dissolves in water. This kind of fiber, found in oats and beans, helps to lower blood cholesterol and thus reduce the risk of cardiovascular disease. Fruits and vegetables contain both kinds of fiber.

Carbohydrates should make up 60 percent of your daily calories. Fewer than 10 percent of your day's calories should come from sugars. It is recommended that you consume between 20 and 35 grams of dietary fiber a day.

dietary fiber:

a subclass of complex carbohydrates with a high ratio of plant material that is not absorbed by the body.

complex carbohydrates:

a subclass of carbohydrates that includes starches, dietary fiber, and glycogen.

fats:

a class of nutrients that supply more energy per gram than carbohydrates or proteins.

saturated fats:

fats that contain single bonds between carbon atoms and the maximum number of hydrogen atoms bonded to carbon.

unsaturated fats:

fats that contain one or more double bonds between carbon atoms and have less than the maximum number of hydrogen atoms bonded to carbon.

Fat Fat is the most concentrated form of energy in food. Along with carbohydrates, fat is an important fuel for the body, yielding 9 calories per gram, or 252 calories per ounce. One tablespoon of fat contains about 13.5 grams of fat, or 120 calories. Like carbohydrates, fat consists of carbon, hydrogen, and oxygen, but these elements are arranged differently. And like glycogen, fat is stored in your body. Fat storage sites are called adipose, or fatty, tissue.

Fat in the diet belongs to a class of compounds called lipids. Lipids are essential for good health. Many hormones, including the sex hormones, are made from lipids. Several vitamins will dissolve only in fat. Fat takes a longer time to digest than either carbohydrates or protein, and it contributes to that sense of fullness that lasts for several hours after a meal.

Just as there are different kinds of dietary carbohydrates, there are also different kinds of dietary fat. They differ in their

chemical structure which affects their physical state at room temperature and their fate in the body.

The long chains of carbon atoms in **saturated fats** have all bond sites filled with hydrogen atoms. Saturated fats are often solid at room temperature, because the carbon chains are straight and can be layered. Animal fats, like butter and lard, are essentially saturated fat. Saturated fats predominate in only two vegetable oils—palm oil and coconut oil. But other vegetable oils can become saturated, either completely or partially, through a process called hydrogenation.

Unsaturated fats are also made of long carbon chains. However these chains consist of multiple bonds between carbon atoms leaving fewer bonds sites available for hydrogen atoms. Therefore, all the carbon atoms are not saturated with hydrogen atoms. Vegetable oils and fish oils are unsaturated by nature. Monounsaturated fats

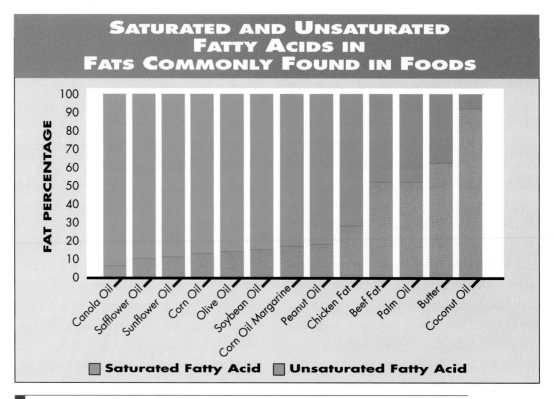

(FIGURE 4-5) **Avoid foods with ingredients that have high percentages of saturated fats.**

are liquid at room temperature, but they harden when refrigerated. Monounsaturated means that the bond between two carbon atoms is not saturated. Polyunsaturated fats have two or more carbon atoms that are not saturated.

Fats can play different roles in the development of disease. Saturated fats are linked to the development of cardiovascular disease and some forms of cancer. Monounsaturated and polyunsaturated oils appear to provide protection against the development of some of these diseases. But vegetable oils that have been hydrogenated are different. During hydrogenation, the bonding between carbon atoms in vegetable oils changes, producing fats called *trans* fats. Trans fats don't spoil rapidly and can be reused longer. However, trans fats behave like any other saturated fat in the body.

To reduce your risk of cardiovascular disease, cancer, and diabetes, limit the total amount of fat in your diet to no more than 30 percent of your day's total calories. Figure 4-7 shows the percentages of calories from fat in various foods. Compare the foods shown with what you normally eat.

Cholesterol **Cholesterol** is a fatlike substance found in some foods of animal origin. It is also produced by the liver. Cholesterol is part of the membrane around a cell, and it provides some protective cover-

ing to nerve fibers in the body. It is essential for the production of vitamin D and bile salts, which are used in the digestion of lipids. Cholesterol is also needed for the production of certain sex hormones. The body makes all the cholesterol it needs.

You may have heard two different terms associated with cholesterol, **high-density lipoproteins (HDL)** and **low-density lipoproteins (LDL)**. HDL is sometimes referred to as good cholesterol because it is thought to provide some protection against heart disease. LDL carries cholesterol and other fats from the digestive system through the blood to the body's cells. The amount of LDL in the blood is regulated by LDL receptors on cells. If there is too much cholesterol in the blood, it can build up on the walls of blood vessels. Eventually, these deposits can clog arteries and restrict the supply of oxygenated blood to the heart, resulting in a heart attack. It is now generally agreed that cholesterol levels in the blood should be below 200 milligrams per deciliter (mg/dL).

Diets that are high in fat increase blood cholesterol levels. Saturated fat is thought to cause the increase in cholesterol level by affecting the LDL cholesterol absorbed by the liver. Therefore dietary guidelines suggest reducing the intake of foods that are high in saturated fat to help lower cholesterol levels.

HDL:

(high-density lipoproteins) com-pounds that remove cholesterol from the blood and transport it back to the liver.

LDL:

(low-density lipoproteins) com-pounds that carry cholesterol to cells for cell processes.

cholesterol:

a fatlike substance that is part of all animal cells and is needed for the production of some hormones and fat digestion.

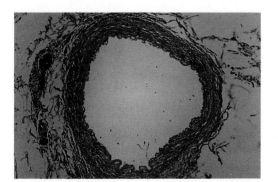 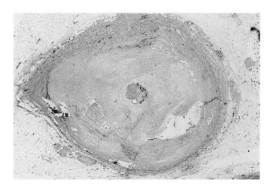

(FIGURE 4-6) **Heart disease resulting from clogged arteries can be the long-term effect of a diet that is high in cholesterol. The artery on the right is completely blocked with plaque. Start now to monitor cholesterol levels throughout your life.**

More than 75% calories from fat

SELECTED FOODS
Avocado
Bacon
Coconut
Cold cuts
Cream cheese
Frankfurters
Nuts
Olives
Peanut butter

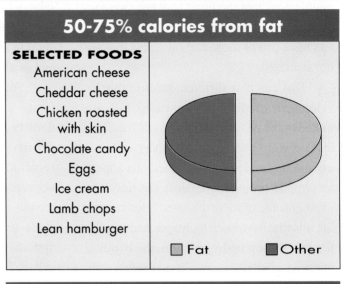

☐ Fat   ■ Other

50-75% calories from fat

SELECTED FOODS
American cheese
Cheddar cheese
Chicken roasted
with skin
Chocolate candy
Eggs
Ice cream
Lamb chops
Lean hamburger

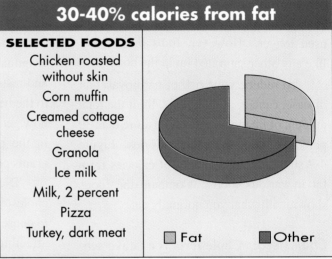

☐ Fat   ■ Other

40-50% calories from fat

SELECTED FOODS
Fried chicken
Sardines
Whole milk
Yogurt

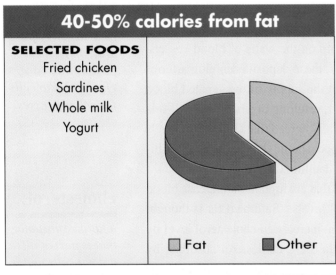

☐ Fat   ■ Other

30-40% calories from fat

SELECTED FOODS
Chicken roasted
without skin
Corn muffin
Creamed cottage
cheese
Granola
Ice milk
Milk, 2 percent
Pizza
Turkey, dark meat

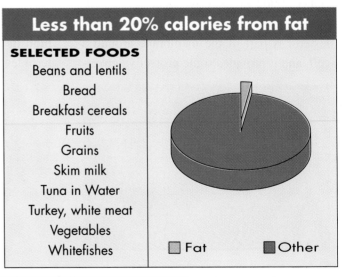

☐ Fat   ■ Other

20-30% calories from fat

SELECTED FOODS
Liver
Pancakes
Low fat yogurt
French toast
Crabmeat
Frozen yogurt

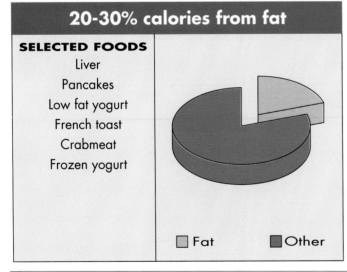

☐ Fat   ■ Other

Less than 20% calories from fat

SELECTED FOODS
Beans and lentils
Bread
Breakfast cereals
Fruits
Grains
Skim milk
Tuna in Water
Turkey, white meat
Vegetables
Whitefishes

☐ Fat   ■ Other

(FIGURE 4-7) **You might be surprised at the amount of fat some foods contain. Learn how to determine these percentages later in this chapter.**

Creating Complete Proteins

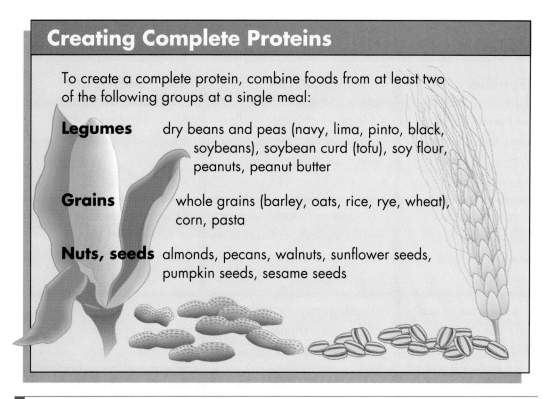

To create a complete protein, combine foods from at least two of the following groups at a single meal:

Legumes   dry beans and peas (navy, lima, pinto, black, soybeans), soybean curd (tofu), soy flour, peanuts, peanut butter

Grains   whole grains (barley, oats, rice, rye, wheat), corn, pasta

Nuts, seeds   almonds, pecans, walnuts, sunflower seeds, pumpkin seeds, sesame seeds

■ (FIGURE 4-8) **When selecting nuts and seeds to create complete proteins, limit the amount you eat because they are high in fat.**

Proteins Like carbohydrates and fats, **proteins** are made of carbon, hydrogen, and oxygen, but they also contain nitrogen. Proteins play a unique role in the growth and repair of body tissues. All cells contain some protein. It is also found in antibodies and some hormones. Enzymes that speed up the rate of chemical reactions in the body are proteins.

All proteins are made of amino acids. There are 20 amino acids; 11 of them can be made in the body and 9 others must be supplied by food. The 9 amino acids that cannot be produced in the body are called **essential amino acids.**

Because proteins perform so many necessary functions, you can see that the foods you select should include good sources of protein. However, the proteins found in the human body are not supplied directly from food. During digestion, proteins in food are broken down to their amino acids. These amino acids are the building blocks of new proteins for growth and tissue repair.

The proteins in food are sometimes classified as complete or incomplete proteins. A **complete protein** is one that contains all nine essential amino acids; an **incomplete protein** contains only some of these nine amino acids. Generally, foods that come from animal products (meat, poultry, fish, and milk products) contain complete proteins. Most proteins that come from plant sources are incomplete. It is possible, however, to get the proper amount of complete proteins from plant sources by selecting various protein sources so that all essential amino acids are supplied. Figure 4-8 contains a recommendation on how to select from a mix of plant foods to achieve a diet that has complete proteins. Proteins should make up about 10 percent of your daily caloric intake for adequate nutrition.

proteins:

class of nutrients consisting of long chains of amino acids, which are the basic components of body tissue and provide energy.

complete protein:

a protein that contains all nine essential amino acids.

incomplete protein:

a protein that lacks one or more of the essential amino acids.

essential amino acids:

a group of nine amino acids that cannot be manufactured by the body and must be supplied by food.

Fat Soluble Vitamins

Vitamin	Function	Sources	Deficiency
A	Maintains healthy eyes, skin, bones, teeth, keeps lining of digestive tract resistant to infection	Milk products, liver, yellow fruits and vegetables, dark-green leafy vegetables	Night blindness, impaired growth
D	Promotes normal growth, works with calcium and phosphorus in building bones and teeth	Fish-liver oils, fortified milk, liver, egg yolk, salmon, tuna	Rickets (inadequate growth of bones and teeth)
E	Prevents destruction of red blood cells; needed for certain enzymes to function	Wheat germ, vegetable oils, legumes, nuts, dark green vegetables	Red blood cell rupture causing anemia
K	Assists with blood clotting, bone growth	Green, leafy vegetables and vegetable oils, tomatoes, potatoes	Slow clotting of blood, hemorrhage

(FIGURE 4-9) **Fat-soluble vitamins can be stored in the body, while water-soluble vitamins (shown on the next page) cannot. It is best to obtain vitamins from food sources rather than from vitamin supplements.**

vitamins:

organic substances that assist in the chemical reactions that occur in the body.

Vitamins **Vitamins** are compounds that help regulate certain chemical reactions in the body. Though vitamins do not supply energy, they are essential for good health. The only vitamins the body can make are vitamins D and K.

Vitamins are grouped into two different categories: those that are fat soluble and those that are water soluble. *Fat soluble* means that the substance dissolves in fat. Fat-soluble vitamins include vitamins A, D, E, and K. Because they dissolve in fat, these vitamins can be stored in body fat. A balanced diet, which you will learn about in the next section, provides the right levels of fat-soluble vitamins and the fats needed to store these vitamins. If a person takes in high levels of fat-soluble vitamins either from food or from vitamin supplements, the excess is stored in the liver or skin and may be harmful. Figure 4-9 lists the fat-soluble vitamins, their sources, and their importance to health.

Water-soluble vitamins like the B group and vitamin C are not stored in the body. Because water-soluble vitamins dissolve in water, any excess is excreted in urine. Therefore, you must have consistent sources of water-soluble vitamins to prevent deficiency diseases. Figure 4-9 also lists the water-soluble vitamins, their sources, and their importance to health. A well-

Water Soluble Vitamins

Vitamin	Function	Sources	Deficiency
B_1 Thiamine	Assists with conversion of carbohydrates to energy, normal appetite and digestion, nervous system function	Pork products, liver, legumes, enriched and whole grain breads, cereals, nuts	Beriberi (inflamed nerves, muscle weakness, heart problems)
B_2 Riboflavin	Assists with nerve cell function, healthy appetite and release of energy from carbohydrates, protein, and fats	Milk, eggs, whole grain products, green leafy vegetables, dried beans, enriched breads, cereals, and pasta	Cheilosis (skin sores on nose and lips, sensitive eyes)
B_3 Niacin	Maintenance of normal metabolism, digestion, nerve function, energy release	Red meats, organ meats, fish, enriched breads and cereals	Pellagra (soreness on mouth, diarrhea, irritability, depression)
B_6 Pyridoxine	Necessary for normal carbohydrate, protein and fat metabolism	Whole grain products, fish, bananas, green leafy vegetables	Anemia, dermatitis
B_{12}	Necessary for formation of red blood cells; normal cell function	Lean meats, liver, egg products, milk, cheese	Pernicious anemia, stunted growth
Folacin	Necessary for formation of hemoglobin in red blood cells; necessary for production of genetic material	Green vegetables, liver, whole grain products, legumes	Anemia, diarrhea
Pantothenic Acid	Assists with energy release from carbohydrates, protein, and fats; used to produce some hormones	Whole grain cereals, liver, green vegetables, eggs, nuts	Reduced resistance to stress
Biotin	Necessary for normal metabolism of carbohydrates and some other B vitamins	Organ meats, egg yolks, green vegetables	Skin disorders, hair loss
C Ascorbic Acid	Needed for normal development of connective tissue, including those holding teeth; wound healing; use of iron	Citrus fruits, melons, green vegetables, peppers	Scurvy (slow healing of wounds, bleeding gums and loose teeth)

minerals:

inorganic substances that are generally absorbed to form structural components of the body.

balanced diet provides enough of each of the necessary vitamins; no vitamin supplements should be necessary.

Minerals Minerals are naturally occurring substances that contribute to the normal functioning of the body. Unlike vitamins, which are produced and found in living materials, minerals are not produced by living organisms. More than 20 minerals are necessary for healthy functioning. Figure 4-10 contains a summary of some essential minerals.

Minerals are divided into two categories: macrominerals, which include calcium, chlorine, magnesium, phosphorus, potassium, sodium, and sulfur; and trace minerals, which include chromium, fluorine, copper, iodine, iron, manganese, selenium, and zinc. Macrominerals are needed in larger amounts by the body, and trace minerals are needed in smaller quantities. All minerals are found in nature in combination with other minerals. Their combinations are known as *salts*. When salts are in solution, they dissolve to form charged particles that are capable of conducting an electric current. These dissolved salts are called *electrolytes*.

Proper electrolyte balance is needed to keep the body's internal environment stable. Sodium and chlorine are two minerals that have received a lot of attention because of their role in regulating fluid balance. An excess of sodium has been linked to high blood pressure.

Ordinary table salt is a combination of sodium and chlorine, and it is a major source of *sodium* in the diet. One teaspoon of table salt provides about 2,000 mg of sodium. The amount of sodium inside and outside of your body cells must be kept in a delicate balance, and a diet high in salt may upset this balance. Health problems linked to high salt intake include high blood pressure, abnormal heart rhythms, fluid around the heart, and overburdened kidneys. For this reason, it is recommended that your daily sodium intake be less than 3,000 mg. Because the link between salt and heart problems has been so publicized, most people watch the amount of salt they use to season food. The bulk of excess salt in the diet comes from packaged foods and fast, convenient foods.

The role of *calcium* and *magnesium* in bone growth and development makes them minerals of major importance. As a teen, you might not worry about your bones thinking that diseases such as osteoporosis only affect older people. But you are building bone now, and the amount of bone that you build before age 35 will influence whether you develop weakened and brittle bones as you age. Calcium and magnesium are two minerals that help build dense, strong bones. Dark green, leafy vegetables are high in magnesium and calcium, and dairy products are high in calcium. These two minerals are also responsible for efficient muscular contraction and relaxation. When you eat a varied diet balanced in both minerals, you will also be consuming other needed minerals.

Growth that occurs during adolescence requires a tremendous amount of energy—to run normal body systems. Iron deficiency anemia, which is due to a lack of iron in the diet and is common in both males and females, can result in fatigue. If you do not eat a lot of foods that are rich in iron, you can improve the absorption of iron by including more vitamin C in your diet. Vitamin C makes the iron in plant foods more available to your body.

Water Water is an essential compound in your diet. About two-thirds of your body

Listing of Important Minerals and Their Function

Mineral	Function	Sources
Calcium	Necessary for normal growth of bones and teeth, transmission of nerve cell impulses, muscle contraction	Milk and dairy products, dark leafy green vegetables
Chromium	Necessary for proper blood sugar regulation and insulin activity	Cheese, plums, apple juice, prunes, peanuts and peanut butter, corn and corn oil, mushrooms
Copper	Needed for normal production of hemoglobin, bone, and melanin (involved in skin color)	Liver, shellfish, legumes, nuts, whole-grain products
Iodine	Essential for production of thyroid hormone	Iodized salt, seafood
Iron	Found in hemoglobin; needed for some enzymes	Organ meats, red meat, whole grains, dark green vegetables, legumes
Magnesium	Needed for chemical reactions during metabolism	Milk, dairy products, green leafy vegetables
Manganese	Used in enzymes for synthesis of cholesterol, formation of urea, normal function of nervous tissue	Whole grain products, leafy green vegetables, fruits, legumes, nuts
Potassium	Helps maintain normal metabolism, nerve and muscle function	Meats, poultry, fish, fruits, vegetables
Selenium	Needed for healthy heart function, protects against heavy metal toxicity	Tuna and other seafood, whole grains, organ meats, molasses, Brazil nuts
Sodium	Essential for proper water balance in cells and tissues; nerve cell conduction	Table salt, high salt meats (ham), cheeses, crackers
Sulfur	Found in several amino acids	Meats, milk, eggs, legumes, nuts
Zinc	Needed for several digestive enzymes; plays a role in respiration, bone and liver metabolism, and healing of wounds	Seafood, meats, milk, poultry

(FIGURE 4-10) **The amount of minerals you need to consume each day measures out to about a tablespoon. You need greater amounts of minerals than vitamins.**

weight is water (65 to 70 percent in males, 55 to 65 percent in females). The percentage of water in the body depends on the amount of body fat a person has. People with high percentages of body fat have lower percentages of body water than normal. Much of this water is found inside your cells. The remaining water is found in the spaces surrounding cells, and in your bloodstream. Most body fluids, such as blood and digestive juices, are 80 percent water. If a 16-year-old male weighs 150 pounds, as much as 105 pounds of that weight is water. Similarly for a 16-year-old female weighing 120 pounds, as much as 78 pounds of that weight is water. The impor-tance of water in the diet becomes obvious when you look at all the ways the body uses water to maintain its stability.

Functions of Water in the Body

1. All body functions are the result of chemical reactions. Most chemical re-actions in the body can occur only in a water medium because substances dis-solve in water.
2. The speed at which some of these chemi-cal reactions occur is affected by how acidic body fluids are. Water helps maintain acidity at the proper levels.

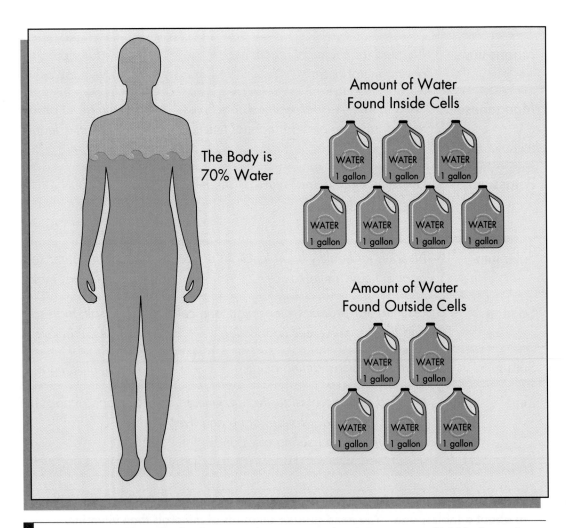

The Body is 70% Water

Amount of Water Found Inside Cells

Amount of Water Found Outside Cells

■ (FIGURE 4-11) **Since the body is mostly water, maintaining proper fluid balance is critical for good health.**

3. Water is a product of the chemical reactions that supply energy to drive your body processes.
4. Water in body fluids provides a medium to transport gases, nutrients, and waste products throughout the body.
5. Water helps regulate body temperature. Water loss through perspiration helps cool the body.

Dehydration Water is so vital that it is rare to live for more than 10 days without water, even though you could live several weeks without food. When the amount of water you excrete exceeds the amount of water you take in, you are in a state of **dehydration.** Dehydration can occur as a result of heavy physical activity or an illness that includes vomiting, diarrhea, or fever. Situations that cause you to sweat profusely can also cause dehydration if you are not drinking enough water. Drinking too much alcohol or eating a high-protein diet can also cause dehydration. A prolonged state of dehydration can lead to kidney failure and death.

We take in water by drinking fluids and eating. Many foods contain large amounts of water. You need to consume at least one-half ounce of water daily for every pound of body weight, which totals at least two quarts. If you are very active or live in a very hot climate, extreme water loss through sweating could interfere with your body's functions.

A simple way to find out if you're adequately hydrated is to check the color of your urine throughout the day. If it is clear and uncolored, your water intake is adequate. If it is colored to any degree, you need to drink more water. If it is highly colored, you definitely need to increase your intake. It is especially important to drink enough water if you are trying to lose weight.

(FIGURE 4-12) **Drinking water after heavy activity replaces fluids lost from sweating.**

Review

1. Describe the importance of complex carbohydrates in the diet.

2. Which nutrient supplies the most calories per ounce?

3. How does a low calcium intake affect the body?

4. Why should you limit the amount of sodium in your diet?

5. Why are saturated fats to be avoided in making food selections?

6. How much of your daily caloric intake should come from carbohydrates, fats, and proteins?

7. Why do you need to have some fat in your diet?

8. *Critical Thinking* Why is it misleading to label peanut butter as having "no cholesterol"?

dehydration:
a state in which the body has lost more water than has been taken in.

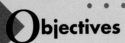
Analyzing Your Nutritional Needs

Objectives

- *Define the nutritional requirements for healthy teens.*

- *Classify foods into the appropriate food groups.*

- *Interpret food labeling to analyze nutritional breakdown.*

- *Make food selections that satisfy nutritional requirements using the Food Pyramid and Dietary Guidelines.*
  - **LIFE SKILLS: Making Responsible Decisions**

- *Identify special nutritional needs of selected populations.*

Knowing about the principles of nutrition is just the first step in improving your health. Putting those principles into action is the next and most important step.

The Dietary Guidelines for Americans were developed to reflect what is currently known about the effect that diet has on health. The guidelines listed in Figure 4-13 provide a profile of a healthful diet and focus on seven eating practices.

Balance of Energy From Nutrients

Recall that three nutrients provide calories—carbohydrates, proteins, and fats. Balancing the calories from these three nutrient groups is the key to improving your diet. When you balance the calories provided by these larger nutrients, many of the nutrients needed in smaller quantities fall into place.

The Daily Reference Values listed in Figure 4-14 describe the percentage of your daily calories that should come from carbohydrates, protein, and fat. These values were designed to help you follow the recommendations of the general guidelines in Figure 4-13. Notice that most of these values can be found in the Nutrition Facts portion of a food label. If you can improve

Dietary Guidelines for Americans

Eat a variety of foods.

Maintain a healthful weight.

Choose a diet that is low in fat, saturated fat, and cholesterol.

Choose a diet with plenty of fruits, vegetables, and grain products.

Use sugars only in moderation.

Use salt and other forms of sodium only in moderation.

For adults who drink alcohol, do so only in moderation.

(FIGURE 4-13) **These recommendations were released in 1990 from the U.S. Department of Agriculture (USDA) and the U.S. Department of Health and Human Services (USDHHS).**

Daily Reference Values (DRVs)

Food component	Daily Reference Value
Total fat	65 g, 30% of total energy requirement
Saturated fat	20 g, 10% of total energy requirement
Cholesterol	300 mg
Total carbohydrate	300 g, 60% of total energy requirement
Dietary fiber	25 g
Protein	50 g, 10% of total energy requirement
Potassium	3500 mg
Sodium	2400 mg

(FIGURE 4-14) **Daily Reference Values are used as the standard for food labels which show the percentages of nutrients suggested for a 2,000 calorie diet.**

(FIGURE 4-15) **Reference Daily Intakes (RDIs) have replaced the U.S. Recommended Dietary Allowances (RDAs), which were once the accepted nutrition standard.**

your diet on a daily basis, then in the long run you'll be making choices about foods that match the dietary guidelines. There may be some days when you find it more difficult to follow the guidelines. One or two-less-than perfect days out of a week don't hurt your efforts to improve your nutrition.

Getting the nutrition you need during your teen years doesn't mean you have to completely give up your favorite foods. But if your favorite foods are high in sugar, calories, and fat, or if your favorite foods are low in fiber or other essential nutrients, you may need to make some changes to your diet to increase its nutritional value and follow the dietary guidelines. As a teen, you have an even greater need for some nutrients because your body is changing.

In some situations, the nutritional needs of a teen differ from those shown in Figure 4-15. For instance, vegetarians, athletes, and teen mothers have additional nutritional requirements that must be met to maintain health.

Some Vitamin and Mineral Reference Daily Intakes (RDIs)

(for adults and children 4 or more years of age)

Mineral/Vitamin	Quantity
Calcium	1 g (gram)
Iron	18 mg (milligrams)
Magnesium	400 mg
Copper	20 mg
Vitamin A	5,000 IUs (international units)
Vitamin C	60 mg
Vitamin D	400 IUs
Vitamin E	30 IUs

How Much Do You Know About Food Selection?

From the statements listed below, choose the best answer. Then check the correct answers below.

1. Cooking practice that increases fat in foods
   baking   broiling   frying   don't know

2. Boiling vegetables reduces vitamins
   yes   no   don't know

3. Salt in peanut butter-and-jelly sandwich compared with a hot dog
   less salt   more   same   don't know

4. Salt in canned vegetables compared with frozen
   less salt   more   same   don't know

5. Fat in frozen yogurt compared with ice cream
   less fat   more   same   don't know

6. Fiber in corn flakes compared with bran cereal
   less fiber   more   same   don't know

7. Fiber in baked beans compared with baked potato
   less fiber   more   same   don't know

8. Eating fatty foods may cause
   cavities   stomach cancer
   heart disease   don't know

9. Eating too little fiber may cause
   colon cancer   high blood pressure
   heart disease   don't know

10. Eating sugar may cause
    heart disease   low blood pressure
    cavities   don't know

11. Amount of iron needed by females compared with males
    less iron   more   same   don't know

12. Amount of calcium needed by teenagers compared to middle-aged women
    less calcium   more   same   don't know

1) frying; 2) yes; 3) less salt; 4) more salt; 5) less fat; 6) less fiber; 7) more fiber; 8) heart disease; 9) colon cancer; 10) cavities; 11) more iron; 12) more calcium

Categorizing Foods— The Food Pyramid

You should know by now that the best nutritional strategies include eating a variety of foods. When you choose a variety of foods, your diet can supply all your daily requirements. One way to select from a variety of foods is by grouping them. The idea of four basic food groups was once used to group foods for nutritional purposes. In May 1992, the U.S. Department of Agriculture provided a new way of categorizing foods called the Food Pyramid, shown in Figure 4-16 on the next page.

Let's look at how the Food Pyramid should be used in planning your diet. The pyramid organizes foods into groups based on the Dietary Guidelines. Notice that the bread, cereal, rice, and pasta group is on the bottom. This placement indicates that foods from this group should be the largest part of your diet. Each day, you should have 6 to 11 servings from this group for good health. Figure 4-17 shows some foods that are part of this group.

As you move up the pyramid, you see that you need fewer servings from the remaining groups to be healthy. For example, you need 3 to 5 servings daily from the vegetable group and 2 to 4 servings from the fruit group. You need only 2 to 3 servings from the milk, yogurt, and cheese group, and the same number of servings from the meat, poultry, fish, dry beans, eggs, and nuts group. Finally, at the top of the pyramid you find fats, oils, and sweets. Foods in this category are not part of a food group. These foods should be selected sparingly as part of your diet.

Bread, Cereal, Rice, and Pasta Group

Foods from this group are made from whole grains and grain products. The term "cereal" is used to describe the food crops— rice, wheat, and corn. These grains supply more than half of the energy humans use

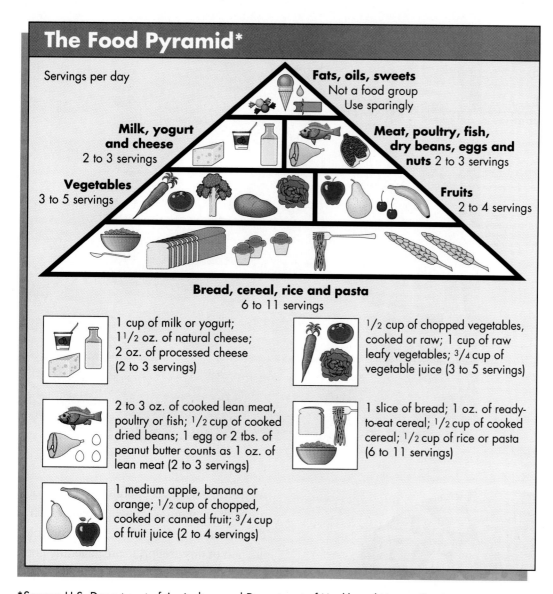

The Food Pyramid*

Servings per day

Fats, oils, sweets
Not a food group
Use sparingly

Milk, yogurt and cheese
2 to 3 servings

Meat, poultry, fish, dry beans, eggs and nuts 2 to 3 servings

Vegetables
3 to 5 servings

Fruits
2 to 4 servings

Bread, cereal, rice and pasta
6 to 11 servings

1 cup of milk or yogurt; 1 1/2 oz. of natural cheese; 2 oz. of processed cheese (2 to 3 servings)

1/2 cup of chopped vegetables, cooked or raw; 1 cup of raw leafy vegetables; 3/4 cup of vegetable juice (3 to 5 servings)

2 to 3 oz. of cooked lean meat, poultry or fish; 1/2 cup of cooked dried beans; 1 egg or 2 tbs. of peanut butter counts as 1 oz. of lean meat (2 to 3 servings)

1 slice of bread; 1 oz. of ready-to-eat cereal; 1/2 cup of cooked cereal; 1/2 cup of rice or pasta (6 to 11 servings)

1 medium apple, banana or orange; 1/2 cup of chopped, cooked or canned fruit; 3/4 cup of fruit juice (2 to 4 servings)

*Source: U.S. Department of Agriculture and Department of Health and Human Services

■ (FIGURE 4-16) **The Food Pyramid replaces the four food groups concept.**

daily. Foods derived from these cereal crops are good sources of complex carbohydrates and dietary fiber. They are generally low in fat and high in B vitamins. ''Generally low in fat'' means you should look at labels to determine if the food selection from this group is low in fat. Recommended serving sizes from this group include one slice of bread, one-half cup of cereal, or one-half cup of pasta.

Foods to Limit: Foods containing a lot of butter or eggs should be limited. For example, the following could be very high in fat, cholesterol, and calories: butter rolls, croissants, cheese breads, egg breads, store-bought donuts, muffins, sweet rolls, and biscuits. Buttered popcorn (including microwave products), foods made with coconut or palm oil, soups made with cream, and high-fat meats should also be limited.

(FIGURE 4-17) **You should have 6 to 11 servings daily from foods in the bread, cereal, rice, and pasta group. Limit sweet bakery in favor of low-sugar, complex carbohydrates.**

(FIGURE 4-18) **Signs in most produce markets remind you to "Eat Five a Day," which means you should eat at least five servings of fruits and vegetables daily.**

Vegetable Group Foods from this group are high in vitamins, minerals, and carbohydrates and very low in fat. All vegetables are part of this group and are generally good sources of dietary fiber. These foods generally supply the best nutrition for the fewest calories.

The size of a serving is a half-cup of cooked or raw vegetables, a cup of raw leafy vegetables, or three-fourths cup of vegetable juice. Select a vegetable or fruit that is high in vitamin C at least once a day. Select vegetables and fruits that are high in vitamin A several times a week.

Vitamin C-rich vegetables: asparagus, broccoli, brussel sprouts, cabbage, greens (mustard, kale, collard, beet), green pepper, potatoes, spinach, and tomatoes.

Vitamin A-rich vegetables: broccoli, carrots, greens, pumpkin, romaine lettuce, spinach, sweet potatoes, tomatoes, and winter squash.

Foods to Limit: Though most fruits and vegetables are low in fat, avocados and olives should be limited, as they are high in fat and therefore high in calories.

Fruit Group Foods from this group are also high in vitamins and minerals while being low in fat. Like vegetables, fruits are also good sources of dietary fiber. The fiber content of raw fruit or dried fruit is much higher than that of fruit juices. If you prefer fruit juice, drink 100 percent juice. Fruit drinks do not have the same nutritional value as juices. If you eat canned or frozen fruits, select those packed in light syrups or natural juices.

The size of a serving is one medium-sized piece of fresh fruit, such as an apple, banana, or orange; one-half cup of chopped, cooked, or canned fruit; or three-fourths cup of fruit juice. In making selections in this group, you should also look for good sources of vitamins A and C.

Vitamin C-rich fruits: tomatoes, cantaloupe, grapefruit, oranges, and tangerines.

Vitamin A-rich fruits: tomatoes, apricots, cantaloupe, mango, papaya, and peaches.

Milk, Yogurt, and Cheese Group All dairy products are found in this group. This group provides the best sources of calcium, good sources of protein, vitamins A and D, and some minerals. Teens and young adults are still building their bones and need the calcium supplied by five servings a day from this group. One cup of milk or yogurt, one and one-half ounces of cheese, or two ounces of processed cheese are recommended serving sizes.

Foods to Limit: Milk products with more than 1 percent fat should be limited. This includes buttermilk and yogurt made from whole milk; condensed milk, evaporated milk, all types of cream, nondairy cream substitutes, and any sour cream sub-

(FIGURE 4-19) **You should have two to three servings daily from foods in the milk, yogurt, and cheese group. Limit cheese and milk products with high fat content. Those items shown are good low-fat selections.**

stitutes with palm oil. Also limit cheeses with more than 2 grams of fat per ounce of cheese, such as cream cheese, creamed cottage cheese, and most processed cheeses.

Meat, Poultry, Fish, Dry Beans, Eggs, and Nuts Group These foods are high in protein and B vitamins, and are also good sources of certain minerals. Foods from this group can be very high in fat and cholesterol. Good choices are the leanest possible cuts of any meat. Skinless poultry and fish are preferred selections over red meat. The new turkey-based products, such as turkey hot dogs, cold cuts, and sausages are the food industry's way of providing foods with less fat than the pork or beef versions. The serving size for this group would be 2 to 3 ounces of cooked lean meat, poultry, or fish. One egg or 2 tablespoons of peanut butter count as 1 ounce of lean meat.

Foods to Limit: Select low-fat meats with no more than 2 grams of fat per ounce

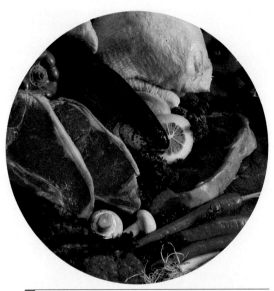

(FIGURE 4-20) **You should select two to three servings daily from foods in this group. Select low-fat ways to prepare meats, fish, eggs, and poultry. Note that nuts and beans are also part of this group.**

of meat. Limit bacon, sausage, corned beef, pastrami, ribs, regular ground meat, goose, duck, and organ meats. Though liver is high in cholesterol, it is very rich in iron and vitamins. Liver provides important nutrients and should be eaten in moderation. Peanut butter and most nuts are high in fat and should be eaten sparingly.

Fats-Sweets The top of the pyramid contains foods that are high in calories, sugars, and fats but are low in nutrients. This section of the pyramid also contains beverages, that are high in sugar, and other drinks, such as coffee, tea, and alcohol, that provide little or no nutrition. Refined sugars and natural sweetners like honey, molasses, and maple syrup and refined sugars are part of this section along with foods high in sugars, such as candy bars, cakes, and pies. Foods high in fat also belong in this section. High-fat diets have been linked to increased risk of heart disease and certain kinds of cancer. In addition, foods from this group contribute to obesity. Therefore, all the foods that fall in this category should be used sparingly. In fact, it is better to go several days without eating foods from this group.

Nutritional Labeling

The food pyramid is a giant step forward in "seeing" what makes a healthful diet. When the food pyramid was introduced, many changes were taking place in the ways government agencies were educating the public about food selection. Unlike other countries where deficiencies of protein and calories still exist, the United States has an abundance of food. The dietary deficiency diseases are rarely seen anymore in our country. But the United States has two primary nutritional problems affecting the health of its children, teens, and adults: consuming too many calories and not getting enough exercise.

One of the most significant changes aimed at educating the public has been the new food label. Figure 4-21 shows you an example of how the label's information can help you make smart food choices and follow the dietary guidelines.

Reading Labels

The new label gives information about the nutrients that make it easier to determine which foods fall within your guidelines for kinds of fat, complex carbohydrates, fiber, and sugar. Few foods are exempt from the labeling requirements. The labeling standards prevent misleading claims about foods advertised as "low fat," "low cholesterol," reduced sugar," or "fat free."

Serving Size—The Basis of Comparison If you eat more or less than the serving size, you'll need to adjust the amount of each nutrient to reflect your serving.

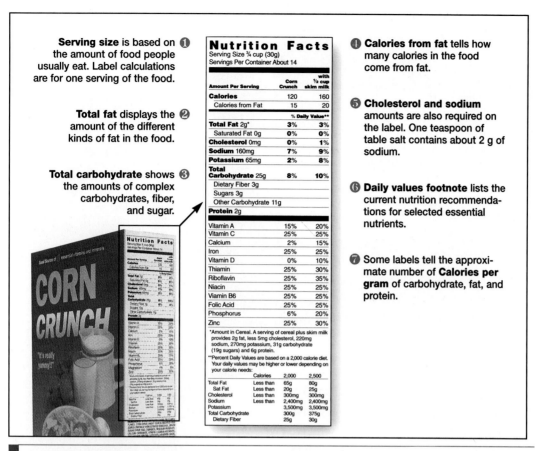

The callout labels around the figure:

Serving size is based on ❶ the amount of food people usually eat. Label calculations are for one serving of the food.

Total fat displays the ❷ amount of the different kinds of fat in the food.

Total carbohydrate shows ❸ the amounts of complex carbohydrates, fiber, and sugar.

Calories from fat tells how ❹ many calories in the food come from fat.

Cholesterol and sodium ❺ amounts are also required on the label. One teaspoon of table salt contains about 2 g of sodium.

Daily values footnote lists the ❻ current nutrition recommendations for selected essential nutrients.

Some labels tell the approxi- ❼ mate number of **Calories per gram** of carbohydrate, fat, and protein.

Nutrition Facts

Serving Size ¾ cup (30g)
Servings Per Container About 14

Amount Per Serving	Corn Crunch	with ½ cup skim milk
Calories	120	160
Calories from Fat	15	20

	% Daily Value**	
Total Fat 2g*	3%	3%
Saturated Fat 0g	0%	0%
Cholesterol 0mg	0%	1%
Sodium 160mg	7%	9%
Potassium 65mg	2%	8%
Total Carbohydrate 25g	8%	10%
Dietary Fiber 3g		
Sugars 3g		
Other Carbohydrate 11g		
Protein 2g		

Vitamin A	15%	20%
Vitamin C	25%	25%
Calcium	2%	15%
Iron	25%	25%
Vitamin D	0%	10%
Thiamin	25%	30%
Riboflavin	25%	35%
Niacin	25%	25%
Vitamin B6	25%	25%
Folic Acid	25%	25%
Phosphorus	6%	20%
Zinc	25%	30%

*Amount in Cereal. A serving of cereal plus skim milk provides 2g fat, less 5mg cholesterol, 220mg sodium, 270mg potassium, 31g carbohydrate (19g sugars) and 6g protein.

**Percent Daily Values are based on a 2,000 calorie diet. Your daily values may be higher or lower depending on your calorie needs:

		Calories	2,000	2,500
Total Fat	Less than		65g	80g
Sat Fat	Less than		20g	25g
Cholesterol	Less than		300mg	300mg
Sodium	Less than		2,400mg	2,400mg
Potassium			3,500mg	3,500mg
Total Carbohydrate			300g	375g
Dietary Fiber			25g	30g

■ (FIGURE 4-21) **The listing of Nutrition Facts on food labels is now required by law. You can use these data to make informed choices about foods so that your diet fits the Dietary Guidelines for Americans.**

Labeling about Calories Excess calories is one reason for weight gain.

Terms You Should Know

Calorie-free: fewer than 5 calories per serving

Low calorie: 40 calories or less per serving

Reduced or fewer calories: at least 25 percent fewer calories per serving than the reference food

Labeling about Sugar Sugar values on the label include naturally occurring sugars, such as milk sugar, and refined sugars added during processing. However, the nutrition label does not account for longer-chain sugars in the food. To keep your sugar intake at or below 10 percent of your day's calories, you'll need to read the ingredient list. Ingredients such as *sugar* (sucrose), *fructose,* *maltose, lactose, honey, syrup, corn syrup, high-fructose corn syrup, molasses,* and *fruit juice concentrate* indicate added sweeteners. If any of these ingredients appears first or second or if several of them appear in the list, the food is probably high in sugar.

Terms You Should Know

Sugar free: there is either no sugar in the food or less than 0.5 gram per serving

No sugar added, Without added sugar: no sugars or ingredients that contain sugars have been added and processing does not increase the sugar content above the amount that is naturally found in the ingredients.

Reduced sugar: contains at least 25 percent less sugar per serving than the reference food

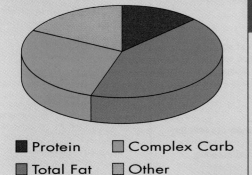

NUTRITIONAL ANALYSIS OF FAST FOOD LUNCH

933 Total Calories

Protein..............13%
Total Fats 42%
Complex Carbohydrates ..28%
Sugar...............16%

■ Protein   □ Complex Carb
■ Total Fat   □ Other

(FIGURE 4-22) **The fast-food diet is high in calories and fat. Compare these values to the guidelines in Figure 4-14.**

Labeling About Fat The label makes total fat and saturated fat values very visible, but reading the ingredients list will give you a more complete picture. The values listed on the label include all naturally saturated fats unless there is less than 0.5 g. If you want to limit your intake of saturated fat from both animal and vegetable sources, read the label and look for the words *hydrogenated* or *partially hydrogenated* used to describe a vegetable oil. Even though these vegetable oils are naturally unsaturated before hydrogenation, they will not be included as unsaturated fat.

Know Your Fat Limit

	Daily calorie level			
	1600	2000	2500	2800
Total fat (grams)	52	65	81	91
Saturated fat (grams)	18	20	25	31

Labeling About Fiber If the labeling claims that the product is high in fiber, either the food must be low in fat or the level of total fat must appear next to the high-fiber claim.

Terms You Should Know
High fiber: 5 grams or more per serving
Good source of fiber: between 2.5 and 5 grams per serving
More or added fiber: at least 0.5 grams more per serving than the reference food

Labeling about Carbohydrates The label will provide values for the amount of dietary fiber, but it will make no distinction between fiber in the food that dissolves or does not dissolve. If you are trying to calculate the number of calories from carbohydrates, don't include the grams of fiber in the calculation. Fiber does not provide calories.

General Labels Food manufacturers sometimes alter food in order to make it more appealing to the consumer, who may be concerned about the number of calories, the sodium level, or the fat content. Two terms, *light* and *lite* are commonly used to compare these altered foods with their reference foods and may mean one of two things:

- the altered product contains one-third fewer calories or half the fat of the reference food, or
- the sodium content of a low-calorie, low-fat food has been reduced to half of its original sodium content.

The American Diet

How does the American diet compare with recommended dietary guidelines? A meal that is fairly standard for teenagers consists of a hamburger, a large order of french-fried potatoes, and a cola drink. According to the Daily Reference Values for a 2000 calorie diet, 200 calories (10 percent) should come from protein. For a 2500 calorie diet, 250 calories (10 percent) should come from protein. In a day, no more than 30 percent of your total calories should come from fats, 10 percent from proteins, and 60 percent from carbohydrates. Figure 4-22 is a summary of the nutritional content of this fast food.

As you can see, this one meal provides more than 46 percent of the caloric intake of a 2000 calorie diet and more than 37 percent of a 2500 calorie diet. This meal contains an appropriate amount of protein, but far too much fat and far too few complex carbohydrates.

Guidelines for Improving Your Food Selections

Now that you have read about basic nutrition principles, you can use the following points to guide you in making nutritious food selections.

1. **Sugars**

   To reduce the amount of refined sugars in your diet you can

   a. reduce the number of soft drinks you have each day.
   b. eat fresh fruit for dessert instead of baked goods.
   c. read food labels and reduce your intake of foods high in sugar.
   d. reduce the amount of sugar you add to foods.

2. **Complex Carbohydrates**

   To increase the percentage of complex carbohydrates in your diet you can

   a. eat more fruits, vegetables, cereals, breads, and legumes at each meal.
   b. eat fresh fruits as snacks.
   c. increase the number of whole-grain products you eat (such as whole-wheat bread rather than white bread).
   d. eat more pasta, noodles, and rice.

3. **Fats**

   To reduce the amount of fat in your diet you can

   a. substitute complex carbohydrates for foods high in fat.
   b. reduce the amount of high-fat meats you eat (for example, regular hamburger, ribs, sausages, and hot dogs).
   c. eat lean meats (for example, white chicken meat roasted without the skin).
   d. increase the amount of fish in your diet as a substitute for meats.
   e. reduce the amount of nuts, peanuts, and peanut butter in your diet.
   f. trim fat from meat before cooking.
   g. limit fried foods.
   h. bake, broil, or cook meats so that fat will drain away from food as it is cooked.
   i. substitute skim or low-fat milk for whole milk.
   j. use low-fat salad dressings.
   k. reduce the amount of butter or margarine you use.
   l. reduce your use of eggs.

Cultural DIVERSITY

Dietary Patterns and Food Selection Tips

Although most Americans eat many of the same kinds of foods, people have some distinct dietary patterns based on their cultural backgrounds.

Jewish Foods Jewish dietary laws originated as the "Rules of Kashruth," and all foods prepared according to these rules were called "kosher." Most of these laws today apply to the methods of slaughter, preparation, and serving of meat products, and to restrictions on the combination of meat, fish, and egg products. There are also special foods to commemorate or celebrate special occasions, such as challah (white bread), gefilte fish (chopped fish), matzoh (unleavened bread), and potato latkes (fried grated potatoes).

African-American Foods The African-American diet includes nutritious items, such as collard greens, sweet potatoes, corn bread, rice, black-eyed peas, lima beans, kidney beans, navy beans, and pinto beans. This selection of foods provides good sources of vitamins A and C, protein, and complex carbohydrates. Fish and chicken are commonly used instead of red meat. Salt, butter, fatback, and salt pork are used in flavoring foods. Limiting items high in salt and fat provides an African-American diet with the nutrients for good health.

Mexican Foods Today's Mexican food customs represent a blend of the food habits of early Spanish settlers in this country and Native-American tribes from the southwest. With this mixing of customs, three foods emerged as important: dried beans, chiles (chili peppers), and corn. Corn is the basic grain for breads and cereals. Masa is a dough made from dried corn that is soaked in water and lime, boiled, then ground into a paste-like dough. This dough is made into tortillas.

Puerto Rican Foods Although Puerto Rico shares a common heritage with Mexico, Puerto Rican foods include many fruits and vegetables not available in Mexico, such as viandas (starchy fruits and vegetables: yams, sweet potatoes, green bananas, and cassava). A typical day's menu might include coffee for breakfast, viandas and codfish for lunch, and rice, beans, and viandas for dinner.

Chinese Foods Chinese cooking is based on enhancing the natural flavor of foods and preserving their color and texture. Chinese prefer to cook fresh foods quickly, stir-frying them. Vegetables are cooked slightly to retain crispness, flavor, and vitamins.

Japanese Foods The Japanese diet contains far more seafood, particularly raw fish, than does the Chinese diet. A traditional Japanese meal might begin with unsweetened tea, followed by tofu or soybean cake served with raw fish (sashimi) or radish (komono), followed by broiled fish, vegetables, steamed rice, fruits, soup, and more tea.

Selecting Foods from Other Cultures

Italian Pasta is a good choice for carbohydrates. Select vegetable sauces without cream, and dishes without a lot of high-fat cheese and meat. Italian ices are good, low-calorie choices for desserts.

Oriental Choose steamed, broiled, or stir-fried dishes rather than deep-fried. Limit your use of soy sauce, which is high in sodium. Select noodle dishes with soft noodles rather than hard noodles, which are fried. Dishes with tofu are high in protein and low in calories.

French Avoid foods with rich sauces like hollandaise and bechamel that are very high in fat and cholesterol. Select foods prepared in wine sauces and ask how the sauce is prepared, to assure that it is low in fat and calories. Foods from southern France are generally prepared with olive oil and with lots of vegetables, which would provide more nutrition with fewer calories.

Greek Select Greek salads, but use the cheese, anchovies, and olives sparingly, as they are high in fat and sodium. Select fish dishes or broiled shish kebab. Avoid dishes with phyllo dough because they are generally made with lots of butter.

Eastern Indian Foods from this culture are generally low in saturated fat and cholesterol. Look for seekh kabob, marinated lamb or chicken, and fish cooked in clay pots. Avoid foods cooked in coconut milk or cream, as they are high in saturated fat.

Mexican Limit tortillas that are fried with lard. Select shrimp or chicken tostadas made with corn tortillas that are baked. Look for dishes without cheese or ask for the cheese on the side. Rice and beans are good choices because they are low in fat and provide complete protein. Limit refried beans as they are often cooked in lard.

Middle Eastern Select dishes made with vegetables, grains, and spices, like couscous or steamed bulgur, topped with vegetables or chicken. Shish kebab is also a good choice as long as it is not basted in butter. Fresh fruits such as melons, figs, and grapes are excellent choices for dessert.

Southeast Asian Limit deep-fried foods and cream soups. Select stir-fried dishes with fresh vegetables and small portions of meat or fish. Grilled meat dishes and hot-and-sour soup are also good low-fat choices.

Checking Your Diet Against the Food Pyramid . . . .

The first step toward developing healthful eating habits is to identify how you're currently eating. Keep a food and beverage diary for three days. Stick to these guidelines when making entries in your diary. For each day . . .

1. Write down everything you eat and drink at each meal, record all snacks. write down the time you eat as well.

2. Be specific when you identify the food at each meal and snack. Is it whole wheat bread or white bread? Is it lowfat yogurt or fat-free yogurt? Instead of writing "hamburger," specify 1 burger bun, 3 ounces of meat, 1 slice of tomato, 1 tablespoon of mayonnaise.

3. Be precise when you record the amounts of food. For instance, write 1 cup of cereal instead of a bowl. You may need to measure to be sure of the exact amount you are eating.

4. Record how the food was prepared. Was it baked, broiled, fried, fresh, or frozen?

Next, make a list of how many servings you should be eating daily from each group in the food pyramid, and compare each day of your log to the list.

How did you do?
Is there one group that is especially high or low?
How could you improve that one group?

Food group	Recommended number of servings	My servings for the day	Number over or under (+ or −)
Bread and cereal group	_____	_____	_____
Vegetable group	_____	_____	_____
Fruit group	_____	_____	_____
Dairy products group	_____	_____	_____
Protein foods group	_____	_____	_____
Fat and sugar group	_____	_____	_____

(FIGURE 4-23) **Snacks are an important part of your diet. The items shown are examples of low-sugar, low-fat snacks.**

Snacks

Snacking is a large part of the American diet. Snacking, in and of itself, is not a bad habit. Some nutritionists actually recommend small meals and snacks rather than three large meals per day. Most weight loss programs include snacks as part of the meal plan. What are nutritious snacks? Where do they fit into your overall diet?

Fruits Fresh fruits, dried fruits, or canned fruits without added sugar provide vitamins and are a quick energy source. Fruit ices and sorbets make good low-calorie substitutes for ice cream.

Vegetables Fresh vegetables are low in fat and low in calories.

Grains Baked tortilla chips, low-fat snack chips (read the labels), pretzels, unbuttered popcorn, whole-grain homemade baked goods (using low-fat ingredients), gingersnaps, newtons, and angel food cake can be low in fat and calories.

Milk products Low-fat or nonfat yogurts and cheeses make excellent snacks.

Foods to Limit: The following are high in sugar or fat and provide little nutrition: all types of candy, store-bought cookies, pies, cakes, coconut, deep-fried chips, desserts with cream or cream cheese, specialty ice creams, and milk shakes made with whole milk and ice cream.

Selecting Foods When Eating Out

There are healthful choices in almost any restaurant, if you take the time to look and give some thought to your choices. Remember the nutritional principles that guide your choices in other settings. Order your meal by selecting a variety of foods from several food groups in the pyramid, and try not to overeat. If you watch what you eat for most of the week, one meal—even one that is high in calories, fat, and sodium—will not cause a problem if you are a healthy person. Rather than avoiding certain things when you eat out, take positive steps.

- If you want salad dressings, toppings, gravies, or other high-fat additions to food, ask for them to be brought "on the side," and use only small amounts.
- When possible, choose low-fat alternatives, such as fish, pasta with vegetables, chicken with its skin removed, low-fat milk or cheese, and baked potatoes instead of fried potatoes.
- Even most fast-food restaurants now offer alternative menus. When possible, choose broiled or baked foods rather than fried foods.
- Choose whole-grain breads or bagels rather than biscuits.

Teenage Nutritional Needs

The onset of puberty brings many bodily changes. During the teenage years maturation speeds up, creating greater demands on body processes. The hormonal changes that control the development of sex characteristics have an important influence on growth and development.

Both boys and girls experience increased demands for energy, protein, vitamins, and minerals to deal with developmental changes. When you snack to get energy, select snacks with nutritional value rather than candy bars or high-fat desserts. You really need protein for muscle growth, along with calcium and iron for other developmental changes. Teens tend to stop drinking milk as they get older. Carbonated beverages do not provide the calcium you need to increase your bone density. Girls must take care to select foods high in iron, since they begin to lose iron when menstruation begins. This iron loss results in fatigue and iron-deficiency anemia. Select foods high in vitamins and minerals.

To summarize, the most common dietary deficiencies seen among teenagers involve a lack of vitamins and minerals such as B, C, A, iron, and calcium.

Nutritional Needs of Pregnant Women As with the teenage years, pregnancy carries with it increased demands for nutrients. The development of the fetus is a period of rapid physical growth from the fertilized egg to a full-term baby. Good nutrition during this time is a major factor in determining the baby's overall health. Pregnant women need to increase the number of calories they consume to meet energy demands and to increase the amount of protein to make tissues. For example, protein is necessary for growth of the placenta, growth of breast and uterine tissue, formation of amniotic fluids, and increased blood volume, all of which provide the right environment for the growing fetus.

Getting adequate nutrition without excessive weight gain is a challenge for the pregnant mother. Eating from all but the top group in the food pyramid will help both the mother and the developing infant.

Vegetarian Diets

Vegetarians choose not to eat meat and meat products. Some also avoid dairy products. The number of vegetarians in this country appears to be increasing each year, and contrary to what many believe, a vegetarian diet can be healthful. However, because plant products do not contain complete proteins, it is important for vegetarians to be aware of protein requirements. Vegetarians must eat a variety of foods to get a mix of proteins that will supply all of the essential amino acids. Since vitamin B_{12} is found only in animals, vegetarians must take a B_{12} supplement if no dairy or meat products are eaten. There are some distinct health benefits of a vegetarian diet, but to be nutritionally successful, it does take some planning within the food pyramid, especially for proteins. It may be wise to work with a licensed dietitian or nutritionist if you are a vegetarian or want to become one.

Nutrition and Athletes

Teens who are athletes need a slightly greater amount of protein than teens who are not athletes. Under ordinary conditions, proteins are not used for fuel like carbohydrates and fats are, but in endurance events some amino acids are actually used for fuel. To use fuel rapidly, an increase in protective nutrients called antioxidants is needed. Leafy vegetables are a good source of antioxidants and should be included in every athlete's diet.

Athletes must be well hydrated if they are to perform their best. For activities lasting under two hours, water can adequately replace any fluid that has been lost. In events lasting longer than two hours, however, both water and electrolytes must be replaced. Sports drinks that are low in sugar are recommended for use during prolonged endurance events. Some newer drinks now include dextrins, carbohydrates that are readily digested and available to the body for immediate use.

Nutrition plays a vital role in successful athletic performance. An athlete can plan what foods to eat in order to store the proper kind of fuel needed for a future event. Short, intense events require plenty of stored carbohydrates, made readily available through the right kind of training. Endurance events require stored fats, stored carbohydrates, and some selected amino acids. Attention to good nutrition year round can help athletes achieve their goals.

Review

1. Describe what is meant by each of the Dietary Guidelines for Americans.

2. To which group on the food pyramid, do you think each of the following foods belongs?
   a. tortilla
   b. rice
   c. bean sprouts
   d. olives
   e. peanut butter
   f. salmon
   g. salsa
   h. bran muffin

3. Look at Figures 4-14 and 4-15.
   a. How much vitamin C do you need per day?
   b. What percentage of your daily calories should come from saturated fat?

4. **Critical Thinking** A beef burrito weighs 206 grams. The burrito supplies 430 calories and has 21 grams of fat. What percentage of the burrito's total calories comes from fat? How does your answer compare with the dietary guidelines?

• • • • •

Objectives

■ *Describe symptoms common to food-borne illnesses.*

■ *Discuss ways to prevent bacterial contamination of foods.*

   ■■ *Life Skills: Being a Wise Consumer*

■ *Locate the "use by" or "sell by" dates on common food items.*

Each year in the United states, millions of cases of food-borne illnesses occur. In most instances, food has been contaminated by bacteria, and the result is an illness that can cause a variety of unpleasant symptoms or—for those who are less healthy—death.

Symptoms of Food-Borne Illnesses

Food-borne illnesses usually affect the stomach and intestines. Common symptoms include diarrhea, cramping, fever, headache, vomiting, and exhaustion. Symptoms may appear as quickly as half an hour after eating, or they may not develop for several days or weeks. They usually last a couple of days or less, but they can last as long as 7–10 days. For most healthy people, food-borne illnesses are not serious, but for very young children, older people, and people who are already ill, food-borne illnesses may be life-threatening. When symptoms are severe, a medical doctor should be seen. For milder symptoms, lost fluids should be replaced and easily-digested meals can be eaten. Some ill-nesses, like botulism, cause nerve problems, and emergency care is essential.

Bacteria and Food-Borne Illnesses

Contamination by bacteria can occur at any point in the food production process, but about 30 percent of all food-borne illnesses result from unsafe food handling at home. A wide range of foods can be affected, including meats, dairy products, unpasteurized fruit juice, fresh pasta, spices, chocolate, seafood, and even water. Other products that can be tainted by bacteria include egg products; tuna, potato, and macaroni salads; and cream-filled pastries. Poultry (usually chicken) is the food most often contaminated by disease-causing organisms.

Safe Food Buying

Preventing food-borne illnesses actually begins during the trip to the supermarket. If any of the items on your shopping list are those that can be affected by bacterial contamination, pick up these foods and frozen foods last. Get them home quickly. Refrigerate or freeze foods right away if they are perishable. Figure 4-24 lists storage guidelines for foods that are commonly served in American homes.

Don't buy bulging cans or jars that are not tightly sealed. Look for "use by" or "sell by" dates, and buy small enough quantities that you can use all of the product before the expiration date. Dairy products and eggs are dated, as are other pasteurized foods, like juices. Place foods that perish quickly in their own bag with like items so their drippings don't contaminate other foods. When buying fish, buy from markets that get their supplies from state-

Cold Storage Periods for Common American Foods

Product	STORAGE PERIOD	
	Maximum Time In Refrigerator	Maximum Time In Freezer
Fresh ground meat	1–2 days	3–4 months
Fresh steaks and roasts	3–5 days	6–12 months
Fresh pork chops	3–5 days	3–4 months
Fresh ground pork	1–2 days	1–2 months
Fresh pork roast	3–5 days	4–8 months
Cured lunch meat	3–5 days	1–2 months
Cured sausage	1–2 days	1–2 months
Gravy	1–2 days	3 months
Lean fish (cod, etc.)	1–2 days	up to 6 months
Fatty fish (perch, salmon, etc.)	1–2 days	2–3 months
Whole chicken	1–2 days	12 months
Chicken parts	1–2 days	9 months
Chicken giblets	1–2 days	3–4 months
Cheese	3–4 weeks	*
Milk	5 days	1 month
Eggs, fresh in shell	3–5 days	do not freeze
Eggs, hard-boiled	1 week	do not freeze

*If cheese is frozen, the texture and taste will be affected.

(FIGURE 4-24) **Labeling foods with a date of purchase can help you better determine when they are no longer safe to eat.**

approved sources rather than at roadside stands or trucks. Check the meat and fish counters and salad bars for cleanliness, and be sure that different foods are kept apart.

Safe Food Handling
The following guidelines can help ensure the careful handling of food to prevent the growth of disease-causing bacteria.

1. Keep foods in the refrigerator no longer than the period shown in Figure 4-24. Hot or cold foods left standing too long at room temperature may provide the climate bacteria need to grow.
2. Cooking foods at too low a temperature or for too short a time may not kill bacteria. Cook eggs well because even though they have a shell they can be infected by bacteria.
3. Knives and cutting surfaces that come into contact with a contaminated food can be a source of contamination to another food if they are not cleaned with hot soapy water. Use a clean platter for cooked meat rather then the one that held it when it was raw.
4. Wash fruits and vegetables well.
5. Always thaw frozen meats in the refrigerator or in the microwave, and then cook them right away.
6. Leftovers should be stored in tightly sealed containers in the refrigerator. Eggs should be stored in their own carton on a shelf in the refrigerator, which is colder than a tray in the door. Avoid overcrowding the refrigerator to allow air to circulate freely.
7. Eat leftovers quickly or discard them.
8. Make it a regular practice to review the "use by" dates for packaged products. Discard any foods that are no longer safe to eat. Look for "refrigerate after opening" directions on labels. Store products accordingly.
9. Mayonnaise and ketchup are best kept in the refrigerator, as their labels direct.
10. When storing canned or dry goods, move older items to the front of the shelf and use them first.

Eating Out Safely
In one of the worst food-poisoning outbreaks ever in this country, contaminated hamburgers made 450 people sick and killed one toddler in 1992. The contamination was caused by a rare strain of *E. coli* bacteria that is normally found in animals. Had the meat been cooked well, the bacteria would have been killed. The Food and Drug Administration now requires that ground meat be cooked to 155°F, well above the pink stage. Ground meats are especially dangerous because the grinding equipment may be contaminated and ground meat has a larger surface area on which bacteria can multiply. It is best not to order a rare hamburger when eating out. In addition, other raw meat dishes and milk can also carry *E. coli*.

Review

1. What are the general symptoms of a food-borne illness?

2. What precautions should you always take when preparing or handling food?

3. **Life Skills: Being a Wise Consumer** Check your refrigerator and other food storage areas in your home. Make a list of at least 10 foods that have been marked with expiration dates.

Highlights

Summary

- Appetite refers to a desire to eat food. Hunger is your body telling you to eat. To get a good balance, appetite and hunger should work together.

- Diet is related to six of the ten leading causes of death in the U.S.

- The six categories of essential nutrients are carbohydrates, fats, proteins, vitamins, minerals, and water.

- The body's primary sources of energy are carbohydrates and fats.

- Cholesterol in the body is measured in two forms: high-density lipoproteins (HDL) and low-density lipoproteins (LDL).

- Water is needed for all body processes, for carrying nutrients to cells and waste to the kidneys, and for temperature regulation.

- The Food Pyramid organizes foods into five categories based on daily nutritional needs.

- The Food Pyramid and the U.S. Dietary Guidelines are guides for a healthful, well-balanced diet.

- Proper food handling practices can protect you from food-borne illnesses.

Vocabulary

carbohydrates a class of nutrients containing simple sugars, starches, glycogen, and dietary fiber.

saturated fats fats that contain single bonds between carbon atoms and the maximum number of hydrogen atoms bonded to carbon.

unsaturated fats fats that contain one or more double bonds between carbon atoms and have less than the maximum number of hydrogen atoms bonded to carbon.

cholesterol a fatlike substance that is part of all animal cells and is necessary for the production of some hormones and fat digestion.

proteins class of nutrients consisting of long chains of amino acids, which are the basic components of body tissue and can provide energy.

vitamins organic substances that assist in the chemical reactions that occur in the body.

minerals inorganic substances that are generally absorbed to form structural components of the body.

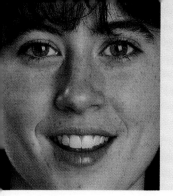

Concept Review

1. List four factors that influence the foods you choose.

2. List the six nutrients, then describe what each one does for the body. Name a food source for each nutrient.

3. What is the difference between simple carbohydrates and complex carbohydrates?

4. What is the difference between saturated fats and unsaturated fats?

5. What is cholesterol and how can it affect your health?

6. What can happen to your body if your diet is deficient in vitamins and minerals?

7. Why is water important to your diet?

8. Identify the five food categories on the food pyramid and list two foods from each group.

9. Explain the organization of the food pyramid.

10. Name four ways to reduce the amount of fat in your diet.

11. What can you do to help prevent osteoporosis?

12. Why do protein requirements increase during pregnancy?

13. List the daily dietary guidelines for fats, cholesterol, carbohydrates, and sodium.

14. In what ways can bacteria contaminate food?

Expressing Your Views

1. Studies have shown that many teenagers in the United States do not make nutritious food choices. Why do you think this is so?

2. Your younger brother loves sweets. He will often eat only a dessert at meal time and you have noticed that he eats sweet snacks all day. He says not to worry because he eats plenty of carbohydrates and they are a source of energy. However, you are concerned that his diet is not adequate. What advice could you give him?

3. Why is making food selections based on calories alone not a good method for planning your diet?

4. Why is it so important to drink at least 8 glasses of water each day?

Life Skills Check

1. Practicing Self-Care
You enjoy eating food from other cultures. You want to make healthful choices when selecting food at restaurants specializing in these dishes. Make a list of foods to avoid when you eat at each of the following restaurants: Italian, Oriental, French, Greek, Mexican, Eastern Indian, and Southeast Asian.

2. Practicing Self-Care
Calculate the percentage of calories from fat for 1 tablespoon of blue cheese salad dressing (about 14 grams). The tablespoon of salad dressing is 77 calories with 8 grams of fat.

Projects

1. Use your detailed food diary from the Life Skills feature to further analyze your diet. Using either a computer software package or a table of food values, analyze your diet for amounts of energy nutrients, fiber, cholesterol, sodium, iron, calcium, and vitamins A and C. What changes do you need to make in your diet?

2. Work with a group to obtain nutritional information from various fast-food restaurants (perhaps by asking for a menu). Analyze this information and decide which foods are the healthiest and most nutritious in each type of restaurant. Write a consumer article for your school newspaper.

3. Bring to class a recipe for a cake, a pie, cookies, or some other dessert. Discuss ways to make substitutions in the recipes to reduce the fat, sugar, and salt. After making these substitutions, develop a ''healthy dessert'' recipe file with the class. Compile all of your recipes into a pamphlet and distribute the pamphlets throughout the school.

Plan for Action

The foods you eat every day have an effect on your overall health. Do you choose healthful foods every day? List five changes you will make in your food selections in order to achieve a more healthful diet.

CHAPTER 5

Weight Management and Eating Disorders

◆ ◆ ◆ ◆

Section 5.1 Metabolism and Ideal Weight

Section 5.2 Eating Disorders

Section 5.3 Disorders Affecting the Digestive System

The focus on being thin has resulted in a major increase in eating disorders like bulimia.

argaret and her best friend, Dale, are 15 years old. Yesterday, Dale was rushed to the local hospital and almost died. When she was admitted to the hospital Dale weighed only 80 pounds. Margaret knew Dale had been dieting for a long time to "get thin." She tried to convince Dale that she was already thin and that she was "starving herself to death." But Dale would not listen. Every time Dale looked in the mirror, she complained about being fat. No one else saw her that way. Dale and her mother argued constantly about eating. It seemed that as Dale got thinner, she ate even less. She exercised all the time. Margaret didn't know how Dale found the strength. What was happening to Dale? Margaret wondered what was causing Dale to feel she had to be so thin, even when she was beginning to lose her health? Why couldn't Dale see that she was already thin? Why was she being so stubborn about eating? What could Margaret have done differently to help Dale? What can Margaret do now to help Dale recover? What can Dale's mother do?

Section 5.1

Metabolism and Ideal Weight

Objectives

- *Describe how to determine your daily calorie expenditure.*
  - **LIFE SKILLS: Assessing Your Health**
- *List the factors that should be used to determine your ideal weight.*
- *Identify the characteristics of fad diets.*
- *Identify the characteristics of healthy weight-loss and weight-gain plans.*

Weight Management Concepts

There isn't a day that goes by that you don't hear something about weight control or dieting. The TV is filled with weight-loss ads. The stores are filled with diet products. Yet many Americans are dangerously overweight. The chances of being overweight at some point during your life are high. Therefore, in this chapter you will study basic information about how your body uses calories and what you can do to maintain a weight that's good for your health. You can control your weight by knowing when and why you eat, and some-

basal meta-bolic rate:

energy needed to fuel the body's on-going processes while the body is at complete rest.

energy-balance equation:

eating the same number of calories that you burn each day.

thing about your body's composition. Look back at the Check Up you answered on page 68. Do you often eat or overeat when you are not hungry?

How Your Body Uses Food Energy

Metabolism describes all the chemical reactions that occur in the body to break down food and build new materials. The body breaks down food so it can be used for energy and other purposes. But how much food do you need? The amount of calories you should consume is determined by two factors: basal metabolism rate and your level of activity. In Chapter 3 you learned

how physical activity affects the amount of energy you expend each day. **Basal metabolic rate** (BMR) refers to the amount of energy it takes to keep your body functioning normally when you are at rest. These functions include breathing, circulating blood throughout the body, and providing energy to maintain cell function. BMR does not include the energy needed to digest food. BMR changes as you age, differs between men and women, and differs depending on your body type. A fit, lean individual will have a higher BMR than someone who weighs the same but has less muscle mass.

If you add your BMR to the energy required for all your activities during a 24-hour period, and to the energy needed to digest the food you have eaten, you end up with the energy your body needs. For example, if your BMR was 1000 calories, and your activity level required another 800 calories per day, your body would need approximately 180 calories to digest food. Your total energy requirement per day to maintain your current body weight is 1980 calories. This concept is called the **energy-balance equation** and is covered in the Life Skills on page 109. You can maintain your current body weight if you balance the number of calories you eat with the number of calories you burn.

Body Composition

The body is made of several kinds of tissue, including fat and **lean mass.** You learned in the last chapter that your diet must include some fat to maintain important body functions. For example, some vitamins can only be used by the body if they are dissolved in fat. The amount of fat that you need for normal functioning is called **essential fat.** Fat intake beyond essential fat is considered excess **storage fat.** Ordinarily, essential fat makes up no more than 3 percent of total

BODY FAT SCALE FOR TEENS

Approx. fat %	Males	Skinfold Caliper Measurement (millimeters)	Females	Approx. fat %
6	Very low	5	Very low	
10	Low	10		11.5
	Optimal	15	Low	15
		20	Optimal	
20		25		
25	Moderately high	30	Moderately high	25
	High	35		29.5
31		40	High	
		45		36
	Very high	50		
		55	Very high	
		60		

(FIGURE 5-1) **If your body fat measurements are outside the acceptable ranges, change your eating habits and level of physical activity.**

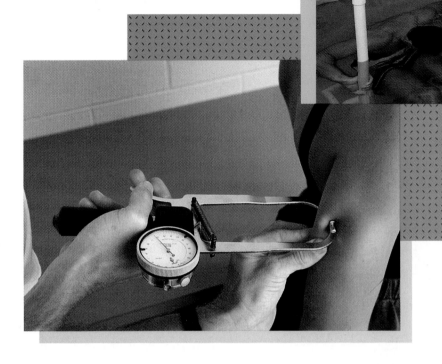

(FIGURE 5-2) **The only way to determine your ideal weight is to start by having your body fat measured. Body fat can be measured using skin-fold calipers or by submersion in a tank of water.**

lean mass:

total body weight minus the weight due to fat.

essential fat:

the amount of fat needed for certain metabolic processes to occur.

storage fat:

excess fat stored in the body.

overweight:

weighing 10 percent more than one's recommended weight.

obesity:

a condition in which one weighs 20 percent more than the recommended weight.

body weight for men, and 10–12 percent for women. Desirable total body fat levels for teens range between 10 and 20 percent for males and between 15 and 25 percent for females. The higher fat composition for females is related to different hormonal needs for the reproductive system. A large percentage of your body weight is made of lean muscle, bone and body fluids.

Figure 5-1 shows the optimal body fat range for teen males and females. There is no fixed ideal body weight for each person. Ideal body weight is based on your age, your sex, and your frame size and bone structure. Height and weight charts are only guidelines. Rather than using height and weight charts, you should have your body fat measured to determine the relationship between fat and lean mass. This is a

better indicator for determining your ideal, healthy weight.

You store a pound of body fat when you eat 3500 calories more than you need. If you weigh 10 percent more than your ideal recommended weight, then you are considered **overweight**. The term **obesity** is used to describe a condition in which one weighs more than 20 percent over an ideal body weight. Being overweight is unhealthy, but being obese is a substantial risk to health and life.

Nathan is 18 years old, 5 feet 8 inches tall and weighs 170 pounds. His close friend Rico is also 18 and the same height, but Rico weighs 180 pounds. A height and weight chart suggests that both Nathan and Rico should weigh about 155 pounds. Nathan and Rico agree to be weighed in an underwater tank to determine their percentage of body fat. Nathan finds that 19 percent of his body weight is fat, while Rico measures 12 percent body fat. What do these measurements mean? To find out, you need to do some math to find Nathan's and Rico's actual body fat. Nineteen percent of 170 pounds is 32.3 pounds for Nathan, and 12 percent of 180 pounds is 21.6 pounds for Rico. Nathan has much more body fat than Rico, even though he weighs 10 pounds less. Now you see why height/weight charts may not be very useful. A person can have too much fat from overeating and lack of exercise, and still not be overweight according to a weight chart.

Body composition is a better predictor of health than height/weight ratios. Rather than losing weight, Nathan could lose fat by improving his nutritional choices and becoming active through exercise. He might actually gain muscle mass while reducing his percentage of body fat. Nathan could be healthier even though he would weigh more.

Weight Gain Can Occur Slowly

There are many ways you can put on weight without realizing it. Suppose your total energy expenditure is 1800 calories per day. Eating that level of calories you would maintain your present weight. Now imagine that you develop a habit of buying a package of pretzels after school and eating them on your way home. The label on the package tells you that this is a relatively low-fat snack with about 100 calories. Eating the pretzels adds 100 calories more each day than you need. Not much? Well, if you do not increase your exercise to compensate for these pretzels each day, by the end of the first week you will have eaten 500 calories more than you needed. In seven weeks this becomes 3500 calories and you gain a pound. By the end of the school year you have eaten enough (just one bag of pretzels a day) to add seven to eight pounds of body fat. Gaining weight over long periods of time does not always mean eating lots of food all at once. Being overweight or obese increases your risks of high blood pressure, diabetes, and elevated cholesterol. When someone is obese, the risk of death from coronary heart disease, cancer, diabetes, and stroke is substantial.

(FIGURE 5-3) **While there is a wealth of information available on losing weight, the guidelines are actually very simple. Avoid programs that promise unrealistic results.**

Calculating Your Caloric Needs . . . .

Your total caloric needs for the day depend on your BMR, your activity level, and the number of calories you need to digest food. The actual measurement of a BMR is very expensive. The formulas given here will give you rough estimates.

1. Calculating BMR Calories

Females
body weight (pounds) × 10 = BMR Calories

Males
body weight (pounds) × 11 = BMR Calories

2. Calculating Activity Levels

Activity Level	% BMR Calories	Multiply by
inactive	30	0.30
average activity	50	0.50
very active (some strenuous activity)	75	0.75

3. Calculating Calories Needed to Digest Food

(BMR Calories + Activity Calories) (0.1) = Digestion Calories

4. Total Calories needed = Step 1 + 2 + 3

Example
Marianne weighs 130 lb. Her activity level is average. Marianne needs 2145 calories to maintain her weight.

$$130 \text{ lb} \times 10 = 1300 \text{ BMR Calories}$$
$$0.50 \times 1300 = 650 \text{ Activity Calories}$$
$$1950 \times 0.1 = 195 \text{ Digestion Calories}$$
$$\overline{ 2145 \text{ Total Calories}}$$

Losing Weight Sensibly

If you determine that you need to lose weight, you should visit your doctor to help you develop a sensible weight loss plan. Your doctor will probably suggest you lose weight by reducing the number of calories you eat and increasing the number of calories that you burn. Your doctor may also tell you that it is possible to lose weight *too* rapidly and may refer you to a registered dietitian. Losing more than one or two pounds per week can be dangerous to your health. That is because during weight loss, stored fats are used for energy. As these fats are transported through the bloodstream to be metabolized, they can clog arteries.

Each year a large number of people try to lose weight. Those who go on diets are rarely successful. As many as 90 percent of the people who lose 20 or more pounds gain them back. However, it is possible to lose weight and keep it off. Here is a sensible plan to lose fat and keep it off.

1. Establish a weight goal based on your excess body fat rather than body weight.

2. Teens are expected to gain weight each year as they are growing, so weight loss should not be extreme and calories shouldn't be cut back excessively. Active teens can safely consume 2000 calories, less active teens should consume no less than 1500 calories daily.

3. A combined program of diet and exercise is the most effective way to lose fat. Begin or maintain a moderate intensity (40–70% of your maximum heart rate) aerobic exercise program five to seven days a week. After 20 minutes of walking, your body uses more fats than carbohydrates for energy. The longer you walk, the more fat you burn.

4. Plan to lose no more than four pounds a month.

5. Use the Life Skills on page 109 to determine the calories you need daily to maintain your current weight.

6. To lose three pounds a month, create a deficit of 300 calories a day. Reduce your caloric intake (eat 150 calories less) and increase your calorie expenditure (burn 150 calories more).

7. Drink enough water daily using the guideline in Chapter 4.

8. Develop eating habits for a lifetime, rather than dieting habits for a short time.

9. Never skip meals. Eat several small meals a day, carefully selecting foods that meet the Dietary Guidelines.

10. Remember that the key to lifelong weight management is regular physical activity balanced against nutritious eating habits that provide adequate calories for health.

Gaining Weight Safely

Many teenagers are unhappy with the way they look. Very thin teenagers may find that being too thin can be stressful. Being too thin and wanting to gain weight can be just as frustrating as being too heavy and wanting to lose weight. The best strategies for overly thin teenagers are much the same as those for obese individuals. Check with a doctor or registered dietitian for safe weight-gain strategies and refer to the points listed for weight control. Modify them slightly to get a reasonable plan for weight gain. Add the following points.

1. Examine your eating patterns. Avoid skipping meals. If you have trouble eating three large meals a day, try eating six smaller meals. Be willing to try new foods. A well-balanced diet is easier to achieve when you eat a variety of foods.

2. Examine your snacking patterns. Do you snack close to mealtime? Snacking increases blood sugar levels, which reduces hunger and appetite. If you snack, do so at least two hours before a meal.

3. If you are sedentary, start to exercise. If you are exercising, increase your activity level. Exercise can increase your metabolism and you will feel less tired.

4. Eat a variety of foods. Look for nutritious foods (such as nuts and dried fruits) that are high in calories.

Remember that it takes an extra 3500 calories to gain one pound. If you can increase your caloric intake by 500 calories above what you burn each day, you should be able to gain about one pound a week.

Fad Diets

Because losing weight takes time and careful planning, many people turn to fad diets for the promise of quick and easy results. A **fad diet** is one that promises quick and unrealistic results. Because being thin seems to be so unrealistically valued in our society, people think being thin is the way to become popular. Obese people are often the subject of jokes and other kinds of discrimination. These are some of the reasons why fad diets are so popular. Fad diets take advantage of people's emotions and give them false hopes. These diets promise a quick fix for obesity and lead you to believe that weight loss takes little effort. Advertisements for fad diets are everywhere—on television, in magazines and newspapers, and on the radio. These ads may appear to be very sound approaches to weight loss. Some will deliver the desired weight loss.

There are two major problems with fad diets. They can be dangerous to your health and the weight that is lost, while using them,

fad diet:

a weight-loss plan that promises unrealistic results.

(FIGURE 5-5) **Fad diets can appear to be sound programs for weight loss. Don't be fooled. People have died from lack of nutrition from some fad diets. Follow a doctor's or dietitian's instructions for a weight-loss plan.**

generally returns when you go back to your old eating habits. Fad diets usually include eating plans that do not provide adequate nutrition. There have been numerous deaths related to fad diets, even medically supervised ones, which do not provide adequate calories and nutrients for healthy body function.

Very low calorie levels also cause a change in the body's metabolic rate. If calories are cut sharply, the body slows its rate of metabolism to function on fewer calories. When the dieting phase ends and the person resumes normal eating habits, more calories are provided so the body stores more fat to prepare for the next state of "starvation."

If you must lose weight because you have a higher than normal percentage of body fat, then ask yourself these questions before you invest the time and energy in a weight loss program: Does the program . . .

• involve qualified nutrition professionals?
• include a safe, personalized physical activity program?

• encourage slow, gradual weight loss?
• include all of the five major food groups in the Food Pyramid?
• fit your lifestyle?
• help you make positive changes in your eating behavior for a lifetime?
• have a weight maintenance program?

A "Yes" to all of these questions indicates a sound program.

*R*eview

1. Calculate your daily caloric need.

2. What factors should be considered in assessing your ideal weight?

3. What are the drawbacks of fad diets?

4. What are the characteristics of a healthy weight-loss plan?

Section

5.2 Eating Disorders

Objectives

- List the health hazards of anorexia, bulimia, and pica.

- Describe the characteristics of individuals most at risk for anorexia or bulimia.

- Explain how eating disorders can be avoided.

back to the Middle Ages), it appears that the percentage of people affected by these disorders is increasing. An estimated one million teenagers are affected by eating disorders. As many as 85 percent of all people with these disorders are female.

There are many reasons why females are more likely to have these disorders. One of the major reasons is that thinness appears to be associated with femininity and sensuality in females. Another reason is that women often think thinness is a factor in being popular.

Dale has carried weight control and dieting too far. She's become attached to a body image that is unreasonable. The only way to achieve that image involves endangering her health.

Think about the body image you would like to have. Does it suit you or is it the image of someone else? Your mind can be flooded with images of young, thin beautiful models as the ideal. As a result, you may feel you are too heavy or unattractive even when you are not.

It is far more important to visualize yourself as a fit, healthy person. Being fit and engaging in healthful behaviors should provide a body image that is right for you. The heavy emphasis on body image in today's society has produced a dramatic increase in the number of people suffering from eating disorders. In this section we want you to explore the emotional and physical effects of these disorders. Let's start by looking at how they come about in the first place. While eating disorders are not new diseases (there is evidence that they date

(FIGURE 5-6) **It is better to see yourself as a fit, healthy person than to try to look like a fashion model.**

Check Up

Are You at Risk for an Eating Disorder?

People with eating disorders will respond with a "yes" to most of the following questions.

1. Do you prefer to eat alone?

2. Are you terrified of being overweight?

3. Do you constantly think about food?

4. Do you "binge" (overeat drastically) occasionally?

5. Are you highly knowledgeable about the calorie content of all the foods you eat?

6. Do you always feel "stuffed" after meals?

7. Are you constantly weighing yourself?

8. Do you eat a lot of "diet" foods?

9. Do you over-exercise to burn all the calories you eat?

10. Do you take a long time to eat meals?

11. Are you frequently constipated?

12. Do you feel guilty when you eat sweet or fattening foods?

13. Do you feel the urge to throw up after eating?

14. Do you feel your life is controlled by food and eating?

If your responses suggest that you may be at risk for an eating disorder, it is suggested that you discuss your situation with an adult or doctor.

(FIGURE 5-7) **One sign of anorexia is excessive exercise.**

ognize when she becomes dangerously thin. She may exercise excessively and will appear to have no appetite. Signs of hunger and appetite are there, but the anorexic does not respond to them.

In dealing with the anorexic, parents and friends may attempt to force the victim to eat. These attempts will generally make the problem worse. The anorexic becomes more determined not to eat. However, on occasion, the anorexic will eat to avoid the hassles of dealing with family or friends. Unfortunately, it is likely that the anorexic will then go to a private place and throw up to get rid of the food.

Anorexia often occurs as a result of emotional problems. The anorexic is generally described as the "perfect" child. These individuals are generally popular. They are characterized as obedient, respectful, and are often good students. Parents or guardians of anorexics may unknowingly be

Anorexia Nervosa

anorexia nervosa:

an eating disorder in which the person refuses to eat because of a fear of weight gain.

Anorexia nervosa is a condition in which a person is constantly dieting and carrying this dieting to an extreme. The anorexic, like Dale in the story, is in a state of starvation. Someone who diets to lose much more weight than is necessary may be anorexic. Dale feels she is overweight. She cannot be convinced to stop dieting because she sees herself as fat. The anorexic is obsessed with becoming thin and doesn't rec-very domineering, or have unreasonable expectations of their child. Control over eating may be the only area where the anorexic feels he or she has firm control in this kind of an environment. Part of the recovery process often involves helping the anorexic gain independence.

Effects of Anorexia Nervosa

The anorexic experiences other physical effects related to the excessive weight loss. Heart rate, BMR, and body temperature all drop to low levels. Because the fat stored in the body is used up, the body begins breaking down muscle tissue for energy. Loss of muscle tissue can cause permanent heart damage. When this disorder occurs during puberty, sexual maturity and growth will stop. Sometimes a girl feels threatened by sexual maturity and will use dieting and weight loss to avoid changes that come with growing up.

The anorexic has low self-esteem, which is generally the cause of the disorder. The state of starvation results in frequent depression. Relationships among family and friends can be strained as the anorexic becomes more and more obsessed with not eating.

Treatment

As many as 10 percent of anorexics die of starvation without treatment. Treatment requires a team of professionals—physicians, nurses, psychiatrists, family psychologists, and dietitians—working together. Mental health counseling is required to successfully treat the disorder. A treatment plan is developed that deals with the physical effects of the disorder and the emotional reasons for its occurrence. Early treatment is essential to prevent permanent damage to one's health. Treatment may sometimes involve forced feeding on a temporary basis. The first priority of treatment is aimed at meeting nutritional deficiencies to prevent long-term medical problems.

Bulimia

Bulimia is a disorder in which a person binges on food. A binge involves eating large amounts of food over a very short period of time. This *bingeing* is then followed by *purging* (either throwing up or using laxatives). Bulimia generally appears from the teen years through adulthood. It is far more common in teenage girls than is anorexia. Bulimics are threatened by being overweight, but derive a lot of pleasure from going on a binge. However, feelings of guilt and fear of weight gain set in and purging occurs.

Effects of Bulimia

A bulimic may throw up daily to purge. Throwing up causes the enamel on the teeth to dissolve from exposure to acid from the stomach. The teeth are more prone to decay. The salivary glands become large from overproducing saliva to prevent dehydration. Frequent throwing up

bulimia:

an eating disorder based on a cycle of bingeing and purging food.

Warning Signs of Bulimia

Recurring episodes of binge eating.

Feeling of a lack of control over eating behavior during the eating binges.

Regular practice of self-induced vomiting, using laxatives, or using diuretics.

Strict dieting, fasting, or engaging in vigorous exercise to prevent weight gain.

An average of two or more binge eating episodes a week for at least three months.

Persistent over-concern with body shape and weight.

(FIGURE 5-8) **Bulimia is diagnosed after careful evaluation of the patient. The signs above are used to make the diagnosis.**

Pam Is in Trouble

Imagine that your best friend, Pam, has been starving herself on a diet for a long time and you think she has gone too far. Every time you say something to her, she tells you that she is too fat. She says everyone makes fun of her because she is too fat and that if you were a real friend you would be supportive of what she is doing.

You have a feeling there is a problem. You have heard about anorexia nervosa. You think Pam is becoming anorexic. Pam gets very angry when you try to talk to her about her weight. It's obvious that your friendship is in trouble. What do you do?

Remember to use the decision-making steps:

1. State the Problem.
2. List the Options.
3. Imagine the Benefits and Consequences.
4. Consider Your Values.
5. Weigh the Options and Decide.
6. Act.
7. Evaluate the Results.

The binge-purge cycle begins to dominate the bulimic's life. Depression is very common. The enormous food habit can be very expensive. A bulimic may have to go to great lengths in order to obtain the money to support a food habit.

Treatment Bulimia can be hard to diagnose because its victims appear to be of normal weight. The disorder becomes apparent only after the person has had the disorder for a long time.

Because the binge-purge cycle dominates the bulimic's eating patterns, some people with bulimia can no longer recognize when they feel full. The chemical signals the body produces to signal fullness may be at very low levels in people who have bulimia. Like anorexia, the emotional basis of this disorder lies in the individual's low self-esteem. Therapy includes training in appropriate nutritional eating habits. Patients are encouraged to engage in activities that develop confidence and build self-esteem.

Anorexia and Bulimia in Combination

About 30 to 50 percent of anorexics also go through binge-purge cycles. Throwing up is one way anorexics maintain their low calorie consumption and keep weight low. Having both disorders just increases the health risks you've read about for each disorder. Professional counseling would almost always be required to successfully treat someone with both disorders.

What Should You Do?

Recognize that eating disorders result from placing too much emphasis on body shape and weight. Because thinness is highly valued in the United States culture, these disorders occur more frequently here than in

can disturb the electrolyte balance in the body and can result in abnormal heart rhythms and kidney damage. Bulimics may also use laxatives. Weight loss caused by using laxatives results from water loss. Excessive use of laxatives disturbs the normal bowel function. The bulimic may then need to continue taking laxatives for the bowels to function at all. The use of diuretics can also alter the electrolyte balance of the body. Excessive use of diuretics can also cause high blood pressure and dehydration.

other parts of the world. The focus on thinness, an obsession with food, and a domineering family situation are prime factors in the cause of these disorders.

Being fit and eating nutritiously will help make you feel good about yourself. When you feel good about yourself, you are less likely to do things that could damage your health. Learn to be comfortable with your body and realize that there is only so much you can do to change it. In trying to be popular, remember that it is your personality that makes you the attractive person that you are.

If you have, or are at high risk for, an eating disorder, seek help now. Talk to an adult you trust. Figure 11-8 on page 235 gives a list of some of the people in your life with whom you could discuss your problem. A visit to the doctor and a complete physical would help you know where to start, if treatment is needed. There are now numerous eating disorder clinics throughout the country. Check the *Hospital* listing in your phone book for places you can call for help.

Treating these disorders is generally a long, slow process. These risky behaviors do not go away overnight and require professional treatment.

(FIGURE 5-9) **Setting a goal to be fit will help boost your self-esteem. When you feel good about yourself, you are less likely to do things that damage your health.**

related to pregnancy, along with changes in food preferences among pregnant women.

The health dangers of pica result from eating harmful bacteria that could be present in clay, soil, or laundry starch. Eating these substances can change the way minerals are absorbed by the body, and mineral deficiencies can result. Eating large quantities of clay can also block the intestines.

Pica

Pica is a little-known eating disorder that involves eating substances not normally considered as food. People experiencing pica have cravings for such things as clay, soil, or laundry starch. This disorder generally occurs among pregnant women. Most pica is reported among pregnant African-American women living in rural areas of the southern United States. The disorder is also found in certain groups living in Australia and Africa. There is some evidence to suggest that pica results from cultural beliefs

Review

1. What are the health risks of bulimia?

2. You think your best friend is bulimic. What signs do you look for to know for sure?

3. How is self-esteem related to some eating disorders?

pica:

an eating disorder in which the person eats nonfood substances like starch, clay, or soil.

Disorders Affecting the Digestive System

Objectives

- List the most common digestive disorders.

- Describe ways to treat constipation and diarrhea.

- Describe the differences between food allergies and food intolerances.

diarrhea:

loose bowel movements that occur when food moves too quickly through the digestive system.

As with many other health-related issues, disorders of the digestive system are frequently related to personal choices, like eating behaviors. Overeating and eating foods that the body has difficulty digesting most frequently cause digestive problems. But digestive problems can also be the result of a specific disease. The most common signs and symptoms of digestive disorders include such things as pain in the chest and abdomen, nausea and vomiting, and constipation and diarrhea.

constipation:

a condition in which bowel movements are infrequent or difficult.

Constipation

Constipation refers to a condition in which a person has difficult or infrequent bowel movements. It usually results when too much water is removed from waste products in the large intestine. This loss causes difficulty in moving waste material through to the rectum. There are many reasons why constipation may occur, including such things as a low-fiber diet, not drinking enough fluids, lack of exercise, stress, or

some disease process. To prevent constipation, your diet should include plenty of fluids, foods high in fiber, and regular exercise. You should try to limit the number of high-fat foods you eat. These foods take longer to travel through your digestive system. If you have a problem with frequent constipation, you should see a physician to rule out the possibility of serious illness.

Diarrhea

Diarrhea occurs when food moves through the digestive system too quickly and there is not enough time for water to be removed. When this happens, the stools are loose and watery, and bowel movements may occur quite often. Usually diarrhea lasts for only a short period of time and stops without treatment. Even though the stools are watery, a person with diarrhea should drink plenty of liquids. The water that is normally removed from digested food in the large intestine is an important source of nutrients for the body. During diarrhea there is a loss of nutrients, and dehydration can occur. When a person has diarrhea for an extended period of time, the large loss of water can be very dangerous to health, or even fatal.

The electrolytes sodium, potassium, and chloride can also be lost during bouts of extended diarrhea—or through any large fluid loss (like heavy perspiration). The proper balance of electrolytes prevents problems resulting from dehydration, such as cramping, heat exhaustion, and heat stroke. Therefore, if diarrhea lasts for more than two days, a physician should always be consulted.

Food Allergies

Allergies brought about by food can cause reactions such as diarrhea, rashes, congestion, sneezing, and itchy, watery eyes. Food allergies are the result of the body's immune system responding to the food as if it were a disease-causing organism. The most common food allergies involve cow's milk, eggs, peanuts, wheat products, shellfish, and fish. The allergic responses are the result of the body's reaction to the foreign proteins in these foods. The most severe food allergy reaction is called anaphylactic shock. The victim of anaphylactic shock experiences severe itching, hives, sweating, tightness in the throat, and difficulty in breathing, followed by low blood pressure, unconsciousness, and eventually death. If you are diagnosed as having a specific food allergy (diagnosis should come from an allergist), you must avoid the food that produces the reaction. This means looking carefully at labels to determine if combination foods are made with substances you are allergic to.

Many allergies begin in infancy and are thought to result from introducing solid foods too early in the infant's diet. It is recommended that cow's milk not be given to infants until they are at least six months of age. Foods that commonly cause allergies should not be given to infants until they are past their first birthday. Certain chemical additives in foods (such as dyes) can also cause allergic reactions.

Food Intolerances

Negative reactions to specific foods that do not involve the body's immune system are called **food intolerances.** Lactose intolerance is one of the most common of these reactions. People with lactose intolerance cannot tolerate milk and milk products. Their bodies do not produce lactase, the

(FIGURE 5-10) **Consuming dairy products containing lactose such as those shown in the top photograph can cause extreme discomfort for individuals with lactose intolerance. The products shown above can be taken by lactose-intolerant individuals to breakdown lactose.**

enzyme that breaks down lactose in milk. Lactose intolerance is high among Asians, Africans, Native Americans, and African-Americans. Drinking milk if you don't produce lactase will cause you to experience bloating, diarrhea, gas, and severe cramps. Fortunately, people who have lactose intolerance can purchase milk already treated with lactase, or add special lactase drops to milk. Lactase tablets can also be used with meals that include milk products. If you have lactose intolerance, you need to be sure you still get an adequate supply of calcium in your diet.

food intolerance:

a negative reaction to food which is not brought about by the immune system.

Common Food Additives and Environmental Contaminants

Additive	Source	Side Effects
MSG	Oriental foods, processed meats	Chest pain, headache, sweating, burning feeling
Coloring agents	Beverages	Allergic reactions: rash, digestive problems
Sodium nitrite	Smoked meats: ham, bacon, sausage, cold cuts	Possible link to cancer
Sulfites (sulfur dioxide)	Potatoes, packaged foods, wine	Allergic reactions including anaphylactic shock
Estrogen	Meats	Possible link to cancer
Lead	Lead-containing paints and glazes	Lead poisoning
Mercury	Contaminated fish	Mercury poisoning

(FIGURE 5-11)

Other common intolerances include the inability to adequately digest substances such as prunes, blueberries, corn, and MSG (monosodium glutamate). MSG can produce a reaction often called "Chinese-restaurant syndrome" (MSG is commonly used in Chinese foods). MSG is an additive in many foods. Reactions to MSG include chest pain, headache, sweating, and a burning feeling.

Figure 5-11 shows some other additives commonly used in foods that can cause the body to react negatively. If you have a food intolerance you will need to check food labels carefully. When eating out, be sure to ask questions about the ingredients used in preparing the food.

Review

1. List the symptoms of a digestive disorder.

2. Why are liquids so important in treating diarrhea?

3. How does a food allergy differ from a food intolerance?

Highlights

Summary

- The number of calories you should consume is determined by basal metabolism rate and your level of activity.

- The body is made of several kinds of tissue, including fat and lean mass. Females have a higher fat content than males.

- A person's ideal weight should be determined by the ratio of fat to lean mass.

- Obesity has serious health risks, including heart disease, cancer, diabetes, and stroke.

- Fad diets are rarely effective and can be dangerous to your health. Regular physical activity is the key to lifetime weight management.

- Anorexia nervosa is a starvation eating disorder that can result in depression, permanent heart damage, and even death.

- Bulimia can cause harmful changes in body organs.

- Some common digestive disorders are constipation, diarrhea, food allergies, and food intolerances.

Vocabulary

basal metabolic rate energy needed to fuel the body's on-going processes while the body is at complete rest.

energy-balance equation eating the same number of calories that you burn each day.

lean mass also known as the lean muscle mass portion of your body. It is your total body weight minus the weight due to fat.

essential fat the amount of fat needed for certain metabolic processes to occur.

storage fat excess fat stored in the body.

obesity weighing 20 percent more than one's recommended weight.

anorexia nervosa an eating disorder in which the person refuses to eat because of a fear of weight gain.

bulimia an eating disorder based on a cycle of bingeing and purging food.

pica an eating disorder in which the person eats nonfood substances like starch, clay, or soil.

constipation a condition in which bowel movements are infrequent or difficult.

diarrhea loose bowel movements that occur when food moves too quickly through the digestive system.

food intolerance a condition in which a reaction occurs to food that is not brought about by the immune system.

Concept Review

1. Your _____ refers to how fast your body burns calories.

2. Rather than using height and weight charts, you should examine your _____ as a better method of determining your ideal weight.

3. Being overweight or obese increases your health risks of _____, high _____, and elevated _____.

4. A simple rule for healthy weight control is to _____ fewer calories than you _____.

5. Fad diets can be dangerous to your health because they require food selections that do not provide adequate _____.

6. A condition called _____ can lead to tooth decay and mineral deficiencies from repeated vomiting.

7. _____ is a condition in which a person is obsessed with becoming thin.

8. To prevent constipation, your diet should include plenty of _____, foods high in _____, and plenty of _____.

9. When a person has _____ for an extended period of time, the large loss of water can be very dangerous to his or her health.

10. A common negative reaction to milk and milk products is called _____.

Expressing Your Views

1. Patricia is 5'5" and weighs 140 pounds. She was surprised when she saw a height/weight chart at the doctor's office that gave her ideal weight as no more than 135 pounds. She is now looking for a diet that promises fast results. What would you advise her? What could you tell her about height/weight charts?

2. Anorexia nervosa and bulimia appear more often in girls than in boys. Why do you think this is true?

3. Daniel has lactose intolerance. How can he be sure his body gets enough calcium?

Life Skills Check . . . . . .

1. Assessing Your Health
You will be traveling next summer on a long road trip. Most of your day will be spent riding in the car. Calculate your total calorie needs for the day. You'll be visiting relatives and you know that their eating habits differ from yours. What can you do to keep your caloric intake and calories burned in balance?

2. Making Responsible Decisions
You have just learned that you are allergic to milk. What kind of changes to your diet will you need to make in order to get the calcium that you need?

Projects . . . .

1. Your genetic makeup plays a role in determining your body composition. Recent evidence indicates that genes may also influence fat storage. In a small group, research what is currently known about the effect of genes on body size, fat storage sites, and weight. Develop a class or school exhibit that shows key facts about the influence of genes on body composition.

2. Locate weight loss programs in your community that advertise for teens. Gather information about each program so that you compare the distinct programs to the characteristics on page 112. Report your findings to the class.

Plan for Action . . . .

Eating patterns and food selection directly affect weight control. List four strategies you will use to help you gain, lose, or maintain your present weight depending on your individual needs.

CHAPTER 6

Personal Care and Appearance

◆ ◆ ◆ ◆

Section 6.1 Skin Care

Section 6.2 Hair and Nail Care

Section 6.3 Teeth and Gum Care

■ Personal care involves more than just how you look. Taking care of yourself makes you feel better too.

The day at the beach was perfect. David and Elena had a great time, swimming and listening to music and watching the waves. When they got home, though, David was red and sunburned all over. Elena told him he looked like a giant tomato. She was teasing, but it wasn't funny. When Elena touched his arm, it felt like a lit match on his skin.

David couldn't understand why he got sunburned and Elena didn't. They both used the same suntan lotion. They put it on at the same time. They were in the sun exactly the same amount of time—from 10:00 A.M. till 4:00 P.M. They both swam for the same length of time. Why did they have such different reactions to the sun?

Section

6.1 Skin Care

Objectives

- *Name the two main layers of the skin.*

- *Recognize skin problems.*

- *Explain how you can reduce your chances of getting acne.*
  LIFE SKILLS: Practicing Self-Care

- *Explain how you can avoid sun damage to your skin.*
  LIFE SKILLS: Practicing Self-Care

David discovered the reason for their different reactions to the sun when he talked with a pharmacist. The pharmacist explained that differences in tanning are due to a substance called melanin in the skin. The more melanin people have in their skin, the darker their skin is and the less likely they are to get sunburned. David is blond, blue-eyed, and fair complexioned, so he sunburned easily. Elena has dark eyes, black hair, and brown skin, so she tanned instead.

In this chapter, you'll learn to protect your skin from the sun and other hazards. You'll also learn how to take good care of your hair, nails, and teeth. And you'll learn that good grooming helps you stay healthy and improves your personal appearance.

Skin Care and How You Look

Care of the skin is an important part of your appearance. This is particularly true during the teen years. Your body has more chemicals called hormones now than when you were a child. Hormones affect your skin and how it looks. Why is it that one day you

How Well Do You Take Care of Yourself?

Which of the following actions do you take to improve your appearance and health?

- Wash skin regularly with soap and water
- Use a sunscreen of at least 15 SPF when outdoors
- Watch any moles for changes in their appearance
- Wash hair regularly
- Limit the use of electric hair dryers and curlers
- Brush teeth at least twice a day
- Floss teeth once a day

have a clear complexion and the next day it's full of pimples? It's because of hormones. You can't do anything to change the hormones in your body, but you *can* improve the look of your skin.

Functions of the Skin

The skin is the largest organ in the body. It is far larger than your lungs or your heart. While you may not think of your skin as an important organ, it actually has some very important functions.

1. to protect the body from germs and injury
2. to regulate body temperature
3. to transmit sensations such as pain or cold
4. to act as a weatherproof cover which can prevent dehydration
5. to excrete wastes
6. to synthesize vitamin D

(FIGURE 6-1) **Having healthy skin helps you look and feel good.**

Structure of the Skin

As you can see in Figure 6-2, the skin has two main layers—the **epidermis** and the **dermis**. Under these two layers is a layer of fatty tissue called the subcutaneous layer. The subcutaneous layer insulates the body from temperature changes and connects the skin to the body.

The Epidermis The epidermis is the top layer of the skin. This is the part of the skin that you see. It is made up of cells that are replaced once a month, which means that none of the skin you see is over a month old.

The epidermis has small openings called pores. Pores are tunnels that lead to the skin surface from below the epidermis. Skin oil and sweat are carried in the pores up to the skin surface.

Melanin, the substance that gives skin its color, is found in the epidermis. Melanin protects the skin from the sun's rays and is produced whenever the skin is exposed to the sun. Melanin does not provide complete protection from the sun, and anyone can be sunburned. Melanin is also the substance that produces freckles.

The Dermis The dermis is the skin layer just below the epidermis. It contains a network of blood vessels that carry heat and nutrients to the surface of the skin. The dermis has thousands of tiny hairs. The root of each hair is surrounded by oil glands. Oil from these glands travels along the hair to the surface of the skin. The oil keeps the skin moist, soft, and waterproof. Overproduction of oil can make the skin feel oily.

The dermis also has thousands of sweat glands that produce sweat to rid the body of excess water, salts, and wastes. When sweat evaporates, it cools the skin. About 1 quart of water is excreted in sweat every day, but most of the time it goes unnoticed. Physical activity causes increased sweating that is, of course, easy to see. Some sweat

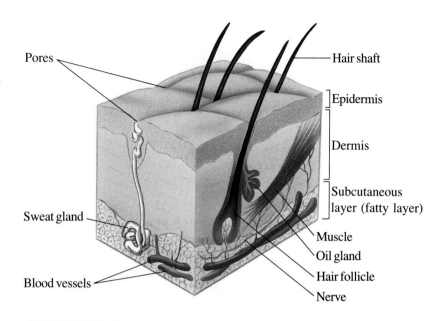

(FIGURE 6-2) **The two main layers of the skin are the epidermis and the dermis. The epidermis is the layer you can see from the outside. The dermis is beneath the epidermis and contains the oil glands.**

glands release their moisture directly to the skin's surface. Other sweat glands release their moisture into a hair follicle in regions such as the armpits and groin. This secretion, rich in proteins and fatty acids, is decomposed by bacteria on the skin's surface, causing a distinct odor. These glands begin to function at puberty. Emotional stress and sexual changes promote secretion from these glands.

Nerves are also found in the dermis, allowing us to sense touch, pain, heat, and other sensations.

Skin Problems

One of the first things people see when they look at you is your skin, so it is especially frustrating when you have skin problems. Some skin problems, like acne, are common during the teen years. Other problems may occur at any time. The following are some of the most common problems.

Skin Blemishes **Acne** is a term that is commonly used to label the skin eruptions

epidermis:

the very thin outer layer of the skin.

dermis:

the second layer of skin; the dermis contains the most important structures of the skin.

acne:

a condition in which the pores of the skin become clogged with oil; acne can take the form of blackheads, whiteheads, or pimples.

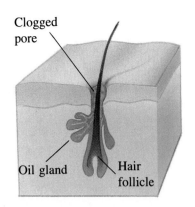
Clogged pore

Oil gland

Hair follicle

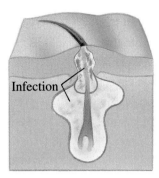
Infection

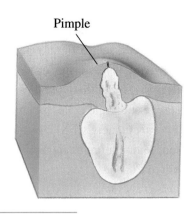
Pimple

(FIGURE 6-3) **A pimple develops when bacteria infect a pore that is already clogged with oil.**

associated with adolescence, but not all skin eruptions are diagnosed as acne, which is a medical condition. Acne is particularly common during the teen years when the skin can produce a lot of oil. There are three other types of skin blemishes: blackheads, whiteheads, and pimples. Blackheads occur when a pore becomes clogged with excess oil and dead skin cells. The combination of oil and dead cells turns black when it is exposed to the air. Whiteheads result from a clogged pore that is not exposed to the air, because the pore is covered by the epidermis. Pimples occur when a clogged pore becomes infected with bacteria. Daily cleansing can reduce the conditions that lead to bacterial infections.

What If You Have Skin Blemishes

Wash your face several times a day with a gentle cleanser to reduce the amount of oil and bacteria on your face.

If you use makeup on your skin, use products that are labeled "water-based." Oily cosmetics can clog the pores.

Do not squeeze or pick at pimples. Squeezing and picking can cause infection and scarring.

Try using an over-the-counter blemish medication containing benzoyl peroxide.

If you have a severe case of blemishes, see a dermatologist — a doctor who specializes in skin disorders. The dermatologist can prescribe medications and offer advice on ways to improve the condition of your skin.

(FIGURE 6-4)

(FIGURE 6-5) **If you have acne, but want to wear makeup on your skin, be sure to buy products that are labeled "water-based." Oil-based products can make acne worse.**

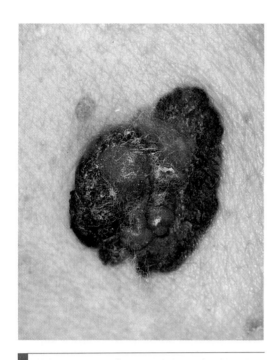

(FIGURE 6-6) **If you notice any changes in a mole, report it immediately to a doctor. A mole can become a malignant melanoma (shown above), a very serious cancer.**

Body Odor When bacteria on the skin attack sweaty secretions, they produce waste with an unpleasant odor. A diet high in animal proteins and animal fats may make this odor even stronger. Daily bathing or showering helps to remove the waste products. In addition, deodorants or antiperspirants may be used. Deodorants kill the bacteria and conceal body odor. Antiperspirants reduce the amount of perspiration and keep the bacteria from growing.

Foot Odor Foot odor can become offensive when the feet perspire heavily. To combat foot odor, be sure to wash your feet thoroughly every day. Wearing cotton socks and open-weave shoes will help reduce foot perspiration, and dusting the feet with plain talc will help absorb moisture. It is also a good idea to alternate pairs of shoes so they can dry out between wearings.

Moles A mole is a small round dark area on the skin. Most moles are not harmful; in fact, they are sometimes called ''beauty marks.'' But just to be safe, report any changes in the size, color, or condition of the mole to a doctor, because these changes may indicate skin cancer.

Warts A wart is a small growth caused by a virus. Although there is no cure for warts, they are usually harmless. Often several warts will appear in the same area. The best treatment for warts is to have them removed by a doctor. If you use an over-the-counter product for wart removal, be very careful. Wart-removal products contain acid that may harm the surrounding skin if they are not applied carefully.

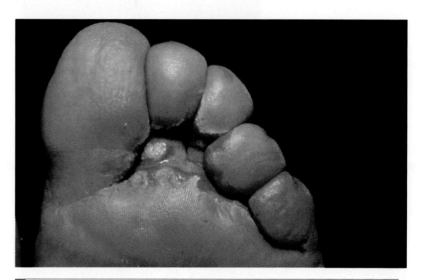

(FIGURE 6-7) **Athlete's foot is caused by a fungus. The symptoms are redness and itching.**

Athlete's Foot and Jock Itch Athlete's foot and other forms of a skin condition called ringworm are caused by microscopic fungi. Athlete's foot gets its name from locker room shower stalls where the fungus may grow and spread to bare feet.

Jock itch occurs in males around the genitals. Symptoms of both athlete's foot and jock itch are redness and itching. Personal cleanliness, using shower shoes, and keeping feet dry will help prevent the spread of the fungus.

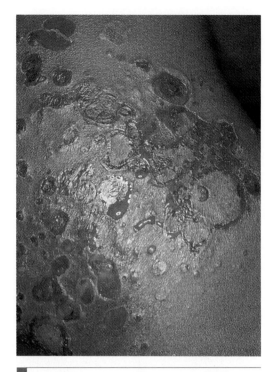

(FIGURE 6-8) **Impetigo is a bacterial infection that causes sores with crusts.**

Impetigo Impetigo is a common infection caused by bacteria, which causes sores with crusts on the skin. It begins in moist areas of the body, in areas where there is friction, and in cuts. Impetigo is most common in children, but may also occur in teenagers and adults. A photograph of impetigo is shown in Figure 6-8. If you think you have impetigo, it is best to seek medical attention.

Poison Ivy, Poison Oak, and Poison Sumac Many people have an allergic reaction to poison ivy, poison oak, or poison sumac. Touching these plants can cause redness, blisters, and severe itching. Each type of plant is shown in Figure 6-9. Memorize how they look so you can be sure to avoid them. Take the following precautions if you touch any of the three plants:

- Immediately wash the skin that came into contact with the plant.

Poison ivy

Poison oak

Poison sumac

(FIGURE 6-9) **Touching these plants can cause a painful allergic rash.**

- If you have a mild allergic reaction, obtain a cream for it from a pharmacy.
- If you have a severe allergic reaction, see a doctor immediately.

Psoriasis Psoriasis is a condition in which red, raised patches appear on the skin. Later the skin becomes dry and flakes off. Areas most commonly affected are the elbows, knees, and scalp. See a doctor for treatment if you have this condition.

Skin and the Sun

Exposure to the sun can be very dangerous by causing damage to your skin now and in the future. Some of the dangers of exposure to the sun include sunburn, wrinkles, and skin cancer.

Sunburn Ultraviolet rays from the sun cause sunburn. Ultraviolet rays that damage skin come in two wavelengths and are known as either ultraviolet A (UVA) or ultraviolet B (UVB) rays. UVB rays burn the skin, so it is easy to see when you have been overexposed to this form of radiation. UVA rays affect the deeper layers of the skin. There is no warning when you have been overexposed. Both kinds of ultraviolet rays are strongest around midday.

10 A.M.

3 P.M.

(FIGURE 6-10) **Ultraviolet rays are at their most intense around midday. This is when you are most likely to get sunburned.**

It usually takes about four to six hours before you can feel the full effects of a sunburn. So even if you feel fine while you are out in the sun, remember that a sunburn won't show up until hours later.

People often have confused ideas about sunburn. Some people think you can get sunburned only on clear days. They don't realize that ultraviolet rays are also present on foggy and cloudy days. In addition, many people think that sunburning is limited to people with light skin. In fact, African-Americans and others with dark skin can also get sunburned.

Wrinkles The skin of people who spend a lot of time in the sun tends to age faster than others. They get wrinkles earlier, and they get more wrinkles as time goes on.

Skin Cancer People who spend a lot of time in the sun without protection or who had severe sunburns during youth are at a higher risk for getting skin cancer. Most skin cancers are easily treatable, but one type called malignant melanoma is very serious. Malignant melanomas are cancers of the cells that produce melanin. If you notice any change in a mole, you should see a physician immediately to make sure you don't have a melanoma.

More information about skin cancer can be found in Chapter 24.

Sun Protection Sunscreens and sunblocks are products that provide some protection from ultraviolet light. A product's ability to block the sun's rays is described by an SPF rating. SPF stands for *sun protection factor*. Figure 6-11 illustrates what different SPF values mean.

Sunscreens partially block UVB rays which burn the skin. Sunblocks partially filter the UVA rays which cause deeper skin damage. Reading the list of ingredients on

Skin cancer is also discussed in Chapter 24.

sunscreen:

a substance that blocks the harmful ultraviolet rays of the sun.

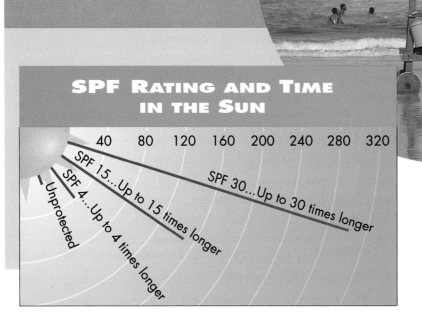

(FIGURE 6-11) **If you usually burn after 10 minutes in the sun, you can stay in the sun for up to 40 minutes (up to four times longer) by using a sunblock with an SPF of 4.**

SPF RATING AND TIME IN THE SUN

40 80 120 160 200 240 280 320

SPF 30...Up to 30 times longer

SPF 15...Up to 15 times longer

SPF 4...Up to 4 times longer

Unprotected

a product's label will tell you whether the product blocks UVA rays as well. Look for titanium or zinc in the ingredients list. If you go swimming, or sweat a lot while in the sun, you may need to reapply the product to be protected.

Wearing protective clothing, such as a hat or long sleeves and pants, also reduces your skin's exposure to the sun.

If you do get a sunburn, you can relieve the pain by applying wet, cool cloths to your burned skin and taking aspirin or acetaminophen. If the sunburn causes blisters or problems with your vision, you should get medical attention.

Review

1. Name the two main layers of the skin.

2. If you had a mole that changed color, what would you do?

3. ▪▪ **LIFE SKILLS: Practicing Self-Care** Why does washing the face with soap several times a day reduce a person's chances of getting acne?

4. ▪▪ **LIFE SKILLS: Practicing Self-Care** Explain how you can avoid sun damage to your skin.

5. **Critical Thinking** What causes the similarity in symptoms between athlete's foot and jock itch?

Section 6.2

Hair and Nail Care

Objectives

- Describe three common hair and scalp problems.

- Explain how to care for your hair.
  LIFE SKILLS: Practicing Self-Care

- Explain how to care for your nails.
  LIFE SKILLS: Practicing Self-Care

Hair is important to not only our appearance but also our health. In the winter, we depend on hair to keep our heads warm. Throughout the year, we rely on the hair in our noses and ears to keep dust out of the body. And every time we blink, our eyelashes, which are specialized hair, protect the eyes.

Structure of Hair

The roots of the hair are in the dermis, where the hair starts growing. But hair cells die when they leave the dermis. That's why it doesn't hurt to have your hair cut—the hair is already dead.

Hair on the head grows for two to six years, then rests for several months. Lots of hair falls out after the rest period, but this is normal and should not cause any concern. It is typical to lose up to a hundred hairs a day, which isn't very many when you consider that most people have 100,000 to 200,000 hairs on their heads.

The part of the hair that we can see is called the hair shaft. The shape of the hair shaft determines whether hair will be straight, curly, or wavy.

Hair color is inherited. It is determined by the kind and amount of melanin in your hair. The melanin in hair decreases as people get older, causing their hair to turn gray and then white. The age at which hair turns gray is determined by heredity.

Thinning of the hair or baldness is an inherited condition affecting mainly men. It occurs with age, but can also result from illness. When hair loss is a result of illness, it is usually only a temporary loss.

Flat hair shafts = curly hair   Oval hair shafts = wavy hair   Round hair shafts = straight hair

(FIGURE 6-12) **The shape of the hair shaft determines whether hair will be curly, wavy, or straight.**

Hair Care Tips

Get a good haircut that fits your lifestyle. Swimmers, for example, may want a short cut that doesn't require much styling.

Brush your hair to get the oil to the ends of the hair. Brushing also stimulates the scalp. It is best to brush with a natural bristle brush and to brush gently. If your hair gets tangled, don't yank at it. Instead, untangle it slowly.

Wash your hair regularly. Washing is good for both the hair and the scalp.

Rather than using a blow-dryer, let your hair dry naturally. Repeated use of blow-dryers can dry out hair. Electric curlers can also dry out hair.

Limit the number of perms you get, since they can damage the hair and scalp. Hair dyes and bleaches can also damage your hair.

(FIGURE 6-13)

Hair Care and Appearance

Taking care of your hair will keep it healthy and looking good. Some tips for keeping your hair in good condition are shown in Figure 6-13.

Keep in mind that you don't need to spend lots of money to have clean hair. Tests of a variety of shampoos have shown that inexpensive shampoos work just as well as the more expensive ones.

Hair and Scalp Problems

The most common problems that affect the hair and scalp can be prevented by good grooming practices. It is most important to shampoo regularly and to avoid sharing combs or brushes.

Dandruff Dandruff is dead skin that flakes off the scalp. People with oily scalps suffer most from dandruff. Washing hair more frequently is the most effective way to control the flaking. Dandruff shampoos with the following ingredients have been shown to be safe and effective for treating dandruff. These include salicylic acid, pyrithione zinc, sulfur, selenium sulfide, and coal tar. It is best to see a doctor for severe dandruff. Seborrhea and psoriasis look like dandruff but they may require prescription medication.

Head Lice Head lice, which are parasites that live in the scalp and hair, are shown in Figure 6-14. They cause almost unbearable itching. Head lice are often spread by the comb or brush of someone who is infected. If you have head lice, ask your doctor or pharmacist about medications that remove the lice. Thoroughly wash or discard clothing and bedding that has come into contact with your head. Do not share combs, brushes, or clothing with others, because this practice spreads the lice.

(FIGURE 6-14) **Head lice are easy to control with the right medication.**

Ringworm Ringworm is caused by a fungus that forms a whitish ring on the skin. It is usually found on the scalp but can also appear on other parts of the body. Ringworm is easily spread to other people by the towels, combs, and brushes of a person who has it. A picture of a ringworm infection is shown in Figure 6-15. If you think you might have ringworm, see a doctor.

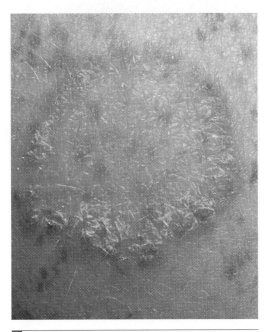

■ (FIGURE 6-15) **Ringworm is spread by sharing towels, combs, and brushes.**

Removing Unwanted Hair

The most common way to remove unwanted hair is to shave it off with a razor. The skin must first be moistened with water and soap or shaving cream. Otherwise the skin can dry out and is also more vulnerable to cuts and sores. Waxing is another hair-removal method, in which a wax is heated and applied to the skin. When the wax has cooled and hardened, it is stripped off, along with the hair. The effects are longer lasting than those of shaving, but waxing can be a bit painful. The only permanent method of hair removal is electrolysis. During elec-

trolysis, an electrical current is sent into each hair follicle. Like waxing, electrolysis can be painful, and it is also expensive.

Nails

Fingernail and manicure services in this country have grown to an estimated $5 billion industry. To improve the appearance of your natural nails, they should be trimmed regularly. The cuticle around the back of a nail can be pushed away and clipped if necessary. And the skin around nails can be moisturized periodically. Toenails can be clipped straight across to prevent ingrown nails. These practices plus a balanced diet can result in attractive nails without the expense of artificial nails. Artificial nails can pose some health risks. Some products used for gluing artificial nails or for removing the glue contain poisonous substances. Common nail problems resulting from the use of artificial nails include infections caused by bacteria, fungi, and the skin viruses that cause warts. Infections usually occur when the nails are left in place too long. If the tools used in a salon are not properly cleaned, they can also spread infections.

> **R**eview
>
> 1. *Describe three common hair and scalp problems.*
>
> 2. ■■ **LIFE SKILLS: Practicing Self-Care** *Explain how to care for your hair.*
>
> 3. ■■ **LIFE SKILLS: Practicing Self-Care** *Explain how to care for your nails.*
>
> 4. **Critical Thinking** *Can a person live in the same house with someone who has ringworm and not get this condition? Explain your answer.*

Section

6.3

Teeth and Gum Care

Objectives

- Explain how dental cavities develop.

- Explain how to care for your teeth and gums.
  ■■ **LIFE SKILLS: Practicing Self-Care**

- Be able to make an appointment with a dentist.
  ■■ **LIFE SKILLS: Being a Wise Consumer**

(FIGURE 6-17) **Having healthy teeth makes it easy to smile.**

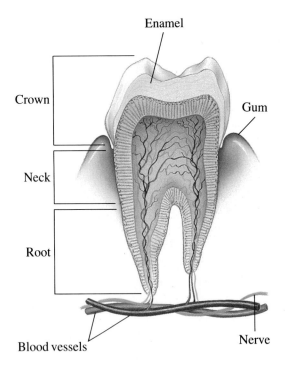

(FIGURE 6-16) **The three main parts of the tooth are the crown, the neck, and the root. The crown is the part that is visible above the gums. Covering the crown is a substance called enamel, the hardest substance in the body.**

Enamel

Crown

Gum

Neck

Root

Blood vessels

Nerve

Have you ever noticed the teeth of people on TV? They almost always look perfect and shiny white. In truth, most of us don't have perfect teeth. In fact, people on TV often have cosmetic dental work done to make their teeth appear whiter and straighter than normal. All of us, however, can have clean teeth that are well cared for. It is simply a matter of good dental care.

Structure of a Tooth

The tooth is divided into three parts, which are shown in Figure 6-16. The crown is the visible part of the tooth above the gum. The neck is just below the gum line where the crown and root come together. The root is the part of the tooth below the gum line.

The part of the tooth that we can see is covered by **enamel,** which is the hardest substance in the body. The only naturally occurring substance harder than enamel is a diamond. Even though it is extremely hard, enamel can still be eroded by decay. Beneath the enamel is soft tissue that contains blood vessels and nerve endings.

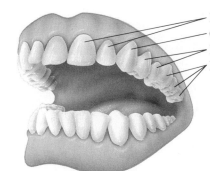

Incisors — Cut and tear food
Cuspids — Tear food into small pieces
Bicuspids — Tear and crush food
Molars — Grind up food

(FIGURE 6-18) **Each of the four types of permanent teeth has a different function in breaking up food before it is swallowed.**

enamel:
the substance covering the crown of the tooth; hardest substance in the body.

Types of Teeth

People have two sets of teeth during their life. First, they have 20 primary teeth—also called baby teeth—that are usually in by age three. These fall out, and permanent teeth start developing around the age of six. By the time people are grown, they have 32 permanent teeth. The four types of permanent teeth and their functions are shown in Figure 6-18.

Dental Problems

Common tooth problems include tooth decay and gum disease. Tooth decay is usually more common in children. Gum disease is usually more common in adulthood. Taking a good care of your teeth can prevent cavities and gum diseases from developing.

Dental Cavity Figure 6-19 shows how a dental cavity develops. A dental cavity results from tooth decay. The decay begins when food is eaten and tiny food particles remain in the mouth. The food particles combine with bacteria and saliva to form

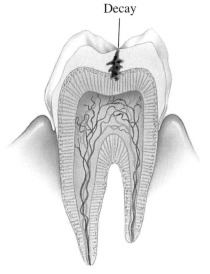

Decay

1. Acid eats through the enamel of a tooth.

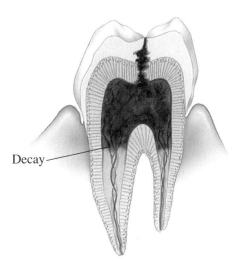

Decay

2. Acid reaches the tissue below the enamel and causes infection.

(FIGURE 6-19) **Bacteria produce acids that eat away tooth enamel, eventually causing dental cavities.**

calculus:

hardened plaque.

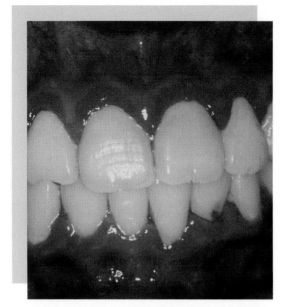

(FIGURE 6-20) **Gum disease is often caused by a buildup of calculus (tartar) on the teeth. If not treated by a dentist, gum disease can cause teeth to fall out.**

plaque:

a film of food particles, saliva, and bacteria on teeth.

plaque, which coats the teeth with a very thin film. The bacteria which grows in the plaque produces an acid that eats through the enamel of the teeth. If the teeth are not cleaned, the enamel is eaten away until a cavity forms in the tooth. Cavities that are very small are not always easy to detect without an X ray, because they are not painful. A toothache may be a sign of decay that has reached the base of the tooth. If the infection spreads to the bone socket, the tooth can become abscessed. Other signs of decay include sensitivity to heat, to cold, and to pressure. If you have any of these sensations, see a dentist immediately. Your tooth will only get worse without treatment.

Bad Breath Most bad breath is the result of plaque, decayed teeth, and gum and throat infections. Mouthwashes may provide fresh breath for a little while, but it will not be lasting. In addition, mouthwashes usually contain alcohol, which can worsen a throat or tooth infection. Sometimes bad

breath results from eating strong-smelling foods—garlic, for example. A coated tongue may also cause bad breath. Most dentists recommend cleaning the tongue by brushing it with a toothbrush.

Gum Disease Gum disease is the leading cause of tooth loss in adults. It begins when a material called **calculus** builds up near the gums. Calculus, which is also known as tartar, is simply plaque that has hardened. Removing plaque at least once every 24 hours prevents it from becoming hard. Calculus must be removed at a dentist's office.

The first sign of gum disease is bleeding when the teeth are brushed. Later, the gums pull back from the teeth and form pockets that may fill with pus. The teeth may then loosen and fall out. Although more common in adults, gum disease can also occur during the teenage years. If treated early, it usually will not cause permanent damage or tooth loss. See a dentist if you think you might have gum disease.

Poor Alignment Usually the top teeth fit exactly over the bottom teeth. When they don't fit correctly, there is an alignment problem. Poor alignment may make it difficult to eat or speak or clean the teeth adequately. Sometimes poor tooth alignment is related to genetics. The bone structure of the jaw may be too small or too large for the teeth. Thumb-sucking may also play a role in poor alignment. Braces and other orthodontic devices are generally used to treat poor alignment, but sometimes tooth extraction and surgery may be required to correct the problem.

Dental Care

Good dental care involves more than just brushing your teeth. The behaviors that are most important to good dental care are: eating nutritious foods, brushing teeth, flossing teeth, and having regular dental checkups.

Eating Nutritious Foods Foods high in sugar and acids can contribute to tooth decay. Eat a balanced diet rich in protein and minerals, along with raw fruits and vegetables. Avoid foods that stick to your teeth as they may promote tooth decay.

Flossing and Brushing Teeth Flossing before you brush loosens food particles so they can be brushed away. Dentists have discovered that harshly scrubbing the teeth may tear the gums and remove tooth enamel. The recommended way to brush is shown in Figure 6-21. You should brush your teeth twice a day. Always brush your teeth after you floss to remove dislodged particles.

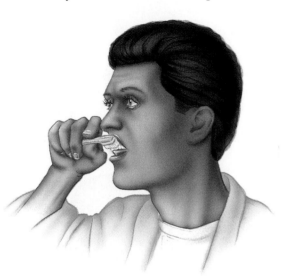

1. Hold the toothbrush at a 45-degree angle to the gums.

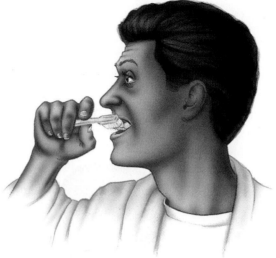

2. Move the brush gently in a circular motion on two teeth at a time. Don't brush hard! Gentle brushing will remove plaque without hurting your teeth.

3. Brush all the surfaces of your teeth, including the backs of teeth.

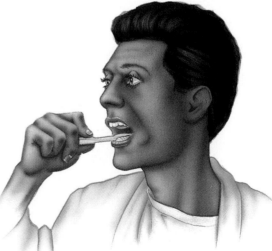

4. Continue until you have brushed all your teeth.

(FIGURE 6-21) **Brush your teeth at least twice a day, immediately after you eat if possible. Use a soft, flat brush that can reach all your teeth.**

dental floss:

a special string that removes plaque from the teeth.

Flossing Teeth **Dental floss** is a special string sold at most supermarkets and drugstores. Flossing once a day will remove most plaque. Flossing is shown in Figure 6-22.

1. Cut off a piece of dental floss about 18 inches long.

2. Wrap the ends of the floss around your middle fingers.

3. Very gently push the floss between two teeth.

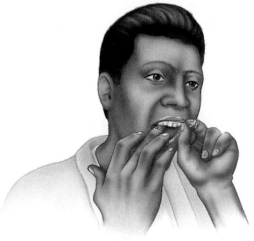

4. Pull the floss around one of the teeth to make a horseshoe shape with the floss. Gently move the floss up and down to clean the sides of that tooth.

(FIGURE 6-22)
Flossing removes the plaque between the teeth. You should floss your teeth every day.

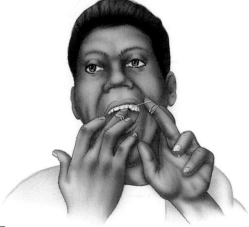

5. Continue until you have flossed all your teeth. Use a clean section of floss on each tooth.

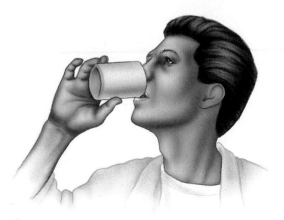

6. Rinse your mouth with water.

Making a Dental Appointment · · · · · · · · ·

Making a dental appointment is something most teenagers haven't had any practice doing. It's actually quite easy to compare dentists and choose the one who suits your needs. You may already have a dentist or know of one you want to see. If not, follow these steps to choose a dentist and make an appointment.

1. Look in the yellow pages of the phone book under "Dentists" and find three dentists who are close to where you live or go to school.

2. Write down their phone numbers and call them.

3. Tell the receptionist who answers that you are just trying to get some information right now—you're not making an appointment. Ask how much an initial visit would cost to examine your teeth and clean them. This price will probably include X-rays of your teeth.

4. Ask when the office would be able to see you. Some dentists have a long waiting period, while others can see people quickly.

5. After calling all three offices, compare the costs of the dentists. Also compare the length of time you would need to wait before seeing each dentist.

6. Now you're ready to make an appointment with the dentist that you have chosen.

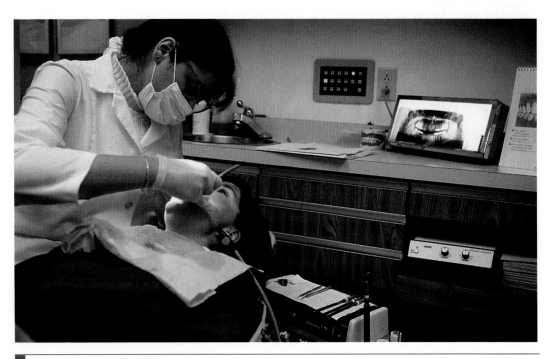

(FIGURE 6-23) **Dentists should always wear gloves and usually wear masks to protect themselves and their patients from infection.**

Dental Checkups How often do you think a person should see a dentist for a checkup?

- Every three months?
- Every six months?
- Every year?
- Every two years?

The answer depends on the person. Some people don't develop cavities or gum disease easily and may not need a checkup more often than every six months. Other people develop calculus even if they floss daily and brush their teeth regularly. They may need to have their teeth cleaned every three months. Most people do not need checkups more often than every six months.

Dentists and dental hygienists clean teeth with tools that look a little like pencils with scrapers on the end. They use these to scrape the calculus off the teeth and polish them. Most people experience very little discomfort with this process and are pleased with the result—nice, clean, polished teeth.

When teeth are flossed and brushed regularly, they usually stay nice-looking during the period between cleanings.

Review

1. Explain how dental cavities develop.

2. What are four things you can do to have healthy teeth?

3. ▪▪ LIFE SKILLS: Practicing Self-Care Describe how to floss the teeth.

4. ▪▪ LIFE SKILLS: Being a Wise Consumer Describe one method of choosing a dentist.

5. Critical Thinking What purpose do you think the enamel of teeth serves?

Highlights

Summary

- The skin functions to protect the body from germs, to regulate body temperature, to transmit sensations such as pain, and as a waterproof cover that holds the body together.

- The epidermis and the dermis are the two main layers of the skin. The dermis contains oil and sweat glands as well as nerves.

- Blemishes, a common skin problem for teens, result when pores in the skin become clogged with oil. They usually can be controlled by washing frequently with soap and water.

- Other skin problems include moles, warts, athlete's foot and jock itch, impetigo, poison ivy, poison oak, poison sumac, and psoriasis.

- Changes in the size, color, or condition of a mole should be reported to a doctor because the changes may indicate skin cancer.

- Exposure to the sun can cause sunburn, wrinkles, and skin cancer. Use of a sunscreen is the most important action you can take to protect your skin from the sun.

- Hair insulates the head from heat and cold. Eyelashes and eyebrows protect the eyes from foreign matter. Hair in the nose and ears keeps foreign matter out of the nose and ears.

- A tooth is made up of a crown, a neck, and a root. The part of the tooth we see is covered by enamel.

- The bacteria in plaque produce acid, which eats through the enamel of teeth and causes decay.

- Good dental care includes brushing and flossing teeth, eating nutritious foods, and having regular checkups.

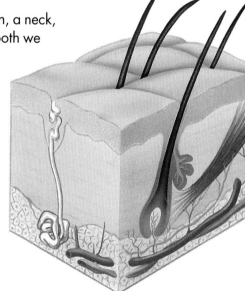

Vocabulary

epidermis the very thin outer layer of the skin.

dermis the second layer of skin; contains the most important skin structures.

acne a condition in which the pores of the skin become clogged with oil; acne can take the form of blackheads, whiteheads, or pimples.

enamel the substance covering the crown of the tooth.

plaque a film of food particles, saliva, and bacteria on teeth.

dental floss a special string that removes plaque from the teeth.

Concept Review . . . .

1. What are three important functions of the skin?

2. Name two things found in each of the two layers of the skin.

3. Name a skin condition caused by fungus; by bacteria; by a virus.

4. When should a mole be checked by a doctor? Why?

5. Why is it important to use a sunscreen? What do the SPF numbers mean on suntan products?

6. How is hair important to our health?

7. Why does dandruff appear? What can you do to control it?

8. Head lice live in the scalp and hair. What are they and what should you do if you become infected with them?

9. Why is it important to take good care of your nails?

10. Name the three parts of a tooth. Which part(s) is above the gum line?

11. What is plaque? How can plaque removal help prevent cavities?

12. What are three things that can cause bad breath?

13. Who usually suffers from gum disease? What causes it and how can it be controlled?

Expressing Your Views . . . .

1. Julie has a mild case of acne. You notice that she wears heavy makeup to cover the pimples, and you often see her picking at her face. How will her behavior damage her skin? How would you advise her?

2. You are embarrassed to remove your shoes in public because when you do you have a very offensive foot odor. What could you do to relieve this problem?

3. You brush your teeth twice a day but lately you have noticed some sensitive areas on your teeth. What might this sensitivity mean? What can you do?

4. Your friend is bothered by unwanted hair on her face. She doesn't want to shave it off because it might make her skin rough and unattractive. What else can she do to get rid of the hair?

Life Skills Check

1. Practicing Self-Care
You took a summer job as a lifeguard at a nearby pool. You have fair skin and you know you will be spending six hours a day in the sun. Should you take extra care to protect your skin from the sun? Why?

2. Being a Wise Consumer
Lamar has just moved to your community and needs to visit a dentist. He doesn't know any of the dentists in town, and he is not familiar with the streets. Explain how you would help him choose a dentist and make an appointment.

3. Practicing Self-Care
Your friend just made the diving team and is concerned about caring for her hair, since she will spend a lot of time in the water. Her shoulder-length hair appears dry and damaged. What advice can you give her?

Projects

1. Work with a group to learn what bacteria cause impetigo. How is this disease spread? How can this disease be stopped and controlled? Find out how your school system handles cases of impetigo. Make a report to your class.

2. Borrow two or three microscopes from the science department to examine the different shapes of hair shafts from you and your classmates. Take turns viewing the different hair structures, then draw and label what you see.

3. Interview a dermatologist or dentist to find out the most common problems he or she encounters with teens. You might ask them what the main causes of the problems are and how they might be prevented. Summarize the information and present it to the class.

Plan for Action

A person's physical appearance reflects a person's health. List five improvements you can make regarding your grooming habits.

Evaluating Media Messages

▼ How In Is Thin?

When Cara told Jennifer, "I love this dress, but it makes me look so fat!" Jennifer just stared at her friend. She wanted to say, "Cara, I hate it when you complain about being fat. You know I'm a lot bigger than you, and when you talk like that, it makes me feel huge!" Jennifer also wanted to tell her friend that she had started to worry about how thin Cara was getting and about what Cara was doing to get even thinner.

Does this sound familiar? Recent studies have shown that very few teenage girls are happy with their appearance, especially their weight. An alarming percentage of these girls report being overweight, even when their weight is healthy by medical standards. One source of such attitudes is the media messages about what is attractive that are found in advertisements, television programs, and movies.

The message to be thin can be both good and bad. Healthy people come in all shapes and sizes.

One of the strongest media messages in our culture is that thin is in and fat is out. Because marketing studies have shown that women's clothes sell better when pictured on thin models, girls get the strongest message to be thin. However, boys are also affected by media stereotypes. For males, attractiveness is usually associated with a muscular, athletic build. While this is a healthy model, a boy can also be healthy and fit without being muscular or athletic. Remember that the primary objective of most media messages is to sell something and that you do not have to look like a media stereotype to be healthy and happy.

When questioned about what they consider attractive, many teenagers automatically agree with the media stereotypes—the ultrathin girl and superjock boy—but only at first. As they continue to express their true attitudes and feelings, they tend to emphasize other, more important qualities:

"What I like most about Chad is that he's never boring. He has a great sense of humor and relates to people really well."

"What I love about Mai is that she knows what she wants out of life and really goes for it."

"Jerry is really sensitive and sweet. He plans to have his own band someday. Because he is also a good student, he should have many options for the future."

When you evaluate your attitudes toward personal appearance, be aware of how media messages influence you. Think about what the messages actually say and why they say what they do. Are they eroding your self-esteem? Are they causing you to engage in potentially harmful behavior? Also be aware of mixed messages. An example of a mixed message is a magazine article about proper nutrition and health that is surrounded by ads featuring extremely thin models. Ask yourself which of these messages is encouraging you to make realistic decisions that are truly in your best interest.

The message to be thin or athletic can be good or bad from a health standpoint. Naturally thin or athletic-looking people can be very healthy. However, these body types are not in the majority. Furthermore, healthy people come in all shapes and sizes. Too often, naturally full-figured people try to achieve the unrealistic goal of a fashion model's thin figure or athletic build by resorting to unhealthy behaviors.

Recently, many well-known personalities, including actors, fashion models, and athletes, have admitted that they engaged in unhealthy eating habits and took dangerous medications to maintain their weight and build. Several of these individuals now promote healthier lifestyles. One very moving appeal for a healthier lifestyle came from Lyle Alzado, a former NFL football player who died of cancer in 1992. Before he died, Mr. Alzado used the media to campaign against the use of steroids by athletes who want to increase their size and weight. He believed that the steroids he took were the cause of his cancer.

Persuasive messages are a fact of life in our society. We can't eliminate them, but we can guard against being manipulated by them. With a clear understanding of your values and a strong sense of self-esteem, you can evaluate media messages and use them to your best advantage by using effective decision-making skills.

Critical Thinking

1. Find a picture of someone you think is really attractive, or describe a favorite actor or actress. Ask yourself:

    - Do I really want to look like this person? Why?
    - Does someone have to look like this person for me to be able to be friends with him or her?
    - Why do I feel like this? Does this really match my values?
    - If someone I cared for gained a lot of weight, would that change my feelings for that person? If I gained a lot of weight, would I understand if a friend tried to break off our friendship?
    - Are my personal appearance and fitness goals realistic and healthy?
    - What will I gain by attaining this goal? (Will I get a boyfriend/girlfriend if I lose five pounds?)
    - What do I have to do to attain this goal? Is the effort worth it?

2. See if you can find an example of a mixed message in an advertisement, television program, or movie.

3. Name a movie or television program that contains characters who are attractive without fitting the stereotypical models of "attractiveness."

HEALTH
AND
YOUR
MIND

CHAPTER

7

Mental and Emotional Health

◆ ◆ ◆ ◆

Section 7.1 Understanding Mental Health and Emotions

Section 7.2 Defense Mechanisms and Positive Strategies

Section 7.3 Types of Mental and Emotional Disorders

Section 7.4 Seeking Help

Emotionally healthy people feel a range of emotions and know how to express them in the right way.

Gena was really scared this time. Kevin had been so angry she was really afraid he would hurt her. Why was this happening? Why was he so mad? She thought about when they first met and started going together. He had been so nice. Lately though, Kevin was really possessive. He didn't like it when Gena talked to any other guys, and now he was beginning to be resentful of her girlfriends.

This last argument seemed so stupid. Gena was talking to Mr. Estrada, her history teacher, when Kevin walked up. That afternoon he told her he didn't want to see her talking to Mr. Estrada again. Gena couldn't believe it. When she tried to explain, he flew into a rage and pushed her against the wall. What was she going to do?

Section
7.1
Understanding Mental Health and Emotions

Objectives

- List the characteristics of a mentally healthy person.

- List qualities that can lead to happiness.
  LIFE SKILLS: Setting Goals

- List ways to manage negative emotions.
  LIFE SKILLS: Coping

People once thought of *mental health* as the absence of mental illness. Now it is defined in much more positive terms. Mental health refers to how you use the various aspects of health to achieve positive feelings about yourself and improve your ability to deal with problems. Do you feel good about yourself and the things you do? Can you cope with problems effectively? Do you have close friendships? Can you work through problems with your friends? If you can answer yes most of the time, you are probably mentally healthy.

It is important to recognize that there will be times when you will not feel good about yourself and times when you will have difficulty resolving problems. While having problems is normal, you can develop skills that will enable you to be more effective in dealing with problems.

The National Association for Mental Health describes someone with good mental health as having the following characteristics:

- feels comfortable with himself or herself
- has good relationships with others
- meets the demands of life

Emotions Are Normal

Emotions are feelings in response to an activity or an experience. Understanding emotions and expressing them effectively are important parts of being mentally healthy.

Everyone has emotions, and they make you feel good or bad. Emotions themselves aren't good or bad, but the way you express emotions can be positive or negative. For example, feeling angry is okay, but expressing your anger by hitting someone is not.

You may feel happy one minute and sad the next. This change in feelings is actually very natural. Your body is changing rapidly, and your hormones can cause mood swings and dramatic changes in your emotions. Drugs and other substances can also have a profound effect on moods. For example, some people become very irritable if they consume too much caffeine. Scientists are studying the relationship between diet and mood.

■ (FIGURE 7-1) **Laughter makes you feel good. Keeping a sense of humor helps you deal with stress effectively.**

• • • • •

152 CHAPTER 7 MENTAL AND EMOTIONAL HEALTH

Expressing Emotions

You learn to express emotions based on past experiences. These experiences include what you learn from your interactions and from seeing how others react. You *model* your reactions on the reactions of someone else. It is important to recognize how to express your emotions in a positive way. Learning how to do this is a continual process. Instead of hitting someone when you're angry, you learn it is better to hit a pillow, or do some strenuous exercise, or tell someone you're angry. One valuable skill in expressing emotions positively is to think of a particular emotion and rehearse what you will do when it occurs.

Kinds of Emotions

We have the ability to feel a wide variety of emotions, from extreme happiness and joy to sadness and misery.

Love Love is the feeling of strong affection or caring for another person. Love can be a very strong emotion that grows deeper and stronger with time. We all have the need to love, and the need to be loved by others.

There are different types of love. You may feel love for the members of your family. You may also feel love for another person. That might be in the form of caring and loyalty to a friend, or in the form of romantic love. Romantic love is different from other forms of love because of the way you feel. Your heart beats faster when you think of the person you love, and you can't stand to be apart. Yet, sometimes it is hard to tell the difference between attraction and love.

Happiness Happiness is a feeling of joy and well-being or contentment. While happiness is an emotion, it is also a goal that drives people. Bookstores are filled with books on how to achieve happiness—how to feel happy. The first step toward achieving this state is to recognize that you have some control over your life. Your attitude about life and how you react to situations are decisions only you make. Adopting a healthy lifestyle by following the guidelines you'll read about throughout this book will put you on the road to happiness. Here are some other things you can do to be happy.

- Establish close relationships with others.
- Work hard at tasks you find meaningful.
- Have a positive attitude.
- Think about what makes you happy and make time for those activities.
- Take good care of your body.
- Be organized, but flexible, so you can adapt to changes as they occur in your life.

Optimism   Feeling optimistic means feeling that life experiences will be positive. It means realistically balancing the ups and downs of life and attempting to keep a positive attitude. Optimism is a healthy emotion that in turn affects your physical well-being. Is optimism part of your range of emotions? Do the following to find out.

Write down all the positive things you expect will happen to you in the future. Then list any of the bad things that you think could happen in the future as well. Now look at your lists. Have you described more positive things or more negative things? How could you revise your lists to look at each negative event with optimism?

Humor   Humor provides a way of expressing some negative emotions in a more positive way. Laughing and finding humor in a stressful situation is a very healthy way of coping. Medical research has found that laughter can increase the effectiveness of your immune system in fighting disease.

Check Up

Assessing Your Mental Health

Answer the following questions and count the characteristics of good mental health that you possess.

1. Are you willing to assume responsibilities appropriate for your age?
2. Do you participate in activities appropriate to your stage of life?
3. Do you accept your responsibilities?
4. Do you solve problems rather than avoid them?
5. Do you make decisions with a minimum of worry?
6. Do you stick with a choice you make until new factors surface?
7. Are you satisfied with your accomplishments?
8. Do you recognize that thinking about a problem is the first step toward taking action?
9. Do you learn from failures or defeats?
10. Do you keep successes in perspective?
11. Do you enjoy working and enjoy playing?
12. Do you say no to negative situations even though they may provide temporary pleasure?
13. Do you say yes to situations that will be positive even though there may be some momentary displeasure?
14. Can you tell others when you are angry?
15. Can you show affection?
16. Can you endure frustration when the source cannot be changed or eliminated?
17. Can you make compromises in dealing with difficulties?
18. Can you concentrate and work at a single goal?
19. Do you recognize the challenges of life?
20. Can you develop and maintain family and intimate relationships?

(FIGURE 7-2) **It is normal to feel anger over an irritating situation. Exercise can provide a good outlet to relieve anger or it can just help you manage anger better.**

Fear Fear is the feeling of danger. When you are afraid, your heart beats faster to supply more blood to muscles. Your muscles become tense and your senses become more alert. All these reactions prepare your body to deal with danger. Your body returns to normal once you have dealt with the situation that caused the fear. It is important to work through fears so that the body doesn't stay in this state of alarm for an extended time.

Fears are often learned from experiences that you had when you were young. If you fell off a horse when you were nine years old, you might now be afraid to go riding. Fears also may be learned from other people, particularly your family. If your mother was robbed, you might be afraid to be alone at night. Some of these fears may be valid, while others may not be. For example, your parents probably told you never to accept rides from strangers when you were young. As a result, you may have developed a fear of strangers as a child that is still useful as you get older. However, as a child you may have been told

not to go outside after dark. If you developed a fear of the dark as a consequence, that is not useful. Some fears, such as a fear of strangers, are useful because they are related to things that can cause you harm. But if a feeling of danger is not realistic, it is important to be able to manage that fear.

Managing Fear Two effective ways to manage fear are self-talk and environmental planning. *Self-talk* is saying things to yourself in order to view a fear more realistically. For example, if you are afraid of the dark, you might make the following self-talk statements:

1. I've never been hurt in the dark before. I probably won't be hurt in the dark now.
2. I sleep in a dark room every night and nothing bad ever happens to me.

3. It doesn't matter whether it's dark or light. It's whether the place or people are dangerous, and since they aren't in this place, there is nothing to fear.

Environmental planning involves re-arranging the environment to reduce your fear. For example, if you are afraid to fly on an airplane you could employ the following environmental planning strategies:

1. Travel with a friend or relative who can comfort you.

2. Bring something to read on the plane to take your mind off the fear.

3. Meditate or engage in some other form of relaxation exercise while flying.

Anger Anger is a strong feeling of irritation. Everyone feels angry at some time. The important thing is how you deal with the anger.

*Life*SKILLS: | Coping

Managing Fears . . . .

Think about something that makes you afraid. With that situation in mind, answer the following questions.

1. What can you say to yourself to be less fearful in that situation?

a. _____

b. _____

c. _____

d. _____

e. _____

2. How can you adjust your environment to be less fearful in that situation?

a. _____

b. _____

c. _____

d. _____

e. _____

If you actually use this plan, it might help you to be less afraid.

Americans' Top Ten Fears

1. Snakes	39%
2. Heights	19%
3. Mice	15%
4. Flying	12%
5. Being closed in a small place	10%
6. Spiders/insects	9%
7. Thunder and lightning	9%
8. Being alone in a house at night	6%
9. Dogs	5%
10. Driving	3%

Anger is not experienced only in your mind. A physical reaction accompanies anger. This reaction varies but may include an increased heart rate and higher blood pressure, headaches, and nausea. It is important to find a positive release for these reactions. That is why exercise is recommended as a way to alleviate angry feelings.

Anger is negative if it is expressed in a violent form. Unfortunately, anger sometimes results in child abuse or spouse abuse. Too often, it also is expressed through aggressive behavior, such as fighting. In the introductory story, Kevin used violence to express his anger at Gena. If such behavior continues unchecked, Kevin will need professional help.

Depression in relation to suicide is discussed in Chapter 11.

Managing Anger It is important to channel emotions appropriately so that anger can be expressed in a positive way. It is helpful to recognize your feelings and the source of the anger. Once you do this, you may wish to talk to the person with whom you are angry. You are likely to have the most positive results from the talk if you do not blame the other person. Keep in mind that other people, even if they make you angry, do not make you *express* your anger in a certain way. Recognizing this simple fact enables you to choose how, when, and to whom you express your anger.

If you are not able to talk with the person to resolve the problem, do something physical to release your anger and relieve some of the physical symptoms. Remember that it is not helpful to keep your feelings penned up inside.

Guilt Guilt is the feeling that you have done something wrong or are responsible for something bad happening. You may feel guilty after you have had an argument with someone you love. Or you may feel guilty if you have done something unintentionally that caused something bad to happen.

Guilt can be your cue to resolve a problem. Guilt may also drive you to do the right thing in a situation. You may be nice to someone you really don't like because you feel guilty if you're mean.

Managing Guilt If you feel guilty about something you've done, think about the source of your guilt. Have you done something wrong, or are you responding to how others see the situation? For example, if you have stood up to others during a conflict, have you allowed a parent or guardian to make you feel guilty for being assertive? Try not to be critical of yourself. If you've made a mistake, correct it and then move on. If you find guilt over an issue or problem to be overwhelming, seek professional help so you can work through the problem.

Depression Depression is a feeling of anxiety, loneliness, and despair. It can interfere with the ability to carry out daily activities. Symptoms of teenage depression may include the following:

- sleeping too much or too little
- feeling tired throughout the day
- lack of interest or lack of ability to concentrate
- loss of appetite
- loss of energy
- withdrawal from a group

Everyone feels sad or depressed occasionally, but extended depression may indicate a need for professional help. Serious depression can lead to suicide.

Several factors are linked to the development of depression.

- *Family History* The tendency for depression appears to be hereditary.

- *Major Life Stresses* Personal traumas such as neglect, abuse, or separation often precede depression.
- *Physical Illness* People who are physically ill are more likely to be depressed.
- *Substance Abuse* Alcoholics and abusers of other drugs have higher rates of depression.
- *Gender* Depression is more likely to occur in women.

Managing Depression When you feel depressed, try to identify why you feel the way you do. Once you do that, you'll be able to put things in perspective, and you may see that they really aren't that bad. Focus on the positive things in your life to keep you from dwelling on the things that aren't going so well. Talk to a trusted friend to help you with your perspective.

Get some exercise. When you get a workout your body produces chemicals that make you feel good. Exercise is a natural way to improve your outlook.

Jealousy Jealousy is the feeling of wanting something that someone else has or the fear of losing something that you have. For example, Mary's parents don't have much money. Mary works after school, but most of her money goes to help pay the family's expenses. Mary sees girls who don't have to work but have lots of nice clothes. Mary is jealous because they have things she would like but can't have.

The situation with Kevin in the introductory story shows an example of jealousy that results from the possibility of losing something. Kevin and Gena have been dating for six months. Gena has started tutoring Jordan after school. Kevin is jealous of Jordan because he has Gena's time and attention. He feels that his relationship with Gena is threatened by Jordan.

Check Up

Are You at Risk for Depression?

Depression occurs in people of all ages. By some estimates, 33 percent of teens are affected by depression. If feelings of depression last more than two weeks, help should be sought. To determine whether you (or a friend) are depressed, answer the following questions.

1. Do you have problems concentrating or making decisions?

2. Are you almost always tired, or do you have problems sitting still because you are so upset?

3. Do you sleep well? Are you sleeping much more or much less than usual?

4. Have you gained or lost a significant amount of weight?

5. Do you find that you no longer enjoy things that used to make you happy?

6. Do you feel worthless most of the time?

7. Do you have thoughts of death?

If you (or your friend) answered YES to five or more of these questions, speak with a mental health specialist.

Managing Jealousy If you are jealous of someone, you should discuss these feelings with the other person involved. Remember that people don't own other people, so they can't "lose" them. Jealousy is an emotion that can be very destructive if it is not controlled. In the introductory story, Kevin's jealousy was driving him to anger. That anger was expressed in a violent way. The jealousy is Kevin's problem, not Gena's. Gena's best course of action would be to stop seeing Kevin until he can get his emotions under control.

(FIGURE 7-3) **Loneliness is a feeling that you can manage by taking some action. Look for ways to interact with people.**

Loneliness Loneliness is a feeling of isolation or alienation. It is not the same as being alone. Being able to enjoy time by yourself is a part of good mental health. Loneliness can be a particular problem for teens, because in trying to become independent, teens sometimes alienate one another.

Managing Loneliness Engage in activities that will make you part of a group. Don't wait to be asked to join in. Take charge of your loneliness. Make the effort to contact your old friends. Get involved in volunteer work as an interest and way of meeting new people. There are times in life when you will be alone. Therefore it is a good idea to start now in being comfortable by yourself.

Shyness Shyness is the feeling of being timid or bashful. Shy people can appear to be less friendly or open. What often happens is that shy people are thought to be snobs or stuck up. Working to improve self-esteem will help in making shyness less of a problem. People who are confident are less controlled by feelings of shyness. Shyness is something that everyone feels at times.

Managing Shyness/Improving Self-Esteem If you are shy, you might try the following.

1. Make a list of your strengths and positive traits.
2. Never say things about yourself such as "What a dummy," or "Boy, am I stupid." These things make you feel inferior.
3. Purposely put yourself in situations with supportive people. As you do, you'll become more confident.
4. Do not spend time with people who make you feel badly about yourself. People who are always putting you down should be avoided. If the person putting you down is a family member and can't really be avoided, keep remembering your strengths and positive traits.
5. Don't be afraid to try new things or be afraid to fail. Failure teaches you lessons that help you grow as a person, and may lead to other opportunities that are successful.

Review

1. How would you know if you are mentally healthy?

2. List four goals you can set for yourself to achieve happiness.

3. Describe some positive strategies for managing anger.

4. **Critical Thinking** List three things you can do to keep from feeling lonely.

Section 7.2

Defense Mechanisms and Positive Strategies

Objectives

• Describe the purpose of defense mechanisms and how they can be helpful.

• Define your self-concept and self-ideal.

■ **LIFE SKILLS: Assessing Your Health**

• Relate Maslow's hierarchy of needs to self-esteem and self-ideal.

Defense mechanisms are techniques you use to protect yourself from being hurt emotionally. They provide a way to deal with problems and maintain self-esteem. However, too much reliance on defense mechanisms is not healthy if they are used consistently to avoid facing an issue. Figure 7-4 is a listing of common defense mechanisms. Look through the list and think of one way to use each mechanism that would be helpful and one way that would be harmful.

Promoting Positive Mental and Emotional Health

Each day you are faced with problems or situations that affect your mental health. While it is easy to let your problems get you down, there are things you can do to stay mentally healthy. The road to good mental health starts with feeling positive about yourself, which means getting to know yourself thoroughly.

Self-Esteem Having high self-esteem is very important in developing and maintaining good mental health. Self-esteem is feeling good about yourself and the things you do. These feelings give you a sense of confidence. Take a moment to consider the positive things about yourself and the things you do well. Make a list of these. Pay particular attention to these positive aspects when you are feeling down. Chapter 8 will give you a number of strategies for building your self-esteem.

Sense of Control Another important factor for staying mentally healthy is acquiring a sense of control. High self-esteem gives you a sense of control. People with low self-esteem feel that events affecting their lives are beyond their control. These people have an *external locus of control.* Others believe they can control at least some aspects of their lives. These people have an *internal locus of control.* If you believe you are in control of a situation, you will do what you need to do to stay in control. If you think what you do influences your grades, you'll find out from your teacher how to do better. If you think you have no control over your grades, you won't bother. The reality is that you always have some control over your life. You need to work out the ways you can influence your future. You cannot solve problems by blaming others and bad luck for your situation.

As a teen, there are certain limits to the control you have. If you want to go to college and you don't have the money, that is a limitation. However, you can set college as a goal and begin to explore possible options

Common Defense Mechanisms

Mechanism	Description	Examples
Compensation	covering a weakness by over-achieving in another area	focusing all your attention on sports because you think you are a better athlete than student
Daydreaming	escaping from an unpleasant situation by using your imagination	in the dentist's chair you focus on the fun you'll have over the weekend with friends because you hate being at the dentist
Denial	failure to accept reality	refusing to accept the death of a close friend or relative; refusing to accept that your relationship with a romantic friend is over
Displacement	the transfer of negative feelings about someone to someone else	you are very angry with your mother and you take out that anger in dealing with your sister or best friend
Projection	putting (projecting) negative feelings on someone else	blaming your teacher for failing a test when you did not study
Rationalization	justifying irrational behavior	not doing your homework one evening because you feel you've spent too much of your time on schoolwork
Reaction formation	expressing emotions that are the exact opposite of what you feel	acting like a clown in a group to hide your shyness
Regression	using childlike ways of expressing emotions like anger or disappointment	throwing a tantrum when you don't get to watch your favorite TV program
Repression	blocking out unpleasant memories	forgetting when you were in the hospital
Sublimation	redirecting bad or unacceptable behavior into positive behavior	channeling your aggression into an athletic sport where aggressive behavior is accepted
Somatization	converting emotions into bodily symptoms	getting stomach cramps every time final exams are scheduled

(FIGURE 7-4)

(FIGURE 7-5) **How closely does your self-concept match how you look and feel? What could you do to improve how you see yourself?**

for getting there. You may be able to seek financial aid or apply for scholarships. To look for ways to take charge of and solve a problem is to be mentally healthy. To give up and run away from your problems is to be unhealthy. If you focus on the negative, you'll be unhappy. If you focus on the positive, you'll be happier. Having a positive outlook will help improve and maintain your mental health.

Self-Concept Rating your level of self-esteem requires a thorough analysis of your **self-concept**, or self-image as it is sometimes called. It means looking realistically at how you see yourself.

Take out a piece of paper and draw a picture of yourself. Now look at the picture. Are you satisfied with the picture you've drawn? What kinds of things can you learn about how you feel about yourself by look- *ing at the picture you've drawn? Do you see yourself as big or small? Did you draw yourself as happy or sad? Does your picture fill up the whole paper or is it off in a corner? Does your picture reflect a positive view of yourself?*

Now think about what you would like your picture to look like. This image represents your **self-ideal**. Your self-ideal can be an image to strive for, as long as it is realistic. For example, if you are short you can't expect to achieve a goal of being tall. If you are sad, you can work at being happy. Your self-ideal should represent your feelings about yourself. Your self-ideal should be based on what you think, not on what your parents think, your friends think, or your teachers think.

Once you have a realistic self-ideal you can set reasonable goals for moving your self-concept closer to your self-ideal.

self-ideal:

your mental image of what you would like to be.

self-concept:

the current mental image you have of yourself.

Maslow's Hierarchy of Needs

Self-actualization	Fulfilling your potential
Self-esteem	Respecting yourself and others
Love and affection	Your ability to give and receive affection; feeling of belonging
Safety-security	Your ability to protect yourself from harm
Physiological needs	Fulfilling your needs for food, water, shelter, sleep, sexual expression

■ **(FIGURE 7-6) According to Maslow, you cannot reach a state of fulfillment without satisfying your basic physiological needs first. Each step in the pyramid requires that the needs in the section below have been met.**

Maslow's Hierarchy of Needs

Focusing on the positive aspects of human behavior was the subject of Abraham Maslow's work on emotional development. Maslow organized human needs by priority in achieving a state of wellness. Maslow's Hierarchy is shown in Figure 7-6. People grow emotionally when they can satisfy their needs from bottom to top of the hierarchy. Reaching the top of the scale represents the fulfillment of one's potential. This stage represents a state of wellness. Self-actualization and fulfillment may be your self-ideal. However, to reach this goal your self-esteem needs must be satisfied. You cannot grow emotionally without self-esteem.

Review

1. *Why do people use defense mechanisms? When are defense mechanisms misused?*

2. *List the phases in Maslow's hierarchy. How is your self-esteem related to self-ideal?*

3. *Critical Thinking List four things you can do to bring your self-concept closer to your self-ideal.*

Section 7.3
Types of Mental and Emotional Disorders

● ● ● ● ●

Objectives

■ Describe the differences among eating, organic, personality, somatoform, mood, and dissociative disorders.

Everyone faces a variety of challenges. It may be the challenge of moving to a new town and making friends. Or it may be the challenge of rejection when you learn that the person you have a crush on doesn't feel the same about you. Most of the time, we are able to face challenges, learn from them, and move forward. Sometimes we are bogged down by them for a time. In these cases, our capacity to cope is exceeded, and the challenge interferes with our ability to function day to day. The inability to function for an extended period of time may be indicative of a mental or emotional disorder. The American Psychiatric Association has categorized mental and emotional disorders according to specific behaviors that people demonstrate. These mental and emotional disorder categories include the information in Figure 7-7. The diagnosis of a mental or emotional disorder should be made by a qualified doctor. People should never attempt to diagnose themselves or others just by reading a short description of a disorder in a textbook. If you are having difficulty, talk to a trusted adult. Counseling may help you deal with your problems. There is nothing wrong with seeking counseling. Seeking help for emotional problems is no different than seeking help for physical problems.

Organic Disorders

Mental and emotional disorders resulting from a *physical* cause are called **organic disorders**. There is evidence that some organic disorders are genetic. Other evidence indicates that these disorders develop as a response to various life experiences. Organic disorders may be caused by a physical illness, injury, or chemical imbalance. Because they involve the body as well as the mind, organic disorders are usually more serious than other types of mental and emotional problems.

An example of a physical illness causing an organic disorder is a brain tumor. A brain tumor can affect mood, speech, and comprehension. These won't improve until the tumor is removed. An example of an injury causing an organic disorder is a severe blow to the head. Brain cells may be destroyed during the injury and the functioning of the brain can be affected.

A chemical imbalance can also cause an organic disorder. For example, drinking alcohol or using other drugs may destroy brain cells, which in turn causes a chemical imbalance. The result can be an organic disorder. Brain cells may also be destroyed by lack of oxygen, such as when someone almost drowns. Chemicals help your brain send messages to your body. An imbalance in chemicals can affect the way you feel and act.

Eating Disorders

In Chapter 5, you learned about the characteristics of the two major eating disorders—anorexia and bulimia. The refusal to eat,

organic disorders:

mental and emotional disorders resulting from a physical cause.

that is characteristic of anorexia, or the binge eating that is characteristic of bulimia are not the actual disorders. Anorexia and bulimia describe behaviors that are the result of deep emotional problems related to self-image and self-esteem.

Eating disorders are included again in this chapter because of their increasing frequency among teens. They are also included here because the cure for these disorders requires psychiatric treatment. The goal of therapy is to find the underlying cause of one's obsession with body image and weight. In some cases, family therapy is needed to provide insights into why the patient has an unrealistic and often negative image of himself or herself. Severe depression and some forms of sexual abuse are often associated with eating disorders.

Anxiety Disorders

You learned in Section 7.1 that fear is a protective emotion that helps you recognize and prepare for danger. It can be beneficial to you on occasions when you should feel afraid. For example, if you are contemplating doing something that is illegal, the fear of getting caught might prevent you from doing the wrong thing. In this case, the fear is helpful.

However, to be constantly afraid of things you should not fear is not normal.

Cultural DIVERSITY

Social Support and African-American Churches

You read at the beginning of this chapter that having good relationships with others—having social support—is an important part of being mentally healthy. Different people find this support in different ways. For many African-Americans, churches serve as an important base of social support.

In fact, African-American churches have a long history of providing support and a sense of community to their members. Almost from the beginning, the churches served as community centers where African-Americans could gather to socialize. In the segregated past, their churches were often the *only* public buildings where they could have large gatherings.

People still come together at churches for services, weddings, baptisms, concerts, suppers, socials, plays, parties, meetings, discussion groups, educational programs, and sports like basketball and softball. Most African-American churches are open at least four nights a week to accommodate all these events.

At times, the support African-American churches give is more than social; families in financial trouble often go to their churches for housing, clothing, and money. Recently, some churches have even begun addressing their members' health-care needs.

Constant fear prevents you from participating in many aspects of a normal life. It can also damage you physically, because your body experiences a number of changes when you are afraid. Your heart rate speeds up, you perspire, and your blood pressure rises. If these changes occur most every day, they can be harmful and become the symptoms of an **anxiety disorder**. Phobias are the most well-known anxiety disorders. A fear of flying in a plane, of riding in an elevator, or of even leaving the house is a very real fear to someone with an anxiety disorder.

Anxiety disorders are the most common mental and emotional disorders. For some reason, anxiety disorders affect a greater percentage of women than men. Anxiety disorders either cause or are a contributing factor in many medical conditions for which Americans seek care.

Dissociative Disorders

A condition in which someone's personality changes dramatically is called a **dissociative disorder**. A person afflicted with a dissociative disorder believes that sometimes he or she is really someone else. People with dissociative disorders separate themselves from their real personality.

anxiety disorder:

a condition in which fear or anxiety prevents one from enjoying life and completing everyday tasks.

dissociative disorder:

a condition in which someone's personality changes to the point that the person believes that sometimes he or she is someone else.

In addition, churches have played a crucial role in the ongoing battle against racial discrimination. In the 1800s, African-American churches were active in the movement to abolish slavery. They were also part of the "underground railroad" that helped escaped slaves find their way to freedom.

Later, black religious institutions furnished much of the leadership for the civil rights movement. Two of the most important leaders of that time, Martin Luther King, Jr., and Malcolm X, began their civil rights work as religious leaders. King was a Baptist minister and Malcolm X was a speaker for the Nation of Islam. Today, African-American churches continue to work for social justice.

Some Mental and Emotional Disorders

Type of Disorder		Characteristics
Eating Disorders	Anorexia	excessive dieting resulting in a state of self-starvation
	Bulimia	bingeing on food then purging to avoid weight gain
Anxiety Disorders	General Anxiety Disorder	constant feeling of anxiety and fear with physical symptoms like increased heart rate, shortness of breath, perspiration, shaking, and diarrhea
	Obsessive-Compulsive Disorder	persistent recurring thoughts accompanied with the need to repeatedly perform some action, such as repeatedly washing one's hands
	Panic Disorder	intense feelings of terror that occur suddenly without cause
	Phobia	persistent fear of something: Hydrophobia-fear of water; claustrophobia-fear of small, enclosed spaces; agoraphobia—fear of public places
Dissociative Disorders	Multiple Personality Disorder	having two or more distinct personalities which can show different physical conditions and are often the exact opposite of each other
	Amnesia	loss of memory
Mood Disorders	Depression	experiencing feelings of sadness, loneliness, and hopelessness for an extended period of time
	Bipolar Disorder (Manic-Depression)	experiencing exaggerated feelings of euphoria, irritability, depression; exaggerated mood swings; reckless behavior
Personality Disorders	Antisocial Personality Disorder	showing a preference to remain distant from others
	Paranoia	consistent mistrust of others for no reason
	Aggression	behavior that displays an inner conflict between being dependent and being assertive which results in erratic moods
Somatoform Disorders	Hypochondriasis	believing and showing signs of serious illness without any physical cause
Schizophrenia	Schizophrenia	impaired perceptions, thinking processes, emotional health, and physical activity

(FIGURE 7-7)

(FIGURE 7-8) **These two pictures of cats, drawn by an artist diagnosed with schizophrenia, show how the disorder can impair perception.**

Dissociative disorders occur infrequently. They are usually the result of a traumatic experience. For example, they may result from severe sexual, physical, or emotional abuse in childhood. These disorders may be the mind's way of avoiding the pain associated with a very unpleasant experience. Amnesia and multiple personality disorder are examples of dissociative disorders.

Mood Disorders

A **mood disorder** occurs when one mood, which is often an unhappy mood, is experienced almost to the exclusion of other feelings.

A mood disorder usually lasts a long time and interrupts a person's ability to complete daily activities. The most common mood disorder is depression. In any given year, severe depression affects 15 million Americans.

Personality Disorders

Traits that negatively affect a person's ability to get along with others are called **personality disorders.** These traits may affect a person's work, relationships, and sense of satisfaction with life. Most personality disorders are very difficult to treat because one's personality is difficult to change.

Somatoform Disorders

People with physical symptoms caused by emotional problems are said to have **somatoform disorders.** However, a person with a somatoform disorder has no actual physical illness. Hypochondriasis is an example of a somatoform disorder—hypochondriacs believe they are ill even though their physical symptoms are caused by psychological factors.

somatoform disorder:

an emotional condition in which there are physical symptoms but no identifiable disease or injury. The physical symptoms are caused by psychological factors.

mood disorder:

a condition in which one mood is experienced almost to the exclusion of other feelings.

personality disorder:

an emotional condition in which a person's patterns of behavior negatively affect that person's ability to get along with others.

Review

1. *How do eating disorders differ from personality disorders?*

2. *What disorders are related primarily to fears?*

Section 7.4

Seeking Help

Objectives

■ *Describe the signs of mental and emotional health problems.*

■ *List community resources that help with mental and emotional problems.*

■ **LIFE SKILLS: Using Community Resources**

■ *Differentiate among types of treatment for mental and emotional problems.*

(FIGURE 7-9) **There are many books written by qualified medical and health professionals that can be of help in trying to deal with an emotional problem.**

Usually you can work through difficult times without outside help. Sometimes, though, you may need to ask for help from friends, parents, or relatives. There may be other times when your problems are so disturbing that it is important to seek professional help. That is when you need the assistance of a mental health specialist.

When to Seek Help for Mental and Emotional Health Problems

You may need to obtain professional help with your problems if you experience any of the following characteristics.

- a prolonged feeling of depression and hopelessness
- a feeling that life is out of control
- the inability to concentrate and make decisions
- difficulty getting along with family and friends
- intense fears
- persistent difficulty sleeping
- emotional problems coping with a physical illness
- inability to stop destructive behaviors like drinking, overeating, and abusing drugs

Mental and Emotional Health Services

If you need help or if someone you know needs help, contact a person you trust. That may be a parent, a teacher, a school counselor, a doctor, or a member of the clergy. Don't wait, thinking that the problems will clear up. Deep problems can only clear up if *you* take some action.

Most communities provide mental and emotional health services. These services may be offered through community mental health centers, local hospitals, and numerous other agencies. Agencies like these in your community are listed in your local telephone book. Look in the phone book under *hospitals, social workers, psychologists, psychotherapists, mental health information,* and *treatment centers.*

In addition, hotline phone services are available in many communities. Where these exist, information and counseling are provided over the phone.

Mental and Emotional Health Therapies

Mental health specialists help people with mental and emotional health problems. For a description of the various types of mental health specialists, see the Career Appendix. The goal of therapy is to help a person work

(FIGURE 7-10) **Support groups such as Al-Anon, Alateen, Alcoholics Anonymous, and many others can provide the support needed to work through specific emotional problems. The Yellow Pages of your phone book can provide information for contacting various support groups in your community.**

(FIGURE 7-11) **There are many sources of help in your community for emotional problems.**

*Life*SKILLS:

Choosing a Therapist . . . .

At some time during your life, you or someone close to you will feel the need to seek professional counseling. In choosing a therapist, consider the following guidelines.

1. Check the background certification, experience, and credentials of the therapist. Does the therapist have a state license?

2. Find out how often you would see the therapist. Do you feel it is frequent enough to meet your needs?

3. Find out if the therapist has experience dealing with problems similar to yours.

4. Use an introductory session to determine whether you feel comfortable with the setting and how the therapist plans to work with you.

5. Look for signs that you are being treated with respect. Do you feel the therapist is concerned about your situation? Do you feel the therapist can be trusted with very personal information about your life? If you are not being treated in an appropriate manner, find another therapist. Do not ever feel you must continue with someone who makes you continually uncomfortable.

6. If during treatment you start to feel very uncomfortable, or if you do not feel you are making any progress, discuss the situation with your therapist. If you cannot resolve the issues, you should feel no obligation to continue with this therapist.

through difficulties so that he or she can return to normal activities and be more capable of dealing with challenges. Different therapies may be used.

Psychoanalysis Psychoanalysis is a form of therapy used to examine unresolved conflicts from the past. For example, Clancy earns extra money by doing odd jobs for people. But he tries to avoid anything that involves climbing over 5 ft. high on a ladder. He could make lots more money if he were not afraid of heights so he decided to undergo psychoanalysis. Clancy discovered during treatment that he had been stranded in a treehouse as a child when the ladder to the treehouse fell down. Although he had forgotten the incident, the fear he experienced made him terrified of heights. The psychoanalyst helped him discover the source of his fear, which may in turn help Clancy overcome his fear of heights.

The process of psychoanalysis was developed by Sigmund Freud. He believed that unresolved conflicts surface as problems later in life. The person examines experiences to improve awareness. The intent is that awareness helps the person understand and resolve the problems.

Behavioral Therapy Behavioral therapy focuses on the patient's behavior rather than on the underlying causes. The therapist helps the patient discover rewards for

(FIGURE 7-12) **Group therapy can provide a supportive environment and a broader view for dealing with problems.**

Chemical Therapy Chemical therapy is the use of drugs to treat mental and emotional disorders. Drugs are prescribed to help control some symptoms of a disorder, such as aggressiveness, or to correct an imbalance of chemicals in the brain that can cause disorders like depression. It is important to note, though, that some drugs can have serious side effects. For example, an antidepressant may work very well in controlling depression in one patient while causing violent or suicidal behavior in someone else. This often is caused by a misdiagnosis or inappropriate use of a drug. As with any prescription medication, the use of chemical-therapy drugs should be closely monitored for serious side effects.

(FIGURE 7-13) **This advertisement is representative of the kind of mental health services provided by counselors.**

desirable behaviors and punishments for undesirable behaviors. This process is called behavior modification. Behavior modification programs help patients learn new ways to respond to situations, ways more effective than the ones they were using.

Group Therapy In group therapy, people with similar problems meet with a therapist to discuss their problems. Both the therapist and the group members suggest solutions, the idea being that the exchange of ideas and input from group members is more helpful than hearing only one perspective from a therapist.

Review

1. How would you know if your best friend or someone in your family needed counseling?

2. List the places in your community where you could go if you were having an emotional problem. List one place you could go if you had an eating disorder. List two places you could go if there was a problem in your family that required counseling.

3. Make a list of four questions you would ask if you were choosing a therapist.

4. How does group therapy differ from behavior modification?

5. **Critical Thinking** If you were suffering from a mental or emotional problem, who would you go to for advice?

CHAPTER 7

Highlights

Summary

- According to the National Association for Mental Health, someone with good mental health feels comfortable with himself or herself, has good relationships with others, and meets the demands of life.

- It is important to express emotions in a positive way.

- Defense mechanisms provide a way to deal with problems and maintain self-esteem. Overuse of these mechanisms is not healthy.

- Maslow believed that all individuals can achieve self-actualization or a state of fulfillment if their basic physio-logical and psychological needs are met first.

- It is just as important to seek help for emotional problems as it is to seek help for physical problems.

- Most difficult times can be worked through without outside help. Some-times, however, you may need to ask for help from friends, parents, or mental health specialists.

- Some therapies that certain specialists practice are psychoanalysis, behav-ioral therapy, group therapy, and chemical therapy.

Vocabulary

self-concept the current mental image you have of yourself.

self-ideal your mental image of what you would like to be.

organic disorders mental and emotional disorders resulting from a physical cause.

eating disorders compulsive eating behaviors caused by emotional problems and an obsession with body weight.

anxiety disorder a condition in which fear or anxiety prevents one from enjoying life and completing everyday tasks.

dissociative disorder a condition in which someone's personality changes to the point that the person believes that sometimes he or she is someone else.

mood disorder a condition in which one mood is experienced almost to the exclusion of other feelings.

personality disorder an emotional condition in which a person's patterns of behavior negatively affect that person's ability to get along with others.

somatoform disorder an emotional condition in which there are physical symptoms but no identifiable disease or injury. The physical symptoms are caused by psychological factors.

Chapter Review

Concept Review

1. Which of the following characteristics define good mental health?
   - fears new experiences
   - has good relationships with others
   - avoids responsibility
   - has a negative attitude
   - meets the demands of life

   Add one characteristic of your own.

2. Identify and describe four emotions most people experience.

3. Why is loneliness a particular problem for teens?

4. In what way can guilt be a positive emotion?

5. Why should you avoid using defense mechanisms too frequently?

6. According to Maslow, when do people grow emotionally? What does reaching the top of the scale represent?

7. Name three possible causes of organic disorders. Are organic disorders more or less serious than other types of mental and emotional problems? Why?

8. Panic attacks and phobias are examples of what kind of disorder?

9. List three factors that are linked to developing depression.

10. Describe four treatments for mental disorders.

11. Why is behavior modification used in treating mental health disorders?

Expressing Your Views

1. Your text states that eating disorders are most often caused by pressure from peers or parents. Do you agree? Why or why not?

2. Martin decided to seek therapy for depression after his grandmother died. His friends have been very critical and told him that anyone who seeks counseling is weak. How should Martin respond to these people?

3. Every time Ruth fails at something she rationalizes her failure. Why do you think she does this? How could this behavior be harmful?

Life Skills Check

1. Coping
You are angry because one of your friends borrowed your car and burned a hole in the seat. Now your friend refuses to help pay for the damage. How could you handle your anger in a positive way?

2. Using Community Resources
Your sister has been acting strangely for the past few months. You are worried about her and think she probably needs help. What advice would you give her? Where could she go for help?

3. Using Community Resources
Find out what 12-step programs are and make a list of those in your area. Include information on how these programs are connected to spiritual health.

Projects

1. Maslow thought Abraham Lincoln, Eleanor Roosevelt, and Thomas Jefferson were self-actualized people. Name someone you would add to Maslow's list and write a one-page essay describing your reasons for choosing this person.

2. Read *One Flew Over the Cuckoo's Nest* by Ken Kesey and note the mental disorders of the characters.

3. Work with a group to compile a list of activities in your school or community that promote good mental health. Suggest other activities that could be offered.

4. Why do you think some music is called the blues? Visit the library to find out the history of the blues. Prepare a brief report and presentation that includes some examples of blues music.

Plan for Action

The things people say about themselves often indicate how they feel about themselves. Write 10 statements about yourself in order to evaluate your self-concept, and devise a plan for improvement.

CHAPTER 8

Building Self-Esteem

◆ ◆ ◆ ◆

Section 8.1 The Importance of Self-Esteem

Section 8.2 How to Build Your Self-Esteem

Everyone does something well. If you make the most of whatever it is you do well, you will build your self-esteem.

Lindsey feels ugly and unlikable. She
compares herself with the models in the fashion magazines and wishes she could be
as thin. When she looks in the mirror, she sees a chubby girl. Yet Lindsey is 5'3" tall
and weighs only 105 lbs. She isn't really chubby at all. She
constantly fantasizes about being popular, but feels that she
doesn't have a chance. She is very shy and doesn't often talk
to other students because she is afraid they won't like her.

Lindsey realizes that many people her age feel the way she
does. However, she has made a silent promise to herself to
find ways to feel better about herself and her life.

The Importance of Self-Esteem

Objectives
• • • • •

- *Define self-esteem.*

- *Describe how self-esteem develops.*

- *Explain how media messages can affect one's self-esteem.*

- *Assess your own self-esteem.*
  LIFE SKILLS: Assessing Your Health

Self-esteem is your pride in and acceptance of yourself. It is your sense of personal worth. When you feel worthwhile, you are able to make good decisions, experience acceptance from others, and give and receive love.

Lindsey has decided to improve her self-esteem. To do so, she must learn to respect herself, consider herself worthy, and avoid comparing herself with others.

Your self-esteem influences your relationships with your family, friends, teachers, and bosses. It affects how you do in school and at work. Low self-esteem can be very damaging, and has been linked to serious problems such as alcohol and drug abuse, eating disorders, suicide, and other self-destructive behaviors.

How Self-Esteem Develops

The development of self-esteem begins at birth. Early on, our feelings about ourselves tend to be a reflection of how we are treated by the people most important in our lives—usually our parents or guardians. We learn to see ourselves as we think they see us.

Most parents love their children and wouldn't knowingly do anything to damage their child's self-esteem. But parents are only human. Sometimes they don't say exactly what they mean. For example, a

self-esteem:

pride in and acceptance of yourself; sense of personal worth.

parent might say, "I don't like you kids much when you're acting like this." The child may think the parent means, "I don't like you." It would be better if the parent said, "I get scared and nervous when you and your brother fight." That way, the parent makes it very clear that it is the behavior that is being criticized, not the worth of the child.

But most parents aren't psychologists. They may not even be aware that their words are so harsh. Most parents honestly want to support and encourage their children and help them feel loved, but they may not always succeed in communicating their support and love.

A more serious situation exists when parents neglect or abuse their children. Jonathan, for example, grew up without the care and attention he needed. He was a neglected child. His mom suffered from depression, and Jonathan remembers many days when she spent the entire day in bed. Jonathan's dad worked long hours, so he wasn't around much. It seemed that the only time his parents paid any attention to him was when he did something wrong. By the time he reached high school, Jonathan had very low self-esteem.

At some point during the first years of life, we make a decision about our own worth based on how we think others see us. The decision may not be a conscious one, but it is a decision nevertheless. After a while, it seems to be reality. We begin to look at our feelings and behaviors and think that's just the way we are.

Because self-esteem is based on a decision, it can be changed by making a new decision later in life. You, like Lindsey, can decide to raise your self-esteem.

body image:

a person's perception of his or her appearance, level of fitness, and health.

Body Image, Media Messages, and Self-Esteem

Your **body image** is your perception of your appearance, level of fitness, and health. Sometimes it is difficult for teens to maintain a positive body image because so many natural physical changes are taking place during the teen years.

The fact that we are constantly exposed to media images that show "perfect" faces and bodies often negatively influences the way we see ourselves. This can lower self-esteem.

Teenage girls have an especially hard time because they sometimes feel that they must look unrealistically thin in order to be attractive. Lindsey looks at advertisements showing extremely thin women, and without realizing it, she accepts these women as a standard against which she must judge herself and her body. This gives her a negative body image.

(FIGURE 8-1) **We make a decision about our own worth early in life based on how we think other people view us.**

(FIGURE 8-2) **Standards of beauty change. In the 1950s, women with curves were considered attractive. A decade later, extremely thin women were fashionable. There is nothing wrong with any body type, but there *is* something wrong with media messages that encourage people to feel bad about their bodies.**

The funny thing about advertising is that the ''perfect'' face and body change over time. Thin bodies for women are fashionable during one decade, and curvaceous bodies are stylish during another one. If you look at old advertisements, you see how ideals of beauty keep changing.

An important thing for Lindsey to remember is that there is nothing wrong with her body type. There *is* something wrong with an advertisement that makes her feel bad about herself. People of all body types can be attractive and accomplished—beauty and success often have more to do with confidence than with actual physical appearance.

Success comes in all kinds of ''packages.'' It comes to people of both sexes, of all ethnicities, and of all body types. Plain people, good-looking people, tall people, short people, and people with physical disabilities can all be successful. Lindsey could think of a well-known person in each of these categories who has developed unique gifts and has become a star in his or her world.

Review

1. Define self-esteem.

2. Describe how a person's self-esteem develops.

3. Explain how media messages can affect a person's self-esteem.

4. **LIFE SKILLS: Assessing Your Health** Describe what you have learned about your own self-esteem.

5. **Critical Thinking** How do you think poverty could contribute to low self-esteem?

Self-Esteem Scale

On a separate sheet of paper, write the letter that most accurately describes how you feel:

1. I feel that I'm a person of worth, at least equal to others.

   a. Strongly agree

   b. Agree

   c. Disagree

   d. Strongly disagree

2. I feel that I have a number of good qualities.

   a. Strongly agree

   b. Agree

   c. Disagree

   d. Strongly disagree

3. All in all, I am inclined to feel that I am a failure.

   a. Strongly agree

   b. Agree

   c. Disagree

   d. Strongly disagree

4. I am able to do things as well as most other people.
   a. Strongly agree

   b. Agree

   c. Disagree

   d. Strongly disagree

5. I feel I do not have much to be proud of.

   a. Strongly agree

   b. Agree

   c. Disagree

   d. Strongly disagree

6. I take a positive attitude toward myself.

   a. Strongly agree

   b. Agree

   c. Disagree

   d. Strongly disagree

7. On the whole, I am satisfied with myself.

   a. Strongly agree

   b. Agree

   c. Disagree

   d. Strongly disagree

8. I wish I could have more respect for myself.

   a. Strongly agree

   b. Agree

   c. Disagree

   d. Strongly disagree

9. I feel useless at times.

   a. Strongly agree

   b. Agree

   c. Disagree

   d. Strongly disagree

10. At times I think I am no good at all.

   a. Strongly agree

   b. Agree

   c. Disagree

   d. Strongly disagree

Scoring. To score the scale and derive a measure of your self-esteem, follow these instructions.

The positive responses for the questions are as follows:

   question 1: (a) or (b)

   question 2: (a) or (b)

   question 3: (c) or (d)

   question 4: (a) or (b)

   question 5: (c) or (d)

   question 6: (a) or (b)

   question 7: (a) or (b)

   question 8: (c) or (d)

   question 9: (c) or (d)

   question 10: (c) or (d)

For each positive answer that you chose, give yourself one point. The range of scores on this self-esteem scale is 0–10. The higher the score, the better your self-esteem.

8.2 How to Build Your Self-Esteem

Objectives

- Name the best way to raise your self-esteem.

- Name at least three other ways of raising your self-esteem.

- Make a plan to improve your own self-esteem.
  LIFE SKILLS: Building Self-Esteem

As you read earlier, self-esteem is a decision we make about our worth as individuals. During childhood, our level of self-esteem is established based on how we see ourselves in relation to the adults around us and on the way we feel about ourselves as a result.

If you have low self-esteem, you can make a new, more accurate, and more positive decision about yourself. You can acknowledge the influence of your past, but resolve to move on. Your self-esteem is now your responsibility. It isn't easy to raise low self-esteem, but it can be done. By deciding to take responsibility for yourself and your own self-esteem, you can make big changes in the way you see yourself. You will be delighted when you discover how much more fun and rewarding your life can be when you feel good about yourself.

Accept Yourself

Learning to accept yourself is the best way to raise your self-esteem. This means learning to appreciate yourself and believing in your worth as a unique and special person.

How can you learn to accept yourself? First, realistically assess your strengths and weaknesses. Don't be modest. No one needs to know what you think your strengths are except you.

Second, try not to judge yourself by unrealistic standards. Don't, for example, compare your looks to those of the actors or actresses you see on television shows and in the movies. When you catch yourself thinking this way, stop and remind yourself of your uniqueness and special talents.

(FIGURE 8-3) **Accepting yourself just as you are is the most important part of raising your self-esteem. Although you aren't perfect, you are a unique and valuable person.**

Third, decide that you are okay as you are, even though there are probably things about yourself you would like to change. Remember that even though you aren't perfect, you are a unique and valuable person. No one else has exactly the same gifts to offer the world. There isn't a single person anywhere who is perfect, and it certainly isn't necessary for *you* to be perfect.

Finally, only expend energy on changing things you have control over. You can't change your height or your body type, for instance, so don't spend time worrying about it. But you can work on developing new skills or interests, which would probably increase your self-esteem.

The more you accept and like yourself, the more others will accept and like you. If you project to others that you like yourself, they will be less likely to judge you or to pressure you to conform to their ideals. And even if they do, you will be less likely to cave in to their pressure.

Use Positive Self-Talk

We are constantly talking to ourselves—not necessarily out loud, but internally. Often this talk is negative. "I'm such an idiot," you might say to yourself. "Why did I do such a stupid thing?" Talking negatively like this can damage your self-esteem over time.

When you use **positive self-talk**, on the other hand, you can raise your self-esteem. Positive self-talk is talking to yourself in a positive way about your characteristics and abilities. An example of positive self-talk might be: "I did a great job on this project. I'm really good at this."

When Lindsey feels nervous and uncomfortable around other students, she usually thinks, "They think I'm no fun," or "Why can't I ever think of anything interesting to say?" Because she feels this way

and talks to herself this way, Lindsey often appears to be awkward and shy.

Suppose that Lindsey decided to use positive self-talk instead. She might say to herself, "Sometimes I'm shy, but I can also be pretty funny, and people usually enjoy my company." If she continues to talk to herself this way and begins to believe what she says, Lindsey will be more likely to converse with other students. As she sees others respond to her more positively, Lindsey's confidence will grow. She will become more comfortable with other people, and her self-esteem will improve.

Be Good at Something

Everyone has something he or she does well. Make the most of whatever it is *you* do well. It might be playing guitar, making up dance steps, working with computers, playing basketball, telling stories, writing essays, making people laugh, being a good friend—the possibilities are endless. Even if it's something as seemingly trivial as being good at bicycle stunts, you'll develop more confidence in yourself if you cultivate your natural ability. Being very good at one thing will also make it easier for you to try new things. If you *know* that you're good at bicycle stunts, you probably won't feel as bad if you find out that you aren't very good at playing basketball.

Use "I" Statements

If you take responsibility for your feelings and words by using "I" statements, you will build self-esteem. People with low self-esteem are often afraid to do this because they fear criticism.

For instance, when Lindsey says, "It is really hard to make friends," she is making a generalization that may not be true for other people. By beginning her statement with the impersonal pronoun "it," she is

positive self-talk:

talking to yourself in a positive way about your characteristics and abilities.

15 Ways to Boost Your Self-Esteem

FIGURE 8-4

1. Make a list of your good qualities and keep it with you at all times. Place extra copies on your mirror, in your school desk, or other places you will see it. Read over the list on a regular basis and at any time when you experience negative thoughts.

2. Avoid wasting time thinking about your negatives.

3. Seek new challenges in your life. Don't be afraid to try new things. Mastering a new task or ability can build self-esteem.

4. Avoid putting yourself down to others or to yourself. Accept compliments with a "thank you" and a smile.

5. Find something that you do very well and work to improve that skill.

6. Reward yourself when you accomplish a task or finish a project.

7. Accept the fact that neither you nor anyone else is perfect. Avoid dwelling on mistakes; laugh them off and continue with the positive.

8. Take a moment to look at yourself in the mirror each day and give yourself a verbal compliment.

9. Keep yourself well groomed, maintain a positive attitude, and develop a sense of humor to handle the difficult situations.

10. Join at least one activity that involves other people. Volunteer for service with an organization or group in your school or community.

11. Associate with other positive thinkers in your school and community. Create your own support group of friends who are a positive influence on you and your self-esteem.

12. Don't fight a fact; deal with it. Try to avoid thinking that people and things in your life that are out of your control should be different. They aren't, and that is the reality.

13. Accept that life does not have to be perfect for you to be happy. Happiness is a way of thinking; a content feeling, not constant euphoria.

14. Remember that sometimes bad things happen that are not within your control. Expect this and try not to let it set you back too much. Do the best you can to change what you can, and avoid dwelling on what you cannot change.

15. Remind yourself that each of us is important and valuable. Try to be the best "you" you can be. Remember, you're the best one for the job.

(FIGURE 8-5) **A support group is a group of people who trust each other and can talk openly with each other. Having a support group can help you build your self-esteem.**

not taking responsibility for her feelings. She could use an ''I'' statement instead: ''I sometimes have trouble making friends.'' She is then talking about *her* feelings only.

When Lindsey said to her brother Scott, ''You made me feel terrible when you told me that Sonya is smarter that I am,'' she was transferring responsibility for her own feelings to Scott. This is not an ''I'' statement—she is saying that *Scott* is responsible for *her* feelings. To take responsibility for her own feelings, Lindsey could say, ''I felt hurt when you said that Sonya is smarter than I am.''

Although it is easier to speak in generalities, it is important to clearly state how you feel.

Develop a Support Group

Few things can be as helpful in maintaining or enhancing your level of self-esteem as knowing people with whom you can share your joys and sorrows—a **support group.** A support group is composed of people in your life whom you trust and with whom you are able to talk openly.

Your support group can consist of friends you trust or family members who care for you. Members of your support group will not exert pressure on you. Instead, they help you to feel good about yourself.

Take a moment to write down the names of five people whom you would like in your support group. In the future, make an effort to spend more time with these people.

Self-disclosure—telling another person meaningful information about yourself—plays a central role in the development of positive self-esteem. When you share your true thoughts and feelings about yourself, you will learn how you are perceived by others through their responses. This process helps you see yourself more accurately. It can help a lot to learn that others often have the same doubts and fears that you do. You can also learn to better appreciate similarities and differences—the diversity among people—by sharing your feelings.

Self-disclosure is usually a gradual process between people. It's important to establish a relationship based on trust and mutual respect before you disclose personal details of your life.

self-disclosure:

telling another person meaningful information about yourself.

support group:

people in your life whom you trust and with whom you are able to talk openly.

Resist Peer Pressure

Individuals who have low self-esteem usually do not have much confidence in their opinions or their decisions. Consequently, they are overly influenced by peers and by peer pressure.

Learning to trust yourself and your values builds confidence. The more you make your own decisions based on what you—not others—believe, the more confidence you will gain. This does not mean that you should ignore the advice or ideas of parents, friends, teachers, or others. It means that you should listen to your inner voice and make decisions based on what it is telling you.

When you make your own decisions, you and you alone are responsible for the outcome of those decisions. Have you ever seen people labor over a decision because their "gut feelings" were different from the advice they received from others?

66 *I'm trying to make my own decisions now and not do things just because my friends are doing them.* **99**

Beatriz

You will notice that they tend to feel miserable afterward if they followed others' advice, only to find that their own path would have been the better one to take.

Act With Integrity

Once you appreciate your own worth, you can better appreciate the worth of other people. People with high self-esteem do not act as if they are only looking out for themselves. On the contrary, they treat others with respect and compassion. They act in ways that will help other people maintain high self-esteem.

It's easy to take advantage of those with low self-esteem by manipulating them or bullying them into doing what you want. But as a person of integrity, it is your responsibility to refrain from doing so.

When you act with integrity and responsibility toward others, you will feel good about yourself, and that will improve your self-esteem even more.

Review

1. Describe the best way to raise your self-esteem.

2. Name at least three other ways to build your self-esteem.

3. ▓ **LIFE SKILLS: Building Self-Esteem** What steps will you take to improve your own self-esteem?

4. **Critical Thinking** Explain why people with high self-esteem do not have to put down other people in order to feel good about themselves.

Highlights

Summary

- Self-esteem is the confidence and satisfaction you have in yourself. It is influenced by the people and events of your early years.

- During childhood, we make decisions about our own worth based on how we think others see us. As we grow older, we become better equipped to make these decisions ourselves.

- Media messages can lower one's self-esteem by presenting unrealistic standards by which we judge ourselves. This can negatively influence our self-esteem because we look or act differently from actors or models.

- Learning to accept yourself is the best way to raise your self-esteem.

- By developing your natural abilities, you will develop more confidence in yourself. Being good at one thing will make it easier for you to take positive risks and develop new skills.

- You can build self-esteem if you take responsibility for your feelings by using ''I'' statements. It is important to state clearly what you mean rather than to speak in generalities.

- Trusting and sharing with a support group can help a person enhance or maintain self-esteem.

- You can improve your self-esteem by trying not to judge yourself by unrealistic standards, by deciding that you are okay as you are, and by trying to change only the things about yourself that are within your control.

- Talking in a positive way to yourself about yourself, and believing it, can improve your confidence and self-esteem.

Vocabulary

self-esteem pride in and acceptance of yourself; sense of personal worth.

body image a person's perception of his or her appearance, level of fitness, and health.

positive self-talk talking to yourself in a positive way about your characteristics and abilities.

support group a group of people in your life whom you trust and with whom you are able to talk openly.

self-disclosure telling another person meaningful information about yourself.

Chapter Review

Concept Review

1. The degree to which a person likes or feels good about himself or herself is _____.

2. Your _____ is your perception of your appearance, level of fitness, and health.

3. Messages from the _____ often cause us to have a low self-esteem by telling us we must look a certain way to be attractive.

4. By deciding to take _____ for yourself and your own self-esteem, you can make changes in the way you view yourself.

5. You can learn to feel good about yourself by accepting your _____ and _____.

6. _____ is talking in a positive way to yourself about yourself.

7. Communication improves when you take _____ for your feelings and words by being specific and using "I" statements.

8. Friends or family members with whom you can speak openly are a _____.

9. You can learn how you are perceived by others by how they respond to you, and you can see yourself more accurately, through _____.

10. People with low self-esteem want to follow the crowd and often allow themselves to be influenced by _____.

11. When you act with _____ and treat other people with respect and compassion, you will feel good about yourself.

Expressing Your Views

1. Some psychologists think that an individual's self-esteem is the most important influence on mental well-being. Why do you think self-esteem is so important?

2. Sylvia hates school because she feels as though she has no friends. She feels shy around other students because she thinks they're all more attractive than she is. What can Sylvia do to boost her self-esteem?

3. Sunday night, Jeremy sneaked out of the house after midnight to ride around and drink beer with his friends. Jeremy didn't really want to go, but he was afraid his friends would think he wasn't "cool." After he got home, Jeremy realized he had been doing a lot of things lately that he didn't really want to do. He decided that from now on he would resist this kind of peer pressure. What could Jeremy do to change?

Life Skills Check . . . . . .

1. Assessing Your Health

You want to be able to accept yourself for what you are, but first you need to evaluate your self-esteem. As realistically as possible, make a personal inventory by listing as many strengths and weaknesses as you can about yourself. If your list of weaknesses is longer than your list of strengths, judge each weakness and decide whether you could view it in a more positive way. List ways you could improve your weaknesses and build on your strengths.

2. Building Self-Esteem

Lee appears to care only for his own feelings and becomes very defensive and upset if anyone criticizes his actions. You don't really consider yourself a close friend of his, but today he told you that he doesn't think anyone likes him much, and that he feels as if he doesn't have one true friend. How would you respond to this statement?

Projects . . . .

1. An essential part of building self-esteem is trying new things. When you volunteer in your community, it gives you a chance to develop your skills while helping other people, and this combination can be very gratifying. Call a local soup kitchen, nursing home, or homeless shelter to find out about ways that you can get involved. You will prob-ably be regarded as a very important addition to the organization.

2. Work with a group to create and produce a skit involving characters with healthy self-esteem and with poor self-esteem. Show how both personalities deal with problems. Then have the audience decide which qualities of healthy self-esteem are missing or are present.

Plan for Action . . . .

An individual's self-esteem has a great impact on his or her mental health. Create a plan to raise your own self-esteem.

CHAPTER
9

Managing Stress

◆ ◆ ◆ ◆

Taking tests is among the many stressors most teenagers face.

Raquel had no idea how she was going to do it—the idea of getting up in front of her English class and giving a speech terrified her. What if she went totally blank and forgot everything she was going to say? Or what if she said something really stupid? What if everyone started laughing at her? What if . . . ? Just thinking about all the "what if's" made Raquel's heart start to pound and her hands start to sweat.

She could pretend to be sick and stay home the day she was supposed to give her speech, but she knew she would have to give it anyway when she went back to school. There wasn't any way out of it, and it was making Raquel a nervous wreck. In fact, she was so stressed-out about it that she couldn't even concentrate on *writing* the speech.

Section 9.1

What Is Stress?

Objectives

- *Define stress.*
- *Describe the stress response.*
- *Name at least four stress-related disorders.*

If you, like Raquel, have had physical reactions to a change in your life situation, you have experienced stress. It is perfectly natural to experience stress. All of us do. The key is learning how to manage stress so that it doesn't make you miserable or sick. In this chapter you'll find out about some techniques that can help you cope with the stress in your life.

Before you can cope with stress, you have to know how it develops. First, a situation arises that is new or potentially unpleasant. This situation is called a **stressor**.

In Raquel's case, the stressor was the speech that she had to give in her English class. Raquel felt anxious, her heart raced, and her hands started sweating when she thought about the speech. What she was experiencing was a **stress response**, the body's reaction to a stressor.

It is important to remember that stressors only have the *potential* to cause a stress response. For some people, giving a speech would not cause a stress response. It's only when a stressor does cause a stress response that stress results. Therefore, **stress** is the combination of the presence of a stressor and the occurrence of a stress response.

Stressors

Stressors can occur in almost every area of life. You may feel stress at home if your parents or guardians are not getting along with each other or if they are getting a divorce. It can also be stressful if one of your

stress response:

the body's reaction to a stressor.

stress:

the combination of a stressor and a stress response.

stressor:

any new or potentially unpleasant situation.

(FIGURE 9-1) **Stressors can come in many forms. If you are having trouble becoming part of a social group, you may experience stress as a result.**

A stressor can be something as simple as trying to get paper clips untangled, getting stuck at a red light when you're in a hurry, or getting a busy signal when you really need to talk with someone. If you let them, these kinds of "daily hassles" can add up and cause a tremendous amount of stress.

Even *positive* situations can be stressors. Getting married is a perfect example. It is a happy occasion, but because it involves a change in one's life situation, it can be just as stressful as a negative event. Making the all-star basketball team is another example of a positive life-changing event that can cause stress.

Having some stressors is perfectly normal and healthy. They motivate us to confront challenges and accomplish things. The ideal balance is to be able to deal with stressors effectively so we don't become ill from too much stress.

parents remarries and you must move in with your new stepmother or stepfather. If you argue with your brother or sister, you might feel stress as a result.

At school, you may experience stress when you try out for a sport or the school play or if you have trouble becoming part of a certain social group. You may feel stress if you don't have the money to buy the clothes you want for a school dance or if other students pick on you.

Many stressors are connected to our self-concept, which is how we think of ourselves. We fear that we will look foolish in front of other people whose opinions we care about. That is why Raquel experienced stress when she had to give a speech. She was worried about other people's opinions, which could affect her opinion of herself. If you have these kinds of self-doubts and fears, be comforted in knowing that you are not alone. People of all ages and all occupations want others to think well of them, and this is just as stressful for them as it is for you.

(FIGURE 9-2) **Even a positive event like getting married can be stressful because it involves a change in one's life situation.**

Life Changes of Teenagers

Life Event	Life-Change Units	Life Event	Life-Change Units
Getting married	101	Beginning to date	51
Being pregnant and unmarried	92	Being suspended from school	50
Experiencing the death of a parent	87	Having a newborn brother or sister	50
Acquiring a visible deformity	81	Having more arguments with parents	47
Going through a parent's divorce	77	Having an outstanding personal achievement	46
Becoming an unmarried father	77	Seeing an increase in the number of arguments between parents	46
Becoming involved with drugs or alcohol	76	Having a parent lose his or her job	46
Having a parent go to jail for a year or more	75	Experiencing a change in parents' financial status	45
Going through parents' separation	69	Being accepted at the college of your choice	43
Experiencing the death of a brother or sister	68	Being a senior in high school	47
Experiencing a change in acceptance by peers	67	Experiencing the serious illness of a brother or sister	41
Having an unmarried pregnant teenage sister	64	Experiencing increased absence from home of mother or father owing to change in occupation	38
Discovering you are an adopted child	64	Experiencing the departure from home of a brother or sister	37
Having a parent remarry	63	Experiencing the death of a grandparent	36
Experiencing the death of a close friend	62	Having a third adult added to the family	34
Having a visible congenital deformity	62	Becoming a full-fledged member of a religion	31
Having a serious illness requiring hospitalization	58	Seeing a decrease in the number of arguments between parents	27
Moving to a new school district	56	Having fewer arguments with parents	26
Failing a grade in school	56	Having a mother who begins to work outside the home	26
Not making an extracurricular activity	55		
Experiencing the serious illness of a parent	55		
Breaking up with a boyfriend or girlfriend	53		
Having a parent go to jail for 30 or fewer days	53		

(FIGURE 9-3) **Major changes in our lives can cause stress, even if they are positive events. To get an idea of how much your life has changed in the past year, add up the life-change units for the changes you experienced during the last 12 months. If your total score is less than 150, your life has changed little. If it is between 150 and 300, you have experienced moderate change. And if your score is over 300, your life has changed significantly.**

The Stress Response

The stress response occurs because of the relationship between your brain and the rest of your body. Your brain recognizes a stressor and evaluates it. If your brain decides that the stressor isn't anything to worry about, nothing happens to your body. But if the stressor is seen as a threat, your brain tells your body to produce certain chemicals that contribute to the stress response. During a stress response, the physical changes shown in Figure 9-4 occur.

Why does the brain tell the rest of the body to respond this way? It doesn't seem as though the stress response would help us at all. It certainly didn't help Raquel prepare for her speech. When could the stress response possibly be helpful to us?

Well, imagine that you are walking down the street and a huge dog suddenly leaps at you from behind a garbage truck, snarling, teeth bared, and ready to bite you. What do you do? Do you try to defend yourself against the dog, or do you run away as fast as you can? Whichever you do—fight the dog or run away—will require you to act immediately and with great physical effort.

The stress response makes it possible for you to protect yourself. Your body produces the hormone called adrenaline, which gives you the rush of extra energy you need. Your breathing speeds up, which helps get more oxygen throughout your body. Your heart beats faster, which increases the flow of blood to your muscles. And your muscles tense up, which prepares you to move quickly.

At the same time these changes are occurring, other changes are also taking place throughout your body. Because all

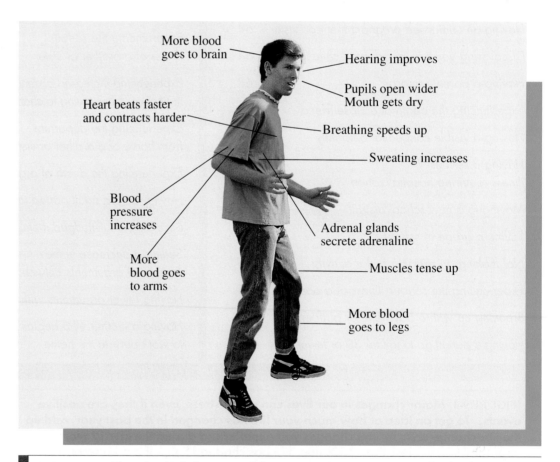

More blood goes to brain

Hearing improves

Pupils open wider
Mouth gets dry

Heart beats faster and contracts harder

Breathing speeds up

Sweating increases

Blood pressure increases

Adrenal glands secrete adrenaline

Muscles tense up

More blood goes to arms

More blood goes to legs

(FIGURE 9-4) **The physical changes of the stress response prepare the body to run away or stay and fight.**

your physical resources are mobilized to help you respond to danger, other body functions may take a back seat. The digestive system, for example, may begin to function strangely, causing diarrhea or constipation. Less saliva is produced, because it is a low priority to your body during times of physical danger. As a result, your mouth becomes dry.

The stress response is sometimes called the ''fight-or-flight'' response because it prepares you to either ''fight'' or ''take flight.'' It prepares you to do something *physical*. So when you are physically threatened and need to respond physically, the stress response is helpful to you.

However, your body also responds the same way to a *nonphysical* threat. For example, giving a speech can cause the same stress response as being attacked by an animal. But giving a speech, unlike defending yourself against an animal attack, does not require you to release stress in any physical way. The stress that is not released can make you physically ill.

Stress Can Make You Sick

It is estimated that from 60 to 80 percent of all physical and mental disorders are related to stress. Not all of these disorders, however, are *caused* by stress. Many of them are simply made worse by stress.

Asthma is a good example of a disorder than can be aggravated by stress. Let's say that you wheeze and you can't catch your breath when you are around cats. In this case, having trouble breathing is a completely physical reaction. It has nothing to do with stress.

Now imagine that you are under a lot of stress. Studies have shown that when you are under stress, especially long-term stress, your immune system suffers. Your asthmatic reaction to a cat may be much worse than it would normally be.

Some of the other diseases and disorders that are suspected of being related to stress include the following:

- **Colds and Flu** Stress can weaken your immune system, the system of your body that defends against infection. As a result, a person under prolonged stress is more likely to become infected with cold and flu viruses. That person may also require more time than others to recover from these illnesses.

- **Tension Headaches** Stress causes the muscles in your neck and head to tense up, which can cause headaches.

- **Backache** Frequent tension in the muscles of the back can lead to backaches.

- **TMJ Syndrome** The joint that connects your upper jaw to your lower jaw is called the temporomandibular joint (TMJ). If stress causes a person to clench or grind the teeth, then pain in the joint, headaches, and dental problems can result.

- **Coronary Heart Disease** Some studies show that prolonged stress may cause changes in your body that may lead to a heart attack. One of these changes is an increased amount of cholesterol in the bloodstream.

  Cholesterol is a fat-like substance that can clog the arteries that supply blood to the heart. If a blockage of blood to the heart occurs, a heart attack may result.

> **"**I used to get a lot of headaches. Now that I'm doing relaxation exercises every day, they don't bother me as much.**"**
>
> ___ Sam

- **High Blood Pressure** Part of the stress response is an increase in blood pressure. High blood pressure results when blood pushes harder than necessary against the inside of the blood vessels. It can eventually lead to the rupture of a blood vessel in the brain. This is called a stroke. A stroke can result in loss of speech and bodily movement, and even in death.

- **Chronic Fatigue** Prolonged stress can cause a person to feel tired all the time. This type of fatigue is different from the feeling one gets after strenuous physical exercise. Chronic fatigue is a *long-term* loss of energy.

- **Depression** Prolonged stress can wear a person down to the point of "burnout" or exhaustion. Depression can occur as a result of an advanced stage of burnout.

  There is even some evidence that people under prolonged stress may be more likely than others to develop cancer.

  Stress can also lead to injuries. When you are under stress, you aren't able to concentrate very well, which could increase your chances of having an accident.

Review

1. *Define stress.*

2. *Describe the stress response.*

3. *Name at least four disorders that are caused by stress or made worse by stress.*

4. **Critical Thinking** *Many businesses offer stress-management programs to their employees. How could a stress-management program increase a company's profits?*

How to Manage Stress

Objectives

- Define stress intervention.

- Explain why physical exercise is a good way to handle stress.

- Use selective awareness to change your interpretation of a stressor.
  ## LIFE SKILLS: Coping

- Practice a relaxation technique that helps you to deal with stress.
  ## LIFE SKILLS: Coping

In this section you'll learn how to manage stressors as they come up on a daily basis by using the stress model shown below. Notice that the stress model consists of a series of steps, each step leading to the next. It is possible for you to take action to *stop* yourself from progressing from one step to the next.

The Stress Model

Step 1: A New or Potentially Unpleasant Situation (The Stressor) A situation which may trigger stress occurs.

Step 2: You Interpret the Situation as Threatening You interpret the situation as threatening, which leads to Step 3.

Step 3: Your Emotional Response You feel anxious, nervous, or insecure, which leads to the physical response in Step 4.

Step 4: Your Physical Response You experience the physical response, which leads to the negative consequences of Step 5.

Step 5: The Negative Consequences If nothing is done to relieve the stress, any number of consequences can result. Schoolwork may suffer, for example, as can a person's relationships with family and friends. A serious illness can also result from untreated long-term stress.

Signs of Stress

Physical Signs	Emotional and Mental Signs
Headaches	Anxiety
Dry mouth	Frustration
Teeth grinding	Mood swings
Shortness of breath	Depression
Pounding heart	Irritability
Indigestion	Nightmares
Diarrhea	Nervous laugh
Constipation	Worrying
Muscle aches	Confusion
Weight change	Forgetfulness
Fatigue	Poor concentration
Insomnia	Loneliness

(FIGURE 9-6) **This table shows some of the signs of stress. How many of these signs do you recognize in yourself? If you have more than a few, be sure to practice the stress interventions discussed in this chapter.**

The following examples will help you understand how the stress model works in a real-life situation.

Stress Sequence	Examples
Step 1. A New or Potentially Unpleasant Situation (The Stressor)	*Someone you are attracted to asks you to go to a movie with him or her.*
Step 2. You Interpret the Situation as Threatening	*You interpret this situation as threatening because you want to make a good impression and be able to go out with this person again. What if you say something dumb? What if this person doesn't think you are any fun?*
Step 3. Your Emotional Response	*During the movie, you start feeling nervous, doubtful, worried, and anxious.*
Step 4. Your Physical Response	*By the time the movie is over, you are sweating like crazy and your heart is racing in your chest.*
Step 5. The Negative Consequences	*You seem very nervous and you can't even talk about the movie later because you were too upset to pay much attention to it. The other person senses your unease and doesn't want to go out with you again.*

(FIGURE 9-7) **If you think positively, a situation such as a date is much more likely to turn out well. You can prevent a lot of stress by changing your interpretation of events and having realistic expectations.**

This scenario can be much different. Imagine that you have the same life situation (being asked out), but this time you decide that you're going to *interpret* the situation positively. "I must be a really fun person," you think. "I must be desirable." Because you think of the situation this way, you won't feel nearly as nervous or insecure, and none of the negative things that happened in the first scenario will occur. You have stopped yourself from progressing from one step to the next.

Think of the stress model as a map of a road that goes through the towns of "A New or Potentially Unpleasant Situation," "You Interpret the Situation as Threatening," "Your Emotional Response," "Your Physical Response," and "The Negative Consequences." As with all roads, you can set up a roadblock anywhere along the way. Stress management is setting up roadblocks that prevent you from traveling to the next "town." The roadblocks you set up are stress interventions. A **stress intervention** is any action that prevents a stressor from resulting in negative consequences.

The following stress interventions, or roadblocks, are helpful in managing stress.

stress intervention:

any action that prevents a stressor from resulting in negative consequences.

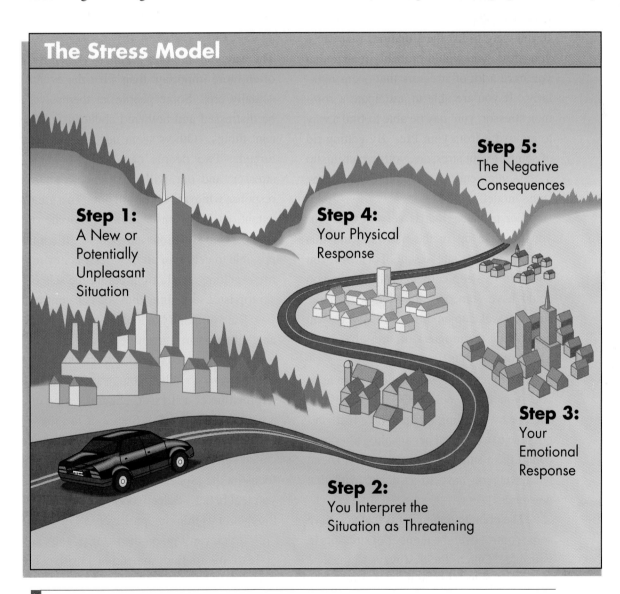

The Stress Model

Step 1: A New or Potentially Unpleasant Situation

Step 2: You Interpret the Situation as Threatening

Step 3: Your Emotional Response

Step 4: Your Physical Response

Step 5: The Negative Consequences

(FIGURE 9-8) **Think of the stress model as a map of a road that goes through different towns.**

Eliminating Some Stressors

If you were to list the situations that cause you stress, you would probably realize that you have a lot of stressors that occur regularly. If you are able to anticipate a common stressor, you may be able to find a way to remove it from your life. By getting rid of some of your stressors, you are setting up a stress intervention in front of Step 1 of the stress model.

For instance, if it is very difficult for you to wake up in the morning and this causes you to be late to school or work, you could go to sleep earlier at night. Or you could have someone you live with make sure you wake up on time. Either way, you would stop the progress of stress by eliminating one of your stressors.

If someone at your school is rude to you, you could eliminate or reduce that stressor by avoiding that person. If it isn't possible to avoid that person altogether, you could make sure that you are with a friend whenever you have to associate with that person.

The point to remember is that you have some control over the number of stressors in your life. One of the best ways to manage stress is to reduce the number of stressors in the first place. Which of *your* stressors can you eliminate?

Changing Your Interpretation of a Stressor

The way you interpret events in your life is often more important than what the events actually are. Some people let themselves be distressed and bothered about insignificant things. Others seem never to be disturbed. Two people can have the same stressor, and one will experience a stress response while the other will not. To a great extent, each person determines how he or she reacts to situations and people. It's impossible to get rid of all the stressors in your life—getting the flu right before the school ski trip isn't something that you can control.

But you can try to look at your unfortunate situation in a positive light—in other words, you can change the way you interpret a stressor. When you change your interpretation of a stressor, you are setting up a roadblock in front of Step 2 of the stress model. To do this, you can use what is called **selective awareness,** or choosing to focus on the aspects of a situation that help you feel better. Selective awareness can be thought of as thinking positively.

If you can't go on the ski trip, you can at least try to find something positive in your situation. If might mean that you will get to spend time with your brother who will be on break from college during the week of

selective awareness:

focusing on the aspects of a situation that help a person feel better ("thinking positively").

the trip. You hardly ever get to see him anymore, and this will be a good chance for the two of you to catch up.

A college student named Tatyana gave her father a good lesson in selective awareness. She wrote him from college that she had fallen out of her dormitory window, cracked her skull, and had been taken to the hospital. She wrote that while she was in the hospital, she fell in love with a man who was on parole from prison for physically abusing his first wife. Tatyana told her father that she and this man were planning to run away to get married.

At the end of the letter, however, she told him that she really hadn't fallen out of a window, hadn't been in the hospital, and hadn't met anyone with whom she had fallen in love. "But," she wrote, "I *did* fail chemistry, and I wanted you to put that in its proper perspective." Tatyana's father was not very upset about her failing chemistry

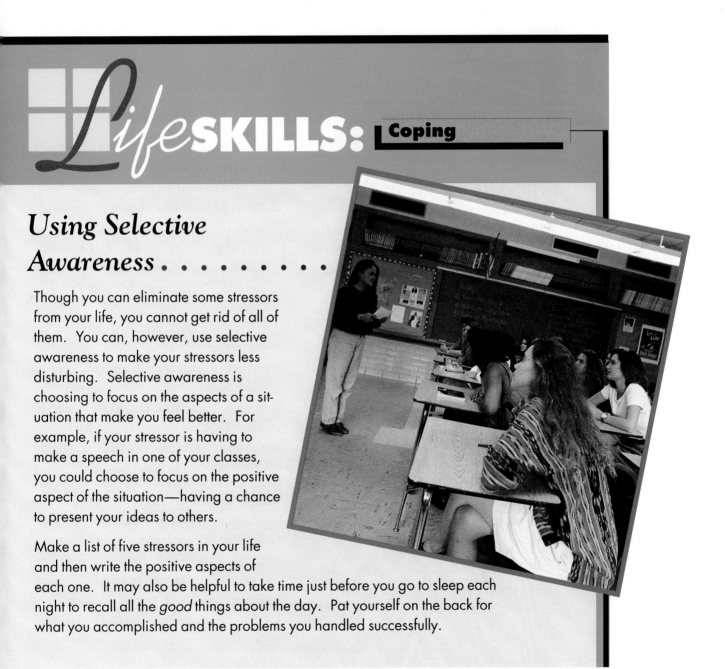

*Life*SKILLS: Coping

Using Selective Awareness . . . .

Though you can eliminate some stressors from your life, you cannot get rid of all of them. You can, however, use selective awareness to make your stressors less disturbing. Selective awareness is choosing to focus on the aspects of a situation that make you feel better. For example, if your stressor is having to make a speech in one of your classes, you could choose to focus on the positive aspect of the situation—having a chance to present your ideas to others.

Make a list of five stressors in your life and then write the positive aspects of each one. It may also be helpful to take time just before you go to sleep each night to recall all the *good* things about the day. Pat yourself on the back for what you accomplished and the problems you handled successfully.

because he focused on the fact that something much worse could have happened. Now *that* is using selective awareness!

The Life Skills activity on page 201 should help you to focus on the positive aspects of your stressors rather than on the negative aspects.

Using Relaxation Techniques

What if you're past the point of changing your interpretation of a situation? What if you are well on your way to becoming upset? One way to relieve your distress is to engage in some method of relaxation. When you do this, you are setting up a stress intervention in front of Step 3.

Different people relax in different ways. Some people like to listen to music. Others find that reading a book, watching television, or playing computer games helps them to relax. These activities have one thing in common: they take a person's mind off problems and hassles by focusing attention on another activity. Anything you do that changes the focus of your mind for a while can be relaxing.

Here are some other relaxation techniques that have been shown to be effective in helping people relax.

Meditation Meditation involves focusing on something that is repetitive or unchanging. You can meditate by doing this simple, yet effective, exercise.
1. Sit down and close your eyes.
2. In your mind, repeat a word you find relaxing—maybe "calm," or "serene," or "one"—every time you breathe out.

After doing this meditation exercise for about 20 minutes, you will probably feel relaxed and energetic.

Progressive Relaxation Some people prefer to be more active while relaxing. Progressive relaxation can meet this need. Here is how you do progressive relaxation.
1. First, tense the muscles in one part of your body. You might tense the muscles in your shoulders, for example. Notice how it feels to have those muscles *tensed*.
2. Then relax the same part of your body that you just tensed. Notice how it feels to have those muscles *relaxed*.
3. Now go from one muscle group to another throughout your body, tensing and relaxing. Many people find that this technique works best when you start at the top of the body and work down to your feet.

This is called progressive relaxation because you "progress" from one part of your body to another. Progressive relaxation is a good technique to use any time you feel tense. It is also a good technique to practice daily, so that when you find yourself in a stressful situation, you can quickly relax the muscles in your body.

Body Scanning Even when you feel tense, there is always some part of your body that feels relaxed. Your shoulders may ache, for example, but your thighs may feel warm and relaxed. When you do body scanning, you search throughout your body for that one relaxed part, and when you find it, imagine the warm, relaxed feeling being transferred to the rest of your body.

Autogenic Training You can relax by imagining that your arms and legs feel heavy, warm, and tingly. When they feel this way, it means that you have let go of muscle tension and dilated the blood vessels in your arms and legs. Once your body is relaxed, think of peaceful images—perhaps a relaxing day at the beach or walking under the stars. Sitting quietly and thinking of certain images can help both your mind and body relax. Although you need to determine for yourself what images are relaxing to you, many people find the following images to be restful:

- the beach
- a park
- green pastures
- blue skies
- a starry night
- a meadow of flowers
- sunshine on your body
- a warm bath
- floating on water

(FIGURE 9-9) **Thinking of peaceful scenes is one effective relaxation technique. Sit quietly and think of images you find restful.**

Check Up

How Tense Are You?

As you begin to read this, *freeze*. Don't move a bit. Now notice how your body is positioned.

1. Can you drop your shoulders? If you can, your shoulder muscles were unnecessarily tense.

2. Can you relax your forehead more? If you can, you were tensing the muscles in your forehead for no useful purpose.

3. Can you relax the muscles in your arms more? If you can, you were unnecessarily tensing them.

4. Check the muscles in your abdomen and legs. Are they contracted more than necessary?

Unnecessary muscle contraction is called bracing. Most of us don't even notice that we are bracing because it has become such a natural response to stressful lives. As a result of bracing, many people develop tension headaches, back trouble, or shoulder pain. Some of the relaxation techniques in this section will help you stop bracing.

Laughing Laughing is one of the easiest and most natural relaxation techniques known. You don't have to be taught how to laugh. Many people find that when they are under a lot of stress, it helps to watch a funny movie or television program or read a humorous book. Some studies have shown that laughing may even strengthen the immune system, and a stronger immune system is better able to fight off infections.

Laughing only works as a relaxation tool when you really think something is funny. Laughing because you feel nervous or embarrassed won't help you reduce stress.

Yelling or Crying Sometimes you just have to go off somewhere private and yell or cry. After a good yell or cry, a person can feel much more relaxed and able to deal with a stressor.

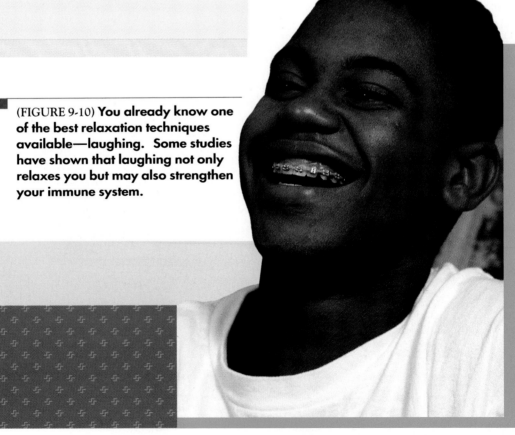

(FIGURE 9-10) **You already know one of the best relaxation techniques available—laughing. Some studies have shown that laughing not only relaxes you but may also strengthen your immune system.**

4 of the model by taking advantage of the body's readiness to do something physical.

Let's say you just had an argument with a friend and you are extremely angry. You can feel muscle tension in your shoulders, and your heart is beating rapidly. If you take a jog around the neighborhood, play basketball, or go for a swim, you use the tension in your muscles and your increased heart rate to do something physical. By exercising, you can use the stress response to your advantage instead of allowing it to hurt you.

Using Physical Exercise

If you don't stop stress from progressing, you could end up with a variety of physical responses, such as muscle tension, a racing heart, or high blood pressure. As you learned in Section 9.1, these changes are the result of the stress response, which prepares you to do something physical. The stress response is harmful to you only if you don't do something physical.

This is where exercise comes in. It sets up a stress intervention in front of Step

Review

1. Define the term stress intervention.

2. ■■ **LIFE SKILLS: Coping** Give one example of a stressor, and explain how a person could use selective awareness to change his or her interpretation of that stressor.

3. Why is physical exercise a good way to relieve stress?

4. ■■ **LIFE SKILLS: Coping** Practice a relaxation technique at least once, and describe how you felt afterward.

5. **Critical Thinking** Regular practice of a relaxation technique helps many people feel more energetic. Offer an explanation of this fact.

Section 9.3 Managing Stress Is a Lifelong Process

Objectives

- *Explain how a support group helps a person deal with stress.*

- *Manage your time by setting goals and prioritizing.*
  LIFE SKILLS: Setting Goals

- *Know how to seek help if you or someone you know is overwhelmed by stress.*
  LIFE SKILLS: Using Community Resources

support group: *a group of people who trust each other and are able to talk to each other about their problems.*

You learned in Section 9.2 how to deal with stressors as they come up on a daily basis. You can also protect yourself from stress by practicing stress-management techniques regularly throughout your lifetime.

Physical Health

Many of the negative consequences of stress can be prevented by taking the following steps to keep yourself physically well:

- Engage regularly in physical activity.
- Eat a balanced diet.
- Get enough rest and sleep.
- Do one of the relaxation techniques discussed on pages 202–204 every day.
- Do not use tobacco, alcohol, or other drugs.

A Support Group

One of the most effective ways to manage stress throughout your lifetime is to talk with other people about the things that bother you. You might be able to discuss your stressors with your family, your friends, or your teachers. Find a few people you can trust and call on them when you need to talk, and be available when they need to talk to someone. A group of people like this is called a **support group.** Sometimes just talking about a stressor with a member of your support group can reduce the stress you're under.

A Spiritual Life

Many people find that having a spiritual life—a sense of connection with something greater than oneself—helps them get through times of great stress. Some people believe in a supreme being who provides

(FIGURE 9-12) **Many people find the support group they need in religious communities such as churches and synagogues. A support group is one of the most effective ways to manage stress throughout your lifetime.**

Managing Your Time by Setting Goals and Prioritizing . . . .

A stressor that almost everyone faces at one time or another is the feeling that you don't have enough time to do everything you need and want to do. The key to using time wisely is to set goals and prioritize them. The following steps will help you reduce the stress of "not having enough time."

1. List your goals for today.

2. Prioritize your goals. Beside each goal, write either an "A," a "B," or a "C." The goals you label "A" are the ones you absolutely must get done that day. The ones labeled "B" are those you would *like* to get done. The goals labeled "C" are not as important and may have to wait until later.

3. During your day, do what is necessary to reach your "A" goals first, then your "B" goals. If you have some time left, you can attend to your "C" goals.

This strategy can be adapted for shorter or longer periods of time than a day. You can develop goals for a single morning, for example, or for a week, a month, and even a year.

The following suggestions may also help you manage your time:

- Learn to say no. Do not take on tasks that you have no time to complete.

- Work on one task at a time. Don't go back and forth between tasks. The time it takes to constantly reorient yourself is time wasted.

- Ask for help from others when you are pressured for time.

comfort and guidance during hard times. And some people feel a strong connection with nature, which gives them a feeling of peace and a sense that they are part of a beautiful world. These are both ways of having a spiritual life. There are numerous other ways, perhaps as many ways as there are people.

Organized religions can help people deal with stress not only by offering spiritual guidance but also by helping people feel like they are part of a community. In this way, members of churches, synagogues, and other religious communities may find the support group they need to cope with the stressors in their life.

Some people would not call themselves ''religious,'' but they know that they have a purpose—to help relieve the suffering of others, for example, or simply to act with honesty and integrity. Believing that one's life has purpose and meaning can help a person through very stressful times.

Getting Professional Help

At times a person can feel overwhelmed by stress. This can happen to anyone, even those who practice stress management. If you ever feel unable to cope with the stress in your life, you can get help from a professional. You might know a minister, priest, or rabbi you can turn to. Your school counselor is someone else who might be able to offer support.

You can also talk to a therapist if you feel overwhelmed by stress. Chapter 7 describes the different types of therapists and how to get in touch with them.

Many stressors cannot possibly be managed without the help of someone else. A person who is being physically, sexually, or emotionally abused should not be expected to deal with that stress all alone. If you are being abused, or if anyone you know is being abused, you should talk with an adult you trust or call the police or the Department of Child Protective Services. You can even report abuse anonymously. Abuse is discussed in greater detail in Chapter 20.

Sometimes stress can be so overwhelming that ending one's life seems like the only way out. If you or someone you know is thinking of suicide, it is very important that you get help immediately. Talk to an adult you trust, or look in the phone book under ''Suicide'' and call your local suicide-prevention hotline. Chapter 11 of this book is devoted to discussing suicide prevention.

R̲eview

1. *How does a support group help a person deal with stress?*

2. ▪▪ **LIFE SKILLS: Setting Goals** *Set your goals for the next week and divide them into tasks you must get done, tasks you would like to get done, and tasks that can wait until later.*

3. ▪▪ **LIFE SKILLS: Using Community Resources** *If you or someone you know were being abused, what could you do to get help?*

4. ▪▪ **LIFE SKILLS: Using Community Resources** *If you or someone you know were thinking of suicide, what could you do to get help?*

5. ***Critical Thinking*** *How could the use of tobacco, alcohol, or other drugs contribute to stress?*

Highlights

Summary

- A stressor is a new or potentially un-pleasant situation.

- A stress response is a reaction of the body to a stressor. Stress responses include release of adrenalin, faster heart rate, faster breathing rate, higher blood pressure, greater muscle tension, and greater blood flow to the brain and legs.

- A stress response is helpful when a person is being physically threatened and needs to respond immediately.

- If not managed properly, stress can cause physical and mental disorders, or make such disorders worse.

- The stress model is a series of steps that describes how stress develops. If you know the way the stress model works, you can stop yourself from progressing from one step to the next.

- Using selective awareness, or thinking

positively, is one way to cope with a stressful situation.

- Changing your focus from your worries for a while can help you relax and reduce stress. Relaxation techniques include listening to music, reading a book, meditating, progressive relaxation, body scanning, and imagery.

- Physical exercise and relaxation techniques can relieve muscle tension caused by stress.

- One of the most effective ways to manage stress is to develop a support system, or a group of people you can talk to about your problems. Support systems usually include family members, friends, teachers, or clergy.

- When a person feels overwhelmed, he or she can get professional help from counselors, therapists, and clergy.

Vocabulary

stressor any new or potentially un-pleasant situation.

stress response reaction of the body to a stressor.

stress the combination of a stressor and a stress response.

stress intervention any action that prevents a stressor from resulting in negative consequences.

selective awareness focusing on the aspects of a situation that help a person feel better ("thinking positively").

support group a group of people who trust each other and are able to talk to each other about their problems.

Concept Review

1. How can stress be both bad and good for you?

2. What changes can occur in your body during a stress response?

3. Can positive situations be stressful? Explain.

4. Explain how stress can make you ill and lead to injuries.

5. Describe at least four other consequences of stress.

6. What are three healthy ways to cope with stress?

7. At the end of a very stressful day, you find yourself unable to sleep. What can you do?

8. Explain why progressive relaxation is a good way to manage stress.

9. What can you do to maintain your physical health during times of stress?

10. What is a support system? How can it help you?

11. What can a person do if he or she feels totally overpowered by stressful situations and has tried all the usual coping techniques?

12. Stress often results from taking on too many tasks. Name three ways to protect yourself from this kind of stress.

Expressing Your View

1. Exam time is always a stressful time for you. While you are studying, you seem to know the material well; but during the exam, your anxiety level is so high that you can't remember anything. What can you do to cope better with the stress so that you can know the material on the next exam?

2. Name five jobs that you think are highly stressful. Name five jobs that you think are not stressful. Do you think everyone would classify these jobs as you did? Why, or why not?

3. Gary has been experiencing muscle tension and a rapid heartbeat. The problem seems to get worse every time he argues with his girlfriend. What can Gary do?

4. Laughter usually has positive results in coping with stress. Describe a situation in which humor might be inappropriate or have a negative effect.

Life Skills Check

1. Coping

Your friend seems very impatient, competitive, and even hostile with her friends lately. You think that she has overburdened herself with activities and responsibilities. Describe some relaxation techniques that might ease her stress.

2. Coping

You just found out that your family will be moving to another city. You know there will be many benefits for your family, but all you can think about are the changes you will have to make. You feel worried and scared. Make a list of five positive aspects of moving that might make you feel better.

Projects

1. Work with a group to make a list of stressors in the everyday lives of people in a certain age category (children, teenagers, adults, or elderly people). Then interview two people in the age category your group chose, to find out what their greatest stressors are. Compare the results to your first list and discuss the results.

2. Write a short essay focusing on findings that show a definite relationship between physical disorders and stress.

3. Find out if you are managing your time wisely by making a pie graph that shows how much time you spend on your daily activities. For example, you might spend 5 percent on chores, 30 percent in school, 15 percent with friends, 10 percent on extracurricular activities, 5 percent on homework, and 35 percent sleeping. Analyze your graph and decide whether managing your time better will reduce your stress.

Plan for Action

List one or two stressors in your life and devise a plan to lower your stress level using the suggestions in this chapter.

CHAPTER 10

Coping With Loss

◆ ◆ ◆ ◆

Section 10.1 Death and Dying

Section 10.2 The Grieving Process

A hospice worker visits a terminally ill person in his home.

Justin's brother, Chad, died last week. Chad had been in and out of the hospital for years with a serious illness; he died at home with his family close by. The funeral is over, and all the relatives have gone home. Now Justin has to go back to school. In a way this will be the hardest part, because he doesn't know how to act around his friends. What should he say? What will *they* say? He doesn't want to make anyone feel bad on his account. But he thinks it might help to talk with a friend about his brother.

Death and Dying

Objectives

- *Describe the five stages terminally ill people generally pass through.*

- *List three reasons why many people choose hospice care when they are terminally ill.*

- *Describe the functions of a living will.*

- *Learn how to be of help to someone who is dying.*
  LIFE SKILLS: Coping

If Justin were your friend, how would you help him? Would you feel embarrassed to say anything to him about his brother, afraid of saying the wrong thing? Most people would. Death is a topic that often makes us uncomfortable. But the more we know about it, the better we'll be able to help other people cope with death, and the better we'll be able to cope with our own losses.

Death is a natural part of life. Although we don't usually stop to think about it, death surrounds us all our lives. Even very young children are exposed to death—usually of pets or other animals. Children also learn about death through the media, especially from television. Those deaths seem remote and far away. By the time people become teenagers, however, most have known someone who has died. Often this is an older person, such as a grandparent, but sometimes it is a friend or brother or sister.

An understanding of death is greatly influenced by a person's age. For example, infants have no real concept of death. From age two to five, children recognize death but do not think it is permanent. They think that death is like sleep. From age five to nine, children come to view death as permanent, but not as something that could happen to them. Around age 10, children realize that death is inevitable and final. They know death happens but have trouble realizing it can happen to anyone at any time. Most people do not have a full awareness of death until adolescence.

When Does Death Occur?

According to the Harvard Medical School, all of the following criteria must be present for a person to be considered dead:

1. Unreceptiveness and unresponsiveness. *The patient is totally unresponsive to applied painful stimuli, such as poking with pins.*

2. Unresponsiveness in breathing. *For over an hour, the patient shows no spontaneous muscular contractions or breathing.*

3. Lack of reflexes. *The knee-jerk reflex is absent, or the pupil does not contract when light is pointed in the eye.*

4. Flat EEG. *For 20 minutes, the patient's brain does not generate an electrical impulse or brain wave.*

(FIGURE 10-1) **According to these criteria, a person who is kept functioning by life-support systems is alive until the machines are shut off.**

When Does Death Occur?

In the past, people considered death to occur when the lungs and heart ceased to function. Scientific and technological advances, though, have made it more difficult to determine when death occurs.

Today, people whose heart and lungs have stopped are sometimes revived by cardiopulmonary resuscitation (CPR) or by a machine. Life-support machines can sometimes keep people "alive" if they cannot breathe or if their heart will not beat on its own. Machines can feed people if they cannot eat, and they can clean the blood if the body's organs cannot do it. Even when people are not emitting brain waves, they can still function artificially. When, then, is a person dead?

The Harvard Medical School has developed a definition of death that attempts to answer this question. According to this definition, the four criteria listed in Figure 10-1 must be met before an individual can be declared dead.

Stages in the Acceptance of Death

People who die suddenly do not have time to prepare for death. However, people who die from a terminal illness often have lots of time to think about death and to prepare for it.

Elisabeth Kubler-Ross, a noted physician, worked for years with patients dying from terminal illnesses. She identified five stages that most terminally ill patients go through when facing death. Understanding these stages can be valuable if you ever need to help a dying friend or relative.

Not all terminally ill people go through these stages in the same order. Some may skip a stage, revert to an earlier stage, or get stuck in one stage. People experience dying with the same individuality that they experience living.

Stage 1: Denial When people learn that they are going to die, their reaction is often to feel shock and denial. Denial acts as a buffer that gives people a chance to think about the news. People may think, "It can't be true, not me." Or they may prefer to believe that a cure will be found for their disease or that they will be the exception to the rule. At this point, it is helpful for patients to get a second opinion from a reputable physician in order to verify their condition. If you have a friend or relative in the denial stage, the best response is just to listen. Even if people who are dying talk about getting well soon, it is better not to contradict them. That could force them to accept their death before they are ready.

Stage 2: Anger When people realize they are really going to die, they are likely to think, "Why me?" and become angry. People may feel as if they are being treated unfairly. They may see someone who is mean and cruel but in perfect health and think, "Why should I have to die while this other person goes on enjoying life?"

In this situation, anger is often directed at medical staff, family, or friends. It is important to let them know they have a right to be angry. If the person gets angry at you, try to accept it without feeling hurt. Recognize that this is simply a stage that will pass. Providing an outlet for the anger can be helpful.

Stage 3: Bargaining Bargaining is a final attempt to avoid the inevitable. People who believe in God may promise to reform their life in exchange for a miraculous recovery.

Stage 4: Depression After passing through the first three stages, dying people often become depressed. Sometimes dying people have worries that it might be helpful for them to discuss—a friend or relative who is dying may ask you to adopt a pet or to visit periodically with his or her children or spouse.

Sometimes dying people are depressed because they feel they are losing everything, especially their friends and loved ones. What may be most helpful is just to be with them, often silently.

Stage 5: Acceptance Accepting your own death is hard to imagine, but most people who have a terminal illness eventually get to a point where they can do so. By this stage, people have usually taken care of all of their personal affairs, including wills,

Check Up

How Do You Feel About Death?

On a separate sheet of paper, answer each of the following questions to determine how you feel about death. Use the following scale:

a = comfortable   c = somewhat uncomfortable
b = somewhat comfortable   d = uncomfortable

1. How comfortable are you talking about death and dying?

2. How comfortable would you feel if you had to visit and support someone you cared about who was terminally ill?

3. How comfortable would you feel if you had to provide support for a friend whose parent had died?

4. How comfortable would you feel about donating your kidneys for use upon your death?

5. How comfortable would you feel about signing a statement requesting that you not be kept alive if in a coma and on life-support mechanisms?

6. If you were legally responsible for someone being kept alive by life-support systems, and you knew the person would not want to remain in that state, how comfortable would you feel about ordering the withdrawal of the life-support equipment?

funeral arrangements, and saying goodbye to special people in their life.

Death With Dignity

One of the most painful things about dying is that it can rob a person of his or her dignity. Recognizing this, the helping professions are exploring ways to allow dying people to have more control over what happens to them and to provide them with the support they need.

will:

a legal document describing what should be done with a person's possessions after the person's death.

hospices:

places that offer housing, medical care, and counseling for terminally ill people and counseling for the family.

What Dying People Need Dying people need to be able to express their feelings, and they need a caring group of family and friends to listen.

Doctors used to be encouraged to withhold bad news from terminally ill patients because it was thought that the patients would be shocked, agitated, or depressed. But knowledge of an impending death can help improve communication and enhance relationships between the dying person and his or her friends and family. When asked, most people say they would want to be told if they had a terminal illness. Even if they are not told, most terminally ill patients know or suspect that they are going to die.

Just like the rest of us, dying people want some control over things that affect them. To have that control, they need honest answers to their questions. Dishonesty not only prevents them from managing their remaining time, but it also damages their trust in others, which is so vital when everything else seems to be falling away.

What kinds of things do people who are dying want to control? They want to decide who their doctors will be, which treatments they will accept, and who will visit them. In addition, they often wish to control their own funeral or memorial service. Decisions such as whether there will be a burial or cremation, who will officiate at the service, and what will be included in the service can be made in anticipation of death. Also, they want to control what will be done with their possessions. Dying people are often comforted by knowing their possessions will be in the right hands after they die. This is best handled through a **will,** which is a legal document describing what should be done after death. It also may contain directions for the care of surviving family members or even pets.

Hospices Many people would rather die at home than in a hospital. **Hospices**—programs that care for terminally ill people—help fill this need. Hospices provide a homelike atmosphere even though the patient is away from home. Although they do not have a hospital's extensive equipment, they can provide a program of medical care and support for the patient, as well as support for the family. Sometimes hospices can provide care in the patient's own home through medical specialists who visit the patient.

The hospice approach has several unique features. For example, medications are freely administered for pain, reflecting the philosophy that the patient's remaining time should be as comfortable as possible. Families visit freely without restrictions on hours or age, and volunteers visit and talk with dying patients.

(FIGURE 10-2) Dying people often want to express their feelings and need a warm group of family and friends to listen.

When hospice care is provided in the patient's own home, families learn to participate in the patient's care. They may administer medications or perform other tasks.

Family members receive counseling to work through their grief and to be better prepared to interact with the dying person. Other hospice services include legal counseling, home nursing care, and support for the grieving family after the patient dies.

People who choose to die in their own homes often prefer hospice care. For example, George Jeffrey, a 78-year-old man, began to feel ill and had extensive tests that showed he had advanced cancer. Mr. Jeffrey was a retired commercial artist who lived with his daughter and son-in-law and his grandchildren. He loved to play golf, spend time with his family, and watch sports on TV.

Mr. Jeffrey and his family chose to receive hospice care in the home. Mr. Jeffrey stayed in the family home and continued to use his favorite easy chair. He continued to watch sports on TV and visited a great deal with his family.

The family was told what to expect throughout the dying process. Nurses from the hospice program made regular visits to Mr. Jeffrey and his family. As the time of death approached, the nurse gently explained to the family what was happening.

When the moment of death was very near, the family's greatest concern was for Mr. Jeffrey. They wanted him to know how much they loved him. They wanted him to know they would be fine and that he could let go and pass from this life.

He died with great courage and dignity. Most of all, he died in an atmosphere of great love.

Living Wills

Many ethical decisions surround the topic of death. Should life be preserved at all costs—even if the person is in a coma or in excruciating pain? Or should death simply be allowed to take its course without intervention?

The **living will** is one way to deal with this complex issue. A living will is a simple statement people can sign that instructs their doctors not to use medical equipment just to keep them breathing and their hearts beating when they have no chance for meaningful recovery. It tells the medical staff to let nature take its course. This takes the burden off their families and lets the medical staff know their wishes. An example of a living will is shown in Figure 10-3. Living wills should not be confused with regular wills. Living wills are concerned with life-support mechanisms, while regular wills deal with the distribution of material goods and instructions for the care of others.

living will

a document expressing a person's wish to be allowed to die in case of terminal illness or incurable injury rather than be kept alive by artificial means.

Review

1. Describe the five stages terminally ill people generally pass through.

2. List three reasons why many people choose hospice care when they are terminally ill.

3. Describe the functions of a living will.

4. **LIFE SKILLS: Coping** You have a friend who is terminally ill and in the hospital. Your friend tells you the doctors are wrong and that he really isn't that sick. He wants to leave the hospital immediately and wants you to help him. What would you do?

5. **Critical Thinking** What types of patients might prefer hospital care to hospice care?

To My Family, Doctors, and All Those Concerned with My Care

I, _____ , being of sound mind, make this statement as a directive to be followed if for any reason I become unable to participate in decisions regarding my medical care.

I direct life-sustaining procedures should be withheld if I have an illness, disease, or injury, or experience extreme mental deterioration, such that there is no reasonable expectation of recovering or regaining a meaningful life.

These life-sustaining procedures that may be withheld or withdrawn include, but are not limited to:

Surgery   Antibiotics   Cardiac Resuscitation   Respiratory Support
Artificially Administered Feeding and Fluids

I further direct that treatment be limited to comfort measures only, even if they shorten my life.

You may delete any provison above by drawing a line through it and adding your initials.

Other personal instructions:

These directions express my legal right to refuse treatment. Therefore, I expect my family, doctors, and all those concerned with my care to regard themselves as legally and morally bound to act in accord with my wishes, and in so doing to be free from any liability for having followed my directions.

Signed _____ Date _____

Witness _____ Witness _____

Proxy Designaton Clause

If you wish, you may use this section to designate someone to make treatment decisions for you if you are unable to do so. Your Living Will Declaration will be in effect even if you have a designated proxy.

I authorize the following person to implement my Living Will Declaration by accepting, refusing, and/or making decisons about my treatment and hospitalization:

Name _____

Address _____

If the person I have named above is unable to act on my behalf, I authorize the following person to do so:

Name _____

Address _____

I have discussed my wishes with these persons and trust their judgment on my behalf.

Signed _____ Date _____

Witness _____ Witness _____

Objectives

- Learn how to deal with your own grief.
  ■■ **LIFE SKILLS: Coping**

- Learn how to give emotional support to someone who is grieving.
  ■■ **LIFE SKILLS: Communicating Effectively**

- List three reasons for having funerals or memorial services.

We experience grief when we suffer a great loss. People can grieve over losses other than death—the loss of a love relationship, for example, or even the loss of a treasured object. But grief is probably most intense when we lose someone through death.

The grief people feel when someone dies is influenced by several factors. For example, the feelings related to a sudden death are different from those resulting from death caused by a long illness. In one case, the death is an unexpected shock. In the other, you have time to prepare. Reactions to death also differ depending upon how close you were to the person who has died. However, regardless of who dies and how close you were to him or her, you will need to wrestle with the feeling of loss. Only the intensity of the loss will vary.

When people know a loved one is dying, they may go through the same stages of accepting death as the dying person. They may deny that death is imminent. They may become angry, sometimes at the patient, especially if they have been dependent on the dying person. They may spend a great deal of time praying and bargaining for the person to recover. They may get depressed. And, ultimately, they may come to accept the death and the need to survive in spite of it.

Dealing With Your Grief

Whether the death of someone close is anticipated or sudden, one thing is certain: expect the unexpected. No matter how much we plan and think about living without someone we love, we never really know how we will react to a death.

The loss of a parent through divorce is discussed in Chapter 19.

The loss of a love relationship is discussed in Chapter 17.

Ways to Deal with Your Grief

Speak to someone you can trust who will respect your feelings and keep your conversation confidential. This might be a close friend, teacher, coach, or school counselor. In some areas, there are support groups for the bereaved that your school counselor or a local hospital might know about.

It is important to get your feelings out. One way to do this would be to use phrases like: "I remember when ...." "What I remember most about ...."

Talking about the future will stress the permanence of death and help with adjustment. For example, you can say: "We're really going to miss ...." "What I will miss the most is ...."

Be honest with yourself and others when discussing your feelings about death.

(FIGURE 10-4)

(FIGURE 10-5)

Ways to Help a Grieving Person

If you have a classmate who has lost someone through death, it is important to express your sympathy as a show of support. You might say: "I was sorry to hear about your brother's death. He was a great guy." But unless you're a close friend, don't ask for details.

Try to put the person in touch with others who are grieving. For example, teenagers who have lost a parent through death can be of great help to another teenager whose parent has just died.

Reassure the person that guilt, sadness, despair, and similar feelings are normal.

Listen to, hold, and touch the grieving person. Let the person share the grief with you.

It is wise not to run away from feelings, because the hurt cannot be denied. It is best to let out the feelings, sharing them with people to whom you feel close. They can help by listening and by serving as a reminder that you are not alone.

During the grieving process, it may help to talk with a good friend about what you are experiencing. If you are a member of a church or synagogue, you may want to talk with your priest, minister, or rabbi. Organized support groups for people who have lost someone through death may also exist in your community. Another alternative is to talk to your school counselor or a therapist. Remember that seeking help is a sign of strength, not weakness. Figure 10-4 has some suggestions that can help you adjust to a death.

Helping Others Deal With Grief

If you know a person who is grieving, you can be of tremendous help. Try to imagine what would help if you were grieving.

What would feel good to you would probably also feel good to someone else.

Communicate your concern. Express friendship. Let the person know you're there if needed. You can show you care by being comforting. Avoid saying things like "Don't cry, you'll get over it." Crying is a healthful way to release feelings of grief. Offer to help the grieving person adjust. You might be able to help with schoolwork or household chores.

As you try to help, let the person set the speed of the recovery. Everyone handles this type of situation differently. Allow the person to decide how you can help. For example, don't insist on giving advice if the person doesn't want it. Respect the grieving person's wishes and take your lead from him or her. And remember that a grieving person often needs support not only right after a death, but also a week, a month, or a year later.

If you are helping someone who is grieving, you might find the suggestions in Figure 10-5 helpful.

Although negative emotions and readjustments accompany death, there are some positive outcomes. When families are close and communicate feelings openly, death can draw the survivors closer together and help them to grow from the experience.

Funerals and Memorial Services

When a person dies, the body is usually buried or cremated. When there is a burial, the body is placed in a casket and buried in a cemetery. In **cremation**, the body is reduced to ashes by intense heat. The ashes may be scattered or placed in an urn.

Within a few days of the death, there is almost always a funeral, which is a ceremony at which others pay respect to the person who has died. Usually the body is in a casket, which is sometimes open, sometimes closed. Often, a service is performed that includes a speech remembering the person who has died. This service may be held in a religious sanctuary or a funeral home.

cremation

the complete reduction of a body to ashes by intense heat.

LifeSKILLS: Communicating Effectively

Helping a Grieving Friend . . .

With another student, role-play the following situation. Alternate roles, so that each of you has an opportunity to play both the grieving friend and the helping friend.

Situation

You are talking with your best friend, whose father just died. Your friend is really sad and needs to express his or her feelings. Using the guidelines in this chapter, talk with your friend and provide your support.

Here's one way you might start.

Friend: It doesn't seem real. I can't stop thinking Dad will come home after work, like he always did.

You: It's really tough, your dad dying. I know you miss him a lot.

(FIGURE 10-6) **Grieving is a way to adjust to the idea that someone we love has died.**

When the body is to be buried, this indoor service is often followed by a short graveside service before burial.

Many times a memorial service is chosen instead of a funeral to pay respect to a person who has died. Memorial services differ from funerals in that the body is not present. Sometimes they take place after the body has been cremated or buried. Some memorial services are similar to funeral services, but others are more informal than traditional funerals.

Funerals and memorial services play an important role in helping people of our culture adjust to their loss and accept the finality of death. They can also assist people in observing the death spiritually.

In addition, these ceremonies provide a way for friends to show support to the grieving family. Seeing friends who knew and loved the person who has died can make the first few days of bereavement a little easier to bear.

Review

1. *Name three ways that funerals and memorial services help grieving people.*

2. **LIFE SKILLS: Coping** *If you were grieving over the death of a loved one, with whom could you talk?*

3. **LIFE SKILLS: Communicating Effectively** *Your friend tells you that she just can't get over the death of her mother, who died two months ago. What would you say to reassure her that her feelings are normal?*

4. *Critical Thinking Your Aunt Cindy's husband died a month ago. She stays home all the time, crying frequently. What do you think would help her most?*

CHAPTER
10

Highlights

Summary

- Most people do not have a full awareness of death until adolescence.

- A person can be declared legally dead if the following criteria are met: unreceptiveness and unresponsiveness, unresponsiveness in breathing, lack of reflexes, and a flat EEG.

- Most terminally ill patients go through specific stages: denial, anger, bargaining, depression, and acceptance.

- A will is a legal document that states what to do with possessions and may contain directions for the care of surviving family members.

- A hospice provides medical care in a homelike environment for a person who is dying. Hospice care might also include counseling for the patient and his or her family.

- A living will allows a person to make the decision to die instead of being kept alive by machines.

- Grieving people may go through the same stages as dying people in accepting death. It may help a grieving person to talk with someone about how he or she is feeling.

- A good way to help a grieving friend is to express your concern and let him or her know that you want to help.

- Funerals help people accept the finality of death, allow friends to show support, and let people observe death spiritually.

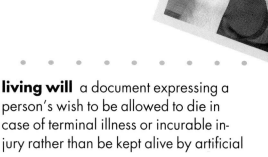

Vocabulary

will a legal document describing what should be done with a person's possessions after the person's death.

hospices places that offer housing, medical care, and counseling for terminally ill people and counseling for the family.

living will a document expressing a person's wish to be allowed to die in case of terminal illness or incurable injury rather than be kept alive by artificial means.

cremation the complete reduction of a body to ashes by intense heat.

Chapter Review

Concept Review

1. Why might some people avoid a grieving person?

2. Describe a child's concept of death at various age levels.

3. List the four criteria for determining when death occurs.

4. Why is it helpful to know the five stages of accepting death identified by Elisabeth Kubler-Ross?

5. What are three needs of a dying person?

6. Why is it important to be honest with a dying person?

7. Describe some unique features of a hospice.

8. How is a regular will different from a living will?

9. How is the grief of a dying person similar to the grief of a survivor or other family member?

10. What factors influence the grief people feel?

11. What can you do during the grieving process to help adjust to a death? How can you help someone else deal with grief?

12. What is one positive outcome of death and grief?

13. How are burials different from cremations? How do funerals and memorial services differ?

Expressing Your Views

1. Your best friend just found out he has a terminal illness. He is convinced that a cure will be found soon and that he is not really going to die. It is hard for you to be around him because you are having trouble accepting the news too, but you want to help your friend if you can. How can you explain your friend's attitude? What would you do?

2. Your neighbor, who has two small children, is terminally ill. She has a full-time nurse at home so she doesn't need any kind of medical assistance. However, you want to help her in some way. What could you do?

3. Manuel has been grieving over his father's death for many months now. His friends don't understand his lingering depression. He is beginning to wonder if the grief he feels after all this time is normal and if it will ever go away. How could Manuel help himself?

Life Skills Check

1. Coping
Beatrice is terribly depressed about her mother's death. She worries that her friends may get tired of hearing about it, but Beatrice does feel the need to share memories of her mother. What could you suggest to her?

2. Communicating Effectively
Your aunt is terminally ill and has been in and out of hospitals for almost a year. She always dreads her hospital stays because she misses her children and pets when she is away from home. What would you suggest to her as an alternative to hospital care? What would you say to explain how the alternative care would be different?

Projects

1. Burial customs vary from culture to culture. Choose another country or culture and research its customs and attitudes toward death. Write a brief essay summarizing your findings and comparing that society's customs with those of our society.

2. Find a newspaper or magazine article about a family that had to make the decision whether to keep a loved one alive by life-support mechanisms, or an article about a situation where a family member carried out a patient's wishes through a living will. Bring the articles to class and discuss them in groups.

3. Invite a grief counselor or mental health professional to your class to lead a discussion about helping people deal with death.

Plan for Action

Friends and family can support a dying person and each other. List three things you can do in the future to help a dying friend.

CHAPTER 11

Preventing Suicide

◆ ◆ ◆ ◆

Section 11.1 Teenage Suicide: A Serious Problem

Section 11.2 Giving and Getting Help

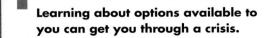

Learning about options available to you can get you through a crisis.

After the divorce, things got really bad for Aaron. He lived with his mother, who was always on his case about something. Aaron knew that she was worried about money because his dad was having trouble paying the child-support payment and they could barely make ends meet.

Aaron was also having a hard time in school. He had flunked three tests in a row, and he knew that if he kept this up, he wouldn't get in to college. Even if he did get accepted, there probably wouldn't be enough money to pay for it. Aaron lay awake at night feeling desperate about his situation, and this made it even harder to concentrate at school.

Then the worst thing of all happened. Aaron's girlfriend, Ashley, who had stayed with him through all his troubles, told Aaron she didn't want to see him anymore. She had started going out with someone else. His whole life seemed so hopeless that he started to think about ending it all. He just wanted to go to sleep and never wake up.

Section 11.1
Teenage Suicide: A Serious Problem

Objectives

- *Define suicide.*

- *Understand how serious the problem of suicide is among teenagers.*

- *Name three possible reasons for the increase in teen suicides.*

- *Name at least three myths and facts about suicide.*

Aaron reacted to the problems in his life by thinking about killing himself—committing **suicide.** He felt trapped. In his despair, he did not recognize that other options existed for him.

If you have ever been depressed like Aaron, you may have considered suicide. This is not unusual. Many people think about taking their own life when they feel extremely unhappy and hopeless. But if you have felt that suicide was the only way out of your troubles, you haven't learned about all the other options that exist.

In this chapter you will learn about the options available to you and your friends if life seems too painful to go on.

The Increase in Teen Suicides

Suicide is an increasingly serious problem among young people. The suicide rate among teenagers has quadrupled in the last 40 years. Suicide is the third leading cause

suicide:

the act of intentionally taking one's own life.

of death among people between 15 and 24. A recent study showed that 27 percent of high school students have considered suicide at least once in their life. Of those who actually attempt suicide, 1 in 50 succeeds. Although the reasons for the increase are not clear, there are several factors that may contribute to teen suicide.

The rising divorce rate and breakup of families has created a situation in which many teenagers feel a sense of isolation and a lack of family support. Only a few decades ago, several generations of a family often lived in the same house. In this situation, young people usually had at least one close relative—a parent, a grandparent, an aunt, an uncle, or a cousin—that they felt they could relate to. Today teenagers live in smaller families, with fewer adults around to offer them the emotional support they need as a natural part of growing up.

Also, people today move from place to place more often than in earlier times. As a result of a parent's job loss or transfer to another city, children and teenagers often lose their old friends and must adjust to new schools. In times of trouble they may not be able to call on friends and relatives, who may be thousands of miles away.

Many teens live in troubled families, and feel that the love and care that they need is simply not there for them. Some teens may also experience physical, emotional, or sexual abuse.

Another factor may be the pressure to succeed in school and in future careers. Young people may feel like failures if they do not live up to their own or their parents' expectations.

The increased use of alcohol and other drugs among teens also contributes to suicides. Although mind-altering substances may provide a temporary escape from emotional pain, they make things worse in the long run. Using alcohol and drugs damages a person's ability to solve everyday prob-

(FIGURE 11-1) **At one time, it was common for several generations of a family to live together. Teenagers in such families usually had at least one close relation to talk to.**

(FIGURE 11-2) **Kurt Cobain, lead singer of the band Nirvana, committed suicide in 1994. Celebrities who commit suicide are sometimes glamorized by the media.**

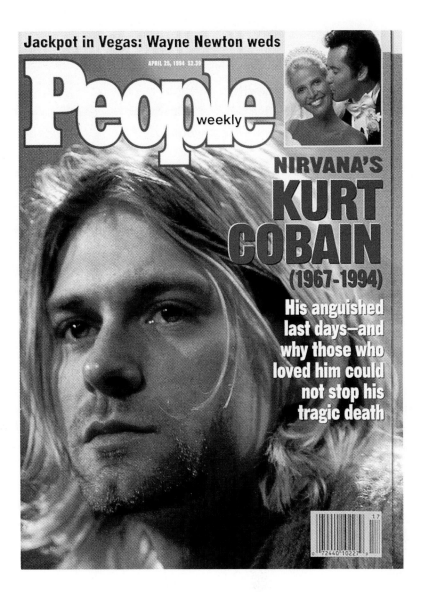

Jackpot in Vegas: Wayne Newton weds

People weekly

APRIL 25, 1994 $2.39

NIRVANA'S KURT COBAIN (1967-1994)

His anguished last days—and why those who loved him could not stop his tragic death

lems. And being drunk or high interferes with a person's judgment, and increases the chance that a person will act on a suicidal impulse.

Finally, the popular media have romanticized suicide to a certain extent. When famous people kill themselves, they are sometimes made to seem like mythic figures. Suicide, such a message may seem to say, is glamorous and romantic. But once a celebrity is dead, he or she is not around to enjoy the romantic image. Suicide is not a glamorous act; it brings only death.

Why Would Someone Want to Die?

The reasons why young people try to kill themselves are many and complicated. Most people don't really want to die—they just want to end the emotional pain that they are suffering.

How can things get that bad? Life as a teenager can seem extremely stressful, especially if a person has low self-esteem. If someone who is already under great stress experiences a crisis, it may make life seem unbearable.

A crisis to one person would not necessarily seem like a crisis to another. To Aaron, losing his girlfriend was the last straw—he felt it pushed him over the edge. His girlfriend provided the only emotional support he had at that time. His father was gone, and his mother seemed preoccupied with earning enough money to pay the bills and keep a roof over their heads.

When a person is depressed, events that at other times would be tolerable might seem impossible to bear. Moving to another town, not making a team or club, or the death of a pet could trigger a crisis in an already depressed person. Even an event that would seem trivial to others—having a bicycle stolen, for example—could be the last unbearable thing for an extremely depressed person.

Myths and Facts About Suicide

Myth	Fact
Suicide usually occurs without warning.	While some suicides may be impulsive, usually the person has thought about suicide for a long time.
People who talk about killing themselves rarely commit suicide.	Most people who commit suicide have talked about it before.
If you ask a person if he or she is considering suicide, you will encourage that person to commit suicide.	You will not cause a suicide by asking if someone is thinking about it. People who are not suicidal will not be influenced by the question. People who are considering suicide will feel relieved that someone cares enough to ask and to listen to their problems.
All suicidal people want to die.	A suicide attempt is often a cry for help. The person may be asking for help to live.
When a suicidal person suddenly seems calm and serene, there is no longer any danger of suicide.	A suicidal person who suddenly acts calm and serene may have decided to commit suicide and therefore feels relief that a decision has been made.
If someone makes a suicidal comment while drunk or high, it isn't very serious.	People who are under the influence of alcohol or other drugs may be at a greater risk of acting on suicidal thoughts because their judgment is impaired and they may be more impulsive.
All people who commit suicide are mentally ill.	Many people who feel suicidal are not mentally ill. They may be in a period of intense emotional crisis.
Once a person is suicidal, he or she will always be suicidal.	Many people consider suicide for only a brief period in their lives. A person who attempts suicide and survives may never attempt it again if proper support and treatment is found.
The tendency toward suicide is inherited and passed from parent to child.	Suicide is a behavior and cannot be inherited. However, depression may have a genetic basis. Severely depressed people may harbor more thoughts of suicide than those who do not suffer from depression.

(FIGURE 11-3) **Because people avoid talking about suicide, many myths have arisen about the subject. Only by openly discussing suicide can people in trouble be recognized and helped.**

• • • • •

(FIGURE 11-4) **Suicide is a permanent response to what is usually a temporary problem.**

When people are in crisis situations, they may become confused and make poor decisions. They may develop "tunnel vision," which is the inability to see all the options available. Aaron thought killing himself was the only way to solve his problems. When someone feels that suicide is the only solution to the problems of living, he or she is said to have a **suicidal mindset.**

But other solutions to problems always exist, even in the worst of situations. If Aaron had committed suicide, it would have been a permanent solution to a temporary problem. Aaron didn't really want to *die*. He just wanted to end his pain and suffering. The key to preventing suicide is getting help from people who can offer alternatives to ending one's life.

Review

1. *Define suicide.*

2. *Where does suicide rank among the causes of death of people aged 15 to 24?*

3. *Name three possible reasons for the increase in teen suicides.*

4. *Name three common myths about suicide and explain why each is not true.*

5. *Critical Thinking Describe some effects of alcohol and other drug use that might increase the possibility that a person would attempt suicide.*

suicidal mindset:

the feeling that suicide is the only solution to the problems of living.

11.2

Giving and Getting Help

Objectives

■ *List at least five warning signs of suicide.*

■ *Learn strategies for dealing with someone who is suicidal.*
  LIFE SKILLS: Solving Problems

■ *Learn how to use decision-making skills to help a friend in crisis.*
  LIFE SKILLS: Making Responsible Decisions

■ *Know what to do if you feel suicidal.*
  LIFE SKILLS: Coping

Because suicide is such a serious and scary issue, it's hard to know how to help someone who is considering it. Do the best you can to help them, but don't feel that the entire burden is on you. You shouldn't feel responsible if a friend commits suicide. If a person kills himself or herself, no one is responsible but that person.

The first step is to try to determine if a friend feels suicidal. Statistics show that 80 percent of the people who attempt suicide have given warning signals. Figure 11-7 on page 233 lists some possible warning signs of suicide.

(FIGURE 11-5) **If you think a friend is suicidal, call a suicide hotline. The staff there will assist your efforts to find help.**

Intervention Strategies: What Should You Do?

Think back to Aaron at the beginning of this chapter. Assume that you are a friend of his and you've noticed that he has seemed really down lately. One night he says to you: ''This may be the last time you will see me.'' Which of the following should you do?

1. Ask Aaron if he is thinking about committing suicide.
2. Avoid mentioning suicide but make an attempt to find out what is bothering Aaron.
3. Keep the talk light so as not to give Aaron any ideas about suicide.
4. Try to joke with Aaron about his problems and about suicide.

The first answer is the best one in this case. If Aaron isn't thinking about suicide, your mentioning it will not do any harm; you aren't going to make him suicidal by asking him if he is. But if Aaron is thinking about suicide, he urgently needs to discuss it. People who talk about suicide, or give any indication they are contemplating it, are often seeking help in the only way they know how.

Most suicidal people reach out to someone for help. In fact, many reach out repeatedly before they actually try to kill themselves.

If you have a friend who is suicidal, let your friend know you are listening and that you understand. Your friend may express feelings of being picked on, different, lonely, ugly, or stupid. Do not try to make your friend feel better by denying the feelings. Don't say, for example: ''Oh, you're just imagining things. Snap out of it.''

Be as understanding and patient as possible. To show you understand, you could say something like: ''It must feel terrible to have all that pain and anguish.''

(FIGURE 11-6) **If a friend seems depressed and possibly suicidal, let him or her know that you're there, and that you care.**

Possible Warning Signs of Suicide

Change in eating and sleeping habits

Withdrawal from friends, family, and regular activities

Violent actions, rebellious behavior, or running away

Use of alcohol or other drugs

Unusual neglect of personal appearance

Marked personality change

Persistent boredom, difficulty concentrating, or a decline in the quality of schoolwork

Frequent complaints about physical symptoms, such as stomachaches, headaches, or fatigue, which are often related to emotions

Giving away favorite possessions

Loss of interest in pleasurable activities

Not tolerating praise or rewards

(FIGURE 11-7) **Eighty percent of people who attempt suicide give warning signs that are a cry for help. If you recognize one or more of these signs in someone, talk with the person about your concerns. If their behavior continues, seek assistance from a professional.**

After discovering that your friend is suicidal, get help. Contact an adult who you feel is caring and in a position to help. This person could be a parent or other relative, teacher, school counselor, school nurse, religious leader, or neighbor. Such a person may be able to help your friend, and may also offer advice on other places to go for help.

You could also call your local suicide hotline. Look in the phone book under "Suicide" or "Crisis." The people staffing these phone lines will find help for you.

You can also call the 911 emergency number or the police department.

Your friend might make you promise not to tell anybody. It may seem like a difficult decision to make—keeping a promise you made to a friend, or going for help. But by confiding in you, your friend is asking for help. To help your friend, you *must* break the promise and notify a trusted adult of the danger that exists.

Remember, though, that you are not responsible for your friend's life. Only he or she can make the decision to live.

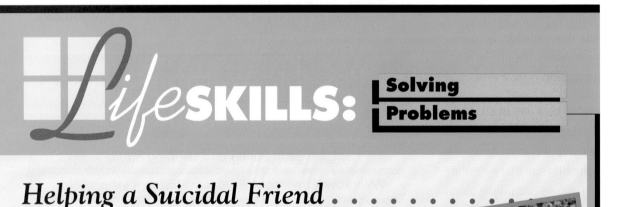

*Life*SKILLS: Solving Problems

Helping a Suicidal Friend . . . .

A friend tells you that he is failing school and feels humiliated because his father is a teacher and has high expectations of him. He says he feels stupid and knows he'll never amount to anything. If that's the way his life is going to be, he says, he might as well kill himself. You listen and let him know you care about him and that you understand how bad he must feel. You offer to help him find assistance.

On a separate sheet of paper, write down the names of as many adults as you can think of who could help your friend.

If You Feel Suicidal

If you ever feel that life is too painful to continue, you must ask for help. The reason you need help is that you are too confused and desperate to see all the alternatives to suicide.

Contact one of the adults listed in Figure 11-8, or any other adult you trust. You might be surprised to find out how much other people care for you and how willing they are to help you.

You may need professional counseling with a psychologist or therapist. At the very least, talk to a therapist to see if counseling is necessary. Therapists can offer options you hadn't thought of before. They can also help you learn new skills so that you can succeed in basic goals like making friends, coping with stress, or getting along with your family. Most important, they may remind you that no matter how bad things may seem, there are things you can do to help yourself feel better.

(FIGURE 11-8) **Help is available for those in crisis. Talk to a trusted adult if you (or a friend) are thinking of suicide.**

What Would You Do ?

Making Responsible Decisions

You Made a Promise

Julia is your best friend. She has been acting depressed lately because her boyfriend broke up with her. Julia came to you and told you that she is thinking about killing herself. But she made you promise you would not tell anyone.

After you talk with her, you begin to wonder if you should tell anyone about Julia's problem. But you *did* promise not to, and she *is* your best friend. What would you do?

Remember to use the decision-making steps:

1. State the Problem.
2. List the Options.
3. Imagine the Benefits and Consequences.
4. Consider Your Values.
5. Weigh the Options and Decide.
6. Act.
7. Evaluate the Results.

Some Adults Who Might Be Helpful in a Crisis

- Parent
- Grandparent, aunt, uncle, or other relative
- Teacher
- School counselor
- School nurse
- Therapist at a mental-health center
- Minister, priest, rabbi, or other religious leader
- Neighbor
- Person who staffs the local suicide hotline, the crisis hotline, or the 911 emergency number
- Person who answers the phone at the police department

(FIGURE 11-9) **You might be surprised to find out how much other people care for you and how willing they are to help you.**

You need to be willing to take a risk—the risk of confronting and resolving your problems. If you are willing to talk openly and honestly about the things that are making you unhappy, you can create options for yourself that do not exist when you remain closed and depressed. Suicide is only one option out of thousands of options that life offers. If you choose it, then you won't have the chance to explore the others.

The teenage years are a difficult time for most people. Many adults who are now living happy lives once considered suicide or even attempted it when they were teenagers themselves.

Remember that with help, you can work through your pain. Don't try to solve a temporary problem with a permanent act like suicide. If you feel like hurting yourself, talk to a trusted adult now.

Review

1. *What are five signs that might indicate someone is suicidal?*

2. ▨ **LIFE SKILLS: Solving Problems** *Describe what you should do if your friend tells you he or she doesn't want to live.*

3. ▨ **LIFE SKILLS: Making Responsible Decisions** *Your friend made you promise that you would not tell anyone he was going to kill himself. Why should you break your promise?*

4. ▨ **LIFE SKILLS: Coping** *If you felt suicidal, how could you help yourself?*

5. *Critical Thinking* *Why do you think a particular situation will cause one person to feel suicidal, while another person in the same situation might not even be depressed?*

CHAPTER 11

Highlights

Summary

- Suicide is one of the leading causes of death among people aged 15 to 24. The suicide rate among teenagers has quadrupled in the last 40 years.

- The following are possible reasons for the increase in teen suicides: (1) the rising divorce rate and breakup of families; (2) families moving from place to place more frequently; (3) absence of parental love and support in some families; (4) pressure to succeed in school and future careers; (5) increasing use of alcohol and drugs; and (6) glamorization of suicide by the media.

- Most people don't want to die but simply want to end the emotional pain they are suffering.

- Crises often seem more stressful if a person has low self-esteem. A crisis to one person may not be a crisis for someone else.

- Depression is a feeling that often accompanies suicide.

- When people are in crisis situations, they may become confused, make poor decisions, and be unable to see all the options available.

- Most people who attempt suicide display one or more warning signs. These signs or threats should always be taken seriously.

- Many adults who are now living happy lives once considered suicide or even attempted it when they were teenagers themselves.

- If you think a friend is thinking about suicide, get help as soon as possible. Contact a caring adult or call your local suicide hotline number.

- If you are in pain and are thinking about suicide, know that counseling is available from mental-health professionals such as psychologists.

- A person who is willing to talk openly and honestly about problems has options that do not exist for a person who remains closed and depressed.

Vocabulary

suicide the act of intentionally taking one's own life.

suicidal mindset the feeling that suicide is the only solution to the problems of living.

Chapter Review

Concept Review . . . .

1. Why is suicide a major problem among young people?

2. Is it true that all suicidal people want to die? Explain.

3. Explain why the breakup of families could contribute to the increase in teen suicides.

4. What makes the depression felt by a possible suicide victim different from the depression most people experience in everyday life?

5. What happens to people who are thinking of suicide when they find themselves in crisis situations?

6. How can you help if a friend is in a suicidal situation? Who are some adults who could help?

7. If a friend who is suicidal confides in you about his or her intentions and swears you to secrecy, should you keep your promise? Explain.

8. If you feel suicidal, how can it be helpful to take the risk of confronting and resolving your problems?

9. If you consider suicide once, will you always be suicidal? Explain.

Expressing Your Views . . . .

1. A good friend of yours has lost a lot of weight pretty quickly. Her grades have been dropping and she seems withdrawn. All of this has happened since her boyfriend broke up with her. You are concerned about her. What should you do?

2. Will's parents have recently divorced, and soon he will have to move to another town. He has been very depressed and has started seeing a psychologist. His friends don't know the whole story, but they say that Will is getting counseling be-

cause he's not strong enough to handle his problems on his own. What would you say to Will's friends?

3. Randall seems antisocial because he is always alone. Twice in the past week he has started strange conversations with you that ended with a suicide threat. When you told a friend what had happened, the friend said not to worry, that Randall threatens suicide all the time just to get attention. What do you think? Should you be concerned?

Life Skills Check

1. Coping

Let's say that during the past year you became terribly depressed. Your spirits were so low that at one point you were thinking about suicide. Instead, you got professional counseling, and now you feel as though you are recovering. As part of your therapy, your counselor has asked you to write down a list of the things that make you happy. What would you include on your list?

2. Solving Problems

Suppose a friend calls you to come over to her house right away. When you arrive, she appears very upset and begins to talk about suicide and death. No one is at home except the two of you. What should you do?

Projects

1. Work with a group to design a suicide-prevention pamphlet, using the information in your textbook. Include myths and facts about suicide, some warning signs of suicide, a list of adults to contact in a crisis, and the free hotline number. Distribute copies of the pamphlet throughout your school or publish it in the school newspaper.

2. Work with a partner to make up a problem situation and then role-play, providing support and receiving support. Devise a positive way to act out how to cope with the situation.

3. Using the library or the Internet to find newspaper and magazine articles, investigate a particular group of people that has a high suicide rate. Document your findings, and then brainstorm to make a list of actions that might help to lower that rate.

Plan for Action

Suicide is one of the leading causes of death among teenagers. Plan how you can prevent suicide in your life and in others' lives.

Ethical Issues in Health

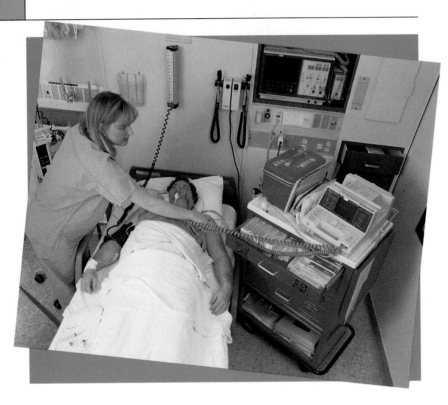

Death is the natural and inevitable end to life. Modern medical techniques, such as CPR and mechanical life support, have made it possible to avert death in situations where once a person certainly would have died. Modern technology is also capable of sustaining a person's life far beyond the point at which natural death would have occurred. Unfortunately, the technology to restore a healthy normal life to most of the people who survive with the aid of life-sustaining equipment does not exist. As a result, thousands of patients with no hope of recovery survive with mechanical support for weeks, months, and even years at great financial and emotional expense to their families and society.

Just as they did when they were healthy, people who are facing death need close relationships, honest communication, personal dignity, and control of their lives. Many people believe that the use of life-sustaining treatments, such as feeding through tubes and using equipment to maintain breathing and circulation, robs terminally ill patients of personal dignity and the right to control their lives. For this reason, many people believe that people with no hope of recovery should have the right to decide to die.

One way that people can retain control of their lives even when they are terminally ill is to establish a "living will." Recognized by most states, a living will is a legal document that allows people to specify what measures they want taken if they should have a serious disease or injury that will ultimately and inevitably result in death. Such a document allows a person to choose between receiving life-sustaining treatment or refusing all life-sustaining treatment so that death can occur naturally. A living will is executed only when the patient becomes permanently unconscious.

Some people want to be able to decide how and when to die, should they become terminally ill. Those who support the legal right to control the conditions of their own deaths make up the "right-to-die" movement. Sometimes terminally ill people request assistance from friends and family in what is often called "assisted suicide" or "assisted death." When a physician helps terminally ill patients die at their request, it is often referred to as "physician aid in dying."

An increasing number of people faced with death, particularly those in the latter stages of AIDS, are asking their friends and physicians to assist them by injecting them with painkillers in large enough doses to cause death. In 1989, the suicide rate among people with AIDS in the United States was six times higher than the rate for other adults. The suicide rate among people with other terminal illnesses is unknown.

The issue of assisted death gained national media attention when Dr. Jack Kevorkian of Michigan was tried for murder after he helped several people die with his controversial "suicide machine." Over the years, there have been several highly publicized court trials of people who caused the death of terminally ill family members suffering excruciating pain.

In the United States, a physician who purposefully causes the death of a terminally ill patient by injecting drugs or writing a prescription for drugs can be charged with murder, even if the doctor's actions were at the request of the patient. A person who is not a physician who helps end a life on request can also be charged with murder. However, very few people who have helped a terminally ill loved one die have been sent to jail. Dr. Kevorkian has been acquitted many times. Laws legalizing assisted death have been introduced in several states, but the idea is still very controversial. In the Netherlands, physicians who assist patients in ending their lives are not prosecuted.

People in the "right-to-die" movement defend assisted death. They argue that the practice is ethical because dying people have the right to have some control over both their lives and their deaths, especially the length of time it takes to die. Those who oppose assisted death say that even those who are dying do not have the right to ask others to participate in an act that is illegal and morally wrong.

Situation for Discussion

Martha is a 35-year-old woman who has cancer. The cancer began in an ovary and has spread to many parts of her body. More than one physician has confirmed that Martha is terminally ill. She suffers excruciating pain and has begun to slip in and out of consciousness. She has asked her doctor to help her die by prescribing a lethal dose of morphine.

a. If Martha's doctor prescribes this medication for her, could he be tried for murder? Research court cases of physicians who have assisted their patients in death. Has anyone been convicted for this action?

b. If Martha's doctor refuses to prescribe the morphine, what steps could she take to assure that she would not be put on machines that would prolong her life?

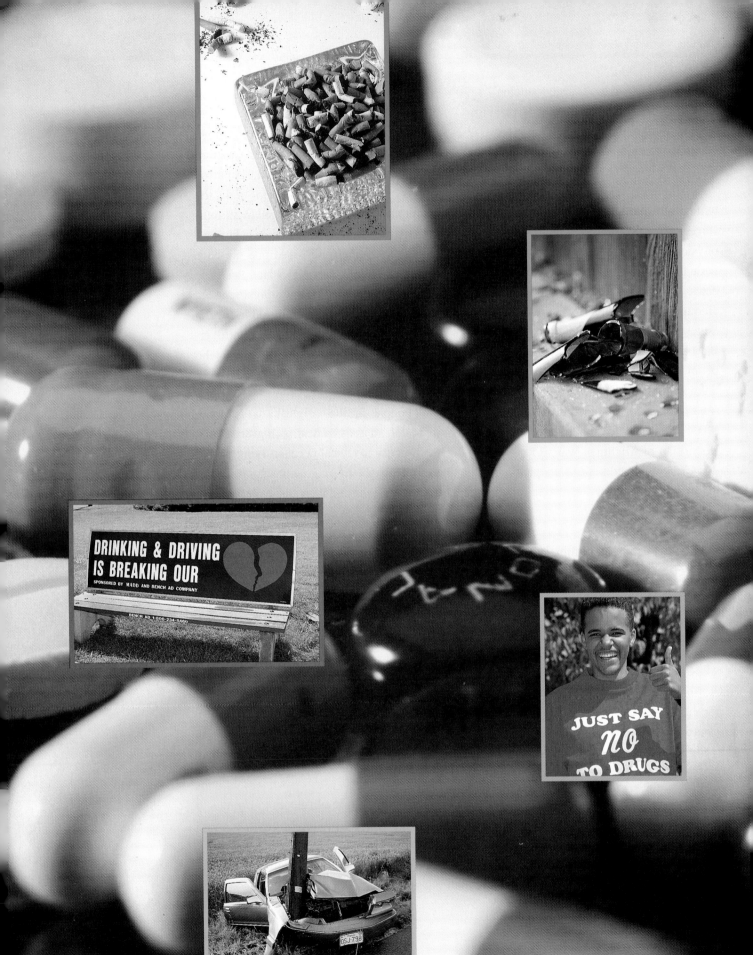

FOUR

PROTECTING YOUR HEALTH IN A DRUG SOCIETY

The Use, Misuse, and Abuse of Drugs

◆ ◆ ◆ ◆

Some people in our society have become very dependent on drugs to solve their health problems.

Everything had gone wrong for Marisa today. The math test was a complete disaster. She had left her health assignment at home. Worst of all, she had a big fight with her best friend. By the time Marisa got home she was crying, and she had a terrible headache.

Without thinking about it, she went to her mother's medicine chest to find a pain reliever for her headache. As she swallowed the pills, Marisa looked at her puffy face in the bathroom mirror. She wished she could take a drug that would make her forget about her bad day.

A Drug-Oriented Society

Objectives

- *Name one problem with living in a drug-oriented society.*

- *Name two ways to treat pain without using drugs.*

- *Know the ways in which drug use, drug misuse, and drug abuse differ from each other.*

We live in a drug-oriented society. The commercials we see on television make this clear. Have a headache? Take a painkiller. Is your stomach acting up? No problem—get some antacids. Feeling tired? Grab a cup of coffee. Want to relax? Have a beer. One reason our society has become so dependent on drugs is that we are constantly hearing about how great they are.

Every year, pharmaceutical companies spend about $25 billion on advertising. The alcohol industry spends an additional $18 billion to $20 billion. As a result, it is hard to find a magazine or a television program that doesn't feature at least one drug advertisement. In addition, many sports events are sponsored by beer manufacturers.

The message we receive from all the advertising is clear: If we take a drug, we'll feel better.

What is so bad about this message? After all, some drugs can save lives. Before the development of effective medicines, there was little relief for severe pain, and even minor infections could become deadly. Today, drugs can prevent, treat, or cure most illnesses. The problem is that many people think drugs can solve *all* their problems.

Healthier Options

Marisa's headache resulted from her stressful day at school. When she got home, she could have done some physical exercise that would have relaxed her, or she could have performed one of the relaxation exercises described in Chapter 9. Chances are, either of these would have made her head feel better.

Next time you have a headache or stomachache, ask yourself if the pain you are feeling has something to do with stress. If it does, see if physical exercise or a relaxation exercise makes you feel better, or just try talking to someone about your anxiety. You may find that the pain goes away without the use of a drug.

If you're feeling depressed or anxious about something, know that drinking alcohol or taking a drug will not solve your problem. The effects of these drugs last for a short period of time, and when they wear off, you might feel worse than you did before. Instead, you might try to find someone you can talk to. A parent, a friend, or a teacher may be able to offer some support.

What Is a Drug?

A **drug** is any substance that causes a physical or emotional change in a person. All drugs can be placed into one of the following seven categories: natural remedies, over-the-counter drugs, prescription drugs, tobacco products, alcohol, illegal drugs, and unrecognized drugs.

drug:

a substance that causes a physical or emotional change in a person.

Cultural DIVERSITY

Medicines From the Rain Forest

People in so-called developing cultures are helping in the development of powerful new medicines. These cultures, which have existed for thousands of years in the tropical rain forests of the world, have already contributed a tremendous amount to the contents of our medicine cabinets. Tropical rain forests, shown in green on the map, are areas along the equator that have great amounts of rainfall and a huge number of different living things.

Quinine is an excellent example of a medicine that came to us from the rain forest. Made from the bark of the *Cinchona* tree in the Andean tropical forest of South America, quinine was long used as a medicine by the native people. Only later did people in more "advanced" societies discover that quinine cured malaria, an often fatal disease transmitted by mosquitoes.

Rain forest cultures introduced us to another important drug called curare. In the South American rain forest, native people extracted curare from woody vines and dipped their arrows into it to paralyze the animals they shot. In our society, curare serves not as a poison but as a muscle relaxant that is used during surgery.

Finally, nearly 70 percent of the plants known to be useful in the treatment of cancer come from rain forests. We know about most of these cancer-fighting plants from the native people who live where the plants grow.

Natural Remedies Natural remedies contain substances that occur in nature and are used to treat or prevent ailments. You should always seek the advice of a trained practitioner before using natural remedies. Some of these substances can be dangerous if misused.

Over-the-Counter Drugs Over-the-counter (OTC) drugs can be legally bought without a doctor's prescription. Two examples of OTC preparations are aspirin and cough medicines.

Prescription Drugs Prescription drugs are drugs that require a doctor's prescription to buy. A **prescription** is a doctor's written order to a pharmacist that a patient be al-lowed to purchase a drug. A prescription includes the drug's name, directions for use, and amount of the drug to be used. Prescription drugs are usually more powerful than over-the-counter drugs.

Tobacco Products Tobacco products contain the drug nicotine. Examples of tobacco products are cigarettes, cigars, snuff, and chewing tobacco.

Alcohol Beer, wine, and distilled liquors all contain the drug alcohol, which is illegal for persons under the age of 21.

Illegal Drugs Illegal drugs are substances that cannot be legally sold, purchased,

prescription:

a doctor's written order for a specific medicine.

Sadly, the rain forests are rapidly disappearing, and along with them the native people who are most knowledge-able about these plants. If we protect the rain forest from destruction, we preserve not only the biological diversity but also the valuable *cultural* diversity of our world.

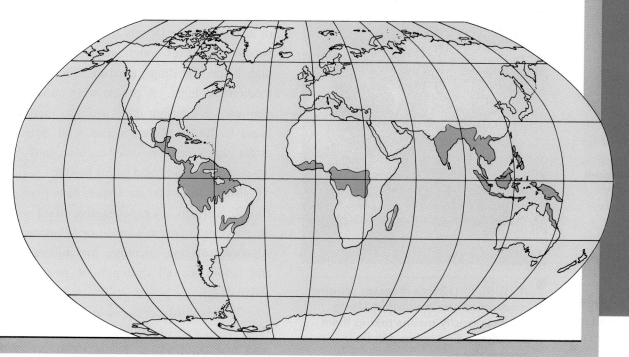

drug misuse:

improper use of a drug.

or used. Powder cocaine, marijuana, crack cocaine, and heroin are all examples of illegal drugs.

Unrecognized Drugs Unrecognized drugs are found in products that are not usually classified as drugs. One example of an unrecognized drug is caffeine. Caffeine is an ingredient in coffee and colas.

Inhalants are another kind of unrecognized drug. Certain substances, when inhaled, cause a lightheaded feeling. Examples of inhalants are gasoline, spray paint, and correction fluid for paper. As you will learn in Chapter 15, inhalants are extremely dangerous.

Drug Use, Misuse, and Abuse

Taking drugs properly and in their correct amounts is called **drug use**. Let's say you wake up one morning with a sore throat and a high fever. You go to the doctor, who

takes a throat culture and tells you that you have strep throat. The doctor gives you a prescription for antibiotics, which fight the bacteria that cause strep throat. When you take the antibiotics as the doctor directs, you are practicing proper drug use.

Drug misuse is the improper use of a drug. One way of misusing drugs is to take the wrong amount of a prescribed drug. If your doctor told you to take two tablets of a certain medicine each day, but you take *four,* you are misusing the drug. Taking too much of a medicine can lead to an overdose, which can be dangerous and even fatal.

Another way to misuse a drug is to stop taking it too soon. If the doctor told you to take two tablets a day until you finished the entire bottle, but you quit as soon as you felt better, you would be misusing the drug.

Taking medicine prescribed for someone else is another example of drug misuse. If you have a sore throat and take the medicine that is prescribed for your sister's sore throat, you are misusing a drug. Taking medicine prescribed for someone else can be very dangerous.

Drug abuse occurs when a person takes a legal drug for a nonmedical reason, or an illegal drug for any reason at all. A person who takes cough medicine to get high is abusing drugs, even though cough medicine is legal. A person who smokes marijuana is abusing drugs because marijuana is illegal. Other instances of drug abuse include smoking crack cocaine, sniffing powder cocaine, and taking heroin.

Many drugs that are abused have psychoactive effects. A **psychoactive effect** is an effect on a person's mood or behavior. Alcohol, caffeine, nicotine, tranquilizers, and heroin are all examples of psychoactive drugs.

The abuse of a drug can lead to **addiction.** When a person becomes addicted to a drug, it means that he or she has developed a

drug use:

taking a medicine properly and in its correct dosage.

drug abuse:

intentional improper use of a drug.

psychoactive effect:

an effect on a person's mood or behavior.

addiction:

a condition in which the body relies on a given drug to help it function.

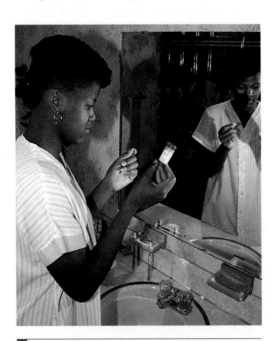

(FIGURE 12-1) **Some illnesses require medications for treatment. Using drugs correctly means taking them exactly as directed and in their proper doses.**

(FIGURE 12-2) **Abusing alcohol or other psychoactive drugs can be deadly.**

physical need for the drug and suffers withdrawal symptoms if unable to take the drug. Some common withdrawal symptoms are nausea, cramps, trembling, and nervousness. Drug abuse and addiction are discussed in more detail in Chapters 13, 14, and 15.

Psychoactive Drug Use and Risk Behaviors

One of the dangers of using psychoactive drugs is that they impair a person's ability to make good decisions. Someone who normally behaves responsibly might not be able to make the right decisions when under the influence of a psychoactive drug.

Joshua, for example, has decided to delay sexual intercourse until marriage. Usually he has little trouble sticking to his decision. But what if he gets drunk or high? Chances are, his decision will be harder to remember and harder to carry out. Not only would Joshua violate his own values if he had sexual intercourse, but he would also increase his risk of causing an unwanted pregnancy or getting a disease that is transmitted sexually. This can be especially

dangerous today, when the risk of getting AIDS can make the wrong decision a life-threatening one.

In addition, studies have shown that the use of psychoactive drugs is strongly associated with an increased risk of serious injury and violence. What this can mean is that you have a much greater chance of getting hurt in an accident or getting into a fight if you are drunk or high.

Review

1. What is one problem with living in a drug-oriented society?

2. What are two ways to treat pain without the use of drugs?

3. Define drug use, drug misuse, and drug abuse. How do they differ?

4. **Critical Thinking** Why might a person who has abused a drug be more likely to get AIDS than a person who has not?

Section 12.2 Over-the-Counter and Prescription Drugs

stimulant:

a drug that speeds up body functioning.

Objectives

- *Describe three types of OTC medicines.*

- *Know why prescription medications require a doctor's prescription.*

- *Name three factors that may influence a medicine's effect.*

- *Know how to read the label on a prescription medicine.*
  LIFE SKILLS: Practicing Self-Care

medicine:

a substance used to treat an illness or ailment.

analgesic:

a medicine that relieves pain.

sedative:

a drug that slows down body functioning and causes sleepiness.

Over-the-counter and prescription drugs are two kinds of **medicines**. Most medicines do at least one of four things: they battle bacteria and other organisms that cause disease; they protect the body from disease; they influence the circulatory system; or they affect the nervous system. For more information on the different types of medicines, see Figure 12-3.

Over-the-Counter (OTC) Drugs

OTC drugs are medicines that you can buy without a doctor's prescription. Three of the most common types of OTC drugs are analgesics, sedatives, and stimulants.

Analgesics are used to relieve pain. Three types of analgesics are aspirin, acetaminophen, and ibuprofen.

Sedatives are drugs that slow down body functioning and make you sleepy. OTC preparations that have sedatives in them include mild sleeping pills.

Stimulants are the opposite of sedatives; they make you more alert. The type of stimulant that is most commonly used in OTC medicines is caffeine. OTC preparations that contain caffeine include some headache remedies, cold remedies, and appetite suppressants.

Most people think that OTC preparations are completely safe. Unfortunately, no drug is free of risk. Aspirin can lead to stomach irritation and bleeding, and it also may be associated with a serious disease called Reye's syndrome. A number of people who have taken aspirin for chickenpox or flu have suffered this illness, which is why doctors now recommend that you use acetaminophen to treat any symptoms of these infections. Salicylates, the ingredients in aspirin that are believed to be linked to Reye's syndrome, are also contained in some other OTC medications. Teenagers suffering from flu and chickenpox should take special care to read all OTC labels carefully and to avoid all preparations that contain salicylates.

In addition, some OTC medicines can be misused or abused. Antihistamines can cause drowsiness and dizziness, which is why a person who has taken them should not try to drive. Over-the-counter appetite suppressants, which contain caffeine and a stimulant drug called phenylpropanolamine (PPA), can cause high blood pressure and increased heart rate.

One final warning about OTC preparations: Remember that sometimes pain is a helpful symptom of infection. By covering up a symptom with an OTC preparation instead of treating its cause, you may be making your infection worse than it already is.

Some Common Drug Types and Their Effects

Type of Drug	Type of Action	Effect	How Available
Vaccines	Protect body from disease	Cause body to set up agents to fight a specific disease before exposure	Doctor's office or clinic
Antisera	Protect body from disease	Provide the body with the antibodies that fight specific diseases after exposure	Doctor's office or clinic
Penicillin (antibiotic)	Battles organisms that cause disease	Kills bacteria by preventing cell wall formation	Prescription
Tetracycline (antibiotic)	Battles organisms that cause disease	Slows down growth and reproduction of bacteria	Prescription
Cardiac Glycoside (Digitalis)	Influence circulatory system	Increases force of heart contractions, corrects irregular heartbeat	Prescription
Diuretics	Influence circulatory system	Relieve body of excess water and salt	OTC or Prescription
Vasodilators	Influence circulatory system	Enlarge veins and arteries to increase flow of blood	Prescription
Antiarrhythmics	Influence circulatory system	Work to correct irregular heartbeat	Prescription
Hypertensives	Influence circulatory system	Work to reduce blood pressure	Prescription
Analgesics (aspirin, acetaminophen, ibuprofen)	Influence nervous system	Relieve pain	OTC or, in some cases, prescription
Stimulants	Influence nervous system	Prevent sleep, heighten awareness	OTC or, in some cases, prescription
Barbiturates	Influence nervous system	Relieve anxiety, insomnia, prevent certain types of seizures	Prescription
Tranquilizers	Influence nervous system	Relieve anxiety, insomnia; frequently milder than barbiturates	Prescription

(FIGURE 12-3) **Medicines can battle diseases and sometimes prevent them completely. Most OTC preparations, however, treat symptoms and do not fight infections.**

Analgesics: Their Effects and Hazards

Analgesic	Effects	Potential Hazards
Aspirin	Relieves pain, reduces fever, reduces swelling	Causes stomach irritation and bleeding, associated with Reye's syndrome in children and adolescents, can cause overdose.
Acetaminophen	Relieves pain, reduces fever	Risk of overdose, may cause liver damage in high doses.
Ibuprofen	Relieves pain, reduces fever, reduces swelling	Can cause stomach irritation and bleeding.

(FIGURE 12-4) **Although analgesics are easily available, they are not without risk. If you must use these preparations, make sure that you take them according to their instructions and in their proper dose.**

Read the labels of all OTC preparations before you buy them. The labels should provide complete information about the correct amount to take and possible undesirable effects.

Prescription Drugs

Prescription drugs are usually more powerful than the medicines you can buy over the counter. For this reason, they cannot be purchased without a doctor's prescription.

A prescription always has a required **dose**—the correct amount of a drug to be taken at one time or at stated intervals. If you are using a prescribed medication, make sure you take the right dose each time. Be sure that you finish the entire prescription, even if the signs and symptoms of your disease have completely disappeared. It is particularly important that you continue taking antibiotics for an infection as long as the doctor instructs. Even though you may start to feel better after a few days, the bacteria that caused the infection may not be completely eliminated. If you stop taking the antibiotics too soon, the remaining bacteria can cause the infection to return.

Finally, prescription drugs can be abused. Some drugs that are prescribed, such as barbiturates and tranquilizers, have very strong psychoactive effects. They can also be addictive, which is why it is very important to take drugs like these only if they are prescribed for you.

It is extremely important that you follow the instructions on the label of any prescription medication. Remember that they are prescribed for a particular person with a particular condition. The only person who should be taking the medicine is the person whose name appears on the label. Even if you and your friend think you have the same

dose:

the exact amount of a drug.

illness, don't take his or her prescription medication. It could be that you don't have the same illness or that you are allergic to the medication offered to you.

Effects of Drugs on the Body

When a drug enters the body, it is absorbed into the bloodstream. Once there, the drug travels to the parts of the body it will affect.

One factor that influences the effect of a drug is the dose that has been taken. The amount of drug that is right for a person will vary according to that person's age, height, weight, and gender, among other factors. In general, the heavier a person is, the higher a dose he or she will require. All medicines have recommended doses.

In addition, the way a drug is administered, or taken, has a very important impact on its effect. Medicines are usually either swallowed or injected. Injected medicines go directly to the bloodstream, which is why they have faster effects than medicines that are swallowed.

Guidelines for Appropriate Use of Medicines

Things You Should Remember About Use of Medicines

Don't mix medications without checking with a physician or pharmacist. When more than one drug is taken the results are often unpredictable.

Don't take a prescription medication unless it was prescribed for you. If you ever have an allergic reaction to a drug or food, make sure you tell a physician before using the same or another medication.

Don't use over-the-counter drugs for long periods of time. You may be delaying diagnosis of a serious problem.

Don't ever conclude that if a little bit of a drug makes you feel good, that more will make you feel better. Never take more of a medication than you are directed to.

Don't use a medicine prescribed for someone else, even if you seem to have the same problem.

Ask the pharmacist to tell you about the drug's purpose, its side effects, and its interaction with food and other drugs, as well as the dosage and length of time you should take the drug.

Keep all drugs away from children.

(FIGURE 12-5) **Keep in mind these basic safety rules for the proper use of medications. Medicines are anything but helpful when they are misused.**

When a medicine is taken orally—by mouth—it is often absorbed into the bloodstream through the stomach lining. This process can take a long time, especially if there is food in the stomach that can slow down the absorption process. The food can also protect the stomach lining from irritation, which is why doctors recommend that certain medicines should always be taken with a meal.

Drug Interactions Sometimes the effect of a medicine can be made either greater or smaller if there is already another drug in your system. This influence, called drug

*Life*SKILLS: Practicing Self-Care

How to Read a Prescription Label . . .

All prescription drugs should have clearly marked labels. If you have a medication prescribed for you, make sure you read the label carefully before beginning your treatment. The prescription number is often at the very top of the label, and your name should be underneath. If your name is not on the label, do not take the medicine. One of the most dangerous things you can do is take a prescription drug that has been prescribed for someone else.

Next to your name, your doctor's name should be listed, along with the date the prescription was filled. Underneath your name are directions explaining how often you should take the drug and how much you should take each time. This is followed by the drug's expiration date—the final date the drug can be safely used—and the name of the drug.

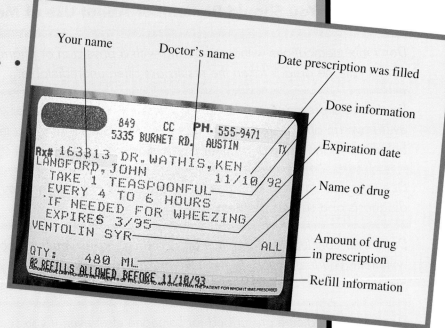

The bottom of the label should list the amount of the drug contained in the entire prescription dose, and should also provide instructions on how many times (if at all) the prescription can be refilled.

Not all labels will follow this exact order, but they all should contain this same information.

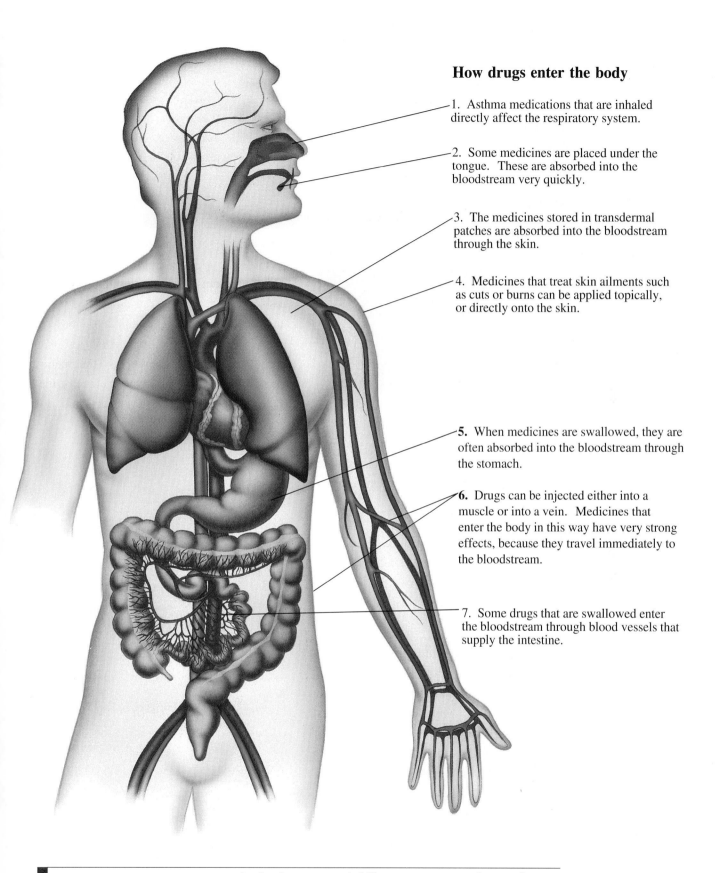

How drugs enter the body

1. Asthma medications that are inhaled directly affect the respiratory system.

2. Some medicines are placed under the tongue. These are absorbed into the bloodstream very quickly.

3. The medicines stored in transdermal patches are absorbed into the bloodstream through the skin.

4. Medicines that treat skin ailments such as cuts or burns can be applied topically, or directly onto the skin.

5. When medicines are swallowed, they are often absorbed into the bloodstream through the stomach.

6. Drugs can be injected either into a muscle or into a vein. Medicines that enter the body in this way have very strong effects, because they travel immediately to the bloodstream.

7. Some drugs that are swallowed enter the bloodstream through blood vessels that supply the intestine.

(FIGURE 12-6) **Drugs can enter the body in several different ways. Medicines that are absorbed into the bloodstream travel to the liver, where they are broken down into simple substances the body can use.**

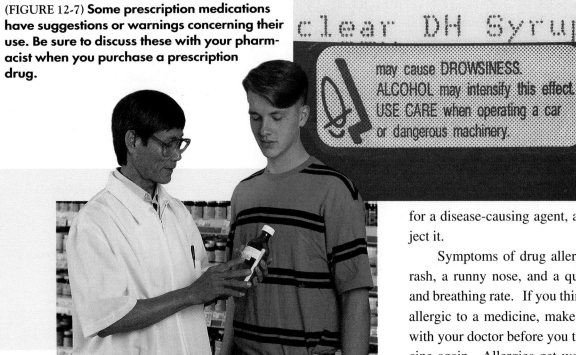

(FIGURE 12-7) **Some prescription medications have suggestions or warnings concerning their use. Be sure to discuss these with your pharmacist when you purchase a prescription drug.**

clear DH Syrup

may cause DROWSINESS.
ALCOHOL may intensify this effect.
USE CARE when operating a car
or dangerous machinery.

interaction, is very difficult to predict. A drug interaction can be dangerous. For example, combining a prescribed barbiturate with alcohol has been known to cause coma or death.

Avoiding a harmful drug interaction is another good reason to read all label information on any OTC or prescription medication you buy. If you have specific questions about how certain medicines interact, ask your doctor.

Side Effects and Allergies If you've ever taken a cold medicine that contains an antihistamine, you may have found that in addition to feeling your nasal passages clear, you felt a bit drowsy. The drowsiness you felt is called a **side effect**, because it is an effect that comes in addition to the drug's desired effect. Other common side effects of medicines include nausea, dizziness, and headaches.

A medicine can also have unpleasant effects when the person taking it has a **drug allergy**. Drug allergies occur when your body mistakes the medicine you have taken

for a disease-causing agent, and tries to reject it.

Symptoms of drug allergies include a rash, a runny nose, and a quickened heart and breathing rate. If you think you may be allergic to a medicine, make sure you talk with your doctor before you take that medicine again. Allergies get worse each time they occur. If their early effects are ignored, they can eventually be fatal.

side effect:

an effect that accompanies the expected effect of a drug.

drug allergy:

an unwanted effect that accompanies the desired effect of a drug.

• • • • •

Review

1. Name three types of OTC medicines.

2. Name two reasons why prescription medicines require a doctor's prescription.

3. What are three factors that can influence the effect of a medicine?

4. ▓ **LIFE SKILLS: Practicing Self-Care** What are three important things to look for on a prescription label?

5. **Critical Thinking** Using your knowledge of drug effects and how they are influenced, explain why it can be dangerous to use a prescription drug that has been prescribed for someone else.

Highlights

Summary

- We live in a drug-oriented society.

- Physical exercise or a relaxation exercise can often relieve pain without drugs.

- Drugs can be classified as natural remedies, over-the-counter drugs, prescription drugs, tobacco products, alcohol, illegal drugs, and unrecognized drugs.

- You can misuse a prescribed drug by taking the wrong dosage, by stopping it too soon, or by taking medicine prescribed for someone else.

- Drug abuse occurs when a person deliberately takes a legal drug for a non-medical reason or an illegal drug for any reason.

- Psychoactive drugs such as alcohol, caffeine, nicotine, tranquilizers, and heroin impair a person's ability to make good decisions. Some of these drugs are associated with an increased risk of serious injury and violence.

- Three of the most common types of over-the-counter drugs are analgesics, sedatives, and stimulants. They should be taken according to the label directions.

- Drugs can sometimes cause side effects or allergies. Nausea, drowsiness, dizziness, and headaches are common side effects. Symptoms of drug allergies include a rash, a runny nose, and a quickened heart rate.

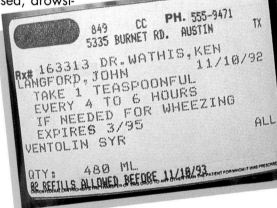

Vocabulary

drug a substance that causes a physical or emotional change in a person.

prescription a doctor's written order for a specific medicine.

drug use taking a medicine exactly as directed.

drug misuse unintentional improper use of a drug.

drug abuse intentional improper use of a drug.

psychoactive effect an effect on a person's mood or behavior.

addiction a condition in which the body relies on a given drug to function.

analgesic a medicine that relieves pain.

sedative a drug that slows down body functioning and causes sleepiness.

stimulant a drug that speeds up body functioning.

Concept Review

1. Give examples of drug use, drug misuse, and drug abuse.

2. Advertisements suggest that drugs make you feel better. How can this be a negative message?

3. Explain two differences between over-the-counter drugs and prescription drugs.

4. What are some ways you can misuse a drug?

5. What are some drugs that have psychoactive effects? What are the risks of abusing these drugs?

6. What does it mean when a person becomes addicted to a drug? How might a person know if he or she is physically dependent on a drug?

7. What are four things that medicines can do to your body?

8. What are some dangers of taking (a) aspirin? (b) appetite suppressants?

9. Why should a person who is taking antihistamines not drive a car?

10. Why is it important to finish a prescribed medication?

11. How are medicines usually administered? How does the method used influence the drug's effect?

12. What can happen if you take a drug when another drug is already in your system?

13. Define drug allergies and name two symptoms of them. What happens if they are ignored?

Expressing Your Views

1. Mario hurt his knee during hockey practice. That night he took some of his friend's prescription medicine for pain. Should Mario have taken this? Why or why not?

2. Your friend has had a fever and runny nose for several days. She has been taking ibuprofen along with an over-the-counter cold remedy to ease her suffering. How is this risky behavior? What would you advise her to do?

3. It seems as if you have had a stuffy nose forever. You have been using a nasal spray for about a month. You realize it is not healthy to take drugs for a long time, but every time you stop using the spray, you can barely breathe through your nose. What do you think has happened?

Life Skills Check . . . . . .

1. Practicing Self-Care
You have had a sore throat and fever for several days. You haven't been eating well because it is painful to swallow. The doctor prescribed a medicine for strep throat, but shortly after you take the directed dosage your stomach starts to hurt. What could be the matter?

2. Practicing Self-Care
Your mother had been having trouble sleeping for a long time. Then her doctor prescribed a sleeping medication, or barbiturate, for her. She's been taking the medication for a week, and has been sleeping better. Last night when you went out to dinner with her, she had a glass of wine. Did she take a risk by drinking alcohol? Explain.

Projects . . . .

1. Select an advertisement for an over-the-counter drug. Analyze the claims and benefits and determine the accuracy of the ad. How does the ad try to sell the drug? Is the drug really needed? Rewrite the ad, giving suggestions for relieving the problem without use of the drug.

2. Invite a pharmacist to the classroom or visit a local pharmacy. Ask the pharmacist about over-the-counter drugs, prescription drugs, warnings, and directions for use.

3. Three common types of over-the-counter drugs are sedatives, analgesics, and stimulants. Go to the store and compare name brands, lists of ingredients, directions, and prices. Record your findings on a chart, and display it in the classroom.

Plan for Action . . . .

You have a choice regarding how much you rely on drugs to relieve symptoms of illness. Devise a plan to restrict your reliance on drugs.

CHAPTER 13

Alcohol: A Dangerous Drug

◆ ◆ ◆ ◆

Section 13.1 Effects of Alcohol on the Body

Section 13.2 Teenagers and Alcohol

Section 13.3 Alcohol Abuse and Alcoholism

Section 13.4 Hope for Recovery

■ Alcohol seriously impairs judgment and reflexes, two properties that are crucial to driving safely.

Navorn was excited. School was out for the summer, and she had a great summer job lined up. Now she was celebrating at an end-of-school-year party, but it was getting late. Navorn saw Billy heading out the back door, and she was about to ask him for a ride home. Then she noticed that he seemed pretty drunk. So she asked a friend who hadn't been drinking for a ride.

The next day she heard the news. Billy had lost control of the car on his way home. It crashed into a ditch and hit several trees. Billy didn't make it. If Navorn had taken a ride with Billy, she might have been killed too.

Section 13.1
Effects of Alcohol on the Body

Objectives

- *Discuss the effects of intoxication.*
- *Name two diseases caused by long-term alcohol abuse.*

Alcohol may be the most misunderstood drug. It is widely advertised and is often consumed at parties and restaurants. But alcohol is also a very dangerous drug that kills thousands of people every year and addicts millions more. It tears families apart and is involved in more than half the violent crimes committed in the United States. And, for Americans under 21, it is an illegal drug.

One reason alcohol is illegal for teenagers has to do with what happened to Billy. In 1994, over 6,000 people died in auto collisions in which teens were driving. Teenage drunken drivers were involved in almost 40 percent of these crashes. These numbers were even higher a few years ago, when some states allowed people as young as 18 to drink. Highway safety experts think the raised legal drinking age is responsible for saving many thousands of lives.

More and more people are deciding not to drink alcohol. They have made this decision not only because they worry about drunken driving, but also because they don't like what alcohol does to their body. Like any drug, alcohol changes the way your body functions. These changes are unhealthy and can be very dangerous.

When Alcohol Enters the Body

Your friend Leo loves beer. He says it's a better thirst quencher than any other beverage, which you find hard to believe. Now Leo is planning to go to Sandra's party, and you're worried that he will get into trouble.

The party is in full swing when Leo arrives. It doesn't take him long to find out where the beer is. From that moment on, Leo's evening is ruined.

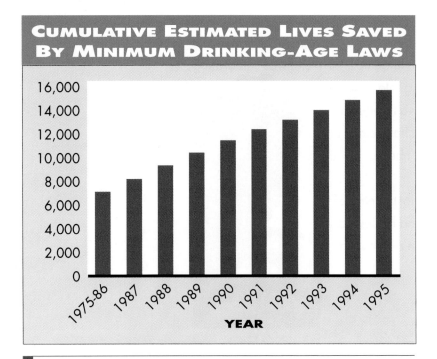

CUMULATIVE ESTIMATED LIVES SAVED BY MINIMUM DRINKING-AGE LAWS

(FIGURE 13-2) **Experts believe that minimum-drinking-age laws have saved more than 15,000 lives.**

blood alcohol level (BAL):

a way to measure the level of alcohol in a person's body.

intoxicated:

being affected by alcohol. Effects of intoxication can range from mild lightheadedness to severe and complete loss of judgment and reflexes.

Each gulp of beer Leo swallows makes its way first into his stomach and then into his small intestine. From his stomach and small intestine, the alcohol is absorbed into his bloodstream. It then travels to all Leo's cells and tissues, including his brain. Within *minutes,* Leo is feeling the effects of the beer.

Eventually the alcohol reaches Leo's liver, which breaks it down into carbon dioxide and water. The more Leo drinks, the harder his liver will have to work to help rid his body of alcohol. In fact, it will take Leo's liver more than an hour to break down the alcohol in each bottle of beer he drinks.

Blood Alcohol Level   One
drink is enough to interfere with a person's judgment and reflexes. And the more a person drinks, the more alcohol interferes with judgment and reflexes.

The percentage of alcohol in a person's bloodstream is called the **blood alcohol level (BAL).** A person's BAL can be influenced by gender, body weight, the amount of food in the stomach, and the rate of drinking.

One drink is enough to raise Leo's BAL to .025 or greater. According to new laws in most states, drivers under 21 are considered legally **intoxicated** at a BAL of .02, and adults are considered legally intoxicated at a BAL of .10. The lower limit for teenagers reflects intolerance for under-age drinking. Even this small amount is enough to impair Leo's judgment and vision. If he keeps drinking, Leo's BAL will keep getting higher.

Short-Term Effects of Alcohol   After a
few beers, Leo starts feeling relaxed. He soon forgets about the rough day he had at school.

His face feels flushed and very warm because the alcohol has dilated, or widened, the blood vessels near his skin. He also has to urinate frequently, as his body tries to get rid of the alcohol in his system.

On his way to the bathroom, Leo knocks over an empty chair. He is too drunk to notice what he did, and when he

(FIGURE 13-3) **A 12-ounce bottle of beer, a 6-ounce glass of wine, and a 1.25-ounce glass of whiskey all have about the same alcohol content.**

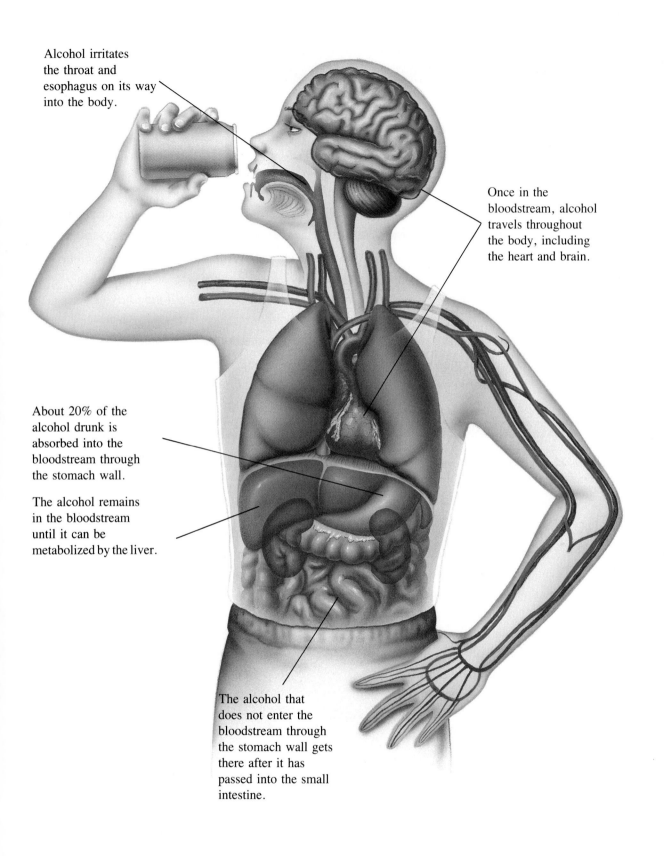

Alcohol irritates the throat and esophagus on its way into the body.

Once in the bloodstream, alcohol travels throughout the body, including the heart and brain.

About 20% of the alcohol drunk is absorbed into the bloodstream through the stomach wall.

The alcohol remains in the bloodstream until it can be metabolized by the liver.

The alcohol that does not enter the bloodstream through the stomach wall gets there after it has passed into the small intestine.

(FIGURE 13-4) **The alcohol in one 12-ounce bottle of beer reaches the bloodstream very quickly. It then remains in the bloodstream until it is metabolized—a process that takes more than an hour for each bottle of beer.**

Myths and Facts About Alcohol

Myth	Fact
You can't get as drunk from beer, wine, or wine coolers as you can from "hard" liquor like vodka and scotch.	A bottle of beer, a glass of wine, and a wine cooler all have around the same amount of alcohol as a shot of a distilled spirit like vodka or scotch. Therefore, they are just as intoxicating.
A person who looks and acts sober is sober.	Not everyone shows the effects of alcohol in the same way. Even people who seem completely sober are dangerous drivers if they have been drinking alcohol.
Alcohol can't be as dangerous as illicit drugs because it is easily available to people over the age of 21.	Even though alcohol is a legal drug for Americans over 21, when it is abused it is just as dangerous as many illicit drugs.

(FIGURE 13-5) **Myths about alcohol not only are untrue, but also can be dangerous to believe—particularly if a person is drinking and driving.**

hangover:

uncomfortable physical effects brought on by alcohol use. Symptoms of a hangover include headache, nausea, upset stomach, and dizziness.

returns from the bathroom he trips over it. Laughing loudly, he struggles to get up from the floor. Leo may find this funny, but his lack of coordination and inhibition has resulted from a serious event; the alcohol in his bloodstream has entered his brain, changing the way it functions.

Leo sees Roberto talking with a girl Leo used to date. The sight enrages him, and he grabs Roberto and shoves him against the wall. Roberto just shakes his head, rolls his eyes, and walks away.

Leo finds some more beer and sits in the kitchen, drinking by himself.

The next thing he knows, Leo is waking up on a kitchen floor—a kitchen floor he doesn't recognize. "Oh yeah," he realizes, "I guess I passed out in Sandra's kitchen." He has a dull headache, a sick stomach, and he feels very dizzy. Leo has a **hangover.** "Just my luck," he says out loud.

Actually, Leo *was* pretty lucky. He could have seriously hurt Roberto or himself if Roberto hadn't ignored him. If Leo had tried to drive home, he could have easily had a wreck.

Leo's hangover lasts until late in the afternoon. (Nothing but time makes a hangover go away.) As a result, he plays poorly at basketball practice. "Okay, so I got drunk last night," Leo tells you when you ask him if he's all right. "What are you—my mother?"

Leo denies that the alcohol has had negative effects. He likes the relaxed feeling he gets while he is drinking. That means he'll probably drink again soon.

Blood Alcohol Level and Its Effects

Number of Drinks in a 1-Hour Period (140-pound person)	Approximate Blood Alcohol Level	Effects on Body
1	.025	Feeling of relaxation, warmth, and well-being; slight impairment of judgment
2	.05	Inhibitions are lessened; judgment impaired, behavior can become impulsive or silly
3	.075	Reflexes and coordination impaired; speech and hearing slightly affected
4	.1	Legally drunk in most states; vision, hearing, judgment, reflexes, coordination impaired
6	.161	Intoxication; coordination seriously affected; vision blurred, speech and hearing severely impaired
8	.215	Intoxication extreme; no control over thoughts and perceptions; walking and even standing become difficult
12	.321	Intoxication severe and dangerous; nervous system may become affected, coma and death can result

(FIGURE 13-6) **This table shows the estimated blood alcohol level and its effects on a 140-pound person. A person's blood alcohol level will vary according to a number of factors, such as weight and gender.**

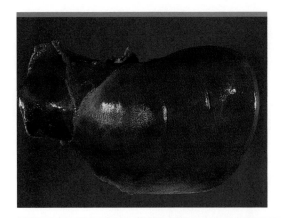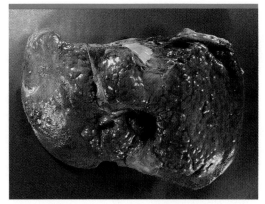

(FIGURE 13-7) **A normal liver (left), and a liver with cirrhosis (right). Cirrhosis is an incurable, untreatable disease caused by alcoholism.**

Long-Term Effects

Over a period of time, the alcohol Leo drinks can seriously damage his body.

First, alcohol can harm his liver. As you now know, the liver works hard to break down the alcohol in his body into carbon dioxide and water. The liver does this job well, but pays a price each time. Studies show that even small doses of alcohol leave fat deposits on liver cells. The livers of alcoholics are often damaged beyond repair.

One liver disease that can result from alcohol abuse is **hepatitis** (hep-uh-TY-tis). Hepatitis is an inflammation or infection of the liver that can cause fever, a yellowing of the skin, weakness, and sometimes death. More information about hepatitis can be found in Chapter 21.

Another liver disease caused by alcohol abuse is **cirrhosis** (sur-OH-sis), which occurs when liver cells are permanently replaced with useless scar tissue. People with cirrhosis often suffer serious digestive problems, because their livers are no longer able to metabolize food properly. Research shows that people with cirrhosis who continue to drink have only about a 50 percent chance of living more than five years.

Alcohol abuse can have many negative effects on a person's health. It causes damage to the heart muscle and increases the risk of heart disease. Alcohol can also increase a woman's risk of developing breast cancer. It interrupts REM sleep, which is a necessary part of the sleep cycle. It can also lower a person's white blood cell count, reducing his or her ability to fight infection.

Alcohol kills brain cells. Unlike those in other parts of the body, the cells in the brain cannot be replaced. Loss of brain cells can lead to irreversible memory damage.

Finally, long-term alcohol abuse can also increase one's chances of suffering cancers of the liver, esophagus, pharynx, and larynx.

hepatitis:

an inflammation of the liver that can be caused by long-term alcohol abuse. Symptoms of hepatitis include high fever, weakness, and a yellowing of the skin.

cirrhosis:

a condition in which liver cells are replaced by useless scar tissue. Cirrhosis can be caused by long-term alcohol abuse.

Review

1. *Explain how a person's behavior changes when he or she is intoxicated.*

2. *Name two diseases caused by long-term alcohol abuse.*

3. ***Critical Thinking*** *What could you say to Leo to persuade him to stop drinking?*

• • • • •

Objectives

■ *Name two reasons why some people drink.*

■ *Name four reasons not to drink.*

■ *Discuss dangers of binge drinking.*

■ *Name at least three ways you could refuse alcohol if a friend offers it to you.*
   ■■ **LIFE SKILLS: Resisting Pressure**

■ *Use the decision-making steps to decide what to do if the person you are riding with has been drinking.*
   ■■ **LIFE SKILLS: Making Responsible Decisions**

If you watch a sporting event on television, or read a magazine, or drive a few miles on the highway, you are certain to see an advertisement for alcohol. Have a drink, the advertisements seem to say, and you can be like the people pictured—cool, glamorous, and sophisticated. Many people believe the ads so they drink to fit the image they see.

Some people think they have to drink to be relaxed, to be social. But as Leo experienced, drinking alcohol can make a person angry and aggressive. In this way, it can make a person *less* social.

Other people may drink to ease emotional pain. You saw how Leo forgot what was disturbing him after he had a few beers. Many teenagers who are having problems at home or at school may be looking for something to help them forget their worries. It's completely understandable to feel this way. But alcohol tends to add to a person's problems, rather than solve them.

Some teenagers drink because it makes them feel independent. Others do so to rebel, or for excitement.

But whatever the reason, if you drink alcohol, you are putting your life on the line.

Drunken Driving

Alcohol severely damages judgment, reflexes, and vision. These effects happen to a person even if he or she doesn't *feel* drunk. In other words a person with a high blood alcohol level may not necessarily be slurring words, reeling, and staggering, but still is in no shape to be behind a wheel.

Blood Alcohol Level and Its Effects on Driving Ability

BAL	Decrease in Driving Ability
.04–.06	12%
.07–.09	23%
.10–.12	30%

(FIGURE 13-8) **A blood alcohol level of .04 or above can severely impair judgment, coordination, and vision, which are all important to safe driving.**

A person doesn't have to be legally drunk in order to be dangerous on the highway. As little as one alcoholic beverage can cause enough impairment to cause a car crash. Figure 13-8 shows how different blood alcohol levels can affect a person's driving ability.

There are things you can do to minimize your risk of getting involved in a drunken-driving incident. First, don't drink. Of all reasons to turn down alcohol, this may well be the most important.

Second, don't accept a ride with anyone who has been drinking, even if he or she swears that you have nothing to worry about. Instead, call a sober person to pick you up. Maybe you can persuade the person you're with to come with you. You may want to show a parent or guardian a copy of the contract prepared by Students Against Driving Drunk (S.A.D.D.). This agreement guarantees that parents or guardians who are called for a ride home will pick up their teenagers—no questions asked. A copy of the contract is shown in Figure 13-10.

Binge Drinking

Remember that alcohol has very serious effects on the body. What you should also know is that alcohol is a poison. If a person drinks enough of it at one time, it can cause immediate death.

Although the amount of alcohol necessary to kill a person varies, a blood alcohol level of about .4 percent is usually enough to put a person in a coma and on the verge of death. For a 140-pound person, that's about 15 to 20 drinks in a one-hour period.

Binge drinking—drinking large amounts of alcohol quickly—can easily cause death by alcohol poisoning. Binge drinking is a very serious problem among teenagers and young adults who take part in drinking games.

Drunken Driving: Facts and Numbers

Among people up to age 34 in the United States, motor-vehicle accidents are the leading cause of death.

Approximately one-third of teenage deaths are the result of motor-vehicle accidents.

The risk of motor-vehicle accidents increases for young drivers who have even a very low concentration of blood alcohol in their systems.

Over 40,000 traffic deaths occur each year, and almost 41 percent of these deaths involve a driver who has been drinking alcohol.

Of the more than 40,000 traffic deaths each year, more than 5,200 involve a teenage driver. Of these deaths, almost 38 percent involve a teenage driver who had been drinking alcohol.

(FIGURE 13-9) **Studies show that drivers between the ages of 16 and 24 are three times as likely to die in a drunken-driving crash as older drivers.**

CONTRACT FOR LIFE

A FOUNDATION FOR TRUST & CARING

By agreeing to this contract, we recognize that SADD encourages all young people to adopt a **substance-free** life style. We view this contract as a means of opening the lines of communication about drinking, drug use and traffic safety to ensure the safety of all parties concerned. We understand that this contract does not serve as permission to drink, but rather, a promise to be safe.

**Young
Adult**

I acknowledge that the legal drinking age is 21 and have discussed with you and realize both the legal and physical risks of substance use, as well as driving under the influence. I agree to contact you if I ever find myself in a position where anyone's substance use impairs the possibility of my arriving home safely. I further pledge to maintain safe driving practices at all times, including wearing my safety belt every trip and encouraging others to do the same.

_____
Signature

**Parent or
Guardian:**

Upon discussing this contract with you, I agree to arrange for your safe transportation home, regardless of time or circumstances. I further vow to remain calm when dealing with your situation and discuss it with you at a time when we are *both* able to converse calmly about the matter.

I agree to seek safe, sober transportation home if I am ever in a situation where I have had too much to drink or a friend who is driving me has had too much to drink. Recognizing that safety belt usage is a vital defense against death and injury on the highway, I promise to wear my safety belt at all times and encourage others to do the same.

_____
Signature

_____
Date

Distributed by S.A.D.D. "Students Against Driving Drunk"

(FIGURE 13-10) **S.A.D.D. published this contract between parents and teenagers for the sake of reducing the amount of drunken-driving incidents. This organization does not approve, however, of alcohol use among teenagers.**

Blood Alcohol Level's Effect on Death Risk

BAL	Chance of Dying
.02–.04	1.5 times as likely
.05–.09	11 times as likely
.10–.14	48 times as likely
.15+	380 times as likely

(FIGURE 13-11) **Drinking alcohol in any amount can put a person's life in danger.**

Breaking the Law

People under 21 break a law every time they have any alcohol (except under special circumstances, such as religious purposes). Like all crimes, getting caught drinking alcohol under the age of 21 can lead to arrest, a fine, and even a criminal record. Many teenagers have decided that they'd rather not risk their futures by drinking alcohol now. In addition, driving while under the influence of alcohol is illegal for people of all ages. A person does not have to be in an accident in order to be caught driving drunk—the driver of any car exceeding the speed limit or noticeably weaving through traffic is subject to inspection and a possible blood alcohol level test.

Losing Control

One of the best reasons not to drink is that alcohol can make a person lose control. Drinking to the point of intoxication can remove inhibitions completely. As a result, drunk people may find themselves doing things they regret.

For example, Krystal and Claudio are the school's most popular couple. Wher-

ever they go is *the* place to be. Whatever they do, everyone wants to do too. It's a secret, but one thing they *haven't* done is have sexual intercourse.

Claudio lives with his grandmother, who happens to be out of town for the weekend. He takes advantage of this opportunity, and throws the year's wildest party. By the end of the night, everyone is very drunk, including Claudio and Krystal. The house is severely damaged: the stereo is broken beyond repair, and part of the carpet has been badly burned.

Claudio doesn't know any of this yet, because Krystal has suddenly decided she's ready to have sex with him. The two of them have stumbled to his bedroom.

Hours later, Claudio wakes up, horrified and ashamed. He hadn't wanted it to be like that. How could he have been so stupid? He knows they both made a mistake and that it's too late to go back now. What if Krystal gets pregnant? What about sexually transmitted diseases? Claudio knows that if they hadn't been drunk, they wouldn't have lost control.

Teenagers who drink are more likely to engage in activities that conflict with their personal and parental values. These actions can result in conflicts with family and friends, feelings of guilt, unwanted pregnancies, sexually transmitted diseases, and damage to public or personal property.

Standards Set by Parents or Guardians

Many teenagers decide not to drink because they want to abide by the standards set by their parents or guardians. Chances are that a lot of students in your class have decided not to drink for this reason.

An Alcohol-Free Life

People who choose not to drink do so because they like being sober. They find that being drunk interferes with a lot of activities they enjoy—like taking part in sports, or going to the movies, or socializing with friends, or reading. Being sober allows them to get the most out of the things that make them happy.

What Would You Do ?

Making Responsible Decisions

Should You Let Him Drive You Home?

You're at a party, and it's getting late. Your friend Cliff, who drove you to the party, says he's ready to drive you home. He tells you he hasn't been drinking, but you're pretty sure he's had at least two or three beers. What would you do?

Remember to use the decision-making steps:

1. State the Problem.
2. List the Options.
3. Imagine the Benefits and Consequences.
4. Consider Your Values.
5. Weigh the Options and Decide.
6. Act.
7. Evaluate the Results.

(FIGURE 13-12) **Life's healthiest and happiest activities never include drinking alcohol.**

Saying No Thanks

You may find yourself in the position of having to turn down a drink at a party. There are a lot of ways to do this, but in general, the less you make of it, the easier it's going to be. If someone asks you if you want a drink, try just saying "no thanks." Remember that you don't owe anyone any explanations.

For many teenagers, saying no to alcohol is a matter of self-esteem. In general, the higher a person's sense of confidence and responsibility are, the better he or she may be at resisting pressure.

See the Life Skills activity below for some situations that test your ability to turn down alcohol.

*Life*SKILLS: Resisting Pressure

To Turn Down Alcohol . . . . .

It's never easy to decide not to do something a lot of other people are doing. Still, resisting pressure to drink alcohol is one of the healthiest decisions you can ever make. If you do have to turn down alcohol, it may help to have some idea of what you want to do or say. On a separate sheet of paper, write down what you would do, say, and feel in each situation.

1. You're at a party, and a friend is about to get herself a beer. She insists that you drink one.

2. You're with a group of friends who are passing around a bottle of liquor. The bottle comes to you, and you realize everyone is watching.

3. Four friends are sitting at a table playing a drinking game. They ask you to join them.

4. Your date buys some sodas at a drive-through restaurant, pulls out a bottle of liquor, and offers to mix some with your soda.

You don't have to make a big deal about the fact that you have chosen not to drink. But be firm about your decision. It is, after all, the right one for you.

(FIGURE 13-13) **Talking about peer pressure and other issues with fellow students often helps teenagers resist the urge to use alcohol.**

Getting Involved

One of the most rewarding things you can do with your spare time is to volunteer for an anti-alcohol cause. This could mean planning an alcohol-free dance or other activities that bring people together without alcohol. You might want to think about organizing a discussion group for students in your school to talk about peer pressure or other things that tempt them to try alcohol.

In addition, look into joining your school or community chapter of S.A.D.D. or Remove Intoxicated Drivers (R.I.D.). Encourage your friends to volunteer with you. If you have trouble persuading them, remind them that drunken-driving crashes kill one teenager every three hours. Any organization that is working to bring that number down is worth the time and effort you put into it.

Review

1. Name two reasons why some people drink.

2. What are two myths a lot of teenagers hear about alcohol?

3. What is the most dangerous consequence of binge drinking?

4. **LIFE SKILLS: Resisting Pressure** Name three ways you could refuse alcohol if a friend offers it to you.

5. **LIFE SKILLS: Making Responsible Decisions** Name two possible short-term negative consequences of accepting a ride with someone who has been drinking.

6. **Critical Thinking** Why are people who are intoxicated more likely to get into automobile crashes than people who are sober? Be specific.

Section 13.3 Alcohol Abuse and Alcoholism

Objectives

- *Know the three phases of alcoholism.*
- *Name the most important risks of alcohol abuse.*
- *Know how alcohol can affect an unborn child.*
- *Know the ways in which a family can be damaged by a family member's alcoholism.*

alcoholism:
the state of being psychologically and physically addicted to alcohol.

According to the American Medical Association, **alcoholism** is a disease just like cancer or heart disease. Most people who have this disease pass through three phases: abuse, dependence, and addiction.

Abuse

When a person who drinks alcohol cannot do so in moderation or at appropriate times, he or she is abusing alcohol. There are more people who abuse alcohol than you may realize. Every person who drives drunk, for example, is abusing alcohol. People who become violent or angry when they are drunk, or do things they wouldn't do when they are sober, are abusing alcohol.

Leo, Claudio, and Krystal are examples of teenagers who are abusing alcohol. In reality, all teenagers who drink alcohol are abusing it because they are doing something illegal.

People who abuse alcohol regularly can suffer in many ways. They often do poorly in school or at their jobs. And they are likely to engage in behaviors that risk the health and safety of themselves and others.

Signs of Alcohol Abuse	
Odor on the breath	*Frequent absences*
Intoxication	*Unexplained bruises or accidents*
Difficulty focusing, glazed eyes	*Irritability*
Uncharacteristically passive or aggressive behavior	*Loss of memory (blackouts)*
Decline in personal appearance or hygiene	*Changes in peer-group associations and friendships*
Decline in school or work performance	*Damaged relationships with family members or close friends*

(FIGURE 13-14)
Every teenager who drinks alcohol is an alcohol abuser.

Risk Factors for Alcoholism

Risk Factors You Cannot Control	Risk Factors You Can Control
Genes	Drinking before the age of 21
Environment	Associating with people who drink
	Bending to peer pressure
	Drinking beyond moderation
	Drinking at inappropriate times
	Drinking alone

(FIGURE 13-15) **Most risk factors for alcoholism can be avoided. For this reason, alcoholism is a preventable disease.**

Dependence

People in the dependence phase of alcoholism feel they need the drug to function properly. They have a very strong and constant desire for alcohol. At this point this desire is a psychological one only, which means that they are not yet physically addicted to alcohol. Even so, alcohol is beginning to dominate their lives.

Addiction

Eventually the dependence on alcohol becomes physical as well as psychological. Those who are physically dependent on alcohol suffer unpleasant withdrawal symptoms if they don't have a regular fix. Studies show that teenagers can become physically dependent, or addicted, much more quickly than adults. Teenagers who use alcohol can become addicted to it in as little as one to two years. It takes most adults about 5 to 20 years of alcohol abuse to become addicted.

Once a person becomes both psychologically and physically dependent on alcohol, he or she is an alcoholic.

Being addicted to alcohol means putting the drug before everything else. Alcoholics often neglect their job, their responsibilities, and even their family because their one focus—the one thing they think about—is getting more alcohol. Sometimes they will substitute alcohol for food, which can lead to serious health problems, such as malnutrition.

They may also be in a constant state of denial. People who are completely addicted to alcohol may resent any suggestion that they may have a drinking problem. They often claim that they can quit any time they want. In reality, such people usually need assistance in order to stop drinking.

Causes of Alcoholism It's not completely clear why some people can drink alcohol without becoming addicted, while others become alcoholics.

fetal alcohol syndrome (FAS):

a set of birth defects that can occur when a pregnant woman drinks alcohol. These defects include low birth weight, mental retardation, facial deformities, and behavioral problems.

Some evidence shows that children of alcoholics are more likely than others to become alcoholics as adults. And some evidence indicates that the likelihood of becoming an alcoholic may be inherited through genes.

But it is difficult to separate the possible effects of genetic traits from environmental factors. Children who grow up in alcoholic families are less likely than others to get their emotional needs met. So when they get older, they may use alcohol to numb their emotional pain.

Alcoholism probably results from a combination of psychological, environmental, and physical factors.

Fetal Alcohol Syndrome

When a pregnant woman drinks alcohol, every bit of the drug in her system passes into the bloodstream of her unborn child. Babies who are exposed to alcohol in this way are at risk of suffering from a set of defects known as **fetal alcohol syndrome (FAS)**. These defects include low birth weight, mental retardation, facial deformities, and behavioral problems.

No one is exactly sure how much alcohol must reach the unborn child in order for FAS to occur, so many doctors advise women not to drink alcohol at all while they're pregnant. Women who are not addicted to alcohol have no trouble following this suggestion. Alcoholic women, however, may have difficulty staying away from alcohol for nine months.

Alcohol and the Family

Dennis's two sons love to be with him when he is sober. That's when he is warm and affectionate—that's when they know that he loves them. It's when he's drunk that everything becomes unpredictable. While drunk, he has beat them more times than they want to remember.

This behavior is not unusual—it is estimated that between 50 and 80 percent of all family violence involves alcohol.

But the damage alcoholism has caused Dennis's family goes beyond physical violence. The two sons don't talk about it, but they know that they must avoid their father when he is drunk. They also must make excuses for him when he is too intoxicated to go to work. They spend their time wondering what Dennis will be like at the end of the day. Will he have gone to work? Will he threaten them? Or will he be kind and loving, and make promises they know he won't keep? Dennis's addiction has taken over his entire family.

(FIGURE 13-16) **Living with an alcoholic family member can be confusing and lonely. But with proper treatment, the families of alcoholics can fully recover—regardless of whether the alcoholic they are living with does.**

(FIGURE 13-17) **Fetal alcohol syndrome is a set of birth defects that can affect the babies of women who drink alcohol while pregnant.**

Being controlled by a family member or a loved one's addiction is sometimes called being codependent. Teenagers who have an alcoholic parent often don't know what to expect when they come home from school. Some have learned that if they don't take responsibility for something, no one in the family will. They may find themselves doing responsible jobs at home, such as making sure the utility bill is paid, that teenagers from nonalcoholic families usually don't have to worry about. And even though they are doing so much for the family, these teenagers often feel as though they are somehow to blame for everything. They may think that they're constantly in the way.

The important thing for them to know is that their parent's drinking is *not* their fault, and that they can get help.

In the next section you'll learn about treatment for alcoholism and about the help available for family members of alcoholics.

Review

1. *What are the three phases of alcoholism?*

2. *What are three dangers of alcohol abuse?*

3. *Explain how a pregnant woman's drinking can affect her unborn child.*

4. *How can a parent's alcoholism affect the children?*

5. ***Critical Thinking*** *What do you think are some psychological and sociological factors that can cause a person to become an alcoholic?*

13.4 *Hope for Recovery*

withdrawal:

the process of discontinuing a drug to which the body has become addicted.

In order to quit drinking, an alcoholic must first admit that he or she is powerless over alcohol. Then the process of recovery can begin. Sometimes a person who is addicted to alcohol can reach this conclusion by himself or herself. Other times it may take intervention by friends and family to get an alcoholic to this point. But no matter how it happens, a person who has admitted this has completed the first step of the recovery process.

Withdrawal

When an alcoholic quits drinking, he or she goes through **withdrawal.** Withdrawal is the process of discontinuing a drug to which the body has become addicted. During withdrawal, a person may suffer extreme

(FIGURE 13-18) **All alcoholics who want to overcome their addiction must first admit that their addiction to alcohol controls their life and that they need to get treatment.**

nervousness, headaches, tremors, or seizures. Ordinarily these symptoms would go away once the alcoholic has some alcohol. But there is no such relief for a person who has decided to quit drinking. The withdrawal phase of recovery usually lasts no more than a few days. Those going through it, however, may want to be under constant medical supervision.

Inpatient and Outpatient Programs

Alcoholics who have gone through withdrawal are no longer physically addicted to alcohol. Now the harder part comes, because they have to stop being emotionally addicted as well. People who have at one time depended on alcohol to help them cope with problems may want a drink whenever times are hard. And because they are alcoholics, having just one drink is likely to make them physically and emotionally addicted once again. That's why patients in treatment programs are not allowed any alcohol at all.

Some recovering alcoholics decide to join hospital inpatient programs, which means that they live at the hospital while receiving treatment. Others choose to move home after completing withdrawal, and to participate in hospital outpatient programs. After going through withdrawal, patients in both programs receive counseling in order to understand why they became addicted to alcohol, and to help them cope with life without it. This may come in the form of individual sessions, or in group therapy, which gives the patient the opportunity to talk to other people going through the same thing. Many hospitals also offer therapy sessions and education classes for families of alcoholics, who are also in a recovery process—living with an alcoholic can be as damaging as being one.

Alcoholics Anonymous

There are many self-help programs for alcoholics. By far the most widely used of these is Alcoholics Anonymous (AA). Many hospital treatment programs require their patients to attend AA meetings. In addition, AA has helped a large number of alcoholics stop drinking without any other form of treatment.

The AA method for recovery involves 12 steps. The first and perhaps most important of these is for the alcoholic to recognize that he or she is powerless over alcohol.

Through regular meetings and shared experience, AA members bring themselves and each other closer to their goal of a life that is free of alcohol, and full of emotional, physical, and spiritual well-being. Such a goal, AA members know, can only be reached one day at a time. For this reason, many recovering alcoholics attend AA meetings every day, and learn to celebrate every day, week, month, and year they conquer without alcohol.

To find out about AA meetings in your area, look in the phone book under "Alcoholics Anonymous."

Al-Anon and Alateen

Having a parent, a sibling, or a spouse who is an alcoholic can make a person feel alone and lost. Al-Anon and Alateen were formed to bring people who are feeling this way together.

Al-Anon is designed to help family members talk about the problems of living with an alcoholic. Alateen was specifically designed to help teenagers cope with the same situation.

Meetings at Al-Anon and Alateen are very much like those of AA. People who feel like talking about their experiences can do so. Those who would rather just listen don't have to say anything. Knowing that

(FIGURE 13-19) **Alcoholics Anonymous is the most widely used and the most successful of the self-help programs. It has helped many alcoholics stop drinking without hospital treatment.**

other people are going through the same thing can make some very difficult situations less painful.

One of the most important goals of groups like Al-Anon and Alateen is to help people realize that they can get help whether or not the alcoholic they are living with gets treatment. Even if the alcoholic keeps drinking, the family members can improve their own lives.

If you want to find out more about Al-Anon and Alateen, look in the phone book under Al-Anon or Alcoholics Anonymous. The person who answers the phone can provide you with meeting information. You may also check the Internet for the Alcoholics Anonymous Web site and the Al-Anon/Alateen Web site.

Review

1. Describe three ways a person can begin recovery from alcoholism.

2. ▪▪ **LIFE SKILLS: Using Community Resources** How could you find out about meetings of Alcoholics Anonymous in your area?

3. ▪▪ **LIFE SKILLS: Using Community Resources** How could you find out about meetings of Alateen in your area?

4. **Critical Thinking** Do you agree with the statement: "Living with an alcoholic can be as damaging as being one?" Why or why not?

CHAPTER 13

Highlights

Summary

- One drink can impair a person's judgment, reflexes, and vision enough to cause an automobile accident.

- Drinking alcohol can cause hangovers, damage the liver and heart, kill brain cells, and increase a person's chances of getting cancers of the liver, esophagus, pharynx, and larynx.

- Minimize your risk of getting involved in a drunken-driving incident by not drinking, and by not accepting a ride with anyone who has been drinking.

- Alcohol can be deadly if a person drinks enough of it at one time.

- Teenagers who drink are much more likely to engage in activities that conflict with their personal and parental values.

- Alcoholics and the people who are close to them can be helped by groups and programs such as Alcoholics Anonymous, Al-Anon, and Alateen.

Vocabulary

blood alcohol level (BAL) a way to measure the level of alcohol in a person's body.

intoxicated being affected by alcohol. Effects of intoxication can range from mild lightheadedness to severe and complete loss of judgment and reflexes.

hangover uncomfortable physical effects brought on by alcohol use. Symptoms of a hangover include headache, nausea, upset stomach, and dizziness.

hepatitis (hep-uh-TY-tis) an inflammation of the liver that can be caused by long-term abuse. Symptoms of hepatitis include high fever, weakness, and a yellowing of the skin.

cirrhosis (sur-OH-sis) a condition in which liver cells are replaced by useless scar tissue. Cirrhosis can be caused by long-term alcohol abuse.

alcoholism the state of being psychologically and physically addicted to alcohol.

fetal alcohol syndrome (FAS) a set of birth defects that can occur when a pregnant woman drinks alcohol. These defects include low birth weight, mental retardation, facial deformities, and behavioral problems.

withdrawal the process of discontinuing the use of a drug to which the body has become addicted.

Chapter Review

Concept Review . . . .

1. How does alcohol affect the mind and body?

2. What is one way that drinking alcohol can make an individual less social?

3. How does alcohol affect a person's driving? What are two consequences of driving drunk?

4. What is S.A.D.D.? What is the purpose of their "Contract for Life"?

5. How is saying "no" a matter of self-esteem?

6. What are some signs that a person has a drinking problem?

7. How is the dependence stage of alcoholism different from the addiction stage?

8. Why can some people drink alcohol without becoming addicted, while others become alcoholics?

9. What does being codependent mean?

10. What is the first step in recovering from alcoholism?

11. What help is available for a problem drinker?

Expressing Your Views . . . .

1. You're about to leave a party with a friend, but you realize that your friend has been drinking alcohol. What should you do?

2. People who drink at parties often try to get everyone else there to drink as well. Why do you think people who drink try to pressure others to drink?

3. Mothers Against Drunk Driving (M.A.D.D.) is an organization that promotes stricter penalties for people who drive drunk. Contact this organization to find out what your state's acceptable blood alcohol level is and what the local and state penalties are for drunken driving. Do you think these penalties are fair and adequate? Why or why not?

Life Skills Check

1. Using Community Resources

Charlie's mother is an alcoholic. Sometimes she's asleep on the living room couch when Charlie comes home from school. Other times she's awake, but impatient with Charlie and quick to get angry over small things. Charlie knows she needs help, and would also like to talk to someone about how his mother's drinking affects him. What can Charlie do to get help?

2. Resisting Pressure

Movies, television, and advertisements often seem to encourage audiences to drink by making alcohol consumption seem appealing and sophisticated. What are they not telling viewers about alcohol?

3. Communicating Effectively

You think your friend may have a drinking problem because she always smells like alcohol, and because she often seems drunk. What could you say to persuade her to contact a group that could help her with her problem?

Projects

1. Make a poster advertising Al-Anon and Alateen meetings. Display these posters throughout the school. Include suggestions and illustrations to help the problem drinker. You might also write to these organizations for any additional information to display.

2. Create a bulletin board to show alcohol's effect on various parts of the body such as the brain, kidneys, liver, stomach, and heart. Include illustrations and labels, along with diseases brought about by alcohol abuse.

Plan for Action

About half of all fatal driving accidents are related to alcohol use. Devise a plan to ensure that you will always drive sober.

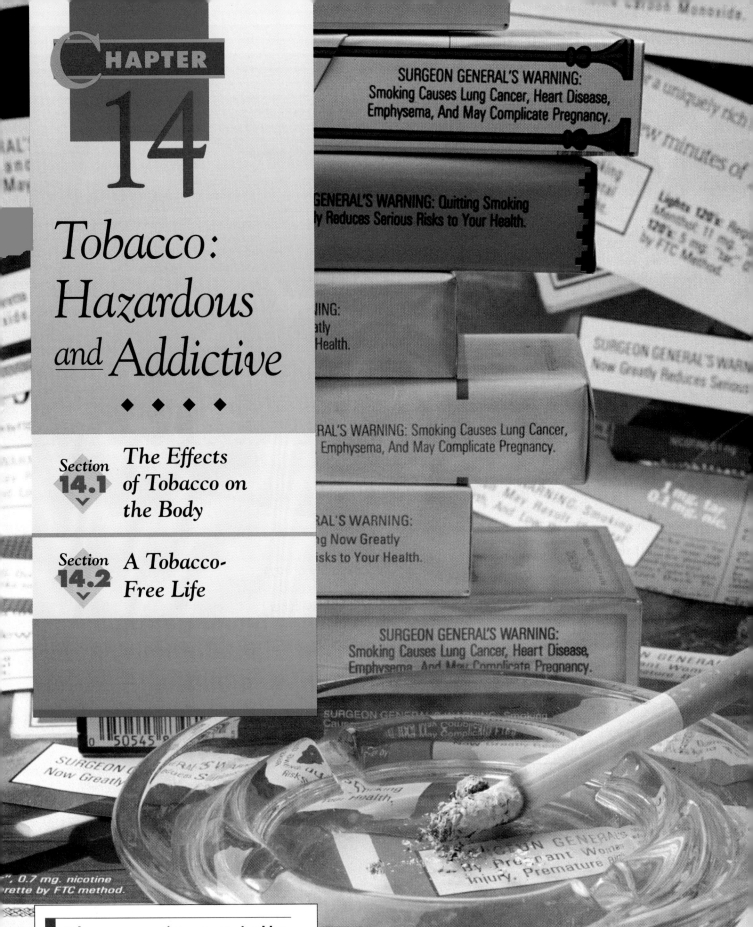

Tobacco: Hazardous and Addictive

◆ ◆ ◆ ◆

Section 14.1 The Effects of Tobacco on the Body

Section 14.2 A Tobacco-Free Life

■ Tobacco companies are required by law to place warnings about the dangers of smoking on all cigarette packages.

Ethan has been smoking a pack of cigarettes every day for the past year. He didn't get hooked right away. In fact, the first few times he smoked, he got really sick. But soon he got used to it, and then he began to enjoy smoking. Now he finds it hard to get through each hour without smoking a cigarette. His girlfriend, Mara, hates his habit. She finds it really unattractive—his hair and clothes always reek of cigarette smoke. More important, she's worried about his health. He's always short of breath, and sometimes he coughs for minutes on end until his throat is raw. Mara knows he has to quit. The problem is, how can she persuade Ethan to give up cigarettes?

The Effects of Tobacco on the Body

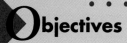

Objectives

- *Name three major chemicals in tobacco.*
- *Name two kinds of diseases smoking can cause.*
- *Name one disease smokeless tobacco can cause.*
- *Know the difference between mainstream and sidestream smoke.*
- *Demonstrate how to ask someone not to smoke in your presence.*
  LIFE SKILLS: Communicating Effectively

- Illnesses caused by smoking kill 434,000 Americans every year. That number is higher than the number of American military deaths during World War II.
- Cigarette smoking is considered the most avoidable cause of death in the United States.
- The death rate from heart disease is 70 percent higher for smokers than for non-smokers, and over 80 percent of lung cancer cases are caused by smoking.
- Tobacco smoke also creates a health hazard for all those around the smoker who rely on the same air supply. Each year an estimated 50,000 nonsmokers die from exposure to tobacco smoke released into the air by smokers.

Mara hopes that if she can teach Ethan enough about the risks of smoking, he'll find the courage and willpower to quit. She found some books and pamphlets on smoking and disease, and she is teaching Ethan some interesting facts. For example:

The Chemicals of Tobacco

Tobacco contains more than 4,000 chemicals. More than 401 of these chemicals are poisonous. When Ethan smokes a cigarette,

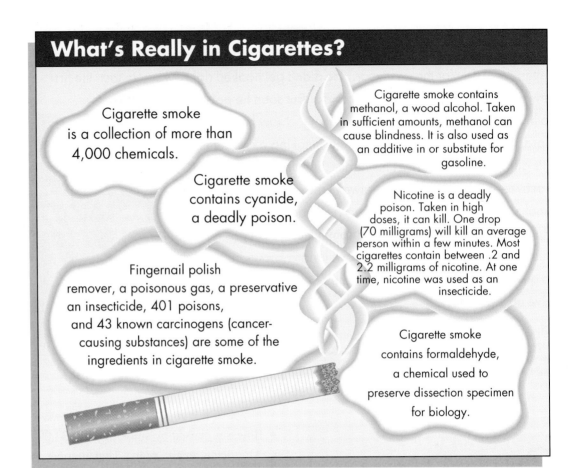

What's Really in Cigarettes?

Cigarette smoke is a collection of more than 4,000 chemicals.

Cigarette smoke contains cyanide, a deadly poison.

Fingernail polish remover, a poisonous gas, a preservative an insecticide, 401 poisons, and 43 known carcinogens (cancer-causing substances) are some of the ingredients in cigarette smoke.

Cigarette smoke contains methanol, a wood alcohol. Taken in sufficient amounts, methanol can cause blindness. It is also used as an additive in or substitute for gasoline.

Nicotine is a deadly poison. Taken in high doses, it can kill. One drop (70 milligrams) will kill an average person within a few minutes. Most cigarettes contain between .2 and 2.2 milligrams of nicotine. At one time, nicotine was used as an insecticide.

Cigarette smoke contains formaldehyde, a chemical used to preserve dissection specimen for biology.

■ (FIGURE 14-1) **It would be hard to find a list of ingredients that are more hazardous than those in tobacco.**

addictive:

causing a physical dependence; a person who is addicted to a drug requires that substance in order to function normally.

tar:

solid material in tobacco smoke that condenses into a thick liquid.

nicotine:

an addictive chemical found in tobacco.

psychoactive substance:

a substance that causes a change in a person's mood and behavior.

• • • • •

he inhales every one of those chemicals and every one of those poisons. Mara did some math and figured out that since Ethan is smoking one pack of cigarettes a day, he inhales these chemicals 70,000 times a year. Three of the most poisonous chemicals in tobacco smoke are tar, nicotine, and carbon monoxide.

Nicotine Nicotine is the psychoactive chemical in tobacco. A **psychoactive substance** causes a change in a person's mood and behavior. Nicotine is also the reason Ethan is hooked on smoking—it is a very **addictive** drug. A person who is addicted to a drug has trouble functioning without it. Because Ethan is addicted to nicotine, if he were to quit smoking, his body would go

through a physical withdrawal. The withdrawal symptoms of nicotine include irritability, headache, restlessness, and anxiety. These symptoms are unpleasant but temporary. Eventually Ethan's body would stop reacting in this way. Ethan is also psychologically dependent on nicotine. This means that he has a constant craving for it. A psychological addiction can be as difficult to overcome as a physical one.

Tar Tobacco smoke contains tiny pieces of solid matter called **tar.** When these tiny particles enter the lungs, they condense and form a sticky coating on the bronchial tubes. The bronchial tubes are lined with tiny hairs called cilia, which beat back and sweep away agents that cause disease. When the cilia are damaged, they can't do their job. Ethan's cigarette habit puts a cup of tobacco tar into his lungs and cilia each year. If Ethan doesn't quit smoking soon, his cilia will be so damaged that they will not be able to protect him from getting a serious respiratory disease.

Carbon Monoxide As the cigarette burns, it releases an extremely dangerous gas called **carbon monoxide**. Carbon monoxide interferes with the blood's ability to carry oxygen. This is why Ethan is always so short of breath—he's not receiving as much oxygen as he should be.

The Effects of Nicotine

Every time Ethan takes a puff of a cigarette, the nicotine he inhales travels to his bloodstream and then to his brain. This entire process takes only seven seconds, so Ethan will start feeling the effects of the nicotine immediately. This means that Ethan's heart will beat more quickly, his blood pressure will increase, and he will begin to feel more alert and energetic. These effects last for only about 30 minutes, which is why Ethan usually craves another cigarette about half an hour after he has finished his last one.

carbon monoxide:

a poisonous gas released by burning tobacco.

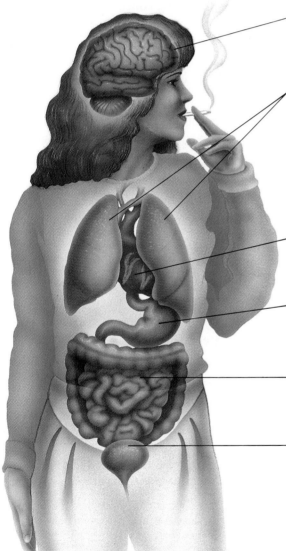

(A) **Brain:** Smoking restricts oxygen flow and causes a narrowing of the blood vessels in the brain, which can lead to stroke.

(B) **Lungs:** Cigarette smoke introduces cancer-causing agents directly to the lung tissue. It also impairs the cilia's ability to clear these and other harmful foreign substances from the lungs, increasing the risk of lung cancer and emphysema.

(C) **Heart:** Nicotine increases heart rate and blood pressure, and constricts the blood vessels, which can lead to a heart attack.

(D) **Stomach:** Cigarette smoke can lead to ulcers.

(E) **Intestines:** Cigarette smoke can also cause ulcers in the small intestine.

(F) **Bladder:** Smoking can cause cancer of the bladder.

(FIGURE 14-2) **Cigarette smoke poses a danger to many major parts of the body.**

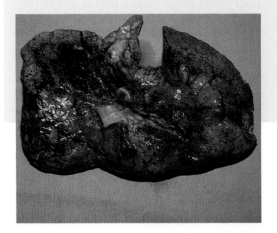

(FIGURE 14-3) **A cancerous lung (left) and a healthy lung (right). The white areas on the otherwise blackened lung show the development of lung cancer.**

cancer:

a disease caused by cells that have lost normal growth controls and that invade and destroy healthy tissues.

Mara discovered why Ethan felt sick the first few times he smoked. When a person's body isn't used to nicotine, a condition called nicotine poisoning can result. Symptoms of nicotine poisoning include lightheadedness, rapid pulse, cold clammy skin, nausea, and sometimes vomiting and diarrhea. "I can't believe you kept smoking when it made you so sick," she told him.

Smoking and Disease

People who smoke put themselves in danger of developing a smoking-related disease. And mothers who smoke risk harming not only themselves but also their newborn and unborn children. For a list of these risks, see Figure 14-4. The risk of getting a smoking-related disease is highest among people who have smoked for a long time, who started smoking at a young age, and who smoke heavily. Mara figures that since Ethan started smoking as a teenager, he'll be at a very high risk of suffering a smoking-related disease if he doesn't quit soon.

Cancer Tobacco is a major cause of several types of cancers. **Cancer** is a dangerous disease with formation and growth of malignant, or deadly, cells that attack and replace healthy cells. This can happen anywhere in the body. One major type of cancer caused by smoking is lung cancer. Lung cancer is the most common cause of cancer deaths among both American men and women and the second most common type of cancer among American men and women.

The bronchial tree, which is the hollow tubing that connects breathing passages from the mouth and nose to the lungs, produces a combination of saliva and mucus called sputum. Over a period of time the chemicals in cigarette smoke may cause changes in the cell genes of the sputum. These changes can lead to lung cancer.

There is no effective treatment for lung cancer. Every year, 120,000 Americans die from this disease. According to studies, cigarette smoking causes more than 80 percent of all cases of lung cancer in the United States.

Other cancers caused by smoking include cancers of the larynx, esophagus, bladder, kidney, and pancreas.

Respiratory Diseases Ethan has a persistent cough because his smoking habit has caused mucus to accumulate in his respiratory tract. Over a period of time this condition can cause a respiratory disease such as chronic bronchitis or emphysema.

Chronic bronchitis is an inflammation of the bronchial tubes in the lungs and the production of excessive mucus. This results in a chronic cough and breathing difficulties. Smokers with chronic bronchitis often wake up in the morning coughing and spitting up mucus. Chronic bronchitis can eventually lead to emphysema.

Emphysema is a disease in which tiny air sacs in the lungs are ruptured, or torn. Under normal circumstances, these air sacs absorb oxygen coming into the body and help push carbon dioxide out of the body. When torn, they lose the ability to do this. This is why a person with emphysema is always short of breath. People with advanced emphysema constantly struggle for air. Sometimes they can't breathe without the help of a special oxygen tent.

Emphysema may last for years and is often fatal. Eighty percent of emphysema cases are related to smoking.

Cardiovascular Disease As you learned earlier in this section, nicotine increases heart rate and blood pressure, and carbon monoxide makes the circulatory system work very hard to deliver oxygen to the body's cells. Over a period of time, both of these chemicals put a great deal of strain on the body's blood vessels and cause cardiovascular disease, or disease of the heart and blood vessels. More than 120,000 smokers in the United States die every year from cardiovascular diseases.

Smoking can lead to atherosclerosis, which is the buildup of fat on the blood vessel walls. This can increase the chance that a blood vessel will become blocked or break

near the heart, resulting in a heart attack. Another type of cardiovascular disease, a stroke, can occur if a blood vessel breaks or becomes blocked near the brain.

Pipes, Cigars, and Smokeless Tobacco

"Maybe," Ethan said, "I could get my fix of nicotine from something else, like a cigar, a pipe, or even chewing tobacco." Mara and Ethan did some research and found that people tend to inhale the smoke from cigarettes more deeply than they do the smoke from cigars or pipes. For this reason, cigarettes are the most dangerous of

chronic bronchitis:

an inflammation of the bronchial tubes in the lungs and the production of excessive mucus.

emphysema:

a disease in which the tiny air sacs of the lungs lose their elasticity.

Reasons Mothers Shouldn't Smoke

There is a greater risk of miscarriage.

The baby might be born too early.

The baby might have a low birth weight or other serious health problems.

The baby might have a slow growth rate.

There is a greater risk of Sudden Infant Death Syndrome (SIDS).

There is a greater risk that the child will develop a respiratory illness.

The baby might receive nicotine from the mother's milk.

The baby could develop learning difficulties.

(FIGURE 14-4) **Pregnant women and mothers who smoke risk harming not only themselves but also their unborn and newborn children.**

chewing tobacco:

a form of smokeless tobacco that is placed between a person's cheek and gum.

the three. However, cigars and pipes have their own serious hazards. Pipe smokers have been known to suffer cancers of the tongue and lip, and certain types of cancers, such as cancer of the stomach and larynx, are more common among people who smoke cigars and pipes than among those who smoke cigarettes.

Smokeless Tobacco Smokeless tobacco comes in two forms. **Chewing tobacco** is placed between a person's cheek and gum. When this tobacco is chewed, it releases juices that contain nicotine and other chemicals. These juices mix with the saliva and are absorbed into the bloodstream.

The second kind of smokeless tobacco, snuff, is ground tobacco that is inhaled through the nose or placed between the cheek and gum. The nicotine and other chemicals are then absorbed into the bloodstream through the mucous membranes of

*Life*SKILLS: Communicating Effectively

A Cigarette With Dinner?. . . . .

Studies show that people who are exposed to sidestream smoke are at risk of suffering the same diseases as smokers. For this reason, new laws have been passed to protect nonsmokers from the dangers of passive smoking. Federal buildings are now smoke-free, and many state, county, and city buildings are smoke-free. Some public places continue to allow smoking but provide designated nonsmoking areas.

Imagine that you and a friend have decided to sit in the nonsmoking section of a restaurant. During the meal, a person at the next table lights a cigarette. The smoke is ruining your meal. Role-play how you could use effective communication and solve the problem.

the nose or mouth. Once in the blood-stream, the nicotine travels to the brain.

Both snuff and chewing tobacco can cause cancer of the mouth and throat, and chewing tobacco can also lead to cancer of the tongue, cheek, and gums.

The Risks of "Passive" Smoking

Mara saved her biggest weapon for last. If Ethan couldn't be persuaded to quit smoking to save his own health, maybe he would do so for hers. "It's dangerous for me to be around you when you smoke," Mara told him. "It could make me sick—it could even kill me."

Mara had learned that a burning cigarette releases two types of smoke:

- **Mainstream smoke** passes through the tobacco and filter when the smoker inhales.
- **Sidestream smoke** rises from the cigarette during the time the smoker is not inhaling.

Almost 75 percent of the smoke that comes from a burning cigarette is side-stream smoke. Sidestream smoke enters the environment and affects anybody who happens to be around. A person who inhales the sidestream smoke of a cigarette is a **passive smoker**. Sidestream smoke contains twice as much tar and nicotine, and three times as much carbon monoxide, as mainstream smoke. After 30 minutes in a smoke-filled room, a passive smoker has inhaled almost as much carbon monoxide as someone who has just smoked a cigarette.

Passive smokers are at an increased risk of suffering both lung cancer and heart disease. Sidestream smoke can also aggravate a person's allergies and cause respiratory infections. When Mara told Ethan these facts, he agreed to quit smoking.

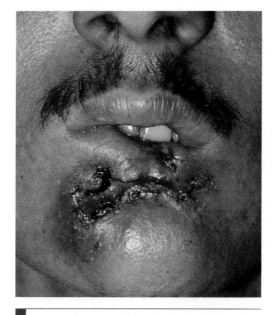

(FIGURE 14-5) **Chewing tobacco can lead to serious facial deformities as well as certain types of cancer.**

Review

1. *What are three major chemicals in tobacco?*

2. *What are two major types of diseases caused by smoking?*

3. *What is one disease caused by smokeless tobacco?*

4. *Define mainstream and sidestream smoke. How do they differ?*

5. **LIFE SKILLS: Communicating Effectively** *What can you say if a person sitting next to you in a nonsmoking area lights a cigarette?*

6. *Critical Thinking If cigarettes did not contain tar, would they be safe to smoke?*

mainstream smoke:

smoke that is inhaled directly into the mouth through a cigarette, pipe, or cigar.

sidestream smoke:

smoke that enters the environment from burning tobacco.

passive smoker:

A nonsmoker who is exposed to the sidestream smoke of a cigarette, cigar, or pipe.

14.2 A Tobacco-Free Life

Objectives

- *Know two reasons why people start using tobacco.*

- *Know three reasons not to use tobacco.*

- *Know two strategies you can use to quit smoking.*

SMOKING POLLUTES YOU AND EVERYTHING ELSE

THERE'S NOTHING MIGHTIER THAN THE SWORD | AMERICAN CANCER SOCIETY

(FIGURE 14-6) **An advertisement from the American Cancer Society. Antismoking organizations are working to destroy the myth that smoking makes people glamorous and attractive.**

Every package of cigarettes and smokeless tobacco carries a warning from the Surgeon General on the dangers of tobacco use. These dangers are well known and well documented. Probably because these risks are so well understood, fewer people today use tobacco than ever before. But even so, more than 72 million Americans ignore these warnings and use tobacco products.

People use tobacco for different reasons. Peer influence and a parent's example may give someone the impression that it's O.K. to use tobacco. For example, Ethan's father has always smoked, and many of his friends smoke as well. If neither his dad nor his friends were smokers, Ethan might never have started smoking.

Another factor that may influence a person's decision to smoke is advertising. Models in cigarette and smokeless tobacco advertisements usually look glamorous and attractive. They can make tobacco use seem very appealing. Some organizations are working to destroy this idea by publishing posters showing the less attractive features of the habit.

Reasons Not to Use Tobacco

Just as peer pressure can tempt you to use tobacco, the influence of friends can help you make the decision *not* to use it. Many teenagers are aware of tobacco's dangers.

Having parents who don't use tobacco can also help a person make the same decision. Most parents realize how harmful tobacco is. They wouldn't want to see their sons or daughters jeopardize their lives by using a dangerous product.

Four Good Reasons to Avoid Tobacco

1. **It's dangerous:** Using tobacco causes cancer and can lead to high blood pressure, cardiovascular disease, and various lung disorders.

2. **It's expensive:** Smoking a pack of cigarettes a day costs more than $800 a year. Chewing a container of tobacco every two days costs about $600 a year.

3. **It leaves an unpleasant odor:** The smell of tobacco lingers on your breath, in your hair, and on your clothes.

4. **It's unattractive:** Tobacco can leave dark stains on your fingers and on your teeth. In addition, many teenagers find the sight of a person smoking or chewing tobacco unappealing.

(FIGURE 14-7)

As Figure 14-7 indicates, using tobacco is an expensive, smelly, and unattractive habit. But the most important reasons not to use tobacco products are that they can damage your health and shorten your life. As you learned earlier in this chapter, the diseases caused by smoking and chewing tobacco are serious and often fatal.

Quitting Smoking

If you avoid smoking altogether, you'll never have to worry about its health risks. But if you are a regular smoker, know that if you quit your habit for good, you can dramatically reduce your chances of getting a serious disease. If Ethan can stay away from cigarettes for five years, his chances of getting lung cancer will decrease by 50 percent. And in 15 years, his chances of suffering *any* smoking-related illness will be almost as low as a person who has never smoked. But even a few days after he stops smoking, Ethan will begin to feel less winded and healthier.

Some smokers are worried that they will gain weight if they stop smoking. In fact, most people don't gain weight. What they do gain is a sense of confidence about themselves. It's a great feeling to overcome a habit that once controlled you.

Even though it is difficult to quit, you can do it. Lots of people do. Here are some strategies that may help you:

Set a Quitting Date Select a date to quit before you actually do so. Choose a time when you can avoid being around other people who smoke and when you won't be stressed by other factors. Taking up a sport or a creative hobby can help distract you from smoking and relieve tension.

Decide Your Approach Different approaches work for different people. Many people prefer the "cold turkey" approach. They decide that, after the quitting date they have selected, they will never smoke again. Others prefer to gradually cut down the number of cigarettes they smoke, until they quit completely.

Prepare Your Environment If you decide to quit cold turkey, throw away all smoking materials and ashtrays in your

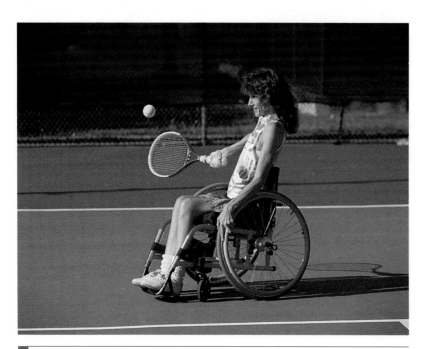

(FIGURE 14-8) **People who don't smoke are able to participate in and enjoy healthy, strenuous activity.**

Find Other Ways to Cope With Stress

Most people who smoke want a cigarette most when they are under stress. There are healthier ways to handle anxiety. Getting regular exercise, for example, can be very relaxing. Try taking a long walk once a day. As your health and your wind improve, you'll be able to exercise for longer periods of time. In addition, the stress-management exercises described in Chapter 9 can help you cope with stress much more effectively than smoking.

After You Quit

Once you have stopped smoking for good, you'll start feeling better, both physically and psychologically. That feeling of being constantly short of breath will go away, and you'll even discover that the food you eat smells and tastes better. Although you may not have realized it, smoking dulls your senses of taste and smell.

In addition, you will enjoy the great sense of achievement that accomplishing a major goal can give you. By quitting smoking, you will have conquered a major addiction and taken a large step toward a long, healthy life.

house and car. If you decide to cut down, keep only one day's supply of cigarettes on hand at a time. If you have decided to smoke eight cigarettes the first day, for example, throw away the rest of the pack or have a friend keep it for you. That way, you won't be tempted to smoke more than you have allowed yourself.

Get Help if You Need It Make sure your family members and friends know that you are planning to quit smoking. You may need their encouragement. Avoid situations that trigger your desire to smoke; it may be helpful to enroll in a workshop or join a support group for people who are giving up smoking. Contact the American Lung Association or the American Cancer Society for information about cessation programs designed for teens.

Some people find that nicotine gum or nicotine patches (squares soaked in nicotine and placed on the skin) help them stop smoking without suffering nicotine withdrawal symptoms. Nicotine gum and patches are available without a prescription.

. . . . .
Review

1. *What are two reasons why people start using tobacco?*

2. *What are three good reasons not to use tobacco?*

3. *What are two things you can do to help yourself quit smoking?*

4. **Critical Thinking** *Why might it be harder for a person to quit if his or her friends and parents smoke?*

Highlights

Summary

- Tobacco smoke contains more than 4,000 chemicals; three of the most poisonous are tar, nicotine, and carbon monoxide.

- Nicotine, the psychoactive chemical in tobacco, leads to both psychological and physical dependence.

- Tar can damage the lining of the bronchial tubes, leaving a person vulnerable to several respiratory diseases.

- Carbon monoxide is a poisonous gas that interferes with the blood's ability to carry oxygen.

- Some diseases caused by smoking include cancer, chronic bronchitis, emphysema, and cardiovascular disease.

- Smoking pipes and cigars can lead to cancers of the lip, tongue, stomach, and larynx.

- Smokeless tobacco can cause cancers of the mouth, throat, tongue, cheek, and gum.

- Passive smokers are at an increased risk of suffering respiratory infections, lung cancer, and heart disease.

- Factors that may cause a person to start using tobacco include peer pressure and a parent's example. The same influences, however, can also help a person make the decision not to use tobacco.

- Once you decide to quit smoking, choose a plan and accept support from friends and family. Substituting other activities will help you cope with your day-to-day stresses.

Vocabulary

nicotine an addictive chemical found in tobacco.

tar solid material in tobacco smoke that condenses into a thick liquid.

carbon monoxide a poisonous gas released by burning tobacco.

chewing tobacco a form of smokeless tobacco that is placed between a person's cheek and gum.

mainstream smoke smoke that is inhaled directly into the mouth through a cigarette, pipe, or cigar.

sidestream smoke smoke that enters the environment from burning tobacco.

passive smoker a nonsmoker who is exposed to the sidestream smoke of a cigarette, cigar, or pipe.

Chapter Review

Concept Review . . . .

1. Which of the following causes the largest number of avoidable deaths in the U.S.?
  a. stress   c. cigarette smoking
  b. SIDS   d. drunken driving

2. Which of the following happens to most people the first few times they smoke?
  a. nausea   c. rapid pulse
  b. clammy skin d. all of these

3. Which is a harmful effect of tobacco use?
  a. respiratory disease
  b. heart disease
  c. cancer
  d. all of these

4. Emphysema is
  a. a deadly respiratory disease.
  b. a cardiovascular disease.
  c. nicotine poisoning.
  d. a form of cancer.

5. Which of the following statements is true about smoking?
  a. Passive smoking carries health risks.
  b. Smokeless tobacco is a safe form of tobacco.
  c. Pipe or cigar smokers are not at risk for developing cancer.
  d. all of these

6. Which of the following statements about tobacco users is NOT true?
  a. Even a light smoking habit can leave a person winded.
  b. Tobacco users often have low blood pressure.
  c. Tobacco users become physically dependent.
  d. Smokers want a cigarette most when under stress.

7. Which of the following may influence people to use tobacco?
  a. peers   c. advertising
  b. parents d. all of these

Expressing Your Views . . . .

1. Yesterday you caught your 13-year-old brother smoking a cigarette. What would you say to him to discourage him from smoking?

2. What would you do if you worked in an area where smoking was allowed? What are some ways to protect nonsmokers from environmental tobacco smoke?

3. You often see certain athletes using chewing tobacco. Why do you think they do this? Do you think the sight of them chewing tobacco will influence young people?

4. Do you think more or fewer regulations should be placed on the advertising of tobacco products? Explain.

Life Skills Check

1. Communicating Effectively

You are going on a long road trip with your aunt that the two of you have been planning for weeks. At the last minute she tells you that a friend of hers, who is a smoker, will be riding for at least half of the trip with the two of you. Cigarette smoke bothers you, especially when it's in a closed area like a car. What would you do?

2. Communicating Effectively

Your friend wants to quit smoking, but she says she's under tremendous stress at school, at her after-school job, and at home. She's afraid the anxiety will be overwhelming. What would you say to her?

Projects

1. Write to your local chapter of the American Lung Association, American Heart Association, or American Cancer Society for information on the effects of using tobacco and about ways to quit using it. Share this information with the class.

2. Find a magazine advertisement for tobacco and display it on one side of a poster board. Beside it, list the facts that the advertiser failed to mention about tobacco use. Display your poster in the classroom or around your school.

3. Research the current cost of a pack of cigarettes and figure out how much money a smoker would spend in a year if he or she smoked a pack a day. Then talk to smokers and ask them to list things they would buy, other than cigarettes, with this amount of money.

Plan for Action

Using tobacco is a very dangerous habit. Design a plan for becoming a nonsmoker or staying a nonsmoker.

CHAPTER

15

Other Drugs of Abuse

◆ ◆ ◆ ◆

The best strategy concerning drugs of abuse is to stay completely clear of them.

Max always looked forward to the weekends. Every Saturday night he would get together with the same four friends, and they would always find something fun to do. Sometimes they'd grab a hamburger and see a movie or go to someone's house and watch a ballgame. Then one night one of Max's friends wanted everyone to smoke marijuana. Max really didn't want to try it, but he did, and didn't like it. Now his friends are smoking pot more frequently and talking about getting some crack. This Saturday night they're supposed to get together and smoke it. This time Max knows he won't be joining his friends—but he doesn't know what to tell them.

Section
15.1

Drug Abuse and Addiction

• • • • •
Objectives

- *Name two important dangers of drug abuse.*

- *Name two ways in which drug abusers can damage society.*

- *Know how a person can become addicted to a drug.*
  LIFE SKILLS: Resisting Pressure

It turned out that Max's friend Troy felt the same way he did. Both of them had been concerned that their friends would think they were weird, and that they would end up being left out of the group.

You may feel uneasy about your decision to not use drugs. At first, a decision to stay away from friends who are abusing drugs can leave you feeling down. A longing for excitement, pleasure, and acceptance from friends can make it hard for teenagers to stay away from drugs. This is especially true when it comes to **psychoactive drugs** of abuse. A psychoactive drug is a drug that affects a person's mood and behavior. Making the decision to abuse them can be deadly.

psychoactive drug:

a drug that affects a person's mood and behavior.

(FIGURE 15-1) **Knowing how to resist peer pressure is an important skill to have—especially when it comes to drug abuse.**

To *use* a drug means to take a medicine exactly as directed. To *misuse* a drug is to take a medication improperly. To *abuse* a drug is to take a legal drug for a nonmedical reason, or an illegal drug for any reason at all.

addicted:
────────
the state of being physically dependent on a drug.

Max was glad that he had the self-esteem and the knowledge necessary to make the right choice. He also felt fortunate that he had Troy to talk to about his decision. It's important to have a high opinion of yourself in order to cope effectively with peer pressure. It's also important to know as much as you can about the risks you would face if you *didn't* make a good decision. Abusing drugs is highly dangerous for two reasons:

1. It can make a person lose control of the ability to make responsible decisions. Many who abuse drugs act irresponsibly, and sometimes violently.

2. It can cause a person to become **dependent**. A person who is dependent on a drug is controlled by a psychological or physical desire for it.

Drug Abuse

On Monday, Max and Troy found out that their friends had stolen a car after smoking crack on Saturday night. They had been caught by the police and were waiting to find out what would happen to them. Max and Troy think their friends would not have stolen the car if they hadn't been under the influence of crack.

People who abuse drugs place themselves, their families, and their society in danger. According to studies, more than 35 percent of all crimes in the United States are committed by people who are under the influence of illicit drugs. That number continues to grow, as drugs like crack have become widespread in many American cities and towns.

Drug abuse also plays a major role in many cases of child abuse and other instances of family violence. Finally, people who drive while under the influence of drugs are just as dangerous to society as those who drive drunk.

The Addiction Process

When a person is **addicted** to a drug, it means that his or her body has grown so used to the presence of the drug that it can't function without it. A lot of people think that drug addiction is something that could never happen to them. They believe that no matter how many times they take a certain drug, they will always have the power to stop when they want to. It's important to know that this isn't so. Addiction is a physical process. No matter how strong and invulnerable people may feel, the truth is that if they abuse addictive drugs, they will become physically dependent.

Just as you couldn't do without getting any sleep for a week, people who are addicted to drugs find it very difficult to function without the substance their bodies have come to demand.

Tolerance The body of a person who regularly uses or abuses a drug will eventually

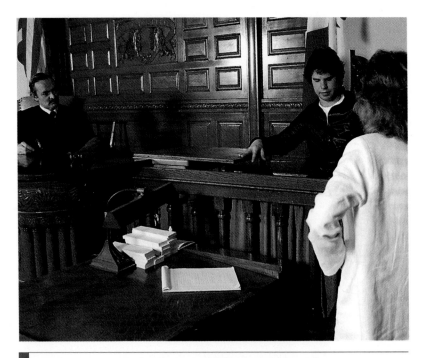

(FIGURE 15-2) **Drug abuse contributes to more than 35 percent of the crimes committed in the United States.**

form a resistance, or **tolerance**, to that substance. This means that higher and higher doses of the drug will be required in order to produce the same effects. If Max's friends were to abuse crack regularly, for example, they would soon discover the need to take more and more of the drug in order to get the same "high" they felt the first time they smoked it.

Crack cocaine is not the only type of drug whose use leads to tolerance. Many people who take prescription medications that relieve pain or anxiety also find that after a while they must increase the amount of drug they take in order to get the same relief that one or two pills used to give them. Tolerance is the first step in the addiction process.

Dependence Many psychoactive drugs will cause a person to become dependent. A drug dependency can be physical, psychological, or both. **Physical dependence**, or addiction, occurs when a person's body comes to expect the presence of a drug. If it doesn't receive the drug it expects, the body will go through a physical **withdrawal**. Common withdrawal symptoms include nausea, chills, depression, and sleeplessness. People who have developed a very high tolerance for a drug may suffer more serious and dangerous withdrawal symptoms, such as seizures. In general, the more addictive and powerful a drug is, the more serious its withdrawal symptoms will be.

A drug doesn't have to lead to tolerance and addiction in order to cause dependence. Many psychoactive drugs can lead to **psychological dependence**. People who are psychologically dependent on a drug are controlled by a constant craving for that substance. Some people with this type of dependency associate certain drugs with a feeling of happiness that they can't seem to find anywhere else.

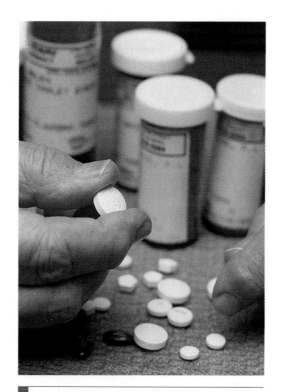

(FIGURE 15-3) **Illegal drugs are not the only substances that can cause addiction. Some prescription medications can lead to tolerance and psychological and physical dependence.**

REMINDER

Alcohol and nicotine are also addictive, psychoactive drugs of abuse.

physical dependence:

a condition in which the body becomes so used to the presence of a drug that it needs it in order to function.

Review

1. What are two important dangers of drug abuse?

2. What are two ways in which drug abusers can damage society?

3. What are two major steps of the addiction process?

4. ▓ **LIFE SKILLS: Resisting Pressure** How would you have told Max's friends that you didn't want to smoke crack?

5. *Critical Thinking* Explain how a person who abuses a drug that is not physically addictive can still become dependent on that drug.

withdrawal:

the body's reaction when it doesn't receive a drug it depends upon.

psychological dependence:

a constant desire to take a psychoactive drug.

15.2 The Effects of Drugs of Abuse

stimulant:

a drug that causes alertness and speeds up the activity of the body.

Objectives

- Know the effects of one category of psychoactive drugs.

- Name two dangers of crack cocaine.

- Know how to avoid inhalant fumes.

- Discuss what you would say to a friend who is thinking of taking anabolic steroids.
  LIFE SKILLS: Communicating Effectively

Psychoactive drugs of abuse fall into several categories according to the effects they have on the body. Of course, different drugs have different effects. A person who has taken cocaine will act very differently, for example, from a person who has taken marijuana. Still, it is important to know that every drug works by influencing a specific part of the body. This means that even if you have convinced yourself that a psychoactive drug you take will not affect you, it will. Once you have taken a psychoactive drug, you have limited control over the effects it has on you. For some information on the effects of specific psychoactive drugs, see Figure 15-9 on pages 308-309.

People who take drugs of abuse often lose control of themselves in certain situations and suffer impaired judgment. Things that require concentration, such as driving a car or making an important decision, can become difficult and often impossible when a person is under the influence of a psychoactive drug.

Stimulants

As you learned in Chapter 12, **stimulants** are drugs that cause alertness. Caffeine is the mildest of the stimulants, which is why it is legal to buy and to use. Other stimulants, such as cocaine and amphetamines, have much stronger effects and can be very dangerous.

Caffeine Caffeine is a naturally occurring stimulant. Aside from over-the-counter medications, caffeine can be found in some colas, in tea, and in coffee. A person who drinks a beverage containing caffeine will feel its effects within about 30 minutes. This is because caffeine is absorbed very quickly into the bloodstream through the gastrointestinal tract, and then travels to every part of the body, including the brain.

There is some evidence that caffeine stimulates the mind and body because it interferes with a chemical the brain produces called adenosine. Adenosine may normally influence certain effects in the brain that make a person weary and tired. Caffeine blocks adenosine from achieving these effects, which means that a person who has taken caffeine will be much more alert and much less tired than someone who has not. In high doses, caffeine can make a person irritable, nervous, and unable to sleep.

There is some evidence that caffeine can lead to tolerance and physical dependence. Regular coffee drinkers who give up their habit have been known to suffer such withdrawal symptoms as headache, irritability, drowsiness, and anxiety.

Cocaine and Crack Cocaine is a stimulant that is derived from the leaves of the

(FIGURE 15-4) **Caffeine is a major ingredient in coffee, tea, chocolate, and certain soft drinks.**

coca plant. Cocaine is a very addictive and dangerous drug. It is sniffed, injected, or smoked (free-base and crack cocaine). Sniffing or snorting cocaine means inhaling the drug through the nose. When sniffed, the chemical enters the bloodstream through the membranes of the nasal passages and travels directly to the brain. Smoking or injecting cocaine allows higher doses to reach the brain faster than sniffing it does.

Cocaine use produces a sense of euphoria because it interferes with the reabsorption of dopamine, the chemical messenger in the brain that is associated with pleasure. The feeling of pleasure lasts 5 to 10 minutes when the cocaine is smoked and about 20 minutes when it is sniffed. Cocaine-related deaths are usually a result of cardiac arrest or seizures followed by respiratory arrest.

One important thing to know about this sense of pleasure is that it is often followed by irritability, anxiety, and exhaustion. These feelings will actually last longer than the pleasurable emotions. Cocaine users find that in order to get the sense of pleasure back, they need to take the drug again.

There are many reasons why cocaine and crack are so dangerous. For one thing, they are extremely addictive. You read that a person who inhales cocaine wants to take more of the drug as soon as the effects wear off. This is true to an even greater extent for crack, since crack's effects are so strong and so immediate. Breaking an addiction to cocaine or crack is very difficult. A person going through cocaine withdrawal may experience an intense and constant craving for the drug and a severe loss of energy, as well as severe depression and anxiety.

In addition, crack and cocaine both cause severe psychological dependence. Many crack and cocaine abusers find that they are happy only when they are high. Ending a psychological dependence can be as difficult as breaking a physical one.

But even without their addictive qualities, crack and cocaine are highly dangerous

Facts on Crack

Crack is a form of cocaine that has been chemically altered so that it can be smoked. Because the process changes the cocaine into a chemical "base," crack belongs to a category of cocaine known as freebase.

Crack looks like small lumps or shavings of soap, but has the texture of porcelain. In some parts of the country crack is called "rock" or "readyrock."

The immediate effects of smoking crack are dilated pupils and a narrowing of blood vessels. Crack also causes increases in blood pressure, heart rate, breathing rate, and body temperature.

Crack can constrict the heart's blood vessels, making it work harder and faster to move blood through the body. In some people, this stress may trigger chest pain or heart attack, even for first-time users.

Crack can cause brain seizures, which are a disturbance of the brain's electrical signals. Some users have suffered strokes after using crack—the increase in blood pressure that the blood causes may rupture blood vessels.

Repeated use of crack without experiencing problems does not guarantee freedom from seizures in the future. The next dose—used in the same amount in the same way—can produce a fatal seizure.

Violent, erratic, or paranoid behavior can accompany the use of crack. Hallucinations are also common. Other psychological effects may include profound personality changes.

Crack is particularly alarming because it causes an intense stimulation of the reward center of the brain by allowing the brain chemical dopamine to remain active longer than normal. This causes changes in brain activity and triggers an intense craving for more of the drug, thus creating a powerful psychological dependence on the drug.

(FIGURE 15-5) **Smoking crack even once can be fatal.**

drugs. Cocaine constricts the body's blood vessels, making it harder for blood to circulate. This can put a strain on the heart, and it can even cause a heart attack. For this reason, trying crack or cocaine even once can be fatal.

Amphetamines In contrast to caffeine and cocaine, amphetamines—another type of stimulant—are not derived from natural substances. They are synthetic drugs, which means they are produced or manufactured in laboratories.

Amphetamine-type drugs are sometimes prescribed for neurological disorders and life-threatening obesity. Amphetamine use can result in tolerance, psychological dependence, and addiction. Withdrawal may cause depression.

Some amphetamines are illegally manufactured in secret labs. This process involves toxic and explosive chemicals that pose a health and safety threat to the surrounding community. Since there are no controls, the resulting drugs can have a wide range of concentrations and impurities.

One particularly dangerous form of amphetamine is called ice. Like crack, ice can be smoked. Remember that when a drug is smoked, it will reach the brain much more quickly than when it is taken orally or injected. Ice is very addictive. Its effects include dilated pupils, short attention span, and extreme talkativeness. Ice stays in the system for a very long time. Unlike those of crack, the effects of ice can be felt for several hours.

Hallucinogens

Hallucinogens such as LSD and PCP are very powerful psychoactive substances because they distort the senses. When the senses are affected in this way, it's not always easy to tell what's real from what is not. This is why people on hallucinogens often forget where they are and may have difficulty keeping track of time. In some cases, hallucinogens have caused people to believe they have special powers. Hallucinogens include LSD, PCP, a designer drug called ecstasy, and some naturally occurring chemicals, such as mescaline, psilocybin, and psilocin.

LSD Lysergic acid diethylamide, or LSD, is made from a type of fungus that grows on rye and other grains. LSD is usually sold in the form of tablets or small paper squares with images on them. The effects of LSD are not always easy to predict. Sometimes the drug will stimulate the body like cocaine. Other times it acts as a **depressant,** which is a drug that slows down body functions such as heart rate and blood pressure.

A person who has taken LSD will begin to feel its effects within about 30 to 90 minutes. The user may see and hear things that are not there. This type of effect is known as a **hallucination.** At the same time, he or she may be experiencing huge emotional swings. People on LSD may be laughing hysterically one moment and violent the next.

Some LSD experiences are extremely frightening. Users can become panicked, confused, and extremely anxious. Some people have become so upset and scared while on the drug that they have killed themselves.

Sometimes a person who has had a bad LSD experience will suddenly start feeling the drug's effects again, long after the experience is over. This is called a **flashback.** People can experience flashbacks without warning, sometimes months after they have taken their last dose of LSD. Flashbacks can be as frightening and dangerous as the bad experiences that prompted them.

PCP Also known as "angel dust," PCP is usually sprayed on tobacco or marijuana cigarettes and smoked. PCP has been known to cause severe mental disturbances that last from a few hours to a few weeks. People on PCP often act violently toward others or toward themselves.

Peyote and Mushrooms The peyote cactus contains the drug mescaline, and certain species of mushrooms contain psilocybin and psilocin. These drugs can cause vomiting and cramping following by hallucinations. Peyote cactus and mushrooms are traditionally used during religious ceremonies of native cultures in Mexico and the southwestern United States. However, concentrated extracts used by drug abusers can cause frightening experiences similar to those of LSD.

Designer Drugs

Some very powerful psychoactive drugs can be created by making slight changes in the chemistry of drugs that already exist. These are called **designer drugs.** One type of designer drug is MDMA, also called ecstasy.

Ecstasy is an illegal drug that is very close in its chemical makeup to amphetamines. Like amphetamines, it causes psychological and physical dependence. People who have used ecstasy say it makes them feel relaxed and happy. It can also cause confusion, depression, sleep problems, and severe anxiety. The physical effects of ecstasy include blurred vision, nausea, faintness, and chills and sweating. Ecstasy has been shown to cause brain damage in laboratory animals.

Marijuana and Hashish

Marijuana and hashish are organic drugs that come from the cannabis, or hemp, plant. It is not certain whether marijuana and hashish are physically addictive, but people have been known to become psychologically dependent on both drugs.

depressant:

a drug that slows body functioning.

hallucination:

imaginary sights and sounds, often induced by the use of a hallucinogen.

designer drugs:

synthetic drugs that are similar in chemistry to certain illegal drugs.

flashback:

an unexpected return to an unpleasant LSD experience, often months after the original experience ended.

hallucinogen:

a drug that distorts a person's senses.

Marijuana and hashish may cause the user to suffer a loss of coordination and have difficulty concentrating. For these reasons, driving a car is very dangerous for people who are high on marijuana or hashish. These drugs can also cause a person to feel anxious or paranoid. Marijuana contains toxins that can damage the lungs, the reproductive system, and the immune system. Marijuana plants grown today yield a much higher concentration of THC than those produced in the 1960s; therefore, the effects are more damaging.

Inhalants

inhalants:

chemicals that produce strong psychoactive effects when they are inhaled.

Inhalants are chemical vapors of solvents and gases that produce strong psychoactive effects. Inhalants include paint thinners, correction fluids, degreasers, glues, gasoline, medical anesthetic gases, aerosol propellants and associated solvents in spray paints and other aerosol products.

narcotic:

a drug with pain-relieving and psychoactive properties that is made from the opium poppy plant.

(FIGURE 15-6) **Many chemical products contain inhalant fumes.**

Inhalants enter the bloodstream and travel to the brain immediately after they are inhaled. A person abusing inhalants will experience an initial feeling of lightheadedness and giddiness. These effects are later replaced by dizziness, nausea, and headache. Repeated use can cause hearing loss, brain and nerve damage, bone marrow damage, and liver and kidney damage. Inhaling high concentrations of these deadly chemicals can cause suffocation and heart failure.

Many chemical products contain dangerous fumes. It's best to avoid these products completely, but if you have to use them, make sure you read the label and follow the instructions.

If you feel yourself getting lightheaded while using one of these products, go outside until the feeling goes away. Make sure that you close all containers after you have finished with them. Inhalants are very powerful drugs of abuse. You wouldn't want to leave yourself or anyone else exposed to their dangers.

Heroin and Other Narcotics

Narcotics, which are drugs that have been derived, or made, from the opium poppy plant, are something of a double-edged sword. Some narcotics serve useful medical purposes because they relieve pain so effectively. Morphine and codeine are two narcotic preparations used in hospitals for patients in severe pain.

On the other hand, narcotics are among the most physically addictive drugs of abuse. All narcotic medications should be taken only under the strict orders and observations of a doctor.

Not all narcotics have medical uses. One type of narcotic, heroin, is a very powerful, very addictive drug that is illegal to buy, sell, or use.

(FIGURE 15-7) **Heroin and other narcotics are all made from the opium poppy plant.**

Like all narcotics, heroin causes tolerance to the drug. People who are addicted to heroin have to keep increasing their doses in order to get the same effects. For this reason they run the constant risk of **overdose.** Large doses of heroin can severely depress the respiratory system. This can lead to a loss of consciousness, coma, or even death.

Heroin is most often bought and sold on the street, which means that it has some additional dangers. For one thing, drug dealers selling heroin often "cut," or mix, the drug with other substances. People who buy heroin never know if the drug they are taking is pure.

In addition, people who use heroin usually inject the drug into their veins. Heroin users who share dirty or contaminated needles run the risk of infecting themselves with hepatitis or AIDS. A growing number of needle-exchange programs are showing some success in reducing this risk.

overdose:

a serious, sometimes fatal, reaction to a large dose of a drug.

A person who has had an overdose needs medical attention immediately. What to do for a person who has had an overdose is discussed in Chapter 28 under **Poisoning.**

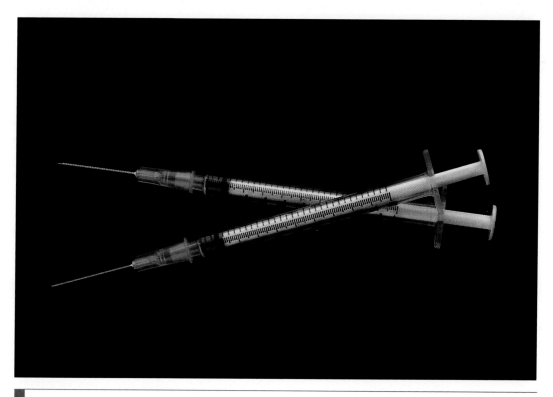

(FIGURE 15-8) **Intravenous drug users who share contaminated needles are at a high risk of contracting HIV.**

Characteristics of Some Drugs of Abuse

Drug	Health Hazards Associated With Abuse
Amphetamines and Methamphetamines	Drug dependence and addiction, elevated blood pressure, increased heart rate, sleep disturbance, fatigue, loss of appetite, stomach pains, abnormal heart rhythms, paranoia, picking at the skin, hallucinations, psychosis, mood swings
Barbiturates	Impaired judgment, loss of muscular control, respiratory depression, anxiety, insomnia, tremors delirium, convulsions, death
Benzodiazepines (minor tranquilizers)	Fatigue, drowsiness, headache, muscle weakness, depression, nausea, confusion, memory loss
Caffeine	Nervousness, irritability, elevated heart rate, sleep disturbance, insomnia
Cocaine, Crack	Brief feeling of euphoria, dysphoric crash, elevated heart rate, fatigue, depression, restlessness, irritability, anxiety, nasal damage, psychosis, death
Heroin	Short-lived euphoria, disorientation, drowsiness, slowed heart rate and breathing, decreased brain activity, depressed appetite, loss of muscle control, increased tolerance for pain, stupor, death
Inhalants	Hearing loss, limb spasms, central nervous sytem damage, bone marrow damage, live and kidney damage, blood oxygen depletion, unconsciousness, death
LSD	Distorted perception, hallucinations, inability to make sensible judgments, anxiety, depression, flashbacks, increased heart rate and blood pressure
Marijuana (THC)	Bronchitis, emphysema, asthma, cancer, increased heart rate, impaired motor skills, increased appetite, cravings, paranoia, reduced short-term memory
MDMA (ecstasy)	Confusion, depression, sleep disturbance, drug craving, anxiety, paranoia, muscle tension, nausea, blurred vision, faintness, chills, sweating, increased heart rate
Mescaline, Psilocybin, Psilocin	Effects are similar to those of LSD; hallucinations, nausea, psychosis
PCP	Numbness, slurred speech, loss of motor control, anxiety, hallucinations, amnesia, mood disorders, paranoia, violent hostility, schizophrenia, false sense of strength

(FIGURE 15-9) **The effects of a particular drug can vary depending on the drug's concentration, the dose, the method of use, and the physical makeup of the user.**

Common Street Names	Methods of Use	Medical Uses
Speed, uppers, crystal meth, crank, ice	Pills, capsules, sniffing	Treatment for narcolepsy and mild depression, treatment for attention deficit disorder in children
Downers, barbs, gangster pills	Pills, capsules, injection	Sedation, induce sleep, prevent seizures
Downers, bennies, V, lib, blue angels	Pills, capsules	Sedation, induce sleep, relieve anxiety, prevent seizures
Joe, java	Beverages, chocolate, pills	Vasoconstrictor, mild stimulant
Snow white, base, caine, coke, line, rock	Sniffing, smoking, injection, ingestion	Was used as a local anesthetic in eye, nose, and throat surgery in the 1880s
Horse, smack, beast, brown	Injection, sniffing, smoking	Was used to treat pain in the late 1800s and early 1900s
Whippets, toncho, buzz bomb, whiteout	Inhalation	Some types used for medical anesthesia
Acid, A, blow, cid, blotters, microdots	Placed on the tongue and absorbed	Has been used to study mental illness
Pot, yerba, bud, chiba, weed, gangster, herb, blunt	Smoking, ingestion, pills	Antinauseant for patients undergoing chemotherapy, appetite stimulant for people with AIDS
Rolling, running, XTC, X, X-ing	Ingestion, sniffing	None
Mesc, cactus, tops, nubs, mushrooms, shrooms	Ingestion	None
Dust, rocket fuel, purple rain, super weed	Ingestion, smoking, injection	Was used as a veterinary anesthetic in the 1960s and 1970s

Sedative-Hypnotics

sedative-hypnotics:

drugs that depress the body systems and cause sleepiness.

Sedative-hypnotics are drugs that depress the body systems and cause sleepiness. Some common names for sedative-hypnotics are tranquilizers, sleeping pills, and sedatives.

The two major kinds of sedative-hypnotics are barbiturates and benzodiazepines. Barbiturates are sometimes prescribed for the prevention of seizures. They are also very addictive, abused drugs that are illegally bought and sold. Secobarbital and pentobarbital (sold under the brand names Seconal and Nembutal) are two common types of barbiturates.

Benzodiazepines (which are sometimes called minor tranquilizers) are prescription medications prescribed to relieve minor anxiety and insomnia. Some common benzodiazepines are diazepam (sold under the brand name of Valium), chlordiazepoxide (Librium), and chlorazepate (Tranxene).

Benzodiazepines and barbiturates are especially dangerous when used with alcohol or other drugs. A user's judgment may be severely impaired, resulting in uncharacteristic and dangerous behaviors.

Q. Can sniffing cocaine kill a person?

A. There have been several instances in which a person has died from sniffing cocaine.

Q. Is marijuana as dangerous as alcohol?

A. Yes. Both alcohol and marijuana impair a person's judgment, lessen coordination, and diminish reflexes. A person who has had alcohol or marijuana should never try to drive. Both substances can also cause long-term damage to the body. Finally, both alcohol and marijuana are illegal substances for teenagers in the United States.

Drugs and Pregnancy

Many drugs a woman takes when she is pregnant pass into the bloodstream of her unborn child. For this reason, women who are pregnant should always check with their doctor before using any medications. This is particularly true during the first several

---

Drugs and Pregnancy Facts

Women who use marijuana when they are pregnant increase the risk that the baby will suffer low birth weight and delayed physiological development.

Women who use cocaine when they are pregnant are at increased risk of suffering hemorrhage (heavy bleeding), premature delivery, and miscarriage.

Heroin use during pregnancy increases the likelihood of stillbirth and infant death.

Babies born to women who are addicted to narcotics are often born with the same addiction.

(FIGURE 15-10) **Women who abuse drugs while they are pregnant endanger the lives and well-being of their unborn babies.**

weeks of pregnancy, when the fetus is especially sensitive to any chemicals that may cause damage.

What if a drug abuser were to get pregnant? Drugs of abuse can pose very serious dangers to the growth and development of an unborn child. Babies born to women who abused drugs when they were pregnant have suffered such damage as facial and body deformities, retardation in growth and learning, brain damage, slowed reflexes, and severe learning disabilities. In addition, there is evidence that babies born to women who are addicted to drugs such as heroin and crack are born with the same addictions as their mothers.

*Life*SKILLS: Communicating Effectively

Should She Use Steroids? . . . .

Jessie hits the swimming pool every morning at 6:00. By the time most people wake up, she has been swimming for an hour. She is captain of the girls' varsity swim team, and she swims the anchor leg on the freestyle and medley relay teams.

Jessie's goal is to swim for a big university team one day. To do this, she needs to win a college scholarship for her swimming accomplishments. Unfortunately, Jessie feels that practice alone will not get her a college scholarship. She insists that her strength and speed will not hold up against larger female competitors. That is why she is thinking about using steroids. She says she knows some swimmers who have used them and have become more competitive.

You know that Jessie is serious and that you have to talk her out of using steroids. What are some good arguments you can use to convince Jessie to stay away from steroids?

Effects of Steroid Use

Physical Changes	Rapid weight gain and muscle development Increased body hair Deepening of voice Acne Hair loss Breast enlargement (males) Elevated blood pressure Stomach upset Heart damage Liver damage Infertility and impotence Aching joints Enlarged prostate Swelling of extremities
Mental Changes	Increased aggression Hyperactivity and irritability Auditory hallucinations Paranoid delusions Manic episodes Depression and anxiety Panic disorders Suicidal thoughts

(FIGURE 15-11) **People who use steroids show certain physical and mental symptoms.**

Anabolic Steroids

One of the most widespread problems in both professional and amateur sports is the use of **anabolic steroids** among athletes. Made to resemble the male hormone testosterone, anabolic steroids were originally developed and used to treat people suffering from certain types of anemia, as well as certain bone and joint disorders.

Because they can help a person gain weight and develop muscles, anabolic ste-

anabolic steroid:

an artificially made, complex substance that can temporarily increase muscle size.

roids have become very popular drugs of abuse. Athletes have used them to help them run or swim faster, or to make them stronger. But the dangers of abusing anabolic steroids far outnumber what some people may think of as benefits.

For example, anabolic steroids can cause liver and heart damage, as well as very high blood pressure. Anabolic steroid abusers have been known to act aggressively and even violently. For more characteristics of anabolic steroid abuse, see Figure 15-11.

Athletes who use anabolic steroids may think they are at an advantage in competition. Anabolic steroids can be easily detected, however, and any athlete caught with anabolic steroids in his or her system is automatically disqualified from most competitions.

Review

1. Explain the effects of one category of psychoactive drugs.

2. Name two dangers of crack cocaine.

3. What is a good precaution to take if you have to use a product with inhalant fumes?

4. ▪▪ **LIFE SKILLS: Communicating Effectively** If your friend wanted to take anabolic steroids to get stronger, what would you say to him or her?

5. **Critical Thinking** Is it possible for a person using drugs for medical purposes to become addicted? Explain your answer.

15.3 Treatment for Dependency

Objectives

- *Name two things everyone should know about treatment for drug dependency.*

- *Know three options for recovering drug abusers.*

- *Know a healthy alternative to abusing drugs.*

Fighting a dependency to any drug is not easy. Most people who are addicted to drugs are psychologically dependent on them as well. The goal of all drug-treatment programs is to help a person battle not only the drug dependency itself but also the reasons why the drug abuse started in the first place. Fortunately, there are many options for people in this situation.

There are two things everyone who decides to seek treatment for a drug dependency should know. First, no one should try to overcome a drug dependency on his or her own. *Everyone* needs help when it comes to addiction or dependence. Another thing to realize about drug dependency is that there is no such thing as a *recovered* drug addict. Even if a person has not abused drugs for years, the chance that the person will relapse by abusing a drug again, and will become dependent again, is always there. Every recovering drug addict learns to take life without drugs one day at a time.

Methadone Maintenance Programs

People who are addicted to heroin have an especially difficult time overcoming their dependence. Their bodies have become so used to the presence of heroin that the withdrawal process can be very painful.

Some heroin addicts choose methadone maintenance to help them go through the withdrawal process. Like heroin, methadone is a narcotic. But its effects are not

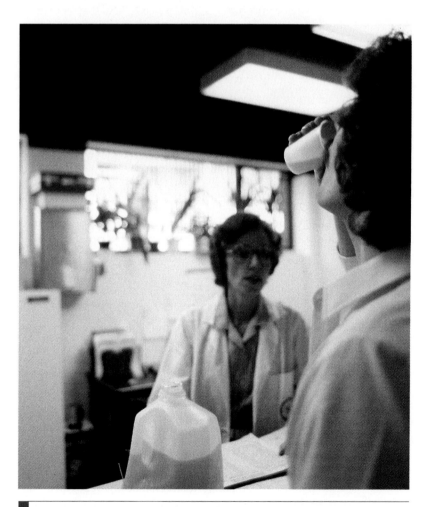

(FIGURE 15-12) **Methadone, a narcotic without the powerful effects of heroin, may help a person endure the painful process of heroin withdrawal.**

nearly as powerful or as appealing. People who go through methadone maintenance are able to provide their bodies with the narcotic they crave. The dosages of methadone are gradually decreased until the withdrawal process has been completed.

Withdrawing from a physical addiction is only the first step in the recovery process. The next hurdle all drug addicts must clear is the psychological dependency they have formed.

(FIGURE 15-13) **Group therapy sessions play an important role in all inpatient and outpatient drug-treatment programs.**

Inpatient and Outpatient Programs

Programs in hospitals and special treatment centers provide help for addicts going through withdrawal. Some recovering drug abusers need to live at the center while they receive treatment. Others will choose to stay at home and participate on an outpatient basis.

Although some programs provide methadone maintenance for recovering addicts, many treatment facilities help their patients go through withdrawal without the use of chemicals.

Inpatient and outpatient programs rely very heavily on education, one-on-one counseling, and group therapy to help recovering patients overcome their psychological dependencies. This is a very important part of the treatment process. In sessions, addicts talk to each other or to a counselor about the reasons why they started abusing drugs, and why they want to stop relying on them now.

Self-Help Programs

There are also programs available for drug abusers who want to quit without the help of professional counselors. Self-help programs like Narcotics Anonymous work in the same way as Alcoholics Anonymous. Participants follow a 12-step program and attend regular meetings, which are held at many times and locations. Members become part of a support system designed to help them change their lifestyle and overcome their addiction. Each person has a sponsor that he or she can call for support.

Options for Teenagers

Many teenagers who abuse drugs want to quit but aren't sure how to go about doing it. Most hospital and treatment-center programs have special divisions for teenagers with drug problems. Even so, some teenagers may find it intimidating to go to a stranger and admit that they have a problem with drugs.

For this reason, many schools now have student assistance programs available for students. Student assistance programs are set up to offer students information and sometimes to refer them to places that can help them overcome a drug dependency. Schools that don't provide student assistance programs usually have guidance counselors to perform the same functions. In addition, many towns and communities have state or local councils on drug abuse that can provide referral services for teenagers seeking treatment. State and local councils on drug abuse should be listed in your yellow pages.

A guidance counselor or student assistance program can also refer students to intervention counselors. If you know someone who is dependent on drugs and who isn't seeking the help he or she needs, you may want to think about using a formal group intervention strategy. Intervention means confronting a drug addict with his or her dependency and strongly encouraging him or her to seek treatment. If you decide that you want to use intervention, make sure you talk to an expert first.

If you have a drug abuse problem, there is nothing to be ashamed or embarrassed about. The important thing is to

(FIGURE 15-15) **School guidance counselors can help teenagers with drug dependencies get proper treatment.**

(FIGURE 15-14) **Sometimes having a friend to talk to can make hard times less painful.**

(FIGURE 15-16) **Life's too short to be wasted on drugs.**

world around them. Why not take a drug, they may think, if it makes things seem easier for a while?

If you have felt this way, you're not alone. But taking drugs is the *worst* thing you can do. Drugs do not help people cope with problems. Their desired effects don't last forever, and when they end, things are usually worse. People who abuse drugs or alcohol often act impulsively and even dangerously. A person who is drunk or high, for instance, is more likely to commit suicide than a person who isn't.

There are people you can talk to about the things that are troubling you. If you don't think you can confide in a parent or close friend, you may want to speak to a coach, a teacher, or a religious leader. If they can't help you, they may be able to refer you to someone who can. The important thing to remember is that life can get better. Drugs may seem like a solution, but in the long run they don't solve problems—they only add to them.

admit you do have a problem and get help. One thing you *shouldn't* try to do is recover by yourself. No one can overcome a drug dependency alone—everyone needs help. Talk to someone in the student assistance program at your school, or call one of the programs listed in the Yellow Pages under ''Drug Abuse and Addiction.'' Once you have admitted that you have a drug problem, you have taken a major step toward recovery.

Finally, if you have thought about abusing drugs, know that there are other options. Life can be very difficult. Many teenagers face struggles in their day-to-day lives—such as poverty, family problems, or depression—that can make it very hard to get through each day. Teenagers in these situations sometimes may feel a sense of hopelessness about themselves and the

Review

1. What are two things everyone should know about treatment for drug dependency?

2. Name three options for recovering drug abusers.

3. What's a healthier way to deal with problems than abusing drugs?

4. **Critical Thinking** Explain the reasoning behind the following statement: ''There is no such thing as a recovered drug abuser.''

Highlights

Summary

- One reason drug abuse is dangerous is that it can cause a person to act irresponsibly.

- Continued drug abuse can lead to psychological and physical dependence.

- Caffeine, cocaine and crack, and amphetamines are all examples of stimulants.

- Hallucinogens such as LSD and PCP are very dangerous psychoactive substances, because they distort the senses.

- Marijuana can impair a person's judgment and coordination.

- Many chemical products contain inhalant fumes that produce strong psychoactive effects when inhaled.

- Narcotics are highly addictive drugs. Some narcotics such as morphine and codeine have some medicinal value. The narcotic heroin, however, has no medical purpose and is illegal to buy, sell, and use.

- Steroid abuse can lead to very high blood pressure and can severely damage the heart and liver.

- No one should ever try to overcome a drug addiction alone.

- There is no such thing as a recovered drug abuser. Even if a person has not abused a drug in years, there is a chance that the person will abuse, and become dependent on, drugs again.

- Methadone maintenance programs, inpatient and outpatient programs, and self-help programs are three options for recovering drug abusers.

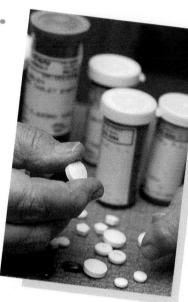

Vocabulary

psychoactive drug a drug that affects a person's mood and behavior.

stimulant a drug that causes alertness and speeds up the activity of the body.

hallucinogen a drug that distorts a person's senses.

narcotic a drug with pain-relieving and psychoactive properties that is made from the opium poppy plant.

sedative-hypnotics drugs that depress the body systems and cause sleepiness.

anabolic steroid an artificially made, complex substance that can temporarily increase muscle size.

Chapter Review

Concept Review

1. A psychoactive drug is a drug that affects a person's _____ and _____.

2. Addiction is a _____ process.

3. _____ is the first step in the addiction process.

4. _____ dependence occurs when a person's body comes to expect the presence of a drug. _____ dependence is a strong desire to repeat the use of a drug for emotional reasons.

5. When _____ is inhaled, it enters the bloodstream, then travels to the brain.

6. Statistics show that 35 percent of all crimes in the United States are committed by people who are under the influence of _____ _____.

7. _____ drugs such as amphetamines are drugs produced or manufactured in laboratories.

8. People on _____ drugs often forget where they are, may have difficulty keeping track of time, and may believe they have special powers.

9. A _____ is an unexpected return to an unpleasant LSD experience, often months after the original experience ended.

10. _____ and _____ are two organic drugs that come from the cannabis, or hemp, plant.

11. Morphine, codeine, and heroin are examples of _____ drugs.

12. Steroids can cause _____ and _____ damage as well as high blood pressure.

13. There is no such thing as a _____ drug addict because even if a person has been off of drugs for years, that person could become dependent again.

Expressing Your Views

1. Your friend Sharon, who has been taking a prescription medication for several weeks, confides to you that she is having to take increasingly greater amounts of the drug in order to get the same pain relief she once got with the recommended dosage. Why is this happening to her? What would you tell her?

2. Your friend Barry takes amphetamines whenever he has to study for a test. "They keep me going," he's told you. But he's been absent from school a lot, and whenever you see him he's moody and anxious. What could be wrong with Barry? How can you help him get the treatment he needs?

Life Skills Check . . . .

1. Communicating Effectively
Your younger brother is planning to attend a party. You found out that several of the people there will be using cocaine and crack. What advice should you give him?

2. Resisting Pressure
While on a camping trip, two of your friends try to persuade you to try PCP. They assure you that the drug's effects will be gone by the time you return home the next day. You feel uneasy about using drugs, but you are also worried about what your friends will think if you refuse—saying no isn't easy. What should you do? What are some good reasons to say no?

Projects . . . .

1. Work with a partner to create a poster that describes information about different types of drugs. The following information could be included: street names, how the drug is taken, the physical and mental effects of the drug, and any other descriptive information. Display your poster in the classroom.

2. Work with a small group. Imagine that all of you in the group are parents. What kind of policies would you set to discourage your children

from abusing drugs? What could you do to encourage your children to follow healthy practices?

3. Certain athletes and other well-known personalities have had highly publicized bouts with drug abuse. Research the experience of one such celebrity. Why do you think this person may have turned to drugs? What other options do you think he or she may have had? Present the results of your research to the class.

Plan for Action . . . .

Life isn't easy for anyone, but people who abuse drugs when times are hard make things even worse for themselves. What are two things a person can do to cope with problems in a healthy way?

Evaluating Media Messages

How Bad Can It Be If Athletes Do It?

Joel and Lucinda were walking home from school when Joel pulled out a pouch of chewing tobacco and put some in his mouth. Lucinda was horrified. "What are you doing with that stuff, Joel?" she cried.

"Oh, come on, Lucinda," Joel said. "It's not like I'm smoking cigarettes—I mean I'm not bothering anyone, and it's not going to give me cancer."

"You're wrong," Lucinda replied. "My uncle used to do it, and he got cancer of the mouth."

"So what?" Joel replied. "Your uncle's probably an old man who would've gotten cancer anyway."

"No, actually he was in his twenties when he got sick."

"Well, look at all the pro athletes who chew tobacco and dip snuff. Those guys are in great shape, so it must be okay."

"Joel, my uncle played college baseball. He was in great shape too," Lucinda informed him.

Joel is one of a growing number of boys who use smokeless tobacco (chewing tobacco and snuff). While smoking has declined among teenagers in the United States, the use of smokeless tobacco has risen. In fact, the number of 17- to 19-year-old males using smokeless tobacco increased by a multiple of 8 during the 1980s. Researchers believe this increase resulted from the skillful marketing efforts directed at teens by tobacco companies.

Advertisers target teenagers because they are aware that teenagers can be very easy to influence. For instance, it is well known that many teens experience low self-esteem and a sense of being powerless. So advertisers portray people in tobacco ads as just the opposite—mature, self-confident, and independent. Such images make using tobacco very attractive to people who are looking for ways to appear more mature, to feel more confident, or to assert their individuality. Teens can fight back, but they must carefully evaluate the media messages in tobacco ads to combat their effect.

When evaluating a media message, it is helpful to refer to a simple model of communication. The SMCR model below breaks communication into four parts.

1. The *Source* of the communication creates a message that can be verbal, non-verbal, visual, or musical.
2. The *Message* is what the source wants to say.
3. The *Channel* is the means by which the message is transmitted. In mass media this could be television, magazines, newspapers, radio, etc.
4. The *Receiver* interprets the message on the basis of his or her individual experiences and values.

Joel's comments to Lucinda indicate how he has been affected by media messages about smokeless tobacco. For example, one message that frequently appears in smokeless tobacco ads is that the product is good because it does not produce smoke, which bothers many people. Joel, the receiver, obviously agrees with the reasoning in this message; but Lucinda objects. "Sure, there's no smoke," she explains, "but when you use that stuff, you still do things that upset a lot of people—like spitting, drooling, and leaving smelly, wet tobacco in soft-drink cans." Joel may not have thought about how other people see these behaviors, because smokeless-tobacco ads don't mention them. Once he has considered Lucinda's remarks, he might evaluate messages about smokeless tobacco differently.

Joel's belief that chewing tobacco can't be very dangerous because athletes do it is an example of association, a very effective marketing tool. It is also an example of how powerful nonverbal communication can be. In using association, the source (an advertiser) makes a connection between something receivers like and the product the source wants to sell. If the channel is television or some other type of visual media, just the picture of a healthy athlete using smokeless tobacco can convey the false impression that the habit is not dangerous. Linking healthy athletes to unhealthy substances such as tobacco is actually a mixed message. When analyzed, mixed messages can be recognized as containing conflicting information.

Tobacco companies employ association not only by using athletes in their ads but also by giving free samples of smokeless tobacco to athletes—particularly major-league baseball players. The free

Media images make tobacco use attractive to people who want to feel more mature and confident.

samples are tremendously effective because millions of fans see their heroes using the products during televised games. To try to eliminate the association of athletes with smokeless tobacco, the National Cancer Institute and the National Institute for Dental Research have recently begun working with major-league baseball teams to help players quit using smokeless tobacco.

Critical Thinking

1. Find several tobacco or alcohol ads and analyze them using the SMCR Model.

2. Identify one product—tobacco, alcohol, antacid, cold medicine, pain reliever, diet pill—that you have bought or wanted to buy because of a media message. Evaluate the message by asking yourself the following questions:

   - Who is the source?
   - What is their message?
   - How will they benefit if I do as they wish?
   - How will I benefit if I do as they wish?
   - What are my values?
   - What is best for me?

3. What can you do to convince a friend who has started using smokeless tobacco to stop?

FIVE

FAMILY LIFE, SEXUALITY, AND SOCIAL HEALTH

Reproduction and the Early Years of Life

◆ ◆ ◆ ◆

A couple embrace their newborn baby.

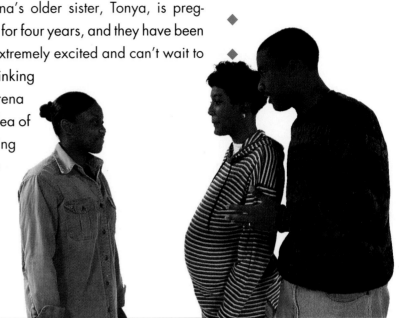

S abrena's older sister, Tonya, is pregnant. Tonya and her husband have been married for four years, and they have been looking forward to having a baby. Sabrena is extremely excited and can't wait to see her new niece or nephew. She has started thinking about what it would be like to have a baby. Sabrena isn't even sure she wants to have children. The idea of being responsible for a child's safety and well-being is pretty frightening. She's glad she doesn't have to make a decision about having children for a long time. Right now, she thinks, she will just enjoy her sister's baby.

Section 16.1 The Male Reproductive System

• • • • • O bjectives

- Name the major organs of the male reproductive system.

- Explain the two functions of the testes.

- Trace the path of the sperm from the testes to the outside of the body.

- Describe how the sperm meets the egg and fertilizes it.

- Describe how to do a testicular self-examination.

  LIFE SKILLS: Practicing Self-Care

Every person who has ever lived is the result of a process that began when a **sperm** cell from a male joined with an **egg** cell, or ovum, from a female. The male and female reproductive systems work together to bring the sperm and the egg together. This union of sperm and egg is called **fertilization.** Each sperm and each egg contains one-half of the instructions needed for the development of a new, unique human being.

The process of producing a new individual is called *reproduction*. In humans, the term reproduction means simply "having children."

One job of the male reproductive system is to produce sperm and transport them into the body of the female. Look at Figure 16-1, which shows the parts of the male reproductive system. The parts that you can see from the outside are the penis and the scrotum. The scrotum is the loose sac under the penis. Inside the scrotum are two testes, which produce the sperm. Connecting the testes and the penis are the two vas deferens, which are tubes through which the sperm travel. Along the way are glands that produce fluids that nourish and protect the sperm.

fertilization:

the union of a sperm and an egg.

sperm:

male reproductive cell; contains one-half of the instructions needed for the development of a new human being.

egg:

female reproductive cell, also called an ovum; contains one-half of the instructions needed for the development of a new human being.

testes:

male reproductive structures that make sperm and produce the male hormone testosterone.

The Testes

The **testes**, which are also called testicles, are two egg-shaped structures that hang inside the scrotum.

The testes have two functions. The first function of the testes is to make the sperm. The testes hang away from the body so that the temperature inside them is slightly cooler than the rest of the body. The temperature in the testes is very important to the sperm-making process. If the temperature is too high, the testes will make defective sperm that cannot fertilize an egg. The testes produce about 50,000 sperm every *minute*.

The second function of the testes is to produce the male sex hormone testosterone. Testosterone is necessary for the production of sperm and also for the development of male sex characteristics.

At puberty, the amount of testosterone in the male body increases, which causes boys' bodies to change. Coarse, curly hair called pubic hair begins to grow on the lower part of the abdomen around the penis. Similar coarse hair grows under the armpits. Teenage boys also begin to grow a beard on the lower part of the face. Some males begin to grow hair on the chest. The hormone testosterone is also responsible for the fact that males have bigger muscles, heavier bones, and deeper voices than women.

The Vas Deferens and the Urethra

The sperm must be able to travel to the outside of the body in order for reproduction to occur. Follow along the red line in Figure

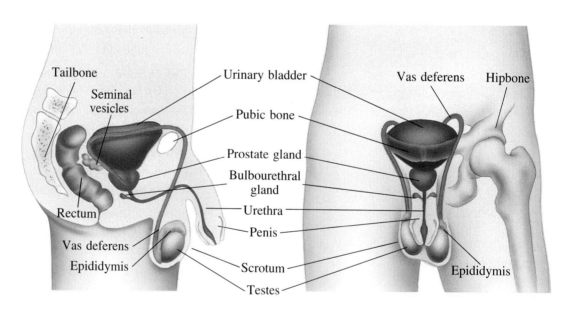

(FIGURE 16-1) **The function of the male reproductive system is to produce sperm that fertilize the egg of the female.**

16-2 to see the route the sperm take to leave the body.

After sperm are made in a testis, they travel to a structure called the epididymis, which is a tightly coiled mass of tubules located at the top of each testis. The sperm become fully mature while they are in the epididymis. After about two to ten days, the sperm leave the epididymis and travel through a tube called the vas deferens. Males have two of these tubes.

The vas deferens tubes lead to the urethra, which is the tube that runs through the center of the penis. The sperm leave the body through the urethra. The urethra is also the tube through which urine leaves the body during urination.

As the sperm travel through the vas deferens and the urethra, they pass by glands that add fluids to the sperm. These fluids nourish and protect the sperm, and enable the sperm to move on their own. The addition of these fluids to the sperm creates the fluid called semen.

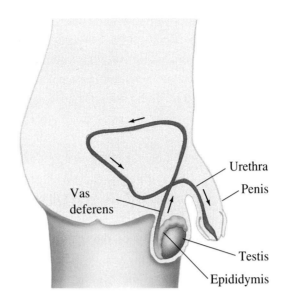

(FIGURE 16-2) **The red line shows the path of the sperm. Sperm originate in the testis, mature in the epididymis, travel through the vas deferens, and reach the outside of the body through the penis via the urethra.**

The Penis

The **penis** is the body part that makes it possible for the sperm to reach the inside of the female's body. When the male becomes sexually excited, the arteries leading to his penis open wider, allowing more blood to flow into the penis. At the same time, some of the veins in the penis close or narrow so that less blood flows out.

The accumulated blood causes the penis to become larger, longer, and firmer and to point upward instead of hanging downward. When the penis is in this state, the male is said to have an erection. An erection makes it possible for the penis to be inserted in the female's vagina.

Ejaculation The process by which semen leaves the male's body is called ejaculation.

During ejaculation, muscles around the urethra and the base of the penis contract. The contraction moves the sperm out of the body. When the male ejaculates, he is said to have an orgasm.

Ejaculation can occur even while a male is sleeping. Especially in teenagers, the levels of testosterone may rise and fall unpredictably. These hormone fluctuations can cause an erection followed by ejaculation during sleep. Ejaculation during sleep is called a nocturnal emission or a "wet dream." Nocturnal emissions are very common in adolescent and adult males.

Pathway to Fertilization

During sexual intercourse, the sperm are deposited inside the female's vagina, a few inches away from the egg. But from a sperm's point of view, this is a long and difficult journey.

penis:

male reproductive structure that deposits sperm inside the female body.

The sperm cell's structure enables it to make the trip. Each sperm has a tail that propels it forward. Also, sperm are streamlined and much smaller than most cells in the human body. Their streamlined shape and small size make it easier for them to swim quickly.

The semen in one ejaculation contains 40 million to 400 million sperm. Why are so many sperm released if only one will join with the egg?

First, the majority of the sperm will never make it to the egg. They will become trapped in mucus or die on the way to the egg.

Second, even though only one sperm can actually fuse with an egg, the presence of many sperm is necessary for this to happen. The egg is protected by a layer of many smaller cells. Sperm contain enzymes that break down this layer of cells. Only after *many* sperm have released their enzymes can *one* sperm make it to the inside of the egg. After one sperm has made it inside, a protective shield forms, which prevents others from fusing with the egg.

Circumcised or Uncircumcised?

Some males are circumcised, and some males are not. Circumcision is an operation in which a fold of skin called the foreskin is cut from around the tip of the penis in order to reduce irritation. Circumcision is usually done when a male is two to eight days old. Parents choose whether or not to have their male infants circumcised.

Figure 16-4 shows the difference between a male who has been circumcised and one who hasn't. Although they look different, circumcised and uncircumcised penises function in exactly the same way.

Males who have not been circumcised should pull the foreskin back when they wash. Cleaning under the foreskin prevents the buildup of a secretion that can cause irritation and odor.

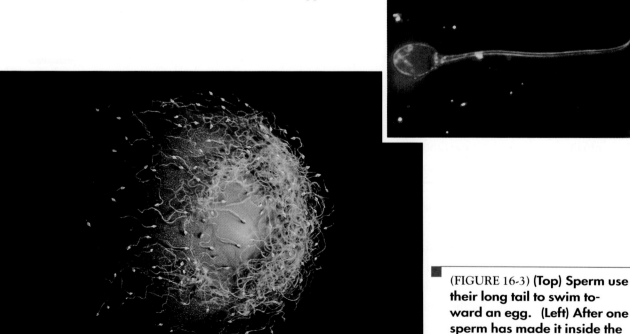

(FIGURE 16-3) **(Top) Sperm use their long tail to swim toward an egg. (Left) After one sperm has made it inside the egg, a protective shield prevents the other sperm from entering.**

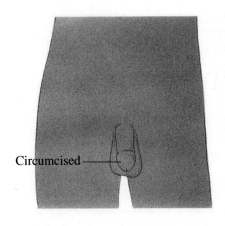 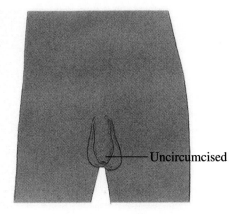

Circumcised — Uncircumcised

(FIGURE 16-4) **Parents decide whether to have their newborn boys circumcised. Although they look different, circumcised and uncircumcised penises function in the same way.**

Disorders of the Male Reproductive System

Even males who take good care of their reproductive system can have something go wrong. However, if a male knows as much as possible about male disorders, he will be prepared to seek the correct treatment.

Testicular Torsion Testicular torsion means "twisted testis." However, that's not exactly accurate. It is the spermatic cord, which suspends each testis in the scrotum and contains many blood vessels, that can become twisted during strenuous exercise or even during sleep. The condition is very rare, but it is an emergency situation, because testicular torsion can destroy the testes. Males who experience pain in the groin should seek treatment immediately.

Undescended Testes When some males are born, one or both of their testes remain inside the body rather than hanging loose in the scrotum. This condition is called undescended testes. If the testes do not descend into the scrotum by the age of two, medical treatment is necessary. Undescended testes are more likely than others to develop cancer. Because this condition interferes with the development of healthy sperm, infertility may result. Any male who thinks he may have this condition should seek medical treatment.

Inguinal Hernia Sometimes part of an intestine protrudes into the scrotum through a weakness in the abdominal wall. This condition is called an inguinal hernia. Inguinal hernias can be painful and usually require surgery to correct.

Infertility The condition of being unable to reproduce is called infertility. Both males and females can be infertile. Infertility in a male means that he has too few sperm or that his sperm are unable to fertilize an egg. Male infertility can be caused by a number of factors, including exposure to harmful drugs or X rays, the development of testicular mumps as an adult, or a genetic defect. Medical treatments are available for many kinds of male infertility.

Enlarged Prostate Gland As men get older, the prostate gland frequently gets larger and obstructs the outlet of the urinary bladder. The result is difficulty with urination. An enlarged prostate gland can be dangerous and uncomfortable.

Prostate Cancer Older men are also more likely to get cancer of the prostate gland, which requires surgical treatment. Prostate cancer is the most common cancer in American males, as well as the second most common cause of deaths due to cancer in American males.

How to Do a Testicular Self-Examination

1. The best time to do the examination is after a warm bath or shower, when the scrotum is relaxed.

2. Stand in front of a mirror and look for any swelling of the scrotum.

3. Check for any lumps, enlargements, tenderness, or changes in texture by rolling each testicle gently between your thumb and fingers.

4. If you notice any abnormalities, report them to your doctor. In order to detect abnormalities as soon as possible, self-examinations should be performed monthly.

(FIGURE 16-5) **If testicular cancer is treated early, there is an excellent chance of recovery.**

Testicular Cancer Testicular cancer is cancer of the testes. It is the most common form of cancer in males between the ages of 15 and 35. The good news about testicular cancer is that if it is detected and treated early, there is an excellent chance of recovery. To make sure that this kind of cancer is detected early, males should do a monthly examination of their testes. See Figure 16-5 for instructions on how to perform a testicular self-examination.

Care of the Male Reproductive System

Males need to follow only a few simple steps to take care of their reproductive organs.

1. Wash the penis and scrotum daily, and check for any sores or bumps.
2. Don't wear extremely tight clothing. Tight clothing over the external reproductive organs can cause pain.
3. Do the testicular self-examination described in Figure 16-5 once a month to detect lumps or other abnormalities.

Review

1. Which male structure makes sperm?

2. Where is the male hormone testosterone produced?

3. What two functions does the male urethra serve?

4. What characteristics of sperm make it possible for them to swim quickly?

5. **LIFE SKILLS: Practicing Self-Care** Briefly describe how to do a testicular self-examination.

6. *Critical Thinking* A vasectomy is an operation in which the vas deferens are cut and tied off. Explain why a vasectomy is a very effective method of preventing pregnancy.

16.2 The Female Reproductive System

Objectives

- Name the organs of the female reproductive system.

- Trace the path of the egg from the ovary to the uterus.

- Explain how the uterus changes during the menstrual cycle.

- Describe how to do a breast self-examination.

  LIFE SKILLS: Practicing Self-Care

The job of the female reproductive system is to produce an egg and to provide a place where the egg and the sperm can join. After the egg and sperm join, the fertilized egg begins its development into a new individual. The female reproductive system provides the new individual with shelter and nourishment for the nine months before birth. And after birth, a woman's breasts are able to provide nourishment in the form of milk. Because of this, breasts are part of the female reproductive system.

The parts of the female reproductive system, except for the breasts, are shown in Figure 16-6.

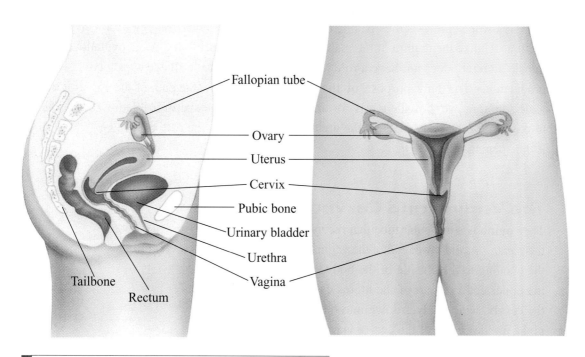

Fallopian tube

Ovary

Uterus

Cervix

Pubic bone

Urinary bladder

Urethra

Tailbone

Rectum

Vagina

(FIGURE 16-6) **The function of the female reproductive system is to produce an egg and provide a place for the egg to be fertilized and to develop.**

ovaries:

female reproductive structures that produce eggs and female sex hormones.

The Vulva

The parts of the female reproductive system that can be seen from the outside are collectively called the vulva.

The bone in the center of the lower part of the torso is called the pubic bone. Women have extra fat in front of the pubic bone that forms padding. The mound formed by the extra padding is called the mons pubis.

The other parts of the vulva are located between the upper part of the thighs. The two larger folds of skin are called the labia majora. At puberty, pubic hair begins to grow on the mons pubis and the labia majora. Inside the labia majora are two smaller folds of skin called the labia minora.

In between the two folds of the labia minora is the clitoris. Like the penis, the clitoris is the source of the greatest sexual excitement and has the capacity to become erect. It is covered by a hood of skin that is connected to the labia minora.

Below the clitoris is the opening of the urethra. Unlike the urethra of the male, the female's urethra does not have a role in reproduction. The only purpose of the female's urethra is to provide a way for urine to pass out of the body. Below the urethra is the opening of the vagina.

The Ovaries

Two **ovaries** are located in the lower part of the abdomen, one on each side of the uterus. Like the testes, the ovaries have two major functions. The first function of the ovaries is to produce the eggs. Ovaries usually produce only one mature egg at a time.

The second major function of the ovaries is to produce sex hormones. At puberty, these hormones cause a girl to develop breasts, wider hips, pubic and underarm hair, and a rounded body shape. After puberty and until a woman is in her 40's or 50's, these hormones control the monthly release of an egg and the menstrual cycle.

Before a female baby is born, her ovaries begin the development of several hundred thousand eggs. All of these eggs remain in the ovaries in a half-mature state until puberty. After the onset of puberty, hormones cause one of the eggs to complete the process of maturing about once a month. The release of an egg from an ovary is called **ovulation**. After ovulation, the egg is able to be fertilized by a sperm.

Follow the path of the egg as it travels to meet the sperm in Figure 16-7. The arrows show the path of the egg.

ovulation:

the release of an egg from an ovary.

vagina:

female reproductive structure that receives the sperm.

cervix:

the base of the uterus, which bulges down into the vagina; has a small opening through which sperm can enter the uterus.

The Vagina and Cervix

The **vagina** is a muscular tube that receives the sperm. At the lower end of the vagina is the opening to the outside of the body. At the upper end is a part of the uterus called the **cervix**, which bulges down into the vagina. In the center of the cervix is a small opening through which sperm can enter the uterus.

During birth, the baby must pass through the cervix and the vagina. For this reason, the vagina is sometimes called the birth canal.

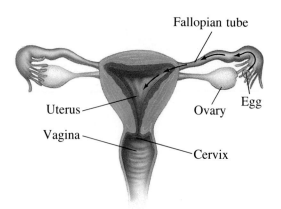

(FIGURE 16-7) **About once a month, an egg leaves a woman's ovary and travels through the fallopian tube to the uterus.**

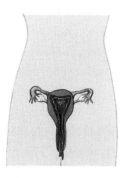

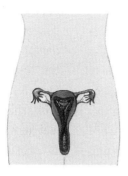

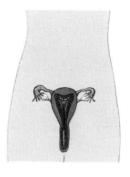

1. Days 1–5 Menstruation begins. Since the lining of the uterus is not going to host a fertilized egg, the uterus sheds the lining, which then flows from the woman's body.

2. Days 5–14 The uterine lining begins to thicken and continues to do so until ovulation occurs, which is around day 14.

3. Days 15–28 The thickened uterine lining awaits a fertilized egg. If the egg is not fertilized, the lining begins to break down.

(FIGURE 16-8) **This diagram shows what happens inside the uterus if the egg is not fertilized. During the menstrual cycle, the uterine lining gets thicker and thicker. If the egg is not fertilized, the uterus sheds the lining, which then flows from the body during the menstrual period. However, if the egg is fertilized, the lining will be maintained, and the uterus will expand to many times its usual size.**

The Fallopian Tubes

When an egg has matured, fluid sweeps it from the ovary into one of the fallopian tubes. It is through a fallopian tube that an egg travels from an ovary to the uterus. A fallopian tube is also the place where fertilization occurs.

If the egg meets the sperm while in the upper third of the fallopian tube, it can be fertilized. If the egg is not fertilized within 12 to 24 hours after it is released from the ovary, the egg begins to break down. Once it begins to break down, it can no longer be fertilized. Whether it has been fertilized or not, the egg continues to travel toward the uterus. It reaches the uterus four or five days after it was released from the ovary. If the egg has not been fertilized, it will dissolve in the uterus. If it has been fertilized, it will implant in the wall of the uterus, where it will grow into an embryo.

The Uterus

The **uterus** is a hollow, muscular organ about the size of a fist. It is sometimes called the womb. The main job of the uterus is to provide a place for the baby to grow before birth. During pregnancy, the uterus is able to expand to many times its usual size.

The Menstrual Cycle

The uterus undergoes cyclical changes (approximately on a monthly basis), which prepare it to receive and nourish a fertilized egg. These changes in the uterus are called the menstrual cycle.

During the menstrual cycle, the inner lining of the uterus thickens, and many tiny blood vessels grow into this thickened lining. The changes in the uterine lining are caused by the female sex hormones. Once these changes have occurred, one of two

uterus:

the hollow muscular organ that provides a place for the baby to grow before birth; also called the womb.

things happens, depending on whether the egg has been fertilized by a sperm.

If the egg *has* been fertilized, hormones are released that tell the uterus to maintain its thickened lining. The female is pregnant.

Most of the time, though, the egg has not been fertilized, and the woman is not pregnant. The thickened uterine lining breaks down, and the female menstruates.

Except during pregnancy, most women release an egg approximately every month from puberty until about age 50. Even if a woman has many children, only a small percentage of her eggs will be fertilized and will result in pregnancy.

Menstrual Fluid If the egg has not been fertilized and the female is not pregnant, the blood vessels of the lining close up and then break. The cells of the lining come loose from the inside of the uterus. Blood from the broken blood vessels helps to wash these cells out of the uterus. This mixture of blood and cells is called menstrual fluid. The amount of menstrual fluid varies from female to female. Some females have a light menstrual flow—only about a tablespoon of menstrual fluid each cycle. Others have a heavy flow—eight or more tablespoons each cycle.

The Menstrual Period The menstrual fluid passes through the opening of the cervix and through the vagina to the outside of the body. The time during which the menstrual fluid flows out of the body is called the menstrual period. Most females have menstrual periods that last from three to seven days.

After the menstrual period is completed, the uterus begins to prepare a new thickened lining. This lining will be ready for the next egg that is released from the ovary and travels down the fallopian tube to the uterus.

The average menstrual cycle lasts about 28 days. This is the time from the first day of a menstrual period until the first day of the next menstrual period. However, the length of the menstrual cycle varies. One female might have a 25-day cycle, while her best friend has a 35-day cycle. Yet another female might have a cycle that is a different length each month. This is called an irregular cycle. Irregular cycles are especially common during the first few years after a female begins to menstruate. In addition, a female who usually has a regular cycle may occasionally have a period earlier or later than usual.

The age at which a female has her first menstrual period also varies from individual to individual. Most females begin to menstruate between the ages of 12 and 14. However, it is not unusual for a female to have her first period as young as age 9 or 10. Other females do not have a period until they are 17 or 18. Beginning menstruation at 10 or 13 or 18, having a regular 28-day cycle or one that's shorter or longer—all of these individual differences are perfectly normal.

Disorders of the Female Reproductive System

Menstrual Cramps Menstrual cramps are a very common problem, especially for teenagers. These are the cramps felt in the lower abdominal area that are caused by the contracting of the uterus as it works to expel its lining. Those who have cramps usually have them the first day or two of their menstrual periods, but sometimes the cramps last longer.

Warm baths and exercise can sometimes relieve cramps. However, medication is usually required for severe cramps. There are a variety of nonprescription pain medicines that are effective in relieving cramps. If an over-the-counter formula is not helpful, a doctor should be consulted. He or she may prescribe medication that alleviates menstrual cramps. Cramps usually decrease in severity as a female gets older unless there is an additional medical problem.

PMS (Premenstrual Syndrome) Some females experience a combination of problems before their menstrual periods called PMS (premenstrual syndrome). PMS seems to be most common in females in their thirties. The physical symptoms include swelling and tenderness of the breasts, a bloated feeling, constipation, headaches, and fatigue. The emotional signs of PMS are depression, crying, anxiety, and anger. A female with PMS may have all of these signs and symptoms, or she may have only a few. PMS usually occurs for one to three days before menstruation, but some females may have PMS for two weeks before each menstrual period.

Researchers do not yet know why some females have PMS and others do not. Nor do they know exactly what causes PMS, although hormonal fluctuations may be responsible.

Some women with PMS find that their symptoms are reduced if they restrict their intake of salt and sugar and completely avoid caffeine (in coffee, teas, colas, and chocolate) and nicotine (in tobacco). Regular physical exercise and relaxation exercises, such as those described in Chapter 9, are also reported to help some women. If a woman feels she has symptoms of PMS, she should seek medical treatment.

Vaginitis An infection in the vagina is called vaginitis. Most women will have vaginitis sometime during their lives. The signs and symptoms include itching or soreness of the vulva, an unpleasant odor, an increase in discharge from the vagina, and

(FIGURE 16-9) **Getting plenty of exercise can help alleviate the pain and tension that sometimes accompany a woman's menstrual period.**

sometimes a burning sensation during urination. Vaginitis can be caused by a fungus, bacteria, or protozoa, and each kind of vaginitis requires a different kind of treatment. Douching for vaginitis is not recommended, because it may aggravate the infection. If a female has any of the symptoms of vaginitis, she should seek medical treatment to get the correct medication.

It is important to know that *most* fluids from the vagina are perfectly normal. If the fluid is clear or whitish and nonirritating, it is probably normal. Many factors besides an infection can create vaginal fluids—sexual excitement and hormonal changes are two examples. All women have these kinds of secretions. It is only when the fluid is irritating, has an offensive odor, or changes color that a woman should become concerned about infection.

Toxic Shock Syndrome Toxic shock syndrome, a rare but dangerous bacterial infection, is associated with the use of highly absorbent tampons. Tampons should be changed frequently (at least every 4–6 hours) to help prevent this infection.

The signs and symptoms of toxic shock syndrome are a high fever, nausea, diarrhea, dizziness, and a sunburn-like rash. The rash is often on the palms of the hands and the bottoms of the feet. A woman who has these signs and symptoms should remove the tampon and go to a hospital emergency room immediately because toxic shock syndrome can cause death.

Ovarian Cysts An ovarian cyst is a growth on the ovary. A woman with an ovarian cyst may experience pain or may have no signs or symptoms at all. Large cysts must be treated medically, but small cysts sometimes disappear without any treatment.

Cancers Cancer can occur in any part of the female reproductive system. The more sexual partners a female has, the greater her risk of developing cervical cancer is. Doctors recommend that all sexually active females, regardless of age, have a yearly pelvic examination to detect cancers early. The earlier the cancer is caught, the more successful the treatment will be. During the examination, the doctor will do what is called a **Pap test**, in which cells from the cervix are removed and tested for cancer. This test saves many lives every year.

Women should also get in the habit of checking their breasts for lumps and other abnormalities each month. Figure 16-10 describes how to do a breast self-examination. Most lumps are found this way and are not cancerous, but any lump should be checked out by a doctor to make sure.

Doctors recommend regular mammograms (an X ray of the breast) beginning when a woman is about 35 years old. If cancer of the breast is detected and treated early, there is an excellent chance of recovery. For this reason, regular breast self-examinations can be lifesaving.

Infertility Females, like males, can be infertile, or unable to have children. The most common cause of female infertility is failure to ovulate—to release an egg. Often, women who are underweight because of an eating disorder or excessive exercise do not ovulate. Another common cause of infertility is scar tissue in the fallopian tubes, which prevents the sperm from reaching the egg. The scar tissue may have been the result of an infection or previous surgery. Sexually transmitted diseases may result in infertility, as can endometriosis, a condition in which tissue from the endometrial lining of the uterus grows somewhere else in the abdomen. Many causes of infertility can be treated medically.

Care of the Female Reproductive System

The female reproductive system may seem more complicated than the male system, but it actually doesn't require much more care. Females should take the following simple steps to keep everything working smoothly:

1. Wash the external reproductive organs daily with a mild, nonirritating soap. Feel for any unusual bumps or sores.
2. Don't use ''feminine hygiene'' sprays. They can cause irritation. If daily washing doesn't keep you clean, you should seek the advice of a health care provider. An unpleasant odor may be a sign of an infection. Remember, though, that for vaginal secretions to have a scent is perfectly normal. As a female gets older, she gets better at telling the difference between the usual healthy scent and an odor that means infection.

Pap test:

a medical procedure in which cells from the cervix are removed and tested for cancer.

Sexually transmitted diseases (STDs) can cause infertility. The relationship between STDs and infertility is discussed in Chapter 22.

3. Don't use douches unless they are medicinal douches recommended for you by your doctor. Like sprays, douches are usually unnecessary, and they can cause irritation.

4. During menstruation, change sanitary pads or tampons often—at least every 4–6 hours. In addition, do not use deodorant tampons, or tampons with greater absorbancy than you need.

How to Do a Breast Self-Examination

Do a breast self-exam once a month. Two or three days after your menstrual period ends is the best time because the breasts are less likely to be tender or swollen.

1. Stand in front of a mirror and look carefully at your breasts. Look for anything unusual, such as a discharge from the nipples or a puckering, dimpling, or scaling of the skin.

2. Clasp your hands behind your head and press your hands forward. Do you notice any change in the shape of your breasts since the last time you did a breast self-exam?

3. Press your hands firmly on your hips and bow slightly forward. Pull your shoulders and elbows forward. Do you notice any change in the shape of your breasts since the last time you did a breast self-exam?

4. Raise your left arm. Use your fingers to examine your left breast. Beginning at the outer edge of your breast, press the flat part of your fingers in small circles, moving the circles slowly around the breast. Make sure to include the area between the breast and the armpit, as well as the armpit itself. Do you feel any unusual lumps under the skin? Repeat the step on your right breast with your right arm raised.

5. Gently squeeze each nipple, and look for any discharge.

6. Lie down and put a pillow or folded towel under your left shoulder. Raise your left arm. Examine your left breast the same way you did in Step 4. Repeat with your right breast.

(FIGURE 16-10) **Breast self-examination should be done once a month to become familiar with the usual appearance and feel of your breasts. Most lumps are not cancerous, but any lump should be checked out by a doctor to make sure.**

Highly absorbent tampons increase the risk of toxic shock syndrome, a rare but deadly disease. Deodorant tampons may cause irritation or infection.

5. Visit a health care provider once a year to make sure that your reproductive system is healthy. A gynecologist is a physician who specializes in caring for the female reproductive system. Young women should start getting yearly gynecological exams at the age of 18, or earlier if they are sexually active.

6. Perform a monthly breast self-examination to find lumps or other abnormalities. (See Figure 16-10.) The best time to do a self-examination is a few days after a menstrual period, when the breasts are less likely to be tender.

Q: I am almost 14 years old, and I still haven't started having menstrual periods. Could there be something wrong with me?

A: It is not abnormal for a girl to be 14 or 15 years old before she begins to menstruate. A girl who has reached the age of 16 and has not menstruated should probably see a doctor to make sure she doesn't have a medical problem.

Q: Someone told me that a woman can't get pregnant the first time she has sexual intercourse. Is this true?

A: No. A woman is just as likely to get pregnant the first time as she is at any other time.

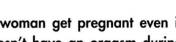

Q: Can a woman get pregnant even if she doesn't have an orgasm during sexual intercourse?

A: Yes. Pregnancy can occur regardless of whether a woman has an orgasm.

Q: Can a woman get pregnant if her partner ejaculates outside her body?

A: Yes. Sometimes fluid containing sperm is released before ejaculation. And when a man ejaculates when his penis is outside the vagina, there is still a chance that sperm can enter the vaginal passage and fertilize the egg, causing pregnancy.

Review

1. Which female structure produces the eggs?

2. In which structure do the egg and the sperm join?

3. What happens to the thickened uterine lining if fertilization does not occur?

4. **LIFE SKILLS: Practicing Self-Care** Briefly describe how to do a breast self-examination.

5. *Critical Thinking* A tubal ligation is an operation in which the fallopian tubes are cut and tied off. Explain why tubal ligation is a very effective method of preventing pregnancy.

Objectives

• List the substances that can pass from the mother to the placenta.

• Describe the events that occur during birth.

• Use self-talk about childhood experiences to increase your self-esteem.

■■ **LIFE SKILLS: Building Self-Esteem**

For most parents, the birth of a child is both exciting and scary. Raising a child can bring parents a great deal of happiness and a sense that they are doing something truly worthwhile. When parents see a bit of themselves in the shape of their child's nose or in their child's way of laughing, they know that a part of themselves will live on after they are gone.

But having a child is also a tremendous responsibility. Parenthood means sacrifices and sleepless nights, losing freedom and gaining worries. The decision of whether to have children is important and shouldn't be taken lightly. This decision will be discussed in Chapter 18. In the rest of this chapter, you'll learn what happens after the sperm and the egg join.

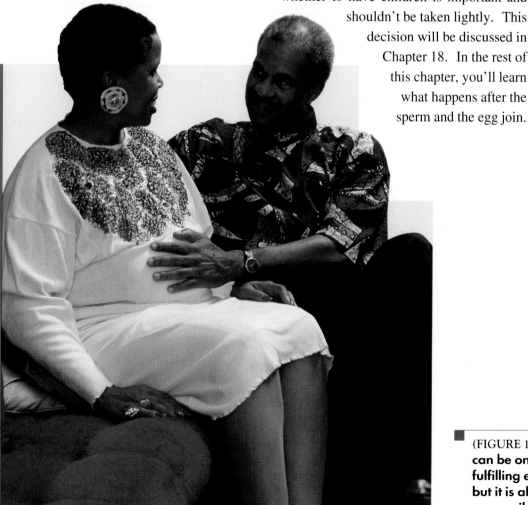

■ (FIGURE 16-11) **Parenthood can be one of the most fulfilling experiences in life, but it is also a tremendous responsibility.**

embryo:

a fertilized egg after it has attached itself to the wall of the uterus.

Implantation

Before fertilization, the sperm and the egg are two separate cells, which each contain *one-half* of the information needed for the development of a new person. After fertilization, there is only one cell, and it contains *all* of the information needed for the development of a new person.

After ejaculation, it usually takes the sperm between 15 minutes and an hour to reach the fallopian tube and fertilize the egg. The fertilized egg then travels toward the uterus. Figure 16-12 shows the path of the egg.

About 30 hours after fertilization, the egg divides into two cells. The two cells then divide into four cells, the four cells into eight cells, and so on. About four days after fertilization, the fertilized egg finally reaches the uterus.

As the fertilized egg comes to rest on the soft, thick lining of the uterus, it begins to burrow into the lining. It is now called an **embryo**. By the 10th day after fertilization, the embryo contains thousands of cells and is completely buried in the uterine wall. This process is called implantation.

From Mother to Baby

As the embryo implants itself in the wall of the uterus, it begins to use up all of the nutrients that were stored in the egg before fertilization. If the embryo is to survive, it must have a way to obtain everything it needs as it grows from the mother. The placenta is the structure that allows the embryo to get what it needs from the mother. The placenta is a disc-shaped organ that is attached to the inner wall of the uterus. It is connected to the embryo by a structure called the umbilical cord.

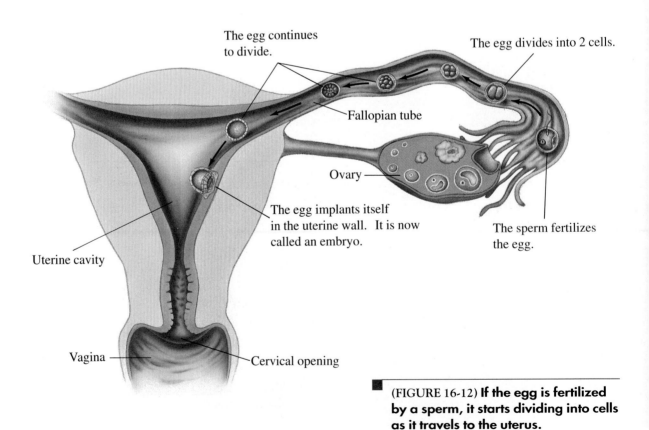

The egg continues to divide.

The egg divides into 2 cells.

Fallopian tube

Ovary

The egg implants itself in the uterine wall. It is now called an embryo.

The sperm fertilizes the egg.

Uterine cavity

Vagina

Cervical opening

(FIGURE 16-12) **If the egg is fertilized by a sperm, it starts dividing into cells as it travels to the uterus.**

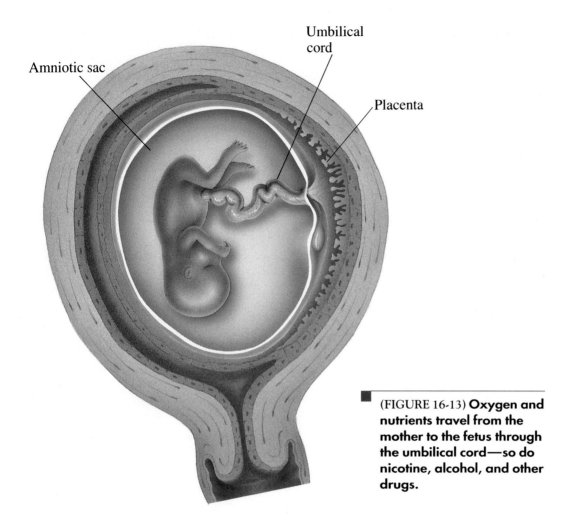

Amniotic sac

Umbilical cord

Placenta

(FIGURE 16-13) **Oxygen and nutrients travel from the mother to the fetus through the umbilical cord—so do nicotine, alcohol, and other drugs.**

The mother's blood does not flow into the baby. Instead, pools of blood are formed in the placenta that bathe the outside of the embryo's blood vessels.

Oxygen, antibodies, and nutrients from the mother's blood diffuse through the walls of the embryo's blood vessels in the placenta. These things then travel through the blood vessels in the umbilical cord to the baby.

Viruses and drugs can also pass from the mother's blood to the baby's blood. Some viruses and drugs can cause the baby to develop abnormally. For this reason, pregnant women should take good care of their health and avoid exposure to diseases. In addition, a pregnant woman should never take any drug without checking with her doctor first. This includes alcohol, nico-tine, and nonprescription drugs, such as as-pirin and cold remedies.

Changes During Pregnancy

Once implanted in the uterus, the embryo grows rapidly. A heart and brain begin to form. Eyes appear and the face takes shape. Small buds on the sides of the body become arms and legs. Internal organs like the lungs, stomach, and liver are developing. The embryo floats in a warm, fluid-filled pouch called the amniotic sac.

Eight weeks after fertilization occurs, the embryo is only 30 mm long (a little over 1 inch). However, all the major organ sys-tems of its body are formed and growing. From the ninth week until birth, it is called a **fetus**.

fetus:

a developing indi-vidual from the ninth week of preg-nancy until birth.

(FIGURE 16-14)

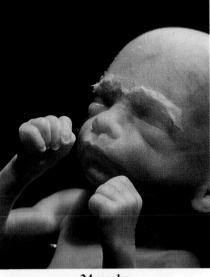

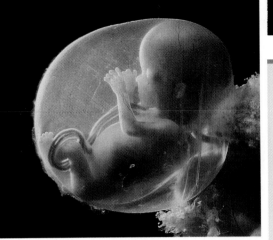

18 weeks

24 weeks

Development Inside the Uterus

By the End of 12 Weeks
- Brain enlarging
- Arms and legs forming
- Bones forming
- Heart and blood system fully functioning
- Digestive system forming
- About 4 inches long

By the End of 16 Weeks
- Mother can feel fetal movements
- About 5 inches long

By the End of 18 Weeks
- Skin begins to grow
- Hair can be detected on upper lip and on eyebrows
- About 6 inches long

By the End of 24 Weeks
- Mouth can open, close, and swallow
- Eyes can open and close
- About 9 inches long

Full Term
- Features, organs fully formed
- 18–22 inches long

16 weeks

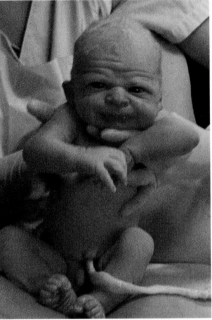

12 weeks

full term

Pregnancy Tests

When a female misses a menstrual period, it is a sign that she *might* be pregnant. However, a number of other factors, like stress and illness, might also explain a missed period. A missed period is not a very reliable indicator of pregnancy.

An accurate pregnancy test detects a hormone called HCG (human chorionic gonadotropin). Three weeks after fertilization, a pregnant female will probably have enough HCG in her blood and urine for a positive test result. Doctors and health clinics can administer these tests.

Pregnancy "test kits" can be obtained at drug stores. These kits also test for the presence of HCG. However, they must be administered correctly to be accurate. If a negative result is obtained, the test should be done again. If the result is positive, the woman should visit a doctor or clinic to do another test to confirm the result.

Childbirth

The stages of the birth of a baby are shown in Figure 16-15. By the time the baby is ready to be born, it has usually moved so that its head is down against the cervix. The cervix is a ring of very strong muscles at the lower part of the uterus. These muscles are able to hold a developing fetus and surrounding fluids inside the uterus without relaxing until the baby is ready to be born.

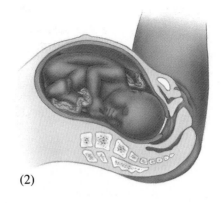

(2)

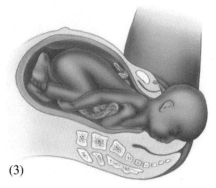

(3)

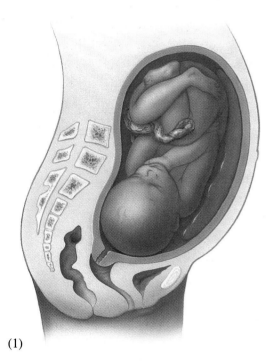

(1)

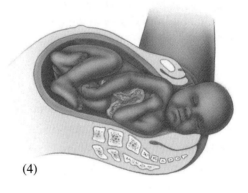

(4)

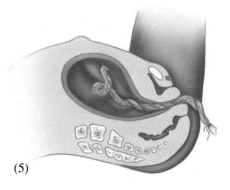

(5)

(FIGURE 16-15)

The birth of a child These drawings show various stages of childbirth. (1) A month or two before birth, the fetus drops to a lower position. (2) In the first stage of delivery (dilation), strong uterine contractions cause the cervix to dilate. (3) By the end of this stage, the cervix has completely dilated, the membranes surrounding the baby have ruptured, and the head has begun to extend into the birth canal. (4) During the second stage (expulsion), the head emerges fully and the shoulders rotate. (5) By the third stage (placental), the baby has been born. The uterus expels the placenta and the umbilical cord.

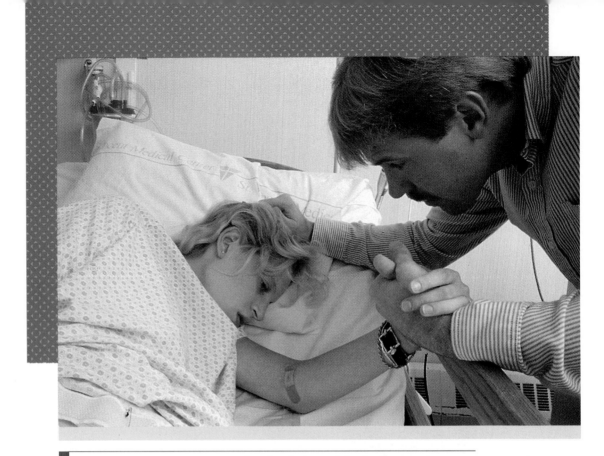

(FIGURE 16-16) **It is common for the father of the baby to take part in childbirth by providing comfort and encouragement to the woman in labor.**

Birth defects are discussed in Chapter 24.

Near the end of the pregnancy, muscles in the walls of the uterus begin to contract. Weak, irregular contractions may occur for several weeks before birth. When it is time for the baby to be born, the contractions become much stronger and last longer. They also start to come at regular intervals, closer and closer together. The final stage of pregnancy, when contractions are strong enough to push the baby out of the mother's body, is called labor. Labor usually takes between five and twenty hours.

Contractions press the baby's head against the cervix. They force the cervix to open wide enough for the baby to pass through. The baby then passes through the vagina and out into the world. Within a few seconds the baby takes its first breath. The baby no longer needs the placenta, so the umbilical cord is cut.

The placenta then separates from the wall of the uterus. Soon after the baby is born, the placenta and umbilical cord are pushed out of the uterus. The process of childbirth is then complete.

More and more hospitals are allowing fathers, friends of the mother, and even brothers and sisters of the newborn to be present at the birth. And some women choose to deliver their children at home with the help of a midwife—a person trained in childbirth—or a doctor. Some women receive pain-relieving medication during labor and delivery. In addition, many women take childbirth classes that help them and their birthing partner prepare for the process ahead.

Though most pregnancies and births go smoothly and normally, complications sometimes occur. Figure 16-17 on page 345 describes some complications of pregnancy and birth.

Complications of Pregnancy and Birth

Complication	Description
Ectopic pregnancy	The pregnancy tissue or embryo becomes implanted in the fallopian tube or somewhere else in the abdomen besides the uterus. The embryo may die and frequently must be removed by surgery.
Miscarriage (spontaneous abortion)	The pregnancy tissue or embryo is expelled from the uterus before it is sufficiently developed. Miscarriages may be caused by a genetic defect, illness in the mother, drugs the mother has taken, or other factors. Miscarriages usually occur during the first three months of pregnancy.
Toxemia	The pregnant woman has high blood pressure, swelling, and protein in the urine. Untreated toxemia can result in convulsions, coma, and the death of both mother and infant. It is most common among teenagers, older women, and women who already have health problems.
Rh incompatibility	A woman's blood produces an antibody that attacks a substance in the infant's blood cells. This may occur if the woman is Rh negative and the infant is Rh positive. The problem can be avoided by injections that prevent a woman's blood from making the Rh antibody.
Premature birth	A baby is born before it is fully developed. A baby is considered to be premature if it is born before the 37th week of pregnancy. Premature babies are placed in a newborn intensive-care unit, where the baby is protected while it continues to develop.
Cesarean section	If delivery through the birth canal is considered to be risky for any reason, an operation called a Cesarean section is performed. An incision is made through the abdomen and uterus, and the baby is taken from the mother's body.
Multiple births	Two or more infants are born together. Two infants are called twins, three are called triplets, and four are called quadruplets. The birth of five infants—quintuplets—is extremely rare.
Stillbirth	An infant that is born dead 22 weeks or more after conception.

(FIGURE 16-17) **Most pregnancies and births go smoothly and normally, but complications sometimes occur.**

(FIGURE 16-18) **Babies who are born before they are fully developed are called premature babies. This premature infant weighed only 1 pound, 14 ounces at birth. Even babies this small respond to a parent's care.**

Infancy Through Childhood

Imagine what it was like living in the womb. You didn't have to eat or breathe, and you didn't have to adjust to different temperatures and different environments. Suddenly, all of that changed. After you were born, food had to be taken into the mouth, and air into the lungs. And you had to let it be known that you needed something (for example, you were cold and needed to be covered with a blanket).

After you were born, you continued to grow and develop. You grew taller and stronger throughout infancy and childhood, and you are probably *still* growing. In addition, you developed in other ways. About a month after you were born, you started to smile when you saw a human face. By six months, you could recognize the familiar people who cared for you, and you probably cried when a stranger tried to hold you. A few months later, you could sit up by yourself and play with simple toys.

(FIGURE 16-19) **You started to smile when you were about one month old.**

_Life_SKILLS:

Using Self-Talk About Childhood Experiences . . . .

Your childhood experiences were probably the most important influences on your self-esteem. Some of the experiences made you feel great about yourself. Others, unfortunately, were painful and made you feel terrible. The following activity will help you understand _why_ you feel the way you do about yourself, and it may help you increase your self-esteem.

1. Make a list of five childhood experiences that made you feel good about yourself.

2. Say positive things to yourself about each experience. If one of your positive experiences was winning an award for a piece of art you made, you could say, "I'm proud that I can draw so well."

3. For the following examples, try to think of something you could say to yourself that might help counteract negative feelings you would have if you were in that situation. For example, if it took Nick longer to read than it takes most kids, he could say to

himself, "Well, at least I learned to read, which is something that a lot of people never learn to do."

a. Felicia's parents got divorced last year, and now she spends the summers with her dad and the school year with her mom.

b. When Rudy was 10 years old, his parents had another child.

c. Kids at school made fun of Laura because she was the tallest kid in her class.

This kind of talking to yourself is called self-talk. Self-talk is a very effective way of making the most of positive experiences and minimizing the effect of negative ones.

(FIGURE 16-20) **Most babies begin to walk when they are about one year old.**

When you were about one year old, you were determined to learn to walk. No one has to teach a baby how to pull itself up onto its own two feet and take its first steps. In fact, it would be difficult to stop a baby from learning to walk.

As a toddler, you were also learning how to talk. The sounds you had been hearing all your life began to have meaning, and you struggled to imitate them. You may have learned that "ba-ba" could cause an adult to give you a bottle of milk or that your mother was delighted when you waved and said "bye-bye."

During your childhood years, you learned how to be more independent. You learned to go to the cabinet for food when you were hungry, rather than sitting in your room and crying until you were fed. You were allowed to go to a friend's house by yourself. You learned how to cross the street safely. You went to school.

School occupied a major part of your day, and you learned a great deal there.

You learned a lot of facts, of course, but you also learned how to get along with people different from you and your family.

These years prepared you for adolescence. Your childhood experiences enabled you to make friends, prepared you to be able to study and learn well, and helped you to be confident that you can make effective decisions.

If you do the Life Skills activity on page 347, it may help you to understand how early experiences can affect your self-esteem.

You also grew *physically* in preparation for adolescence. Your height and weight increased quite a bit, and your coordination improved. These and other physical changes became even more dramatic as you approached puberty. In the next chapter, you'll learn about the changes that occur during adolescence.

Review

1. *What substances pass through the placenta from the mother to the fetus?*

2. *Describe how the uterus and the cervix change during labor.*

3. **LIFE SKILLS: Building Self-Esteem** *Think of one aspect of yourself that you really like. Practice self-talk by stating a positive conclusion that you've made about yourself.*

4. *Critical Thinking AIDS is caused by a virus. Explain how this virus, HIV, may be transmitted from a pregnant woman to her developing child.*

Highlights

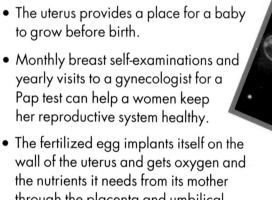

Summary

- The union of sperm and egg is called fertilization.

- The testes, vas deferens, urethra, and penis are the major organs of the male reproductive system.

- The testes make sperm and produce the male hormone testosterone. The amount of testosterone increases at puberty, causing boys' bodies to change.

- Even though only one sperm can fuse with the egg, the presence of many sperm is necessary for this to happen.

- In the female, the vagina, the ovaries, the fallopian tubes, and the uterus make up the internal reproductive system.

- The ovaries produce eggs and sex hormones. After puberty, these hormones control the monthly release of an egg .

- The egg and sperm join in one of the fallopian tubes.

- The uterus provides a place for a baby to grow before birth.

- Monthly breast self-examinations and yearly visits to a gynecologist for a Pap test can help a women keep her reproductive system healthy.

- The fertilized egg implants itself on the wall of the uterus and gets oxygen and the nutrients it needs from its mother through the placenta and umbilical cord.

Vocabulary

sperm male reproductive cell; contains one-half of the instructions needed for the development of a new human being.

egg female reproductive cell, also called an ovum; contains one-half of the instructions needed for the development of a new human being.

fertilization the union of a sperm and an egg.

testes male reproductive structures that make sperm and produce the male hormone testosterone.

ovaries female reproductive structures that produce eggs and female sex hormones.

uterus the hollow muscular organ that provides a place for the baby to grow before birth; also called the womb.

embryo a fertilized egg after it has attached itself to the wall of the uterus.

fetus a developing individual from the ninth week of pregnancy until birth.

Chapter Review

Concept Review . . . .

1. Sperm are made in the
a. urethra.
b. testes.
c. penis.
d. testosterone.

2. When a sperm joins with an egg, it is called
a. ovulation.
b. premenstrual syndrome.
c. ejaculation.
d. fertilization.

3. A disorder of the male reproductive system is
a. circumcision.
b. toxic shock syndrome.
c. undescended testes.
d. epididymis.

4. The female reproductive system includes
a. the ovaries.
b. the fallopian tubes.
c. the uterus.
d. all of these.

5. Egg cells and female sex hormones are produced in the
a. ovaries.
b. cervix.
c. vagina.
d. vulva.

6. When the uterus sheds its lining, it is called
a. premenstrual syndrome.
b. ovulation.
c. vaginitis.
d. menstruation.

7. Which of the following behaviors provides good screening for young women against breast cancer?
a. monthly self-examinations
b. loose-fitting clothing
c. yearly mammograms
d. body cleanliness

8. From the mother, the fetus can receive
a. viruses.
b. oxygen.
c. nutrients.
d. all of these.

Expressing Your Views . . . .

1. Keeping in mind that an embryo or fetus receives all of its nourishment from the mother through the placenta and the umbilical cord, list some practices you think a pregnant woman should avoid.

2. Millions of sperm are released in one ejaculation. Why do you think so many are released if only one is needed to fertilize an egg?

Life Skills Check

1. Practicing Self-Care
A friend has confided in you that he has been having soreness and swelling in his testes. He is hesitant to visit a doctor. What advice would you give him?

2. Building Self-Esteem
Most people have sides to their personality that they would like to change in order to feel better about themselves. Think of one aspect of your personality you think you would like to change. How could you change this trait or at least develop it to be more positive?

Projects

1. Go to the local library to look for information about the immunities passed from mother to baby in breast milk. Take notes on your findings, and present them to your teacher.

2. If you are male, find out if there are any risk factors for testicular cancer, and write a one-page report about your findings. If you are female, write a one-page report about behaviors or environmental factors that are associated with breast cancer.

Plan for Action

Males and females need to follow only a few basic steps to take care of their reproductive organs. Plan a daily, monthly, and yearly routine to ensure a healthy reproductive system and to prevent disorders from occurring.

Adolescence: Relationships *and* Responsiblities

◆ ◆ ◆ ◆

Section 17.1 Changes During Adolescence

Section 17.2 Communicating Effectively

Section 17.3 Relationships With Peers

Section 17.4 Sexuality and Responsibility

Section 17.5 Skills for Responsible Sexual Behavior

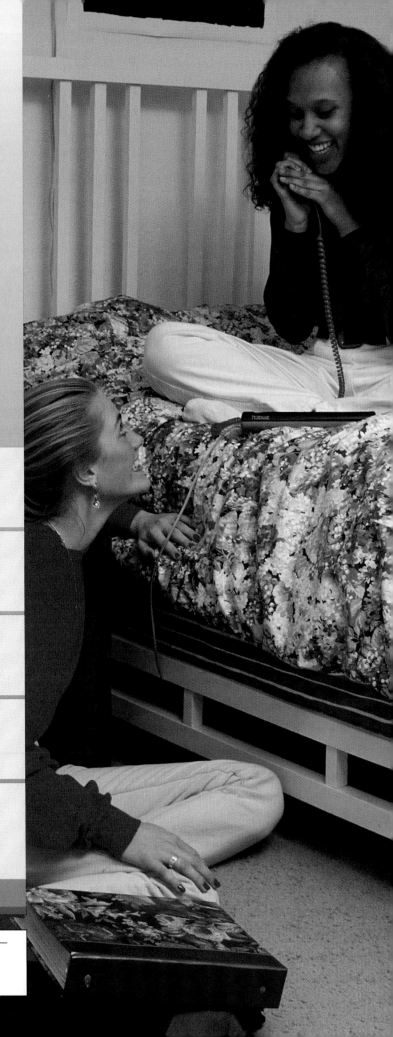

■ **Social interactions become very important during the adolescent years.**

"She'll never want to go out with me,"
Martin mutters as he shoves his books into his locker. Every time he gets up the nerve
to say hello to Caitlyn, he can't think of anything to say if she says
"Hi" back. He ends up just standing there feeling like a fool.
Martin's never really felt like this about anyone before—he's so
attracted to Caitlyn that he's almost afraid of her. Really he's afraid
that she wouldn't find him attractive. He figures, "Why would she
when I act so weird around her? If I did get up the courage to
ask her out, my heart would be beating so fast and my palms
would be so sweaty that she probably wouldn't want to
have anything to do with me anyway." Although many
people Martin's age go through the same thing, he is
convinced that he is the only one with these problems.

Section 17.1 · Changes During Adolescence

Objectives

- *Describe how puberty affects the male body.*

- *Describe how puberty affects the female body.*

- *Describe the nonphysical changes that occur during adolescence.*

Martin doesn't realize it, but virtually everyone suffers similar discomforts during adolescence. If he could read Caitlyn's mind, he would probably find that she, too, has many of the same feelings.

Adolescence is a time of change—changing body, changing emotions, changing mental abilities, and changing social life. All these changes can cause feelings of awkwardness. It helps to know as much as possible about what is going on, and it also helps to realize that the changes are perfectly normal.

(FIGURE 17-1) **People go through puberty at different rates. Don't worry if you are maturing faster or slower than your friends.**

puberty:

the period of physical development during which people become sexually mature and are able to produce children.

hormones:

chemical substances, produced by the endocrine glands, which serve as messengers within the body.

REMINDER

The endocrine glands are discussed in greater detail in the Body Systems Handbook on pages 677–679.

Physical Changes

The most dramatic changes during the adolescent years are the physical ones. You grow taller and larger, and enter the time of life called **puberty.** Puberty is the period of physical development during which people become able to produce children. Both males and females go through puberty. The age at which people begin puberty varies widely, from as young as 8 to as old as 16. It usually takes from two to four years for all of the changes of puberty to be completed.

Puberty is triggered by the release of specific **hormones**. Hormones are chemical substances, produced by the endocrine glands, which serve as messengers within the body.

The pituitary gland, located in the brain, releases hormones that send the message to other endocrine glands that it is time for them to begin releasing the hormones that cause puberty.

In males, the pituitary gland releases hormones that cause the testes to manufacture increased amounts of the hormone testosterone. Testosterone causes many of the changes of puberty. A male notices that his testes and penis begin to grow larger and that pubic hair appears around them. He gets taller and stronger. Later, hair grows

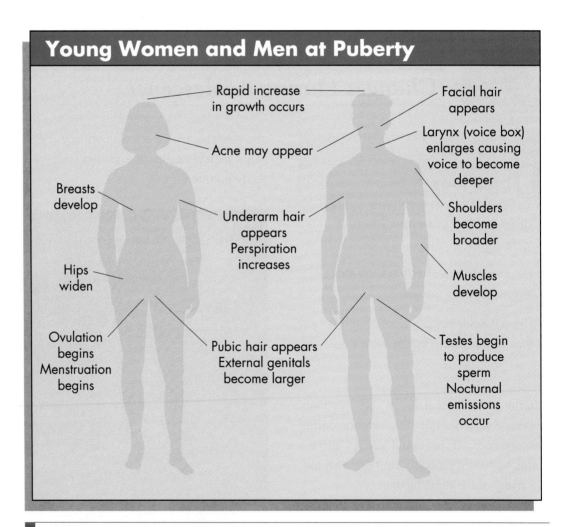

Young Women and Men at Puberty

Rapid increase in growth occurs

Acne may appear

Facial hair appears

Larynx (voice box) enlarges causing voice to become deeper

Breasts develop

Underarm hair appears
Perspiration increases

Shoulders become broader

Hips widen

Muscles develop

Ovulation begins
Menstruation begins

Pubic hair appears
External genitals become larger

Testes begin to produce sperm
Nocturnal emissions occur

(FIGURE 17-2) **Puberty is the time of life in which people become sexually mature and are able to produce children.**

under his arms and on his face. Testosterone also causes the larynx (voice box) to enlarge, resulting in the lower and deeper male voice. Before the voice stabilizes, however, it may break unpredictably for a while.

These types of changes may be welcome, but another aspect of puberty usually isn't. The increase in testosterone levels causes the oil glands to increase their production of oil. When these glands become clogged, acne can result.

An important part of male puberty is the beginning of sperm production by the testes, when boys start to experience **nocturnal emissions** ("wet dreams"). Nocturnal emissions are ejaculations of semen that occur during sleep. They are perfectly normal and no cause for alarm. Once sperm production has begun, a male is capable of causing pregnancy in a female.

In females, the pituitary gland releases hormones that cause the ovaries to produce the hormones estrogen and progesterone, the major female sex hormones. The female sex hormones cause female changes at puberty. The uterus, fallopian tubes, vagina, clitoris, and vulva grow in size. The breasts also start to grow, and pubic hair appears around the genitals. A female grows taller, and her hips widen.

During puberty, a female begins to ovulate and have menstrual periods. The first menstrual period usually occurs between the ages of 12 and 14, but it is not unusual for a girl to have her first period as young as 9 or as old as 17. Once a female has begun ovulation and menstruation, she is capable of becoming pregnant. As a result of hormonal changes during puberty, both males and females experience an increased sex drive and may find that they feel sexually aroused around some people.

Teenagers tend to develop at the same rate as their parents did. That does not mean, however, that all teenagers develop at the same rate. If you are developing at a faster or slower rate than other people your age, don't worry. You are almost certainly developing normally. If you are concerned, speak to a health professional or other trusted adult.

Q: Is it possible for a girl to get pregnant before she has had her first menstrual period?

A: Actually it is possible, but only if she has had her first ovulation. Ovulation occurs two weeks before menstruation. A girl does not always feel ovulation and may not know when she is ovulating. So she could become pregnant if she has sexual intercourse after her first ovulation but before her first menstrual period.

Q: Lately I've noticed that one of my testes is larger than the other. I've heard that testicular cancer is the most common kind of cancer for males my age, and I'm wondering if there's something wrong with me. Should I see a doctor?

A: Having one testicle that is larger than the other is very common, and it is usually nothing to worry about. However, hard lumps or an enlargement of the testes are things you should watch out for. It's always a good idea to perform the testicular self-examination on a regular basis and consult a doctor about anything that concerns you.

REMINDER

Ovulation is the release of an egg from an ovary.

nocturnal emissions:

ejaculations of semen that occur during sleep.

(FIGURE 17-3) **Your mental abilities improve during adolescence, allowing you to think and reason in a logical, abstract manner.**

Other Changes

At the same time that your body is developing, your emotions, mental abilities, and social abilities are also changing.

As you mature, you experience emotions for different reasons, or perhaps you feel them more intensely. Things that didn't bother you when you were younger might cause you distress now. At the same time, you might be totally unaffected now by things that you used to feel strongly about.

With maturity, you can better recognize and control emotions. Controlling your emotions helps to keep them from having a negative effect on you. For example, when you feel angry, you should be able to control yourself so that you don't hurt yourself or someone else.

Emotional growth is influenced mainly by your environment, especially by the adults with whom you interact. Parents and other family members set examples, and you are likely to learn their ways of dealing with emotions. If they can control their emotions, you probably will learn how to control yours too. If they cannot, you may have to work harder at this aspect of emotional growth.

During adolescence, you also grow mentally. You begin to think and reason in a different way. Your thinking becomes more logical and abstract. You are able to ask such questions as, "Why is this correct?" or "Can this be done another way?"

You can deal with more complex problems. For example, you are able to consider the immense size of the sun and its constant chemical changes. As a child, you may have understood only that the sun provides light and heat.

Your improved mental abilities also allow you to make realistic plans because you can imagine the consequences of actions and think about alternatives. You can evaluate the results of decisions and learn from your successes and mistakes.

You also grow socially during adolescence. You move from being totally dependent on other people to being more independent. At the same time, you develop an increased awareness of the feelings of others, and you desire their approval.

Review

1. Describe how puberty affects the male body.

2. Describe how puberty affects the female body.

3. Describe the nonphysical changes that occur during adolescence.

4. **Critical Thinking** How might the changes of puberty affect a person emotionally?

Communicating Effectively

Objectives

- *Learn how to use "I" messages instead of "you" messages.*
  - **LIFE SKILLS: Communicating Effectively**

- *Learn active-listening skills.*
  - **LIFE SKILLS: Communicating Effectively**

- *Learn a method of verbally resisting pressure.*
  - **LIFE SKILLS: Communicating Effectively**

- *Learn a method of resolving conflict.*
  - **LIFE SKILLS: Communicating Effectively**

As a teenager, you are beginning to learn how to communicate in a more adult way. If you learn effective communication techniques now, you'll be much more successful in your interpersonal relationships throughout your life.

Levels of Communication

There are four levels of communication, each of which is appropriate for different situations:

1. Information giving
2. Directing or arguing
3. Exploring
4. Self-disclosing

An example of Level 1 communication, information giving, is talking about the weather. Another example might be telling someone what you plan to wear to the football game on Friday night. Most casual conversations are conducted at Level 1, the least risky level of communication.

You might use level 2 communication, directing or arguing, when you tell a driver not to switch lanes because a car is there, or when you disagree with a statement another person has made.

Level 3 communication, exploring, is a safe way to find out how someone feels about something. For example, you might ask how your boyfriend or girlfriend feels about your relationship. Since you have not told the other person how you feel, you do not risk exposing your feelings. If the other person says your relationship is great, you can agree. If the person says he or she doesn't see much future together, you can also agree. Level 3 communication provides you with a safe way to explore another person's feelings, but it is not completely honest. The other person may never know how you really feel.

Level 4 communication, self-disclosing, is the deepest and the riskiest way of communicating. When you self-disclose, you reveal your feelings before you know how the other person feels. You might tell a friend, for example, that you really like her and want to spend more time with her. Her response might be positive or negative—she may tell you she feels the same way, or she may tell you that she doesn't share your feelings. Either way, you should have a good idea of where you stand, as a result of risking Level 4 communication. Self-disclosing can be a very honest and mature way of communicating.

"You" and "I" Messages

A "you" message is a blaming or shaming message, which is likely to put the other person on the defensive. Unfortunately, most people use "you" messages without thinking when they are upset. Jeremy, for instance, sent a "you" message to Angelique when she forgot to call him.

Jeremy: *You are so inconsiderate! How could you forget to call me when you promised? I'm not going to sit around waiting for you to call ever again!*

Angelique is likely to respond negatively to this "you" message. The conversation will probably go downhill without much chance of getting better.

*Life*SKILLS: Communicating Effectively

Sending "You" and "I" Messages . . .

Using "you" messages can lead to misunderstandings and arguments. We would get much better results if we translated our "you" messages into "I" messages. Practice this skill by thinking of "I" messages that could replace each of the following "you" messages:

"You" Messages

1. You jerk. You ruined another one of my tapes.

2. No, I'm not going to give you a ride because you always make me late.

3. You are so lazy. All you do is lie around watching T.V. while I clean the house.

4. How could you forget my birthday again? You are so thoughtless.

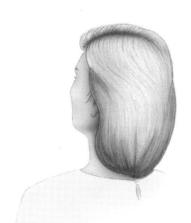

(FIGURE 17-4) **You send messages through your body language without even being aware of it. In the top drawing, the girl is very interested in what the other person is saying. In the bottom drawing, she is showing very little interest.**

An "I" message, on the other hand, is much more likely to be successful because it doesn't put the other person on the defensive. The "I" message has three basic parts: the event, the results of the event, and feelings about the event.

Jeremy could have sent the following "I" message when Angelique forgot to call. Jeremy: *When you forgot to call me* (the event), *I wasted time waiting for you* (the result), *and I felt really angry with you* (feelings about the event).

Angelique is now likely to apologize to Jeremy, rather than snap at him defensively.

You can practice sending "I" messages by doing the Life Skills activity on page 358.

Nonverbal Communication

Words are important, but they are not the only messages we send. We also communicate through our behavior, through **nonverbal communication**. This kind of communication involves eye contact, facial expression, and body positions. Sometimes we communicate more with nonverbal com-

munication than with verbal communication. If you are interested in something, you may lean forward in your chair and make direct eye contact. If you are bored, you may look around the room and lean back in your chair. You send messages about your feelings without even being aware of it.

If you pay attention to the nonverbal communication of your friends and family, you will have a better idea of how they are feeling. A friend, for example, may take his ring on and off when he is nervous. When you see him do this, you will know that he feels nervous.

nonverbal communication:

nonverbal behavior, such as eye contact, facial expression, and body position, that communicates information.

mixed message:

a message that is sent when the verbal and nonverbal communications do not match.

A **mixed message** is sent when the verbal and nonverbal communications do not match. If Cynthia says she is interested in working with you on a project, but has a frown on her face and sits at the back of her chair with her arms crossed, she is sending a mixed message. When people receive mixed messages, they are more likely to believe the nonverbal communication than the spoken words.

Active Listening

Colleen was watching TV when her mom came home from work. Her mom asked Colleen about her day and continued talking to her. Colleen kept watching TV and didn't pay much attention, other than to grunt an occasional "ya" or "na." Finally her mom came into the room and asked Colleen if she had been listening. "Sure, Mom," Colleen answered.

Actually, Colleen was hearing the words her mother said, but she wasn't really listening to them. Consequently, her mother felt that Colleen didn't care about what she was saying.

You can improve your communication skills by practicing **active listening.** Active listening is the process of hearing the words of the speaker and clarifying anything that you find confusing. Here is how to practice active listening.

active listening:

the process of hearing the words of the speaker and clarifying anything that is confusing.

- Give the speaker your full attention. This means that you should not think about something else or about what you are going to say next.
- Try to identify the main concepts and ideas that are being communicated.
- Make eye contact with the speaker.
- Indicate you are listening by nodding your head or saying "um-hmm."
- Provide feedback to the speaker. Ask questions, or repeat in your own words

the speaker's comments to make sure you understand. For example, you might say, "If I understand you correctly, you are saying . . ."

- Wait until the speaker is finished before you start talking. Do not finish sentences for the speaker.

Resisting Pressure

The ability to resist pressure is extremely important to staying well. A person who cannot resist pressure to smoke cigarettes, for instance, or to take a ride with a person who is drinking, runs serious health risks. It is possible to resist pressure to do things that you don't want to do and still keep your friends.

Resisting Verbally Li's friend Kirsten got drunk last Saturday night and insisted that she drive Li home. Li knew she shouldn't ride with Kirsten, but she didn't know how to turn her down without looking stupid. Here is a five-step method of verbally resisting pressure that would have helped Li.

Step 1: Identify the problem.
Step 2: State your feelings about the problem.
Step 3: State what you would like to happen instead.
Step 4: Explain the results if the requested change is made.
Step 5: Explain the results if the requested change is not made.

Using this method, Li could have said to Kirsten:

When you want to drive me home after you've been drinking (identify the problem), *I'm afraid that we'll have a wreck* (state your feelings). *I'd like to drive you home or get someone else to take us home* (state what you would like to happen in-

(FIGURE 17-5) **The best way to resist pressure to do something you don't want to do—like taking a ride with someone who has been drinking—is to state your feelings clearly and honestly.**

stead). *If you take my suggestion, I will feel good about going to other parties with you and I won't worry about you being hurt in a wreck—that's very important to me because I like you so much* (state results if change is made). *But if you insist on driving after you've been drinking, I won't ride with you and I'll think less of your judgment* (state results if change is not made).

In this way Li does not place herself in a dangerous situation, and she probably won't lose Kirsten's friendship either, because she let Kirsten know how much she cares about her.

Resisting Nonverbally If Li's nonverbal communication didn't reinforce what she said, Kirsten probably wouldn't take Li seriously. What if Li refused to look Kirsten in the eyes, shifted her weight back and

forth, and laughed nervously as she spoke? Kirsten might feel that she could bully Li into doing what she wanted. To be effective in your resistance, you must look the other person directly in the eyes, stand straight and steady on both feet, and speak with confidence and sincerity.

Reasserting Your Resistance Sometimes people will continue to pressure you even after you've used the five-step method for resisting pressure. Then it's time to use other communication techniques. There are two that are particularly effective.

• The Broken Record—If the other person keeps pressuring, keep stating your resistance, like a broken record. Eventually, the other person may believe you are serious about resisting.

- Separating Issues—Imagine that Kirsten said, "If you were really a good friend, you'd let me drive you home." Li can counter by separating the "good friend" issue from the "driving home" issue. Li could say, *I think I am a good friend because I spend a lot of time with you, especially when you need someone to talk to. But I don't want to put myself in a dangerous position by letting you drive me home after you've been drinking.*

If nothing works and you are truly in danger, you may have to resist physically. If someone were trying to pull you into a car against your will, for instance, physical resistance would be entirely appropriate.

Resolving Conflicts

Conflicts are a natural part of life. It would probably be impossible to go for a week without some sort of conflict arising with someone. But conflicts can usually be resolved if people show respect for each other. The following is an example of how not to resolve a conflict. Trina and Ronnie have been dating for a long time, but sometimes their tastes in friends are not the same.

Trina: *Let's go to Jenny's party tonight. I hear it's going to be great.*

Ronnie: *Are you kidding? Jenny's friends are boring. No way I'm going to that party!*

Trina: *Oh come on. How can you say Jenny's friends are boring? You're not the most exciting person in school, you know.*

Ronnie: *Who do you think you're talking to? I don't have to take that from anyone. Go out with yourself tonight. In fact, don't bother calling me again.*

Trina: *Don't worry about me calling you. No chance!*

When this conflict began, Trina and Ronnie wanted to spend the evening together. When it ended, not only did they not want to spend the evening together, but they had decided never to see each other again. The couple's predicament resulted from a lack of conflict-resolution skills.

Trina and Ronnie could have used the following RESPECT method for resolving conflicts, which requires that you show respect for the other person and for yourself.

1. **Recognize** that there is a difference of opinion.
2. **Eliminate** from your mind any thought of what you want for the time being. You'll get back to it later.
3. **Scan and listen** to what is being communicated by the other person in words and feelings.
4. **Paraphrase** what was communicated in words and state the feelings you believe the other person is experiencing.
5. **Express** what you want and describe your reasons for wanting it.
6. **Collect** several alternative solutions that meet both your needs.
7. **Try** the best of the alternative solutions.

Imagine that Trina had used the RESPECT method:

Trina: *Let's go to Jenny's party tonight. I hear it's going to be great.*

Ronnie: *Are you kidding? Jenny's friends are boring. No way I'm going to that party!*

Trina: (She recognizes there is a conflict and eliminates her own desires for the moment). *You sound as though you wouldn't be comfortable with Jenny's friends and wouldn't have a good time.* (Trina scans Ronnie's words and paraphrases them. She also paraphrases any feelings she thinks he might have, even those that were not expressed verbally.)

Ronnie: *That's right! All those people ever talk about are the honors and scholarships they're getting and the places that they travel to over summer vacation. I always feel out of place when they do that.*

Trina: *I know what you mean. Sometimes I feel out of place, too. But I like parties where I can dance and listen to music. I had a rough week, and I want to wind down tonight.* (Trina expresses what she wants and why she wants it.) *Let's see how many alternatives we can think of in which you feel comfortable and I can wind down.* (They collect several alternative solutions.)

Ronnie: *Well, maybe we could stay just a little while at the party.*

Trina: *Or we could go to the party but stay to ourselves. We really don't have to talk to anyone there, except to say hello. That way I can listen to music and you can be more comfortable there.*

Ronnie: *And I guess another possibility is for us to do what you want this time and for me to get my way next time we disagree.*

After generating several other alternatives, they try one. Using RESPECT, Trina and Ronnie both get what they need. If you respect the other person's needs, that person will be more likely to respect your needs.

Review

● ● ● ● ● ●

1. ■■ **LIFE SKILLS: Communicating Effectively** Write a "you" message you might use and then translate it into an "I" message.

2. ■■ **LIFE SKILLS: Communicating Effectively** During a debate, each debater is thinking about his or her reply while listening to the other debater. Explain why this is not an example of active listening.

3. ■■ **LIFE SKILLS: Communicating Effectively** A friend is pressuring you to go to a party where you will see the person who broke up with you last week. You feel that you are not yet ready to socialize with this person. Using the five-step method of verbally resisting pressure, write down the words you would use in talking with your friend.

4. ■■ **LIFE SKILLS: Communicating Effectively** Daniel and his buddy Josh get together every Tuesday night to watch their favorite television show. Then the show is canceled. Daniel wants to continue getting together on Tuesday, but to play pool instead. Josh wants to switch to Monday nights and watch a different television show. Suggest several alternatives that could resolve their conflict.

5. **Critical Thinking** Name one situation in which Level 1 communication, information giving, would be inappropriate. Explain your answer.

17.3 Relationships With Peers

Objectives

- *Describe how to make and keep a friend.*
- *Name three functions that dating serves.*
- *Name three actions you can take that will help you cope with a breakup.*
  - **LIFE SKILLS: Coping**

relationship:

a connection between people.

A **relationship** is a connection between people. It can be long-lasting and strong, such as a relationship between a parent and child, or it can be shorter and fairly superficial, such as a relationship between a supervisor and a summer employee. It can involve romance, as a dating relationship does, or it can be linked to friendship.

Each of us has a variety of relationships, including those with peers. Because you spend so much time with your peers, it is crucial for you to understand the nature of peer relationships.

Friendships

A friend is someone you know and like. Most friendships are based on common interests and values. You may have different friends for the different things you like to do. Perhaps one friend is fun to play basketball with, and another is good to talk with on the telephone. If you were going on a class field trip, another friend might come to mind. As friendships grow, they provide opportunities for emotional closeness.

How to Make a Friend Some people are able to make friends easily. If you are shy, however, you may have difficulty making and keeping friends. Especially if you've just moved to a new town or started attending a new school, you may find yourself feeling lonely. It is possible that you have *no* friends. If you would like to make some new friends, you will have to take some positive risks.

First, look at the people around you and think about a person you would like as a friend. Try to find someone you think you would feel comfortable with, someone you wouldn't have to impress. Think about someone you would like to spend time with that you could trust. You may notice someone who seems to be alone a lot; that person may also be shy and would be happy to have a new friend. Don't try to fit in with people who don't show much interest in you, no matter how popular they are. It isn't much fun to be one of the "hangers-on" of an "in" group.

No matter how shy you are, you can find people who really like you and want to be your friend. After you've looked around, decide on one person you think would make a good friend for you.

Then approach the potential friend. Yes, this is a frightening prospect. What if the person looks at you like you're an idiot? What if the person just ignores you? These are definite possibilities, but you must risk rejection if you want to make friends. You can make it easier on yourself by first talking casually with the person about a class or other activity you share, or about something else that is happening in school. If that con-

(FIGURE 17-6) **If you want to make new friends, you may have to take the first steps. After you've found someone you think would be a good friend, approach that person and start a conversation.**

versation goes fairly well, you can later invite your potential friend to do something with you—to go with a group of friends somewhere, for example, or to come over to your home to study.

If the person doesn't respond positively, don't take it too hard. Try not to think that you weren't "good enough." Everyone gets rejected sometimes. It is a fact of life that some people will like you and some people won't, no matter who you are. If you are rejected, just think to yourself, "It's their loss." If your first potential friend doesn't work out, try again with someone else, and keep trying until you find someone who responds positively. Eventually you'll find someone you like who also likes you.

How to Keep a Friend "You have to be a friend to have friends," goes an old saying. Different people, require different qualities in friends, but there are some qualities that almost everyone values.

One of the most important qualities of a good friend is trustworthiness. It's very important that your friends know you won't tell other people personal things about them or any secrets that they have shared with you. It's also important that you don't criticize a friend to other people.

The way you talk with your friends is also critical to maintaining a friendship. Be honest, but temper your honesty with kindness. It would be better to tell someone that she looks best in blue, for example, instead of saying that she looks terrible in red.

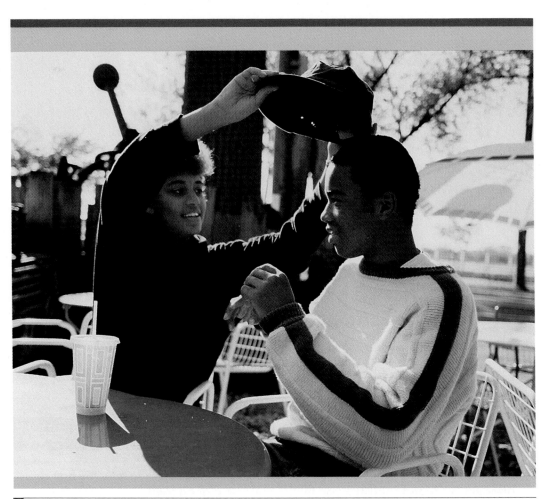

(FIGURE 17-7) **Besides just being fun, dating serves important functions in a person's social development.**

empathy:

the ability to understand how another person feels.

Show **empathy** when talking with your friends. Empathy is the ability to understand how another person feels; it involves putting yourself in your friend's place. For example, if your friend just found out that he didn't get a part in a school play, you could show empathy by saying: "I'm really sorry you didn't get that part. I know how rotten that feels." On the other hand, be sure to show your support when your friend succeeds, too.

If you have hurt someone's feelings, don't be afraid to say that you are sorry. The ability to admit that you are wrong demonstrates that you are mature, which is part of becoming an adult.

Try to be tolerant of any differences between you and a friend. The more tolerant you are of your friends, the more likely it is that they will be tolerant of you.

Finally, don't try to pressure someone else into doing something he or she feels uncomfortable doing. Just as you don't want to be pressured, others don't want to be pressured either.

Groups of Peers Peer groups provide you with a sense of belonging, support, and friendship. In a group of friends and acquaintances, you can learn how to present yourself to others and how to lead and follow others. You can talk about your values and what you believe is important. These experiences will allow you to compare your values and goals with others, as you decide what kind of adult you want to be.

Your contact with peer groups probably started when you were a preschooler with a circle of friends. You learned about the give-and-take of relationships and began to practice social skills, such as learning how to compromise.

Sometime between the fourth and sixth grades, cliques start to form. Cliques are small groups of three to eight people who exclude others from the group. If you are in a clique, you probably don't mean to be deliberately exclusive. The result, though, is that many people are left out of your group.

Teenagers often belong to a crowd, which is a loosely knit group of peers. A crowd starts to form when cliques begin to interact with each other. A crowd helps its members become familiar with different types of people. If the crowd is diverse—that is, if it includes people of different genders, ethnicities, cultures, and religions—it is beneficial to be in a crowd. Toward the end of high school, crowds begin to break up, as dating becomes more important.

Dating and Romantic Relationships

Dating is a great way for teens to get to know each other. When young people start dating, it's often just a group of friends going out together. In a group, there is usually less awkwardness than in a one-on-one dating situation.

Though dating provides positive, enjoyable experiences for many people, not all people begin dating as teens. Some teenagers find that other activities provide a full life without dating.

Friends or Dates? It is common in elementary school for close friends to be of the same sex. In the teen years, however, close friendships often form with members of the other sex. Two people may not be interested in each other romantically, but they still enjoy being together. For example, a boy may find that he can relax with a certain girl because the relationship doesn't have the demands of a romantic relationship. Friendships like these are said to be "platonic" relationships.

Crushes Whether they are called crushes, infatuations, or puppy love, the short-lived romantic feelings many teenagers experience can be intense. Someone experiencing a crush may daydream about the other person and become fascinated with details of his or her life. The other person, however, may not even know about the crush.

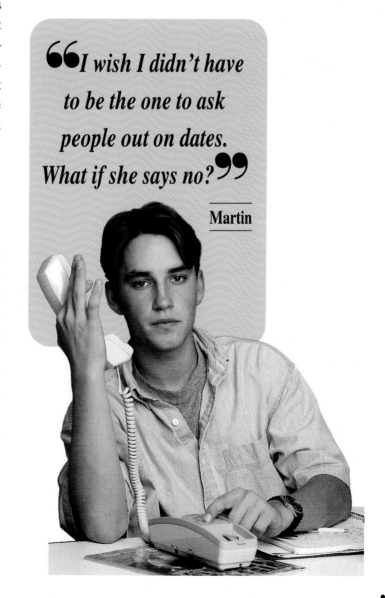

66*I wish I didn't have to be the one to ask people out on dates. What if she says no?***99**

Martin

Such one-sided relationships are part of learning to love. Since the other person is not required to respond, a crush lets you explore romantic relationships in a safe way.

Beginning to Date It's normal to feel both excitement and fear about dating. And it's completely normal to be unsure about who to ask for a date. The qualities you look for in a friend are also good qualities to look for in a date.

In the past, it was almost always the boy who asked the girl out. But in recent years, it has become more common for girls to initiate dates.

As you begin to date, you learn how to talk and act with members of the other sex.

Suggestions for Successful Dating

Don't give up on yourself if you're rejected. It hurts if the person you like doesn't want to go out with you, but keep trying. You'll eventually find people you like who also appreciate you.

Have courage to date someone you like even if others don't agree with your taste.

Don't break a date unless you absolutely must. It is not acceptable to break a date just because something better came along.

Show up on time. If you must be late, call.

Don't expect every date to be wonderful.

Let your date know if you had a good time. Saying something like, "Thanks, you're fun to be with," is all it takes.

Don't accept bad treatment from your date. If your date is inconsiderate, don't go out with him or her again.

(FIGURE 17-8)

You might feel as though others are judging every move you make, but that's probably not true. In fact, they are probably more concerned about how they appear to you.

Besides just being fun, dating serves important functions in a person's social development. It provides an opportunity to learn skills such as being able to talk easily with others, cooperate with them, and be considerate of them. Through dating, you learn what characteristics you like in others and what kind of people you are compatible with. And knowing that you are attractive to someone else helps you gain confidence.

As a dating relationship develops, you can share your thoughts and feelings. You can have a companionship that doesn't necessarily lead to a long-term commitment.

As in other relationships, communication is crucial for success. Clearly communicating your feelings and expectations gives you a better chance for understanding each other. See Figure 17-8 for other ways to make your dates more successful.

Two people sometimes decide to date only each other. One advantage of "going steady" is the opportunity to get to know the other person very well. But there are also some disadvantages. Going out with only one person limits a person's opportunity to meet other people, and if the relationship ends, it might be difficult to begin dating other people.

Breaking Up When two people are going together, they usually don't think about the relationship ending. Yet in reality, most romantic relationships developed during adolescence end in a breakup. Even though breakups are so common, they can be very painful.

Usually the first stage of a breakup is shock and numbness. A person who has been rejected may find it difficult to believe the other person really wants to break up.

There is a tendency to deny the other person's words. It is easy to think the other person will want to get back together.

When the reality of a breakup is accepted, there may be anger. The other person's faults may be magnified. If the other person has started going with someone else, the anger may be directed at that person also, especially if the person was a friend.

A breakup can cause self-doubt, resulting in negative thoughts such as ''If only I had been more fun'' or ''If only I were better looking.'' But it is better not to dwell on and give in to negatives. Instead, try to be very good to yourself.

If a relationship you were in has just ended, think of things you especially like to do and indulge yourself a little. Stay in contact with your friends. Remember that you are in the middle of a healing process and that the pain will end eventually. However, if you feel seriously depressed for more than a few weeks, seek help. Talk with a parent or guardian, or a school counselor, teacher, or coach.

Just remember that you will recover, that you will pick up your life and keep going. Although breaking up with someone is painful, it can also lead to personal growth. Your judgment about people becomes more reliable as you learn to evaluate people more realistically. Everything you have learned in this relationship will help you when you develop a deep and lasting relationship that doesn't break up. The suggestions in Figure 17-9 may help you cope with a breakup.

If you are the person who is ending the relationship, act with sensitivity and integrity. Tell the other person plainly that you want to break up. Don't just avoid the person and hope that the message is communicated. Be honest about your feelings, but don't say unnecessarily hurtful things.

Coping With a Breakup

Be very good to yourself. Do things you especially like to do, and stay involved with your friends.

When you start thinking or reminiscing about your ex-boyfriend or ex-girlfriend, command yourself to "Stop!"

Don't look at his or her photograph, reread old letters, or play "your song."

Ask trusted friends or family members if you may call them when you feel like calling your ex-boyfriend or ex-girlfriend.

If you are seriously depressed for more than a few days, seek help from a trusted adult.

Remember that you will recover from your loss.

Remember that you will find someone else.

(FIGURE 17-9)

Review

1. Describe how to make and keep a friend.

2. Name at least three functions that dating serves in a person's social development.

3. **LIFE SKILLS: Coping** Name at least three actions you can take that will help you cope with a breakup.

4. **Critical Thinking** Look at your answer to Question 2 of this Review. What activities other than dating could serve each function you listed?

Objectives

- Describe the difference between sexual and emotional intimacy.

- Name three possible consequences of teenage pregnancy.

- Describe the advantages of sexual abstinence.

- Consider how a pregnancy now would affect your life goals.
  LIFE SKILLS: Setting Goals

The adolescent years are a time of emerging sexuality. During this time a person's interest in sexual matters increases dramatically. This increased interest is a completely normal part of becoming an adult. Another important part of maturing is making responsible decisions about sexual behavior. The ability to use good judgment is crucial, not only to your current and future romantic relationships, but also to your health.

What Is Sexuality?

People often use the word "sexuality" as a synonym for "sexual activity." But sexuality is not just a physical act. It includes everything that makes someone a sexual person. Sexuality involves how we feel about our bodies, our desire for physical closeness with others, and all the thoughts and feelings we have about sexual intimacy. In fact, sexuality encompasses everything about being a male or female person. It isn't necessary to "have sex" to be a sexual person. In fact, people who abstain from

heterosexuals:

people who are sexually attracted to those of the other sex.

homosexuals:

people who are sexually attracted to those of the same sex.

sexual intimacy are just as sexual as those who don't. Everyone has sexuality, and everyone is a sexual being.

Most people are **heterosexuals**, people who are sexually attracted to those of the other sex. Some people are **homosexuals**, people who are sexually attracted to those of the same sex. Homosexual men are called gay men, and homosexual women are called gay women or lesbians. People who are attracted to members of both sexes are referred to as bisexual.

It is possible for adolescents to have sexual feelings for those of the same sex but be heterosexual as adults. Similarly, some people who are homosexual as adults have had sexual feelings for members of the other sex. It is the predominant sexual attraction—to those of the other sex or to those of the same sex—that determines whether a person is said to be heterosexual or homosexual in orientation.

No one knows for certain why some people are heterosexual and others are homosexual. Much of the evidence from recent studies indicates that homosexuality may result from a combination of biological and environmental factors.

Everyone—regardless of his or her sexual orientation—deserves to be treated with respect and dignity and without discrimination.

Influences on Sexuality As you grow up, your sexuality is influenced to a large extent by the people around you and the things you see, hear, and read. The earliest influences come from your family. If the people who raise you are comfortable showing affection through touch, you have a

Myths and Facts About Sexual Intimacy

Myth	Fact
Becoming sexually intimate shows a couple is really in love.	Although sexual intimacy can be an expression of love, it doesn't prove that a couple is in love. Couples become sexually intimate for reasons other than being in love: curiosity, trying to hang on to a partner, proving to themselves that they are sexually normal, or because one partner wants to. It is possible for couples to express their love in ways that do not include sexual intimacy.
If a person has been sexually intimate once, there's no reason to say no to being sexually intimate again.	Many people are intimate once and decide there are many reasons not to do it again: fear of pregnancy or diseases, moral or religious beliefs, waiting for the right person, or wanting to wait until it can be a very satisfying experience.
One way to keep a boyfriend or girlfriend is to be sexually intimate.	Sexual intimacy doesn't guarantee a boyfriend or girlfriend will stay. Sometimes sex will keep a partner for a period of time because of a sense of duty or feelings of guilt. Sometimes a relationship will end after sexual intimacy because the challenge is gone or because a partner feels tied down and doesn't want to be.
If a male is a virgin when he graduates from high school, he's probably homosexual.	Many heterosexual males don't become sexually intimate until after high school because they believe they should wait for marriage. Others aren't ready for commitment, while still others don't want to jeopardize their plans for education and financial security.
The best way to get to know someone is to be sexually intimate with him or her.	Sexual intimacy is only one way of getting to know someone. There are many facets of a person's character one does not learn during sex. If sex replaces talking, spending time with mutual friends, and enjoying activities together, a couple may never truly get to know each other.

(FIGURE 17-10)

(FIGURE 17-11) **If the people who raise you are comfortable showing affection through touch, you are likely to feel comfortable with physical affection as well.**

sexual intimacy:

genital touching and sexual intercourse.

emotional intimacy:

sharing thoughts and feelings, caring for and respecting the other person, and gradually learning to trust one another.

pretty good chance of growing into a person who also shows physical affection easily. On the other hand, if your family is reserved and does not show affection readily, you may also be reluctant to show physical affection.

How your family talks about sexuality also can influence your attitudes about the subject. In some families, sexuality is openly discussed, and in others, there is an unspoken rule that it should not be discussed at all. Most families fall somewhere in between.

As you get older and enter adolescence, your peers become more important as sources of information about sexual matters. You hear what they think about sexuality and what they say they do. However, teenagers often misrepresent their sexual activities to impress others, so peer information may not be the most reliable.

An increasingly important influence on your sexuality is mass media—television, movies, magazines, and newspapers. Most of the information you get from the media is designed to sell you something. The more viewers a television show gets, the more it can charge for advertising time. And the more movie tickets are sold, the more money a movie makes. That's why the sex scenes in television shows and movies are usually so unrealistic: the more graphic the scenes are, the more money is made. Realistic sexual and emotional intimacy is rarely shown on the screen. What you see is what sells.

Sexual Intimacy Versus Emotional Intimacy Sexual intimacy and emotional intimacy are often confused. **Sexual intimacy** involves genital touching and intercourse. **Emotional intimacy** involves sharing thoughts and feelings, caring for and respecting the other person, and gradually learning to trust one another. It is entirely possible to have one kind of intimacy without the other.

"Casual sex" is an example of sexual intimacy without emotional intimacy. When people have casual sex, they are often using the other person for gratification without regard for the person's feelings. In this way they are treating the other person as an object rather than as a human being.

Sometimes a person who is lonely or uncomfortable around others will offer sexual intimacy in an effort to achieve emotional intimacy. This can be a painful experience and can be harmful to that person's emotional (and physical) health.

When people are sexually intimate, they allow themselves to be vulnerable, and for that reason it is very important to trust the other person a great deal. Trust is established over a period of time and requires commitment. When this type of lasting commitment exists between two emotionally mature, loving, and trusting people, sexual intimacy can be one of the best experiences in life.

Risks of Teenage Sexual Intimacy

Though sexual intimacy is a positive, pleasurable part of adult life, it can be harmful if it starts too soon. The risks of teenage sexual activity include conflicts with personal and parental values, sexually transmitted diseases, and unwanted pregnancy.

Conflicts With Personal and Parental Values Everyone must consider his or her own values—what he or she strongly believes—when making decisions about sexual behavior. Actions that conflict with one's own values can cause feelings of guilt and low self-esteem.

(FIGURE 17-12) **As people become emotionally intimate, they share their thoughts and feelings, care for and respect the other person, and gradually learn to trust one another.**

Teenage Pregnancy Facts

Each year, almost one million teenage females—11% of all females aged 15 to 19 and 20% of those who have sexual intercourse—become pregnant.

85% of teen pregnancies are unplanned, accounting for about one-quarter of all accidental pregnancies annually.

6 in 10 teen pregnancies occur among 18- to 19-year-olds.

Teen pregnancy rates are much higher in the United States than they are in many other developed countries—twice as high as in England and Wales or in Canada, and nine times as high as in the Netherlands or in Japan.

Among sexually experienced teens, about 8% of 14-year-olds, 18% of 15- to 17-year-olds and 22% of 18- to 19-year-olds become pregnant each year.

(FIGURE 17-13) **The United States has a higher teen pregnancy rate than does any other developed nation in the Western world. (Source: The Alan Guttmacher Institute)**

(FIGURE 17-14) **Caring for a child is a 24-hour-a-day responsibility. Teenage parents often find that they don't have time to do things they used to enjoy doing.**

Many teenage pregnancies occur because teens tend to think: "It won't happen to me." But in fact, it does happen to about one million adolescent girls in the United States each year. This works out to 1 out of every 10 girls, the highest rate of teen pregnancy of any industrialized nation in the Western world.

A teenager who has become pregnant, or who has gotten someone pregnant, must face the consequences of his or her actions. Being a parent is hard for everyone, but it is especially difficult for teenagers, who are still developing the ability to make responsible decisions.

Because teenagers often delay making a decision about their pregnancies, they may not get adequate prenatal care. Partly as a result of less prenatal care, teenagers are more likely than older women to have health problems during a pregnancy. In fact, the risk of death due to complications is 60 percent higher for girls younger than 15 than for mothers who are older than 20. Many of these deaths are caused by a condition called toxemia, which is characterized by high blood pressure and fluid retention. Teenage mothers are also more likely to give birth to premature babies and to babies who weigh less than normal.

In addition to suffering health problems, teenage mothers experience educational, economic, and social disadvantages. They are less likely to finish high school, and once out of school, they are less likely to become employed. In addition, few teenage mothers marry the father of their children, and half of those who do are divorced within five years.

These dry facts, of course, do not begin to describe the emotional consequences to a teenager facing early parenthood. It can be very stressful to care for a helpless baby. The 24-hour-a-day responsibility, including middle-of-the-night feedings and diaper

Adolescents must also consider the values of their families. When you are part of a family, your decisions affect not just you, but other family members as well. If your parents believe, for example, that sexual intimacy before marriage is wrong, they would be disappointed and hurt if you became sexually active.

Sexually Transmitted Diseases A sexually active person risks contracting sexually transmitted diseases (STDs), including AIDS. Chapters 22 and 23 deal with STDs.

Teenage Pregnancy Adolescence is a time of coming of age—of emotional, social, and intellectual growth—and all this can be jeopardized by a pregnancy. A person may not be able to reach his or her goals in life because of a teenage pregnancy.

STDs are fully discussed in Chapter 22.

HIV infection and AIDS are the subjects of Chapter 23.

changing, exhausts the mother and takes its toll on her emotional resources.

When teenagers become parents, they usually find that they simply do not have enough time to do the things they previously enjoyed—going out with friends, for example, or dating or going to the movies. The constant care that a new baby requires can make something as simple as relaxing at home difficult for a new parent.

Teenage mothers are not the only ones who suffer the emotional consequences of premature parenthood. Teenage fathers may also experience major difficulties. They often feel guilty and depressed. They may find the sudden responsibility overwhelming. And like the mothers, teenage fathers are less likely to finish high school and are less successful financially than their peers who are not parents.

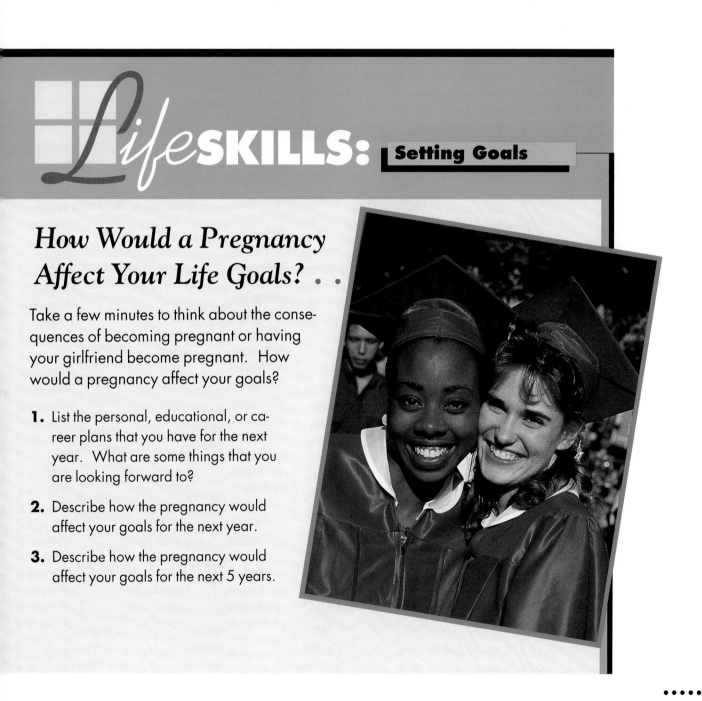

LifeSKILLS: Setting Goals

How Would a Pregnancy Affect Your Life Goals? . .

Take a few minutes to think about the consequences of becoming pregnant or having your girlfriend become pregnant. How would a pregnancy affect your goals?

1. List the personal, educational, or career plans that you have for the next year. What are some things that you are looking forward to?

2. Describe how the pregnancy would affect your goals for the next year.

3. Describe how the pregnancy would affect your goals for the next 5 years.

Some Consequences of Teenage Pregnancy

Greater chance of suffering health problems during pregnancy

Greater chance of giving birth to premature babies

Difficult choice among pregnancy options

Stress of caring for an infant

Increased family conflict

Possible depression, guilt, and sense of isolation

Both mothers and fathers are less likely to finish high school

Both mothers and fathers are less successful financially

(FIGURE 17-15)

sexual abstinence:

delaying or refraining from sexual intimacy.

In addition, according to federal law the father must take financial responsibility for his child. This means that a male who fathers a child will be expected to pay for the support of that child for approximately 18 years. What if a male who fathers a child claims that he is not the father? In most states the mother can take legal steps to establish the paternity—who the father is—of her child without the father's permission. Once the paternity is established, the father is legally bound to support the child financially.

A teen pregnancy affects different people in different ways. The Life Skills activity on page 375 will help you get an idea of how a pregnancy would affect your life.

Although the consequences of teenage pregnancies are felt most deeply by the individuals directly involved, society as a whole also pays a cost. Teen pregnancies cost taxpayers an estimated $20 billion annually in public support.

Abstinence

A person who delays or refrains from sexual intimacy is practicing **sexual abstinence**. Being abstinent is a positive, responsible decision that allows you to avoid teenage pregnancy and sexually transmitted diseases.

Abstinence is the most responsible choice for a teenager because it allows you to delay sexual intimacy until you are in a stable, committed relationship, such as a marriage. Teenagers who practice sexual abstinence grow by acting responsibly and by learning to develop relationships that are not based on sexual intimacy. As adults, they may be better prepared to build strong, lasting relationships based on mutual trust and respect.

If you have already become sexually intimate, you can still choose to delay further intimacy and become abstinent until you know you are capable and ready to accept the consequences of sex.

Review

1. Describe the difference between sexual intimacy and emotional intimacy.

2. What are the advantages of delaying sexual intimacy until marriage?

3. ■■ **LIFE SKILLS: Setting Goals** How would a pregnancy now affect your life one year from now?

4. **Critical Thinking** Name one love scene in a movie, television program, or book that seems unrealistic to you, and explain why it is unrealistic.

Section
17.5 Skills for Responsible Sexual Behavior

Objectives

- Learn how to resist internal pressure to become sexually intimate.
  LIFE SKILLS: Resisting Pressure

- Learn how to resist external pressure to become sexually intimate.
  LIFE SKILLS: Resisting Pressure

- Apply the decision-making model in this textbook to decisions about your own sexual behavior.
  LIFE SKILLS: Making Responsible Decisions

Choosing to refrain from sexual intimacy is a sound, responsible decision. It doesn't help to decide to delay sexual intimacy, however, if you haven't developed the skills necessary to carry out your decision. In this section, you'll learn some valuable skills for responsible sexual behavior.

Resisting Internal Sexual Pressure

A person must first acknowledge sexual feelings before he or she can deal with them. The sex drive can be especially powerful during the teen years, when hormonal changes occur rather suddenly and an increased awareness of sexuality develops. The natural sex drive can make sexual inti- macy a very strong temptation, especially when you are in love.

The best way to deal with the internal pressure to be sexually intimate is to exer- cise self-control. You can also learn to express your romantic love for another per- son in ways other than sexual intimacy.

Other Ways to Show Love There are many ways to show love for another person while delaying sexual intimacy. Showing consideration for each other's feelings, doing special favors, hugging, kissing, and laughing together—all of these things show love.

A good way to think of ways to express love without sexual intimacy is to think of how you would want someone to show love to you. What could another person do that would make you feel cared for?

Practicing Self-Control We exercise power over our lives by practicing self- control. When you practice self-control, you make rules for yourself and act on them. It helps to think ahead about temptations and plan what you will do about them. For instance, you may feel that you are not ready for sexual intimacy. If you have given some thought to what your personal reasons for abstinence are, then it might be easier to remember to stick to your decision in a situation where you are tempted. In such a situation, you should ask your- self, What are the rules I have set for myself pertaining to sexual relationships?

Dealing With External Pressures

External pressures come from outside you. They include pressures from your boyfriend or girlfriend, your friends, or from media messages. Sometimes the external pressures can become internal pressures. If, for instance, you get the idea from television programs that virtually everyone your age is sexually active, you might begin to put pressure on yourself, telling yourself that something is wrong with you if you have not yet experienced sexual intimacy.

Old-fashioned stereotypes of male and female sexual behavior can contribute to the external pressures. Young men may feel that they are expected to be the sexual aggressor, to push for a greater degree of sexual intimacy, whether or not they really

(FIGURE 17-16) **You can show your love for someone in nonsexual ways through gestures such as cooking a meal.**

want to. And a young woman may think that to please a boyfriend she must go further than she is emotionally ready to.

The most important thing to know is that you have a right to refuse sexual intimacy, anytime, for any reason. If you are not sure you are ready to be sexually intimate, you probably aren't. If someone tries to make you feel guilty or "no fun" because you don't want to do a certain thing with your body, that person probably doesn't respect you. Being pressured into sexual intimacy with someone who doesn't respect you is almost certainly going to be harmful to your self-respect, not to mention "no fun" for you.

Resisting Sexual Pressure Lisa and Jamal have been going out for about two months. They spend a lot of time together, talking and kissing, and things are starting to get serious. Lisa loves being with Jamal, and sometimes it's hard for her to keep from going further. Jamal, for his part, isn't even trying to restrain himself. He wants to have sexual intercourse, and the sooner the better. Though he hasn't tried to make Lisa feel bad about not going further, he has told her that he's extremely frustrated. Lately he's become insistent, making it more and more difficult for Lisa to resist.

Lisa genuinely cares for Jamal and wants to continue seeing him, but she doesn't feel ready for sexual intimacy. Deep down, it just doesn't feel like the right thing to do at this time in her life. Plus, she doesn't want to jeopardize her future by becoming pregnant or getting a sexually transmitted disease.

The resistance skills discussed in Section 17.2 could help Lisa avoid a degree of sexual intimacy she doesn't want, in a way that won't make Jamal feel that he has been attacked. The same conversation could work for a male who is being pressured by a female.

The five-step method of verbally resisting pressure is:

1. Identify the problem.
2. State your feelings about the problem.
3. State what you would like to happen instead.
4. Explain the results if the requested change is made.
5. Explain the results if the requested change is not made.

Here is how Lisa could express her feelings to Jamal:

The problem is that I don't want to go as far sexually as you do (identify the problem). *I like you a lot, and I want to keep going out with you. I'm also sexually attracted to you and love what we've been doing together, but I feel uncomfortable about going any further* (state your feelings). *I'd like you to respect my feelings about this and not pressure me* (state what you would like to happen instead). *If you do respect my feelings and back off, I'll keep seeing you, because I think you're great* (state results if change is made). *But if you keep pressuring me, I won't go out with you anymore* (state results if change is not made).

Lisa has stated how she feels and what she wants in a way that leaves no doubt about what she means. To be certain that Jamal gets a clear message, Lisa must reinforce her verbal statements with her nonverbal communication. She must look him straight in the eyes and speak confidently.

Sometimes we are in a situation in which we don't know what we want. If someone is putting on the pressure, we might do what he or she wants because we think we have to answer yes or no on the spot. But actually, we don't have to make a decision at that moment. We can say, ''Let me think about it.'' Learning how to say this simple sentence can be a lifesaver.

What Would You Do

What if You've Already Become Sexually Active?

Making Responsible Decisions

Last night Sandra and Dylan had sexual intercourse for the first time. It seemed like the right thing to do—from stories Sandra had heard she thought that she and Dylan would become closer as a result. But Sandra doesn't feel any closer to him. In fact, now she feels really uncomfortable around Dylan. Things were fine before this happened, but now Sandra is thinking that she made a mistake.

By the end of the day, she's convinced that she doesn't want to continue the sexual intimacy. The problem is, Sandra and Dylan have plans to be together this weekend. She doesn't know whether to cancel the plans and risk ruining their relationship, or tell Dylan about her feelings. What should she do? What would you do?

Remember to use the decision-making steps:

1. State the Problem.
2. List the Options.
3. Imagine the Benefits and Consequences.
4. Consider Your Values.
5. Weigh the Options and Decide.
6. Act.
7. Evaluate the Results.

What if you've already become sexually intimate with someone and then you realize that it was a bad decision? You have the right to change your mind. Just because you've done something once doesn't mean you have to continue doing it. It is always your right to say no even if you've previously said yes.

Respecting Others Just as it is your right to resist pressure to do things with your body that don't feel right, it is also your

(FIGURE 17-18) **Participating in group activities is a healthy way to avoid the risk of unwanted sexual intimacy.**

obligation to respect the rights of others. People often don't realize when they are putting unfair pressure on others, especially in intimate situations.

If someone tells you that he or she doesn't want to do something sexually, back off. If the person appears reluctant but doesn't say anything, pay attention to the nonverbal signals. It's often difficult for people to admit that they feel uneasy about sexual intimacy. You might say something like, "You seem uncomfortable. Do you want to stop?"

High-Risk Situations Once you have chosen to delay sexual intimacy, avoiding situations that can make abstinence more difficult will help you stick to your decision.

The main things to avoid are drinking alcohol or using other drugs. These substances impair your judgment and self-control, making sexual activity more likely. Any party at which alcohol and other drugs are present is a high-risk situation.

Spending a lot of time alone with someone is also risky. Avoid being at home together when no one else is there, as well as parking in cars in isolated spots. Group ac-

tivities such as going to the movies and playing sports are best if you want to avoid sexual intimacy.

Review

1. **LIFE SKILLS: Coping** *Describe how a person can deal with internal pressures to become sexually intimate.*

2. **LIFE SKILLS: Resisting Pressure** *Name the five steps of verbally resisting pressure.*

3. **LIFE SKILLS: Making Responsible Decisions** *If you made a decision to remain sexually abstinent, what steps would you take to ensure that you followed through on your decision?*

4. **Critical Thinking** *Why might it be difficult for a person to admit that he or she feels uneasy about sexual intimacy?*

Highlights

Summary

- Adolescence, which is the gradual transition from childhood to adulthood, is a time marked by physical, emotional, mental, and social changes.

- Puberty is a period of physical development during which people become able to have children.

- Four types of communication are information giving, directing or arguing, exploring, and self-disclosing.

- Communication skills can be improved by using "I" instead of "You" messages, practicing active listening, and showing respect for the needs of others when conflicts arise.

- Most friendships are based on common interests and values. One of the most important qualities of a good friend is trustworthiness.

- Peer groups provide a person with a sense of support and friendship.

- The risks of teenage sexual activity include conflicts with personal and parental values, sexually transmitted diseases, and unplanned pregnancy.

- Pressures to be sexually intimate can be overcome by exercising self-control, learning to express romantic love in ways other than sexual intimacy, and avoiding high-risk situations.

Vocabulary

hormones chemical substances, produced by the endocrine glands, which serve as messengers within the body.

nonverbal communication nonverbal behavior, such as eye contact, facial expressions, and body position, that communicates information.

mixed message a message that is sent when the verbal and nonverbal communications do not match.

active listening the process of hearing the words of the speaker and clarifying anything that is confusing.

heterosexuals people who are sexually attracted to those of the other sex.

homosexuals people who are sexually attracted to those of the same sex.

sexual intimacy genital touching and sexual intercourse.

emotional intimacy sharing thoughts and feelings, caring for and respecting the other person, and gradually learning to trust one another.

sexual abstinence delaying or refraining from sexual intimacy.

Chapter Review

Concept Review

1. The period of physical development in which the body becomes able to produce children is called
a. adulthood.
b. childhood.
c. puberty.
d. adolescence.

2. Revealing your feelings before you know the feelings of another is the level of communication called
a. self-disclosing.
b. directing or arguing.
c. information giving.
d. exploring.

3. The process of hearing the words of the speaker and clarifying anything that is confusing is known as
a. nonverbal communication.
b. active listening.
c. mixed messages.
d. "you" and "I" messages.

4. The RESPECT method is used to
a. resist pressure.
b. listen actively.
c. resolve conflicts.
d. communicate nonverbally.

5. A friend is someone
a. you feel comfortable with.
b. who is trustworthy.
c. who shows empathy.
d. All of these.

6. Which of the following is not a high-risk situation if you have decided to delay sexual intimacy?
a. group activities, such as movies and sports
b. parties where alcohol is served
c. using drugs on a date
d. studying at home alone with your boyfriend or girlfriend

Expressing Your Views

1. In your opinion, what is the most difficult thing about adolescence? What would make it easier?

2. Some people find it hard to make and maintain friends. Why do you think this is true?

Life Skills Check . . . . . .

1. Communicating Effectively

Last week you told one of your friends something in confidence, and you just found out that your secret was shared with someone else. Using the method found on page 359, communicate an ''I'' message to let your friend know how you feel.

2. Coping

Your family is planning to attend the yearly family reunion. You can't imagine anything more boring than listening to the same old family stories. All you can think about is the upcoming school dance and whether your new friend will ask you out. You feel as if you must go to the reunion. What could you do to make your family day pleasant?

Projects . . . .

1. Select a biography or historical story about someone and note what you can about this person's teenage years. Look for events, circumstances, and behaviors that were different from the experiences of your adolescent years. Report your findings in writing.

2. Write *age 5*, *age 9*, and *age 14* across the top of a poster board. Under each age, list games and activities you enjoyed as well as any responsibilities you might have had

at that particular time in your life. Evaluate why the list changed from age to age and report this information to the class.

3. Choose three letters from an advice column dealing with teenage relationship problems. Without looking at the advice offered, write your own responses to the problems. Then compare your responses to the ones given in the paper. Bring the letters and both sets of responses to class for discussion.

Plan for Action . . . .

The period between childhood and adulthood is an intense time of change that can be very difficult. Create a plan to help you cope with this period of transition.

CHAPTER 18

Adulthood, Marriage, and Parenthood

◆ ◆ ◆

Section 18.1 Adulthood

Section 18.2 Marriage and Parenthood

Deciding whether to get married is a major choice, usually made during young adulthood.

Carmen had a pretty strange dream last night. She dreamed it was her wedding day but she hadn't bought a dress. She also hadn't chosen a place to live, a job she wanted to do, or even the person she was going to marry. When she awoke, Carmen laughed out loud. But she also had to admit that she was relieved she would not have to make those kinds of decisions for several more years. Being an adult, she thought to herself, can't be all that easy.

Section

18.1 Adulthood

Objectives

- Know the three stages of adulthood.

- Define emotional maturity.

- Name three concerns an elderly person might have.

- Identify the difficulty of coping with a grandparent who has Alzheimer's disease.

  ■■ **LIFE SKILLS: Coping**

It may seem as though you'll be young forever. The thought of being an adult might bring a mixture of excitement and anxiety. How will you know what choices to make? Will you want to get married, or remain single? What kind of parent will you be? As you leave your teenage years and enter your twenties, many of these questions will become clearer to you. Even so, every day of your adult life you will be faced with decisions—some obvious, others more difficult.

In that way, adulthood doesn't differ too much from adolescence. Decision making is never easy, but your adult years will offer you the opportunity to accomplish the goals that you are setting for yourself now, as well as the freedom to pursue your dreams.

The Stages of Adulthood

How will you know when you're an adult? Will you wake up one morning and just feel different? In the United States, a person is legally an adult when he or she turns 18. That doesn't mean, of course, that the person you are on your 18th birthday is the person you'll be for the rest of your life. In fact, you are likely to change just as much during your adulthood as you do during your teenage years. Adulthood is divided into three stages: young adulthood, middle adulthood, and older adulthood.

Young Adulthood Even though Americans are considered legal adults at the age of

young adulthood:

the period of adulthood between the ages of 20 and 40.

middle adulthood:

the period of adulthood between the ages of 41 and 65.

emotional maturity:

the capacity to act independently, responsibly, and unselfishly. Being emotionally mature requires having compassion, integrity, and self-esteem.

18, a person who is 18 is still technically a teenager. According to most guidelines, a person between the ages of 20 and 40 is in the stage of **young adulthood.** Young adulthood has its own series of decisions and challenges. Most people who marry, for example, do so during this stage of adulthood. You will most likely choose the career you want to pursue early in your adulthood as well. In addition, the friendships you form during your young adult years may be the longest lasting of your life.

Decisions such as these require a certain degree of maturity. There are two types of maturity. The first, physical maturity, is usually an automatic part of growing up. Being physically mature simply means being fully developed and fully grown. This happens to most people by the time they are in their early twenties. The second type of maturity, **emotional maturity,** is not as automatic. People who are emotionally mature have the capacity to form close

relationships, yet act independently. They are able to make decisions that are responsible and unselfish. Being emotionally mature requires having the self-esteem to recognize your own strengths, even when times are hard.

No one can be emotionally mature all the time—everyone makes mistakes. But being equipped with a degree of emotional maturity will help you make better decisions throughout your life. For that reason, attaining emotional maturity should be a major goal during young adulthood.

Middle Adulthood The **middle adulthood** years, the period between the ages of 41 and 65, are, for some people, the most enjoyable time of adult life. Some of life's most difficult choices—about marriage, career, and parenthood, for example—have been made during the young adult years. Middle age can be a time to savor and appreciate the results of those choices.

(FIGURE 18-1) **Finding the right job is one of the most important challenges young adults face.**

(FIGURE 18-2) **Middle adulthood is often a time to savor the romance of a good marriage and the satisfaction of a happy life.**

Middle adulthood does involve a series of physical and emotional changes. Hair may turn gray, some wrinkles may develop, and a few pounds will probably be gained. Most women stop menstruating during the middle adult years. Once a woman permanently ceases to menstruate, she can no longer bear children. Some women find this change, known as menopause, disheartening. Others welcome the end of their menstrual cycle. Middle-aged men and women who are unhappy in their career may begin to question whether the choices they made during young adulthood were the right ones. In addition, middle-aged adults often find themselves confronting the death of a spouse, a parent, or a close friend, a painful reminder that everyone's life ends at some point.

Parents in the middle-adult stage may also experience ''empty-nest syndrome''— feelings of sadness when their children become adults and leave home. Although a change like that requires adjustment, some parents find that it returns romance to their relationship.

Older Adulthood Living to the age of 65 was once an almost miraculous accomplishment—a person born in the year 1900 had a life expectancy of only 47 years! Now, turning 65 simply marks the beginning of the **older-adulthood** stage. In fact, older adults are the fastest-growing segment of the population.

(FIGURE 18-3) **Older adults often find that they have more time for leisurely and healthy activities, such as exercise.**

older adulthood:

the period of adulthood past the age of 65.

A Family Member With Alzheimer's Disease . . . .

At first Nate wasn't especially upset by his grandfather's forgetfulness. That just happens when people get old, he thought to himself. Then one night Nate's mother got a call from the police. Nate's grandfather had been found wandering around his neighborhood, lost. "How could Grandpa be lost in his own neighborhood?" Nate asked his mom, who was equally puzzled.

Nate's mom took his grandfather to a doctor. After doing some tests, the doctor asked Nate's family to come in for a meeting.

The news wasn't good. Nate's grandfather has Alzheimer's disease, an incurable illness that gradually destroys a person's memory. Eventually a person with Alzheimer's will not be able to remember how to do things that once came naturally—like reading and writing. The names of family members may be forgotten—many Alzheimer's sufferers don't recognize their own spouses or children.

In the several months since he was diagnosed, Nate's grandfather has gotten progressively worse. Sometimes he stares at Nate for long periods of time without speaking. Other times he'll yell at him for no reason.

The illness has been hard on Nate's mom, too. She spends time every day caring for her father. Sometimes he'll recognize and respond to her. Other times he won't. She has to help him get dressed—he no longer remembers how to do it himself. Soon she'll have to decide whether to put him in a nursing home, or hire 24-hour care for him.

Nate spends time every day thinking about his grandfather. He's also shared some memories of his grandfather with his friends from school. His friends know that Nate needs to talk about his grandfather, but they're not always sure what they should say to him. What would *you* say?

Many people think of older adulthood as a time characterized by physical and mental deterioration. It's true that the older a person is, the more likely he or she is to get certain illnesses and conditions. Someone who is over 65 is much more likely to suffer from cancer, heart disease, or arthritis, for example, than a person who is 21. (These problems are discussed in greater detail in Chapter 24.) **Alzheimer's disease,** an incurable illness characterized by a gradual and permanent loss of memory, and **Parkinson's disease,** which causes a gradual loss of muscle function, are two other serious diseases that most commonly affect older adults.

However, many people remain happy and healthy well into their eighties and even nineties. For these individuals, older adulthood provides an opportunity to enjoy their family, relax, and reflect on their rich, fulfilling lives.

Aging

To a large extent, the choices you make now will affect your health as you grow older. For example, a person who exercises and eats regular, nutritious meals is much more likely to enjoy good health as an older adult than an inactive person who eats foods high in fat and cholesterol.

Common Concerns Physical well-being is an essential concern of aging, but it is not the only one. Jesse's grandparents, for example, had a happy life together for 40 years. But when Jesse's grandfather died last year, his grandmother was left alone. During the past year her health has gotten progressively worse. Jesse's parents are worried about her and have asked her to move in with them. But whenever they bring the subject up, Jesse's grandmother gets angry and defensive. "You don't trust me to take care of myself," she says.

Cancer, heart disease, and arthritis are discussed in greater detail in Chapter 24.

Alzheimer's disease:

an incurable illness characterized by a gradual and permanent loss of memory. Alzheimer's disease most commonly affects the elderly.

Parkinson's disease:

an incurable disease characterized by a gradual loss of control of muscle function. Parkinson's disease most commonly affects the elderly.

Myths and Facts About Aging

Myth	Fact
Most older people are sickly and unable to take care of themselves.	The majority of older people are fairly healthy and self-sufficient.
Intelligence declines with age.	People may become more knowledgeable as they age if they continue to exercise their mind.
Older people should stop exercising and get a lot of rest.	Exercise at any age strengthens heart and lung function. Older people can benefit as much from exercising as anyone else.
People's personalities change as they get older.	People's circumstances may change when they become older adults, but their personalities don't.

(FIGURE 18-4)

One afternoon after school when Jesse stops by to say hello to his grandmother, she tells him that she's beginning to worry about finances. Her utility bills keep rising, and she's concerned that if she were to become very ill she wouldn't be able to afford good medical care.

"Why don't you move in with us?" Jesse asks her. "We'll take care of you." But his grandmother worries about that too. She doesn't want to burden her children. "You and your family have your own home and your own life," she tells Jesse. "You're not going to want to take care of a helpless old woman."

Jesse's grandmother's concerns are not at all unusual. As people get older, they must consider and cope with circumstances that younger people don't have to worry about. For example, most Americans stop working at some point during their sixties. This often results in financial strain, less contact with the outside world, and an abundance of free time.

Filling the sudden increase of time with fulfilling activities can be a challenge. Some people pursue options such as volunteer work, and some travel with enthusiasm. Others, though, find the sudden freedom overwhelming and depressing.

Cultural DIVERSITY

Growing Old in China

"I dread getting old," you hear people say. It seems that in our society, getting old often means losing much of what we value, such as independence and respect. But in other cultures, growing old has an entirely different meaning.

In many cultures, the older members of society are considered to be the most knowledgeable. They know how the weather affects crops, for example, or they know the habits of domesticated animals. They are the repositories of knowledge. To exclude older people in these cultures would be akin to destroying libraries in our society.

Though many cultures have shown great respect for the old, ancient China was extreme in this characteristic. Respect for older people was one of the

Loneliness can also be a problem for elderly people. Jesse's grandmother is luckier than many older adults—even though she has lost a spouse, she has a loving family who wants her to move in with them. The death of a spouse can leave some elderly people completely alone and isolated.

Another problem older people sometimes face is age discrimination. Also called ageism, age discrimination occurs when a person is judged solely on the basis of his or her age. If, for example, a company chooses to hire a young person rather than an older person who is just as qualified for the job, that company is practicing age discrimination.

Like all prejudices, age discrimination results, at least in part, from ignorance. Judging a person on the basis of age is just as wrong as deciding not to like someone because of his or her race, religion, sexual orientation, or physical impairment.

Needs of the Elderly Jesse's grandmother used to love to cook. Recently, however, she has lost interest in preparing foods. She doesn't even enjoy eating any-

most important tenets of the Confucian system of ethics. The tradition of revering the elderly was so strong that, in large measure, it survived the communist revolution of the 1940s and the Cultural Revolution of the 1960s.

The respect that Chinese people owed their parents was called *xiao*. To show *xiao* meant to obey one's parents, to be extremely polite to them, and to care for them in their old age. It was thought that nothing could repay parents for the gift of life, but *xiao* was at least a meager attempt.

Older people were considered so special that only they could have birthday celebrations. A birthday was not considered to be noteworthy unless it was a 60th, 70th, 80th, 88th, or 100th birthday.

Even though the influence of old people is not quite as absolute in contemporary China as it was in the past, it is still understood that younger generations will care for their aging parents; very few elderly people live in nursing homes. In this way, the concept of *xiao*— a feeling of respect and obligation toward the aged—remains to tie the generations together.

more. Jesse's grandmother might be losing her sense of taste, which sometimes happens as a person gets older. She may need to eat specially prepared foods that are highly seasoned in order to enjoy meals again. Some organizations, such as Meals on Wheels, serve hot, specially prepared foods to people such as Jesse's grandmother, who are confined to their homes.

Another common need among elderly people is appropriate housing. Like Jesse's grandmother, most older adults prefer to live in their own homes for as long as they can. Modifications and adjustments can be made to make this possible. Special ramps, lighting, and wider doorways, for example, can make it possible for a person in a wheelchair to be mobile around the house.

If living at home becomes too difficult, though, a choice must be made. People who can afford to do so may choose to live in retirement communities, which offer special care and companionship.

Another option for people in this situation is to move in with family. Jesse's grandmother finally decided to do this. At first Jesse was surprised at how many adjustments had to be made. He could no longer listen to his radio late at night—it kept his grandmother awake. Sometimes he had to come straight home from school to care for her when no one else was around. But eventually Jesse grew to love living with his grandmother. She had great stories to tell, and she always had time to listen whenever something was troubling him.

Sometimes an elderly person will almost completely lose mental or physical functioning. When this happens, a nursing home may be the best option. A nursing home is a facility that offers special attention and long-term care for those who require it. Only a small percentage of elderly people in the United States live in nursing homes.

Stress-management techniques are discussed in detail in Chapter 9.

Tips for Healthy Aging The most important thing you can do now to stay healthy in the years to come is to practice good health habits. You learned earlier that getting regular exercise and eating a healthy diet decrease your risk of suffering certain diseases when you get older. Getting regular physical checkups, seeing a dentist regularly, and practicing good hygiene are some other things you can do to help yourself remain healthy during the years to come.

Avoiding tobacco, alcohol, and other drugs can also help you stay healthy throughout your life. Some people turn to these drugs to help them handle stress. When not managed properly, stress can cause physical disease, but there are better ways to manage stress than to use drugs. The techniques discussed in Chapter 9 can help you do this.

Review

1. Name the three stages of adulthood.

2. Define emotional maturity. How does it differ from physical maturity?

3. Describe three things an elderly person might be concerned about.

4. **LIFE SKILLS: Coping** What could you say to a friend who has just found out that his or her grandfather has Alzheimer's disease?

5. **Critical Thinking** Why do you think Jesse's grandmother reacted the way she did when Jesse's parents asked her to live with them? How do you think you would react?

18.2 Marriage and Parenthood

• • • • •
Objectives

- *Name two reasons why people get married.*

- *List three ingredients that can help a marriage be successful.*

- *Name three difficulties teenagers who marry may face.*

- *Name three responsibilities of parenthood.*

Carmen, the girl discussed in the beginning of this chapter, has been seeing Danny for about two months. They really like being together—Carmen has feelings for Danny she's never had for anyone else. For that reason, she was kind of disturbed that Danny wasn't in her dream about getting married.

But the more she thought about it, the more she realized that it was pretty silly to think about marrying Danny—or anyone else, for that matter—at this time of her life. In fact, she wasn't all that sure she ever wanted to get married. As for having children—well, that can wait a while, too.

Why People Get Married

Carmen isn't certain how she feels about it yet, but when she gets older she may very well decide that she does want to get married. More than 90 percent of American adults have made that decision. There are several different reasons why people get married. The best reason for two people to get married is that they want to make a life-long commitment to be with the person they love and respect. Some people get married because they want to have children or because they seek the close companionship that marriage can provide. Others get married because they are seeking financial security. Still others marry because it is expected of them or because they are scared they will end up alone.

Successful Marriage

The most important ingredients two people can bring to a marriage are love and respect. Marriage often involves putting another person's needs before your own and making difficult sacrifices for the sake of your spouse's happiness. It takes a great deal of love and respect to do these things.

Other factors needed for a successful marriage are emotional maturity and the ability to compromise. The decisions you make when you are married affect both you *and* your spouse. What if a certain job you want involves moving across the country? What if you want to have children, but your spouse doesn't know if he or she wants them? A person who is not emotionally mature would probably have a difficult time making the kinds of compromises that are required to sustain the type of partnership that is necessary for a healthy and successful marriage.

One more ingredient that makes marriage successful is the ability to communicate effectively. Two people who are in a

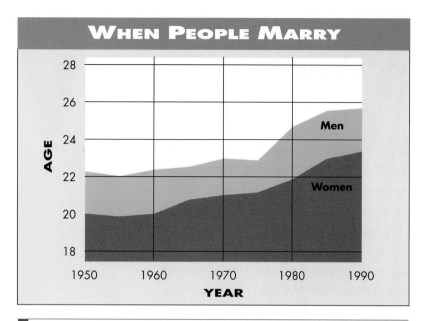

WHEN PEOPLE MARRY

(FIGURE 18-5) **Studies show that men and women are getting married at an older age than they once did.**

People who have very busy jobs that require extensive travel or whose jobs require that they move often may also choose not to marry. It's not always easy to juggle a busy, demanding career with marriage, although it can be done.

Some people decide not to get married simply because they prefer to remain single. The decision to remain single is the right one for many people. Those who don't marry usually have more time for friends and career and are generally able to be completely independent and self-sufficient. Marriage, they may feel, would jeopardize these freedoms.

lifelong partnership must be able to tell each other how they are feeling and what they are thinking. As they do in all relationships, conflicts will inevitably arise in marriage. People who are in a good marriage are able to resolve these conflicts through communication and respect. Conflict-resolution skills are discussed in some detail in Chapter 17.

When two people are willing to make the commitment marriage requires, the result can be a rewarding, fulfilling relationship, well worth the work and compromise it requires.

Conflict-resolution skills are discussed in Chapter 17.

Reasons People Don't Get Married

Like all of life's choices, marriage is not for everyone and is not right for every partnership. Two people who enjoy being together but are not willing to make necessary compromises, for example, probably would not be happy married to each other.

Teen Marriage

In addition to the challenges of every marriage, a marriage between teenagers has its own set of difficulties. It is almost impossible for teenagers who are still in school to support each other financially. In order to make ends meet, married teenagers often find that they must leave school to work full time.

Having enough money to live on becomes more important—and more difficult to accomplish—if the couple has a child to support. Married teenagers who are also parents will find it practically impossible to find the time and energy to do the things they once took for granted, such as going to the movies, eating out, or just being with friends.

The emotional responsibilities of marriage can also take their toll on teenagers. No one finds it easy to make the compromises and selfless decisions required for a successful marriage. But it can be especially difficult for teenagers, who are still developing emotionally and who are probably not ready to put another person's needs before their own.

Divorce and Remarriage

Unfortunately, not all marriages are successful. When a marriage falters, some couples try living apart for awhile. Such an arrangement is called a separation. If one or both partners decide that the marriage is over, they will generally seek a divorce. A **divorce** is the legal end of a marriage.

A divorce can be very painful emotionally, not only for the two people going through it, but also for their sons and daughters. Sometimes, divorced people decide to marry again. Remarriage can also be difficult, particularly when there are children involved. Chapter 19 examines divorce and marriage in greater detail and offers some advice on ways to cope with the stress of divorce.

Parenthood

The decision to have children may be the most important one you will ever make. The commitment you make to a child is lifelong. Parenthood is rewarding and exciting, but it isn't easy. In fact, being a parent is a job that requires care and attention 24 hours each day, 7 days each week.

Family Planning If married couples don't want to start a family, they can prevent pregnancy by using contraceptives every time they have sexual intercourse. A **contraceptive** is a device or method that prevents the fertilization or implantation of a woman's egg. Some methods of contraception are more effective than others. Using a condom with spermicidal foam, for example, is a more effective method of con-

Chapter 19 discusses the effects of divorce and remarriage on teenagers.

divorce:

the legal end to a marriage.

contraceptive:

a device or method that prevents the fertilization or implantation of a woman's egg.

(FIGURE 18-6) **Dating is an exciting and pleasurable activity for many teenagers. But teenagers who decide to get married must contend with some very difficult circumstances.**

For information on fertilization and conception, see Chapter 16.

traception than simply using a condom. For definitions and reliability of different forms of contraception, see Figure 18-7.

Responsibilities of Being a Parent

Being a parent means caring for another human being completely. It means putting the welfare of your children before everything else. It means being able to support your children both financially and emotionally. It means feeding your children when you would rather be sleeping, laughing at their jokes when you've heard them thousands of times before, and letting them know you love them when they are convinced they are unlovable.

In other words, being emotionally mature is the most important key to being a

Actions and Effectiveness of Some Contraceptives

Method	Action	Effectiveness
Birth control pill	Temporarily stops a woman from ovulating and prevents the implantation of an ovum into the uterine lining; women take one pill every day.	97–99.9%
Condoms	Thin sheath that fits over penis and collects sperm.	88–98%
Diaphragm	Rubber cup that covers cervix and prevents sperm from reaching egg; most effective when used with spermicide.	72–94%
Spermicidal foams, creams, jellies, vaginal suppositories	Chemicals that are inserted inside the vagina to kill sperm and prevent sperm from entering the uterus; for greater effectiveness, should be used with a condom.	75–90%
IUD (intrauterine device)	A small device inserted by a health-care provider into the uterus, where it remains and prevents pregnancy for several years.	94–97%
Hormone implants	Six small capsules implanted in the skin of a woman's arm; releases a contraceptive hormone called progestin; effective for up to five years.	99.96%
Rhythm method	Requires that a couple determine when the woman is ovulating and abstain from sexual intercourse during that time.	80–86%

(FIGURE 18-7) **When used incorrectly, contraceptives offer no protection against pregnancy or sexually transmitted disease. Even when used correctly, no method of contraception is as effective as abstinence.**

Check Up

Are You Ready to Be a Parent?

Answer the following questions to determine how ready you are to be a parent.

1. Could you handle a child and a job at the same time? Would you have time and energy for both?

2. Would you be willing to give up the freedom to do what you want to do, when you want to do it?

3. Would you be willing to decrease the time spent on your social life and spend more time at home?

4. Could you afford to support a child?

5. Would you want to raise a child where you now live? If not, can you afford to move? Are you willing to move?

6. Would a child fit into your career plans or educational plans for the future?

7. Are you willing to devote about 18 years of your life to the complete care of a child?

8. Do you understand how a child grows and develops or what children can be reasonably expected to understand?

9. Do you have the patience to cope with the noise and confusion that come with caring for a child?

10. Are you able to control your anger so that you won't take it out on a child?

11. Would you be able to discipline a child without being too strict?

12. Are you willing to take responsibility for a child's health and safety?

13. Would you be able to accept a child who developed values and ideas that are different from your own?

14. Would it matter to you whether the child you have is male or female?

15. Would you be as loving and accepting of an unhealthy child as you would be of a healthy child?

The more "Yes" answers you gave, the better parent you would probably be. Remember that becoming a parent is a serious responsibility. It is unfair—to you and to the child— to conceive a child without having considered your reasons for wanting to become a parent. Having a child doesn't make you "adult"; acting responsibly does.

(FIGURE 18-8) **Parenting requires time, patience, love, and a great deal of emotional maturity. But the rewards it offers are plentiful.**

Chapter 17 discusses the difficulties of teenage parenting.

successful parent. As you now know, emotional maturity is not a quality you can acquire overnight. It takes years of growth and experience to become a mature adult. This is one reason why teenage parents, who are still growing physically and emotionally, so often find their responsibilities overwhelming. The difficulties of being teenage parents are discussed in greater detail in Chapter 17.

Being financially secure also makes the job of parenting more manageable. Every state requires parents to support their children until the children reach age 18 (in some states it is 21). Clothing, feeding, and educating a child for 18 years is extraordinarily expensive.

It is also important for good parents to provide discipline. It is not easy to reprimand or punish a child for making mistakes. Some parents may remember making the same mistakes when *they* were younger. On the whole, discipline that is accompanied by compassion and love is the surest way to help a child understand what is right and what is wrong.

For all its difficulties and challenges, being a parent is one of life's most satisfying experiences. How good a parent do you think you'd be? Read the Check Up feature on page 397 to find out.

Review

1. *What are two possible reasons why people get married?*

2. *Name three ingredients that can help a marriage be successful.*

3. *What are three difficulties teenagers who marry may face?*

4. *Name three responsibilities of parenthood.*

5. ***Critical Thinking*** *What do you think is the most important quality a parent can have? Explain your answer.*

CHAPTER 18

Highlights

Summary

- Adulthood is divided into three stages: young adulthood, middle adulthood, and older adulthood.

- Decisions made during your adulthood require a certain degree of emotional maturity. For that reason, emotional maturity is a major goal to attain during young adulthood.

- Some middle-aged people may experience feelings of sadness when their children leave home, but middle adulthood also presents an opportunity to savor happy experiences.

- Common needs among elderly people include companionship, proper meals, and appropriate housing. As people grow older, they may elect to modify their own homes, move in with family,

or live in retirement communities or nursing homes.

- The most important ingredients two people can bring to a marriage are love and respect.

- Marriage is particularly difficult for teens because they are still developing emotionally and may not be ready to put another person's needs before their own.

- Being emotionally and financially secure are important keys to being a successful parent. Good parents should also provide discipline accompanied by compassion and love.

Vocabulary

young adulthood the period of adulthood between the ages of 20 and 40.

middle adulthood the period of adulthood between the ages of 41 and 65.

older adulthood the period of adulthood past the age of 65.

emotional maturity the capacity to act independently, responsibly, and unselfishly. Being emotionally mature requires having compassion, integrity, and self-esteem.

Alzheimer's disease an incurable illness characterized by a gradual and permanent loss of memory. Alzheimer's disease most commonly affects the elderly.

Parkinson's disease an incurable disease characterized by a gradual loss of control of muscle function. Parkinson's disease most commonly affects the elderly.

contraceptive a device or method that prevents the fertilization or implantation of a woman's egg.

Chapter Review

Concept Review

1. The period between the ages of 20 and 40 is known as _____ .

2. Age does not necessarily reflect _____ maturity.

3. Menopause occurs during _____ .

4. _____ and _____ are two incurable diseases that affect the elderly.

5. _____ occurs when a person is judged solely on the basis of his or her age.

6. A _____ may be recommended as housing for elderly people who lose almost complete mental and physical functioning.

7. Perhaps the best reason people get married is that they want to make a _____ to someone they love and _____ .

8. An important ingredient that makes a marriage successful is the ability to _____ effectively.

9. If one or both partners decide that the marriage has failed, a _____ will usually result.

10. Discipline that is combined with _____ and _____ is the best way to help a child understand what is right and what is wrong.

Expressing Your Views

1. Your grandparents are in their mid-seventies, and they are considering moving to a community of retired adults. It would provide a lot of opportunities for them, like tennis, book clubs, a new group of friends, and on-site health care, but it would mean they would have to give up their home. What do you think they should do?

2. What are some advantages of being middle-aged? What are some disadvantages?

3. Your friend Jed is planning to drop out of school and get married. He has asked you for your opinion of his decision. Explain how you would answer your friend.

4. Explain why you think compromise plays such an important role in the success of a marriage.

Life Skills Check . . . . . .

1. Setting Goals

Think of two long-range goals you have for the next five years. Then list ways these goals would be affected by marriage and by parenthood. How can you help yourself stay on track and achieve your goals? Share your thoughts about the impact of marriage and parenthood on one's life with the class.

2. Coping

Your grandmother has just been placed in a nursing home. You know it is the best place for her because she is too sick to stay at home. You have always been close to your grandmother and you want to continue the close relationship; however, you feel uncomfortable visiting her in the nursing home. What should you do? How can you maintain a strong relationship with her?

Projects . . . .

1. Develop a questionnaire for adults. Interview three adults, one from each of the three age groups. Include the following questions: What are your goals now? How are they different from the goals you set during your teenage years? Share your results with the class.

2. Write a creative essay in which you describe yourself and your life at age 35 and at age 70. Include a

discussion of your work, your family life, and your leisure time.

3. Work with a group to plan a budget for a newlywed couple. Include expenses such as rent, utilities, food, clothing, insurance, transportation, and entertainment. Consider who would be responsible for paying the bills and what would be done to cover emergency expenses.

Plan for Action . . . .

Marriage and parenthood are two of the most life-changing events that you can experience. Create a plan that you think would help you become better prepared for decisions regarding these actions.

CHAPTER
19
Families

◆ ◆ ◆

Section 19.1 *Understanding Family Relationships*

Section 19.2 Coping With Family Problems

Families serve important functions.

After Braylon's mother died he moved in with his grandparents. Since his father lived thousands of miles away, Braylon got to see him only a few times a year. It was a rough time—he loved his grandparents, but he also really missed his mother and father. His grandparents took good care of him though, and they were always ready to listen when he had something on his mind.

Things gradually started to settle down, and Braylon was able to concentrate on school again. Then his Uncle William moved back home, and Braylon had to share a bedroom with him! William was in his twenties—what right did he have to move back home and mess up Braylon's room with all his stuff? Braylon decided to talk to his grandfather about how he was feeling. Maybe his grandfather could help him cope with all of the changes.

Section
19.1
Understanding Family Relationships

Objectives

- *Name the three main functions of healthy families.*

- *Explain how families have changed in recent years.*

- *Name the characteristics of healthy families.*

- *Consider what your own family will be like when you are an adult.*
  LIFE SKILLS: Setting Goals

Most of us grow up in some type of family. Your family may be the traditional kind, composed of a father, a mother, and one or more children. Or like Braylon's family, it may be less traditional.

Whatever kind of family you have, it probably means a lot to you. Healthy families provide us with love and support. They also teach us lessons about family relationships, which we use when we establish our own families. When people begin their own families, they tend to model them after the family relationships they experienced when they were children. If you grew up in a healthy family, this tendency to reproduce your childhood experience can have very positive effects.

Functions of Healthy Families

Although there is great diversity among families, all healthy families have similar functions. Whether a healthy family consists of just a parent and child, or if it also includes grandparents, a stepparent, and halfbrothers and sisters, it serves three basic functions.

First, families help provide basic physical needs such as food and shelter. When a family member is ill, the family provides the necessary care.

Second, families provide emotional support. The members of a supportive family know they can turn to each other when they have problems. Emotional bonding occurs in healthy families through shared experiences and close communication.

Third, families help provide structure for our lives. Your family helps you organize your activities and schedule your time.

You might want to stay up late at night, for example, but your parents or guardians probably require that you go to bed early so you will be rested the next day. A healthy family looks out for your best interests by providing structure.

Types of Families

The great variety of family types makes it difficult to define the word *family*. But regardless of who is included in the family structure, any family can be healthy and happy.

The traditional structure of a mother, father, and one or more children is known as

Cultural DIVERSITY

Extended Families of Hispanic Americans

Hispanic Americans are the second largest ethnic minority group in the United States. Immigrants and their descendants from Mexico, Cuba, Puerto Rico, Central and South America, and other Spanish-speaking areas make up this culturally diverse group. Despite their differences, Hispanic cultures share one important characteristic—the importance of family.

In Hispanic cultures, the word *familia* means not just the nuclear family but an extended network of parents, brothers and sisters, grandparents, aunts, uncles, cousins, and in-laws. Godparents, too, are considered to be members of the extended family. Through the custom called *compadrazgo*, a *compadre* (godfather) or *comadre* (godmother) has real responsibility for the spiritual, emotional, and material welfare of the godchild.

a **nuclear family.** At one time, the father typically worked outside the home and the mother worked inside the home, taking care of the children and the household. Now, parenting roles are no longer so divided. This pattern is becoming less common as more women work outside the home and men take a more active role in parenting.

The nuclear family tends to go through the following four stages: beginning stage, parenting stage, empty-nest stage, and retirement stage.

The focus of the beginning stage is the establishment of the household by the new couple. They are adjusting to each other and are planning the things that will be important to them in their life together.

The parenting stage begins with the birth or adoption of the first child and lasts until the youngest child leaves home.

The empty-nest stage takes place when the children leave home, which used to be when the parents were middle-aged. It may now be later than middle age for parents who have children later in life or for parents whose children live at home for a while as adults. Some parents experience adjustment problems when their children leave home, especially if their children were the center of their activities. Others manage

nuclear family:

a family in which a mother, a father, and one or more children live together.

A child who grows up in such a family therefore has the benefit of a great deal of social support.

Grandparents are highly respected members of traditional Hispanic families. As esteemed authority figures, they play a large role in the family decision-making process. The elders also make significant contributions to the family by helping with household tasks and child care.

A strong family system like this promotes good health by providing social support and an atmosphere of mutual respect.

(FIGURE 19-1) **Single-parent households are becoming increasingly common.**

couple family:

a family in which only a husband and a wife live together in the home.

single-parent family:

a family in which only one parent lives with the children in the home.

extended family:

an emotionally close family that includes relatives outside the central family unit.

perfectly well and, in fact, welcome the freedom to make decisions and to use their time without having to consider their children at home.

It is becoming more common for grown children to live at home with their parents. Many young adults cannot afford to live on their own, so they continue to live with their parents until they have the money to move. Others move out, find out they can't afford their own place or miss the emotional support of home, and move back in with their parents.

In the retirement stage, people adjust to changes associated with leaving the work force. They also deal with the changes that are part of aging.

An **extended family** includes relatives who are not part of the central family unit but who are emotionally close. They may be grandparents, grandchildren, aunts, uncles, or cousins. Years ago, it was very common for extended families to live together, but it is less common now.

A **couple family** has only the husband and wife living at home. Some couples never have children. They may choose not to have children, or they may be unable to reproduce or to adopt children. Others may have children who are living with someone else—a former spouse, a grandparent, or another relative.

A family in which only one parent lives with the children is called a **single-parent family.** The single parent may be divorced, never married, or widowed. Most single-parent families are headed by women, although many are headed by men. The single parent manages all aspects of the household alone, which can be extremely difficult if the parent also works outside the home. Juggling home and work responsibilities is not easy.

Sometimes divorced parents spend equal amounts of time with their children. In one arrangement, the children may spend one week with one parent and the next week with the other. Or the children may spend three or four days with one parent and then three or four days with the other parent. The important consideration for parents in this situation should be what is best for the child.

A **blended family** results when divorced or widowed parents remarry. The parents and their children from previous marriages combine to form the blended family. The parents may decide to have more children together. The parent who is not a child's biological father or mother is known as a stepparent. Some stepparents legally adopt their new spouse's children.

The members of a blended family face unique problems. They often must deal with changes in the family rules, for example, or they must work out arrangements in which unrelated children share a bedroom.

Some families don't fit any of the descriptions but are families nevertheless. A grandparent may take care of one or more grandchildren, for instance, or a child may live with a foster family. Sometimes people who aren't married or related choose to live together to support and care for one another. These people grow into a family, too.

How Families Have Changed

In recent years, families have changed a great deal. The typical family of the 1950s and 1960s was defined as a working father, a mother who stayed home, and two children. Today, only about 10 percent of families in the United States fit that description.

Years ago, women were expected to stay at home, care for their children, and tend to the household chores. But circumstances have changed. Today, most women with children work outside the home. Some women work primarily because of the

blended family:

a family that results when divorced or widowed parents remarry. The parents and their respective children from previous marriages live in the home together.

(FIGURE 19-2) **Blended families bring two households together.**

(FIGURE 19-3) **It is important for all family members to have responsibilities.**

satisfaction they receive from their accomplishments in the workplace. Others prefer not to work outside the home but must do so to support themselves and their family. Still other women prefer to stay at home and are able to do so. It is both challenging and rewarding to care for a family and a home. One of the benefits of recent changes in society is that many options are available to women, and each can be very satisfying.

Another major difference between today's families and those of the past is the number of single-parent families. Mostly as a result of the high divorce rate, single-parent families are much more common today than they were in earlier times. There are also many more blended families since most divorced people remarry.

Today's families are smaller in comparison with the families of the past. Before, having many children was beneficial if a family owned a farm or business; the children contributed to the material success of the family by working from an early age. Now, very few people in this country rely on their children for the family's economic survival. Even people who own a farm or business do not depend on their children as parents did years ago. These people usually hire other people to work in the business or on the farm and expect their children to help out only occasionally. Another reason for smaller families today is the high cost of raising children. It now costs a minimum of $100,000 to raise and educate one child through high school.

Characteristics of Healthy Families

Healthy families have certain characteristics in common. These include respect for family members, shared responsibilities, good communication, emotional support, and the ability to manage change.

Respect for Family Members Respect for family members is essential to a healthy family—this includes respect for privacy, property, and feelings. Respect means that you value what is important to another person. A brother might show respect for a sister, for example, by controlling an urge to read her diary. In this way he is respecting her privacy. A father might show respect for a teenage son by not criticizing his son's color choices in clothing. In this way he is respecting his son's current sense of fashion. If family members are not treated with respect, they might withdraw from the family.

Shared Responsibilities Responsibility helps us feel important and valuable. It is important that all family members have responsibilities, though they should be appropriate to each person's age and abilities. The responsibilities of a 4-year-old should be different from those of a 14-year-old, which should be different from those of a 40-year-old.

Good Communication Good communication is a vital ingredient of successful family relationships. People need to be able to express their feelings in an open and supportive environment. One of the most important communication skills is listening. Sometimes the best thing you can do for someone is simply to listen.

Effective communication can go a long way toward helping families work through their problems. Without it, the problems will probably get worse.

Communication skills are discussed in Chapter 17.

*Life*SKILLS: Setting Goals

Your Future Family . . . . . .

What will your own family be like when you are an adult? You can start thinking about it now by answering the following questions.

1. Do you want to get married? If your answer is yes, when do you think you will be ready for marriage?

2. Will you work outside the home? Explain.

3. Will you want your spouse to work outside the home? Explain.

4. Do you want to have children? Explain.

5. If you want to have children, how many would you like?

6. Who will watch your children before they enter kindergarten? You? Your spouse? Another family member? A day-care center? Someone else?

(FIGURE 19-4) **Good communication is an important characteristic of a healthy family.**

adjust to maintain good relationships. Space must be shared, new responsibilities must be assumed, and the family rules might have to be changed.

If a family member becomes disabled, the family must change to accommodate the disability. The physical structure of the apartment or house may have to be altered, and other family members may be called on to assist the disabled person, and to help him or her adapt to a new situation.

Disability and the addition of new family members are examples of dramatic changes that a family must adjust to. Most changes are less dramatic and occur over a longer period of time. As individual family members grow older, they develop new interests and begin to follow different life paths. Such changes are a completely normal part of life. Members of healthy families are usually able to accept and adapt to these new situations.

Emotional Support A healthy family provides emotional support to its members. For example, a teenager in a healthy family could turn to the family for support if he or she didn't make the track team or failed a test. A husband or wife can seek support from a spouse when going through a difficult time at work.

Ability to Manage Change Changes occur frequently in families. A healthy family can manage the variety of changes that occur during its members' lifetimes.

When family members are added to a household, the relationships between members may become more difficult, simply because it's a new situation. Living arrangements change when a baby is born, a grandparent moves in, a parent remarries, or grown children move back home after living on their own for a while. These changes aren't bad; they just mean the family has to

Review

1. *Name the three main functions of healthy families.*

2. *Explain how families have changed in recent years.*

3. *Name the characteristics of healthy families.*

4. **LIFE SKILLS: Setting Goals**
Describe the kind of family you would like to have when you are an adult. What actions can you take now to help your plans succeed?

5. **Critical Thinking** *What social changes have caused the shift in attitudes about women working outside the home?*

19.2 Coping With Family Problems

Objectives

- Describe the common emotional reactions of a child to parents' divorce.
  ■ **LIFE SKILLS: Coping**

- Name two actions a person can take to cope with parents' divorce.
  ■ **LIFE SKILLS: Coping**

- Describe the effects on a child who grows up in a dysfunctional family.

- Name two actions that could help a teenager cope with living in a dysfunctional family.
  ■ **LIFE SKILLS: Coping**

- Apply the decision-making model to a family problem.
  ■ **LIFE SKILLS: Making Responsible Decisions**

Although it would be wonderful if all families lived happily ever after, we know this is not the case. All families have problems. Some problems are temporary, and the family either copes with them or solves them. Other family problems are more serious and long lasting. As a teenager, you are not in a position to solve your family's problems, but you can find ways of coping with them.

If Your Parents Divorce

Each year, more than 1 million children experience the divorce of their parents. Although divorce is extremely common, it can be a shattering experience for all members of a family. When parents divorce, their children have to make major adjustments to cope with the changes that result.

(FIGURE 19-5) **If your parents divorce, you will have to make adjustments to cope with the changes that result.**

Emotional Reactions After parents divorce, children often see less of the parent who moved out. They may see that parent only on holidays or during the summer. In some extreme cases, they never see that parent again. This creates a tremendous sense of loss for children who want to be close to the parent they no longer live with. It is natural to have strong emotional reactions—they are part of the grieving process.

At first, there may be anger at the parent who left; the child may feel betrayed and abandoned. There also may be anger at the parent who stays—a feeling that this parent has somehow caused the other parent to leave. It is common to take sides with one parent, but rarely does either parent deserve all the blame for a divorce. Because marriage is a very personal relationship, others outside the relationship cannot understand all the underlying reasons for the divorce.

Sometimes children feel very guilty after a divorce and blame themselves for their parents' decision. A person whose parents are divorcing may think, "If only I had been better, this would never have happened." But it's important to realize that getting married is a decision for adults, and therefore ending a marriage is also a decision for adults. Children are *not* responsible for their parents' divorces, although they may feel like they are.

Children of divorced parents may also experience anxiety about the future. Often there is anxiety about money or about whether the family will have to move. Again, these are matters for adults. Children are not responsible for their family's financial situation. They may, however, have to make some sacrifices to help make ends meet, especially during the initial adjustment period.

Another very common emotional reaction is depression. When parents divorce, the children may have problems sleeping and may find it harder to concentrate in school. They may have a poor appetite or feel generally listless and down. It is normal for children to experience a sense of sadness and loss when their parents divorce. If they are sad for more than a few weeks,

What Would You Do ?

Making Responsible Decisions

Should You Move Back Home?

Imagine that you graduated from college a year ago, and got a job as a copywriter at a small advertising company. You hope to work your way up the ladder there. In the meantime, you bought a used car and began sharing an apartment with two of your friends.

Then you discover that you never have enough money to make it from one paycheck to the next. You're constantly having to borrow money from your parents. Finally your father suggests that you just move back home until you make enough money to live on your own.

In a way, his idea is tempting; you have missed the refrigerator full of food and a washer and dryer in the house. But on the other hand, you have worked very hard to be self-sufficient, and you worry that others might think less of you for not "making it" in the real world. What would you do? What are your options?

Remember to use the decision-making steps:

1. State the Problem.
2. List the Options.
3. Imagine the Benefits and Consequences.
4. Consider Your Values.
5. Weigh the Options and Decide.
6. Act.
7. Evaluate the Results.

they should seek professional help. They could start by talking with a parent or a school counselor, who could refer them to a therapist or support group.

One good way to deal with your emotions is to communicate them to people you trust. In a situation like divorce, you might want to spend more time talking with your friends, especially those who have had a divorce in their family.

Another thing you could do is get involved in a new hobby or sport. Find something that absorbs your interest and takes your mind off problems that you cannot solve.

It's important to realize that attempting to escape from emotional pain by using alcohol or other drugs will not help, nor will expressing anger through violence or abuse. These behaviors create more serious problems and prolong the pain.

After children come to accept their parents' divorce, they will be able to look at the situation and evaluate it more objectively. A happy single-parent family suits some people better than an unhappy two-parent family.

Remarriage At some point, divorced parents may begin dating and eventually remarry. The remarriage of a parent can create new feelings of loss for the children. It might be the first time that a child has to abandon the dream that his or her family will someday get back together. The new stepparent may take away some of the attention a child was used to receiving from a parent. The stepparent may have children, and later there may be half-siblings, all of whom could threaten the child's sense of security in terms of how the parent spends his or her time and how money is distributed.

It takes some time to build a new family. If you are in this situation, be realistic, and recognize that adjustments may be difficult. But also be aware that second marriages are often quite successful and that a happy, united family can emerge. Try to do your part to bring this about—be patient, and understand that all family adjustments take time to be successful—and you may find that, rather than losing a parent, you have gained valuable family members.

Dysfunctional Families

A family that fulfills the basic functions of a healthy family—to meet the basic physical needs of family members, to provide emotional support, and to provide structure—can be thought of as a functional family. A family that does not fulfill these basic functions is known as a **dysfunctional family.**

In some dysfunctional families, children may not be physically cared for. They may not be fed, clothed, or sheltered properly. In most dysfunctional families, however, the basic physical needs of children are met, but their emotional needs are not. Children might be neglected or abused. In some dysfunctional families children are rigidly controlled, while in others very little structure is provided.

Most dysfunctional families are a direct outgrowth of troubled parents. The parents may have an unhappy marriage, problems with alcohol or other drugs, or emotional problems. Usually, the parents grew up in troubled families. These parents don't intend to be inadequate parents; they are simply overwhelmed by their own problems and are therefore incapable of meeting their children's needs.

But regardless of parents' intentions, their behavior has a profound and lasting effect on children. Children who do not receive adequate parenting may develop low self-esteem, and grow up ashamed of their family and themselves. They often

dysfunctional family:

a family that does not fulfill the basic functions of a healthy family.

(FIGURE 19-6) **Many forms of help are available for troubled families.**

While you do what you can to improve your situation, remember that you are a valuable person, even if your parents don't treat you that way. You are lovable, even if it sometimes seems that your parents don't love you. It isn't your fault that you are part of a troubled family.

When things seem especially bad, remind yourself that when you reach adulthood, you will have much more control over your life. You will be in a position to heal the old hurts and create the kind of life you want for yourself.

Emotional, physical, and sexual abuse are discussed in Chapter 20.

feel that they don't belong anywhere and that they are not "good enough." As a result, they may be angry or depressed.

If Your Family Is Dysfunctional If you have grown up in such a family, know that help is available. Talk with an adult you trust about getting counseling. It would be most helpful if your entire family received counseling, but if that is not possible, don't hesitate to go by yourself.

It will also help to seek out adults who care about you and who will give you some of the emotional support you are missing. Do you have a relative—a grandparent, an aunt or uncle, or a brother or sister—that you can turn to for support? Perhaps there is a teacher, a religious leader, or another adult who would be willing to listen to you and help you.

Review

1. Describe the common emotional reactions of a child to parents' divorce.

2. ▓ LIFE SKILLS: Coping Name two actions a person can take to cope with parents' divorce.

3. Describe the effects on a child of growing up in a dysfunctional family.

4. ▓ LIFE SKILLS: Coping Name two actions that could help a teenager cope with living in a dysfunctional family.

5. ▓ LIFE SKILLS: Making Responsible Decisions What are the advantages and disadvantages of continuing to live at home after high school graduation?

6. Critical Thinking How could a person who grew up in a troubled family avoid making the same mistakes with his or her own family?

Highlights

Summary

- Families help meet basic physical needs and provide emotional support and structure for our lives.

- There are a variety of family forms, including nuclear families, extended families, single-parent families, and blended families. Some families don't fit into any of these categories.

- In recent years the number of nuclear families has decreased, while the number of single-parent and blended families has increased.

- Healthy families have certain characteristics in common: respect for family members, shared responsibilities, good communication, emotional support, and the ability to manage change.

- A family that does not fulfill the basic functions of a healthy family is known as a dysfunctional family. In most dysfunctional families, physical needs are met, but emotional needs are not.

- Children who grow up without adequate parenting may have low self-esteem, be ashamed of their families and themselves, or be angry or depressed.

- Children of dysfunctional families can be helped through counseling or by seeking emotional support from other trusted adults.

Vocabulary

nuclear family a family in which a mother, a father, and one or more children live together.

extended family an emotionally close family that includes relatives outside the central family unit.

couple family a family in which only a husband and a wife live together in the home.

single-parent family a family in which only one parent lives with the children in the home.

blended family a family that results when divorced or widowed parents remarry. The parents and their respective children from previous marriages live in the home together.

dysfunctional family a family that does not fulfill the basic functions of a healthy family.

Concept Review . . . .

1. When people begin their own families, they tend to model them after the family relationships they experienced as _____ .

2. Emotional bonding occurs in healthy families through shared _____ and close _____ .

3. A nuclear family tends to go through stages. The _____ stage takes place when the children leave home.

4. Grandparents, uncles, aunts, and cousins make up an _____ _____ .

5. A _____ family is a household in which only one parent lives with the children. Most of these families are headed by _____ .

6. Today, most women with children work _____ the home. Also, today's families are _____ in size.

7. _____ for family members, which is essential to a healthy family, means that you value what is important to the other person.

8. It is important that all family members have _____ , but they should be appropriate to each person's age and abilities.

9. One of the most important communication skills for a successful family is _____ .

10. _____ and _____ are examples of changes that a family must adjust to.

11. In most dysfunctional families, the _____ needs of the children are met, but their _____ needs are not.

12. Most dysfunctional families are the result of _____ , _____ , or the emotional problems of the parents.

Expressing Your Views . . . .

1. How are your family responsibilities helping you prepare for independent life?

2. How can teenagers whose parents have divorced help other family members cope? How could they help friends experiencing a family breakup?

3. Many family problems are worked out through communication. Why do you think it is sometimes difficult for family members to communicate with each other?

4. What are some advantages of living within an extended family structure? What are some disadvantages?

Life Skills Check

1. Setting Goals

Sometimes just listening to someone is the most helpful thing you can do. How good are your listening skills? For a week, try to practice really listening to at least one person every day. Then evaluate your efforts. Set a goal to increase the amount of time you spend listening to people who are important to you.

2. Coping

Simira's mother is planning to remarry, and her mother's future husband has two small children. Simira and her mother have lived alone for almost all of Simira's life. Now Simira is afraid that she will never get to spend time with her mother, and she's worried that her new stepbrothers will complicate her life. What could you say to Simira to help her adjust to the change?

Projects

1. Working with a partner, research and compare the family structures of two different cultures. Give an oral report on your findings.

2. Work with a group to prepare a skit involving a family with two working parents, one teen, and one eight-year-old child; the family is trying to set up a schedule for household responsibilities and tasks. After pre-senting your skit, evaluate how successful and fair the family was with the schedule.

3. Work with a group to create a bulletin-board display entitled "Healthy Families." Include family photographs, magazine pictures, or original art showing a variety of family types.

Plan for Action

A strong society depends on healthy family structures. Healthy families develop skills to work through problems. Devise a plan to help your family work out its problems and to help promote your family's health.

Preventing Abuse and Violence

◆ ◆ ◆ ◆

By the age of 18, the average person has seen approximately 250,000 violent acts on television.

Naomi and Carolyn are best friends, and they have always told each other everything. But Carolyn has a new boyfriend and is reluctant to tell Naomi about the time she spends with him. And instead of being happy about her new relationship, Carolyn is becoming quiet and withdrawn, and Naomi rarely sees her anymore. Although Carolyn insists that everything is fine, Naomi is beginning to think that something is very wrong.

A couple of weeks ago, Carolyn had a big bruise on her arm, but she had a very believable explanation when Naomi asked her about it. Last Sunday Naomi noticed that Carolyn had a swollen lip and some bruises on her leg. Naomi is beginning to think that Carolyn is being abused by her boyfriend. She has decided to confront her friend about her suspicions.

20.1 Abusive Relationships

Objectives

- *Name and define four different types of abuse.*

- *Use a decision-making model to decide what you would do if you suspected child abuse.*
  - **LIFE SKILLS: Making Responsible Decisions**

- *Know at least two ways you could report an abusive situation.*
  - **LIFE SKILLS: Using Community Resources**

How would you react if you thought a friend was being abused? Would you intervene? What if someone was subjecting you to abusive behavior? These are some very difficult questions to answer.

This chapter is devoted to helping you understand the types of violent and abusive behaviors and their consequences. The behaviors take many forms: domestic abuse, sexual assault and harassment, homicides, and even terrorism. Through constant exposure to violent images on television and in the movies, we become numbed to the significance of violent or abusive behavior. Because these images don't shock us, we are more likely to accept them as a part of life. But think about these statistics:

- The United States ranks first among developed countries in deaths due to violent acts.
- The total number of deaths by firearms in the United States is higher than the totals of the next 17 countries combined.
- Homicide is the second leading cause of death among 15–24 year olds, and the murder rate among teens is increasing. On a typical day in the United States, 9 teenagers will be murdered, and 13 teens will commit murder.

All abuse—physical abuse, sexual abuse, emotional abuse, and neglect—is against the law, which means that the police or other authorities can intervene. They can arrest the offender or otherwise make sure that the abuse does not continue.

Physical Abuse

Physical abuse occurs when a person inflicts bodily harm on another person. An abused child or adult may suffer scratches, bumps, bruises, broken bones, burns, or chipped teeth.

Though some cases of physical abuse are obvious, others are hard to detect. An abuser may be careful to hit a child, girlfriend, or wife in areas that are usually covered by clothing or may try to attribute the injury to an accident. It's likely that the abused adult or child may also try to conceal evidence of the mistreatment, which can make abuse even more difficult to detect.

Sexual Abuse

Sexual abuse is sexual behavior between an adult or adolescent and a nonconsenting person. (A minor is legally unable to give consent.) Sometimes sexual abuse is called molestation. It usually involves the touching of private parts, but it can also include the watching or the photographing of sexual acts. It can involve force on the part of the abuser, but it is usually limited to threatening. Sexual abuse is most often inflicted upon girls between the ages of 12 and 14 by a father, stepfather, other relative, or friend of the family.

Though young girls are the most common victims of sexual abuse, boys are also frequently sexually abused. It is difficult to estimate how many boys are sexually abused because they are less likely to tell anyone about the abuse.

It is rare for any child to report sexual abuse. As a result, it is very difficult to get an accurate estimate of the extent of sexual abuse. However, some experts estimate that as many as 40 million people in the United States have been sexually abused.

Programs have been developed in schools and other community settings to make sure that children and adolescents understand these important principles:

- Sexual abuse is against the law.
- Children and adolescents have the right to refuse any sexual contact and to run away and yell if they are being abused.
- It is illegal to have sex with a minor.
- In most states, you are required by law to report abuse if you suspect it.
- Children and adolescents should tell a trusted adult if they are being abused.
- Even if they did not seek help, children and adolescents should not blame themselves for what happened.

People who have experienced sexual abuse often have great difficulty forming close friendships and other intimate relationships. It is extremely important that people who have been sexually abused receive counseling so they can be assured that the abuse was not their fault.

Neglect

Few people realize that **neglect** is a form of abuse. Neglect is the failure of a parent or guardian to provide for the basic needs of a person in his or her charge. Failure to feed a child or provide adequate supervision are examples of neglect.

physical abuse:

bodily harm inflicted on another person.

sexual abuse:

sexual behavior between an adult or adolescent and a nonconsenting person.

neglect:

failure of a parent or legal guardian to provide for the basic needs of a person in his or her charge (child or adult).

(FIGURE 20-1) **One of these people appears to be an abuser and the other a victim. In reality, however, most adults who abuse children were also the victims of child abuse.**

Emotional Abuse **Emotional abuse** is emotional mistreatment of another person. A parent may continually criticize a child or fail to show love and affection. Although the effects of emotional abuse aren't as visible as those of physical abuse, they can be just as devastating. One of the worst effects of emotional abuse is low self-esteem. Children or adolescents who are emotionally abused should report the abuse to a trusted adult or call 911 for help.

Child Abuse

The term **child abuse** refers to the mistreatment of children or adolescents. Child abuse can take the form of neglect or physical, emotional, or sexual abuse. Although some children are abused by people outside the family, more than 90 percent of child abuse is inflicted by family members.

Many abused children and adolescents run away from home. They hope that living on the streets will be better than living at home. But tragically, many runaways survive by prostitution and other behaviors that endanger their lives. They also run the risk of being victims of a violent crime.

There are many reasons why parents abuse children. Lack of money, unemployment, or alcohol or drug abuse can make a parent angry or frustrated. Some parents take out their frustration on their children.

Abusive parents may expect more mature behavior from a child than is reasonable. When the child isn't able to perform as the parent expects, the parent may become abusive.

People who were abused as children are most likely to abuse their own children. They may not even realize what they are doing. To them, excessive force or mental cruelty may seem like normal discipline. It's important to remember, however, that people who were abused as children can

emotional abuse:

emotional mistreatment of another person.

child abuse:

illegal treatment committed by an adult against a child that involves use of physical, sexual, or emotional force, cruelty, or neglect.

Making Responsible Decisions

A Case of Child Abuse?

You have agreed to baby-sit for a family that you have never met before. They got your phone number from one of the other families that you baby-sit for.

When you get to the couple's house, you are told that their three-year-old son is asleep and shouldn't give you much trouble. But shortly after the couple leaves, the child starts screaming. You decide to pick him up and walk with him until he goes back to sleep. As you are lifting him out of bed you notice very large black-and-blue marks on both arms, and on looking further, you see huge welts on the child's back. You don't know what could have caused the injuries, but you are sure the boy is in a lot of pain.

You've just learned about child abuse in school. You think this child may have been beaten, but you aren't sure. What would you do? Use the decision-making steps found on page 25.

prevent the cycle of abuse from continuing with their own children. They can stop the destructive patterns by learning appropriate parenting skills.

Spouse Abuse

Physical abuse of one's husband or wife is known as **spouse abuse** or spouse battering. When violence occurs between spouses, it is usually a woman who suffers injuries because of differences in strength. Approximately 20 percent of women in the United States are victims of spouse abuse at some point in their life, and about 2,000 women die each year as a result of abuse from their partner. Pregnant women are at the greatest risk. Between 3.9 percent and 8.3 percent of women in the United States are abused during a pregnancy.

A male abuser is usually a controlling person who becomes easily frustrated. Male abusers were often victims of abuse as children. In the majority of battering cases, the man had been drinking or using other drugs.

It may be difficult to understand why an abused woman would stay with her spouse. Experts think that many abused women have low self-esteem and believe they deserve the abuse. They may feel that abuse is normal in marriage, especially if they observed their own mothers being abused. Another reason abused women stay in the relationship is that they often don't have enough money to move out and live on their own. But the most common reason is that battered women are often more afraid to leave than to stay. In many cases the batterer has threatened to kill her or the children, to kidnap the children, or to harm himself if she leaves.

Some victims of this form of abuse do decide to leave their spouse. Many communities have established shelters for such people. The shelters provide a temporary home and help people find jobs or other means of financial support. In most communities, shelters for abused spouses are listed in the White Pages of the telephone book under "Battered Women."

Elder Abuse

Elder abuse is the abuse of an elderly person. As with other kinds of abuse, family members who abuse elders are often frustrated with their lives and take their frustrations out on someone else. When a case of elder abuse is reported, trained professionals will probably require that the family participate in some type of counseling. The elderly person may be placed in another living arrangement if the counseling does not end the abuse.

spouse abuse:

abuse of one's husband or wife.

elder abuse:

abuse of an elderly person.

Peer Abuse

At the beginning of every school year, there are stories in the news about high school students or college students who have been injured or killed as a result of hazing. *Hazing* is defined as any physical or psychological abuse associated with initiation into a club or team. It includes whipping, beating, striking, branding, electronic shocking, sleep deprivation, excessive drinking, and the use of other drugs. Although most campuses have policies forbidding hazing, it is still a common practice because the nature of initiation involves secrecy. Hazing should be reported to the administration of the institution where it occurs. No club or organization is worth endangering your life.

Help for Victims of Abuse

No one deserves to be abused, whether the abuse is physical, emotional, sexual, or in the form of neglect. It is important to report abuse immediately. If you suspect abuse or are a victim of abuse, you can anonymously report the abuse to a trusted adult, the police, or the Department of Child Protective Services.

Families in which abuse and violence occur need professional help to break the cycle of abusive behavior. It is best if help is sought voluntarily, but it can be mandated by law.

Many victims feel responsible for the abuse. They believe that they are bad people who did something to deserve the abuse. Victims of abuse often need to undergo counseling to help them realize that they are not responsible for what has happened to them.

Counseling is available at many community health agencies for parents and children. The fees for counseling are usually based on ability to pay; if an individual has very little money, he or she will be charged very little or nothing for the counseling. Counseling with a private therapist will usually involve a set fee, but sometimes an agreement based on ability to pay can be arranged.

People who abuse children or fear they will do so can obtain help through Parents Anonymous, a national organization that helps parents cope without using violence. Many cities have local chapters of Parents Anonymous. Parents can call their local chapter of Parents Anonymous when they feel they are losing control. The people who answer the phones at the hotline number are trained to defuse the immediate situation and encourage parents to get ongoing help.

Review

1. Name and define four different types of abuse.

2. ▪▪ LIFE SKILLS: Making Responsible Decisions If you knew that a two-year-old child was frequently left alone for hours at a time, what would you do?

3. ▪▪ LIFE SKILLS: Using Community Resources To whom could you report a case of elder abuse?

4. Critical Thinking Why do you think sexually abused children often have trouble making friends?

Section
20.2 Sexual Assault

bjectives

- *Define sexual assault.*

- *Define acquaintance rape.*

- *Discuss how young men can avoid committing acquaintance rape.*

- *Know what a victimized person should do to get help after a sexual assault.*
  - **LIFE SKILLS: Using Community Resources**

- *Define sexual harassment.*

sexual assault:

any sexual contact with a person without his or her consent.

Sexual assault is any sexual contact with a person without his or her consent. Sexual assault is a violent way to show dominance or anger. It includes the sexual abuse of children, forced sexual intercourse (rape), and sexual harassment. Approximately 75 percent of sexual assaults are committed by people known to the victim.

Each year, women are the victims of more than 5 million violent crimes, including approximately 500,000 rapes or other sexual assaults. Every 46 seconds a woman in this country is raped. It is difficult to know exactly how many assaults against women are committed—women victimized by people they know are not likely to report the crime because they are afraid of being victimized again—but approximately one out of every four women in the United States will be sexually assaulted.

Rapists do not discriminate on the basis of age, marital status, or physical ap-

pearance. Though most victims are female, males are also sexually assaulted, usually by heterosexual men.

Taking Precautions Against Sexual Assault

A person who is sexually assaulted is never responsible for what happened. It doesn't matter if the assaulted person left the doors or windows unlocked, wore ''provocative'' clothing, hitchhiked, or went out on a date with the assailant; the victim was not responsible for the assault.

A woman can *minimize* her chances of being assaulted, though, by taking the following precautions:

- Avoid walking alone in deserted areas.
- Have your keys ready for the car or the front door.
- Make sure that no one is in the rear seat of the car before getting in.
- Keep entrances and doorways to your house or apartment brightly lit.
- Use deadbolt locks on the doors of your house or apartment.
- Keep all windows and doors locked.

It is not possible to recognize a sex offender by their outward appearance. There are, however, some behaviors that are known to be associated with sex offenders. Be wary if someone does the following:

- acts as if he knows you better than he does
- stands too close to you and seems to enjoy your discomfort
- blocks your way
- grabs or pushes you

Myths and Facts About Rape

Myth	Fact
Only young, beautiful people are raped.	Rape victims include people of all ages and appearances.
People who hitchhike or wear sexy clothing are asking to be raped.	No one asks to be sexually assaulted; nor does any victim's behavior justify or excuse the crime.
Most rapes occur in dangerous places.	More than half of all rapes occur in the home. The next most common place is in an automobile.
Most rapes occur because the rapist is sexually starved.	Most rapes occur because the rapist has a desire to overpower and humiliate someone else.
Most rapes are committed by someone unknown to the victim.	Most rapes are committed by a person known to the victim.
It is common for a woman to falsely accuse a man of rape.	There are no more false reports of rape than of any other crime. Most victims do not even report the rape.
Men are never raped.	Men are raped, usually by heterosexual men. However, men are less likely to report a rape.

(FIGURE 20-2)

The best protection is to act quickly when someone's behavior seems strange. It might require causing a scene in public, but that's better than being assaulted. Begin with a loud yell, which can intimidate the aggressor and give you confidence.

Physical resistance, including running and fighting, is entirely appropriate if you are in danger of being assaulted. It is also important to know, however, that a person who has been sexually assaulted and did not try to resist or run away has also acted appropriately. Anything a person does to stay alive during such an attack is absolutely acceptable and is nothing to be ashamed of.

Many people take self-defense classes to learn how to protect themselves. If you would like to do this, choose a class that deals specifically with self-defense in real-life situations, not martial arts such as judo and karate. Martial arts increase strength and build confidence, but they don't provide the kind of experience a person needs to defend against a sexual assault.

A Case of Acquaintance Rape

How Amy Described What Happened	**How Jim Described What Happened**

I first met Jim at a party. He was really good looking and he had a great smile. I wanted to meet him but I wasn't sure how. I didn't want to appear too forward. Then he came over and introduced himself. We talked and found we had a lot in common. I really liked him. When he asked me over to his place for a drink, I thought it would be O.K. He was such a good listener, and I wanted him to ask me out again.

When we got to his room, the only place to sit was on the bed. I didn't want him to get the wrong idea, but what else could I do? We talked for a while and then he made his move. He started by kissing. I really liked him, so the kissing was nice. But then he pushed me down on the bed. I was so startled. I tried to get up, and I told him to stop. He was so much bigger and stronger. I got scared and I started to cry. I froze and he raped me.

It was terrible – he was so rough. When it was over he kept asking me what was wrong, like he didn't know. He had just forced himself on me, and he thought that was O.K. He drove me home and he said he wanted to see me again. I'm so afraid to see him. I never thought it would happen to me.

I first met her at a party. She looked really hot, wearing a sexy dress that showed off her great body. We started talking right away. I knew that she liked me by the way she kept smiling and touching my arm while she was speaking. She seemed pretty relaxed so I asked her back to my place for a drink. When she said yes, I knew that I was going to get lucky!

When we got to my place, we sat on the bed kissing. At first, everything was great. Then, when I started to lay her down on the bed, she started twisting and saying she didn't want to. Most women don't like to appear too easy, so I knew she was just going through the motions. When she stopped struggling, I knew that she would have to throw in some tears before we did it.

She was still very upset afterwards, and I just don't understand it! If she didn't want to have sex, why did she come back to the room with me? You could tell by the way she dressed and acted that she was no virgin, so why she had to put up such a struggle I don't know.

(FIGURE 20-3) **These are two accounts of an acquaintance rape that occurred at a college. Notice that Jim has no idea he raped Amy. Whenever someone is forced to have sex, a rape has occurred.**

Preventing Acquaintance Rape

Acquaintance rape, which is sometimes called "date rape," occurs when a person is forced or coerced into sexual intercourse by an acquaintance or date. The force or coercion may be verbal pressure, threats, physical restraint, or physical violence. Any time a person's protests against engaging in sexual intercourse are ignored, a rape has occurred.

Acquaintance rape is partly the result of the way many men think they are supposed to behave with women. Some men assume they should always be aggressive and in control.

Some men see sexual intimacy as a competition between the man and the woman. As in playing sports, some young men might feel that they should "win" at any cost. Even the slang of sexual conquest is similar to that of sports: men speak of "scoring" with a woman. One young man described the situation this way: "A man is supposed to view a date with a woman as a premeditated scheme for getting the most sex out of her. He's supposed to constantly pressure her to see how far he can get. She is his adversary, his opponent in a battle. . . ."

Most women, however, have not been socialized to think of sexual intimacy as a contest. Nor have they been encouraged to be assertive in resisting things they don't want to do. As a result, they may be unprepared to resist this type of aggression.

Read the two accounts of an acquaintance rape in Figure 20-3. The account on the left was given by a female college student who was raped. The one on the right is the account given by the male college student who committed the rape. Notice how differently each interprets the events.

As with any sexual assault, the burden of responsibility for preventing acquaint-ance rape lies with the offender, not the potential victim. It requires a fundamental change in the way many men view sexual encounters.

Males can avoid committing acquaintance rape by remembering that if someone says "no" at any point, they are obligated to accept "no" as the answer. If a woman voluntarily engages in some degree of sexual intimacy, it is not the same as agreeing to intercourse. One thing does not necessarily lead to another. No matter how quietly a woman objects, she still means "no."

It is important that young women communicate their limits clearly and assertively to the other person. It will help to review the discussion about resisting pressure on pages 378–379 in Chapter 17. As in any kind of sexual assault, running away or physically resisting is entirely appropriate.

After a Sexual Assault

After any sexual assault, a victimized person should contact the police as soon as possible. It is also helpful to call the local rape-crisis hotline, which can provide counseling and emotional support, as well as assistance with the judicial system. In addition, a medical examination will probably be necessary to collect legal evidence of the assault and to screen for possible sexually transmitted diseases and pregnancy. It is important that a victim of an assault get examined before washing or using the bathroom if at all possible. A worker from the rape-crisis center can accompany the person throughout this crisis and can provide assistance even if the person chooses not to report the crime to the police.

Unfortunately, most rapes are not reported because victims of a sexual assault often feel humiliated and ashamed. They may feel that reporting the crime might prolong their feelings of anguish and that it may be better to try to forget what happened and

acquaintance rape:

the forcing or coercion of a person into sexual intercourse by an acquaintance or date.

(FIGURE 20-4) **Help for victims of sexual assault can be obtained by calling a local rape-crisis hotline.**

- staring at a person's body
- telling sexually-oriented jokes, stories, or remarks
- describing sexual acts or posting suggestive pictures or written material
- making unnecessary physical contact
- exerting pressure on someone for dates or sexual activity
- making unwelcome calls or writing unwelcome letters with sexual overtones
- making demands for sexual favors with implied threats related to benefits or opportunities

Any unsolicited conduct that fits these descriptions is sexual harassment. It is important that the victim communicates to the harasser that the conduct is unwelcome and must stop. Make sure you know the policies and procedures of your school or workplace so you know how to best handle a harassment situation.

get on with life. These feelings are completely understandable, but it is also important to know that rape is a serious crime. No matter whether the rape occurred between strangers, acquaintances, or even friends, the person who committed the rape is a criminal and deserves to be punished.

Sexual Harassment

sexual harassment:

unwanted, unwelcome, or offensive sexual behavior.

Sexual harassment is unwanted, unwelcome, or offensive sexual behaviors. Like rape, it has more to do with power than sex.

A male or female can be the victim or the perpetrator of sexual harassment. It most commonly occurs in school or the workplace. Each of the following are examples of sexual harassment:

- making demeaning remarks about a person's clothing, body, or activities

Review

1. Define sexual assault.

2. Define acquaintance rape.

3. Discuss how young men can avoid committing acquaintance rape.

4. Define sexual harassment.

5. ■■ **LIFE SKILLS: Using Community Resources** What can a victimized person do to get help after a sexual assault?

6. **Critical Thinking** Review the two accounts of a rape in Figure 20-3. What were the fallacies in Jim's thinking that led to his committing an acquaintance rape?

20.3 *Preventing Violent Conflict*

Objectives

- *Name the three major risk factors associated with homicides.*

- *Discuss the reasons why some teenagers join gangs.*

- *Know how to prevent your anger from turning into violence.*
  ■■ **LIFE SKILLS: Coping**

- *Know how to resolve conflicts without violence.*
  ■■ **LIFE SKILLS: Solving Problems**

- *Define peer mediation.*

It is estimated that by age 18, the average youth has watched 250,000 acts of violence and 40,000 attempted murders on television. These figures don't even include the violent acts depicted in movies, books, and magazines. Violence in the media often appears exciting and glamorous. Even grisly cult murders are presented in gory detail. It seems that violence has become so commonplace that we hardly react to it anymore. The lesson that many learn from all this is that if you have a problem, you solve it with violence.

What we know about violence in our society seems to indicate that too many people are attempting to solve their problems with violent acts. **Homicide**—a violent crime that results in the death of another person—is the second leading cause of death of all people aged 15 to 24.

One of the major risk factors related to homicide is the use of alcohol or other drugs. Substance abuse is a factor in almost half of all homicides in this country. Alcohol alone is involved in more than half of all violent crimes committed in the United States.

Another major risk factor is possession of a gun, since the most common weapon used to kill people is a firearm. A recent survey of high school students showed that approximately one out of 20 students had carried a gun at least once during the 30 days preceding the survey. Clearly, many deaths of young people could be prevented if people did not carry guns.

Arguments are also a major risk factor associated with homicide. As you can see in Figure 20-5, the most common event associated with a homicide is an argument. If

homicide:

a violent crime that results in the death of another person.

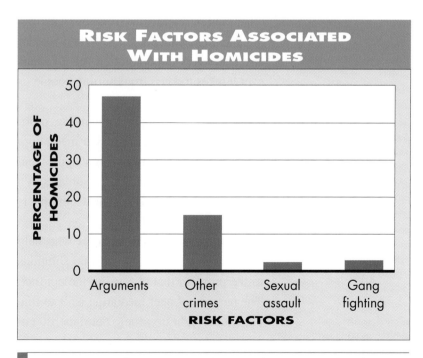

(FIGURE 20-5) **The event most commonly associated with a homicide is an argument.**

we can prevent violent arguments, especially when they occur between people who have been abusing drugs and who are carrying guns, many homicides can be avoided.

Managing Anger

Anger is a natural and even healthy emotion. Unfortunately, people often let this natural emotion change to violence. We all feel anger from time to time, and we will continue to do so throughout our life. But by learning to manage angry feelings and express them in healthy ways before they get out of control, we can help to prevent emotional and physical abuse.

Physical signals that you are getting angry are pretty easy to recognize: your heart starts to beat faster, your muscles automatically tense up, and you start to breathe more rapidly. Once you recognize what's happening, there are several things you can do.

Talking to someone about the way you are feeling is often the best way to work things out. But sometimes you need another kind of release, like running, walking, or punching a punching bag. When you are angry, it's very important that you do whatever it takes to keep from hurting people or damaging property.

Another technique for solving problems that lead to violence is peer mediation. This is a process for resolving disputes and conflicts in which a neutral person acts as a mediator for the process. This technique is often used in a school setting.

The mediators are students who help their classmates identify and find solutions to the problem that is causing the conflict. The purpose of peer mediation isn't to find out who is right or wrong, but rather to encourage students to learn how to get along with each other. The students who are in conflict are asked to tell their stories and ask

questions. The mediators help students identify ways to solve the conflict.

Situations involving name-calling, rumors, bumping into students in the hallways, and bullying are best dealt with through peer mediation. You'll find the steps of mediation in the Life Skills section on the facing page.

Resolving Conflicts Without Violence

The best way to deal with potentially violent conflicts is to avoid them. If someone seems to be picking a fight with you, walk away if you can.

If you cannot avoid the conflict, do what you can to keep the conflict from becoming violent. Take some deep breaths, stay calm, and do not raise your voice. Try to think of a way to compromise with the other person.

Gangs

Gang-related violence is increasing in this country, and more and more teenagers are becoming involved. Although many gang-related crimes are directed at enemy gang members, these crimes do not constitute the majority of gang incidents. Most of the time, people with no gang affiliation are the ones who are killed or assaulted.

Why do teenagers join gangs? Poverty and poor job prospects contribute to the proliferation of gangs. Gangs also provide a sense of family and a feeling of belonging that is lacking in many young people's lives. Michael, a former gang member who is serving time in prison, said that after his parents split up he didn't get the attention he needed. Then he joined a gang. ''There I got a little attention—from the other gang members,'' Michael said. ''I felt they loved me and they were a family.''

But there are many clubs and organizations for teens that can also provide a feeling of belonging to a family without the goal of violence. Recreation centers generally sponsor youth groups, and many schools have athletic, academic, and social clubs for interested students. Check your phone book or your school guidance counselor's office for possible options.

The desire for status is another reason some people join gangs. Gang members may get ''respect'' from others. The media may also contribute to the appeal of gangs. A radio ad for a malt liquor, for example,

LifeSKILLS: Solving Problems

Nonviolent Conflict Resolution . . . .

For the situation described below, explain how you might use peer mediation to prevent a violent conflict.

A group of people at your school have accused a student of covering a wall with graffiti. The person who has been accused claims that he didn't do it. He says he thinks he might know who did but doesn't want to say. How could peer mediation help in this situation?

Guide to Peer Mediation

Participants should be willing to	Mediation Steps
Solve the problem	Agree upon the ground rules
Tell the truth	Each student tells his or her story
Listen without interrupting	Verify the stories
Be respectful	Discuss the stories
Take responsibility for carrying out agreements	Generate solutions
Keep the situation confidential	Discuss solutions
	Select a solution
	Sign a contract

(FIGURE 20-6) **In recent years, drive-by shootings and other incidents of gang violence have become more common on the streets of our cities.**

refers to a gang tradition and compares the drink to a certain type of gun.

The status that members get from gangs is often short lived. Gang members are extremely vulnerable to homicide. A gang member who was locked up in a juvenile security camp in Los Angeles County described his life: ''I've been stabbed four times, shot three times, and locked up and beaten up so many times that it's hard to keep count. The only thing left for me is to die, but I've been ready for that every day since I turned 13, and I'm 16 now.''

There is hope for gang members; they can leave their gang and make a new life for themselves. After losing five friends in street warfare, Michael is learning to weld, and he hopes to get married and have kids when he gets out of prison. He said, ''The guys in my neighborhood, I'll always love them. . . . But I don't want that life anymore.''

- - - - -

Review

1. *Name the three major risk factors associated with homicides.*

2. *Discuss the reasons why some teenagers join gangs.*

3. *Define peer mediation.*

4. ▣ **LIFE SKILLS: Coping** *If you felt yourself becoming extremely angry at a stranger, how could you prevent your anger from turning into violence?*

5. ▣ **LIFE SKILLS: Solving Problems** *If a fellow student stole your jacket, what could you do to resolve the conflict without using violence?*

Highlights

Summary

- Abuse can take the form of physical, emotional, and sexual abuse, as well as neglect.

- People who were abused as children are more likely to abuse others.

- Alcohol and other drug abuse is a factor in most cases of spouse abuse. When violence does occur between spouses, it is usually the woman who suffers injuries, because of differences in size and strength.

- Many abused women who stay in abusive marriages do so because they have low self-esteem.

- It is important to report abuse immediately. Families in which abuse and violence occur need professional help to break the cycle of abuse.

- Sexual assault is less a sexual act than a way to show dominance over or anger toward the victim. Most sexual assaults are committed by someone the victim knows.

- To avoid acquaintance rape, men should accept that when a woman says "no" she means "no." It's also important for women to communicate their limits clearly and assertively.

- The best way to deal with potentially violent conflicts is to avoid them.

- Poverty, poor job prospects, the desire for status, and the need to belong are factors that cause youths to join gangs.

Vocabulary

physical abuse: bodily harm inflicted on another person.

sexual abuse: sexual behavior between an adult or adolescent and a non-consenting person.

neglect: failure of a parent or legal guardian to provide for the basic needs of a person in his or her charge (child or adult).

emotional abuse: emotional mistreatment of another person.

child abuse: illegal treatment committed by an adult against a child that involves use of physical, sexual, or emotional force, cruelty, or neglect.

sexual assault: any sexual contact with a person without his or her consent.

acquaintance rape: the forcing or coercion of a person into sexual intercourse by an acquaintance or date.

sexual harassment: unwanted, unwelcome, or offensive sexual behavior.

Chapter Review

Concept Review

1. Why is it sometimes difficult to detect abuse?

2. What are three factors that might cause a parent to abuse a child?

3. Name three kinds of family violence.

4. Why do abused wives have trouble leaving their spouse?

5. List three behaviors that are known to be associated with sex offenders.

6. Why is a medical examination necessary after a sexual assault?

7. Which type of self-defense class is recommended for people wanting to learn how to protect themselves?

8. How prevalent is homicide in our society?

9. What signs does your body give you when you are getting angry?

10. How do gangs provide a sense of family?

Expressing Your Views

1. Do you think all forms of sexual assault should be reported? Explain.

2. Why do you think emotional abuse should not be ignored even though the effects aren't visible?

3. Your friend confides to you that her uncle has been sexually abusing her for over a year. She refuses to tell her parents because she thinks it was her own fault for being too friendly with her uncle. How could you help her?

4. Patty works late three nights a week and must walk across a large parking lot to her car. What precautions would you encourage her to take?

Life Skills Check · · · · · ·

1. Using Community Resources
Your cousin confided that she often feels as if she is losing control with her children and that she is afraid she might hurt them. What could you advise her to do?

2. Making Responsible Decisions
Katie's parents seem to criticize everything she does. They are hardly ever at home, and when they are, Katie never hears one kind or encouraging word from them. The situation has gotten so bad that she is thinking about running away. What alternatives does Katie have?

3. Coping
You like Ray a lot and enjoy some degree of sexual intimacy, but you do not want to have intercourse with him. The last time you were on a date, he assumed that because you enjoyed kissing him, you didn't want him to stop—you had to be really firm. The two of you are supposed to go out tonight. What should you do?

Projects · · · · · · · · · · · · · · · · · ·

1. Most child-care centers are very reliable. However, child abuse does occasionally occur at these facilities. Interview a parent whose child attends a child-care center. How did the parent choose the center? What does the parent do to make sure no abuse is taking place? What would he or she do if child abuse were suspected? Share your findings with the class.

2. Work with a group to develop a puppet show to teach young children about child abuse and how to report it. Try to obtain permission to present the show to first- or second-graders in your school district.

Plan for Action · · · · · · · · · · · · · ·

Crime is one of the major health problems facing Americans today. List 10 ways to reduce your risk of becoming a victim of violent crime.

▼ Violence and the Media

Andy couldn't believe it. Ten extra laps! What had he done this time? It didn't seem to matter; no matter what he did, the coach always managed to find something wrong. Kurt, on the other hand, could get away with anything. Andy didn't really blame Kurt—after all, they were good friends—but it did seem completely unfair. The more Andy thought about it, the angrier he got. By the time he started to step into the shower, he was ready to explode. At that moment, Kurt showed up and, with a grin, popped Andy with a towel. It took Andy only a split second to react. His arm shot up, and without thinking, he shoved Kurt against the wall.

Andy and Kurt were both stunned. Andy slowly lowered his hand, struggling to

calm down. "I'm sorry, Kurt," Andy said. "I don't know what made me do that."

Andy is not the only teenager who has reacted violently to frustration and anger. Over the past several years, the incidence of violence has increased among young people to the point that homicide is now the second leading cause of death for people 15 to 24. Although aggressive and violent behavior can result from a number of factors, many psychologists and educators believe that mass media have had an enormous effect on the increase in these behaviors. From television programs to rock concerts, mass media too often depict people taking violent actions. It is possible, therefore, that Andy's behavior in the locker room could be linked to the amount of violence he has witnessed through mass-media channels.

One of the most powerful ways that mass media influence people is by providing role models. Like many living things, people learn much of their behavior by copying what they see. Someone whose behavior is copied is a role model. If the role model is an admired person, like a popular actor or athlete, association makes the role model an even more powerful factor in influencing behavior. Therefore, when a person (receiver) sees a role model coping with a problem by asking for help and

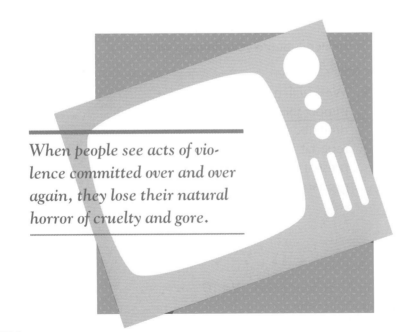

When people see acts of violence committed over and over again, they lose their natural horror of cruelty and gore.

talking about it calmly, he or she is likely to behave this way. And studies have shown that when people watch others using violence in movies or on television, their behavior tends to become more aggressive.

Another way media messages influence people is by attempting to teach attitudes and values. Unfortunately, too few of the situations used to teach values are based in reality. For instance, a Harvard University study found that many of today's cartoons represent the world as a very fearful place, where the criminals are so evil that the only way to deal with them is to destroy them completely. Even though the heros usually win, the world they live in and the solutions they use are not realistic. As a result, viewers cannot easily apply the values presented in these cartoons to real-life situations. In addition, the pain and humiliation that real victims of violence experience is generally missing from the media's treatment of violence. By not showing the negative consequences of violence, the source of a media message omits an important part of the values lesson—a reason for not using violence.

Seeing violence in the media also affects viewers in another, more subtle, way. When people are repeatedly exposed to stressful events, especially while in pleasant surroundings, the stress reaction is reduced. Consequently, when people see acts of violence over and over again, they lose their natural horror of cruelty and gore. Even news programs have this effect.

It is possible to reduce the amount of violence seen in mass media if you remember that receivers of media messages have power over the sources of those messages. Most media experts agree that violence is prevalent in the media because it attracts attention and sells products. But in a way,

people who buy albums that advocate violence or who watch violent movies and television programs are endorsing the destructive messages they contain.

As members of a major consumer group, teenagers have more power to affect the media than they realize. To help reduce the use of violence in the media and in society, think twice about spending money on something that uses violence as a marketing tool.

Critical Thinking

1. Think about how you usually react when someone makes you angry.

   - Have you always reacted this way?
   - Do people you admire behave this way? Who?
   - What kinds of things have influenced your behavior?

2. When you watch your favorite television programs tonight, take notes on how many times disagreements are handled with nonviolent solutions.

3. Analyze a movie or television program that contains violence by answering the following questions.

   - What is the source of the message to use violence?
   - What was the reason for making this movie or television program?
   - How do I benefit from the messages in this show?

4. Automobile accidents are the leading cause of death for teenagers. How do you think the scenes of car chases in movies and television programs might contribute to reckless driving and accidental deaths among teenagers?

5. Homicide is the second leading cause of death for people 15 to 24. How do you think media messages might affect violent behavior among teenagers?

DISEASES AND DISORDERS

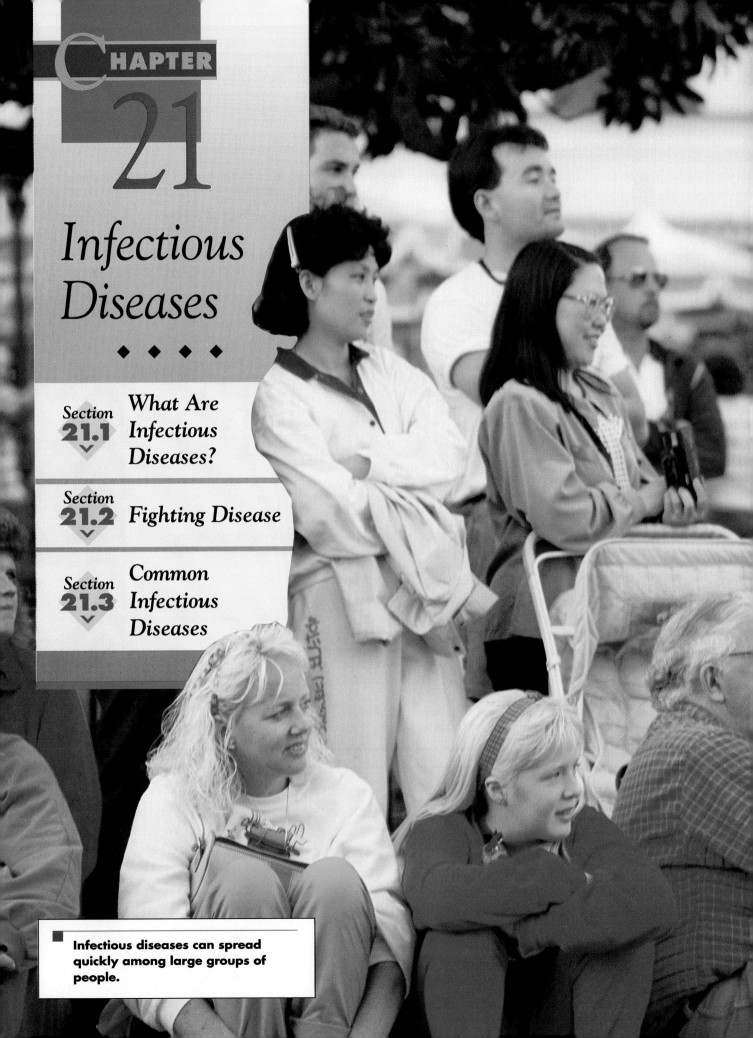

CHAPTER 21

Infectious Diseases

◆ ◆ ◆ ◆

Infectious diseases can spread quickly among large groups of people.

The clock radio beside Tanita's bed suddenly blares out rock music, as it does every school morning at 6:30. But as she reaches out to turn down the volume, she realizes something is wrong. When she went to bed the night before, she thought she felt more tired than usual. She feels more than tired now. Her throat hurts and she feels feverish.

Tanita's best friend, Clarissa, has been out of school the past two days with the flu. Now it's Tanita's turn. She spends most of the day sleeping. When she's awake she drinks a little water and lies still, feeling queasy. Over the next several days, she gradually feels better. She's able to eat some soup and crackers, to watch TV, and to read a magazine.

Finally Tanita is well enough to go back to school. There's a history test to make up and she's way behind in her homework, not to mention the dance she missed last Friday. Being sick is no fun.

Section 21.1
What Are Infectious Diseases?

Objectives

- Describe the causes of infectious diseases.

- Identify the ways in which diseases are spread.

The disease that Tanita had is influenza, which is often called ''flu'' for short. If you have had influenza, you know that it makes you feel pretty miserable for a few days. But after resting and taking care of yourself, you soon feel like your old self again.

Influenza is an example of an **infectious disease.** An infectious disease is one that is caused by an agent that can pass from one organism to another. Influenza is also a contagious or **communicable disease**, an infectious disease that is passed from one person to another. Tanita feels sure that she ''caught'' the flu from Clarissa, and most likely she is right.

Not all diseases are infectious diseases. Illnesses like cancer and heart disease are not spread from one person to another. No one knows exactly why one person gets cancer or has a heart attack and another person does not. Researchers have found that certain factors—like smoking, a high-fat diet, and lack of physical activity—can increase your chances of getting these kinds of diseases. But you don't ''catch'' these diseases from another living thing.

communicable disease:

an infectious disease that is passed from one person to another.

infectious disease:

a disease caused by an agent that can pass from one living thing to another.

pathogen:

any agent that causes disease.

microorganism:

a living thing that can be seen only with a microscope.

bacterium:

a type of microorganism that can cause disease.

What Causes Infectious Diseases?

Infectious diseases are caused by agents called **pathogens.** In the United States, the most common pathogens are bacteria and viruses. Bacteria and viruses are two different things, but they are sometimes grouped together and called germs.

Other pathogens include fungi, protists, and parasitic worms. Bacteria, protists, and many fungi are too small to be seen without a microscope. For this reason, they often are called **microorganisms.**

Some of the pathogens that can cause disease are shown in Figure 21-1.

Bacteria Bacteria are very simple living things. Each **bacterium** is a single cell, much smaller than the cells that make up your body. The vast majority of bacteria are harmless.

A few types of bacteria, however, are a real problem for people. They can spoil food or cause diseases. Common diseases caused by bacteria are strep throat, food poisoning, and urinary-tract infections.

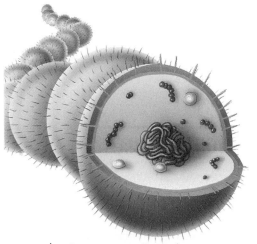

A. Streptococcus Bacterium
Causes strep throat

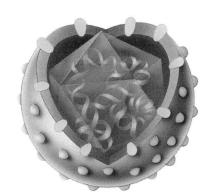

B. Herpes Virus
Causes chickenpox, herpes, and shingles

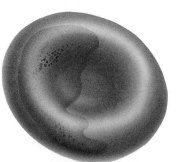

C. Plasmodium
(in red blood cell)
Causes malaria

D. Roundworm Parasite

(FIGURE 21-1) **Four causes of infectious diseases are bacteria, viruses, protists, and parasitic worms. Any agent that can cause an infectious illness is called a pathogen.**

Viruses A **virus** is a microscopic disease-causing particle consisting of genetic material and a protein coat. Viruses cannot reproduce without first invading a living cell. Once inside a living cell, the virus's genetic material acts as a program that directs the cell to make more viruses. After the cell makes new viruses, it often dies and releases the viruses. These viruses spread to new cells, which also die.

Viruses are specialized to infect only certain types of cells. For example, some viruses attack only plant cells, while other viruses attack certain animal cells. If you have a dog, you know your pet needs to be immunized against certain diseases that affect only dogs. You also have your pet immunized against rabies, a viral disease that both humans and dogs can get.

Some common diseases caused by viruses include the common cold, the flu, cold sores, and measles.

How Are Infectious Diseases Spread?

You have seen that all infectious diseases are caused by pathogens that can be passed from one organism to another. In order for you to catch an infectious disease, a pathogen must first leave the body of a living thing and then enter your body. There are several ways that this can happen.

Through the Air Clarissa was sick with the flu because influenza viruses were invading cells in her respiratory system, mainly in her nose and throat. The viruses then moved from Clarissa to Tanita, and Tanita got sick.

How did the viruses get from Clarissa to Tanita? Influenza viruses usually travel through droplets in the air. When you sneeze, thousands of tiny drops of mucus and saliva are sprayed into the air, as shown

(FIGURE 21-2) **The viruses that cause influenza are spread through droplets in the air.**

in Figure 21-2. If your nose and throat are infected with viruses, some viruses are carried out into the air in the droplets. Someone nearby who breathes in the droplets can then become infected with the viruses.

Contact With Contaminated Objects

A person who is sick may leave bacteria or viruses on objects like doorknobs, drinking glasses, toothbrushes, towels, or combs. Some agents of disease do not live for long outside of the human body, but other pathogens are tougher. These types of pathogens may be passed from one person to another when the second person opens the same door, shares a glass, or uses the sick person's toothbrush.

Person-to-Person Contact

Sometimes the agents of disease are spread by direct person-to-person contact. For example, you can get some illnesses by shaking hands, kissing, or touching the ulcers or sores of a sick person. Some infectious diseases are spread by sexual contact. These diseases are discussed in more detail in Chapters 22 and 23.

virus:

a microscopic disease-causing particle consisting of genetic material and a protein coat.

Sexually Transmitted Diseases are discussed in Chapter 22. AIDS and HIV are discussed in Chapter 23.

• • • • •

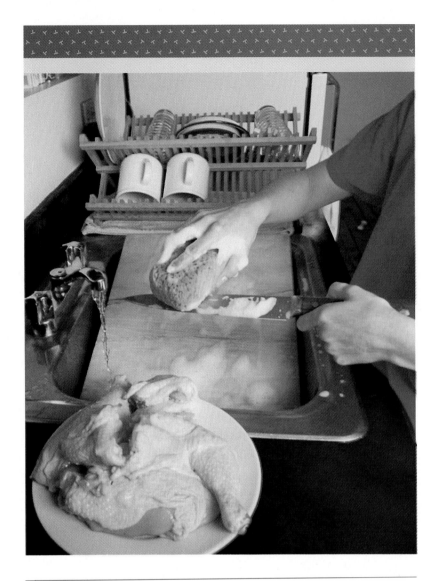

(FIGURE 21-3) **To help protect against food poisoning, always cook meat and eggs thoroughly and wash working surfaces, utensils, and hands with hot, soapy water after contact with meat.**

Food and Water Eating contaminated food or drinking contaminated water can also spread disease. Diseases that affect the digestive system are often spread when feces from an infected person or animal contaminate food or water. This is why people who work with food are required by law to wash their hands thoroughly after every trip to the bathroom. For the same reason, fresh fruits and vegetables, particularly those that grow on the ground, should be washed thoroughly before they are eaten.

Large numbers of bacteria growing in food can cause food poisoning. Symptoms of food poisoning include nausea, vomiting, and abdominal pain. The best way to prevent this type of infection is to refrigerate food except while it is actually being prepared or served, keep hands and utensils clean while preparing foods, and cook food thoroughly to kill any bacteria present.

In the United States, drinking tap water is safe. But campers and hikers who drink water from streams must purify the water first, either by boiling or by using water purification tablets or special filtering systems, to protect themselves from disease.

Animals That Spread Disease Some infectious diseases are spread by animals. Humans can get a fungus called ringworm from handling an infected dog or cat. It is possible for people to get rabies from the bite of an infected animal. A type of encephalitis, or inflammation of the brain, is spread by mosquitoes. Lyme disease, a serious bacterial infection, is carried by ticks. Hantaan virus, which causes a deadly hemorrhagic fever, can be transmitted through contact with feces from infected rodents.

Review

1. Name four types of pathogens, and give an example of each.

2. What are three ways in which infectious diseases can be spread?

3. **Critical Thinking** Is there anything that Tanita could have done to avoid catching the flu from Clarissa?

Fighting Disease

Objectives

- Distinguish between infection and disease.

- Name four ways the body resists infection.

- Explain how an immunization can prevent disease.

Bacteria, viruses, and other agents of disease are everywhere around us. They are found in the air you breathe, on surfaces you touch, and even on your own skin. So why aren't you sick all the time?

Remember that in order for you to get sick, a pathogen must not only leave another organism, but also enter your body. Even if it enters your body, it cannot make you sick unless it survives, multiplies, and somehow causes damage to your system. Most of the time, pathogens are quickly destroyed or swept away before they have a chance to multiply in your body.

Infection and Disease

If pathogens do enter your system and begin to spread and reproduce, then you are infected. Being infected is not the same as having a disease, or actually being sick. Even after pathogens begin to multiply, your body can mount such a good defense against them that they can be destroyed or made harmless before they cause any actual damage. If this happens, you will probably never know that you have been infected. But if you are infected with certain disease-causing agents, you *can* pass them to someone else.

Disease   If your defenses cannot stop the pathogen quickly enough, you may begin to feel sick. A disease is any harmful change in your body's normal activities. A pathogen can cause disease when it is able to multiply in your body and cause damage to your cells and tissues.

Signs and Symptoms   The effects of a disease are called signs and symptoms. A sign of a disease is something another person can see or detect. Tanita had a fever,

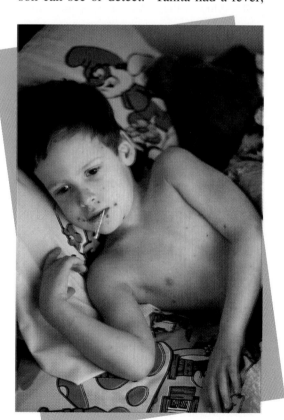

(FIGURE 21-4) **The effects of a disease are called signs and symptoms. One sign of the chickenpox is fluid-filled blisters.**

which is a sign of influenza. Other diseases might have signs like sneezing, coughing, looking pale or flushed, or having skin eruptions like those shown in Figure 21-4.

A symptom is any feeling of pain or discomfort that you experience when you are sick. Tanita's sore throat, tiredness, and queasy stomach are all symptoms of influenza. Other symptoms of disease might include itching, tenderness, cramps, headache, or dizziness.

Defenses Against Infection

Your body has many ways of coping with disease-causing bacteria, viruses, and other pathogens.

Skin One of the functions of your skin is to protect the rest of your body from invasion by agents of disease. The outer part of your skin is very well designed for this job. The lower layers of this part of the skin are tightly joined so that it is difficult for anything to penetrate the skin and enter the tissues beneath it.

The upper layers of the skin are made of dead skin cells filled with a tough waterproof protein. Every day, millions of dead skin cells are shed from the surface of your skin and are replaced by new cells from the layers below. When you shower or bathe, you wash off even more skin cells. As the dead cells come off, they take any bacteria, viruses, or other pathogens that have settled on your skin with them.

Chemical Warfare on Germs Many of the chemical substances your body makes for its activities also act to destroy pathogens. For example, sweat and oils produced by your skin contain acids that can kill bacteria. Enzymes in tears and saliva also kill bacteria.

mucous membranes:

the tissues that line the openings into your body; pathogens can enter the body through the mucous membranes, although many are trapped there.

(FIGURE 21-5) **Every time you shower you remove dead skin cells from your body. Any agents of disease that have formed on these cells are washed away as well.**

Mucous Membranes The tissues lining the openings into your body, such as your mouth and nose, are different from the skin on the outside of your body. These tissues are called **mucous membranes** because cells in these tissues secrete a coating called mucus.

When you breathe through your nose, pathogens in the air are trapped in the sticky mucus that coats the passages of your respiratory system. The cells that line these passages have tiny projections on their surfaces called cilia, shown in Figure 21-6. In your nasal passages, the cilia sweep the mucus downward. In the tubes that lead to your lungs in the lower part of your respiratory system, the cilia sweep the mucus upward.

All of the mucus ends up in your throat and is swallowed, along with saliva from your mouth. This is a natural cleansing process that helps keep your respiratory passages free of microorganisms that might cause disease. Unless you have a disease that causes you to produce extra mucus, like a cold, you might not even be aware of it.

Stomach Acids Not all microorganisms enter your body through your respiratory system. A pathogen might get into your system through your mouth when you touch your fingers to your lips, breathe through your mouth, or bite your nails. Most microorganisms that enter your body in these ways are swallowed, and eventually they end up in your stomach.

Most of the microorganisms that reach the stomach are destroyed there. This is because your stomach contains acids that are 10 times stronger than the acid in pure lemon juice. The acids not only help digest your food, but they also help protect you from disease.

Helpful Microorganisms Remember that most microorganisms are harmless to humans. Many of these microorganisms,

(FIGURE 21-6) **The cells that line the passages of your respiratory system contain tiny projections called cilia, which help sweep disease-causing agents out of your body.**

especially bacteria, live on the skin and mucous membranes of every normal, healthy person. Within minutes after you were born, these microorganisms began to make themselves at home both on you and in you.

These microorganisms actually help protect you from pathogens. The harmless bacteria living in your mouth, for example, take up most of the space and use up most of the food available. When a pathogen is breathed in or eaten with a bite of food, it cannot multiply because there is simply no room for it.

Inflammation If you have ever had an infected cut, you may have noticed that it was swollen, red, painful, and warm to the touch. These are the signs of inflammation, which is caused by the body's defense reaction to the invasion by pathogens.

Your skin and mucous membranes are very effective at protecting the tissues underneath them from infection by pathogens. However, when you cut or burn yourself, pathogens are sometimes able to cross these protective barriers.

Fortunately, another set of defenses against pathogens is waiting in the tissues underneath the skin and mucous membranes. Any damage to these tissues results in the release of several different kinds of chemicals. The purpose of these chemicals is to act as signals for mobilizing the disease-fighting defenses.

First, small blood vessels expand to bring more blood to the injured area. Fluids from the blood and the white blood cells, called phagocytes, pour out of the blood and into the surrounding tissues. Then the phagocytes attack, eat, and destroy any microorganisms that they find in the vicinity. The extra blood and fluid cause the injured area to become swollen and warm and appear red or changed.

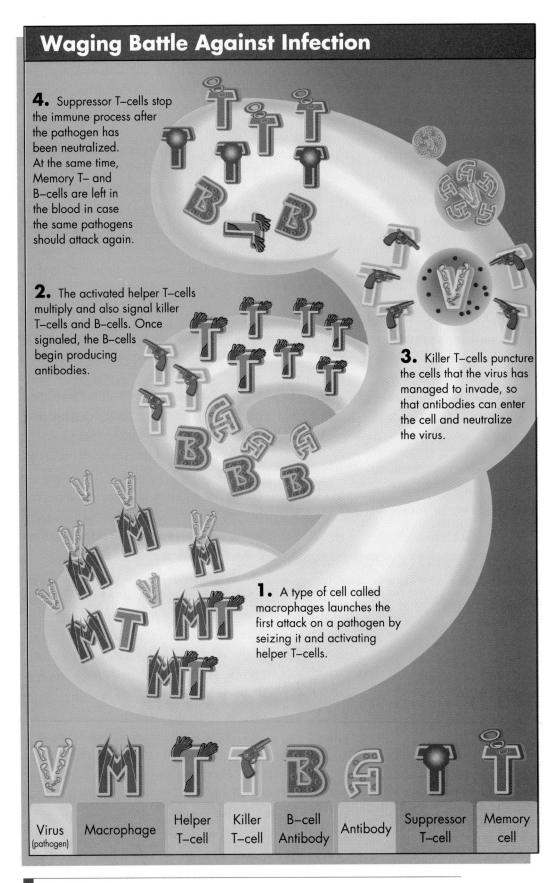

Waging Battle Against Infection

4. Suppressor T–cells stop the immune process after the pathogen has been neutralized. At the same time, Memory T– and B–cells are left in the blood in case the same pathogens should attack again.

2. The activated helper T–cells multiply and also signal killer T–cells and B–cells. Once signaled, the B–cells begin producing antibodies.

3. Killer T–cells puncture the cells that the virus has managed to invade, so that antibodies can enter the cell and neutralize the virus.

1. A type of cell called macrophages launches the first attack on a pathogen by seizing it and activating helper T–cells.

| Virus (pathogen) | Macrophage | Helper T–cell | Killer T–cell | B–cell Antibody | Antibody | Suppressor T–cell | Memory cell |

(FIGURE 21-7) **Your immune system launches an all-out war every time a pathogen invades your system.**

The Immune System All of the defenses that you have learned about so far will attack and destroy any and all possible agents of disease. In addition, your body has a complex system of fighting specific invaders. For example, if a measles virus gets past your other defenses, your body will launch an all-out war on measles viruses throughout your body.

The weapons your body is using to fight the measles virus work only on measles viruses. They have no effect on any other kind of pathogen. When the body mobilizes its defenses to fight one specific type of invader, the process that is activated is called the immune response. The cells and organs that fight the war against specific invaders are called the **immune system.**

Weapons of the Immune Response

Before a baby is born and during the first years of its life, the immune system produces millions of different kinds of immune cells. Each of these cells can attack a molecule of a certain shape. Such a molecule might be a protein in the outer coat of a virus or a poison molecule made by a bacterium. When an immune cell comes into contact with a molecule that is the right shape, biologists say that the immune cell "recognizes" that molecule.

There are millions of different kinds of these cells, and each kind recognizes a different shape of molecule. So no matter what kind of pathogen might invade your body, there are some immune cells ready to fight it. There are two main types of immune cells that are able to fight any pathogen that might come along.

T-Cells One type of immune cell is called **T-cells**. Certain T-cells mobilize to fight pathogens directly. These T-cells are called killer T-cells. When a pathogen invades your body, its molecules will be recognized by some of your killer T-cells. These cells will divide into many cells that then kill the invaders.

Another class of T-cells, called helper T-cells, get the immune response going by activating killer T-cells, phagocytes, and other immune cells. Helper T-cells are activated by macrophages, which are cells that form the first line of defense against a pathogen. Suppressor T-cells turn off the immune response after the pathogen has been defeated.

Antibodies The other main type of immune cell is called **B-cells.** Their job is to produce antibodies. **Antibodies** (AN tee bahd eez) are Y-shaped molecules that stick to and cover foreign molecules in the body. When a pathogen invades, the B-cells that recognize that pathogen divide rapidly and produce thousands of antibody molecules apiece. When a bacterium or virus is covered with antibodies, it has great difficulty attacking body cells.

Immunity

You may know that after you have had certain diseases, you can't catch them again. For example, after a person has had the mumps, that person doesn't have to worry about getting the mumps a second time.

You probably never had the mumps, however. Most people your age have been immunized against mumps and so never get this disease even once.

In other cases, it doesn't seem to count for anything if you've already had a disease. You may have had two colds this year alone, not to mention the one you had last year, and the one two years before that.

Why the difference? How can you be protected against some diseases entirely by an immunization, get other diseases only once, and get still others over and over?

B-cells:

cells in the immune system that produce antibodies against infection.

antibodies:

substances that stick to the surface of pathogens, slowing their action.

immune system:

the system that protects the body from disease.

T-cells:

cells that regulate the action of the immune system.

immunization:
injection of a small amount of a pathogen that will provide protection against an infectious disease.

Protection against developing a certain disease is called immunity. There are three basic types of immunity.

Innate Immunity You are immune to certain diseases just because you are who you are. First of all, you are a human being. You will never have to worry about diseases that affect only fish or rose bushes or horses. In addition, some people seem to inherit resistance to certain human diseases.

Active Immunity Once your body has launched an all-out war against a specific invader, it remains armed and ready to fight that same invader much more quickly and effectively if that same invader should ever show up again.

This happens because when the B- and T-cells that fight a specific invader multiply while they are fighting a pathogen, some of these cells are set aside as "memory cells." Any subsequent time that specific pathogen tries to invade your body, your immune system is ready for it. Memory cells multiply quickly and produce huge numbers of antibodies in a very short time. The invaders are defeated and destroyed so quickly that they don't have time to make you sick. You never even know that they were ever present in your body.

There are two ways that you can acquire active immunity. One way is by actually having the disease. For example, the cells of Tanita's respiratory system were attacked by an influenza virus. Some of her immune cells recognized the proteins on the outside of the viruses. Those T-cells and the B-cells then began to divide and fight the infection.

At the same time, Tanita's immune system set aside memory T- and B-cells that recognize this flu virus. If that exact same influenza virus ever attempts to invade Tanita's body again, her immune system will fight it off before she even knows it.

But people sometimes get the flu more than one time in their life. Why is that? Influenza viruses slowly change over time. After a while, a strain of flu may come along that is very different from the one Tanita is immune to. Her memory cells won't recognize this new flu virus, and she could get sick with the flu again.

Another way to acquire active immunity is through **immunization.** Sometimes called vaccination, immunization is a way of tricking your body into thinking that it has already had a disease. When you get an immunization, dead or weakened pathogens, or sometimes just parts of a pathogen, are injected into your body. These pathogens can't multiply and cause damage to your body, so they don't make you sick. However, your immune system recognizes them as foreign invaders and mobilizes the immune response to the pathogen.

You may be able to feel your immune system at work. For example, your immune system causes your temperature to go up when it is working hard. A slight to moderate fever is an immune response. When fever goes over a temperature of about 104°F, it may begin to do more harm than good. Some people get a little feverish and achy after an immunization—for example, after a diphtheria booster. This does not mean, however, that they got diphtheria from the immunization. It just means that they can feel their immune system going to work.

Just like actually having a disease, an immunization can leave memory cells behind. If you are effectively immunized against polio viruses, you cannot get polio. If polio viruses enter your body, your memory cells destroy them—and you don't even know that you have been infected.

Many serious pathogens do not change much over time. Having the disease or being immunized against it, like the person shown in Figure 21-8, will give many years of protection, although periodic boosters are sometimes needed. It is also possible to be immunized against diseases that do change, like influenza. However, every time a new strain of flu virus appears, a new vaccine must be developed to protect against it.

Why isn't there a vaccine for the common cold? The virus that causes the common cold changes even more rapidly than the influenza virus. There may be several different cold viruses being passed around at any one time, and they are changing all the time. Plus, the common cold is not a very serious disease. A vaccine for the common cold would be a waste of time and money. By the time it was ready, the strain going around would have changed so much that the vaccine would be useless. Research into new vaccines is much more useful if it is focused on preventing really serious diseases like hepatitis and AIDS.

Passive Immunity A third type of immunity to disease is called passive immunity. If you have passive immunity to a particular disease or infection, it means you have received antibodies from another person—or sometimes an animal—that have made you resistant to disease or infection.

Before you were born, some of your mother's antibodies passed from her to you. These antibodies gave you passive immunity that helped protect you from disease in the first few months of your life, until your immune system was mature enough to take care of your own body.

Antibodies are also injected into people who have been exposed to certain serious diseases. These antibodies may be extracted from the blood of humans or animals that have been exposed to the particular disease or venom. A person bitten by a dog with rabies is treated with injections of rabies antibodies. A person bitten by a poi-

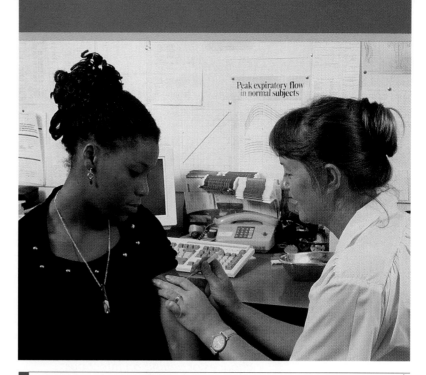

(FIGURE 21-8) **Immunizations, such as this one for tetanus, trick the body into thinking it already has had a specific disease. When this happens, the body produces memory cells that will automatically destroy the pathogens that cause that illness.**

sonous snake is treated with snake venom antibodies.

Passive immunity lasts for only a short time. Eventually the antibodies break down and are removed from your bloodstream.

Review

1. What's the difference between being infected and having a disease?

2. Name four ways that the body resists disease.

3. How does an immunization work to prevent disease?

4. *Critical Thinking* Is it always a good idea to take a medication that lowers fever? Why or why not?

• • • • •

Objectives

■ *List four common diseases caused by viruses.*

■ *Explain which kind of diseases antibiotics can cure, and which kind they can't.*

■ *Know some ways to decrease your chances of getting an infectious disease.*

LIFE SKILLS: Practicing Self-Care

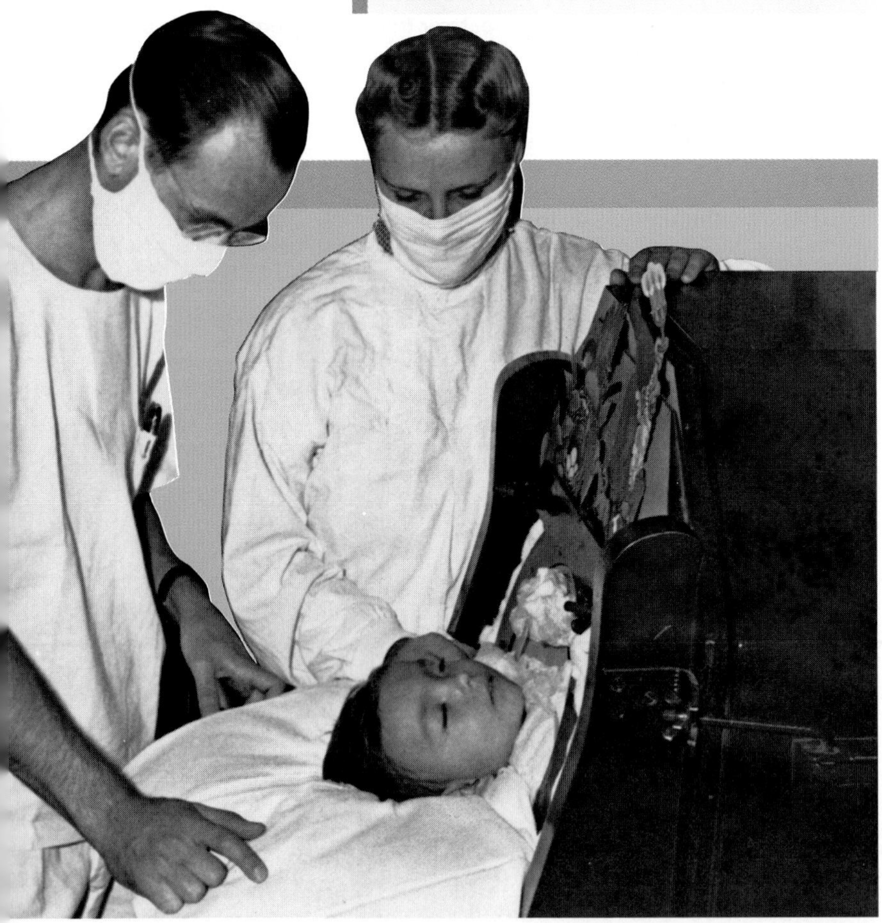

You know now that diseases are caused by bacteria, viruses, fungi, protists, and other parasites. It's not always easy to avoid some infectious diseases, particularly those that are easily spread. But in general, the more you know about preventing an individual illness, the better your chances are of avoiding it. When you are sick, it's always a good rule of thumb to see your doctor. Keep in mind that even diseases that are not serious can have complications.

Viral Diseases

Some of the most common infectious diseases in the United States are caused by viruses. These include the common cold, influenza, cold sores, warts, mononucleosis, chickenpox, and AIDS.

Preventing Viral Disease A number of viral diseases that were common when your parents and grandparents were young are now quite rare in the United States. In the 1940s and early 1950s, a polio epidemic left many children paralyzed. Some polio victims were unable to breathe on their own, like the child shown in Figure 21-9. Until the 1960s, almost everyone got measles, mumps, and rubella (sometimes called German measles) when they were children.

Today, almost all children are immunized against these diseases, which are now rarely seen. One exception is measles. Recently there have been several outbreaks of measles among high school- and college-aged young adults. Because of this, many people in this age group have had to get extra booster immunizations. In contrast,

■ (FIGURE 21-9) **Polio, a viral disease that reached epidemic proportions during the 1940s and 1950s, left thousands paralyzed and unable to breathe without the help of an iron lung.**

the immunization campaign against small-pox, a disease that killed thousands of people several centuries ago, was so successful that smallpox has been eliminated.

The most deadly viral disease in the United States today is AIDS. So far, there is no vaccine to prevent AIDS, but researchers in many laboratories are working hard to develop one.

Curing Viral Diseases Most of the time when you recover from a viral disease, it is because your immune system has destroyed the viruses in your body or made them harmless.

Antibiotic (an tee by AHT ik) drugs like penicillin and tetracycline work by preventing the growth and cell division of living bacterial cells. Eventually the bacteria die. Viruses, however, cannot be killed by antibiotics.

What follows is a list of the most common viral infections. For symptoms, vaccine information, and treatment suggestions for each type of infection, see Figure 21-11.

The Common Cold The common cold should really be called the common colds. That is because more than 200 different viruses can cause the cold. A cold may make you feel really miserable, but it usually lasts only two or three days.

Each year, Americans spend more than $500 million on cold remedies. None of these remedies can actually cure a cold, but they can make you feel better while you are waiting to get well. Some over-the-counter drugs can help clear a stuffy nose or ease aching muscles.

Although there is no way to cure the common cold, there are some things you can do to reduce your chances of getting one. For one thing, try to avoid people who are sick with a cold. Colds are very contagious, especially through person-to-person contact. Washing your hands often will reduce

(FIGURE 21-10) **There is no immunization against the common cold. Fortunately, most colds last for only a few days.**

antibiotics:

drugs that kill or limit the growth of bacteria.

your risk of being infected with a cold virus.

If you do get a cold, rest, eat nutritious foods, and drink plenty of water. Studies show that a diet rich in vitamin C can lessen the severity of your symptoms.

Influenza Like the common cold, influenza is caused by a viral infection of the respiratory tract. The flu usually lasts longer than an ordinary cold. A cold usually lasts only two to three days, while it may take 7 to 10 days to feel like your old self again after having the flu.

Most people who are basically healthy recover from the flu without any serious problems. However, influenza may have serious complications and can be life threatening for the elderly and people with respiratory problems. These people may choose to be immunized against influenza.

Common Viral Diseases

Disease	Signs and Symptoms	Treatment
Common Cold	Sneezing, stuffy nose, sore throat, aches, fever, fatigue	Rest, fluids
Influenza	Chills, fever, sore throat, muscle aches, fatigue, cough, weakness	Rest, fluids
Chickenpox	Blisters, rash, fever, muscle soreness	Rest, fluids
Mononucleosis	Swollen lymph nodes, fatigue, fever, sore throat, enlarged liver and spleen	Rest, fluids, balanced diet
Hepatitis	Fever, weakness, loss of appetite, nausea, jaundice (yellowing of skin)	Gamma globulin, interferon, rest
Measles	Rash, high fever, sore throat, conjunctivitis, swollen lymph nodes	Gamma globulin, fluids, rest

(FIGURE 21-11) **The best way to treat most viral diseases is to get plenty of rest and to drink lots of fluids.**

If you do get the flu, check with your doctor if your symptoms become severe—for example, if you experience difficulty breathing or have a high fever.

Chickenpox Chickenpox is caused by one of the herpes viruses. It is usually a mild disease and treatment is limited to relieving the itching and fever. Aspirin should not be used because of the possible link to Reye's syndrome, a rare but serious disease that affects the brain and the liver.

Chickenpox can be dangerous for children who suffer from other diseases. It can also be serious for people who are infected as adults. A vaccine is now available, but the duration of the immunity provided is uncertain. People who get chickenpox won't get it again, but they might have a flare up of the virus later in life. This condition is called shingles.

Measles One of the most serious viral diseases is measles. Without proper care, measles can lead to complications such as encephalitis and meningitis (an infection of the brain and spinal cord).

Like influenza, measles can spread through droplets in the air that can enter the body through the eyes, nose, and throat.

Mononucleosis Mononucleosis, often called mono for short, is caused by the Epstein-Barr virus, or EBV. This virus is usually spread by contact with the saliva of an infected person. Children are usually exposed to EBV at an early age and have symptoms so mild that the illness is mistaken for a brief cold or flu. These children develop immunity and can continue to transmit the virus through out their life.

Mononucleosis seldom lasts for more than three or four months. If symptoms last more than six months, the illness might more appropriately be described as chronic fatigue syndrome, or CFS.

Hepatitis Hepatitis is a viral disease that can cause serious damage to the liver. There are three main types of hepatitis— Type A, Type B, and Type C hepatitis. These three diseases are caused by three different viruses. Type A hepatitis is usually spread by food contaminated with feces. The most effective way to prevent hepatitis A is to wash your hands frequently when you prepare or serve food.

Hepatitis B is more serious than hepatitis A. It is usually spread through infected blood, semen, or saliva. Therefore, it can be spread through intravenous drug use,

sexual contact, or tattoo needles and ear-piercing equipment that are not sterile. Hepatitis C is most often spread through blood transfusions. It is also very serious. Studies show, though, that hepatitis C can be treated with an antiviral agent called interferon.

A vaccine for Type B hepatitis has recently been developed. In addition, people exposed to hepatitis are often treated with an injection of gamma globulin, which is the part of the blood that contains antibodies. Therefore, gamma globulin injections can provide some temporary passive immunity for hepatitis.

Common Bacterial Diseases

Immunization can prevent some bacterial diseases, such as tetanus. In addition, antibiotics are very effective against bacterial diseases. If left untreated, however, bacterial diseases can be serious. That's why it's

(FIGURE 21-12) **Mononucleosis is spread through contact with the saliva of an infected person.**

Tips on Preventing Infectious Diseases . .

To decrease your chances of getting an infectious disease and increase your chances of staying healthy, you can do the following things:

1. Try to avoid close contact with other people who might be sick. When you must be exposed to people who are sick, wash your hands often. Do not share personal items like hairbrushes and toothbrushes. Avoid sharing food or drinks with other people.

2. Reduce the amount of refined sweeteners in your diet. Follow the nutrition principles described in Chapter 4. A balanced diet is a key factor in strengthening your immune system.

3. High stress levels can decrease the efficiency of your immune system. Practice the effective stress management skills discussed in Chapter 9. Make time for rest, and participate in relaxing activities that you enjoy.

4. Drink 8–10 cups of water a day— more if you are very active or live in a hot climate. Water is vital for your immune system.

5. Make sure you are up-to-date on your immunizations.

6. Get regular checkups by doctors and dentists.

7. Design and maintain an appropriate exercise program as outlined in Chapter 3.

a good idea to see a doctor if you think you have a bacterial disease.

Strep Throat

A sore throat caused by the *Streptococcus pyrogenes* bacterium is not a very serious disease in itself, but it can have serious complications. These complications include permanent heart and kidney damage. Unlike sore throats caused by the cold or flu viruses, strep throat can be easily cured by taking antibiotics.

Any severe sore throat, or a sore throat that lasts more than two days, should be checked by a doctor. A simple test that takes only a few minutes in a doctor's office can show if your sore throat is caused by a *Streptococcus* bacterium. If so, you will need to take antibiotics to avoid serious complications.

Tuberculosis

The bacteria that cause tuberculosis, or TB, attack the lungs and cause fluid to build up there. Not surprisingly, people with tuberculosis suffer severe coughing spells. Other symptoms of TB include high fever, weakness, and loss of appetite.

Tuberculosis is another disease spread through droplets in the air. Fortunately, it is not easy to become infected, even if you inhale these droplets. Unless you are in close contact for a prolonged period of time with a person who has TB, chances are you won't catch the disease. In recent years tuberculosis cases have increased dramatically, partly because people with AIDS are very vulnerable to it. Other factors that have contributed to the increase of tuberculosis include malnutrition and alcohol and

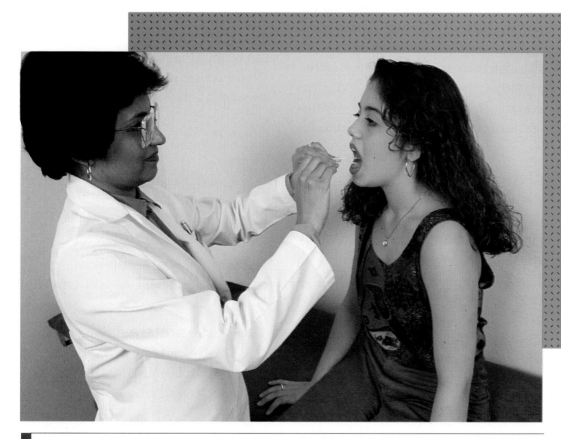

(FIGURE 21-13) **A teenager gets tested for strep throat. If you have a sore throat that lasts for more than two or three days, see your doctor. Strep is easily cured with antibiotics, but it can have serious consequences if left untreated.**

(FIGURE 21-14) **Malaria, which strikes 200 million people every year, is spread from person to person by mosquitoes.**

drug abuse. Tuberculosis can be effectively treated with antibiotics, although some strains of the disease have proven to be resistant to treatment.

Sinus Infections A cold, flu, or allergy that leads to heavy mucus production can lead to a bacterial infection in your sinuses. The most common signs and symptoms of a sinus infection are thick, greenish mucus, headaches, and sinus pain. A doctor can determine if you have a bacterial infection that needs to be treated with an antibiotic.

Other Diseases

Remember that there are diseases caused by pathogens other than bacteria and viruses. Fungi, protists, and animal parasites may also be agents of disease.

Three common conditions caused by fungi are athlete's foot, jock itch, and ringworm. These are discussed in Chapter 6.

Diseases caused by protists (which are complex, one-celled organisms) are not widespread in the United States, although they are common in other parts of the world. The most widespread and serious of these diseases is malaria. Each year, as many as 200 million people suffer from malaria, and one to two million people die from it.

Malaria is caused by a protist that is carried from one person to another by mosquitoes.

Diseases can also be caused by animal parasites. Animals like hookworms, flukes, pinworms, and tapeworms can live inside the human body and cause disease. One kind of parasitic roundworm causes a disease called trichinosis. This roundworm can be found in the muscle tissue of pigs. For this reason, pork must always be cooked thoroughly before it is eaten.

Review

1. *What are four common diseases that are caused by viruses?*

2. *What kind of diseases can antibiotics cure? What kind can't they cure?*

3. ▪▪ *LIFE SKILLS: Practicing Self-Care Name four ways you can lower your chances of getting an infectious disease.*

4. *Critical Thinking What do polio and AIDS have in common? How are they different?*

Highlights

Summary

- Infectious diseases are diseases that pass from one organism to another. Communicable, or contagious, diseases are infectious diseases that pass from one person to another.

- In the United States, the most common infectious diseases are caused by bacteria and viruses. Other disease-causing pathogens are fungi, protists, and parasitic worms.

- A sign of a disease is something another person can observe, such as a fever, cough, sneeze, or rash. A symptom of a disease is any feeling of pain or discomfort a person experiences with a disease.

- Some of the body's defenses against disease are skin, mucous membranes, stomach acids, and body chemicals.

- The immune system is a complex system of organs and cells that fight specific agents of disease.

- A person can acquire active immunity to a disease by having the disease or by getting immunized, or vaccinated, against it.

- The common cold, influenza, hepatitis, mononucleosis, chickenpox, and AIDS are diseases caused by viruses.

- Strep throat, tuberculosis, and sinus infections are common bacterial diseases.

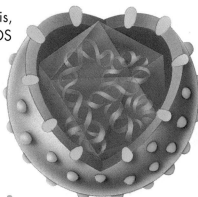

Vocabulary

infectious disease a disease that is caused by an agent that is passed from one living thing to another.

communicable disease an infectious disease that is passed from one person to another.

pathogen any agent that causes disease.

bacterium a type of microorganism that can cause disease.

virus a microscopic disease-causing particle consisting of genetic material and a protein coat.

immune system the system that protects the body from disease.

immunization injection of a small amount of a pathogen that will provide protection against an infectious disease.

antibodies substances that stick to the surface of pathogens, slowing their action.

antibiotics drugs that kill or limit the growth of bacteria.

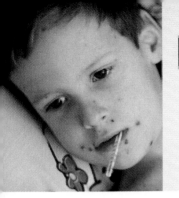

Chapter Review

Concept Review

1. Food poisoning and urinary tract infections are diseases caused by _____.

2. _____ and _____ are two diseases that affect humans but are spread by animals.

3. Refrigerating, cooking foods thoroughly, and washing hands and utensils help prevent _____ _____.

4. The _____ acts as a barrier to protect the rest of your body from pathogens.

5. If an infected cut is swollen, red, painful, and warm to the touch, it is a sign of _____.

6. The _____ _____ produces special kinds of cells that attack pathogens.

7. The three basic types of immunity are _____, _____, and _____.

8. Sometimes called a vaccination, _____ is a way of artificially acquiring immunity.

9. Measles and influenza are diseases caused by _____.

10. Bacterial infections can be cured with _____ drugs.

11. _____ is the most serious and widespread disease caused by a protist.

Expressing Your Views

1. Dion and Sam are planning to visit a foreign country that has poor living conditions. Do you think they will be at an increased risk of getting a disease? Why or why not?

2. Buddy is home with a sore throat. He says he can't afford to miss any more work, so he plans to stock up on throat lozenges and go back to work. Do you think that is a wise thing for Buddy to do? Why or why not?

3. Last night you had a party and had a lot of leftover food. You were too tired to put all the food away so you left most of it out all night on the counter. What should you do with the leftover food now? Explain.

Life Skills Check . . . . . .

1. Practicing Self-Care
You are drinking a soda when a close friend comes over and asks you to share. You would really like to share but are concerned about spreading germs. What should you do?

2. Practicing Self-Care
You were immunized against measles and mumps when you were an infant. You thought the immunizations were good for life, but you just read that there is an outbreak of measles at the local college. What should you do?

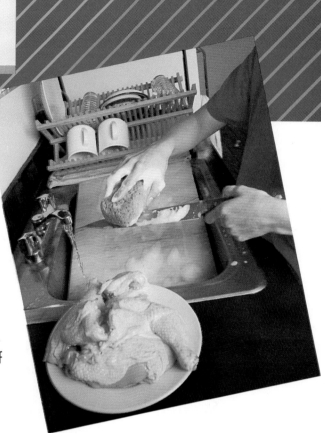

Projects . . . .

1. Choose a common infectious disease and create a poster containing information about it. Show the causes, symptoms, method of transmission, long-term effects, and treatments of the disease. Display your poster at a suitable place in your school.

2. Contact your doctor or school nurse and ask for a copy of your immunization record. The record should have vaccinations you have received during your life and the date when each was given. Make a list of diseases you have been vacci-nated against, and record the date when your next booster shots, if any, are due.

3. Work with a partner to collect information about natural remedies and preventive measures for common illnesses. Use library references or call a naturopathic doctor for information about alternatives to over-the-counter drugs. Find out how the substances are taken and how they affect the body. Write a report that includes the benefits and the possible side effects of the alternative medicines.

Plan for Action . . . .

There are several strategies a person can take to control the spread of infectious diseases. What are some things you can do to help keep infectious diseases from spreading?

CHAPTER 22

Sexually Transmitted Diseases

◆ ◆ ◆ ◆

Section 22.1
What Are Sexually Transmitted Diseases?

Section 22.2
Preventing Sexually Transmitted Diseases

■ **Education is the first step toward preventing sexually transmitted diseases.**

Vanessa and her best friend, Han, agree that sometimes it seems like everybody takes it for granted that all teenagers are sexually active. In movies and on TV sitcoms the teenage characters joke about birth-control pills and losing their virginity. The songs on the radio are pretty explicit. It all adds up to a lot of pressure to have sex. At the same time, worrying about diseases that you could get makes sex seem pretty scary.

One evening Han was having supper with Vanessa and Vanessa's mother at their apartment. Han was surprised when Vanessa asked her mother about these diseases. Vanessa's mom is a nurse, so she was able to tell the girls a lot of what they wanted to know. Vanessa's mom said that AIDS is the most deadly disease you can get through sexual activity, but that there are others that are also dangerous. Some of them can cause infertility, the inability to have children. Vanessa didn't intend to get pregnant any time soon, but she had always assumed that some day she would have children. Finding out that a disease might make it impossible to have children made her realize that these diseases are serious.

What Are Sexually Transmitted Diseases?

Objectives

- *Define the term sexually transmitted disease.*

- *Know the names of four common sexually transmitted diseases.*

- *Know how sexually transmitted diseases are spread from one person to another.*

- *Know the signs and symptoms of sexually transmitted diseases.*

Each year, about 2.5 million teenagers are infected with sexually transmitted diseases. A **sexually transmitted disease,** or **STD** for short, is a disease that is passed from one person to another during sexual contact. These diseases used to be called venereal diseases (VD). Some of these diseases are merely uncomfortable, while others can be quite serious.

The most dangerous STD is AIDS. It cannot be cured and is eventually fatal. Because AIDS is such a serious threat, the next chapter will be devoted entirely to AIDS and the virus that causes it. This chapter will tell you about other diseases that are spread by sexual activity.

sexually transmitted disease (STD):

a disease that is passed from one person to another during sexual contact.

HIV infection and AIDS are discussed in Chapter 23.

Check Up

How Much Do You Already Know About STDs?

1. Can someone have an STD and not know it?
2. Are STDs common among sexually active teenagers?
3. Do birth-control pills prevent STDs?
4. Can STDs be prevented by washing carefully after sex?
5. Can the use of latex condoms greatly reduce the risk of getting an STD?
6. Can a person get an STD from oral sex?
7. Is it easy to tell if someone has an STD?

1. yes 2. yes 3. no 4. no 5. yes 6. yes 7. no

gonorrhea:

an STD caused by bacteria that can infect the mucous membranes of the penis, vagina, throat, or rectum.

REMINDER

Antibiotics are drugs that kill or limit the growth of bacteria.

Gonorrhea

One of the most common STDs is **gonorrhea** (gahn-uh-REE-uh). Gonorrhea is an infection caused by a bacterium. The gonorrhea bacterium attacks mucous membranes. It can infect the mucous membranes of the penis, vagina, throat, or the rectum.

About one million cases of gonorrhea are reported each year. Because many cases are not reported, however, the actual number is probably closer to three million cases each year.

What Are the Signs and Symptoms of Gonorrhea?
As you learned in Chapter 21, a sign of a disease is something another person can see or detect. A symptom of a disease is any feeling of pain or discomfort you may experience. As many as 80 percent of women who have gonorrhea have no signs and symptoms or have signs and symptoms that are so mild that they aren't noticed. Because of this, most women with gonorrhea do not even realize that they have the disease.

One sign of gonorrhea in females is irritation of the vagina that is accompanied by a discharge. Since a female may have a vaginal discharge for other reasons, this is not a sure sign of gonorrhea. Females with gonorrhea may also have pain in the lower abdomen. But since this pain is usually mild, it is a symptom that is often ignored.

Unlike women who have gonorrhea, men infected with gonorrhea usually have signs and symptoms. One sign of gonorrhea is a heavy yellow discharge of pus from the penis. Symptoms of gonorrhea include frequent, painful urination, tenderness in the groin or testicles, and swelling of the lymph nodes in the groin. These signs and symptoms usually appear about 2 to 10 days after infection. Sometimes the signs and symptoms go away, but that doesn't mean that the infection is gone.

One reason why gonorrhea is such a common disease is that a large number of people who are infected do not have signs or symptoms. These people may not realize that they have gonorrhea, but they can still pass the bacteria to their sex partners.

How Can a Person Become Infected with Gonorrhea?
Gonorrhea is spread by sexual contact or from mother to infant at delivery. The gonorrhea bacteria can be passed from one person to another only by moving directly from one warm, moist body surface to another. It is not true that gonorrhea can be caught from dirty toilet seats, cups, or towels. This is because these bacteria must have the right combination of temperature, humidity, atmosphere, and nutrients to grow. A gonorrhea bacterium on a toilet seat would live for only a few seconds, because it dies when it is exposed to the air.

What Happens if Gonorrhea Is Not Treated?
Gonorrhea can be completely cured by the appropriate antibiotics.

Myths and Facts About STDs

Myth	Fact
Birth-control pills prevent STDs.	Birth-control pills provide no protection against STDs.
Washing the genitals after sex prevents STDs.	Washing is not an effective way to prevent STDs.
It is best to see if an STD goes away on its own before going to a doctor.	STDs do not go away on their own. Even if the symptoms go away, it does not mean the STD is cured.
The medicine prescribed for one kind of STD will cure any STD.	Each STD requires different treatment. A doctor must be consulted for proper treatment.
As soon as a person feels better, he or she can stop taking the medicine prescribed for an STD.	All of the medicine prescribed by the doctor must be taken, even if a person starts feeling better before the medicine is all gone.
If one sex partner is treated for an STD, it isn't necessary for the other partner to be treated.	Both sex partners must be treated so they will not continue to reinfect each other.
It is easy to tell when a person has an STD.	Some people show no signs of illness even though they have an STD.

(FIGURE 22-1) **A national survey, *The National Adolescent Student Health Survey*, showed that many teenagers have misconceptions about STDs that could endanger their health.**

However, untreated gonorrhea in females may spread to the reproductive organs inside the pelvic cavity. Infection of the uterus and fallopian tubes is called **pelvic inflammatory disease (PID).** PID can be caused by several different kinds of microorganisms, including the bacterium that causes gonorrhea. The signs and symptoms of PID may include painful sexual intercourse, uterine bleeding, vaginal discharge, abdominal pain, and fever. PID can be a very serious disease. It must be treated with powerful antibiotics and may even require hospitalization. PID can cause scarring of the fallopian tubes, resulting in infertility.

A woman with untreated gonorrhea can also pass the gonorrhea bacterium to her baby at birth. This can cause blindness in the infant. To reduce this risk, it is standard procedure to treat the eyes of babies with medicated eyedrops immediately after birth.

pelvic inflammatory disease (PID):

an infection of the uterus and fallopian tubes often caused by STDs; if untreated, may result in infertility.

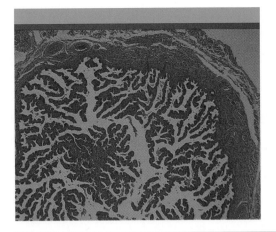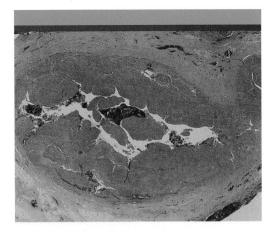

(FIGURE 22-2) **The photograph on the left shows normal tissue from a woman's fallopian tube. The photograph on the right shows the effects of pelvic inflammatory disease (PID). Some sexually transmitted diseases can cause PID and result in infertility.**

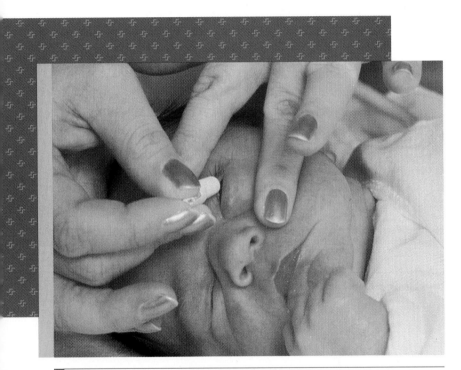

(FIGURE 22-3) **A newborn baby's eyes are treated with medicated eyedrops. This is standard procedure to prevent possible STD infections that could cause blindness.**

chlamydia:

the most common STD in the United States; caused by bacteria.

A male who has been infected with gonorrhea may suffer serious complications in a short period of time, sometimes in just two to three weeks. Infection can spread quickly throughout the male reproductive system and cause pain, fever, and urinary problems. Eventually, the man may become infertile as a result of scarring of the reproductive organs.

Chlamydia

Chlamydia (klam-ID-ee-uh) is the most common STD in the United States. There are from 3 to 10 million new cases each year. Chlamydia is caused by a small bacterium. It is not a new disease, although it has become more common in recent years.

What Are the Signs and Symptoms of Chlamydia? Like gonorrhea, chlamydia does not cause signs and symptoms in the majority of women who are infected. Also, about one-fourth of infected men do not get signs and symptoms. In people who get them, the signs and symptoms of chlamydia will usually appear one to three weeks after exposure.

In males, the signs and symptoms of chlamydia infection include painful and difficult urination and a white or yellow watery discharge from the penis. In females, signs and symptoms may include painful urination, vaginal discharge, pain in the lower abdomen, and bleeding between menstrual periods.

How Can a Person Become Infected With Chlamydia? Chlamydia is transmitted from one person to another through sexual contact. One reason chlamydia is such a common STD is that it is often spread by people who don't know that they have the disease.

What Happens if Chlamydia Is Not Treated? In women, the bacterium that causes chlamydia is another microorganism that can cause PID. Like PID caused by gonorrhea, PID caused by chlamydia can damage a woman's reproductive system, making her infertile. In men, an untreated chlamydia infection can also result in infertility.

Women with chlamydia are more likely to have problems during pregnancy, and babies born to women with chlamydia may get eye infections or pneumonia. Because of this, pregnant women should be screened for chlamydia even if they have no signs and symptoms.

Genital Herpes

Infection with the herpes simplex virus in the genital region is called **genital herpes** (HUR-peez). Two types of the herpes simplex virus exist—type I and type II. Usually, type I is found above the waist, appearing as a cold sore or fever blister on the mouth. Type II is usually found below the waist. There are more than 40 million Americans with genital herpes. About 500,000 more become infected each year.

What Are the Signs and Symptoms of Genital Herpes? Only about 25 percent of people infected with genital herpes have signs and symptoms. The other 75 percent still have the disease and can give it to someone else.

If there are signs and symptoms, they usually take from 2 to 10 days to develop. In females, painful blisters may appear on the cervix, vagina, or vulva. In males, blisters and ulcers may appear on the penis. Pain may also be experienced when urinating. In both sexes, redness and blisters may appear at any site of contact.

In addition, some people experience itching, tingling, or burning sensations just before the sores appear. Other symptoms of herpes may include a sluggish feeling, fever, and flulike symptoms.

There is no cure for herpes. Once you are infected with the virus that causes herpes, you are infected for the rest of your life. If you do not have signs and symptoms, or when they go away, the herpes-causing virus stays inactive in the nerves. The virus may be reactivated by anything that stresses the immune system.

genital herpes:

an STD caused by a virus that often causes painful blisters or ulcers; cannot be cured.

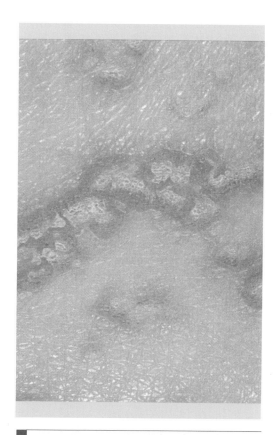

■ (FIGURE 22-4) **Painful blisters like these are the result of genital herpes. However, most people infected with genital herpes have no symptoms.**

Sexually Transmitted Diseases

STD	What Causes It?	How Is It Spread?
Gonorrhea	Neisseria gonorrhoese bacterium	Sexual contact; mother to infant at birth
Chlamydia	Chlamydia trachomatis	Sexual contact; mother to infant at birth
Genital herpes	Herpes simplex virus	Sexual contact; contact between sores and mucous membranes or break in skin; mother to infant at birth
Syphilis	Treponema pallidum bacterium	Sexual contact; contact between chancre or rash and mucous membranes or break in skin; mother to infant before birth
Nongonococcal urethritis (NGU)	Several causes, such as chlamydia, ureaplasma, mycoplasma, trichomonas, herpes	Most often spread by sexual contact, but some microorganisms can be spread by other means
Genital warts	Virus	Sexual contact
Vaginitis	Several causes, such as candida, gardnerella, herpes, trichomonas, mycoplasma	Often spread by sexual contact, but some microorganisms can be spread by other means
Hepatitis B	Hepatitis B virus	Sexual contact; sharing needles; sharing items like razors, toothbrushes, eating utensils; mother to infant at birth
Pubic lice	Insect	Sexual contact
Scabies	Mite	Sexual contact

(FIGURE 22-5) **A sexually transmitted disease (STD) is a disease that is passed from one person to another during sexual contact. AIDS is another STD, and is discussed in Chapter 23.**

What Are the Signs and Symptoms?	How Is It Treated?
Females: often no signs or symptoms; vaginal irritation and discharge; pain in lower abdomen **Males:** frequent, painful urination; heavy yellow discharge of pus from penis; tenderness in groin or testicles; swollen lymph nodes on groin	Antibiotic
Females: usually no signs or symptoms; painful urination; vaginal discharge; pain in lower abdomen; bleeding between menstrual periods **Males:** often no signs or symptoms; painful, difficult urination; white or yellow discharge from penis	Antibiotic
Females: usually no signs or symptoms; painful blisters on cervix, vagina, vulva, thighs, or buttocks; sluggish feeling; fever; flulike symptoms; lymph node enlargement **Males:** usually no signs or symptoms; blisters on penis, thighs, or buttocks; painful urination; sluggish feeling; fever; flulike symptoms; lymph node enlargement	No cure but acyclovir can ease symptoms
First sign: small, red bumps at the point of infection, which becomes an open sore oozing fluid (called a chancre) **Later signs and symptoms:** a rash; a dull, depressed feeling; fever, joint pain; hair loss; large moist sores around the sex organs or mouth **Final stage:** Blindness; brain damage; paralysis; can cause death	Antibiotic
Painful urination; discharge	Antibiotics or other drugs depending on cause
Warts in the genital or anal area	No cure; trichloracetic acid; podophyllin; laser; liquid nitrogen; surgery
Itching or pain in vaginal area; vaginal discharge that is yellowish or has an unpleasant odor	Antibiotics or other drugs depending on cause
Flulike symptoms; dark urine; yellowing of skin	No cure; interferon and gamma globulin can ease symptoms; vaccine available
Intense itching and possible rash in genital area; occasional swelling of lymph nodes in the groin	Medicated lotions and shampoos
Intense itching in genital area, under the breast, in the armpits, between the fingers, or elsewhere	Medicated lotions and shampoos

22.1 WHAT ARE SEXUALLY TRANSMITTED DISEASES? **469**

How Can a Person Become Infected With Genital Herpes? Herpes is almost always transmitted by sexual contact. However, any direct contact with a herpes sore can cause infection with herpes. The tiny blisters that form during a herpes outbreak are filled with a clear fluid that contains the virus. When blisters appear, the disease is in its most infectious state. That is the time when genital herpes can most easily be transmitted to another person. The open lesions will eventually crust over as the healing begins.

This does not mean that you cannot get herpes if you do not see herpes blisters on your partner's genitals. For one thing, although herpes is most contagious when blisters are present, it can also be transmitted when there are no blisters—for example, right before an outbreak of blisters. Also, blisters may be present but not seen. For example, if the infection were on a female's cervix, it would not be seen. Still, it could infect her sex partner.

What Happens if Genital Herpes Is Not Treated? Some people who have genital herpes will never experience signs and symptoms. Some may have signs and symptoms when they are first infected and never have them again. Still others may have herpes signs and symptoms that come and go. The signs and symptoms may appear once every few years or as often as every few weeks.

Although there is no cure, there is a drug that can be helpful to people with herpes. For people whose signs and symptoms return again and again, the drug acyclovir is used. Although acyclovir does not cure herpes, it can reduce the pain of the signs and symptoms and cause them to go away sooner than they would have without treatment. Acyclovir is available in capsules or as a cream.

The most important serious effects of genital herpes are the long-term problems. First, living with an incurable condition that can flare up at any moment can cause much stress and worry. Second, if a pregnant woman has an outbreak of herpes during childbirth, a Caesarean section may be necessary to prevent the baby from being born infected. Herpes infections in newborn babies are very serious. Fifty percent of newborns infected with herpes die, and half of the surviving babies will have severe brain or eye damage.

Syphilis

Syphilis (SIF-uh-lis) is caused by a bacterium. Syphilis is a very serious disease because it can spread through the bloodstream to any organ of the body. More than 120,000 new cases of syphilis are reported each year.

What Are the Signs and Symptoms of Syphilis? The first sign of syphilis is a painless sore called a chancre (SHANG-ker). The chancre starts out as a small red bump that later becomes an open sore that oozes fluid filled with syphilis bacteria. The chancre forms at the part of the body where the infection occurred.

A chancre on the penis or on the lips of the vagina is most likely to be noticed. However, the chancre may also form on the cervix, inside the vagina, in the mouth, in the throat, or in the rectum. Since the chancre is small and painless, it is usually not noticed if it forms in these areas. A chancre on the lips may be mistaken for a cold sore. While the chancre is present, the infected person has primary syphilis.

It usually takes about three weeks for the chancre to appear after infection, although it may appear as soon as 10 days after infection. In some people it may not appear for as long as three months. Before

syphilis:

an STD caused by bacteria, that can spread through the bloodstream to any organ of the body.

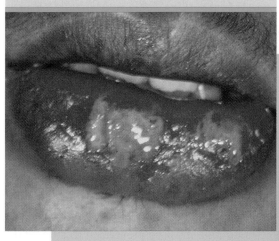

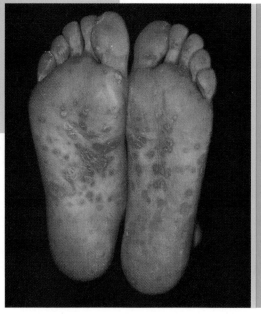

the chancre forms, a blood test for syphilis may be negative even though the bacterium is present in the body and the disease is progressing.

The chancre disappears with or without treatment within one to five weeks. However, disappearance of the chancre does not mean the disease is cured. It is just progressing to the next stage.

The next stage of the disease is called secondary syphilis. The signs and symptoms of secondary syphilis appear about two to six months after exposure. The most common sign of secondary syphilis is a rash that appears on the body. Sometimes the rash appears on the palms of the hands and the soles of the feet. The rash does not itch, and it goes away without treatment after a few weeks, although it may come back and go away again several times.

A person with secondary syphilis may also have a dull depressed feeling, fever, sore throat, joint pain, or hair loss. Large, moist sores sometimes develop around the sex organs or in the mouth. Like the chancre that is characteristic of primary syphilis, the signs and symptoms of secondary syphilis disappear without treatment. Syphilis then enters the latent stage.

Latent syphilis has no signs and symptoms. This stage may last for a few years or for an entire lifetime. However, latent syphilis may progress to tertiary syphilis. Tertiary syphilis is the stage of the disease in which the syphilis bacteria cause severe damage to parts of the body such as the skin, blood vessels, heart, bones, spinal cord, and brain. Tertiary syphilis can cause blindness, brain damage, paralysis, and, in some cases, even death.

How Can a Person Become Infected With Syphilis?

The bacterium that causes syphilis is very frail and cannot survive drying or chilling. It dies within a few seconds after exposure to air. Therefore, as with gonorrhea, you cannot get syphilis from toilet seats or dirty towels. Syphilis is usually transmitted during sexual contact. The bacterium is passed from the chancre or rash of

The Spread of STDs

STD	Approximate New Cases Each Year
Gonorrhea	1–3 million
Chlamydia	3–10 million
Genital herpes	500,000
Syphilis	120,000
Genital warts	1 million

(FIGURE 22-7) **Sexually transmitted diseases are spreading at an alarming rate. One reason for the rapid spread is that many people do not have signs and symptoms of disease and unknowingly infect others.**

genital warts:

an STD caused by the human papilloma virus, or HPV; causes warts in the genital and anal areas and has been linked to cervical cancer and penile cancer.

an infected person to the mucous membrane of the vagina, penis, mouth, or rectum of the other person. It is also possible for syphilis to be transmitted from a chancre or rash to an open wound or sore. An infected woman can also pass syphilis to her unborn child during pregnancy.

What Happens if Syphilis Is Not Treated?

Syphilis can be cured at any stage by using the right antibiotics. Treatment for the disease is easiest during the first year of infection.

After a year, syphilis can still be successfully treated, but the medication must be taken for a longer period of time.

If syphilis progresses to the final tertiary stage, treatment can stop the progression of the disease but cannot reverse the damage that has already occurred. As you already read, tertiary syphilis can cause blindness, paralysis, and even death.

Other STDs

The most common STDs are the ones already discussed. However, there are other STDs as well.

Nongonococcal Urethritis (NGU) Any infection of the urethra—the tube that carries urine from the bladder to the outside of the body—that is not caused by gonorrhea is called nongonococcal urethritis. Several different organisms cause NGU, but most cases are caused by chlamydia. The proper antibiotic must be prescribed to cure NGU.

Genital Warts **Genital warts** may be the fastest growing STD in the United States. There are more than one million new cases each year. Warts may appear in the genital and anal areas.

Genital warts are caused by the human papilloma virus (HPV). HPV is not curable, but its symptoms may be treated with drugs, lasers, liquid nitrogen, or surgery. HPV is associated with penile and cervical cancers, so people who have been infected should be screened for cancer regularly.

Vaginitis Vaginitis is any inflammation of the vagina. Signs and symptoms may include itching or pain in the vaginal area or any unusual vaginal discharge. It is normal for the vagina to secrete a small amount of clear liquid. It is also normal for the amount and thickness of the secretion to vary somewhat during the monthly cycle. However, if the discharge is yellowish, if it has an unpleasant odor, or if there is much more than usual, it is a sign of vaginitis.

Vaginitis can be caused by the gonorrhea or chlamydia bacteria, as well as by other microorganisms. Trichomoniasis (also called "trick") is caused by a one-celled organism that burrows under the mucus in the vagina. It is often transmitted through sexual intercourse. It can also be contracted by exposure to moist objects containing the organism. For example, this could happen if you used someone else's wet towel or bathing suit.

Vaginitis can also be caused by a fungus called candida. This kind of infection, candidiasis, is commonly known as a yeast infection. A yeast infection is not necessarily sexually transmitted. Any imbalance in the normal environment inside the vagina can give candida a chance to grow and to cause problems.

Hepatitis Hepatitis (hep-uh-TY-tis) is an inflammation of the liver that can be caused by several different viruses. The type of hepatitis that is called hepatitis A is not usually transmitted sexually, but it can be passed from one person to another by oral-anal contact.

The hepatitis B virus, on the other hand, is easily transmitted through sexual contact. It may be present in the body fluids—saliva, urine, blood, semen, and vaginal secretions—of an infected person.

But sexual contact is not the only way hepatitis B is spread. Practices such as sharing toothbrushes, razors, or needles with an infected person can also transmit the disease.

Hepatitis B is a serious disease. It can cause damage to the liver and result in serious health problems. Early signs and symptoms may be similar to those of the flu and may also include dark urine and yellowing of the skin and the whites of the eyes. If you are exposed to hepatitis B, it is important for you to seek treatment right away.

A vaccine is now available that prevents hepatitis B. If you are concerned about this type of hepatitis, talk to a doctor or another health professional about receiving the vaccine.

Parasitic Infections Pubic lice ("crabs") and scabies can be spread by either casual or sexual contact. Pubic lice are small insects that live in the pubic hair and attach their eggs to hair shafts. Pubic lice grip the pubic

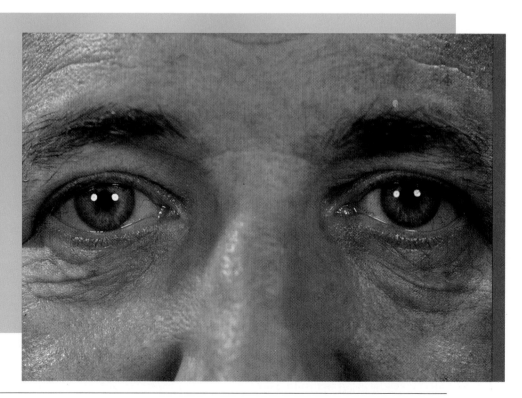

(FIGURE 22-8) **One of the early signs of hepatitis B is yellowing of the skin and the whites of the eyes.**

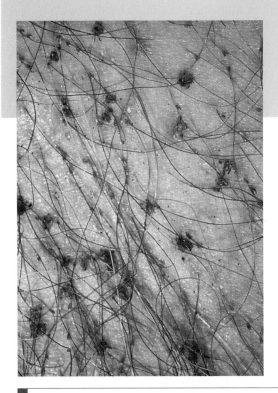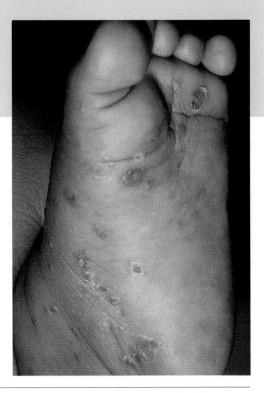

(FIGURE 22-9) **Pubic lice [left] live in the pubic hair, causing irritation and itching. Scabies is caused by a tiny mite that burrows under the skin.**

hair and feed on tiny blood vessels of the skin. The lice irritate the skin and cause itching and occasional swelling of the glands in the groin.

Scabies (SCAY-beez) is caused by a tiny mite that can barely be seen. The mite burrows under the skin and causes intense itching and the formation of pus. In addition to the genital area, scabies may appear under the breasts, in the armpits, between the fingers, and elsewhere.

Special medicated shampoo is used to treat pubic lice, and medicated lotion is used to treat scabies. However, pubic lice and scabies can be found in clothes and bed linen. Therefore, all clothing and bed linen must be washed in hot water and either dried in a hot clothes dryer or dried in bright sunshine in order to eliminate these parasites.

Review

1. What is a sexually transmitted disease?

2. Name four common sexually transmitted diseases.

3. Name two ways that chlamydia can be transmitted.

4. What are the signs and symptoms of genital herpes?

5. **Critical Thinking** Is it possible for someone to transmit an STD to another person without realizing it? Explain.

22.2 Preventing Sexually Transmitted Diseases

Objectives

- Know what you can do to decrease your chances of getting an STD.

- Name 10 ways you can show love for someone without sexual intimacy.
  - **LIFE SKILLS: Communicating Effectively**

- Know where to go for testing and treatment for STDs.
  - **LIFE SKILLS: Using Community Resources**

Vanessa said that she thought these diseases must be pretty rare. After all, she had heard a lot of people talking about sex, but she had never known anyone personally who had gotten one of these diseases. But her mother pointed out that most people who get an STD are embarrassed about it. They aren't likely to go around telling everybody that they have one of these diseases.

Han said that she thought the people who got STDs were probably very promiscuous, with many sex partners. Vanessa's mom said that it's true that the more sex partners you have, the more likely you are to get one of these diseases. However, you can get an STD by having sexual contact just once, if your partner is infected.

Staying Healthy

STDs can be prevented by making responsible decisions. You can stay healthy by refusing to take part in behaviors that put you at risk for STDs.

Delaying Sexual Intimacy Many of these diseases are transmitted only by sexual contact or mainly by sexual contact. If you are not sexually active, you will probably never have to worry about getting gonorrhea, syphilis, or chlamydia.

Although it is theoretically possible to get genital herpes, trichomoniasis, pubic lice, or scabies in other ways besides sexual contact, it is very unlikely. You can reduce your risk of these diseases to practically zero if you avoid sexual contact and also practice good hygiene. That means not sharing towels, clothing, or bed linen with anyone else unless those items have been thoroughly washed. In addition, you must avoid direct contact with any open sores another person might have.

(FIGURE 22-10) **If two people abstain from sexual activity until marriage and remain faithful to each other, they will be protected from STDs.**

As you already learned, delaying or abstaining from sexual intimacy is called sexual abstinence. If you decide to practice abstinence until you are older, that doesn't mean that you will not have sexual feelings for someone in the meantime. There are many safe ways to express sexual affection for someone. Talking, hugging, and holding hands, for example, are the safest possible expressions of feelings.

In spite of the messages you may be getting from music, movies, TV, or even your friends, the truth is that many teenagers are not sexually active. Teenagers choose to delay sexual intimacy for a variety of reasons. For some teens it is a matter of avoiding sexually transmitted diseases and pregnancy. For others, the primary reason for delaying intimacy involves personal goals and values. People are generally happier when they live up to their values and accomplish their goals.

Remember, if two people abstain from sexual activity until marriage and remain faithful to each other, they will be protected from STDs.

Life SKILLS: Communicating Effectively

Showing Love Nonsexually . . . .

The teenage years are a time of strong sexual feelings. Even though you know that choosing abstinence is the best way to avoid STDs, you may want to show your affection for someone by becoming sexually intimate.

When you are in love and really care for someone, it's natural to want to show it. But sexual intercourse is not the only way to show affection. For example, one of the nicest things you can do for a person is to listen to what he or she has to say with genuine interest. This shows that you take the person seriously and that his or her thoughts and feelings are important to you.

On a separate sheet of paper, write down at least 10 other ways besides sex that you can show you love your girl-friend or boyfriend.

Staying in Control Using alcohol and other drugs can be harmful to your health in more ways than their direct effects on your body. Drinking or doing drugs can also increase your risk of getting an STD. How? Drugs and alcohol interfere with your judgment and decision-making abilities. With drugs or alcohol clouding your thinking, it is much easier to convince yourself that it's okay ''just this once.''

Besides avoiding drugs and alcohol, it can also help to avoid situations where you might be pressured to participate in sexual activity. For example, group dating with friends who share your values can make it easier to avoid temptation. Also, getting involved in sports, after-school clubs, hobbies, or volunteer work can reduce your need to alleviate boredom or find satisfaction through sex.

Reducing the Risk of STDs There are some sexual practices that—although they are not completely safe—can reduce the risk of getting an STD during sexual contact. For example, the **latex condom,** a covering for the penis, helps protect both partners from sexually transmitted diseases and helps prevent pregnancy. For a condom to be effective though, it must be used properly. The condom must be put on before any physical contact and must be worn until contact has ended. When putting the condom on, the reservoir tip at the top of the condom must be pinched as the condom is unrolled to the base of the penis. To prevent the condom from slipping off inside the vagina, the penis must be withdrawn while still erect while the condom is held snugly to the base of the penis. High temperatures weaken latex, so condoms should never be stored in a car or in a wallet carried in a hip pocket. Also, condoms weaken over time, so remember to check the expiration date printed on the package. Using a spermicide can give added protection against STDs and pregnancy. Although water-based lubricants do not protect against STDs or pregnancy, they do reduce the risk of condom breakage. Caution: Any oily substance can weaken the latex and cause the condom to break.

Breaking the Cycle of Infection Sexually transmitted diseases have become epidemic in the United States. One reason why so many people have them is that STDs are spread from one sex partner to another in a seemingly endless chain by people who don't know that they have a disease, who do not get proper treatment for the disease, or who don't inform their partners.

As Figure 22-11 shows, if an infected person passes an STD to two sex partners and those people pass it to two partners, and so on, the disease can spread from one person to many people in a relatively short time.

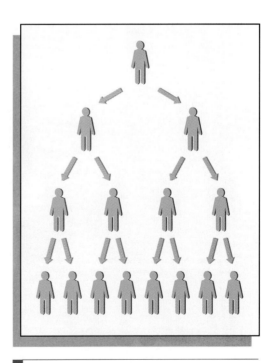

(FIGURE 22-11) **This diagram shows how rapidly an STD can spread if each infected person passes it to two sex partners.**

latex condom:

a covering for the penis that, when used correctly, helps protect both partners from sexually transmitted diseases and helps prevent pregnancy.

If you think you might have an STD, it is very important that you break this chain of infection. If you do not act responsibly to stop the disease, there could be serious consequences to your own health. You could also be responsible for the infection of many other people.

If You Think You Might Have an STD

If you have any reason to think you have been exposed to one of these diseases, you must find out for sure if you have it even if you do not have signs or symptoms. Only a doctor or a health professional at a clinic can diagnose STDs.

Where to Go for Help   You have several choices about where to go for proper diagnosis and treatment. You can go to your family doctor or to another private doctor. Remember, doctors have a professional duty to keep information regarding their patients confidential.

If you don't have a private doctor, or if you cannot afford to pay for private treatment, there are public health clinics that offer free or low-cost treatment. To find the number for a public clinic, look in the local government section of the Blue Pages under "Health and Human Services." Other clinics that offer testing services are listed in the Yellow Pages under "Clinic—Medical."

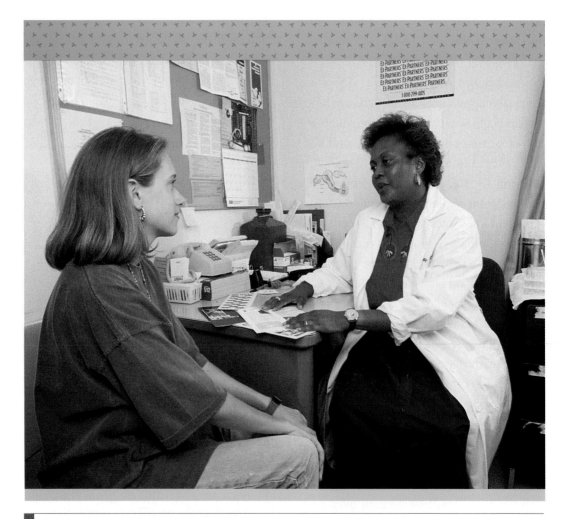

(FIGURE 22-12) **Public health clinics will keep your name, your diagnosis, your treatment, and any other information about you completely confidential.**

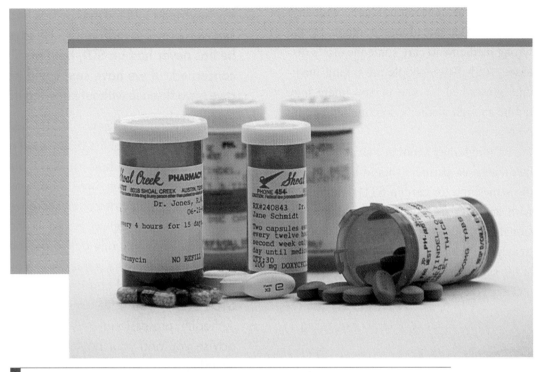

(FIGURE 22-13) **People with STDs should take all the medicine they are prescribed and follow the doctor's orders exactly.**

You can also call the National STD Hotline number, which is listed with Directory Assistance, to find out where in your area you can go for STD testing and treatment. The people staffing the hotline can answer any questions you have about STDs.

It is the law in most states that anyone can be treated for a communicable disease. This means that anyone who seeks treatment for a sexually transmitted disease can receive it.

Don't worry about the health workers in the clinics being shocked or upset that you might have an STD. Remember, dealing with STDs is just part of their daily routine. Their goal is to stop the spread of these diseases. Public health workers are more likely to be upset by people who do not get treatment and who continue to spread the disease. Public health clinics will keep your name, your diagnosis, your treatment, and any information you give them completely confidential.

If you are diagnosed with certain STDs, workers at the clinic may ask for the names of your sex partners. They do this so that they can inform your partners of possible exposure to the disease. For many people, telling their partners is the hardest part of dealing with an STD. If a person with an STD wishes, a health clinic worker will contact the sex partners but not reveal the name of the person with the STD.

Treatment for STDs Different STDs require different treatments, so a visit to a health professional is necessary to receive the correct treatment.

Many people think they have to take their medicine only until they feel better. This is not true! Once a person feels better and is not so worried, it may take some effort to keep taking the medicine until it is gone. However, it is very important to do so. People with STDs should take all the medicine they are prescribed and follow the doctor's instructions exactly.

REMINDER

〰〰〰〰〰

Bacteria can develop immunity to any antibiotic that is not taken as directed.

Medicine must not be shared with anyone else. For one thing, it might be the wrong medicine to cure someone else's disease. And if two people are taking medicine prescribed for one person, there may not be enough medicine to completely cure both people.

Though they shouldn't share the same medicine, sex partners should be treated at the same time for certain STDs. A person with an STD should ask a health professional if his or her partner should also be treated. If both sex partners are not treated at the same time, they can continue to reinfect each other.

Q. A friend told me that the best way to avoid STDs is to take a shower right after having sex. He said that if you can't take a shower right away, you should at least wash off the best you can. Is this true?

A. No. Washing after sexual contact will not prevent STDs. If you have unprotected sexual contact with an infected partner, disease-causing microorganisms can cross mucous membranes and enter your body before you can wash them off.

◆◆◆

Q. Is it true that taking birth-control pills can prevent STDs?

A. No, definitely not. Birth-control pills prevent pregnancy but do nothing to prevent STDs.

◆◆◆

Q. My boyfriend told me that he has had sex with previous girlfriends. He says he has never had an STD, but I'm still concerned. If we have sex, could he give me a disease without knowing it?

A. Not everyone who gets an STD has signs or symptoms of the disease. If a previous girlfriend had an STD but failed to inform your boyfriend, you are at risk. People are often secretive about STDs, so getting tested is the best way for a sexually active person to find out if he or she is infected. You and your boyfriend can be tested for STDs even if you have no symptoms. A health professional will probably advise you and your boyfriend to be tested now, and then again after a waiting period.

Review

• • • • •

1. *Name four actions you can take that will eliminate or reduce your risk of getting an STD.*

2. ▣▣ **LIFE SKILLS: Communicating Effectively** *Name 10 ways you can show love for someone without becoming sexually intimate.*

3. ▣▣ **LIFE SKILLS: Using Community Resources** *If a friend told you that he thought he might have an STD but didn't know where to go to find out for sure, how could you help him?*

4. **Critical Thinking** *What do you think will happen if a patient being treated for a bacterial STD does not take all of the antibiotic?*

CHAPTER 22

Highlights

Summary

- The most dangerous STD (sexually transmitted disease) is AIDS. It cannot be cured and is eventually fatal.

- Some other serious STDs include gonorrhea, chlamydia, genital herpes, syphilis, and HPV.

- Gonorrhea is an infection caused by a bacterium. Many people with gonorrhea do not have symptoms but can pass the bacteria to their sex partners.

- Genital herpes is caused by a virus; there is no known cure. Fifty percent of newborns infected with herpes die, and half of the surviving babies will have severe brain or eye damage.

- Syphilis is caused by a bacterium and progresses in stages. It can be cured at any stage with the right antibiotic, but if it progresses to the final stage, the damage that has occurred cannot be reversed.

- Other common STDs include genital warts, hepatitis, and pubic lice.

- When used properly, a condom and spermicide can reduce the risk of getting an STD. Safe lubricants for a condom are "water-soluble" ones.

- Confidential diagnosis and treatment for STDs can be obtained from a private doctor or a public health clinic.

- Sexual partners should be treated at the same time for STDs, but they shouldn't share the same medicine.

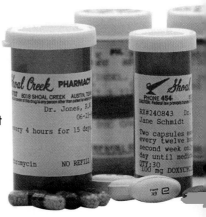

Vocabulary

sexually transmitted disease (STD) a disease that is passed from one person to another during sexual contact.

gonorrhea an STD caused by bacteria that can infect the mucous membranes of the penis, vagina, throat, or rectum.

pelvic inflammatory disease (PID) an infection of the uterus and fallopian tubes often caused by STDs; if untreated, may result in infertility.

chlamydia the most common STD in the United States; caused by bacteria.

genital herpes an STD caused by a virus that often causes painful blisters or ulcers; cannot be cured.

syphilis an STD caused by bacteria that can spread through the bloodstream to any organ of the body.

genital warts an STD caused by the human papilloma virus, or HPV; causes warts in the genital and anal areas and has been linked to cervical cancer and penile cancer.

Concept Review . . . .

1. An incurable STD is
   a. gonorrhea.   c. syphilis.
   b. herpes.   d. chlamydia.

2. An STD that can cause sterility and pelvic inflammatory disease is
   a. syphilis.   c. vaginitis.
   b. genital warts.   d. chlamydia.

3. How are some sexually transmitted diseases commonly spread?
   a. from mother   c. by using dirty
      to infant   toilet seats
   b. by closed-mouth   d. all of these
      kissing

4. An STD associated with cancer is
   a. vaginitis.   c. scabies.
   b. NGU.   d. genital warts.

5. Hepatitis B can be spread by
   a. sharing tooth-   c. sharing needles.
      brushes.
   b. sexual contact.   d. all of these.

6. Special medicated shampoos or medicated lotions are used to treat
   a. genital warts.
   b. PID.
   c. parasitic infections.
   d. genital herpes.

7. Which of the following behaviors provides the best protection against STDs?
   a. using a condom
   b. using a condom with spermicide
   c. practicing abstinence
   d. getting tested for STDs

8. To find out if you have an STD, you should
   a. talk to a counselor.
   b. visit a doctor or clinic.
   c. talk to your sex partner.
   d. get an over-the-counter drug from the pharmacist.

Expressing Your Views . . . .

1. Your friend has confided to you that she has genital herpes. Her boyfriend does not use a condom during sexual intercourse. She says she will not infect her boyfriend as long as she doesn't have an outbreak of blisters. How would you respond to this statement?

2. You have a friend who has been diagnosed as having a sexually trans-

mitted disease. He has received treatment but is too embarrassed to tell his sex partners about his problem. He keeps telling himself that he didn't have sexual intercourse with them often enough for them to be infected. Why is it important for him to inform his partners?

3. Why do you think sexually transmitted diseases continue to spread?

Life Skills Check . . . . . .

1. Communicating Effectively

Write a script for a play to be acted out by members of your class in which one character informs his or her sex partner that they are most likely both infected with an STD. Include conversations the two characters might have with friends and relatives about the situation. End the play with the couple deciding on a course of action to resolve their problem.

2. Communicating Effectively

You have noticed a small, painless, leaky sore in your mouth. Ordinarily you would dismiss it as a cold sore. But lately you have been behaving in a way that would put you at risk for a sexually transmitted disease, and you wonder if that is what it could be. How could you find out for sure in a confidential manner?

Projects . . . .

1. Use telephone books and library research to compile a list of telephone numbers and addresses of local agencies that could provide information, counseling, and testing for sexually transmitted diseases. Display the lists in the classroom and around the school.

2. Work with a group to create a bulletin board describing the STDs covered in this chapter. Include symptoms, dangers, and treatments of each disease.

3. Design a cartoon illustrating a way for people to cope with a risky situation or peer pressure.

Plan for Action . . . .

STDs are a major health concern because of their increase among teens and young adults. Make a plan to protect yourself and to help control the spread of these diseases.

CHAPTER
23

HIV
Infection
and AIDS

◆ ◆ ◆ ◆

Section 23.1
What Is HIV Infection?

Section 23.2
Transmission of HIV

Section 23.3
How to Protect Yourself From HIV

Section 23.4
HIV Infection and Society

Talk About AIDS

AIDS Is Scary, But A Zit Is Real. Right

A young man takes positive action against AIDS by staffing an AIDS information hotline.

Michael and Bryan had been friends since the fourth grade. So Michael noticed immediately that something was really bothering Bryan; he was quiet and looked sad. But Bryan wouldn't talk about what was wrong.

Finally, Michael lost his patience and told Bryan he needed to know what was bothering him. Bryan said he'd think about it, which kept Michael wondering what the problem could be. A couple of days later, Bryan told Michael that his older brother Aaron had tested positive for HIV. Michael felt like he had just been punched in the stomach. He had no idea what to say. "Does that mean Aaron has AIDS?" he blurted out, and then he wanted to kick himself for asking that question. But Bryan didn't seem surprised. He told Michael that so far Aaron didn't seem sick. Then Bryan said that he trusted Michael not to tell their other friends.

Michael was in a daze for the rest of the day. Was Bryan's brother going to die? How did he get infected? Was there any possibility that Bryan could be infected by the AIDS virus? Michael decided he needed to find out more about AIDS.

Section 23.1

What Is HIV Infection?

Objectives

- Define AIDS.

- Describe how HIV works in the body.

- Describe the three phases of HIV infection.

- Find out where to get an HIV-antibody test.
  - **LIFE SKILLS: Using Community Resources**

Michael sat down at a computer to search for information about HIV infection and AIDS. In this chapter, you'll learn what Michael learned as he read the information he found.

The most important thing to know about HIV infection is that it is preventable. You can keep from getting it by learning about how it is spread and then avoiding behaviors that might allow you to be infected. In other words, you can choose responsible behaviors to protect yourself. And you can relax about behaviors that don't put you at risk.

AIDS:

a disease, caused by a virus, that cripples a person's immune system; AIDS is classified as a sexually transmitted disease, but it can also be spread in other ways, such as through sharing infected equipment for injecting drugs, tattoing, or ear piercing. AIDS is the last phase of HIV infection.

REMINDER
〰〰〰

A virus is a microscopic agent that can cause disease.

HIV:

(human immuno-deficiency virus) the virus that causes AIDS; also called the "AIDS virus."

■ (FIGURE 23-1) **The virus that causes AIDS is called HIV (human immuno-deficiency virus).**

AIDS, the last phase of HIV infection, is considered to be a sexually transmitted disease because it is most often spread through sexual contact. The name **AIDS** stands for Acquired Immune Deficiency Syndrome. When you break the name of the disease down into its parts, the name makes sense.

Acquired means that a person gets AIDS during his or her lifetime, rather than inheriting it from parents (although a pregnant woman with HIV infection can pass the virus on to her baby).

Immune Deficiency means that the body's immune system, the system that defends the body against infection and disease, is no longer able to do its job. In other words, the immune system becomes deficient.

Syndrome refers to the many diseases and conditions that result from having AIDS.

AIDS is caused by a kind of virus called **HIV** (human immunodeficiency virus). HIV is often referred to as the

"AIDS virus." You can see a diagram of one of these viruses in Figure 23-1.

HIV actually attacks the body's immune system, making it difficult for the immune system to defend the body against infection. What this means is that infections that normally wouldn't be very dangerous can kill a person with AIDS.

There is still no cure for HIV infection. Once the virus is able to enter a person's body, there is no way to remove it. There is currently no form of vaccination that can keep you from getting infected with HIV. That's why it's important to read this chapter carefully and take precautions to protect yourself from HIV infection.

The Spread of HIV Infection

The first cases of AIDS were diagnosed in the United States in 1981. Since that time, the number of people with AIDS has grown tremendously, as you can see in Figure 23-2. At the end of 1981, there were 379 cases of AIDS in the United States. Ten years later, the number had increased to more than 200,000. By the end of 1995, the number of cases was well over 500,000 and 62 percent had already died.

There are probably many more people that are infected but don't know it yet because they show no symptoms of the disease. The World Health Organization estimates that 18 million adults and 1.5 million children have been infected with HIV.

Many of the people who first had AIDS in the United States were homosexual men. As a result, some people thought that only homosexuals could get AIDS. That is now known to be a myth. Anyone who engages in risky behaviors can get HIV, whether that person is homosexual or heterosexual. Heterosexual contact is becoming an increasingly common method of transmission. In fact, in some parts of the world, heterosexuals make up the largest group of people with AIDS.

Something that is particularly disturbing about the spread of HIV is the large number of people in their twenties who have it. Since it often takes years from the time of infection until a person actually gets sick, this means that many people were in their teens when they were originally infected with HIV. Among people 15 to 24 years of age, AIDS is now the sixth leading cause of death.

How HIV Works

Among people aged 25–44, AIDS is now the leading cause of death in men and the third leading cause of death in women. If you know the way in which HIV works in the body, you'll understand why certain behaviors increase your chances of being infected with the virus.

Check Up

How Much Do You Already Know About HIV Infection?

1. Can you get HIV by drinking from a glass that someone with HIV has once used?

2. Can you get HIV by holding hands with a person with HIV?

3. Can you get HIV by having sexual intercourse with a person with HIV?

4. If a restaurant cook with HIV sneezes on your food, could you get HIV?

5. Can a woman with HIV infect her baby during delivery?

6. Can you get HIV by donating blood?

7. Can you tell by looking at someone whether he or she has been infected with HIV?

8. Is there a blood test that shows whether a person has been infected with HIV?

1. no 2. no 3. yes 4. no 5. yes 6. no 7. no 8. yes

Note: Any time the blood of an infected person can enter another person's bloodstream through an open cut, sore, or other wound, the potential for infection exists.

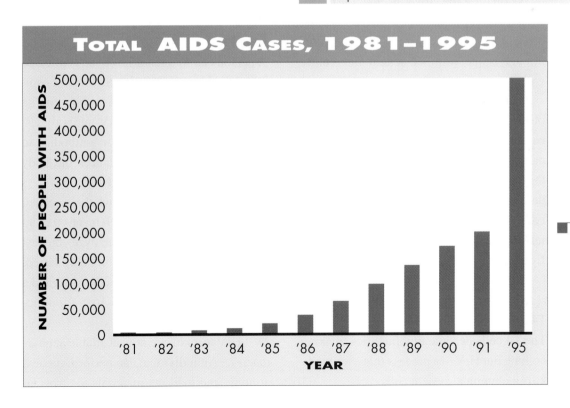

TOTAL AIDS CASES, 1981–1995

NUMBER OF PEOPLE WITH AIDS

YEAR

(FIGURE 23-2) **The total number of people diagnosed with AIDS has grown tremendously since 1981.** (Source: U.S. Centers for Disease Control, Atlanta, Georgia.)

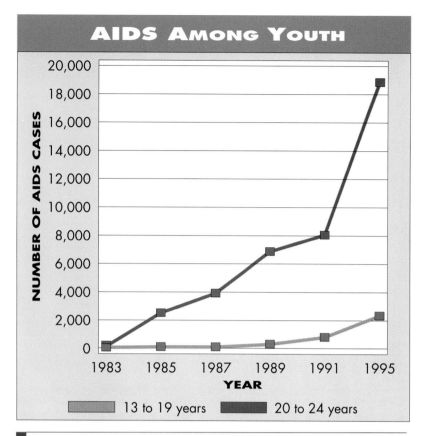

AIDS AMONG YOUTH

NUMBER OF AIDS CASES (y-axis: 0, 2,000, 4,000, 6,000, 8,000, 10,000, 12,000, 14,000, 16,000, 18,000, 20,000)

YEAR (x-axis: 1983, 1985, 1987, 1989, 1991, 1995)

■ 13 to 19 years ■ 20 to 24 years

(FIGURE 23-3) **The graph shows the alarming increase in the number of teens and young adults with AIDS.**

The newly made viruses then go on to target and attack other T4 cells. As more and more cells are destroyed, the person's immune system gets weaker and weaker. Without a working immune system, a person's body is defenseless against other viruses, bacteria, fungi, and cancer cells. These other infections and cancers are what kill a person with AIDS, not HIV itself.

There are two main points to remember about how HIV works. First, the virus has to get into a person's bloodstream before it can cause infection. What this means to you is that you have to avoid doing things that might let HIV into your bloodstream.

Second, HIV can be in a person's body for years before any signs or symptoms of illness appear. Sometimes more than 10 years can pass before an infected person has any outward signs of the disease. That means you can't tell by looking at someone whether he or she has been infected with HIV. Someone who carries the virus but is not sick can still infect others.

First, HIV must get into a person's bloodstream. The virus can enter the bloodstream directly through shared needles or syringes, or the virus can be transmitted through some form of sexual intercourse with an infected person.

In the body, HIV targets a special kind of blood cell—white blood cells called T4 cells. T4 cells are an extremely important part of a person's immune system because they are the cells that coordinate the body's defense against infection. The attack on T4 cells is what makes HIV so dangerous—it targets the cells that are most important in fighting off infection.

The virus enters the T4 cells and slowly destroys them. The virus forces the T4 cell to make thousands of copies of HIV. The T4 cells become tiny factories, making nothing but HIV—a process that eventually kills the immune system cells.

HIV-Antibody Tests

A person can find out if he or she is infected with HIV by going to a health clinic, hospital, or doctor's office and asking for an **HIV-antibody test.** The HIV-antibody test checks a person's blood for antibodies to HIV. Antibodies are substances the body makes to fight infectious agents.

Many clinics offer what is called "anonymous" testing, which means that no one at the clinic or lab that analyzes the test knows the name of the person being tested. Instead the person being tested is assigned a number. Testing is usually free at public-health clinics.

HIV test kits are now available at pharmacies. An individual can perform the test at home and mail the materials to a special

HIV-antibody test:

a test used to determine whether a person has been infected with HIV.

lab for analysis. The test materials are labeled by number, so the people in the lab do not know the identity of the person taking the test. The test results are made available when the person calls the lab and provides the identification number. A positive test result should be followed up immediately by a visit to a doctor for confirmation of the results because there may be other reasons why the results could show up positive.

Myths and Facts About HIV Infection

Myth	Fact
HIV and AIDS are the same thing.	HIV (human immunodeficiency virus) is the name of the virus that causes AIDS. AIDS is the last phase of HIV infection.
People who are infected with HIV look very sick.	Although people with advanced AIDS may look very sick, many people with HIV look perfectly healthy. You can't tell by looking at people whether they have the virus. Even HIV-positive people who look healthy can infect others.
A person who is young and healthy cannot be infected with HIV.	Anyone can be infected with HIV. Unfortunately, many teenagers see themselves as "immune" to misfortunes such as HIV infection.
Birth control pills can prevent the transmission of HIV.	Birth control pills have no effect whatsoever on the spread of HIV.
A person who uses a new latex condom each time he or she has intercourse runs no risk of getting HIV.	Although latex condoms provide good protection, they are not 100 percent effective in preventing HIV transmission. Condoms sometimes tear or are used incorrectly.
Sharing needles to inject insulin, antibiotics, or steroids is not risky for HIV transmission.	Sharing needles for any purpose is risky, even if the injected drugs are legal.
It is possible to get HIV by donating your blood.	Donating your blood does not put you at risk for HIV. Blood-donation centers use a new, sterile needle with each donor.
If a mosquito bit someone with HIV and then bit you, you could get HIV.	There have been no cases of HIV transmission by an insect or any other animal.
It is possible to get HIV by eating food that a person with HIV has handled.	There have been no cases of HIV transmission through food or beverages.

(FIGURE 23-4)

The HIV antibody test has one major drawback. It takes a while for an infected person's body to make enough antibodies to show up on the test—usually from 6 to 12 weeks, but sometimes up to 6 months. If a person gets tested immediately after possibly being infected, the test results will be negative. So even when the test results are negative, there is still some chance that a person could be carrying HIV.

There are two very compelling reasons to be tested if you think you might be infected with the virus. First, it may be possible to slow the progress of the disease with early treatment. Early treatment can prolong life if an individual starts medication before he or she gets sick. The second reason is that if you know you are infected, you can take precautions not to infect others.

Phases of HIV Infection

There isn't a timetable for the progression of HIV infection, but people tend to go through the following three phases.

Phase 1: Infection With No Signs or Symptoms of Illness Some people—infants, people who already have chronic diseases, and older people, for example—show signs and symptoms of infection very quickly. Others can be infected with HIV for years, sometimes 10 years or longer, without any noticeable illness. They seem perfectly healthy and wouldn't even know they were infected if they hadn't tested positive on the HIV-antibody test.

People who have been infected with HIV are said to be **HIV-positive.** It's important to remember that people can be HIV-positive and not have AIDS. People who are HIV-positive will probably get sick eventually; however, researchers might

find a way to prevent the disease from progressing. The main thing to remember now is that people who are infected with HIV but don't show any signs or symptoms of illness can still transmit the virus to other people.

Phase 2: Infection With Signs and Symptoms of Illness During the second phase of HIV infection, a person's immune system will begin to fail. A person in this phase may have one or more of the following signs and symptoms:

- swollen lymph glands in the neck and armpits
- extreme tiredness
- fever
- diarrhea
- severe weight loss
- excessive sweating during the night
- white patches on the inside of the mouth

You might be thinking to yourself, "I've had some of those signs. Does that mean I might be infected with HIV?" Remember that these signs and symptoms can also be caused by other infections, such as a cold or the flu. If you have these signs and symptoms, it doesn't necessarily mean that you're infected with HIV. One difference between the signs and symptoms of an HIV infection and a cold or flu is that the signs and symptoms of HIV infection tend to last a lot longer. If you have any of the signs or symptoms for more than two weeks, it's a good idea to see a doctor just to be on the safe side.

In addition to these infections, females can develop problems of the reproductive system. Often the first symptom of a weakened immune system in women is a series of severe vaginal infections.

Phase 3: AIDS According to the Centers for Disease Control and Prevention, there are two ways in which an HIV-infected person is considered to have AIDS. As it is clinically defined, a person has AIDS when

HIV-positive:

the condition of being infected with HIV.

the level of T4 cells in his or her blood is fewer than 200 cells per microliter, which is less than 14 percent of the white blood cells in the blood. This level indicates that a person's immune system has been severely damaged.

The second factor that doctors look for in diagnosing AIDS is the development of serious conditions that result from long-term damage to the immune system. Among these serious conditions are opportunistic infections. They are called opportunistic infections because they take the "opportunity" created by a weakened immune system to attack a person's body.

One of the most common opportunistic infections affecting people with AIDS is a kind of pneumonia called *Pneumocystis carinii pneumonia,* which causes difficulty in breathing, chest pain, and coughing. Another common opportunistic infection is *Kaposi's sarcoma,* which is a rare form of cancer that causes purple patches or bumps on the skin and on the internal organs. It is very unusual for someone who does not have AIDS to get Pneumocystis carinii pneumonia or Kaposi's sarcoma because a normally functioning immune system can successfully defend against these infections. Pulmonary tuberculosis is another opportunistic infection. This type of tuberculosis and a low T4 count are used to diagnose AIDS. HIV-infected women are more likely than other women to get cervical cancer.

People with HIV who have a large number of functioning T4 cells often appear healthy. They are energetic for long periods of time and can work or go to school. Those with fewer T4 cells are more likely to become ill and develop opportunistic infections and cancers.

There is still no cure for AIDS, but researchers continue to develop new treatments that can help people with AIDS lead longer, healthier lives.

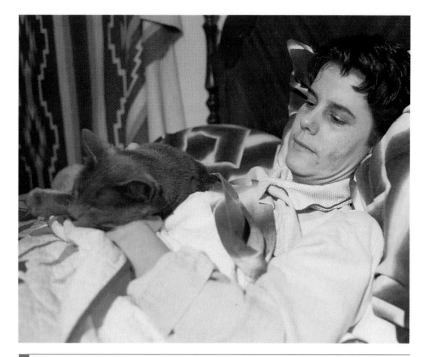

(FIGURE 23-5) **People with AIDS are more susceptible to infections and cancers than people who have fully functioning immune systems.**

Review

1. Define AIDS.

2. Define HIV.

3. Can a person infected with HIV who shows no outward signs of illness infect another person? Explain your answer.

4. **LIFE SKILLS: Using Community Resources** Make a list of the resources in your community that you can consult to find out more about AIDS.

5. **Critical Thinking** Is it possible for a person who was infected with HIV at the age of 14 to have no outward signs of illness at the age of 19? Explain your answer.

23.2 Transmission of HIV

Objectives

■ Name the four body fluids that may contain enough HIV to infect another person.

■ List the four behaviors that put you at risk for HIV infection.

■ Name at least five behaviors that don't put you at risk for HIV infection.

■ Find out where you can get answers to any questions about HIV that are not covered in this chapter.
▪▪ **LIFE SKILLS: Using Community Resources**

Fortunately, HIV is not transmitted like the viruses that cause the common cold or flu. Cold and flu viruses are transmitted easily by contact between two people. If you shake hands with a person who has a cold or flu, for example, and then you touch your mouth, you are very likely to catch the virus from that person. HIV is much harder to catch because it is not transmitted through the air. By far, the most common way that HIV is transmitted from one person to another is through body fluids. Only some of these fluids contain enough of the virus to infect someone else. The following body fluids can contain enough HIV to infect another person:

- blood
- semen
- vaginal secretions
- breast milk

▪ (FIGURE 23-6) **You can't get AIDS from being around a person in an ordinary, every-day kind of way.**

Transmission of HIV

Risky Behaviors	Safe Behaviors ("Casual Contact")
• Sharing equipment for injecting drugs, tattooing, or piercing	• Working at the same place or going to the same school
• Anal intercourse with an infected person	• Living in the same home
• Vaginal intercourse with an infected person	• Shaking hands, holding hands, or hugging
• Oral intercourse with an infected person	• Sharing a toilet or using a public toilet
• Having multiple sex partners	• Using the same locker room
• Exercising poor judgment regarding sexual activity as a result of using alcohol or other drugs	• Using the same telephone
	• Using the same water fountain
	• Swimming in the same pool
	• Being breathed on, coughed on, or sneezed on
	...and any other ordinary, everyday kind of contact

(FIGURE 23-7) **Risky behaviors involve the exchange of blood, semen, or vaginal secretions. Safe behaviors don't involve those body fluids.**

Remember that HIV must enter a person's bloodstream for infection to occur. It must go from the blood, semen, vaginal secretions, or breast milk of an infected person into the bloodstream of another person. But how does HIV get into the bloodstream?

First, HIV can be transmitted directly from an infected person's blood into another person's bloodstream when needles and syringes used to inject drugs are shared.

Second, HIV can enter the bloodstream through the **mucous membranes** of the body. Mucous membranes are moist, pink tissues that line the openings to the body—the mouth, the vagina, the anus, the rectum, and the opening at the tip of the penis. If there are sores or tiny breaks in the mucous membranes, there is a simple pathway for HIV to enter the bloodstream. But even if a person has no breaks in the mucous membranes, documented cases show that HIV can still enter the body through the mucous membranes during sexual intercourse.

mucous membranes:

moist, pink tissues of the body; includes membranes of the mouth, vagina, anus, rectum, and the opening at the tip of the penis.

Actions That Put You At Risk

People used to talk about HIV risk groups—groups of people who are more likely than others to get HIV. Now we know that anyone who takes part in certain risky behaviors is at risk of contracting HIV.

Sometimes it is hard to talk about risky behaviors because it involves discussing intimate sexual matters and illegal activities. But knowing about HIV transmission is a life-or-death matter, so it is necessary for you to be aware of any actions that put you at risk of contracting the disease.

There are four behaviors that put you at risk of HIV infection. By choosing to avoid these behaviors, you can protect yourself from infection.

> **66** *I was really scared about AIDS until I took this health class. I'd heard all kinds of wild stories about how you could get it.* **99**
>
> **Mei**

Sharing Equipment for Injecting Drugs, Tatooing, or Body Piercing

Any sharing of needles or other equipment for injecting drugs, tatooing, or body piercing is very risky behavior. When people use the same needle to inject drugs, blood from the first person can go directly into the second person's body. If the blood on the needle contains HIV, the virus is injected along with the drugs. It does not matter what kind of drug is injected—cocaine, heroin, or steroids. Even injecting vitamins, insulin, or antibiotics can expose a person to HIV if the needles or syringes are shared.

Body piercing has become increasingly popular among teens. Body piercing increases a person's chance of contracting many infections. It is an extremely risky behavior if unsterilized needles are used for piercing. A safer option is to go to a licensed practitioner who performs body piercing using sterilized equipment.

Sexual Intercourse With an Infected Person

Vaginal intercourse is one kind of sexual intercourse. It is the most common kind of intercourse between a man and a woman. During vaginal intercourse, a man puts his penis into a woman's vagina.

HIV can be transmitted during vaginal intercourse. If the man is infected with HIV, the virus in his semen can be transmitted into the woman's bloodstream through the mucous membranes in her vagina.

If the woman is infected with HIV, the virus can be transmitted from the fluids in her vagina to her partner through the mucous membranes around the opening at the tip of his penis.

Although either partner can transmit the virus to the other, women are at a greater risk than men because the mucous membranes of the vagina have a much larger surface area, resulting in more exposure to the virus. Also, because semen may remain in a woman's vagina for some time after intercourse, the likelihood of infection is increased. More women are infected with HIV from vaginal intercourse than men.

During oral intercourse, also called oral sex, the virus can be passed to either partner through tiny cuts or through the mucous membranes of the mouth or genitals.

During anal intercourse, it is possible for either partner to transmit the virus to the other. HIV can pass through the mucous membranes of the anus, the rectum, or the opening in the penis.

Other Methods of Transmission

Although transmission of the virus through body fluids is most common, there are other ways people have contracted AIDS that have nothing to do with risky behaviors. Nearly all children who are HIV positive contracted the virus from their mothers while still in the womb or during the birth process. Any woman who has had sex with someone at risk for HIV or who has a history of intravenous drug use should be tested for HIV before thinking about becoming pregnant.

*Life*SKILLS: Using Community Resources

Getting HIV Information . . . .

You may have questions about HIV infection that haven't been answered in this chapter. Don't worry; you can get answers to your questions. You may be comfortable talking to a parent or teacher, or you may prefer to call someone who doesn't know you. After you do the following exercise, you'll be able to get the information you need.

1. Look in the phone book under "AIDS" and write down the name of every organization you see.

2. Write down the phone number of the local AIDS hotline.

3. Find the CDC Web site for HIV infection and AIDS. Make a list of some of the information that is available.

4. Where could you call to talk to someone about whether you are at risk of being infected with HIV?

5. Write down the name and phone number of a place where you can get an HIV-antibody test. (You may have to call one of the phone numbers you've already looked up to get this information.)

Some health-care workers have contracted the virus while working with infected patients. If a worker has cuts or other breaks in the skin which come in contact with infected blood, they can be infected. Cases have been reported in which health care workers have been stuck accidentally with needles used to draw blood from an infected patient. Health-care workers now use "universal precautions" which are a set of guidelines for handling all patients to reduce the risk of a worker's exposure to the virus. These precautions apply to dental workers as well.

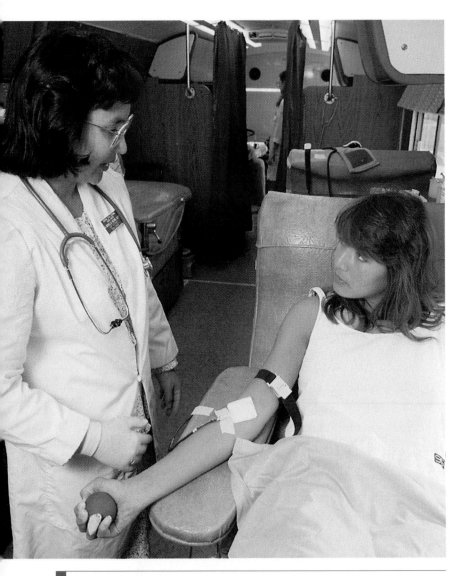

■ (FIGURE 23-8) **All blood that is donated in the United States is tested for HIV, and all blood that is infected is discarded.**

Before 1985, people contracted the virus while receiving blood transfusions or other blood components that were contaminated with HIV. People with hemophilia (a blood-clotting disorder) were particularly at risk. Because their blood does not clot, people with hemophilia may often need transfusions. The blood components in those transfusions often came from many different donors. Because the risk of transmission in blood was not known at the time, many people who received life-saving transfusions in hospitals later found out that they had contracted the virus. There are also reported cases of HIV transmission resulting from organ transplants and artificial inseminations from infected donors.

Since 1985, all blood donated in the United States is tested for HIV, and any HIV-infected blood is discarded. If you know in advance that you will need to replace lost blood, for example, after major surgery, you can donate your own blood for a later transfusion. All donated tissue is now tested for the virus before it is made available for transplant. Unfortunately, you should be aware that there are reported cases of HIV transmission where tissue samples were HIV negative at the time of donation or transplant.

You can see that transmission of the virus occurs in very specific ways. The list of all the ways you can't get HIV is much longer than the list of ways that you can get HIV. You can't get HIV by having what is called "casual contact" with someone who tests HIV positive. In other words, you can't get HIV by being around an infected person in ordinary day-to-day contact. There has not been a single case of transmission of the virus through casual contact with an infected person. Even family members and friends who live with people with AIDS and help care for them have not been infected with HIV through casual contact.

Q and A

Q: Is it possible to get HIV from kissing?

A: You can't get HIV from a "simple" kiss, the kind in which people just put their lips together. If you could, a lot of people would already have been infected this way. There have been no reported cases of this happening. But it is theoretically possible for the virus to be transmitted through "French" kissing—deep, open-mouth kissing—since HIV has been found in the saliva of infected people. HIV researchers think it usually takes many viruses to cause infection, however, and saliva contains very few viruses. And here again, there have been no reported cases of HIV being transmitted in this way.

Q: Isn't it true that you can get AIDS if you donate your blood?

A: No, absolutely not. This is something that many people are confused about. Blood-donation centers use a new, sterile needle with each donor. Don't let a myth like this keep you from donating blood to those who need it.

Q: I've heard people say that you could get HIV if a mosquito bites a person with HIV and then bites you. Is that true?

A: No. If mosquitoes could transmit HIV, there would already be many cases of that happening by now. In fact, there

are no reported cases of HIV being transmitted by any kind of insect or other animal.

Q: What should I do if I think I might be infected with HIV?

A: Talk to someone you trust about getting an HIV-antibody test—a parent, teacher, coach, school nurse, counselor, doctor, or someone at a health clinic. You can also call an AIDS hotline number to find out where you can go for HIV testing and counseling.

Review

1. *Name four body fluids that can contain enough HIV to infect another person.*

2. *Name the four behaviors that put you at risk for HIV infection.*

3. *Name at least five behaviors that don't put you at risk for HIV infection.*

4. **LIFE SKILLS: Using Community Resources** *Name two people you could talk to about whether a certain behavior could put you at risk for getting HIV.*

5. *Critical Thinking Could you get infected with HIV by wiping away the tears of a baby with HIV? Explain your answer.*

Skills for delaying sexual intimacy are discussed in Chapter 17.

Objectives

- *Discuss abstinence as the most effective way to prevent the sexual transmission of HIV infection.*

- *Practice resisting pressure to be sexually intimate.*
  LIFE SKILLS: Resisting Pressure

- *Explain how to reduce your risk of HIV infection if you are sexually active.*
  LIFE SKILLS: Solving Problems

In this section you'll learn exactly how to reduce your risk of becoming infected with HIV. Protecting yourself requires knowledge about HIV and the skills to put your knowledge to use.

Abstinence

The only way to be 100 percent safe from getting HIV sexually is to avoid the three kinds of sexual intercourse that were discussed in Section 23.2. When a person decides against taking part in sexual intercourse, that person is said to be choosing abstinence.

Being abstinent doesn't mean that a person has no sexual feelings. Everyone has sexual feelings—they are a perfectly natural and pleasurable part of being human. It's just that people who choose abstinence decide not to act on their sexual feelings in ways that could endanger them. There are many ways to show affection for

(FIGURE 23-9) **People who are sexually abstinent can show affection for each other in ways that don't put them at risk for getting HIV.**

other people that don't put you at risk of getting HIV. The Life Skills activity below will prepare you to resist the pressure to do things you really don't want to do or take risks you really don't want to take.

One final note about abstinence: You will have a harder time sticking to your decision to remain abstinent if you drink or use other drugs. Any resolutions can be ignored or forgotten when a person is drunk or high.

Monogamy

The only sexual intercourse that is completely safe from HIV infection is sexual intercourse between two disease-free adults

*Life*SKILLS: Resisting Pressure

Saying No . . . .

One of the ways to keep from doing things that put you at risk for HIV is to become resistant to pressure. See if you can think of a resistant response to each of the statements below.

1. "We'll just play around some. We can stop whenever you want."

2. "If you really loved me, you would make love to me."

3. "You must not have any sexual feelings at all."

4. "But I hate using condoms. It takes all the fun out of it."

5. "I'll pierce your ears and then you can pierce mine."

Although it helps to think of responses to certain statements, remember that you aren't required to have a reason. If you don't want to explain, all you have to say is "I don't want to." You don't have to debate what to do with your own body.

monogamy:

when two people have intercourse with only each other for their entire lives.

who practice safe behaviors and who are emotionally mature enough to be faithful to each other for their entire life. When two adults have sexual relations with each other over a lifetime, they are said to be practicing **monogamy.**

What if someone says that he or she has never had any form of sexual intercourse before. Can you assume that this person does not have HIV? The answer is a definite no. Unfortunately, people do not always tell the truth when it comes to sexual matters. For example, studies show that people have lied to their sexual partners about past encounters in order to have sexual intercourse.

All too often, a person has intercourse out of fear of losing a boyfriend or a girlfriend. It is difficult to resist this kind of pressure, especially when it comes from someone you love. However, if your partner truly loves you, that love would not be used to pressure you to do something that you don't feel ready for. A young woman named Amy Dolph has some advice to share about this problem. She says you should not allow another person, even someone you love, to determine when you will die. ''Do you want to put your life in that other person's hands?'' she asks. ''Is that boy or girl worth dying for? I doubt it.'' Amy contracted HIV during high school from a boyfriend.

The risk of HIV infection is something that extends well beyond your teen years. During your adult life, you will be exposed to many of the same risks you may now encounter. Remember that when you become an adult, the risks are still there. During adulthood, the following two steps should

(FIGURE 23-10) **Group activities such as team sports can help teenagers form close relationships without the risk of sexual intimacy.**

be taken to reduce your lifelong risk of HIV infection:

1. **Practice Monogamy** The fewer sex partners a person has, the less likely he or she is to have intercourse with someone who is HIV-positive. But remember that it takes only one HIV-infected partner to infect a person with the virus.

2. **Use Latex Condoms During Intercourse** Sex partners must use latex condoms to reduce their risk of HIV infection. Condoms are not 100 percent effective in preventing the spread of HIV, but when used properly they can make sexual intercourse less risky. To be effective in protecting against HIV, a condom must be made of latex (a kind of rubber). No other material provides the same degree of protection in preventing the spread of the virus from one partner to the other. If a condom is made of latex, it will say it on the package.

    It is important to remember that a condom must be used the whole time—from start to finish—during intercourse. Condoms can not be reused. A new condom must be used each time a person has intercourse. If the outside surface of a condom touches the tip of the penis, semen can be deposited there. This condom should be discarded because it no longer provides protection against HIV or pregnancy.

Don't Inject Drugs

If you haven't used injected drugs, don't start. If you do use them, seek treatment to help you quit. See Chapter 15 for information about drug-treatment programs.

Sharing needles to inject drugs is one of the major causes of HIV transmission. Even when all equipment is cleaned with bleach-and-water solution before and after each use, the possibility for infection still exists.

What If You've Already Engaged in Risky Behavior?

What if you haven't followed these guidelines? Should you just forget about it because it's already too late? No, absolutely not. You haven't necessarily been infected, even if you know you've engaged in risky behavior with an HIV-infected person.

If you think there is a chance you've been infected, get an HIV-antibody test immediately. Protect yourself, and protect other people.

R eview

1. What is the best way to prevent the transmission of HIV through intercourse?

2. ▪▪ **LIFE SKILLS: Resisting Pressure** If your friend wanted the two of you to give each other tattoos, what would you do or say to protect yourself against the possibility of HIV infection?

3. ▪▪ **LIFE SKILLS: Solving Problems** If you have decided to have intercourse, how could you reduce your risk of becoming infected with HIV?

4. *Critical Thinking* Explain the reasoning behind this statement about the transmission of HIV: "When you have intercourse with someone, you're also having intercourse with everyone that person has ever had intercourse with."

23.4 HIV Infection and Society

Objectives

- Describe medical treatments available for HIV infection.

- Name at least two actions you can take to help people with HIV infection.

HIV doesn't just affect individuals. It affects society. Millions of dollars are being spent searching for new treatments for HIV infection, even as discrimination against people with HIV continues.

(FIGURE 23-11) **AIDS activists have pressured government agencies to increase spending on HIV research and on programs to help those with the disease. Elizabeth Glaser worked tirelessly for this cause until her death from AIDS in December 1994. She contracted the disease from a transfusion during the birth of her last child.**

But a society is made up of individuals. Each individual can do his or her part to eliminate the disease and care for the people affected by it.

Medical Advances

Recent medical advances have made it possible to ease the symptoms of HIV infection and perhaps delay the onset of illness. Researchers discovered that combinations of drugs such as AZT (zidovudine), ddI (dideoxyinosine), and nevirapine show promise in postponing symptoms in people who have tested HIV-positive but are not yet sick. AZT, ddI and other similar drugs slow down the rate at which the virus reproduces inside the body. Combinations of drugs are generally used because the virus has the ability to adapt and change rapidly in response to a single drug.

Because of the development of drugs and other treatments, HIV infection is now considered to be a chronic condition that can be managed for many years. Researchers continue to search for a cure for HIV infection. They also hope to develop a vaccine to prevent infection in the first place. But because the virus can change quickly, developing a vaccine is very difficult; it may take many years before the attempts are successful. In the meantime, your first line of defense against HIV is you.

(FIGURE 23-12) **Dawn Marcel was infected with HIV when she was a senior in high school. She is now a speaker for an AIDS-education program in San Francisco. "I've been on AZT for three years," Dawn said. "I take it for one month, then go off it for one month because it destroys my liver. I don't look sick. I'm chubby, or I think I'm chubby. People don't imagine that I could be sick, but you can't tell by looking at someone."**

Teens and Risk

Teens have special needs when it comes to HIV prevention. It is normal for teens to experiment and be eager to try new things. Much of this experimentation is a healthy part of the maturation process. But studies show that teens often engage in activities that put them at great risk. When it comes to HIV, teens who have intercourse or experiment with injected drugs are risking their lives and the lives of their friends. A study done in 1995 indicates that 53.1 percent of high school students have engaged in sexual intercourse. Among sexually active high school students, 45.6 percent had not used a condom the last time they had intercourse. Fortunately, the study shows much smaller numbers of students are injecting drugs. But it should be obvious that teens are ignoring tremendous risks by engaging in these activities.

In Chapter 17, you learned that part of growing up means accepting responsibility

for your actions. Plan now to protect yourself as well as those you care about by taking what you have learned in this chapter seriously. If you have placed yourself at risk from intercourse or drugs, get tested. Resolve to change your life to ensure that you will be able to keep on living.

Living With HIV Infection

People often avoid and isolate people who have HIV infection. When the people in Ryan White's town found out he had AIDS, for example, they made life rough for him. "Lots of kids in school flattened themselves against walls when I walked by," Ryan said. "When I went to restaurants, people would get up and leave. Even in church, no one would shake my hand."

Michael's friend Bryan was afraid that he would lose his friends if people found out that his brother had HIV. Bryan knew only too well that some people think they can

(FIGURE 23-13) **Earvin "Magic" Johnson, former Los Angeles Lakers basketball star, discovered in 1991 that he was HIV-positive.**

(FIGURE 23-14) **You can help people with HIV infection by doing volunteer work for AIDS organizations. These teens are working at an AIDS education center in Massachusetts.**

become infected with HIV just by being around someone who is HIV positive. Even though this is not true, people with HIV infection may face discrimination at work, at school, and in their personal relationships. They are forced to face this discrimination at the same time that they are fighting a deadly disease.

Taking Positive Action Against HIV

You have already learned what you can do to protect yourself against HIV infection. But what else can you do to stop the spread of this disease?

You can educate others. If someone says something that is not true about HIV, you can give him or her the correct information. You can be a tremendous help to people with HIV infection by helping others overcome their prejudices based on misinformation.

You can treat people with HIV infection as you would treat any person who has a life-threatening illness—or anyone else, for that matter—with respect, compassion, and acceptance.

Review

1. Describe medical treatments that may delay the onset of HIV symptoms.

2. Why are teens at greater risk for HIV infection than adults?

3. Why has it been difficult to develop a vaccine for AIDS?

4. **Critical Thinking** Why do many people with HIV infection choose not to tell their fellow students or co-workers about their HIV test results?

5. **Critical Thinking** What are some ways you could help people with AIDS?

CHAPTER 23

Highlights

Summary

- AIDS is a sexually transmitted disease that is caused by a virus.

- The virus that causes AIDS is called HIV (human immunodeficiency virus).

- AIDS is the last phase of HIV infection.

- Even though an HIV-infected person appears healthy, he or she can still transmit the virus to another person.

- The four behaviors that put a person at risk for getting HIV are: 1) sharing equipment for injecting drugs, tattooing, or ear piercing with an infected person; 2) having anal intercourse with an infected person; 3) having oral intercourse with an infected person; and 4) having vaginal intercourse with an infected person.

- The behaviors that are most effective in preventing HIV infection are abstinence from sexual intercourse and abstaining from drugs.

- Properly using latex condoms reduces the risk of sexual transmission of HIV.

- People with HIV infection must struggle with discrimination at the same time they are fighting a deadly disease. They do not want to be thought of as passive "victims."

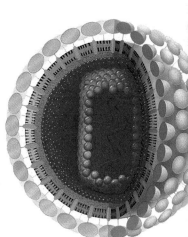

Vocabulary

AIDS a disease, caused by a virus, that harms a person's immune system; AIDS is classified as a sexually transmitted disease, but it can also be spread in other ways, such as through sharing infected equipment for injecting drugs, tattoing, or ear piercing. AIDS is the last phase of HIV infection.

HIV (human immunodeficiency virus) the virus that causes AIDS; also called the "AIDS virus."

mucous membranes moist, pink tissues of the body; HIV can enter the body through the mucous membranes of the mouth, vagina, anus, and rectum, and the opening at the tip of the penis.

monogamy when two people have sex with only each other for their entire lives.

latex condom a covering for the penis that helps protect both partners from sexually transmitted diseases and also helps to prevent pregnancy.

Chapter Review

Concept Review

1. When a person has HIV infection, it means that he or she
   a. has AIDS.
   b. can infect other people with HIV.
   c. has Kaposi's sarcoma.
   d. has used injected drugs.

2. A person can find out if he or she has been infected with HIV by
   a. getting an HIV-antibody test.
   b. calling the AIDS hotline.
   c. asking all previous sexual partners if they are HIV-positive.
   d. talking with a school counselor.

3. Which of the following behaviors can put a person at risk for HIV infection?
   a. sharing needles to inject steroids with an HIV-infected person
   b. shaking hands with an HIV-infected person
   c. sharing an elevator with an HIV infected person
   d. all of the above

4. Which of the following types of sexual intercourse with an HIV-infected person is risky for HIV infection?
   a. vaginal intercourse
   b. oral intercourse
   c. anal intercourse
   d. all of the above

5. Which of the following behaviors provides the best protection against HIV infection?
   a. practicing abstinence from sexual intercourse
   b. using condoms
   c. showering every day
   d. practicing French kissing

6. Which of the following actions would help people with HIV infection?
   a. raising money for agencies that help people with HIV infection
   b. treating people with HIV infection no differently from anyone else who had a life-threatening illness
   c. both of the above

Expressing Your Views

1. You are planning to get your ears pierced. One of your friends offers to pierce your ears for free. What problems could develop in accepting your friend's offer?

2. At a party your best friend gets drunk and confides to you that he or she is going to "do it" tonight. What do you think you should do?

3. Why do you think some people are prejudiced against people who have HIV infection?

Life Skills Check . . . . .

1. Using Community Resources

Debra needs to find out if something that she is doing puts her at risk for HIV infection. She feels that she cannot talk to her parents or any of her teachers or counselors. In fact, she feels that she cannot talk to anyone who knows about this. How might Debra get the information she needs?

2. Resisting Pressure

You are being pressured by your boyfriend or girlfriend to have sexual intercourse. In talking about this situation with a friend, she tells you that you have nothing to worry about if you use a condom. How would you respond to this statement?

Projects . . . .

1. Design a survey to find out how much other students in your school know about HIV infection. Think of five questions to ask in your survey, and work in a group of 3-4 students to collect responses from the whole student body. Tabulate your results and present your data and conclusions to your class.

2. Work with a group of students to come up with a plan to inform the students in your school about HIV prevention. Present your group plan to the principal.

3. Have a health fair at your school in which a variety of health topics are introduced, including HIV infection.

Plan for Action . . . .

HIV infection is a communicable disease that can be prevented. Devise a plan to protect yourself from getting infected with HIV.

Noninfectious Diseases and Disorders

◆ ◆ ◆ ◆

■ **Monitors enable diabetics to test their blood sugar and make sure they are taking the right amount of insulin.**

Shawn's pretty lucky; he had ear infections and a case of the chickenpox when he was very young, but during the last few years the only disease he's had to worry about has been an occasional cold. Some of the people he knows, and even some people in his own family, have had much more serious illnesses. His mother has high blood pressure. His cousin has sickle cell anemia. And two years ago, his grandfather died of lung cancer. Shawn has some questions about these diseases.

For example, is there any need to worry about being around people who have these diseases? Are any of them contagious? Could he inherit high blood pressure from his mother, or lung cancer from his grandfather? Is there anything he can do to avoid getting these diseases?

Hereditary and Congenital Diseases

REMINDER

A microorganism is a living thing that can be seen only under a microscope.

Objectives

- *Define noninfectious disease.*
- *Distinguish between hereditary and congenital diseases.*
- *List three factors that may cause congenital disease.*

High blood pressure, sickle cell anemia, and cancer are all examples of **noninfectious diseases.** A disease is a condition that prevents your body from functioning normally. When a disease is noninfectious, it means that you can't catch it from viruses or microorganisms that pass from another person or other organism. A cold is an infectious disease. You can "catch" a cold from your

best friend, when viruses pass from your friend's body to yours from casual contact. You can't catch sickle cell anemia or cancer because these diseases are not spread by viruses or microorganisms.

There are many different noninfectious diseases. Some people are born with a disease such as sickle cell anemia or cystic fibrosis and are affected by the disease throughout their life. Other noninfectious diseases, like cancer and heart disease, usually show up later in life. When you say that a person was "born with" a certain disease, you are referring to either a hereditary or a congenital disease.

Hereditary Diseases

A **hereditary disease** is a disease caused by defective genetic information passed from one or both parents to a child. In order to understand how this happens, it is important

noninfectious disease:

a disease that a person cannot catch from another person or any other organism.

hereditary disease:

a disease caused by defective genes inherited by a child from one or both parents.

chromosomes:

cell structures that carry hereditary information.

gene:

a short segment of a DNA molecule that serves as a code for a particular bit of hereditary information.

to know something about heredity. Many of your characteristics, such as the way you look and certain talents you have, were passed on to you from your parents. This kind of information is carried from your parents to you in the form of tiny structures within the body's cells known as **chromosomes**. Chromosomes contain the hereditary material deoxyribonucleic acid, better known as DNA.

Each chromosome is made up of thousands of genes. A **gene**, which serves as a code for a particular bit of inherited information, is a short segment of the DNA in a chromosome. The genes that you inherited from your parents determined many of your characteristics; for example, whether you have blue, green, or brown eyes. Tens of thousands of genes determine the inherited characteristics of an individual. Genes don't always carry correct information,

however. If one single gene does have incorrect information, it can cause a hereditary disease.

Sickle Cell Anemia One hereditary disease that occurs when genes carry incorrect instructions is sickle cell anemia, the illness Shawn's cousin Nelson has. The genes that carry incorrect information in Nelson's body affect the construction of a protein called hemoglobin. This protein, which is found inside the body's red blood cells, carries oxygen from the lungs to the other tissues in the body.

Because the hemoglobin inside Nelson's red blood cells isn't constructed correctly, the hemoglobin forms long, stiff chains. This causes the red blood cells—normally smooth, round disks—to sickle, or become spiky, such as those that are shown in Figure 24-2.

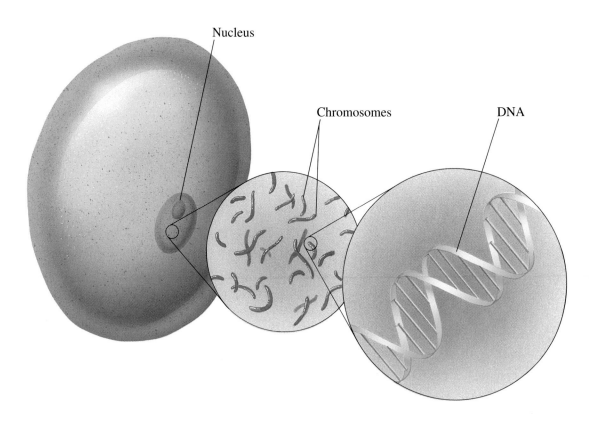

Nucleus

Chromosomes

DNA

(FIGURE 24-1) **Each chromosome in the cell nucleus contains a DNA molecule. The genes that determine all your inherited characteristics are segments of a DNA molecule.**

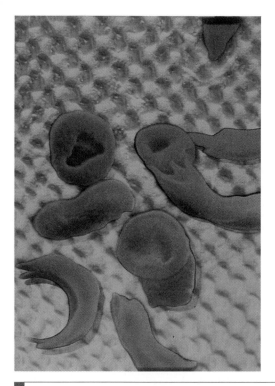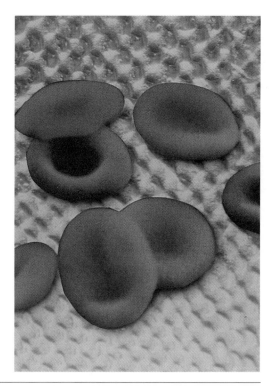

(FIGURE 24-2) **The red blood cells of a person who has sickle cell anemia (left) become long, spiky, and sickled. Note how different they look from normal red blood cells (right).**

Anything that reduces oxygen in Nelson's body, such as stress, respiratory disease, or strenuous exercise, can cause a sickle cell crisis. During the crisis, a high percentage of red blood cells sickle. Spiky, sickled red blood cells rupture easily and tend to stick inside the smallest blood vessels, the tiny capillaries. Intense pain and damage to vital organs may result.

For a person to have sickle cell anemia, he or she must inherit two copies of the sickle cell gene, one from each parent. People who have inherited only one sickle cell gene from one parent are usually quite healthy. Almost 10 percent of African-American people carry the gene for sickle cell anemia.

Cystic Fibrosis The most common serious inherited disease among white Americans is cystic fibrosis. Cystic fibrosis is a hereditary disease that results in the secretion of very thick mucus in the lungs and digestive tract.

Unlike normal mucus, which is regularly cleared from the lungs, the thick mucus produced by people with cystic fibrosis builds up and blocks small air passages inside the lungs. This makes breathing difficult and increases the likelihood of lung infections. Mucus in the digestive tract interferes with the action of digestive enzymes. Because of this, people with cystic fibrosis have difficulty getting adequate nourishment from food.

The symptoms of cystic fibrosis can be treated with physical therapy and drugs that loosen mucus in the lungs. These drugs may be delivered to the lungs by using a vaporizer, like the one shown in Figure 24-3. Unfortunately, this treatment provides only temporary relief. Cystic fibrosis is a very serious, and eventually fatal, disease.

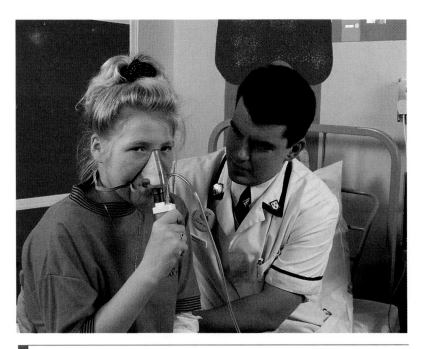

(FIGURE 24-3) **Cystic fibrosis causes mucus to build up and block air passages in the lungs. Vaporizers that deliver special medications to clear these air passages can help people with this disease breathe more easily.**

Like sickle cell anemia, cystic fibrosis strikes only those who have inherited two cystic fibrosis genes—one from each parent. About one in twenty white Americans carries one gene for cystic fibrosis.

Tay-Sachs Disease Tay-Sachs disease is a condition caused by a defective gene that causes fat to accumulate in the brain, destroying normal brain tissue. Although babies born with Tay-Sachs seem normal at first, by the time they are a few months old, symptoms begin to appear. These symptoms include seizures, mental retardation, and blindness. Death generally occurs by the age of three or four.

The gene that causes Tay-Sachs disease is most common in families of eastern European origin.

Muscular Dystrophy Muscular dystrophy refers to several genetic diseases that cause muscles to weaken and degenerate. One of the more common forms, Duchenne muscular dystrophy, affects only boys.

Children with this form of muscular dystrophy develop normally at first, but between the ages of two and ten, they become clumsy and uncoordinated as their muscles begin to weaken. As the disease progresses, they have difficulty standing and they fall frequently. By their teens, people with muscular dystrophy must use a wheelchair. The disease is fatal when it progresses to the point that the muscles that control breathing fail. This usually occurs when patients reach their early twenties.

There is currently no cure for muscular dystrophy. However, the gene that is responsible for Duchenne muscular dystrophy has been identified. Researchers hope that better understanding the functioning of the gene will lead to an effective treatment for this disease.

Type II Diabetes Diabetes is a disease that results when a hormone called insulin is lacking in, or is not used properly by, the body. Hormones are chemicals produced in the body to regulate body functions. Insulin helps blood sugar enter the body's cells. Blood sugar is the body's major source of energy, even for people who don't eat many sweets. Starchy foods like potatoes contain sugars that are broken down and used for energy. But when insulin is lacking or cannot be used properly, as is the case in people with diabetes, the body's cells are unable to use the sugar that is in the blood.

When sugar cannot enter a person's cells to provide energy, the cells begin to use fats and proteins for energy. Breaking down large amounts of fats and proteins produces dangerous levels of toxic waste products. For this reason, diabetes that is not treated is often fatal.

The most common form of diabetes, called Type II diabetes, usually appears in middle age. People with Type II diabetes do produce insulin; however, their bodies cannot use it properly. There is evidence that Type II diabetes is hereditary. Studies have shown that if one identical twin has Type II diabetes, there is a 100-percent chance that the other twin will have the disease. Other factors that may contribute to the onset of Type II diabetes include age and obesity. Type II diabetes can sometimes be controlled by a strict, healthy diet (most Type II diabetics are obese) and exercise. Drug therapy such as insulin is often needed as well.

Type I diabetes is a more serious form of the disease that usually begins during childhood. Only about 10 percent of diabetics have Type I diabetes. Unlike Type II diabetes, Type I diabetes does not appear to be an inherited illness. People with Type I diabetes must take daily injections of insulin to replace this substance, which is missing from their body. You'll learn more about Type I diabetes in the next section.

Allergies Allergies affect about one of every seven people in the United States—more than 35 million Americans. An al-

lergy is the overreaction of a person's immune system to a common substance—such as dust, pollen, certain foods, mold spores, or animals—that has no effect on nonallergic people. A person can inherit a tendency to have allergies.

Allergic reactions take many forms. When an inhaled substance triggers an allergic attack, the person may experience a stuffy nose, red itchy eyes, and sinus pain. Allergies to foods or certain drugs sometimes cause hives, itchy welts, or bumps to develop on the skin.

Although allergies are generally not life-threatening, they do make life miserable. If you have an allergy, the best way to treat it is to avoid the thing that you're allergic to. For example, if you are allergic to cat dander and saliva, as many people are, you'd be wise to choose another kind of pet.

(FIGURE 24-4) **(Left)** A person who is allergic to a substance that is inhaled may experience red eyes, a stuffy nose, and sinus pain. **(Right)** An allergy to a food or drug can cause hives or welts to develop on the skin.

(FIGURE 24-5) **Specially prescribed inhalers can prevent asthma attacks or lessen their severity.**

these types of allergic reactions are not really serious. However, about 15 million people suffer from asthma, which is a very serious disease that is often a form of allergic reaction.

Take a deep breath. The air you just inhaled travels through a series of air passages that branch into smaller and smaller tubes inside your lungs. These tubes are encircled by small muscles that adjust the width of the tubes.

Changing the diameter of the tubes is one of the ways in which your body adapts to allow you to take in more air when you are exercising, and less air when you are sitting quietly.

During an asthmatic attack, these muscles overreact, causing the air passages to become constricted. Taking in enough air becomes very difficult. To make matters worse, the linings of the air passages may swell and become filled with mucus. Sometimes the small tubes collapse and make it even more difficult to exhale than it is to inhale.

An asthmatic attack can be life-threatening. More than 6,000 people a year die from asthma, and the number is increasing. Fortunately, there are effective treatments for asthma. Most deaths from asthma occur because the person had not been diagnosed or was not getting proper treatment.

Once they understand that asthma must never be taken lightly, asthmatics can usually lead normal, healthy lives, provided they faithfully follow the treatment prescribed by a doctor. Drugs breathed into the lungs from an inhaler, like the one shown in Figure 24-5, can often prevent asthmatic attacks or reduce their severity.

Such treatments have made it much safer for people with asthma to participate in athletic activities. In fact, not only is exercise beneficial for most people with

If you're allergic to house dust, on the other hand, you will suffer much less if you live in a house that has wood or tile floors rather than carpeting.

Sometimes it is simply impossible to avoid the substance causing the allergic reaction. In that case, medicines called anti-histamines can help relieve the allergic symptoms. Histamine is the substance released by the immune system that causes the unpleasant effects of an allergy. Antihistamines work by interfering with the action of histamine. Some allergies can also be treated by a series of injections that reduce the sensitivity of the allergic person to a particular substance.

Asthma Even though hay fever or hives can make a person very uncomfortable,

asthma, but many people with this condition excel at sports.

A person with asthma who does perform strenuous exercise, however, must follow certain precautions. For some people, this may mean avoiding exercise in cold, dry air or when air pollution levels are high. To prevent attacks, most asthmatics must take medication before engaging in strenuous exercise.

Down's Syndrome: An Inherited Disorder

One in every 800 to 1,000 babies born each year in the United States has a disorder called Down's syndrome. Down's syndrome is caused by the presence of an extra chromosome in body cells.

Normally, cells in the human body contain 46 chromosomes. The exceptions are sperm and egg cells, which each contain 23 chromosomes. When the sperm and egg unite at fertilization, the fertilized egg has the normal complete set of 46 chromosomes. Sometimes, however, a sperm or egg with 24 chromosomes is produced. Sperm with extra chromosomes are usually so abnormal that they are unable to fertilize an egg. For this reason, it is unlikely that sperm with extra chromosomes will contribute to the formation of an abnormal embryo. However, an egg with an extra chromosome can be fertilized.

An extra chromosome always causes serious problems in the development of an embryo. In most cases, the deformities caused by the extra chromosome are so severe that the embryo dies before birth. Survival is possible, however, if the extra chromosome is one of the smaller ones. Down's syndrome results when there is an extra copy of chromosome 21, one of the smallest chromosomes.

(FIGURE 24-6) **Down's syndrome results from an extra copy of chromosome 21 in body cells.**

All people born with Down's syndrome show some degree of mental retardation. The severity of the impairment varies from person to person. Other effects of Down's syndrome include defects in the thyroid gland and heart. Heart defects are fairly common, and they are often fatal during infancy. People with Down's syndrome can live a long and healthy life if the effects of the syndrome are not severe.

Genetic Screening Sophisticated genetic testing and prenatal screening can help couples with family histories of hereditary disorders. A couple planning to have a child can find out if they are at risk for passing defective genes to their unborn child. Tests can determine the presence of genes that may carry Tay-Sachs disease, cystic fibrosis, or sickle cell anemia. Parents can then be made aware of the likelihood of passing on a disease based on its inheritance pattern.

Pregnant women who are at risk of having a child with a hereditary disorder can undergo specific tests that can detect some genetic defects in the fetus. For example, women over the age of 35 are at a higher risk than younger women for giving birth to a child with Down's syndrome. Many doctors recommend that pregnant women over the age of 35 undergo a test called amniocentesis. This test is given at the end of the woman's first timester of pregnancy. Amniocentesis can detect the presence of Down's syndrome, as well as other chromosomal defects.

Congenital Diseases

A **congenital disease** is a disease that is present from birth but is not inherited. In other words, a congenital disease is not caused by an abnormal gene present in the egg or sperm at the time of fertilization, but by an accident or incident that occurs during fetal development or birth. For example, if a woman contracts rubella (German measles) during pregnancy, her baby may be born with cataracts or heart defects. Besides exposure to certain diseases, exposure to certain drugs or to environmental dangers such as radiation or pollution, during pregnancy can cause a congenital disease. It is therefore very important for a pregnant woman to carefully read the labeling of any medication she may consider taking during her pregnancy.

Fetal Alcohol Syndrome One drug that can cause a serious congenital disease is alcohol. A woman who drinks heavily during pregnancy risks having a baby with fetal alcohol syndrome. The effects of this congenital disease include low birth weight, mental retardation, facial deformities, and heart defects.

Many doctors believe that drinking smaller amounts of alcohol during pregnancy causes a mild form of fetal alcohol syndrome that may result in mental retardation with less obvious physical deformities. For this reason, pregnant women are generally advised to refrain from drinking alcohol during pregnancy.

Cerebral Palsy Cerebral palsy is caused by damage to the brain. This damage results in a form of paralysis that makes it impossible for a person to control his or her muscles. The muscles may be limp and unresponsive or may contract randomly and uncontrollably. Random contraction of the muscles is known as spastic paralysis.

People with cerebral palsy sometimes find it difficult to walk or talk because of the difficulty of controlling their muscles. Although some people with cerebral palsy are mentally retarded, many are of completely normal intelligence and are as capable of achievement as those born without the disease.

Fetal alcohol syndrome is also discussed in Chapter 13.

congenital disease:

a disease that is present from birth, but is not inherited.

The brain damage that causes cerebral palsy can result from several factors. Lack of oxygen during birth is one possible cause. Exposure during pregnancy to radiation, certain drugs, or some diseases can also be a factor.

Epilepsy Epilepsy is a disease in which electrical activity in the brain becomes abnormal for short periods. Epilepsy is not mental retardation. People with this disorder have the same mental abilities as people who are not epileptic.

Epilepsy takes different forms, depending on which type of abnormal brain activity occurs. The periods of abnormal brain activity are called epileptic seizures.

The most serious form of epilepsy is grand mal epilepsy. During a grand mal seizure, the person loses consciousness, and may fall to the floor and thrash about. The movements can be so forceful that people have been known to injure themselves by hitting objects such as desks or other furniture.

A grand mal seizure is often very frightening to witness. If someone around you should have a grand mal seizure, the best thing you can do to help the person is to move furniture out of the way to reduce the risk of injury. Do not try to touch or move the person while he or she is having a seizure. Grand mal seizures usually last only a few minutes. After the seizure, the person will probably sleep for a short time.

Grand mal seizures are also frightening for the person who experiences them. The person may feel disoriented and confused after a seizure. Many epileptics are embarrassed by their seizures or feel guilty because of the disruption and worry they have caused. It is very important that people who witness a seizure be understanding and supportive.

Fortunately, medication helps most people with grand mal epilepsy avoid having seizures. Once the proper drug therapy is prescribed, an epileptic may go for many years, or for the rest of his or her life, without a seizure.

There are two other forms of epilepsy. Petit mal epilepsy causes a person to simply ''go blank'' for a minute or two. Convulsions do not occur. This form of epilepsy usually occurs during childhood and disappears by adolescence. Psychomotor epilepsy causes seizures in which the person does not fall or have convulsions but may repeat simple movements over and over. Epilepsy may be a hereditary or congenital disease, or it may be caused by a head injury or a tumor later in life.

People with epilepsy, or with any type of congenital or hereditary disease, should be treated the same way as anyone else: with compassion and respect.

Review

1. What is a noninfectious disease? How does it differ from an infectious disease?

2. Define hereditary disease and congenital disease. How do they differ?

3. List three factors that can cause a congenital disease.

4. **Critical Thinking** Should a person born with fetal alcohol syndrome be able to sue his or her mother for damages if it can be proven that the mother used alcohol during pregnancy, knowing of its risks? Why or why not?

24.2 Autoimmune Diseases

Your immune system consists of an amazing set of specialized cells that destroy potentially dangerous viruses, microorganisms, and poisons that enter your body. Cells of the immune system constantly patrol your blood and tissues, checking out every cell and substance they meet. When an immune system cell recognizes a cell or molecule, it leaves it alone. But an immune system cell will attack and destroy anything that it does not recognize.

You could not survive without this patrol system. However, in some people, the immune system mistakes a cell type or a certain kind of body tissue for a foreign invader and attacks it. When a person's immune system attacks and damages an organ of his or her own body, the person has an **autoimmune disease.**

What Causes Autoimmune Disease?

There seem to be several factors that trigger the immune attack. Some tissues in the body are not normally patrolled by, or exposed to, the immune system. An example is the thyroid gland. If an injury or infection brings immune cells into contact with thyroid cells, the immune system behaves as if this "new" tissue is foreign.

Sometimes a virus or bacterium contains molecules that are very similar to molecules found in the human body. If a person is infected by one of these viruses or bacteria, the immune system fights the infection in the normal way. However, after the infection is over, the immune system then goes on to attack the similar molecules in the body. For example, molecules on heart valves are similar to molecules found in the streptococcus bacterium that causes strep throat. After a strep throat infection, the immune system may attack the heart valves and damage them. This autoimmune disease is called rheumatic fever.

Even though autoimmune diseases are disorders of the immune system, it is important not to confuse them with HIV infection or AIDS. Infection with HIV leads to the gradual destruction of the immune system until it is unable to defend the body against invaders. With autoimmune disease, the immune system is strong and effective against foreign invaders, but it also attacks some part of the "self."

The most important distinction between AIDS and autoimmune diseases is that AIDS is a communicable disease. That is, it is passed from one person to another. Autoimmune diseases are noncommunicable diseases. You do not have to worry about "catching" them from someone else.

Multiple Sclerosis Multiple sclerosis (MS) is classified here as an autoimmune disease because it is often the result of an immune system attack on the fatty coverings of nerves. The resulting nerve damage affects different parts of the nervous system

autoimmune disease:

a disease in which a person's own immune system attacks and damages an organ of his or her own body.

in each patient. Early symptoms include vision disturbances, stiffness and fatigue in limbs, dizziness, and emotional disturbances. Complete paralysis, numbness, double vision, speech problems, general weakness, difficulty in swallowing, and other problems may occur in the advanced stages.

The exact trigger for the autoimmune attack is unknown. The disease usually shows up in early adulthood. One characteristic of multiple sclerosis is the cycle of temporary recovery from symptoms followed by periods when the disease gets worse. There is no cure for the disease, and the periods during which the symptoms are less severe make it very difficult to judge the value of any particular treatment.

Type I Diabetes You have already learned how important it is for the body's cells to be able to use sugars for energy, and that in order to use the sugars, the body must have insulin. Insulin is a hormone that is made by the pancreas.

Type I diabetes, which is sometimes called juvenile diabetes, is believed to be caused by an autoimmune attack on the insulin-producing cells of the pancreas. Once their insulin-producing cells are destroyed, people with Type I diabetes must receive insulin every day. There is no ''insulin pill'' that works, because the insulin would be destroyed by acids and enzymes in the digestive tract. The insulin must be delivered directly to the bloodstream, either by injections (''shots'') or by an insulin pump. Diabetics must carefully monitor the level of sugars in their blood to make sure that they are taking the right amount of insulin. Some diabetics use a device like the one shown at the beginning of this chapter.

Some symptoms of diabetes are excessive thirst, excessive hunger, excessive urination, unexplained weight loss, slow healing of cuts and bruises, low energy, intense

(FIGURE 24-7) **People with Type I diabetes must take insulin every day.**

itching, vision changes, and pain in the extremities. If these symptoms appear, a doctor can perform a urine or blood test to determine whether the person has diabetes.

When a diabetic does not get enough insulin, a diabetic coma may occur. A person about to enter a diabetic coma may develop a fever, appear quite ill, complain of thirst, and vomit. A diabetic who receives too much insulin may suffer from insulin shock. Weakness, moist pale skin, and tremors or convulsions are all symptoms of insulin shock. Sugar (orange juice, soft drinks, granulated sugar on the tongue) may be given if the person is conscious.

Although diabetes is a serious disease, treatment is very effective. Diabetics who monitor and control their intake of insulin carefully, maintain a healthy, specially designed diet, get regular exercise, and avoid tobacco can lead healthy lives.

(FIGURE 24-8) **Former First Lady Barbara Bush suffers from Graves' Disease, a disorder that causes irregular heartbeat and a protruding of the eyeballs.**

Rheumatoid Arthritis Rheumatoid arthritis occurs when the immune system attacks the membranes that line the spaces between joints. Eventually, the joints may be destroyed and the bones may even fuse together. Unlike osteoarthritis, which is very common in older people, rheumatoid arthritis usually shows up at a younger age. It is more common in women and often first appears between the ages of 30 and 40.

Rheumatoid arthritis may also cause other problems, like anemia and heart disease. It is treated with anti-inflammatory drugs and gentle exercise.

Hashimoto's Thyroiditis and Graves' Disease Hashimoto's thyroiditis and Graves' disease are both caused by an immune attack on the thyroid gland, but oddly, they have opposite effects. In the case of Hashimoto's thyroiditis, the immune system destroys tissues of the thyroid gland and not enough thyroid hormone is produced. People with this disease must take thyroid hormone pills every day to replace the missing hormone.

In Graves' disease, the immune system attacks the thyroid, and the thyroid gland is tricked into making too *much* thyroid hormone. The usual treatment for this disease is to remove the thyroid or destroy it with radioactive iodine. Then the person takes thyroid pills to restore and maintain a normal level of the hormone.

Review

1. *Name three common autoimmune diseases.*

2. *What is an important distinction between AIDS and autoimmune diseases?*

3. *Critical Thinking Why is it so important for a person to monitor the amount of insulin he or she takes?*

Degenerative Diseases

• • • • •

Objectives

- Describe what happens to arteries during the development of atherosclerosis.

- Explain the relationship between atherosclerosis and high blood pressure.

- List three kinds of cancer to which tobacco use contributes.

- Name four things you can do to reduce your risk of cardiovascular disease.
  ▪▪ LIFE SKILLS: Practicing Self-Care

- Name two things you can do to reduce your risk of getting cancer.
  ▪▪ LIFE SKILLS: Practicing Self-Care

Degenerative diseases are diseases that result from gradual damage to organs over time, and that are more likely to occur as a person gets older. In this section, you will learn about three degenerative diseases: osteoarthritis, cardiovascular disease (disease of the heart and blood vessels), and cancer.

Osteoarthritis

Osteoarthritis is very different from rheumatoid arthritis, the autoimmune disease. Osteoarthritis seems to be caused by wear and tear on joints over time. Osteoarthritis is very common among the elderly, although the age at which it appears varies from person to person. Some people begin to feel its effects in middle age or even earlier, while other people in their seventies or eighties are free of it. Some researchers think that the age at which osteoarthritis appears is determined by your genes, but that everyone who lives long enough would eventually get it.

Osteoarthritis is usually treated with aspirin or ibuprofen. Gentle exercise, which is often prescribed by a doctor or therapist, can slow the progression of the disease, relieve stiffness and pain, and prolong freedom of movement.

Cardiovascular Disease

Progressive damage to the heart and blood vessels is called **cardiovascular disease.** Damage to blood vessels usually occurs slowly, over many years. It may even begin in childhood. In the early years of the disease, it causes no pain or other symptoms, which means that some people in their teens and early twenties are suffering from cardiovascular disease and don't know it.

Although the early stages of cardiovascular disease don't have symptoms, the effects of the illness can be deadly. Heart disease is the leading cause of death in the United States. Stroke, which is also caused by cardiovascular disease, is the nation's third leading killer.

Atherosclerosis **Atherosclerosis**, the most common cause of cardiovascular disease, is a narrowing of the arteries caused by a buildup of fatty material. Arteries are blood vessels that carry blood away from the heart. Atherosclerosis begins with a small injury to the inner wall of an artery.

cardiovascular disease:

progressive damage to the heart and blood vessels.

degenerative diseases:

diseases that result from gradual damage to organs over time.

This triggers the cells lining the artery to multiply and take in certain substances circulating in the bloodstream. One of these substances is cholesterol.

Cholesterol is found only in animal cells. A certain amount of cholesterol is essential for your body to function normally. Cholesterol makes up part of your cell membranes and provides the raw material for certain essential hormones. Your body can make all the cholesterol it needs. Even strict vegetarians who do not eat eggs, meat, or cheese do not show any cholesterol deficiency. If your diet includes cholesterol, your body will make less and use some of the cholesterol in your food to supply its needs. However, the average American eats far more cholesterol than the body is able to use.

A diet high is saturated fats can also increase a person's cholesterol to an unhealthy level. When this occurs, more fatty deposits or plaque are deposited on the inside the artery walls. There is more information on fats, plaque, and cholesterol in Chapter 4.

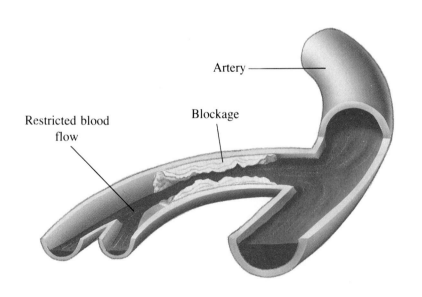

Artery

Blockage

Restricted blood flow

(FIGURE 24-9) **Fatty material that accumulates in the arteries can interfere with or block blood flow.**

The regions in arteries where plaque is deposited tend to thicken over time, narrowing the opening through which blood flows, as shown in Figure 24-9. Eventually, the arteries stiffen because of the accumulation of calcium, which restricts blood flow even further. When the disease becomes this severe, it is called **arteriosclerosis,** which means "hardening of the arteries."

People who have high cholesterol levels can develop atherosclerosis at an early age. In addition to eating foods high in cholesterol and fat, high levels of cholesterol in the blood can be increased by smoking, lack of exercise, or heredity—or in most cases, by several of these factors combined.

High Blood Pressure Another major cause of cardiovascular disease is high blood pressure. As you now know, your blood circulates from your heart to the rest of your body through tubular blood vessels called arteries. Your blood travels through your arteries in much the same way that water travels through a garden hose. Just like water in a garden hose, the blood in your arteries is under pressure. Imagine that you turn the water faucet connected to your garden hose on and off repeatedly. The pressure rises when water rushes out of the faucet and then falls when you turn the water off.

A person with a strong, healthy heart and flexible, healthy arteries should have a blood pressure reading of about 120/80 or less. A blood pressure measurement greater than 140/90 is considered high. These numbers represent the highest and lowest pressure inside your arteries.

While your heart contracts, squeezing blood into your arteries, the pressure inside your arteries is at its highest. This pressure is your systolic blood pressure, which is what the first number represents. When the heart muscle relaxes, the pressure in your arteries falls. The lowest pressure—the

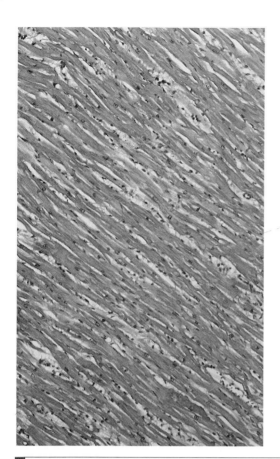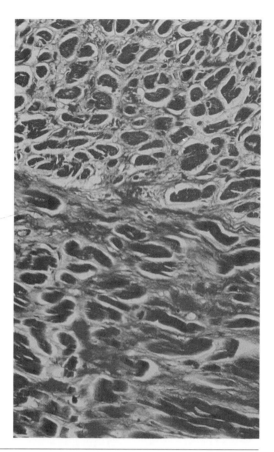

(FIGURE 24-10) **A heart attack does permanent damage to the heart by replacing healthy muscle (left) with scar tissue (right).**

pressure of the blood in between contractions of the heart—is the second number. This is called your diastolic blood pressure.

High blood pressure can damage the inner walls of arteries and accelerate the process of atherosclerosis. As fat is deposited and arteries narrow, the heart must pump harder in order to push blood through the body. Blood pressure rises even higher, causing even more damage to blood vessel walls.

Heart Attack The heart is the hardest working muscle in your body. It contracts continually throughout your life, never resting, not even when you sleep. A plentiful, oxygen-rich supply of blood is essential to the health of your heart.

Since the heart is filled with blood, you might think that the blood inside the heart

supplies the heart muscle with all of the oxygen and nutrients that it needs. However, this is not the case. In fact, the inner lining of the heart actually acts as a barrier to the transfer of oxygen and nutrients.

When blood leaves the heart, it is pumped out through the largest artery in the body, the aorta. However, before blood is carried to any other part of the body, some of the blood detours into small blood vessels leading off from the aorta, where it connects to the heart.

These vessels on the outside of the heart are the coronary arteries. They have one of the most important jobs in the entire blood vessel system—that is, to supply blood to the heart muscle itself.

If the coronary arteries have been narrowed by atherosclerosis, a spasm in the muscle layer of the artery—or a tiny blood

The circulatory system is discussed in greater detail in the Body Systems Handbook.

The symptoms of a heart attack are discussed in Chapter 28.

clot—can block the coronary artery. Part of the heart muscle receives no oxygen and begins to die within a few minutes. When this happens, a heart attack has occurred. If the damaged region of the heart is not too large, and the person receives medical treatment quickly, there is a good chance that the heart attack victim will survive. After recovery, however, the damaged heart muscle will be replaced by scar tissue.

Stroke Like the heart, the brain needs blood and the nutrients it carries in order to survive. When a region of the brain is cut off from its blood supply, a **stroke** occurs. Some strokes result when blood traveling through blood vessels damaged by cardiovascular disease can't reach the brain. A stroke can be caused by a blood clot, by a broken blood vessel if it swells and puts pressure on the brain, or when the artery that supplies blood to the brain is severely narrowed by atherosclerosis.

Nearly 150,000 people die each year of stroke. If you think someone you're with is having a stroke, call a doctor immediately and describe the symptoms. If a physician is unavailable, call an ambulance or take the person to the hospital immediately.

The symptoms of stroke are discussed in Chapter 28.

Cancer

Your body makes millions of new cells every day. Normally, this is a controlled process in which cells divide to provide replacement cells for the ones that are worn out. Sometimes, though, cells divide and multiply in an uncontrolled way.

Cancer is a disease caused by cells that have lost normal growth controls. These irregular cells accumulate rapidly. They can invade, compress, and destroy the surrounding healthy tissue. These cells may form a solid mass called a tumor. A benign tumor does not invade the surrounding tissues. Most tumors are benign and may be safely ignored, whereas others will need to be removed through surgery. When a tumor spreads to the surrounding tissues it eventually damages vital organs. A malignant tumor consists of cells that can spread the cancer.

Cells in almost any part of the body can become cancerous. When a cancer arises, it usually grows for a while in the part of the body where it began—sometimes for years. Eventually, however, some of the cancer cells may metastasize, or move to other parts of the body. The cancer cells often travel through the blood or lymph fluid and give rise to new malignant tumors.

cancer:

a disease caused by cells that have lost normal growth controls and that invade and destroy other tissues.

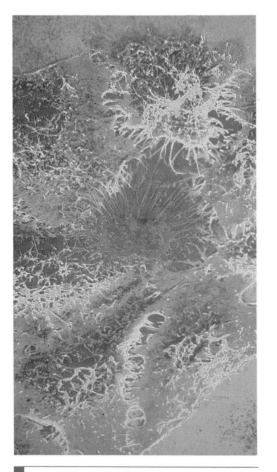

(FIGURE 24-11) **Cancer results when cells that have undergone a rapid and uncontrolled growth invade other cells and body tissue.**

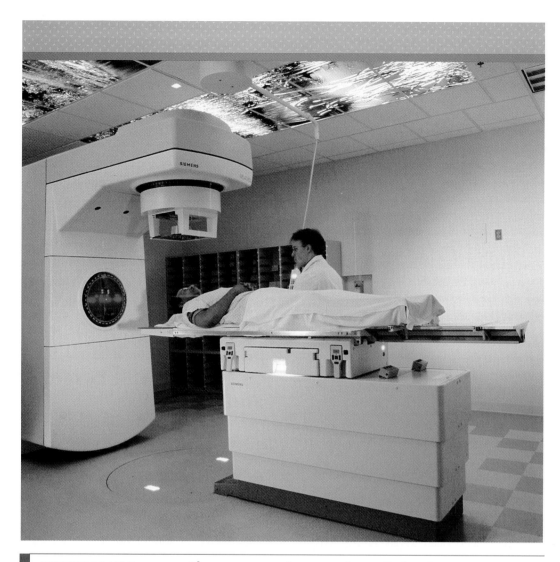

(FIGURE 24-12) **Persons with cancer sometimes require radiation therapy.**

Cancer Treatments At one time, the vast majority of cancers were incurable. Today, many cancers can be controlled, and often cured. Even so, cancer remains a very serious disease. It is the second leading cause of death in the United States.

The first step in treating cancer is usually to surgically remove the cancerous growth. Surgery is most effective in the early stages of cancer. A small cancer that has not spread to other parts of the body can be completely removed in this way. Some skin cancer surgery is performed with lasers, which can cut through the cancerous tissue without causing damage to the surrounding tissue.

Some cancer patients receive radiation treatments or chemotherapy, either alone or in addition to surgery. The purpose of radiation therapy is to kill any cancer cells near the original tumor that were not removed by surgery. The goal of chemotherapy, which is treatment with special anti-cancer drugs, is to destroy cancer cells that have traveled to other parts of the body.

When cancer is not diagnosed until after it has grown and spread into vital organs such as the lungs, the pancreas, or the brain, surgery is often useless. Radiation or chemotherapy may be used to treat advanced cases of cancer. In these cases, a cure is very unlikely. However, treatment

Seven Warning Signals for Cancer

Change in bowel or bladder habits.

A sore that does not heal.

Unusual bleeding or discharge.

Thickening or lump in breast or elsewhere.

Indigestion or difficulty in swallowing.

Obvious change in wart or mole.

Nagging cough or hoarseness.

(FIGURE 24-13) **Having one or more of the above signs and signals does not mean that you have cancer. But to be on the safe side, see a doctor.**

Complete information on breast and testicular self-examinations is provided in Chapter 16.

sometimes reduces the size of tumors, reduces pain, and prolongs life.

Early Detection of Cancer It is important that everyone know the early warning signs of cancer. Remember, cancer caught early is very often completely curable. You can begin protecting yourself by learning the seven warning signals for cancer that have been developed by the American Cancer Society, listed in Figure 24-13. If you have one of these warning signals, see your doctor immediately.

Some cancers do not have symptoms that you can feel or see in their early stages, yet they can be detected by certain diagnostic tests. This is one reason why regular checkups are so important. Regular self-examination of breasts or testicles is the most effective way to detect cancer in these regions at an early stage. See Chapter 16 for more information regarding these important self-exams.

Preventing Cardiovascular Disease and Cancer

It's not always easy to determine the exact reason why a particular person gets cardiovascular disease or cancer. There is evidence that a person can inherit a tendency to suffer a certain degenerative disease from his or her parents, and it is also known that older people are more likely to get degenerative diseases than are younger people.

Risk Factors for Degenerative Disease

Factors You Can't Control	Factors You Can Control
Gender	Poor Dietary Habits
Heredity	High Blood Pressure
Age	Lack of Exercise
	Smoking
	Drinking Alcohol

(FIGURE 24-14) **Most of the risk factors for degenerative disease are within your control.**

(FIGURE 24-15) **Some studies have shown that certain foods contain nutrients that may reduce a person's chances of suffering cancer.**

Age and heredity are two disease-causing factors a person can't do anything about. But there are things you *can* do to decrease your chances of getting certain diseases. The decisions you make concerning the care of your body—starting now—can have a very strong influence on your health as you grow older.

By making healthy choices, you may be able to avoid getting a certain degenerative disease. Even if you don't avoid the disease entirely, you may be able to postpone the age at which a disease shows up, or reduce its severity.

Cardiovascular Disease
It may not seem especially important to think about preventing cardiovascular disease while you're still a teenager. But in fact, the choices you make now about diet, exercise, tobacco, and alcohol are already affecting your heart and blood vessels. For some measures you can take to reduce your risk of

getting cardiovascular disease, read the Life Skills feature on pages 528–29.

Preventing Cancer
In order for cells to become cancerous, a series of changes must occur in cells in a particular sequence. These changes cause the cells to lose their normal growth controls. Scientists have discovered several factors that cause some of these changes in cells. Regular exposure to these factors increases your risk that some of the cells in your body will undergo the unlucky combination of changes that results in cancer.

High doses of radiation and certain very toxic chemicals are known to cause cancer. Fortunately, you are unlikely to be exposed to these factors. However, many people are concerned that low doses of less toxic chemicals common in the environment may also be causing cancer in some people. Research continues to explore the relationship between environmental factors and cancer.

Reducing Your Risk of Cardiovascular Disease

Here are some steps you can take—starting now—to reduce your chances of getting cardiovascular disease.

1. *Don't smoke.* Smoking cigarettes or using any other form of tobacco increases your risk of heart attack and stroke more than any other factor that you can control. Smokers are two to six times more likely to have a heart attack than are nonsmokers. Smokers who have heart attacks are more likely to die from them. The best thing that you can do to maintain good health is to never start smoking. If you have started, quit. For some suggestions on ways to stop smoking, see Chapter 14.

2. *Have your blood pressure checked regularly.* Most people with high blood pressure can bring their blood pressure down to normal levels and greatly reduce their risk of heart attack and stroke. Many people return to normal blood pressure readings simply by quitting smoking, not drinking alcohol, maintaining a normal weight, and getting regular exercise. Some people also need to take medication to lower their blood pressure.

3. *If you are diabetic, be sure you follow medical advice to control it.* Diabetics develop more severe atherosclerosis earlier in life. If you have diabetes, be sure that you see a doctor regularly, and follow his or her instructions regarding insulin shots and general self-care. In addition, a healthy lifestyle is even more important for you than for nondiabetics.

4. *Eat healthy foods.* Eating a healthy variety of foods in moderate amounts reduces your risk of obesity, which in turn reduces your risk of suffering cardiovascular disease. You should make a special effort to avoid foods that are high in fat. Chapter 4 offers specific information on choosing a nutritious diet.

5. *Exercise regularly.* Regular aerobic activity can strengthen the heart and has been shown to increase the internal diameter of arteries, allowing more blood to pass through. Exercise can also lower blood cholesterol. If you don't exercise, not only will you lose these protective effects, but you will find it much more difficult to maintain normal weight.

6. *Learn how to manage stress.* Everyone suffers from stress now and then. But having a continuous amount of high stress can contribute to heart disease. Learning how to manage the stress in your life can make you not only happier, but healthier too. Some specific approaches for stress management are discussed in detail in Chapter 9.

7. *Schedule regular medical checkups.* An examination by a health professional can let you know if you are developing risk factors such as high blood pressure, diabetes, or high blood cholesterol levels. You can then treat these conditions before they cause serious damage to your heart and blood vessels.

Another thing you can do to help protect yourself from cancer is to avoid overexposure to the sun. Ultraviolet rays from the sun are known to cause skin cancer.

Some forms of skin cancer are easily treated and rarely fatal. However, one form of skin cancer that is on the rise, melanoma, can be incurable unless detected early. A single case of sunburn in childhood serious enough to cause blisters can dramatically increase the risk of melanoma.

If you do spend time in the sun, be sure to use a sunscreen with a high sun protection factor number. For more information on selecting a proper sunscreen, see Chapter 6.

(FIGURE 24-16) **Too much sun can cause skin cancer. If you do spend time in the sun, be sure to cover up as much as possible and to use proper protection.**

There are several proven measures you can take to decrease your risk of getting cancer. First, don't use tobacco. Smoking cigarettes is the number-one cause of lung cancer in this country. Chewing tobacco and snuff can cause cancers of the bladder, pancreas, and kidney. Long-term tobacco use is associated with a higher risk of liver, esophagus, larynx, and pharynx cancers. By avoiding tobacco, you can significantly lessen your chances of getting any of these diseases.

It is also important to follow a healthy diet and exercise plan. Eating low-fat foods and getting plenty of exercise can help you maintain a healthy body weight and reduce your chances of getting many diseases—including cancer. In addition, some evidence indicates that certain nutrients are anticarcinogens, which are substances that can prevent cancer.

Review

1. *Explain the ways in which the arteries are affected by atherosclerosis.*

2. *Describe the relationship between atherosclerosis and high blood pressure.*

3. **LIFE SKILLS: Practicing Self-Care** *List three kinds of cancer that tobacco use can cause.*

4. **LIFE SKILLS: Practicing Self-Care** *Name four things you can do to reduce your risk of cardiovascular disease.*

5. *Name two things you can do to reduce your risk of getting cancer.*

6. **Critical Thinking** *A friend of yours who smokes cigarettes and eats a diet high in fats tells you it's stupid to worry about cardiovascular disease while you're still a teenager. What could you say in response?*

Highlights

Summary

- Diseases that are not transmitted from one organism to another are called noninfectious diseases. Hereditary, congenital, autoimmune, and degenerative diseases are all types of noninfectious diseases.

- Hereditary and congenital diseases are diseases people are "born with."

- Genes are responsible for transmitting hereditary characteristics. Some hereditary conditions are sickle cell anemia, cystic fibrosis, Tay-Sachs disease, Down's syndrome, muscular dystrophy, Type II diabetes, allergies, and asthma.

- Exposure during pregnancy to some drugs, environmental factors, and certain diseases can cause congenital diseases. Some congenital diseases are fetal alcohol syndrome, cerebral palsy, and epilepsy.

- Autoimmune diseases are disorders of the immune system. The most important distinction between AIDS and autoimmune diseases is that AIDS is an infectious disease, and autoimmune diseases are not.

- Three types of degenerative disease are osteoarthritis, cardiovascular disease, and cancer.

- Many types of cancer and heart disease can be prevented by avoiding certain environmental and lifestyle risks. Early detection and treatment can cure some types of cancer and control cardiovascular disease.

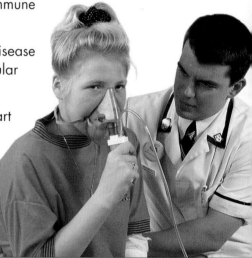

Vocabulary

noninfectious disease a disease that a person cannot catch from another person, animal, or other organism.

hereditary disease a disease caused by defective genes inherited by a child from one or both parents.

congenital disease a disease that is present from birth but is not inherited.

autoimmune disease a disease in which a person's own immune system attacks and damages an organ of his or her own body.

degenerative diseases diseases that cause gradual damage to organs over time.

cardiovascular disease progressive damage to the heart and blood vessels.

cancer a disease caused by cells that have lost normal growth controls and invade and destroy other tissues.

CHAPTER 24

Chapter Review

Concept Review

1. High blood pressure, sickle cell anemia, and cancer are all examples of _____ diseases.

2. The characteristics that were passed from your parents to you are carried on tiny structures within the body's cells known as _____.

3. _____ is a hereditary disease that results in breathing and digestive difficulties caused by the secretion of thick mucus in the lungs and digestive tract.

4. _____ is caused by the presence of an extra chromosome in the body cells.

5. When a person's immune system attacks and damages an organ of his or her own body, the person has an _____ disease.

6. The most common cause of cardiovascular disease is _____, a narrowing of the arteries caused by a buildup of fatty materials.

7. A _____ tumor is called a benign tumor.

8. _____ is one form of skin cancer that is on the rise and can be fatal unless detected early.

9. The choices you are making now concerning _____, _____, alcohol, and tobacco are already affecting your heart and blood vessels.

Expressing Your Views

1. Your uncle, who has just returned from jogging, says he has an uncomfortable feeling of pressure in the middle of his chest and then becomes short of breath and dizzy. What might he be experiencing, and what should he do?

2. Your new friend, Wendy, has just told you that she suffers from epilepsy. Would you ask her any questions about her disease? What would you do if she had a seizure when you were alone with her?

3. Your father just found out that his cholesterol level is dangerously high. What things would you suggest he do to bring his cholesterol level down?

4. Do you think most people would want to know if they had possibly inherited a fatal disease? Explain.

Life Skills Check . . . . . .

1. Practicing Self-Care

On a hot summer day, you and your friends plan to go to the beach. You are sure you will spend all day there and you are worried about sunburn. What could you do to protect yourself?

2. Practicing Self-Care

You have recently been diagnosed as having asthma. Does this mean you can no longer participate in athletic activities? What can you do to minimize your attacks?

3. Practicing Self-Care

Since your family moved to a new house, you have had a stuffy nose, itchy eyes, and frequent sneezing. What might you be experiencing? What could you do to relieve your misery?

Projects . . . .

1. Research the cause and nature of a given noninfectious disease. Then prepare an oral report that describes the disease, its prevention, and its treatment, and that identifies any behaviors that could minimize the risk of getting the disease.

2. Work with a group to write public service announcements that inform the public of ways to prevent cancer. Deliver your announcements to the class.

3. Work with a group to create a bulletin board that illustrates ways to lower your chances of developing cardiovascular disease.

4. Several cultures around the world have low rates of heart disease. Work with a partner to research the diet of one of these cultures. Prepare a meal that is representative of the foods they eat.

Plan for Action . . . .

Early habits and attitudes play an important role in the prevention of cardiovascular disease and cancer. Create a plan to reduce your chances of getting one of these diseases.

&thical &ssues in &ealth

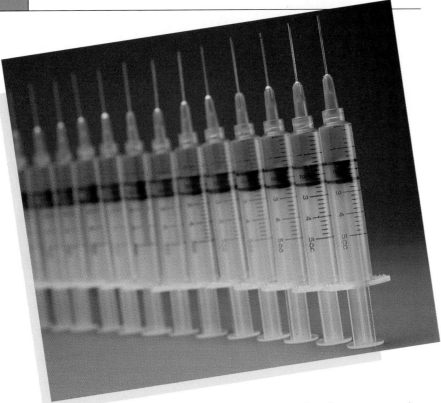

Intravenous drug use has become a major factor in the spread of AIDS because of a very dangerous practice—sharing needles. According to the Centers for Disease Control and Prevention, 23 percent of AIDS cases reported in the United States in 1992 resulted from intravenous drug users sharing needles contaminated with HIV.

Public-health authorities have proposed a method to slow the spread of HIV infection by intravenous drug users. The method involves distributing clean needles and supplies such as bottles of bleach and water for cleaning needles and syringes.

These items are included in a "survival kit." The popular name for such an effort is "needle exchange program." Reactions to this method have sparked national and international debate.

Those who oppose needle exchange programs argue that the programs will increase intravenous drug use and encourage youngsters to use drugs. Some opponents also argue that intravenous drug users will not take advantage of programs to protect their health. They believe that by using drugs, users show a lack of concern for themselves.

Advocates of needle exchange programs contend that most persons addicted to drugs are concerned about AIDS and will take steps to prevent HIV infection, if they are assisted in doing so. Supporters also argue that making clean needles available will not increase the use of drugs but will improve the relationship between public-health workers and people addicted to drugs. This improved relationship, they believe, will increase the likelihood that people with addictions will get into treatment programs.

During a two-year experiment in New Haven, Connecticut, researchers at Yale University collected information about the effects of a needle exchange program. Their data showed that the program had several positive effects. First, the needles returned for exchange were in circulation for a shorter length of time than needles in circulation before the program began. This indicates that fewer people used each of the needles. Second, the percentage of needles infected with HIV dropped by one-third. Third, referrals to drug treatment centers increased.

The Yale study showed that in New Haven, drug use did not increase when a needle exchange program was begun, as many had feared. In fact, it may have decreased somewhat. In addition, the chief of police in New Haven reported a 20-percent decrease in the area's crime rate. He speculated that the reason for the drop may have been an improved relationship between public-health workers and the drug-using community. Since the average participant in the program was 35 years old and had been shooting drugs for an average of seven years, the Yale study also suggests that the New Haven program did not encourage more adolescents to use drugs.

Currently, there are many legal barriers to conducting needle exchange programs. In some states, it is just as illegal to carry needles and syringes as it is to use or possess drugs. Public-health workers who distribute ''survival kits'' in these states often risk being arrested.

State and federal lawmakers who support needle exchange programs have begun to address the legal barriers. On the local level, several city governments have authorized needle exchange programs despite unanswered legal questions. These cities have obtained police cooperation to prevent the arrest of health workers and needle recipients.

One group that could benefit from needle exchange programs is children. Seventy percent of all AIDS cases among children are linked to intravenous drug use by a parent. These children were infected with HIV before birth. One mayor who had opposed a needle exchange program in his city changed his mind and became an advocate after seeing HIV-infected newborns in a hospital.

◁Situation for Discussion

Ben is a 28-year-old married man who has used intravenous drugs for more than 10 years. He frequents a ''shooting gallery'' where needles are shared. Ben is aware of the danger of HIV infection and the possibility of infecting his wife and future children, but his wife is unaware of his addiction and wants to start a family. Ben wants to get treatment for his addiction but worries that he will be fired if he uses the insurance his employer provides. He has heard about a needle exchange program near the shooting gallery but fears he will be arrested for carrying needles if he participates.

a. What course of action is open to Ben? What keeps him from getting help? What are some positive and negative aspects of participating in the needle exchange program?

b. If you were a public official, would you support or oppose a needle exchange program? What data would you gather to support your position? What steps would you take to start or stop such a program?

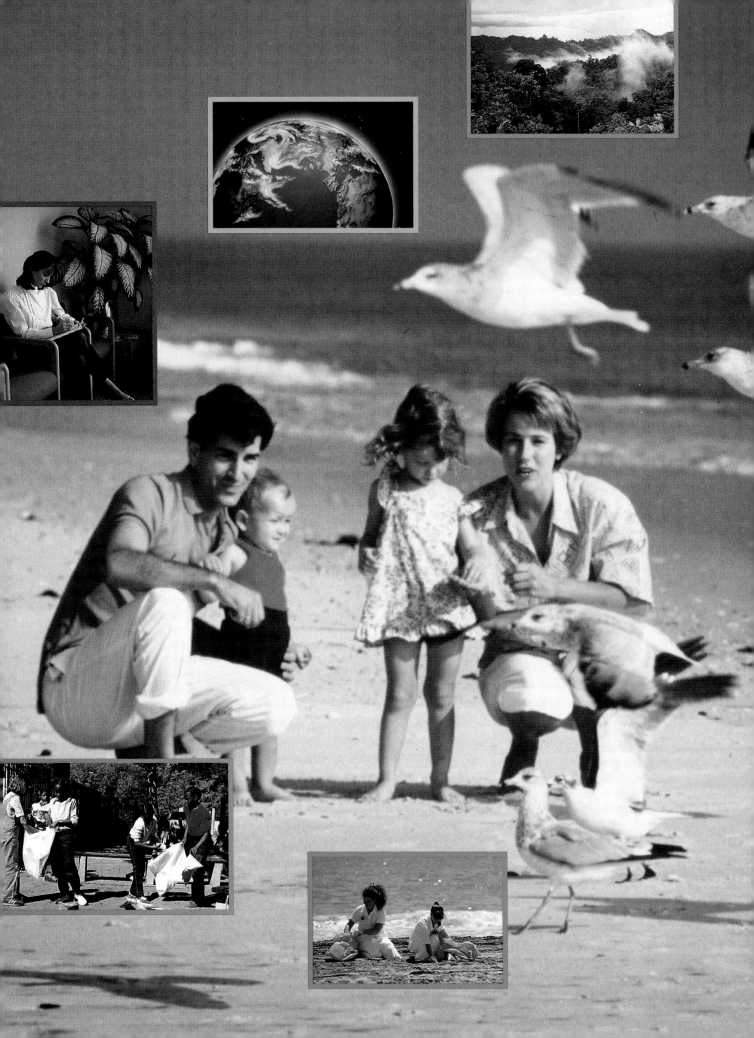

HEALTH AND SOCIETY

CHAPTER

25

Environmental *and* Public Health

◆ ◆ ◆ ◆

For many people, enjoying the outdoors is part of a healthy lifestyle. But even if you don't enjoy outdoor activities, a healthy environment is essential to your health and to the health of all people.

The trouble started when Teresa's sister wound up in the hospital with pains in her abdomen. Before long, several other people in the neighborhood began to have the same symptoms. People were upset because the doctors at the local clinic hadn't been able to figure out what was making everyone sick. Eventually, officials from the health department were called in to help solve the mystery.

Within a few weeks, health officials announced that Teresa's sister and her neighbors were suffering from gasoline poisoning. Small amounts of gasoline in the neighborhood's drinking water had caused liver and nerve damage. In other words, the environment in the neighborhood was unhealthy. To inform as many people as possible of the danger, a neighborhood meeting was arranged. Teresa decided to go to find out what was going on.

Section 25.1

The Environment and Health

Objectives

- Identify the characteristics of an ecosystem.

- Describe the components of a healthy environment.

- Identify the consequences of overpopulation and pollution.

At the meeting, several environmental and health specialists spoke to people from Teresa's neighborhood. As she listened to the speakers, Teresa began to get a better idea of how all living things are related to their environment. Teresa learned that a healthy environment promotes good health, and that when the environment is damaged, the health effects can be enormous.

Discussing the environment in health class may seem strange, but a healthy environment is an important element in both personal and public health. Every year thousands of people—like the people in Teresa's neighborhood—find out how important the environment is to their health. In this chapter, you will discover how the environment is important to your health.

Ecosystems

Every living thing is part of an **ecosystem**, which consists of many groups of living things and their physical surroundings (environment). For example, a lake and all the organisms (living things) that live in it make up an ecosystem. All the living things on Earth and the places where they live make up a worldwide ecosystem. From the smallest to the largest, all ecosystems have several things in common.

ecosystem:

a system made of living things and their physical surroundings.

Interactions One characteristic of an ecosystem is that its living and nonliving parts interact with one another. Some living things feed on others. Living things also take the water and nutrients they need from the environment and then return the materials that are needed by other living things. For example, you inhale oxygen and exhale carbon dioxide. Plants take in carbon dioxide and give off oxygen. In other words, each living thing provides something that other living things need.

Nonliving materials interact as well. For example, oxygen reacts chemically with certain elements to form new compounds. The rusting of iron represents this type of reaction. Another example of interaction between nonliving parts of the environment is the effect that carbon dioxide has in the atmosphere. Carbon dioxide helps maintain the temperature of our surroundings by trapping heat from the sun inside our atmosphere.

Interdependency Consider what could happen if most of the Earth's plants died. For one thing, there would be less oxygen and more carbon dioxide. Both you and the environment would be affected. Your body would have to adjust to having less oxygen. The extra carbon dioxide might make the climate warmer—imagine summertime temperatures 10 to 20 degrees warmer than they are now. This could happen if certain human activities (such as releasing large amounts of carbon dioxide by burning oil and gas and clearing away large areas of the world's forests) are not reduced.

You can see that whatever happens to one part of an ecosystem affects other parts. In other words, the parts of an ecosystem are interdependent. The water, air, land, and climate, plus the kinds of organisms and the size of their communities, are all important to the health of an ecosystem. If one part of an ecosystem is damaged, the environment in the ecosystem could become unhealthy.

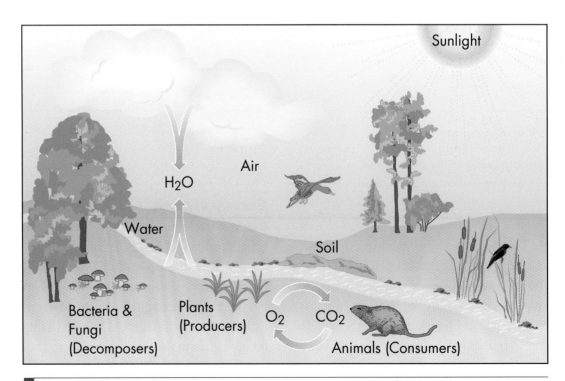

(FIGURE 25-1) **The parts of an ecosystem interact and are independent. Here you can see how living and nonliving elements of an ecosystem affect each other.**

(FIGURE 25-2) **In addition to the many everyday activities for which we use water, each of us uses about 40 gallons of water per day just for personal washing and toilet flushing.**

Change and Homeostasis Fortunately, living things are able to adjust to changes in their environment. When it's cold, for instance, you shiver and get goose bumps. This is an automatic change your body makes to warm you up. Organisms rely on such changes to maintain a balance inside their bodies. Maintaining this balance is called **homeostasis**.

Ecosystems also change constantly. For example, the temperature changes from day to night and from season to season. Materials such as water and air, as well as the living things, constantly come and go. In healthy ecosystems, there is a balance between the materials that are entering and leaving. The internal balance that exists in an ecosystem also represents a type of homeostasis.

Elements of a Healthy Environment

Even though living things can adjust to many of the changes in their surroundings, there are limits to this ability. The environment provides certain materials and conditions that are essential for the healthy existence of living things. Among these essentials are water, air, and adequate food and living space.

Water Water is one substance that is vital to all living things. It is home to many organisms (living things). But more important, all of the body processes that sustain life require water. In fact, most of an organism's body is water. For instance, water makes up as much as 65 to 70 percent of your body as a whole, and 80 percent

homeostasis:

the tendency of any living thing to maintain a balance in its inner systems.

food chain:

a sequence of organisms that begins with a food producer and continues with one or more organisms, each of which eats the one before it.

of your brain. Human activities require a great deal of water as well. In addition to the water we must drink daily to maintain good health, we also use water for personal and household cleanliness, food preparation, and recreation. Agriculture and industry use huge amounts of water to grow food, process food and raw materials, and manufacture other necessities.

Unfortunately, less water is available for our use than most people realize. Almost 97 percent of Earth's vast water supply is salt water. Most of the remaining 3 percent is frozen in the polar icecaps and glaciers. This means that only about 0.5 percent of the Earth's water supply is fresh water that is suitable for use by humans and the other organisms that require fresh water.

Air Air is another substance that is vital to all living things. Without it, you could survive for only a few minutes. Oxygen is the most important gas you get from air. It allows you to obtain energy from your food. Other gases, such as carbon dioxide and ozone, are also important to you. In addition to trapping the sun's heat, carbon dioxide is used by plants to make the food on

which all animals depend. The ozone layer of the atmosphere protects living things from the damaging ultraviolet rays in sunlight.

Other Essentials Nutrients (food and minerals) are another requirement for living that comes from the environment. All living things are part of a **food chain**. In a food chain, an organism, such as a frog, eats another organism, such as a dragonfly. The frog may then be eaten by a fish, and the fish may be eaten by a human. As you can see in Figure 25-3, all food chains begin with a life form, such as a plant, that makes its own food out of nonliving materials from the environment.

If something affects one of the life forms in a food chain, the others are usually affected as well. For example, if all of the frogs disappeared, there would be more dragonflies. And because the fish would have less food, there would be fewer fish, which would mean there would also be less food for the humans.

Living things also require a certain amount of room in which to live. The amount of space needed by a particular type

(FIGURE 25-3) **A typical food chain.**

plant ➡ mosquito larva ➡ dragonfly ➡ frog ➡ fish ➡ human

of organism depends on many things, such as the type of shelter it needs and the amount of light, water, air, and food it requires for living. These factors help determine how many individuals of a certain kind can be supported by the environment of a particular area.

Upsetting the Balance

If you have ever had food poisoning from eating contaminated food or become dehydrated from perspiring too much, you know how bad you can feel when your homeostasis is disrupted. Your health suffers when your internal balance is upset. Likewise, the health of the environment is threatened when the homeostasis of an ecosystem is disturbed. **Overpopulation** and pollution are two factors that disturb the healthy balance in an ecosystem.

Overpopulation If you had been born in 1900, you could have expected to live about 47 years. Babies born in the United States in the 1990s are expected to live about 76 years. Better health care and cleaner living conditions are primary reasons for this dramatic increase in *life expectancy* (the average length of time a person is expected to live). However, as life expectancy has increased, the number of people living on Earth has also increased.

The world's population is currently growing at a rate of about 255,000 people per day, or 93 million people per year. At this rate, the world's population will double in about 60 years. Such a rapidly growing population places a burden on natural resources. When the population of a region becomes too large to be supported by the available resources, overpopulation has occurred.

The effects of increasing population are serious. At its worst, overpopulation results in poverty and starvation when food production cannot keep up with population

(FIGURE 25-4) **Overpopulation has resulted in a shortage of food in Dhaka, Bangladesh. These conditions have made it necessary for the people there to wait in long lines just to get a small ration of milk for their children.**

growth. In addition, there are severe shortages of usable land and other natural resources. Currently, Earth's **nonrenewable resources** such as petroleum and mineral ores such as coal are being used at an alarming rate. Even **renewable resources** such as timber and seafood are being consumed at a much faster rate than they are currently being replaced.

overpopulation:

the point at which the population of an area is so large that it can no longer be supported by the available resources.

nonrenewable resources:

natural resources such as coal and oil that cannot be replaced once they are used.

renewable resources:

natural resources such as trees that can be replaced continually.

Consequences of Pollution and Removal of Resources

Extinction of life forms, such as the passenger pigeon.

Destruction of ecosystems, such as the tropical rain forests of Central and South America.

Climate changes, such as global warming due to the greenhouse effect.

Shortages of food and clean water, which lead to famine and disease.

(FIGURE 25-5) **Since the parts of the environment are interrelated, any one of these events could trigger the others.**

Pollution The balance in an ecosystem is also disturbed when one or more of its parts is damaged by pollution. Pollution occurs when substances that are harmful to living things contaminate the air, water, or soil. Such substances include poisonous chemicals, garbage, and radioactive wastes. Even excess amounts of otherwise beneficial materials such as carbon dioxide can also be considered as pollutants (substances that cause pollution). It is difficult to predict how pollution will ultimately affect Earth and its inhabitants, but it has already greatly affected human and environmental health. In Figure 25-5, you will find some of the many possible consequences of pollution.

(FIGURE 25-6) **When properly managed, forests like this one can be renewable resources. What are some of the other natural resources that can be renewed?**

Review

1. List the characteristics of an ecosystem.

2. What do living things need from their environment for a healthy existence?

3. How do overpopulation and pollution affect an ecosystem?

4. **Critical Thinking** Do you think that humans are a part of the natural ecosystems on Earth? If so, what responsibility, if any, do you think humans should take for the other parts of ecosystems?

Environmental Pollution

- Identify the main cause of environmental pollution.

- Describe the environmental consequences of air pollution.

- Identify health problems caused by various types of pollution.

The situation in Teresa's neighborhood is just one example of how pollution can damage the environment and affect human health. You have probably heard or read about many other incidents that are similar, or even more serious. In this section, you will learn about several forms of environmental pollution and discover how they may affect your health.

Although Teresa had learned a lot at the neighborhood meeting, she was still upset. "Did you hear?" Teresa asked her boyfriend, Jaime. "The health department found out there's gasoline in our drinking water! That's what made my sister and our neighbors sick. They say the gasoline's coming from some gasoline storage tanks in our neighborhood."

"I heard," Jaime said. "My dad works for a company that owns some of those tanks. That's all he talked about last

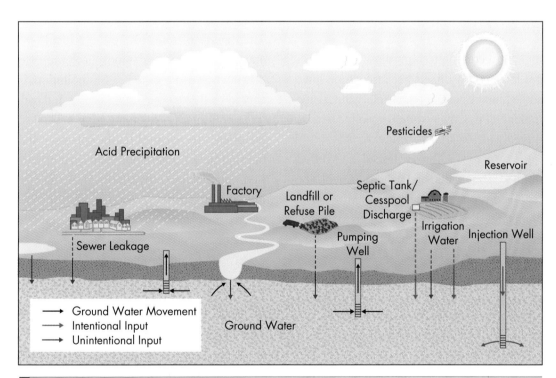

(FIGURE 25-7) **Sources of water pollution. Public drinking water comes from two main sources: surface waters (precipitation that collects in rivers, lakes, and reservoirs) and ground water (precipitation that seeps into the ground). The quality of drinking water varies, depending on its source and its exposure to pollutants.**

Genetics and the Environment: How Do They Relate?

Like height or eye and hair color, physical disorders can be inherited. Some people have a genetic predisposition for certain illnesses or diseases. This means that a person is predisposed (inclined) to develop a certain physical condition because he or she has inherited genes related to that condition. Whether a person will actually develop symptoms of a disease or illness he or she has a predisposition for depends on many factors.

Environmental pollution is a good example of something that triggers physical illness. It not only aggravates asthma and allergies but also increases the risk of activating certain diseases for which people may have a genetic predisposition. Leukemia and breast cancer are two examples of such diseases.

You can see again that environmental factors play important roles in our health. If you are aware of your surroundings and of how they affect you, you can use this information to your best health advantage.

(FIGURE 25-8)

night. According to him, those tanks can't be leaking gasoline, because they have some kind of pollution controls. But, come to think of it, I always smell gasoline when I drive by the tank farm.''

"Me too," Teresa agreed. "Well, I think we should demand that all the tanks be removed from our neighborhood! Those companies don't have the right to make everybody in our neighborhood sick by polluting the water!''

Water Pollution

Our increasing need for water, combined with the pollution of our water supply, is moving us steadily toward a health disaster. Part of our limited supply of fresh water is already too polluted for human use. As a result, many communities, like Teresa's,

have health problems due to polluted drinking water. Entire populations of some countries suffer from life-threatening health problems caused by severe shortages of clean, fresh water. Imagine what life would be like if you did not have enough water for drinking, bathing, cooking, or washing clothes.

Industry, agriculture, and our everyday activities create a vast amount of waste water that contains many dangerous chemicals and disease-causing organisms. Although cholera and typhoid (two diseases spread by polluted water) have been virtually eliminated in the United States, chemicals such as lead, gasoline, oil, fertilizers, and disinfectant byproducts impose many health risks. These and other hazardous chemicals increase the risk of cancer and birth defects, as well as nerve, stomach, kidney, and liver disorders.

Air Pollution

The quality of our air and the critical balance of gases in our atmosphere are also threatened by pollution. Air pollution is caused by the release of toxic gases and particles into the atmosphere by automobiles, factories, power-generating plants, and burning trash. These pollutants can be carried long distances by the wind or can rise into the upper levels of the atmosphere, where they can cause major worldwide problems.

Many health problems are linked to air pollution. The Environmental Protection Agency (EPA) blames air pollution for at least 2,000 new cases of cancer each year. There is also evidence that polluted air is a factor in birth defects and many other health problems. Young children, the elderly, and people who suffer from allergies or respiratory diseases such as asthma, bronchitis, and emphysema are especially at risk.

Destruction of the Ozone Layer

Ozone is an unstable form of oxygen. In the lower atmosphere, ozone is an undesirable gas that contributes to air pollution and is often a major component of smog. But the ozone found in the region of the upper atmosphere called the ozone layer is vital to living things.

The ozone layer completely surrounds the planet and protects living things from the ultraviolet (UV) light rays of the sun. UV light is dangerous to living things because it damages cells. In the early 1970s, scientists discovered a hole in the ozone layer over Antarctica. In the early 1990s, another hole was detected over the Northern Hemisphere. These holes in the ozone layer allow more of the damaging UV light to reach the Earth's surface.

Chemicals called chlorofluorocarbons (CFCs) have been linked to the destruction of the ozone layer. Sunlight causes these chemicals to break down. When they do, chlorine that is released from CFCs breaks down ozone molecules. Aerosol sprays (such as hairspray and deodorant) and chemicals used for cooling in air-conditioning systems and refrigerators are the main sources of ozone-damaging CFCs. However, coolants containing CFCs are slowly being phased out, and the ultimate goal is to have a total ban on CFCs by the year 2000. In addition, new regulations have been passed regarding the disposal of ozone-depleting chemicals.

Increased exposure to UV rays has been linked to an increase in several health problems, including skin cancer. Each year over 500,000 new cases of skin cancer are diagnosed.

Global Warming and the Greenhouse Effect

A greenhouse is a great place to be when it's cold outside, but not such a great place to be in the summer when it's hot.

Precautions you can take to avoid overexposure to the sun are discussed in Chapter 6.

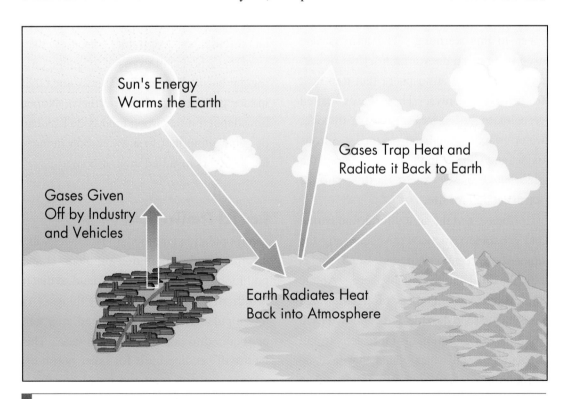

Sun's Energy Warms the Earth

Gases Trap Heat and Radiate it Back to Earth

Gases Given Off by Industry and Vehicles

Earth Radiates Heat Back into Atmosphere

(FIGURE 25-9) **The greenhouse effect causes warming of the atmosphere. Many scientists predict that as the concentration of greenhouse gases in the atmosphere increases, global warming (an overall rise in the Earth's temperature) will result.**

Some Indoor Air Pollutants

Formaldehyde *chemical used in making furniture, foam insulation, and pressed wood—can cause dizziness, headaches, nausea, and burning eyes and lungs.*

Asbestos *fibrous mineral once used in insulation—linked to lung cancer and other respiratory diseases.*

Radon *radioactive gas that occurs naturally in certain kinds of rocks—linked to lung cancer.*

Carbon monoxide *invisible, odorless gas that escapes from faulty furnaces—causes drowsiness and death.*

(FIGURE 25-10) **Your home, school, or workplace could contain one or more of these indoor air pollutants. Your local health department can help you find out how to determine if any of these pollutants are present in your home.**

greenhouse effect:

the trapping of heat from the sun by certain gases in the atmosphere called greenhouse gases.

The glass or plastic that covers a greenhouse traps heat from the sun's rays, warming the inside. The **greenhouse effect** is the name given to this warming. The term is also used to describe the warming effect of certain gases in the atmosphere that trap heat from the sun's rays. These gases, called greenhouse gases, include carbon dioxide, water vapor, methane, ozone, nitrous oxide, and CFCs. In the right amounts, the greenhouse gases keep Earth's surface warm enough for life.

Today, certain agricultural, industrial, and consumer practices are increasing the amount of greenhouse gases—such as carbon dioxide—in the atmosphere. At the same time, vast numbers of trees, which consume carbon dioxide, are cut down each year. Water pollution also threatens to kill algae and small water plants that take up carbon dioxide and give off oxygen. The overall effect of these changes may be a gradual increase in the temperature of the planet—**global warming**.

global warming:

long-term increase in temperature that is related to air pollution and the greenhouse effect.

Already, global warming has resulted in a rising sea level and the erosion of many coastal areas. Experts believe that by the year 2100, increasing temperatures could melt many glaciers and raise the sea level another two to seven feet. A seven-foot rise of sea level would flood 50 to 80 percent of our coastal wetlands (bays and swamps) and cause extensive destruction of coastal property, wildlife, and beaches.

Indoor Air Pollution Most of us are exposed daily to air pollution in our homes, schools, and workplaces. In tightly sealed buildings, air pollutants may be more concentrated than they are outdoors. In general, air pollution tends to aggravate health problems such as asthma, bronchitis, heart disease, and emphysema. Certain pollutants can cause cancer and other serious illnesses.

Tobacco smoke is a common indoor air polluter. You learned in Chapter 14 that if you smoke or live with a smoker you are more likely to develop cancer, cardiovascular disease, or respiratory diseases than someone who is not exposed to smoke on a regular basis. Figure 25-10 lists some other indoor pollutants and their effects. Notice how dangerous a carbon monoxide leak can be—it's important to have carbon monoxide detectors installed in your home.

Land Pollution

Overpopulation and modern technology are creating another pollution problem. Land pollution is the spoiling of the land so that it is unfit to be inhabited by living things. As the population grows, more land area will be required to house the human race. This land will become unfit for other purposes, such as growing food and supporting wildlife. But an even greater land-pollution problem is the accumulation of wastes that are produced and discarded by humans.

Solid Wastes Solid wastes include all of the materials that humans discard. In the United States, agriculture, manufacturing, mining, health care, and just everyday living produce more than 150 million tons of solid wastes each year. Each one of us generates about four pounds of trash per day. Figure 25-11 shows the type of materials that the average American throws away.

The most common way of dealing with solid wastes has been to dump them "as far away as possible" so that they could be forgotten. But open dumps (where wastes are left on the ground) are breeding grounds for odors and disease-carrying insects and rodents. Today, the amount of solid wastes has grown so much that finding a safe place to put them is a serious problem.

Most solid wastes are now placed in sanitary landfills, where they can take years to decompose (break down). At these sites, the wastes are covered with a layer of soil to prevent the spread of disease. However, materials often escape from landfills and pollute the air and water. Some wastes are burned in incinerators (industrial plants where solid wastes are burned). Unfortunately, burning waste can pollute the air.

Sanitary landfills and incinerators are healthier than open dumps. However, all of these methods take up land that could be used for other purposes, and none are completely safe for human and environmental health. This is why it is so important for us to focus our efforts on reducing the amount of trash we generate.

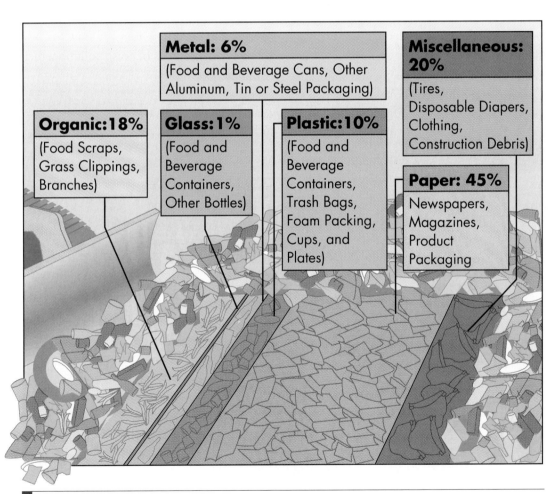

Metal: 6%
(Food and Beverage Cans, Other Aluminum, Tin or Steel Packaging)

Miscellaneous: 20%
(Tires, Disposable Diapers, Clothing, Construction Debris)

Organic: 18%
(Food Scraps, Grass Clippings, Branches)

Glass: 1%
(Food and Beverage Containers, Other Bottles)

Plastic: 10%
(Food and Beverage Containers, Trash Bags, Foam Packing, Cups, and Plates)

Paper: 45%
Newspapers, Magazines, Product Packaging

(FIGURE 25-11) **Do you know what's in your trash? Some of these figures may surprise you.**

hazardous wastes:

wastes that are dangerous to the health of living things or that are harmful to the environment.

Hazardous Wastes Certain types of wastes are classified as **hazardous wastes** because they may cause injury, illness, or death. Heavy metals, such as lead and mercury, and many chemical wastes, such as paint, paint removers, automobile fluids, pesticides, herbicides, and even batteries, are all examples of hazardous wastes. These substances are toxic (poisonous) to living things and are responsible for a lot of human health problems, including many birth defects and cases of cancer. Even plastic bags and balloons are considered hazardous wastes. When swallowed by wildlife, they can block the digestive system, causing starvation or disease.

Nuclear wastes are another type of hazardous waste. These highly dangerous radioactive materials result from nuclear-weapons research and production, nuclear-power generation, and medical treatments. It takes 10,000 years for some dangerous radioactive elements to decay into safe substances. Exposure to a large dose of radiation from nuclear wastes can be deadly. Even small amounts of radiation have been shown to cause bone marrow damage, skeletal abnormalities, and cataracts, as well as leukemia and other types of cancer.

Noise Pollution

The average amount of sound in our environment doubles every 10 years. Each day, you are exposed to many sources of noise pollution, including cars, trucks, heavy equipment, and jet aircraft. Sounds from radios, televisions, stereos, and loud concerts are also major noise pollutants.

Loud or constant noise can not only damage your hearing, but also cause stress, fatigue, irritability, anger, and anxiety. Prolonged exposure to loud sounds can even rupture your eardrum and may cause permanent hearing loss. Figure 25-13 shows some sources of noise pollution, their volume, and the type of damage they may cause.

(FIGURE 25-12) **Live rock concerts often produce sound levels that can cause some people pain and may even result in hearing loss.**

LOUDNESS OF COMMON SOUNDS

THE DECIBEL SCALE. The decibel (dB) is the unit of sound loudness. It is based on the faintest sound people can hear. The decibel scale is exponential, which means that an increase of 10 dB produces a sound that is ten times louder. Therefore, an increase from 20 dB to 40 dB does not double the loudness of sound—it increases it 100 times. The graph below compares the loudness of some common sounds.

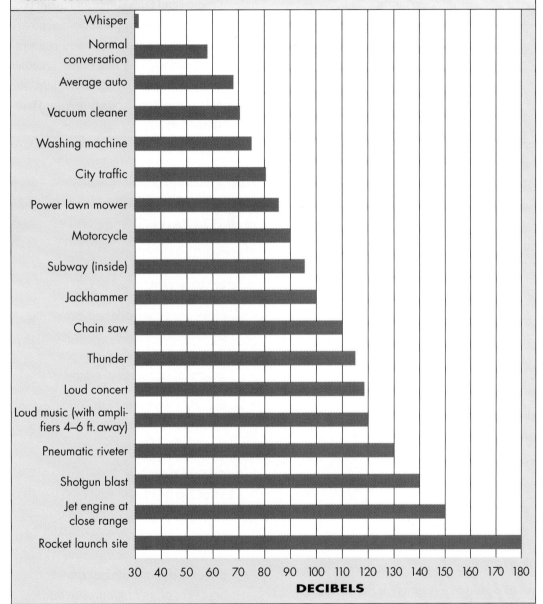

(FIGURE 25-13) The slightest sound that the human ear can detect has a loudness of 0 decibels (dB). Sounds in the 40–60 dB range are considered comfortable. Constant exposure to sounds above 70 dB (10 million times louder than the slightest sound) can be annoying and may begin to damage your hearing. Serious damage to hearing occurs with exposure to sounds of 120 dB. Sounds of 140 dB or more can cause pain, and at 180 dB, immediate and irreversible hearing loss occurs.

Check Up

Are You Protecting Your Hearing?

There are several ways that noise can increase your anxiety level or permanently damage your hearing:

- prolonged exposure to sounds above 70 dB (increased anxiety level),

- 8 hours of exposure to 90 dB or more (hearing damage),

- short-term exposure to 120 dB or more (serious hearing damage),

- or exposure to 150 dB or more for any length of time (eardrums may rupture). Damage may occur with or without apparent symptoms.

Use Figure 25-13, Loudness of Common Sounds, as a guide, and evaluate your potential for hearing loss by responding "yes" or "no" to the following questions. Write your answers on a separate sheet of paper.

1. Do you attend loud concerts?

2. Do you frequently go to places that play loud music?

3. Do you listen to your stereo, videogames, or T.V. with the volume turned very high?

4. Do you use earphones when you listen to music?

5. Do you live or work around sources of loud noises, such as construction, airports, or major industry?

6. Do you sit up front when you go to:
movies?
concerts?
other places that play loud music?

7. Do you hunt with a rifle or a shotgun or practice using firearms at a shooting range?

8. Have you ever been exposed to extremely loud noises (above 120 dB)?

If you responded yes to any of the questions above or if you frequently have trouble hearing certain sounds, you may have suffered some hearing loss. You should seriously consider changing your behavior so you do not further damage your hearing.

Some teenagers have already damaged their hearing. Studies indicate that many college freshmen suffer some degree of hearing loss. Much of this damage occurs during the middle school and high school years, in spite of the fact that hearing can easily be protected. Turning down the volume of radios and televisions and using protective earplugs when operating machinery and firing guns are ways that you can protect your hearing. To determine whether your hearing is damaged, complete the "Check Up: Are You Protecting Your Hearing?" to the left.

Review

1. What is the main cause of environmental pollution?

2. How does air pollution cause the greenhouse effect? destruction of the ozone layer? What are the potential dangers of each?

3. List five ways in which solid and hazardous wastes are harmful to the health of living things.

4. *Critical Thinking* Recently, smoking has been banned or restricted in most public places—schools, transportation systems, the workplace, and restaurants. This poses a difficult ethical question. Smokers often feel unfairly treated and resentful when they are not allowed to smoke. Nonsmokers usually find the smell of cigarette smoke very unpleasant. It is also hazardous to their health. How do you think this problem could be handled?

25.3 *What Can You Do?*

Objectives

- Describe the benefits of responsible waste management, recycling, and conservation.

- List specific ways each individual can help reduce pollution.

- Make a recycling and reuse plan for your household.
  - **LIFE SKILLS: Setting Goals**

After what they had learned about the effects of environmental pollution on health, both Teresa and Jaime wanted to know what they could do to protect their health. By collecting brochures and reading books and articles on the subject, they found that there are many ways to protect environmental and personal health.

Protecting Natural Resources and the Environment

As you learned in Section 25.1, the environment provides the materials that living things need for survival. This includes the many materials that people use for manufacturing the growing number of products and appliances they depend on. Currently, many natural resources are being used at an

(FIGURE 25-14) **Strip mining is one way that natural resources such as copper and coal are gathered. Frequently, these methods are very harmful to the environment.**

alarming rate, while the manner in which they are used pollutes the environment. If we don't reverse this trend, we will be left with an environment that can no longer support life as we know it. Fortunately, there are healthier and more responsible alternatives to the activities that are endangering the health of our environment.

Conservation **Conservation** is the protection and wise use of natural resources. By taking fewer natural materials from the environment, particularly those that are nonrenewable, we can help ensure that these resources will continue to be available in the future. One example of a pressing need for conservation efforts is in the way we produce energy. Much of our electricity is generated by burning coal and oil. Gasoline is burned to power most motor vehicles.

conservation:

the wise use and protection of natural resources.

However, burning fuels such as coal, oil, and gasoline is very harmful to the environment. In addition, supplies of these fuels are limited. Using less electricity and driving less helps to extend the supplies of burnable fuels and slow down the rate of pollution. It also helps each of us save money.

Conservation also means protecting the environment from pollutants by using products that are less toxic (safer). Safer alternatives to many toxic products are available. For example, pump sprays do not contain CFCs and do not damage the ozone layer. Low-phosphate and no-phosphate laundry detergents are less polluting to the water than high-phosphate detergents. Safer alternatives to burning fuels for energy include solar power, wind power, and water power. These energy sources are also renewable.

Recycling and Reusing Many of the materials that we discard can be reused. Ways of reusing materials include:

- recycling—the reusing of materials either directly or indirectly by making them into another product (For example, glass bottles can be used again or ground up and remelted to make a new item.)
- composting—the converting of organic matter into fertilizer by allowing it to be broken down by the action of bacteria
- pulverizing and compacting—the pounding of solid wastes into bricks that can be used in constructing landfills, roads, or other structures

About 80 percent of the solid waste produced is reusable. The advantages of reusing these materials include reducing the volume of solid waste and slowing down the rate at which resources are removed from the environment. Unfortunately, it costs more in many instances to recycle items than to produce them from scratch. As a

(FIGURE 25-15) **Many products that are sold in aerosol cans are available in pump sprays, which do not contain CFCs or damage the ozone layer.**

result, less than 10 percent of reusable solid wastes is actually being recycled, but researchers are actively striving to develop low-cost methods of recycling. Most cities and towns now have centers that will accept recyclable items. Since some recycling centers pay for the materials, this is a good way to clean up the environment and raise money for a good cause.

Reducing Personal Pollution

There is much that each individual can do to limit the amount of pollution that enters the environment. Teresa and Jaime decided to list easy ways that they could begin to make their environment cleaner and safer. The following are some of the things they listed as personal goals.

Preserving the Air To help keep the air as clean as possible, we will:

- Walk, bicycle, use public transportation, or carpool whenever possible.
- Purchase safer alternatives to products sold in aerosol cans.
- Choose not to smoke or spend time with those who do.
- Keep the car well tuned, and have the exhaust system checked frequently.
- Avoid purchasing products that contain formaldehyde or CFCs.
- Use less electricity.
- Plant trees by participating in a community program.

Preserving the Water To conserve water and help keep it cleaner, we will:

- Use only biodegradable, low-phosphate detergents.
- Fix leaky faucets and toilets quickly.
- Put displacement devices in all toilet tanks. (See Figure 25-17 to find out how to make a displacement device out of common household products.)

(FIGURE 25-16) **Community recycling centers accept a variety of recyclable materials. These materials must be separated according to their type. It's a good idea to do this ahead of time if you plan to recycle.**

- Take shorter showers, use less water in the tub for baths, and replace shower heads with water-conserving models.
- Fertilize and water lawns sparingly.
- Avoid using pesticides, and use the least-toxic products available when they are necessary.
- Dispose of all hazardous household chemicals safely. (Contact the local EPA office or city sanitation department for instructions and disposal sites in your community.)

Reducing Solid and Hazardous Waste
To help reduce pollution and preserve nonrenewable resources, we will:

- Recycle and reuse whenever possible.
- Reduce household trash by purchasing reusable items and products with minimal packaging.

(FIGURE 25-17) **You can reduce the amount of water used in flushing the toilet by placing a displacement device into the tank. A plastic milk or juice bottle filled with water and a few rocks to weight it down is ideal for this purpose. Your city water board should be able to give you more information on how to conserve water.**

- Join or support the efforts of environmental groups such as the Sierra Club, Friends of the Earth, the Wilderness Society, and the Nature Conservancy.
- Call problems to the attention of those who can help, such as conservation groups, newspapers, and city hall.
- Help attorneys prosecute violators by identifying sites of pollution and providing evidence such as photos.
- Participate in the law-making process by voting and by writing or talking to elected officials about your concerns.
- Encourage the school to obtain and use programs that build environmental awareness: Project WILD, Project Learning Tree, and the National Wildlife Federation CLASS PROJECT.

- Start a compost pile for biodegradable garbage.
- Limit the use of chemical fertilizers and pesticides.
- Purchase environmentally safe cleaning products.

Other Ways to Make a Difference

In addition to adopting personal behaviors that reduce pollution, there are many ways people can work together to promote a cleaner, safer environment. Some of the ways you could help are listed here.

R• • • • •eview

1. *What are the benefits of recycling and conservation?*

2. *List three ways individuals can help reduce each of the following: water pollution, air pollution, and land pollution.*

3. ▪▪ *LIFE SKILLS: Setting Goals Find out where the recycling centers are in your community and what materials they accept. Then outline a recycling and reuse plan for your household and plan to carry it out.*

4. *Critical Thinking How would you label hazardous and nuclear wastes so that someone living 10,000 years in the future would be able to understand their danger even though they may not speak your language?*

25.4 Public Health

Objectives

- Define public health.

- Describe four public-health activities.

- Compare the public-health concerns of developed and developing countries.

- Discover what the major public-health issues are in your community, and find out where to get help for a public-health problem.
  - **LIFE SKILLS: Using Community Resources**

In most of the chapters in this book, your attention is focused on your personal health. However, your health and well-being are affected by the health and well-being of other people. For example, infectious diseases (diseases caused by bacteria, viruses, or other parasites) cause many people to suffer poor health. And communicable diseases (infectious diseases that are passed from person to person) spread when people who are sick come in contact with healthy people. In fact, certain infectious diseases are among the leading causes of death. And as Teresa and Jaime learned, environmental problems can also affect the health of large numbers of people.

(FIGURE 25-18) **Because the people living together in a community interact with one another, they affect each other's health and well-being.**

What Would You Do ?

You're Sick but You're Needed at Work

Making Responsible Decisions

Imagine that you work at a popular fast-food restaurant near a high school. Lots of kids go there every day for lunch. One day you get really sick with a stomach flu and call as soon as possible to report why you cannot make it to work. Your supervisor insists that they can't handle the lunch crowd without you and tells you that you have to come in, sick or not. What would you do?

Remember to use the decision-making steps:

1. State the Problem.
2. List the Options.
3. Imagine the Benefits and Consequences.
4. Consider Your Values.
5. Weigh the Options and Decide.
6. Act.
7. Evaluate the Results.

epidemic:

an occurrence of disease in a particular area that affects many more people than expected.

public health:

the health of a community as a whole; the organized efforts of a community to promote the health and well-being of all its members.

Controlling the spread of infectious disease and problems like the one in Teresa's neighborhood are public-health concerns. **Public health** is the health of the people in a community. The term is also used to refer to the actions a society takes to protect and promote the health of its people.

Public-health problems cannot be solved by individual efforts alone. Cooperation is needed. Through government and privately sponsored activities, individuals can work together to create a healthier environment for everyone. In this section, you will learn about public-health activities and some of the agencies that deal with public-health problems.

Public-Health Activities

For most of human history, public health was endangered because of a lack of healthy, clean living conditions and because people did not understand how they got diseases. As the human population grew, large numbers of people died during repeated **epidemics**, or widespread occurrences of infectious disease. A variety of public-health activities developed out of a desire to control the spread of disease.

Sanitation Sanitation is the practice of providing pure drinking water, sewage disposal and treatment systems, waste-disposal sites, and clean living and working conditions. It was the first community wide method of controlling the spread of infectious disease. From collecting garbage to inspecting the food-preparation and storage areas of restaurants for sanitary conditions, modern sanitation efforts play an important role in protecting public health.

Hygiene Practicing personal hygiene (cleanliness) in one way you can play an important part in protecting public health. For instance, simply washing your hands is the most effective practice for controlling the spread of communicable diseases. It not only protects your own health, but also helps keep you from passing certain communicable diseases to others.

Quarantine The practice of quarantine (separating the sick from the healthy to stop the spread of disease) is another public-health activity that was begun to combat massive epidemics. People, as well as animals, plants, and agricultural crops, may be placed in quarantine if they are suspected of carrying an easily transmitted infectious disease. The period of separation lasts until the disease-causing agents are no longer infectious or until they can be destroyed by antibiotic or chemical treatments.

Immunization and Antibiotic Treatments Two of the most important public-health activities are immunization and antibiotic treatments. Before you entered school, for instance, you were required to have immunizations against several infectious diseases. Such requirements have eliminated the deadly diseases of smallpox and polio in the United States and greatly reduced the occurrence of other serious diseases such as whooping cough and measles.

Although immunization programs have completely or nearly eliminated several serious diseases, such programs must be continued to prevent the return of these diseases. Recently, the number of measles cases has been on the rise in the United States. This rise has been blamed on poor immunization rates and the high cost of health care. More information about antibiotic drugs and the process of immunization is found in Chapter 21.

Public-Health Goals

Even though great progress has been made in protecting public health, modern methods are not available in all parts of the world. As a result, public-health problems and priorities are very different in different parts of the world.

Developed Countries In developed countries such as the United States, modern health care (including immunization programs and antibiotic treatments) and modern sanitation systems have greatly reduced the number of deaths from traditional infectious diseases. As a result, chronic noninfectious diseases, new infectious diseases, and the problems of homelessness have become greater public-health concerns. Heart disease, for instance, the number-one cause

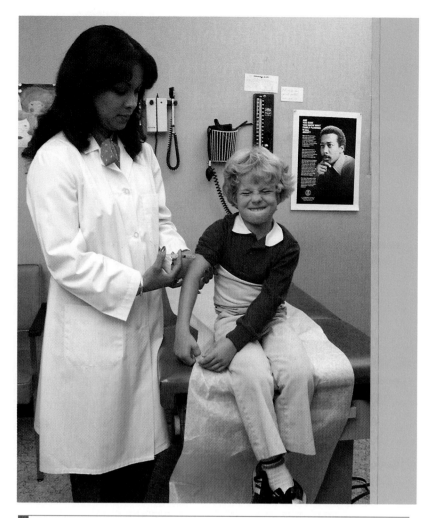

(FIGURE 25-19) **Immunizations given in doctors' offices and public-health clinics like this one protect the health of the individuals in a community. Although some serious diseases have almost been eliminated, they could return if people do not take advantage of the immunizations that are available.**

of death in developed countries, is linked to lifestyle choices. Therefore, encouraging people to eat less fat and get more exercise has become a public-health priority.

A list of some of today's major public-health priorities is found in Figure 25-20. Although disease prevention is still a priority in developed countries, effective public-health efforts must address all of these issues. The ultimate goal of public-health programs in developed countries is to create an environment in which each member of a community can enjoy a healthy and productive life.

Major Public Health Priorities and Selected Examples

Maternal, Infant, and Child Health
  prenatal care
  nutrition
  detection of birth defects and risks
  reduction of infant mortality rates
  immunization programs

Adolescent and Adult Health
  teen sex and unplanned pregnancy
  sexually transmitted diseases, including HIV
  teenage smoking; alcohol and other drug abuse
  accidental injury
  violence and homicide
  suicide

Aging and the Elderly
  physical activity and fitness
  mental health and mental disorders
  diseases of aging

Environmental Health
  community injury control
  community water and waste management
  housing
  control of disease-carrying insects
  air and noise pollution

Access to Health Care and Rehabilitation Resources

Community Mental Health, Stress, and Violence

Communicable Disease Control

Lifestyle and Health Promotion

(FIGURE 25-20) **Public-health programs today are aimed at solving a variety of problems in an attempt to provide a healthier, more productive life for all. Some of the public-health problem areas that are currently being targeted by public-health agencies in the United States are listed above.**

Our nation's goals for public health are stated in a lengthy report that was prepared through a joint effort sponsored by the U. S. Public Health Service. The report, which is titled *Healthy People 2000*, lists several hundred specific health objectives. But the major goals of this report can be summarized as follows.

- Increase the healthy life span of all Americans.
- Reduce the health disparities among different ethnic groups in America.
- Provide access to preventive services and care to all Americans.

The objectives listed in *Healthy People 2000* are being used by various agencies to plan public-health activities that will improve the overall health of Americans. A sample of these objectives appears in Figure 25-21.

Developing Countries Adequate health care and sanitation are not facts of life for many people in the world. As a result, infectious disease remains a leading cause of illness and death in many of the world's developing (unindustrialized) countries. Achieving effective disease control in developing countries depends on:

- financial resources—to provide the necessary health-care supplies, facilities, and professionals.
- political stability—so that public-health efforts can be carried through.

Unfortunately, developing countries are often characterized by poverty, unstable governments, and a lack of resources. Along with growing populations, these conditions have led to famine (a severe lack of food) in many of these countries. Therefore, in addition to infectious disease, starvation and malnutrition are major public-health problems in developing countries.

Selected Health Objectives From *Healthy People 2000*

Reduce deaths due to heart disease to no more than 100 per 100,000 people. (In 1987, it was 135 per 100,000. By 1995, we had significant improvement, with about 60% of the goal achieved.)

Reduce the percentage of overweight people to no more than 20% of people aged 20 and older and no more than 15% of adolescents aged 12–19. (From 1976 to 1980, it was 26% of people aged 20 to 74—24% for men and 27% for women—and 15% of adolescents aged 12–19. By 1995 results were discouraging: the percentage of those aged 20–74 who were overweight had increased by more than 100%.)

Increase to at least 30% the percentage of people aged 6 or older who engage regularly (preferably daily) in light to moderate physical activity lasting at least 30 minutes. (In 1985, 22% of people aged 18 or older were active for at least 30 minutes five or more times per week. By 1995, we had made progress and were closer to the year 2000 goal.)

Reduce cigarette smoking by teens and pre-teens so that no more than 15% have become regular cigarette smokers by age 20. (In 1987, 30% of youths had become regular cigarette smokers by ages 20–24. By 1993, some minimal progress had been made. In 1995, the percentage of smokers in this age group had been reduced to 27%.)

Increase to 60% the percentage of women cigarette smokers who quit when they become pregnant and maintain abstinence for the remainder of their pregnancy. (In 1985, 39% of Caucasian women aged 20–44 quit at some point during pregnancy. By 1995, we were moving in the wrong direction, with only 31% of women quitting smoking during pregnancy.)

Reduce to no more than 20% the percentage of children aged 6 and younger who are regularly exposed to tobacco smoke at home. (In 1986, 39% of households with children in this age group had a smoker in the home. By 1993, progress had been made toward this goal; fewer than 27% of households with children in this age group still had a smoker in the home.)

(FIGURE 25-21) **These are a few of the specific health objectives from** *Healthy People 2000.* **An evaluation of these objectives was completed in 1995.**

Public-Health Agencies

Promoting and protecting public health require the coordinated efforts of government agencies and private organizations. Public-health agencies work at local, state, national, and international levels.

Local and State Agencies   Public-health activities are usually carried out by state and local agencies. Each state has a board of health, which is made up of several elected officials. The board establishes laws and regulations that direct the public-health activities of local health departments, public-health clinics, and state hospitals throughout the state. When Teresa called the local health department to find out what services it provides for the community, she was given a long list. Figure 25-22 contains some of the major public-health activities occurring in most communities.

Public Health Activities in a Community

Regulation of community food, water, and milk supplies as well as medication, toys and recreational equipment.

Prevention of communicable and chronic diseases.

Planning the development, availability, and quality of health facilities, personnel, and services.

Maintaining and analyzing vital records systems.

Educating and motivating the public in personal and community health.

Scientific, technical, and administrative research.

Control of environmental pollution.

(FIGURE 25-22) **Local public-health agencies protect the health of the people in a community in a variety of ways.**

National Agencies   The primary public-health agency of the United States is the Department of Health and Human Services (USDHHS). USDHHS underwent a major revision in its structure in March of 1996, eliminating what was once one of the most well-known government agencies—the Social Security Administration. Now, three remaining agencies, the Administration for Children and Families (ACF), the Administration on Aging (AOA), and the Health Care Financing Administration (HCFA), oversee all government entitlement programs. These programs provide support to people who qualify for certain services by belonging to a specific group or by demonstrating a certain level of need. Examples of entitlement programs include Medicare, Medicaid, and Temporary Assistance to Needy Families.

Most of the federal government's public-health activity is handled by the remaining agencies in the United States Department of Health and Human Services. These agencies and their functions are described in Figure 25-23.

International Public Health

Because similar health problems can affect many nations at the same time, an organized system that conducts public-health activities across many nations is necessary. AIDS, tropical diseases such as malaria, diarrheal diseases, and environmental pollution are international health problems that require international efforts. Other critical issues affecting international health are poverty, natural disaster, war, and famine. Several government and private organizations are attempting to deal with the massive health problems that exist internationally.

Public Health Service Agencies

Substance Abuse and Mental Health Services Administration *(SAMHSA)—focuses on problems related to alcohol and drug abuse and mental health issues.*

The National Institutes of Health *(NIH)—directs and conducts basic research on the prevention, diagnosis, and treatment of diseases.*

The Centers for Disease Control and Prevention *(CDC)—works directly with state health departments to monitor health status, detect health problems, and control epidemics.*

The Health Resources and Services Administration *(HRSA)—is concerned with such issues as access to and equity, quality, and cost of health care.*

The Food and Drug Administration *(FDA)—is responsible for assuring that food is safe and wholesome; drugs, biologicals, and medical devices are safe and effective; and radiological equipment is used appropriately and safely.*

The Indian Health Service *(IHS)—provides hospitals, health centers, and health stations for American Indians and Alaska Natives.*

The Agency for Health Care Policy and Research *(AHCPR)—administers several research programs designed to identify problems and solutions to provide adequate access to health care for all Americans.*

The Agency for Toxic Substances and Disease Registry *(ATSDR)— monitors and provides information to the public regarding exposure to hazardous substances in the environment.*

(FIGURE 25-23) **The Public Health Service, a division of the Department of Health and Human Services, conducts most of the public-health activities of the United States government. The PHS is divided into eight smaller agencies. Each of these agencies concentrates on a separate area of public health.**

The United Nations The United Nations (UN) plays a major role in international public health. The UN is an alliance of over 170 nations dedicated to working together for the purpose of preserving world peace and human dignity. Several agencies established by the UN have had an impact on the health of the world's inhabitants. Among these agencies are:

- The United Nations Children's Fund (UNICEF)
- The United Nations Educational, Scientific and Cultural Organization (UNESCO)
- The Food and Agricultural Organization (FAO)
- The World Food Program (WFP)
- The World Health Organization (WHO)

The World Health Organization The primary health organization of the United Nations is the World Health Organization. It was created after World War II to deal with the devastation and disease that the war brought to Europe. Today, the goals of the WHO are worldwide prevention of disease and attaining a level of health that will permit all people of the world to lead socially and economically productive lives.

The main targets of WHO programs are developing countries. WHO programs provide the citizens of these countries with access to health care by training health-care professionals, building hospitals and clinics, and sponsoring a variety of preventive health-care services.

The WHO is also involved in fighting the AIDS pandemic (an epidemic that affects many countries at the same time). In 1987, WHO began the Global Strategy for the Prevention and Control of AIDS. Other WHO activities include working toward universal childhood immunization and organizing effective family-planning programs.

Other International Agencies The United States government sponsors several international health efforts, especially in developing countries. The Peace Corps, for example, sends volunteers to these countries to provide education and assistance with agriculture, construction, sanitation, and health services. The Agency for International Development (AID) has provided billions of dollars in emergency assistance to regions such as Africa that have serious problems with famine. With UNESCO and other international organizations, AID also sponsors programs for immunization and oral rehydration therapy (the giving of fluids to a person who is dehydrated from excessive diarrhea or vomiting).

(FIGURE 25-24) **The WHO coordinates many activities that are designed to combat the spread of AIDS. Here, Dr. Kristina Baker and her assistant are distributing information about AIDS to a group of Zambian school children and helping them start an anti-AIDS club. The activities of more than 260 such clubs are teaching the children of Zambia how to avoid getting AIDS.**

Being Aware of Public-Health Issues in Your Community . . . .

Teresa and Jaime became aware of public-health issues in their community through personal experience. You may or may not have had a similar experience. The public-health problems in your community are probably very different, but problems do exist. There are also places in your community where you can get help for problems related to public health.

To make yourself better aware of the public-health problems and resources in your community, follow your local newspaper for two weeks. Look for any articles that have to do with health issues, especially in your community. On a piece of paper, complete the following activity.

1. List five public-health problems that exist in your community. How have these problems affected the quality of life in your community? How have these problems affected your friends and relatives?

2. Choose one of these problems and write down your thoughts about the problem. What is the reason for the problem? How do you think it could, or should, be solved? What may happen in the future concerning the problem?

3. Find out which public-health agencies or organizations in your community can help with the problem you choose. Call or write to one of these groups for more information about the problem and the group's public-health programs.

Private Organizations Private organizations also provide important public-health support around the world. One such organization is the International Red Cross, which was originally created in 1859 to provide assistance to soldiers and others during war. Since then, it has expanded its relief efforts to include natural disasters such as floods and earthquakes.

Goodwill Industries of America is another privately funded public-health and assistance organization. This international nonprofit organization collects and distributes reusable materials to the poor and provides job training and rehabilitation services to the disabled.

The Salvation Army is yet another international organization that performs a valuable public-health service. Salvation Army volunteers help provide shelter and health services to the homeless and the poor worldwide. Figure 25-25 lists several other private health organizations.

Private organizations depend on donations and volunteers to fund health research, education, and support services. They also offer many types of support groups for those who suffer from a particular health problem or have friends or family who do. These support groups provide an opportunity for people to meet, discuss the frustrations they feel, and share positive skills and experiences. Private volunteer health agencies also provide excellent opportunities for young people to become actively involved in the health of their communities.

Private Health Organizations

The American Cancer Society
The American Diabetes Association
The American Foundation for the Blind
The American Heart Association
The American Lung Association
The American Red Cross
The Arthritis Foundation
The Cystic Fibrosis Foundation
The Epilepsy Foundation of America
The March of Dimes
The Multiple Sclerosis Foundation
The Muscular Dystrophy Association
The National Council on Alcoholism
The National Hemophilia Foundation
The United Cerebral Palsy Association

(FIGURE 25-25) **Private and voluntary health agencies such as these play a vital role in solving many public-health problems.**

Review

1. Define public health.

2. Describe three types of public-health activities that control the spread of communicable disease.

3. What are four of the major public-health problems in developed countries today? in developing countries?

4. **LIFE SKILLS: Using Community Resources** What public-health agencies would play an active role in resolving problems like the one in Teresa's neighborhood? Write to one of these agencies to get more information on the public-health programs they provide.

5. **Critical Thinking** Could the massive public-health problems of developing countries affect public health in developed countries? Explain.

CHAPTER 25

Highlights

Summary

- All living things are part of a world-wide ecosystem. If overpopulation or pollution damages that ecosystem, all forms of life are threatened.

- Human activities are the primary cause of environmental pollution.

- Pollution can be controlled or prevented by conserving resources, choosing safer alternatives to toxic chemicals, and recycling materials.

- The ultimate goal of public-health programs is to create an environment in which each member of a community can enjoy a healthy, productive life.

- Modern health care and sanitation systems have greatly reduced the number of deaths from infectious diseases.

- Government and private public-health agencies work at local, state, national, and international levels.

Vocabulary

ecosystem a system made up of living things and their physical surroundings.

homeostasis the tendency of any living thing to maintain a balance in its inner systems.

food chain a sequence of organisms that begins with a food producer and continues with one or more organisms, each of which eats the one before it.

overpopulation the point at which the population of an area is so large that it can no longer be supported by the available resources.

nonrenewable resources natural resources such as coal and oil that cannot be replaced once they are used.

renewable resources natural resources such as trees that can be replaced continually.

greenhouse effect the trapping of heat from the sun by certain gases in the atmosphere called greenhouse gases.

global warming long-term increase in temperature that is related to air pollution and the greenhouse effect.

hazardous wastes wastes that are dangerous to the health of living things or that are harmful to the environment.

conservation the wise use and protection of natural resources.

public health the health of a community as a whole; the organized efforts of a community to promote the health and well-being of all its members.

epidemic an occurrence of disease in a particular area that affects many more people than expected.

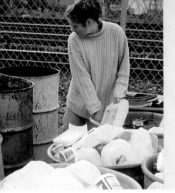

Chapter Review

Concept Review

1. What is an ecosystem?

2. Name two factors that disturb the healthy balance in an ecosystem.

3. What are the major causes of water pollution? What are some important health problems caused by water pollution?

4. How is destruction of the ozone layer linked to skin cancer?

5. How can a landfill cause water pollution and air pollution?

6. What are three sources of nuclear wastes? Why are they so dangerous?

7. Identify three alternatives to burning fuels for energy. Why are these alternatives safer?

8. List three ways to reuse materials. What are the advantages to reusing materials?

9. What are three ways in which individuals can help make a difference in protecting the environment?

10. In the past, why was public health endangered? What was the first community-wide method of controlling the spread of infectious diseases?

11. What is famine, and how does it affect public health? What causes famine in developing countries?

12. Three federal government agencies oversee entitlement programs. What do these programs provide? What are two examples of entitlement programs?

Expressing Your Views

1. Why is pollution an international problem?

2. Who do you think should be responsible for protecting the environment: individuals, industry, local governments, or the federal government?

3. Do you think quarantine is a violation of personal freedom? Why or why not?

Life Skills Check . . . .

1. Communicating Effectively

Write a letter to one of your local legislative representatives describing an environmental concern and what you would like him or her to do about it.

2. Setting Goals

Someday you will move into a place of your own. Suppose you were to design your house or apartment. What are some things you would put in your plans that would be energy efficient and foster environmental protection? Include plans for landscaping, materials for building the house, and plumbing fixtures.

3. Using Community Resources

You would like to provide public-health support by doing volunteer work. You don't really want to work with a government agency. Who else might need your help? What could you do for them?

Projects . . . .

1. Write a brief report about your community's trash disposal system. Does your community have a sanitary landfill? If not, how does your community dispose of trash? Is the system environmentally safe? If your community has a landfill, does the landfill prevent environmental pollution? How? If possible, include pictures with your report.

2. By reading the newspaper or watching the local news, monitor the "pollution index" of your area for a week. Then find out what the pollution index was six months ago. (You can do this by looking up old newspapers in the library.) Compare the numbers. What do they mean? How could they affect your health? Report your findings to your class.

Plan for Action . . . .

The responsibility for your community's environment ultimately rests with the individuals of the community. Devise a plan to adapt your behaviors in order to promote a healthy environment in your community.

Being a Wise Consumer

◆ ◆ ◆ ◆

■ **The right doctor is critically important to maintaining good health.**

Cam sat in the middle of the living room looking at all the boxes that surrounded her. Books were strewn across the floor, and her cat was having a great time running through the maze. Cam could hear her parents in the next room hanging pictures. It seemed they had been here longer than just two days.

All of a sudden, Cam began to wheeze from all the dust in the room. "Oh, no," she thought. "I hope I don't get an asthma attack *now*. Not when we just moved to this town. We don't even have a doctor yet."

Section
26.1

What You Can Expect in Health Care

Objectives

- *Develop a plan to select a physician.*
  - ■■ **LIFE SKILLS: Being a Wise Consumer**

- *Learn how to communicate with medical personnel.*
  - ■■ **LIFE SKILLS: Communicating Effectively**

- *Understand your rights as a patient.*

Like Cam and her family, practically everyone needs a **primary care physician** (family medicine physician). Although the right doctor is critically important to maintaining good health, many people don't know how to find a good doctor. People often seem unconcerned with how they choose their physician. In fact, some studies indicate that the average American spends more time selecting a mechanic than in selecting a doctor. In this chapter, you'll learn how to se-

lect a doctor and how to communicate with doctors. You'll find out what your rights are in dealing with them. And you'll learn about some of the plans that are available to pay for the costs of health care.

primary care physician:

a family physician, a pediatrician, or a general internal medicine physician.

(FIGURE 26-1) **It is important that you feel free to be direct and assertive with your doctor and to ask any questions that concern you.**

The Selection Process

As an adult, you will need to decide who your doctor will be. You may decide to keep the same physician you have always had. If you decide to change doctors, it's best to go ahead and make the change while you are healthy.

There are several ways to go about finding a new doctor. One way is to ask your relatives and friends about their physicians. Another method is to locate a medical school that is affiliated with a nearby hospital. Then, call the school, and ask for a list of its staff physicians. The county medical society can also provide you with a list of physicians.

After making your choice, call the doctor's office to find out if he or she is accepted by your medical plan and to make sure new patients are welcome. Check on hours and fees as well.

During your first appointment, your doctor will record your reason for coming in, your specific signs and symptoms (temperature, blood pressure, heart rate, type of pain, etc.), medication you are taking, and your diet and exercise habits. Information about previous illnesses, surgery, treatment, allergies, and reactions to medications will also be needed to establish your medical history. During the examination, you can help by pointing out pains, lumps, growths, or previous injuries that cause pain or concern. Keep in mind that your doctor is trying to learn and record as much about you as possible to aid diagnosis and treatment.

It is important for you to feel comfortable enough with your doctor that you are able to be direct and assertive, and to ask questions. You might ask, How long will it take to heal? Will the medicine produce any side effects? Should I take the medicine with food or on an empty stomach? When should I come back? Can I exercise and go to soccer practice? You should expect answers to all of your questions, no matter how trivial they may seem. Some people like to write down their questions and bring the list with them. You may also want to write down any special instructions the doctor gives you during the office visit. Do not allow the doctor to rush you or brush you off to get to the next patient. Avoid making a final decision about a new doctor until after a few visits. If you are hurried, treated like a child, cannot get direct answers, sense questionable business prac-

(FIGURE 26-2)

Patient's Bill of Rights

As a patient, you have the right to:

considerate and respectful care.

obtain complete information concerning your diagnosis, treatment, and prognosis in language you can understand.

information (risks, benefits, alternative treatments) you need in order to give informed consent before treatment.

refuse treatment, once you are aware of the facts, to the extent permitted by law.

privacy (refusal to be examined in front of people not involved in your case) and confidentiality of records.

a reasonable response when you ask for help.

information about any possible conflicts of interest (hospital ownership of labs, professional relationships among doctors who are treating you).

be told if the hospital plans to make your treatment part of a research project or experiment.

an itemized explanation of your hospital bill.

know what hospital rules apply to your conduct as a patient.

expect good follow-up care.

(FIGURE 26-3) **You and your family may have to consult a team of doctors if someone close to you has a major illness and requires long-term medical care.**

tices, or do not feel comfortable, then change doctors.

Remember that you have a right to get the opinion of another doctor at any time. This can be especially important when surgery or another major procedure has been recommended. The recommendation of the second doctor is called a "second opinion."

Patient's Bill of Rights

The basic rights of human beings include freedom of expression, the right to make one's own decisions and to act upon them, and the right to maintain one's personal dignity. These rights should be preserved for you when you are a patient. If you are hospitalized for any reason, you should receive your copy of the Patient's Bill of Rights, shown in Figure 26-2. Although it is not a legal document, it does set forth standards that hospitals are expected to follow. Becoming aware of your rights as a patient is your first step toward getting quality health care. It is your own personal responsibility to look out for yourself, insisting on good care and freely expressing your needs and concerns.

Review

1. **LIFE SKILLS: Being a Wise Consumer** *List three ways to select a physician.*

2. **LIFE SKILLS: Communicating Effectively** *This is your third visit to your doctor about the headaches you have been having. Your doctor hasn't told you what is causing the headaches or whether they will go away. Write down four questions you can ask your doctor to get clear information on your condition.*

3. **Critical Thinking** *Why should a hospital tell you if it plans to make your treatment part of an experiment it is conducting?*

Section

26.2 *Financing Your Medical Costs*

defensive medicine:

use of numerous and sometimes unnecessary diagnostic tests to avoid a lawsuit.

premium:

payment a person makes to an insurance company in exchange for coverage.

Objectives

- *Understand why health-care costs in the United States are rising.*

- *Know the advantages and disadvantages of traditional private health-care insurance and HMOs.*
  - **LIFE SKILLS: Being a Wise Consumer**

- *Learn how to locate free health care in your community.*
  - **LIFE SKILLS: Using Community Resources**

- *Learn how to recognize quackery.*
  - **LIFE SKILLS: Being a Wise Consumer**

We are spending more and more each year for personal health care as physician costs, dental costs, and hospital-care costs rise rapidly. You can see this trend in Figure 26-4. High tech equipment, organ transplants, the AIDS epidemic, malpractice insurance, and **defensive medicine** (use of numerous and sometimes unnecessary diagnostic tests to avoid a lawsuit) are some of the causes, and they will continue to increase costs in the future. Unless something is done to reduce these costs, the number of Americans unable to afford medical or dental care will continue to grow.

The U.S. government and businesses are exploring ways to make medical care affordable for everyone by examining proposals for socialized medicine (health care paid from tax dollars), shared-cost programs, and managed care.

Your Family Health Insurance Plan

A good health insurance plan is an absolute necessity in the United States today. Employees of major industries, the government, and other companies often pay a fee, called a **premium**, for their insurance coverage. For an additional fee, they may add family members. Unfortunately, many small businesses and other employers have no such plans, and their employees cannot afford the high health insurance premiums of individual policies. High medical costs have also forced many companies to reduce their benefits and to increase premiums, especially for employees with unhealthy lifestyle behaviors such as smoking. The monthly insurance premium is taking a big-

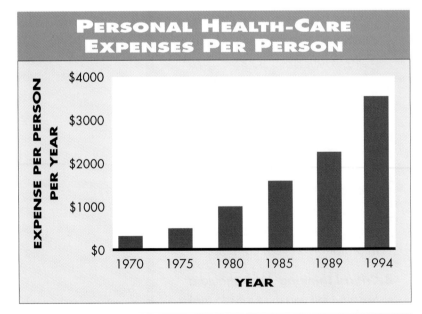

(FIGURE 26-4) **The cost of health care in the United States has been rising rapidly, making it difficult for many people to obtain health care. (Source: U.S. Bureau of the Census.)**

Check Your Insurance Coverage

(FIGURE 26-5)

Can you choose any physician, or is there a limited list of providers?

Is there a deductible? That is, do you have to pay anything before the insurance company begins paying?

What deductible amount is suited to your family income and predicted health needs?

Is disability or lost-income protection provided? Is there a lump-sum payment to dependents in case of death?

Is full coverage provided for hospital, medical, and surgical costs? Can you go outside the plan and still be covered?

Is major medical insurance available for serious illness and accidents?

Are expenses for care during pregnancy and delivery covered?

Is this a "commercial policy" (one that can be canceled if the holder becomes a bad risk after the claim for a current illness is paid)?

Is a group policy available? These are less expensive.

Is coverage provided for mental and emotional disorders?

Is coverage provided for dental care?

Are dependents covered?

Do any restrictive clauses eliminate coverage of pre-existing conditions or require a waiting period before such conditions are covered?

What happens if I am covered by a group policy at work and I get fired or resign? Could I keep my insurance, or would the policy be canceled?

ger and bigger portion of the employee's take-home pay. In addition, health insurance pays only part of the bill. For those who are stricken with a serious illness, family savings are often quickly drained.

Traditional Policies Traditional private health insurance policies have advantages and drawbacks. One big advantage is that the insurance company will pay for treatment by any doctor or hospital the insured person chooses. This can be very important if a person has had the same physician for a long time and does not want to change.

One drawback is that the insured person must pay for any doctor visits or medical expenses up front, and then fill out a claim form in order to be reimbursed.

Another disadvantage is that the insured person must pay a yearly **deductible,**

deductible:

the amount of medical costs an insured person must pay before the insurance company begins paying.

HMOs (health maintenance organizations):

organizations that offer subscribers complete medical care in return for a fixed monthly fee.

PPOs (preferred provider organizations):

organizations that offer subscribers discounted medical care when they use preselected health-care providers.

(FIGURE 26-6)

or set fee, before the insurance company begins paying for any of the costs. And routine checkups at a doctor's office are usually not reimbursed—only office visits for illness or injury. Insurance companies reimburse only a percentage of office visit costs, usually 80 percent. The remaining amount is paid by the insured person. Insurance companies also pay only a percentage of hospital costs, usually 80 percent as well.

Before purchasing a traditional health insurance policy, it would be helpful to find out the answers to the questions in Figure 26-5. You might also find it helpful to call your state insurance department for assistance. A representative can analyze any policy, explain its terms, and provide information on how to get reimbursed for claims.

HMOs and PPOs A more recent type of health-care plan is an **HMO (Health Maintenance Organization),** a group of health-care providers who offer complete medical care in return for a fixed monthly fee. In addition, some HMOs charge a small fee for office visits and prescriptions.

HMOs have several advantages. First, patients do not have to submit claim forms for reimbursement. Another advantage is that HMOs practice preventative medicine. Because HMOs receive almost the same amount of money from members no matter how many times members use their services, it is financially advantageous for HMOs to have healthy members. Therefore, HMOs emphasize checkups, immunizations, and other ways of staying healthy.

A big drawback of HMOs is that you can't freely see any doctor of your choice. If you see a specialist outside an HMO without the consent of the HMO, you must pay for the services yourself.

There is another type of health-care plan that combines features of both traditional policies and HMOs—**Preferred Provider Organizations (PPOs).** As a

Traditional Insurance Policies Versus HMOs

Traditional Insurance Policies	HMOs
Focus is on treatment	*Focus is on prevention*
Regular checkups usually not covered; only a percentage (usually 80 percent) of hospital costs and office visits reimbursed; reimbursement doesn't begin until costs exceed the deductible	*Most health-care costs paid, except for a small fee (copayment) charged by some HMOs for office visits or prescriptions*
Can see any primary care physician you choose	*Must use one of the HMO's participating primary care physicians*
Can see any specialist you choose	*Must have the HMO's consent to see a specialist, or the HMO will not pay costs*

member of a PPO, you may either select your health-care provider from a pre-approved group, the "preferred providers," or you may choose to be in the care of someone outside of the group. However, the insurance company has arranged to have services performed by a preferred provider at a discounted rate. What this ultimately means is that although you can go to any doctor you want, it will cost you less money if you choose to go to a doctor that your PPO has selected.

$\mathcal{L}ife$SKILLS: Being a Wise Consumer

Traditional Policy or HMO?

Someday you will need to select a health insurance policy of your own. Get some practice now by evaluating the following situation.

At your new job, your take-home pay is $1,100 a month. You're married and have a small child. Your spouse does not have health insurance at work, but you can get either a traditional policy or join an HMO where you work.

The traditional policy would cost you $71 per month. It would cost you $22 per month to add your spouse and child. The traditional policy has a $250-a-year deductible for you, or $500 for you and your dependents (spouse and child), and it pays 80 percent of hospital costs.

You would pay $56 per month for the HMO. It would cost $22 per month to add your spouse and child. In addition, each time you or a member of your family visited the doctor or bought a prescription medicine, you would pay a $5 copayment. There would be no copayment required of you if you or a member of your family entered the hospital.

Everyone in your family is enjoying good health right now. Your child will need a checkup at least once a year. You are happy with the pediatrician who cares for your child. You and your spouse, however, have not yet chosen a primary care physician.

Which family members would you insure? Would you choose the HMO or the traditional policy? Why?

How to Find and Use Free Health Services

Most states and communities have some form of free or reduced-cost health care. Medicaid, which is funded by every employed person in the United States, provides federal aid to the blind, disabled, low-income families with dependent children, and those who live at or below the federally designated poverty level. Medicare provides federal aid for the elderly.

Community health resources are also available to the public. State health departments and county or city health units exist to help residents with specific health problems. Immunization centers for disease control, special clinics for sexually transmitted diseases, and maternal and child health services are generally available. Some places charge small fees for their services.

"Free clinics" have also been established in most cities to treat or counsel people for unplanned pregnancies, sexually transmitted diseases, and drug abuse. Many of these clinics also treat other types of ailments for those people who are unable to afford medical care.

Cultural DIVERSITY

Native Americans and Health Care

The United States health-care system is enormous. It includes a large number and variety of hospitals, health-care centers, doctors, nurses, and other health professionals. Some people find that the options available within this system meet their health needs quite effectively. Others, however, have customs and beliefs that lead them to seek different sources of treatment, called "alternative" health-care systems. Native American cultures are examples of cultures that provide alternative health systems for their people.

According to the philosophy of these cultures, all elements of the world—inanimate objects as well as living things—have life, spirit, power, and specific roles to play. Each element is related to the others, and each affects the entire universe. When there is harmony among these elements, a state of well-being results. But an imbalance among the elements can cause illness.

When such an imbalance occurs, a Native American may seek the help of a traditional healer. Healers are trained men and women who perform ceremonies to right the imbalance and in so doing heal the illness. Such healing ceremonies may include prayers, rituals, special medicines, and the use of visual symbols.

Though the practices of Native American healers may seem quite differ-

However, funding for these clinics is usually low, so they must restrict the medical services they offer to a small number of patients and limit the services provided. Check the yellow pages for a list of health-care clinics that are in your area, or call your state, county, or city health department.

Quackery

Quackery—the promotion of medical services or products that are worthless or unproven—can endanger your health.

Worthless so-called miracle remedies for weight loss, arthritis, cancer, epilepsy, and other serious disorders flood the market and confuse the public. Fake treatments and worthless medication may delay accurate diagnosis and appropriate treatment until the problem is very serious.

And even when worthless treatments don't actually endanger your health, such as creams that are advertised as breast enlargers, they waste your money.

It is often very difficult to know which health products and services to purchase for special problems and which ones to avoid. Television, radio, magazine, and mail advertising is designed to get you to buy vari-

quackery:

the promotion of medical services or products that are worthless or unproven.

ent from those of medical doctors, there are similarities. Like medical doctors, Native American healers must undergo years of special training. They must learn the right ceremonies and rituals to perform for the different types of imbalance. Also like medical doctors, Native American healers sometimes specialize in certain kinds of health problems. The healers may refer a patient to another healer or to a medical doctor if an illness is not within their area of expertise.

The alternative health-care systems of Native Americans are perhaps the best known, but they are by no means

the only ones. Some African-Americans, Asian-Americans, Hispanic-Americans, and people who live in the Appalachian Mountains also practice alternative health care.

ous products. Each media message does its best to convince you that its product is the absolute best way to eliminate a particular health concern.

Quackery is not always practiced by dishonest people. Some people who sell worthless products or services truly believe in what they are selling.

Your best protection is to analyze carefully every product or treatment method you are considering. You may have to contact your physician or a reputable agency or nonprofit organization for advice. One good resource for information on drugs and cosmetics is a book called *The Medicine Show*, an unbiased report on numerous products by the editors of *Consumer Reports* magazine. Other sources of health-related consumer information are the National Health Council, the World Health Organization, the Food and Drug Administration, the Department of Health and Human Services, and various nonprofit associations, such as the American Heart Association and the American Lung Association. Any time you are in doubt, check the product out before you purchase it. Figure 26-7 gives you some tips to help identify a quack or an unsound product.

Are You Dealing with a Quack?

If you encounter the following, you may be dealing with a quack:

The promise or guarantee of a quick cure

The use of a "secret remedy" or an unorthodox treatment

The use of advertising to gain patients

Testimonials by patients who have been cured

Claims that a product will cure a wide variety of ailments

Claims that sound too good to be true

Request for a large payment in advance

Claims by the manufacturers or sponsors of the product that the medical profession is persecuting them

(FIGURE 26-7) **Spectacular claims are often a sign that you're dealing with a quack.**

Review

1. List three reasons why health-care costs are rising in the United States.

2. ■■ **LIFE SKILLS: Being a Wise Consumer** You have a chronic condition for which you've been seeing the same doctor for years. You have a great deal of confidence in your doctor and don't want to change. Would you choose a traditional insurance policy, an HMO, or a PPO? Explain why.

3. ■■ **LIFE SKILLS: Using Community Resources** List three groups of people who can receive health care through Medicaid.

4. ■■ **LIFE SKILLS: Being a Wise Consumer** You are considering buying a health product that guarantees a quick cure for your condition. Name two groups you could consult to determine whether you are dealing with a quack.

5. **Critical Thinking** Which people in the United States are least likely to have access to good health care?

Highlights

Summary

- When choosing a doctor, ask friends and relatives about their physicians, or obtain a list of the staff physicians at a nearby hospital.

- It is important to feel comfortable and to be able to communicate well with your doctor. You should ask any questions that concern you and insist that the doctor explain special instructions clearly.

- As a patient, you have the right to get another doctor's opinion at any time.

- An advantage of a traditional private health insurance policy is that the insured person can choose any doctor. Disadvantages are that the insured person must pay a yearly deductible and usually must pay medical fees before being reimbursed. Also, tradi-

tional health insurance does not reimburse the cost of preventative practices.

- Two advantages of HMOs are that their practitioners stress preventative medicine and patients do not have to submit claim forms for reimbursement. One drawback of HMOs is that patients can't always see a doctor of their choice.

- PPOs combine aspects of traditional policies and HMOs, and discount the services of preselected doctors.

- Many community health resources are available to the public. Some services are free, while others require small fees.

Vocabulary

primary care physician a family physician, a pediatrician, or a general internal medicine physician.

defensive medicine the use of numerous and sometimes unnecessary diagnostic tests to avoid a lawsuit.

premium the payment a person makes to an insurance company in exchange for coverage.

deductible the amount of medical costs an insured person must pay before the insurance company begins paying.

HMOs (health maintenance organizations) organizations that offer subscribers complete medical care in return for a fixed monthly fee.

PPOs (preferred provider organizations) organizations that offer subscribers discounted medical care when they use preselected health-care providers.

quackery the promotion of medical services or products that are worthless or unproven.

Concept Review

1. What types of information make up a medical history?

2. What is included in a routine physical examination?

3. What is a "second opinion"? When might a patient need one?

4. When would an individual receive a copy of the Patient's Bill of Rights? What does it do?

5. Are health-care costs rising or falling? Why? What is the outlook for health-care costs in the future?

6. What are two approaches being considered by the U.S. government and businesses to make medical care affordable for everyone?

7. Why have many companies had to reduce the health insurance benefits they provide for employees?

8. Name one advantage and one disadvantage of traditional private health insurance policies.

9. Who can you contact to help you choose a traditional health insurance policy? How can they help you?

10. What is an HMO? Describe its service.

11. Name three types of health services that are available through state health departments and county or city health units.

12. What kind of treatment or counseling do "free clinics" provide? Who do they treat?

13. Name four instances in which a health consumer should suspect quackery.

Expressing Your Views

1. You need to select a primary care physician. What professional and personal characteristics of a doctor are important to you? What would you do if, after you found a doctor, you were not satisfied with him or her?

2. Your primary care physician has recommended that you have surgery. You are wondering if you should see another doctor for a second opinion. What advantages are there to getting an opinion from another doctor?

3. Why do you think some people continue to buy worthless products?

Life Skills Check

1. **Communicating Effectively**

   You have your first appointment with your new primary care physician concerning a recent health problem. What information should you take to the doctor with you? What are three questions you could prepare to ask the doctor?

2. **Being a Wise Consumer**

   Your family has been offered a fantastic deal on a traditional health insurance policy. What questions should you ask the insurance agent before purchasing the policy? Where else could you check to be sure the company is sound and that the policy is a good one for your family?

Projects

1. Some countries have a national health insurance program. Many people think we should have such a program in the United States. Work with a group to research the national health insurance program of another country and compare that program with the health services available in our country. Organize a class debate on whether our federal government should institute national health insurance.

2. Work with a partner to create a short skit about quackery. The skit can be humorous or outrageous. One partner should pretend to be a quack using some of the common practices listed in Figure 26-7. The other partner should pretend to be a consumer. Lead the audience to see the possible negative consequences of being misled by quackery.

Plan for Action

A health-care system cannot be expected to care for your health if you are not willing to do your part in caring for yourself. Make a plan to find a doctor if you do not have one and list three local health-care facilities you could use if necessary.

Ethical Issues in Health

There are times in everyone's life when the attention of family is required. When you were a baby, for instance, you needed constant care. Chances are that a parent or guardian remained at home for a period of time to provide that care for you. Even after you started school, someone probably stayed home to take care of you when you were sick. You may also remember a time that a family member helped out when a serious injury, illness, or death occurred in your family. Such physical and emotional care is an important function of families.

For many families, caring for each other is also a financial necessity. Today's soaring medical costs make hospital care unaffordable for many people, especially when they require continuous care for a long period of time. For example, someone who has been seriously hurt in an accident may require 24-hour care for weeks, months, or even years. People who have

Parkinson's or Alzheimer's disease also require constant care. Since the number of older persons in our society is rapidly increasing, family members will be called on more and more in the future to care for older adults suffering from cancer, heart disease, arthritis, loss of memory, or muscle disease. Unfortunately, people with full-time jobs often find it impossible to work and still provide regular care for a family member in need.

Employers can make such situations easier to manage by allowing employees to take a leave of absence from their jobs—as they would if they were sick—to take care of family members. This type of leave is usually called family leave. Some companies continue paying an employee's salary and insurance premiums while he or she is on family leave. Others simply provide assurance that the same job, or a similar one, will be available when the employee is able to return to work. Child-care leave is a specific type of family leave that many companies provide for women who have just had babies. In some companies, child-care leave is available to new fathers as well.

Many people believe family and child-care leave should automatically be part of the benefits and rights for all employees. These advocates contend that government and the business community have a responsibility to help families cope with the consequences of birth, death, illness, and disability. They stress that home care is better and much less expensive than the care given in a hospital, day-care center, or nursing home. Since health-care costs are often paid for by the insurance plans provided by employers or by tax dollars (as with Medicare and Medicaid), some experts predict that family leave would reduce the overall cost of health care.

In one of the first acts of his administration, President Clinton signed into law the Family and Medical Leave Act. This legislation requires all businesses with more than 50 employees to provide up to 12 weeks of unpaid family leave to all employees who have worked at the company at least one year and who work at least 25 hours per week. Employers must also offer the same job or a comparable job to employees returning from leave and must pay employees' health insurance costs while they are on leave. Several states have laws that require smaller companies to provide family-leave benefits as well.

Opponents of family-leave laws argue that a company should be responsible only for providing its employees fair salaries and reasonable benefits. They argue that a company should not have to take responsibility for the well-being of an employee's entire family. They predict that if employers are required to provide family-leave benefits, some private businesses could be driven out of existence as a result.

Those who oppose family-leave laws also predict that such policies would increase taxes, as well as the price of products and services. Taxes would increase because the large number of government employees would receive family-leave benefits. Prices of products and services would increase because the cost of temporarily replacing an employee is high. In order to survive, many companies will have to add this cost to the prices customers pay.

Situation for Discussion

In the Garcia family, both parents work at a small company in order to support their four children, who range in age from 8 to 16. Mrs. Garcia's 78-year-old father, Mr. Peña, lives alone in an apartment near the family's home. Several months ago, Mr. Peña was diagnosed with bone cancer. Although he has been able to care for himself until now, he is about to undergo a series of chemotherapy treatments that will make it necessary for him to have constant care for at least a couple of months.

a. How can the Garcia family manage this situation? What choices do they have?

b. If Mr. Garcia or Mrs. Garcia could take family leave, should the company hold a job until he or she returns, or hire a person who is equally qualified for the job? Should the company pay full salary during the leave? What would the company have to do to continue normal operations during the leave?

c. Should the government reimburse a company for the cost of family leave?

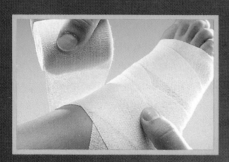

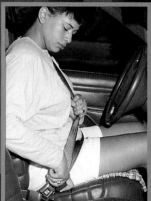

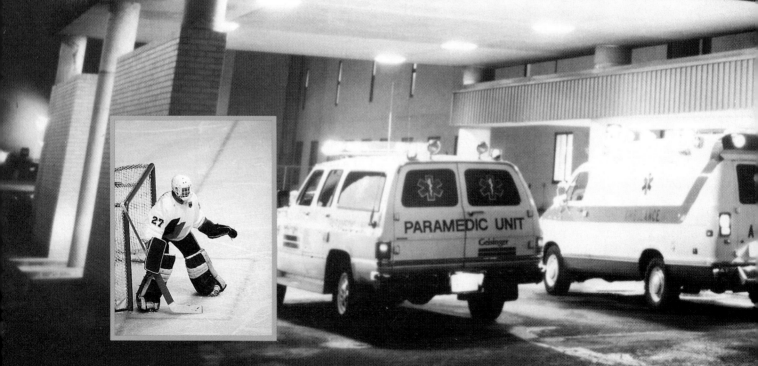

SAFETY
AND
EMERGENCY
CARE

CHAPTER 27

SAFETY AND RISK REDUCTION

CHAPTER 28

FIRST AID AND CPR

CHAPTER 27

Safety and Risk Reduction

◆ ◆ ◆ ◆

Physical activity is an important part of good health, and some activities are more dangerous than others. Rock climbers follow certain procedures and use the proper safety equipment to reduce their risk of injury and have fun at the same time.

Sarah hung up the telephone and turned toward her mother. "That was Jan, Mom. Her little brother, Billy, just got back from the emergency room. He flipped off his bike today and broke his wrist. The lace of his sneaker jammed the bike chain and he was thrown over the handlebars."

"Poor Billy, he won't have much of a summer vacation this year," said Sarah's mother.

"It could've been a lot worse," said Sarah. "He hit his head on the curb, but his bicycle helmet cushioned the blow. The doctor told his mother that if he hadn't been wearing a helmet, Billy's injuries would've been more serious."

Sarah thought of her younger sister, Lynette. "Mom, I think it's time we bought a bike helmet for Lynette."

"And what about you, Sarah? Can you be sure that you'll never take a fall from your bike?"

Section 27.1 *Accidents and Risks*

Objectives

■ *Recognize that accidents are the leading cause of death for people between the ages of 15 and 24.*

■ *Recognize that risky or careless behaviors are factors in most accidents.*

■ *Identify ways in which your personal behavior can be modified to reduce your risk of accidents.*
  ■■ **LIFE SKILLS: Practicing Self-Care**

Billy's broken wrist was the result of an **accident.** In this chapter, you will learn that even though they are unexpected, many accidents can be prevented.

Accidental Deaths

Accidents are the number-one cause of death in the United States among people aged 15 to 24. Among people of all ages, accidents are the fourth leading cause of death. Figure 27-1 on the next page breaks down the number of deaths that occur each year because of specific types of accidents. Notice that motor-vehicle accidents are responsible for the greatest number of accidental deaths—approximately the same amount as all the others combined.

Different age groups tend to have different types of accidents. Among 15- to 24-year-olds, for example, most fatal accidents involve motor vehicles or alcohol, or both. Very young children and elderly people are more likely to be injured or killed in falls. Children under five account for many cases of accidental poisoning.

accident:
_____

any unexpected event that causes damage, injury, or death.

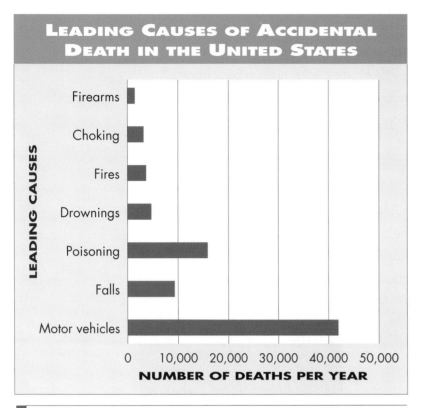

LEADING CAUSES OF ACCIDENTAL DEATH IN THE UNITED STATES

LEADING CAUSES (y-axis): Firearms, Choking, Fires, Drownings, Poisoning, Falls, Motor vehicles

NUMBER OF DEATHS PER YEAR (x-axis): 0, 10,000, 20,000, 30,000, 40,000, 50,000

(FIGURE 27-1) **Accidents are currently the fourth leading cause of death in the United States. For young adults 15 to 24, they are the leading cause of death.**

risk:

an action that is potentially dangerous; the chance of injury.

safety awareness:

knowledge about risks and how to reduce them.

Risks and Carelessness

Sometimes a person has no control over the things that lead to an accident. For example, when an earthquake causes bricks to fall from a building, someone may be injured. Such events, however, make up a minority of accidents.

Most accidents result from the actions, or inactions, of people. Have you noticed that certain people seem to have more accidents than others? You've probably also heard or used phrases such as ''He is an accident waiting to happen'' and ''She's accident prone'' many times. Such phrases suggest that the person may be at least partly responsible for many of the accidents that happen to him or her. A person's behavior may greatly affect his or her chances of being involved in an accident. Understanding why accidents occur can help you avoid most accidents.

Taking Risks One type of behavior that increases the likelihood of having an accident is taking risks. A **risk** is an action that involves danger of some kind. Many everyday activities involve risk. Every time you cross a busy street, for example, you are taking a risk. But your chances of being injured are fairly low if you pay attention and obey traffic signals.

Many people, however, take unnecessary risks. Dodging traffic to cross the street in the middle of the block is far more likely to lead to an accident than crossing at the corner. Drinking alcohol and taking drugs increase the risk of accidents because these substances impair a person's ability to make good judgments, alter his or her perceptions, and impede normal physical skills.

The high number of accidents among teenagers is related to the fact that they take more risks than older people. You can minimize risk by making responsible decisions.

Being Careless Putting dishes away, as the boy in Figure 27-2 is doing, is not, by nature, dangerous. But notice that by not paying attention to his task, the boy has managed to push a bowl off the shelf—and possibly onto his head! His behavior is not risky—it is careless. Carelessness is a lack of concern about the possible effects of one's actions, or not paying attention while performing a task. As with taking unnecessary risks, carelessness can lead to accidents that could have been avoided.

Safety and Behavior

Avoiding unnecessary risks and being attentive are important to your safety. **Safety awareness** is knowing about risks and how to reduce them. Assuming that they don't wish to be injured, why do so many people lack safety awareness? There are several answers to this question.

*Life*SKILLS:

Analyze Your Safety Awareness . . . .

The teens in this photo are demonstrating their safety awareness by buckling their seat belts. You can protect yourself from many accidental injuries by being safety-conscious and practicing behaviors that promote safety as well.

To analyze your safety awareness and behavior, answer the following questions on a separate sheet of paper. Thousands of 10th-graders answered similar questions when they took the *National Adolescent Student Health Survey*, a project developed by health educators and funded by agencies of the U.S. Department of Health and Human Services. Later in this chapter, you will discover how your behavior and safety awareness compare to that of these 10th-graders.

1. How many times in the past month did you ride with a driver who had used alcohol or drugs?

0 times	7–10 times
1–3 times	11–20 times
4–6 times	Over 20 times

2. Did you wear a seat belt the last time you rode in an automobile?

Yes   No   Don't remember

3. How often do you wear a helmet when riding a bicycle?

Never	Usually
Rarely	Always
Sometimes	

4. How often do you warm up before exercising?

Never	Usually
Rarely	Always
Sometimes	

5. How often do you swim alone or in a restricted or unsupervised area?

Never   Sometimes

Once you have identified behaviors that place you at risk of being injured in an accident, work on modifying these risky behaviors to protect yourself.

(FIGURE 27-2) **Not paying attention to what you are doing is a factor in many accidents.**

Ignorance and lack of caution can lead to dangerous situations. For example, Rob is on the school swimming team. While out with friends, he decided to swim across a small river to show his ability. Rob assumed the current was not very strong. However, he was swept downstream and had to be rescued by people fishing from a small boat. Rob did not know the strength of the current. He exercised poor judgment and was not cautious. Among young people, such lack of caution can stem from the feeling that "it can't happen to me."

The use of alcohol and other drugs increases risky behavior and carelessness as well. A person is far more likely to attempt a foolish—even dangerous—act if he or she is under the influence of alcohol or other drugs.

A person's emotional state can also contribute to risky behavior. For example, someone who is angry is likely to act on impulse and with little or no regard for what might happen. Such a person may drive over the speed limit, putting himself or herself and others at risk. Someone suffering from depression may also be indifferent to personal safety and may act in a way that could lead to an accident.

Peer pressure can influence individuals to take unnecessary risks. For example, Meda was with a group of friends when they found a fallen tree that made a bridge over a deep gorge. Her friends took turns walking on the tree to cross the gorge. Meda could see the tree wasn't steady, but her friends dared her to cross and she did. Everyone, at some point, has been dared to do something dangerous. Taking a dare, even though the results could be fatal, becomes a test of one's courage, but it is neither mature nor responsible behavior.

Personal responsibility is the key to avoiding accidents. To discover whether your behavior demonstrates safety awareness, complete the Life Skills activity on page 591.

Review

1. What is the leading cause of death among young people 15 to 24?

2. Name and describe the two factors that contribute to avoidable accidents.

3. **LIFE SKILLS: Practicing Self-Care** This week, eliminate or modify at least one behavior that contributes to your likelihood of having an accident.

4. **Critical Thinking** Can infants and toddlers engage in risky behaviors that lead to accidents? Support your answer with examples.

27.2 Vehicle Safety

- Recognize factors that contribute to motor-vehicle accidents.

- Identify behaviors that reduce the risk of being injured in a motor-vehicle accident.

- List some ways to maintain a bicycle for safety.

- Identify behaviors that reduce the risk of being injured in a bicycle accident.

Riding in or on any vehicle involves risk. And because of their size, weight, and the speed at which they travel, motor vehicles have great potential for doing damage. Now look again at Figure 27-1 and recall that motor-vehicle accidents account for more deaths than any other kind of accident. For these reasons alone, vehicle safety should be a priority for you.

As a teenager, you may already have a license and be driving. You probably also ride with friends. Unfortunately, drivers under the age of 24 have more accidents than drivers in other age groups. There are also more deaths from motor-vehicle accidents among 15- to 24-year-olds than in any other age group. In fact, three-fourths of all accidental deaths in this age group are related to motor vehicles. Half of these deaths also involve alcohol. By learning to avoid certain risky behaviors, you could avoid having an accident that could result in injury or death.

Behavior and Auto Accidents

As with accidents in general, motor-vehicle accidents are usually linked to human behavior. The automobile in Figure 27-3 was demolished in an accident, and the driver and passengers were injured. Quite possibly, the driver's behavior was at fault.

Using alcohol or other drugs is a behavior that is a factor in many motor-vehicle accidents. In Chapters 13 and 15, you studied some of the effects of these substances: reaction time is slowed, judgment is impaired, and general awareness is lowered. Thus, a person driving under the influence of alcohol or other drugs is not in full control of a vehicle that can be a deadly weapon.

The effects of alcohol and other drugs on the body are discussed in Chapters 13 and 15.

(FIGURE 27-3) **Alcohol is a factor in at least half of all automobile accidents.**

Other behaviors that increase the risk of having an accident are speeding and reckless driving. Mark is a high school senior who enjoys driving his own car. But in three months he has received three speeding tickets. His response is, "What's the big deal? I like to drive fast." This attitude is dangerous to Mark and to others.

For several reasons, speeding increases the risk of accidents and injuries. One reason is a driver's reaction time (the time between deciding to apply the brakes and applying them). Although reaction time is usually less than one second, a car moves some distance in that second. And a car traveling at 45 mph goes much farther in that time than a car traveling at 25 mph. Furthermore, a car traveling at a faster speed has a longer braking distance and takes more time to stop. Finally, the faster a car is traveling upon impact, the more likely it is that people will be seriously injured. So speeding increases both the likelihood that an accident will occur and the risk of serious injury or death.

Reckless driving is careless behavior. Being distracted from driving for just a moment—tuning the radio, talking to a passenger, reading signs or a road map, or trying to get a wasp out the window—can get you into trouble. Even more serious are deliberate actions, such as not obeying traffic rules and signs, trying to turn or pass with too little time, or running a light.

Reducing Auto Injuries

Avoiding automobile accidents is the best way to reduce your risk of injury. The first step is never drink and drive or ride in a car with a driver who is under the influence of alcohol or other drugs. If you know someone is under such influence, try to keep him or her from driving.

Obeying traffic laws, including posted speed limits, will also reduce your risk of being involved in an auto accident. If you know someone who disregards safe driving practices, is careless, or takes chances behind the wheel, don't ride with that person.

10th Graders Who Rode With Drivers Who Had Used Alcohol or Other Drugs

Number of Times	Male	Female	Total
0 times	57.0%	54.0%	55.6%
1-3 times	23.4%	30.8%	27.0%
4-6 times	7.6%	7.1%	7.4%
7-10 times	4.5%	4.5%	4.5%
11-20 times	3.1%	1.8%	2.5%
over 20 times	4.4%	1.8%	3.2%

(FIGURE 27-4) **This is how the 10th-graders who participated in the *National Adolescent Student Health Survey* responded to the question: "How many times in the past month did you ride with a driver who had used alcohol or other drugs?"**

Seatbelt Use Among 10th Graders

Wore Seat Belts	Female	Male	Total
Yes	39.9%	40.3%	40.1%
No	58.3%	57.6%	57.9%
Don't Remember	1.8%	2.1%	1.9%

(FIGURE 27-5) **This is how the 10th-graders who participated in the *National Adolescent Student Health Survey* responded to the question: "Did you use a seat belt the last time you rode in a vehicle?"**

When you drive, practice **defensive driving** to avoid accidents. Defensive driving involves expecting other drivers to drive recklessly, like changing lanes suddenly or turning from the wrong lane. You will be better able to handle such situations if you assume they might happen.

Wearing a seat belt is the best way to reduce your risk of being injured or killed in a car accident. Forty-six percent of people killed in auto accidents were not wearing seat belts.

Safety and Other Motor Vehicles

Motorcycles, minibikes, snowmobiles, and all-terrain vehicles (ATVs) are other types of motor vehicles. They are fun to ride, but they can also be dangerous. In accidents involving these vehicles, the risk of serious head injury is very high. Approximately 60 percent of 10th-graders surveyed reported having recently ridden on a motorcycle or minibike, but less than 30 percent reported that they always wore a helmet.

To protect yourself from injury, take the following safety measures when riding on one of these vehicles. Always wear a helmet to reduce your risk of suffering a serious head injury. Wear goggles to protect your eyes, especially if the vehicle has no windshield. Sturdy, close-fitting clothing can also help prevent an injury in the event of an accident. Obey all traffic laws as you would when driving a car. Don't use alcohol or drugs or ride with someone who has.

Bicycle Safety

As with any vehicle, there are hazards involved in bicycle riding. And once again, risky behavior and carelessness—the human factors—contribute to many bicycle accidents.

When Billy's shoelace got caught in his bicycle chain, it resulted in an accident. Clothing catching in the chain or wheels is a leading cause of bicycle accidents. The sudden jamming of the chain or wheel can cause the rider to be thrown from the bike. When riding a bicycle, make sure your laces are tucked into your shoes or tied so that they hang toward the outer side of your shoes. It is also best to wear clothing that is closefitting.

Losing control of a bicycle can also result in an accident. Hitting a hole or turning suddenly to avoid a person walking can cause a rider to lose control. As with motor

defensive driving:

driving as though you expect other drivers to drive recklessly.

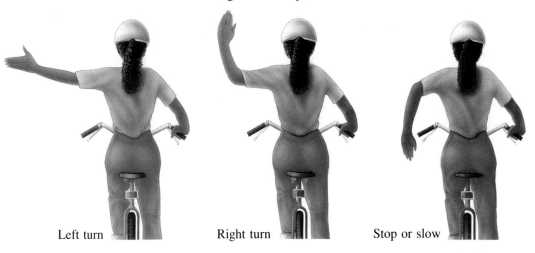

Left turn   Right turn   Stop or slow

(FIGURE 27-6) **By warning the traffic behind you that you intend to change direction or speed, you can help to protect yourself from being injured in an accident while riding a bicycle.**

(FIGURE 27-7) **Serious cyclists wear specialized equipment to reduce their risk of having an accident or being seriously injured in an accident.**

vehicles, maintain control by not speeding and ride defensively.

Bicyclists must generally obey the same traffic laws as other vehicles. A bicycle, for example, should be ridden in the direction that traffic flows. Hand signals, as shown in Figure 27-6, should be used to signal a change in direction or speed. If you ride at night, your bicycle should be equipped with lights and reflectors.

Sometimes bicycle accidents are caused by mechanical problems with the bicycle. Maintaining the bicycle in a safe condition is important. Keep the fenders, spokes, pedals, and handlebars undamaged and tightly attached. Adjust the saddle height and handlebars for comfortable fit. Keep the chain lubricated, and be sure it is in good condition. The bell or horn, lights, and reflectors should be working perfectly. Keep the tires filled with air, and check them for wear, leaks, or embedded pebbles and nails.

The cyclists in Figure 27-7 are skilled riders—they race bicycles. Notice that they are wearing helmets. But as Figure 27-8 indicates, 10th-grade bicycle riders

Bicycle Helmet Use Among 10th Graders

Helmet Is Used	Female	Male	Total
Never	94.3%	89.2%	91.6%
Rarely	2.9%	5.2%	4.1%
Sometimes	1.4%	3.4%	2.5%
Usually	0.7%	1.7%	1.3%
Always	0.7%	0.4%	0.6%

(FIGURE 27-8) **This is how the 10th-graders who participated in the *National Adolescent Student Health Survey* answered the question: "How often do you wear a bicycle helmet when riding a bicycle?"**

almost never wear helmets. Head injuries account for the majority of fatal injuries in bicycle accidents. Deciding to wear a helmet will reduce your risk of being seriously injured or killed in a bicycle accident.

Pedestrian Safety

People riding in motor vehicles are not the only victims of motor-vehicle accidents. People are often struck and killed by motor vehicles while crossing the street. Some accidents occur when young children run from between parked cars into the street. In other accidents, people are hit by a vehicle when they cross a busy street carelessly. Don't assume that a car will stop for you or that it will turn if its turn signal is on. Frequently, impairment from alcohol or other drugs is a factor in these accidents.

Only about one-third of 10th-graders questioned said that they always or usually cross busy streets at the corner. At busy intersections, pedestrian walk signs may be provided, and there is usually at least a painted crosswalk. Once again, the behavior you choose affects the probability that you will be involved in an accident.

Review

1. Describe two factors that contribute to motor-vehicle accidents.

2. What are some ways that a person can reduce his or her chances of being injured in a motor-vehicle accident?

3. List some ways to maintain a bicycle for safety.

4. What are some ways that a person can reduce his or her chances of being injured in an accident while riding a bicycle?

5. **Critical Thinking** Some drugs, such as stimulants, increase awareness and may cause a person to react more quickly. Why, then, would a person who is under the influence of such a drug still be a hazard when driving a motor vehicle?

27.3 Safety at Home and at Work

Objectives

- Recognize the relationship between accidents that frequently occur in the home and personal behavior.

- Identify potential accident hazards in the home and in the community.

- Recommend steps to reduce the potential for accidents in the home and in the community.
  ■■ LIFE SKILLS: Problem Solving

- Identify ways to maintain safety in the workplace.

People spend much of their time at home. Most adults and some teenagers also spend part of their day at the place where they work. Unfortunately, accidents are common in both places. This section contains tips that will help you reduce your risk of accidental injury at home and at work.

Safety Around the Home

Look again at Figure 27-1. Many of the types of accidents listed are likely to occur at home. Most falls, which are the cause of the second greatest number of accidental deaths, do not occur outdoors while hiking or climbing but in the home. Accidents involving fires and poisons are also most likely to occur at home. So making sure that your home is a safe place to be is extremely important.

Falls About 50 percent of fatal accidents that occur in the home are due to falls. The chances of dying in a fall increase with age. In fact, for people over 65, falls make up from one-third to one-half of all accidental deaths! Young children are also more likely to be injured or killed in falls, often as a result of climbing onto or off of furniture and other items.

Many falls occur on staircases. Surprisingly, however, falls on level surfaces are more numerous and cause more fatalities. Examine the photos in Figure 27-9 for hazards that could lead to falls. Notice the objects on the floor at the top of the staircase. Anyone could stumble over one of these objects and fall down the stairs. The curled rug is another hazard that could lead to a fall. Finally, that highly polished floor may look very nice, but it could easily cause someone to slip and fall. Check your home for such hazards when you go home today.

The following are some measures that can be taken to help reduce the risk of falls:

- If you have staircases, the handrails should be sturdy and the steps should have nonslip treads or flat carpeting.
- Floors should be kept free of clutter—toys, electrical cords, or books—that could cause someone to trip.
- Frayed rugs and broken floor tiles should be repaired.
- The bottom of the bathtub should have a nonskid texture. If elderly people live in the house, there should be handrails on the walls beside the bathtub as well.
- Floor mats in the bathroom should also be nonskid to prevent slipping when stepping into and out of the tub or shower.

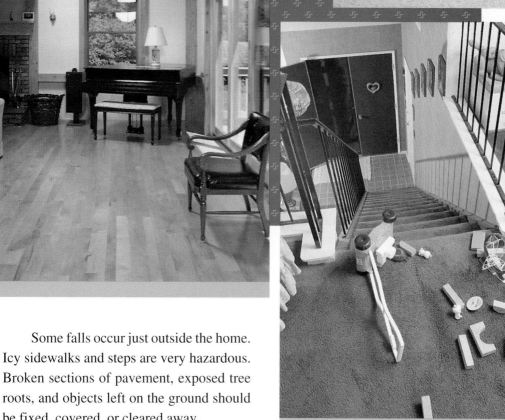

Some falls occur just outside the home. Icy sidewalks and steps are very hazardous. Broken sections of pavement, exposed tree roots, and objects left on the ground should be fixed, covered, or cleared away.

Fires Fires are the third most common cause of accidental death in the home. Careless smoking, often in connection with alcohol use, is a leading cause of home fires. Other causes include faulty electrical wiring and faulty heating units, cooking accidents, children playing with matches, and improper use of fireplaces.

Carelessness, whether while cooking, smoking, or using electricity, contributes to many household fires. Use the following list to check your home for fire hazards:

- Do not overload electrical outlets.
- If you have fuses, use only fuses of the specified amperage. If you have circuit breakers, keep them in good working order.
- Have the heating system inspected regularly by a professional.
- If you have a fireplace, use a protective metal screen and have the chimney cleaned regularly.
- Keep the kitchen stove free of grease.

All homes should have smoke detectors and fire extinguishers. But in a recent study, about 20 percent of students questioned reported not having smoke detectors in their homes. Smoke detectors should be located on every floor and should be tested regularly to make sure they are working. It's a good idea to make a chart showing the dates smoke detectors have been checked. Fire extinguishers should be placed in kitchens, basements, and storage areas to deal with small fires.

Finally, you should have a plan for escape in case of fire. The plan should be practiced, and all family members should take part in fire drills. If a fire does break out in your home, observe the following safety precautions:

- If possible, alert the other members of your household, and leave by one of the exits established in your escape plan.

- If there is smoke, cover your nose and mouth with a wet cloth, drop to the floor, and crawl toward the prearranged exit.
- If a closed door is warm to the touch, do not open it. There could be fire on the other side of the door.
- Close doors behind you, if possible.
- Once outside, call the fire department from the nearest phone.
- If your hair or clothing catches on fire, stop, drop, and roll to extinguish the flames. Do not run.

Electrical Safety Faulty electrical wiring and improper use of fuses can result in fires. Electricity also presents an additional danger. **Electrocution** is death resulting from the passage of electric current through the body. About 1,000 people are accidentally electrocuted each year.

Many electrical accidents involve appliances that are not installed or used properly. Any electrical appliance that is not working properly should be unplugged right away. It should be repaired by a qualified

electrocution:

death resulting from the flow of electrical current through the body.

technician, or it should be replaced. Never attempt to fix an appliance that is plugged into an outlet!

Careless use of electrical appliances around water is very dangerous. Because water is a good conductor of electricity, someone who is wet or has wet hands can become a pathway for electric current. Avoid using hair dryers and other appliances in the bathroom. Never place a radio or other electrical device near a tub or sink. Bathroom outlets should have built-in circuit breakers.

A worn electrical cord is both a fire hazard and an electrocution hazard. Inspect the electrical cords in your home. Tell a parent or guardian about any defective wiring that you find.

Electricity is especially dangerous to young children. They should not be allowed to play with electrical cords or appliances nor permitted to plug in or unplug

(FIGURE 27-11) **This outlet has a built-in ground fault protector to break the circuit automatically in case an electrical appliance comes in contact with water.**

such appliances. Outlet caps should be placed over electrical outlets to keep young children from sticking objects into the holes.

Poisoning Most cases of accidental poisoning involve children under five. These children may swallow medicines, cleaning chemicals, pesticides, or other poisons. Improper storage of poisonous substances or failure to put them away after use are the most common ways that poisons get into the hands of youngsters.

To make your home safer for children, all medicines should be placed in cabinets that are out of a child's reach. Cleaning fluids and other poisonous materials should not be stored under sinks or in closets where children can reach them. A locked cabinet is the best storage location. Since basements are often collection places for a variety of dangerous chemicals, they should be inspected carefully and childproofed.

Older children and adults can also be victims of accidental poisoning. Storing liquids in plastic soda bottles is a very dangerous practice that can lead to someone accidentally drinking a poisonous material. Always store materials in their original containers, and make sure they are clearly marked.

Sometimes people are accidentally poisoned when handling pesticides and weedkillers. Before using any of these chemicals, read the label carefully and follow the instructions given. When using such products, you should wear gloves. If you spray pesticides indoors, the windows should be open, and it is a good idea to go outside afterward. If you need to spray outdoors, do not do so on a windy day.

Accidental poisoning can also result from taking medicine that was prescribed for someone else. Since your present health condition can affect how you react to a drug, you should take only medicines that were

Carbon Monoxide: A Deadly Poison

Each year in this country, as many as 1,500 people die from accidental exposure to carbon monoxide (CO), an odorless, colorless, tasteless gas, and 2,300 people use it to commit suicide. Carbon monoxide poisoning is generally the result of defective heating and cooking systems, the burning of certain fuels and solid waste products, or cigarette smoke. The following steps will reduce your risk of CO poisoning:

Never leave a car running in the garage, especially if the garage door is closed or if the garage is attached to your house.

Put carbon monoxide detectors in your home.

Make sure fuel-powered equipment is working correctly and is properly ventilated.

Keep your car windows rolled up when you are in heavy traffic, especially if you are in enclosed space, such as a tunnel.

(FIGURE 27-12) **Carbon monoxide causes more deaths in the United States than any other environmental poison. You can take a few easy measures to protect your family. (Source: Wayne State University School of Medicine.)**

prescribed for you. Combining drugs is another risky behavior. It can result in a drug interaction that is dangerous to your health. Such a situation is also a case of accidental poisoning.

Everyone should inspect his or her home for poison hazards and take steps to poisonproof it. One step that is a must is to have the telephone number of the nearest Poison Control Center next to your phone. By calling that number, you can get instructions for helping someone who has been poisoned.

Safety in a Disaster

An event that seriously affects the lives and health of the people living in one or more communities is called a **disaster.** Many disasters, such as storms and earthquakes, are acts of nature. People have no control over such events. However, it is possible to reduce your risk of injury from these events.

disaster:

an event that affects the lives and health of people in one or more communities.

Thunderstorms Thunderstorms are powerful but short-lived events that are most common in spring and summer. Although

most thunderstorms would not be considered disasters, strong winds that sometimes accompany thunderstorms can blow objects around and cause widespread damage as well as injuries.

The most dangerous aspect of any thunderstorm is the lightning. Lightning is a gigantic discharge of electricity. It often strikes the tallest object in the area. However, the electricity can move from an object to your body if you are nearby. More people are killed each year by lightning than by any other weather-related event.

To reduce your risk of being injured during a thunderstorm, observe the following precautions:

- If you are outdoors, try to find shelter in a building or car.
- If you are on or in water, such as a lake or swimming pool, leave the water immediately. High winds, waves, and lightning are dangerous to boaters and swimmers.
- Never stand under a tall, isolated tree or other tall object.
- If you are in an open area, discard anything that might attract lightning, such as a large metal belt buckle, metal-frame backpack, or golf club. Crouch down to avoid being the tallest object in the area.
- If you are indoors, close the windows and stay away from them. Do not use the telephone, computer, or other electrical appliances. If lightning strikes a nearby electrical transmission line, the electricity can be transferred to you.

Tornadoes Like thunderstorms, tornadoes are most common in the spring and summer. Although they are fairly brief, the winds in tornadoes can be as high as 300 mph. Thus, tornadoes are able to destroy homes and send objects, including cars, flying through the air. The following are some safety tips to follow if a tornado is sighted or a warning is issued in your area:

- Try to get indoors, then go to the lowest part of the building. Basements and interior bathrooms, closets, and hallways on the ground floor will provide the most protection.
- Stay away from windows and doors. Windows may be shattered by the winds. Doors can be ripped from their hinges and thrown about.
- If you are in a vehicle or mobile home as a tornado approaches, get out of it and go to a safer place. A tornado can overturn most vehicles and mobile homes. If you cannot get indoors, lie in a ditch or the lowest place you can find.

Hurricanes Hurricanes are strong tropical storms that occur most often in late summer and fall. Hurricane winds range from 75 to more than 150 mph, and the rain from a hurricane is usually very heavy. Hurricanes are very large storms that may travel great distances. Fortunately, there is usually some time to prepare for a hurricane. Observe the following precautions if a hurricane is forecast for your area:

- If you live along the coast, be prepared to leave if local officials advise it. The huge ocean waves and flooding produced by a hurricane do great damage to coastal areas and are a major cause of injuries and deaths from these storms.
- Have a supply of canned food, drinking water, flashlights, fresh batteries, candles, and first-aid materials in your home.
- If possible, board up windows or tape the inside of each pane. Place indoors all objects that might be blown away if left outside, such as lawn chairs or bicycles.
- Remain indoors until authorities advise that the storm is over. Once outside, avoid downed electrical wires and flooded areas.

(FIGURE 27-13) **Severe thunderstorms, like the one shown here, can produce dangerous lightning, damaging winds, hail, heavy rain, flash flooding, and even tornadoes. If you live in a part of the country that is prone to these types of storms, learn to recognize the signs of an approaching storm, and know what to do to protect yourself from storm-related injuries.**

(FIGURE 27-14) **This building collapsed during an earthquake in San Francisco, CA. In earthquake-prone areas, building codes now specify earthquake-resistant designs.**

Earthquakes An earthquake is a sudden movement of Earth's crust. Earthquakes are brief, lasting only a minute or two. However, one earthquake can mean others will occur over the next few days. Powerful earthquakes and their aftershocks can cause great damage and loss of life. In North America, most serious earthquakes occur near the West Coast. Safety during an earthquake is often a matter of thinking quickly. The following are suggestions that could save your life:

- If you are outdoors, get away from buildings and other tall objects. Material falling from them could injure or kill you.
- If you are in a car, pull over but remain in the car.
- If you are indoors, stand in a doorway between rooms or get under a heavy table. Stay away from windows, doors with glass panes, and objects that might shake loose from walls.

Other Disasters Although many disasters are caused by nature, some, such as gas explosions and forest fires, often result from the activities of people. During any disaster, follow the instructions of the emergency workers in charge. It is a good idea to listen to the emergency information on a local radio station so that you know what to do.

Assaults

A personal attack in which you are threatened or harmed is called an **assault.** Many assaults occur in connection with robberies, but some assaults, such as sexual assaults, are often committed by people known to the victim. Therefore, to reduce your risk of being assaulted, take precautions and be alert when you are alone with someone you are acquainted with as well as when interacting with strangers. Consider the following safety precautions:

assault:

a personal attack in which you are threatened or harmed.

Ways to avoid being a victim of violence are discussed in Chapter 20.

- When at home, keep doors locked both day and night. Never unlock the door for a stranger. If a service person comes to the door, have the person show identification at a window.
- Never let a stranger know that you are home alone, even if the stranger is on the telephone. If you receive a threatening or obscene phone call, hang up and then call the police.
- Do not walk outside alone, particularly at night. Even when you are with friends, avoid deserted areas, alleys, and poorly lighted parks.
- When in a car, keep the doors locked. At night, keep the windows partially rolled up. If a stranger approaches your car, drive away.

If you are attacked, let good judgment determine your actions. Escape if you can. If your attacker has a weapon, do not try to resist unless you think that your life is in immediate danger. Afterward, report the attack to the police.

Occupational Safety

Many people are injured or killed each year in job-related accidents. According to a study by the National Safety Council, personal behavior—such as being careless and disregarding safety requirements—is a factor in 82 percent of these accidents. Close to 20 percent of work-related accidents are caused wholly by such behavior. Faulty machinery and unsafe working conditions also contribute to many injuries and deaths.

As a student, you are preparing for your future occupation. Some occupations, such as mining and the manufacturing of chemicals and explosives, are obviously risky. But as the graph in Figure 27-15 indicates, agriculture, construction, and transportation can also be considered risky occupations.

What Would You Do ?

Making Responsible Decisions

Your On-the-Job Safety Is Threatened

Suppose that you work for a company that uses hazardous materials in its everyday operation. You like the job and the people you are working with. Then one day, one of your co-workers shows you a copy of the *Material Safety and Data Sheet* for a chemical that you use frequently, saying that you should read it carefully.

Material Safety and Data Sheets are government publications that contain information about the hazards of chemicals and the types of protective clothing and equipment that are needed for handling them safely. After reading the data sheet, you realize that you have not been provided with the proper protective equipment. What would you do?

Remember to use the decision-making steps:

1. State the Problem.
2. List the Options.
3. Imagine the Benefits and Consequences.
4. Consider Your Values.
5. Weigh the Options and Decide.
6. Act.
7. Evaluate the Results.

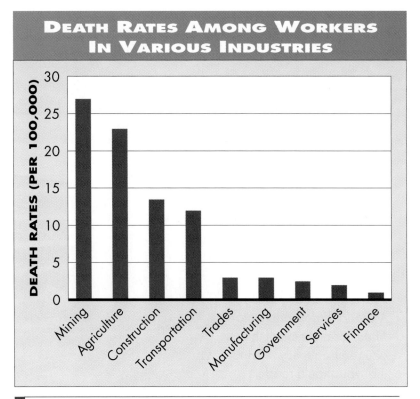

DEATH RATES AMONG WORKERS IN VARIOUS INDUSTRIES

DEATH RATES (PER 100,000)

30

25

20

15

10

5

0

Mining
Agriculture
Construction
Transportation
Trades
Manufacturing
Government
Services
Finance

(FIGURE 27-15) **This data supplied by the Bureau of Labor Statistics indicates the most hazardous occupations. Remember that both you and your employer are responsible for your safety.**

The Occupational Safety and Health Administration (OSHA) is a federal agency that sets safety standards in the workplace. State and local governments may also set standards for safety in various occupations. Fire safety, requirements for storing large amounts of chemicals, and the types of safety equipment that workers must wear are examples of factors the government regulates. In industries that expose workers to dangerous materials such as poisonous vapors and radiation, the government sets limits on how much exposure a worker is permitted to have.

Work-related illnesses and injuries affect close to two million Americans each year. Many workers once employed in the asbestos industry developed serious lung diseases as a result of contact with asbestos. Illnesses caused by contact with irritating or toxic materials continue to affect the health of many workers each year. To practice protecting yourself at work, complete the "What Would You Do?" activity on page 605.

Although the accident rate in the workplace has, in general, been declining, such accidents are still an important factor in the total number of accidental injuries and deaths. The same principles that apply to accidents in general also apply in the workplace. Both employers and employees are responsible for ensuring safe working conditions and preventing accidents.

Review

1. Cite some examples of how careless behavior can contribute to accidents in the home.

2. What unsafe conditions can you identify in your home that might lead to accidental falls? to electrical accidents?

3. ■■ **LIFE SKILLS: Problem Solving** Review the fire safety of your home. Then develop a plan to improve it. Discuss your plan with a parent or guardian. With his or her assistance, put your plan into action.

4. What federal agency oversees the safety of workers? List three ways this agency helps protect workers from injury on the job.

5. **Critical Thinking** Choose one of the occupations shown on the graph in Figure 27-15. What potential hazards associated with that occupation might be regulated by government agencies to help ensure the safety of the workers?

27.4 Recreational Safety

Section

Objectives

- *Recognize potential hazards in recreational activities.*

- *Identify ways to reduce the risk of accidents in recreational activities.*
  ■ **LIFE SKILLS: Problem Solving**

Activities such as swimming, hiking, and playing baseball provide fun and exercise, and can reduce stress. Recreation also involves risk, but there are things you can do to reduce the risk of accidents and injury.

Sports and Safety

The student in Figure 27-16 is on a high school track team. But right now he is not running; he is warming up. Figure 27-17 gives information about warm-up practices among 10th-graders who exercise or play sports outside of school.

Warming up stretches ligaments and tendons—tissues that connect bones and hold muscles to bones, respectively.

(FIGURE 27-16)
Warming up protects against sports injuries.

Warm-up Practices of 10th Graders

Warm Up Before Exercises	Female	Male	Total
Never	9.8%	14.9%	12.5%
Rarely	11.1%	14.1%	12.7%
Sometimes	20.7%	18.1%	19.3%
Usually	22.7%	20.7%	21.6%
Always	35.7%	32.1%	33.8%

(FIGURE 27-17) **This is how the 10th-graders who participated in the *National Adolescent Student Health Survey* answered the question: "How often do you warm up before exercising?"**

(FIGURE 27-18) **In-line skaters wear helmets, kneepads, and other protective gear to reduce their risk of injury.**

The importance of warming up properly is discussed in greater detail in Chapter 3.

The most serious injuries in sports often occur because of the misuse—or lack of use—of protective equipment, such as helmets and mouthguards. As with riding bicycles and motorcycles, playing sports often requires the use of safety equipment. Batting helmets are required in Major League Baseball. No player in the National Football League would head onto the field without his helmet and his mouthpiece. Professional athletes reduce their risk of injury by using such equipment. Unfortunately, amateurs don't always take the same precautions.

In-line skating, which has become very popular, is a sport that causes many broken bones and other injuries. Notice the types of protective equipment being worn by the skater in Figure 27-18. If you participate in this activity or a similar activity, such as roller-skating or skateboarding, be sure you are protected against accidental injury—wear protective equipment.

Warming up also slowly increases the flow of blood, and thus oxygen, to muscles. Beginning physical activity without first warming up can result in pulled ligaments and muscles and in muscle strains. Such injuries are common among people who participate in sports.

Water Safety

As you might suspect, the recreational activity that results in the greatest number of accidental deaths is swimming. Figure 27-1 shows that drowning is the fourth leading cause of accidental death. This is partly because a great number of people head for the water on hot summer days.

Swimming and Diving Many drownings occur in home swimming pools. Because of carelessness, young children are frequently the victims. Children should never be left unattended in or near a pool. Many communities require pools to be fenced so that youngsters cannot wander into them.

Older children and adults, including those who can swim, are also victims of drowning. In many cases, risky behavior contributes to an accidental drowning.

Water Safety Among 10th Graders

Behavior	Never Do	Sometimes Do
Swim alone	62.0%	38.0%
Swim in restricted/ unsupervised area	70.7%	29.3%

(FIGURE 27-19) **This is how the 10th-graders who participated in the *National Adolescent Student Health Survey* answered the question: "How often do you swim alone or in restricted or unsupervised areas?"**

Swimming alone and swimming in an unprotected area are two such behaviors. Figure 27-19 shows that approximately one-third of 10th-graders surveyed engage in such risky behavior at least some of the time. To reduce the risk of drowning, you should always swim with a friend and swim where there are lifeguards.

Learning how to swim will reduce your risk of drowning. But if you are in trouble in deep water and no immediate help is available, a technique called **drown proofing** can help keep you afloat. The steps in drown proofing are as follows:

- First, take a deep breath and relax, allowing your face to enter the water. Let your legs hang down in the water and your arms float forward.
- Next, slowly exhale underwater. Then move your arms downward as you kick with your feet to raise your head above the surface.

- Take a breath and begin again.

Diving into water requires caution. Learn to dive from someone who knows how. Diving into an unknown area or into water of unknown depth is a very risky behavior. Hitting bottom can cause serious head, neck, and spinal injuries. Paralysis or death often results from such accidents.

Boating Safety Some drownings occur as a result of boating accidents. The girls in Figure 27-20 are reducing their risk of drowning by wearing life jackets. All boaters, regardless of their swimming ability, should wear a life jacket *at all times.*

Boating accidents usually result from carelessness or risky behavior. As with a car, speeding in a boat can result in loss of control. Alcohol is another factor in many boating accidents. Ignoring warning buoys and other markers and weaving unnecessarily can also result in accidents. Sudden

**drown
proofing:**

a technique to stay afloat that can be used even by those who cannot swim.

(FIGURE 27-20) **As these girls are demonstrating, every person in a boat should have his or her own life jacket.**

(FIGURE 27-21) **This is one safe way to manage a campfire. Campfires should not be left unattended and should be extinguished completely before the last person leaves the area.**

storms and overloading a small boat with people and equipment can result in capsizing, or turning the boat over. If you use a boat, learn how to handle it. Also learn the rules of boating safety.

Wilderness Safety

Hiking, camping, and hunting are outdoor activities enjoyed by millions of people. Although some people are injured by animals such as bears and snakes, such incidents are rare. Hazards such as getting lost, losing control of a fire, and being injured with firearms are far more common.

Hiking in the woods involves thinking ahead. For example, when Gary and Lien planned to hike for a day, they bought a trail map of the area, studied it, then let their parents know where they were going and when they expected to return. As they hiked, Gary and Lien followed the marked trail. They did not try to cut across the forest to reach their destination. Carrying a map and staying on the trail helped Gary and Lien avoid getting lost. Letting people know where they were going hiking was

another good precaution to take in case something went wrong.

Careless handling of campfires and other fires results in many forest fires each year. Damage runs into the millions of dollars, and loss of life can result. Like the campfire in Figure 27-21, a campfire should be built only in a fire ring of metal or stone, or in a stone fireplace. Using inflammable liquids to start a fire or get it burning better is a risky behavior that can result in injuries. A fire of any kind must never be left unattended. If the fire danger in the area is high, it is unlikely that campfires will be permitted.

Hunting accidents often result from carelessness. If you hunt, wear bright red or orange clothing so that you are visible to other hunters. When preparing to shoot, be sure that your target is the intended animal. If you are not certain about what you are shooting at, don't shoot. Firearms should always be stored and transported unloaded. But when you are handling a firearm, always assume that it is loaded until you have checked it!

Review

1. *In what ways do careless and risky behaviors contribute to accidental drowning?*

2. **LIFE SKILLS: Problem Solving** *Discuss some ways to reduce injuries resulting from participation in sports.*

3. *Critical Thinking Review your recreational activities for potential hazards. Identify actions that you can take to reduce the risk of accidents.*

Highlights

Summary

- To reduce the risk of accident or injury in a motor vehicle, wear seat belts, obey traffic laws, drive defensively, and never drive after using alcohol or other drugs or ride with a driver who is under the influence of alcohol or other drugs.

- To reduce the risk of accident or injury on a bicycle or motorcycle, wear a helmet and proper clothing, avoid speeding, ride defensively, obey traffic laws, and keep bikes in good working order.

- To prevent injury from fire, install fire extinguishers and smoke detectors; properly maintain heaters, stoves, fireplaces, and electrical wiring; and have a home evacuation plan.

- To reduce the risk of accidental poisoning, keep medicines and other poisonous substances out of the reach of children, store them in properly marked original containers, and follow the directions for their proper use.

- To reduce the risk of carbon monoxide poisoning, install CO detectors in your home and make sure fuel-powered equipment and cars are working and are properly ventilated.

- To reduce the risk of being assaulted, keep doors locked, avoid strangers and deserted areas when alone, and when in a car, keep the doors locked.

- To reduce the risk of accidental injury or death when engaging in outdoor activities, use the proper safety equipment and follow the safety rules for each activity, tell someone where you are going and when you will be back, and never go alone.

Vocabulary

accident any unexpected event that causes damage, injury, or death.

risk an action that is potentially dangerous; the chance of injury.

safety awareness knowledge about risks and how to reduce them.

defensive driving driving as though you expect other drivers to drive recklessly.

electrocution death resulting from the flow of electrical current through the body.

disaster an event that affects the lives and health of people in one or more communities.

assault a personal attack in which you are threatened or harmed.

drown proofing a technique to stay afloat that can be used even by those who cannot swim.

Concept Review

1. Knowledge about risks and how to avoid them is called _____.

2. _____ accidents account for more deaths than any other kind of accident.

3. You can reduce your risk of being involved in a motor-vehicle accident by not riding with a person who _____.

4. _____ involves expecting other drivers to do the unexpected.

5. Wearing a _____ when riding a bicycle or motorcycle can reduce your chances of suffering a serious injury.

6. For people over 65, _____ cause from one-third to one-half of all accidental deaths.

7. Two types of devices that reduce the risk of injury from a fire are _____ and _____.

8. Electrical appliances should never be used around _____.

9. _____ have the highest risk of being poisoned by improperly stored medicines and poisons.

10. _____ and _____ are the most dangerous aspects of a thunderstorm.

11. The two most risky occupational fields are _____ and _____.

12. The recreational activity that results in the greatest number of accidental deaths is _____.

13. All boaters should wear a _____.

14. For safety, firearms should be stored and transported _____.

Expressing Your Views

1. Why do you think so many teenagers fail to use safety equipment such as seat belts and bicycle helmets, as indicated by the tables in Figures 27-5 and 27-8?

2. Many states have laws that require passengers in cars to wear seat belts and motorcyclists to wear helmets. Do you think people should be required by law to wear such equipment? Why or why not?

3. If your one-year-old cousin were coming to your house for a visit, what changes would you make in your home to assure his safety?

Life Skills Check

1. Practicing Self-Care
You just got a late-night job at a restaurant downtown, about eight blocks from your house. What safety precautions could you take to make sure you get home safely each night?

2. Making Responsible Decisions
Your friend tries to talk you into going swimming and diving with him in a water-filled quarry late one night. You try to persuade your friend to do something less dangerous, but he won't listen. What should you do?

3. Problem Solving
Tornadoes, hurricanes, and earthquakes are natural disasters. What could you do at home and at school to prepare for each of these disasters?

Projects

1. Divide a sheet of poster board into four parts. Create a "What Is Wrong?" picture in each part, showing an important safety rule being violated. Present these to the class and have volunteers guess what is wrong in each picture.

2. Working with a group, contact your local police department, hospital, or EMS squad to find out the numbers and types of accidents that are most common in your community. Ask if any prevention programs are being used to reduce these problems. Present your findings to the class along with your suggestions for ways to limit these accidents.

3. Develop a fire-escape plan for your home. On a floor plan of your home, diagram the escape routes for every member of your household, and make a list of the directions to share with your family.

Plan for Action

The home is a place where people spend much of their time, and unfortunately, it is a place where accidents are common. Create a plan to help reduce the risk of accidents in your home.

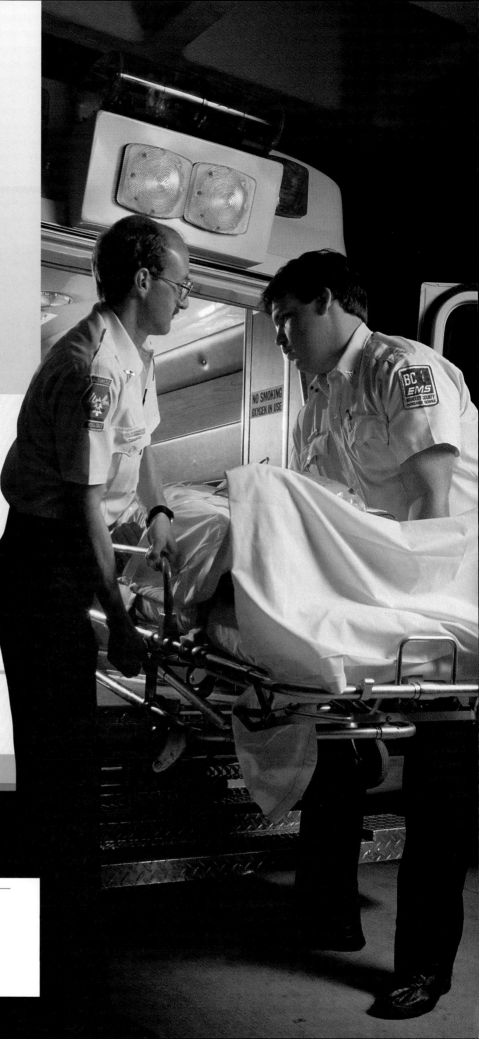

CHAPTER 28

First Aid and CPR

◆ ◆ ◆ ◆

People who are not physicians but are trained to give emergency medical care often help save lives. With training in First Aid and CPR, you may someday be able to save a life as well.

The late afternoon sun hung low in the sky as Sonya walked home, her jacket collar pulled up against the chill autumn air. She heard the swish of leaves behind her, and Masahiko streaked past her on his bicycle.

While Sonya watched in horror, a driver pulled out of a parking place directly in front of Masahiko. Unable to brake in time, Masahiko crashed into the side of the car and flew off his bike. His head slammed into the curb.

Looking around for help, Sonya saw no one. She was on her own. What should she do first? How could she tell whether Masahiko was injured seriously? How should she treat his injuries?

Section 28.1 — *Emphasis* **Emergency Priorities**

Objectives

- *Name the first steps that should be taken during an emergency.*
  - **LIFE SKILLS: Intervention Strategies**

- *Describe the procedure for rescue breathing.*
  - **LIFE SKILLS: Intervention Strategies**

- *Describe the procedures for stopping or controlling bleeding.*
  - **LIFE SKILLS: Intervention Strategies**

- *Describe the signs of shock and its treatment.*

- *List two facilities that might offer CPR training.*
  - **LIFE SKILLS: Using Community Resources**

You never know when an emergency may occur, or in what form. You could be needed to help the victims of a hurricane, earthquake, car collision, or sporting accident. A classmate could be wounded in metal shop, or a person near you at a concert could collapse from a drug overdose.

In this chapter you will learn how to respond in an emergency when lives could depend on what you do next. You will learn what to do first and about treatment priorities. After studying the chapter, you will know how to treat many medical emergencies. To find out how to get specialized training, complete the Life Skills activity on page 617.

First Aid: The Difference Between Life and Death

First aid is the immediate care given until professional medical personnel arrive at the

first aid:

emergency care given to an ill or injured person before medical attention is available.

scene of an accident or sudden illness. Sonya knew that appropriate first aid could mean the difference between life and death or between recovery and permanent injury. If Masahiko was seriously injured, Sonya had only seconds to act. Prompt medical attention was essential.

Sonya made an effort to compose herself, then ran to Masahiko. He wasn't moving. The car's driver, a man of about 50, seemed unhurt but was almost hysterical. He was beating his fists on the steering wheel and crying, ''What have I done?'' Grabbing the man by the arm, Sonya asked him to calm down, find a telephone, dial 911, report the emergency, and then come back to tell her when the ambulance and paramedics would arrive.

Sonya then turned to Masahiko, tapped him on the shoulder, and asked in a loud voice, ''Masahiko, are you all right?''

Masahiko still did not move, but he groaned and muttered ''No.''

Steps To Take in a Medical Emergency

1. Survey the scene.

2. Rescue the person if necessary to prevent further injury.

3. Send for help.

4. Treat life-threatening conditions.

5. Go for help yourself if nobody has done so.

6. Identify other injuries, and provide first aid.

7. Remain with the victim until medical help arrives. Monitor breathing and heart rate, and prevent further injury.

(FIGURE 28-1) **Follow these steps if you are the first person to arrive at the scene of a medical emergency. Do not risk your safety to rescue or give first aid to someone else.**

First Steps in a Medical Emergency

If you are the first person to arrive on the scene of a medical emergency, there are certain steps you should take. Figure 28-1 summarizes these steps. Do not, however, risk your own safety in order to rescue or provide first aid to another person.

Survey the Scene First, evaluate the situation and the area for possible danger to you or to the victim. Determine what happened and how many people are injured. Look for and call out for bystanders who can help you.

Rescue If you can do so safely, your next step is to rescue anyone whose life is endangered. For example, a victim in deep water or a burning car will need to be moved to a safer place before you can even begin to check for injuries. Otherwise, *never* move an injured person until medical help arrives. Moving someone who has a head, neck, or spine injury could cause further serious, or fatal, injury. Instead, do what you can to protect the person from further injury.

Because of the nature of Masahiko's accident, Sonya knew that he could have suffered a head or neck injury. Until she knew the full extent of Masahiko's injuries, moving him would risk making his injuries worse. Luckily, a motorist stopped to help. Sonya asked her to park her car crosswise in the street, providing a barrier to protect Masahiko from oncoming traffic. This was Sonya's rescue step.

Send for Medical Help If others are available, send them for medical help. If not, shout ''Help!'' Do not leave the injured person, even to go for help, until you have checked for and treated life-threatening conditions. People who call for help in an emergency should use the procedure given at the top of page 619.

First Aid and CPR Training . .

You never know when you may be called upon to give emergency care to help save a life, prevent further injury, or simply lessen discomfort. People in certain professions are required to study emergency care. For example, boat captains, flight attendants, police officers, and firefighters all need to be certified in first aid and cardiopulmonary resuscitation (CPR). Knowledge of emergency care can also be extremely important for anyone who spends time in the wilderness. On a hunting or backpacking trip, for instance, people may be miles from the nearest vehicle or medical facility. First aid may be the only care an injured person receives for hours, days, or even weeks.

First-Aid Training If you have not already taken a first-aid course, you may wish to do so. The course will give you hands-on experience that will help you remember the techniques described in this book. First-aid courses are given by the American Red Cross, local community colleges, and hospitals.

CPR Training Someday you may be able to save a life if you are trained in CPR. A local chapter of the American Red Cross or the American Heart Association will be able to tell you where training is available.

1. To find out where you can receive training in first aid or CPR, call a hospital, college, or organization such as the American Red Cross or the American Heart Association.

2. Find out when the courses are given.

3. Ask if there is a charge for the course.

• Caution: If you haven't had CPR training, *do not* attempt to administer CPR. If done improperly, CPR can cause further injury or even death.

Rescue Breathing:

1. Open the airway by tipping the head back and lifting the chin.

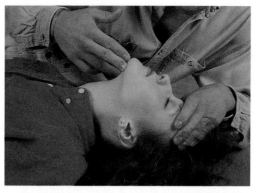

2. Check for breathing by placing your cheek next to the person's nose and then listening and feeling for breath.

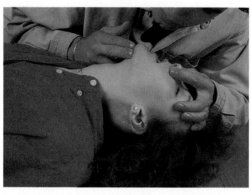

3. If the victim is not breathing, pinch the nose closed with one hand while keeping the airway open by holding the chin up with the other hand.

4. Tightly seal your mouth over the victim's mouth and blow air into the victim's lungs, or hold the mouth closed and blow into the nose.

5. After two breaths, check for a pulse and signs of breathing.

6. Continue to give one slow breath every 5 seconds until medical help arrives, you are too exhausted to continue, or the victim begins to breathe.

For young children and babies:
1. Blow into the mouth and nose at the same time.
2. Give one breath every 3 seconds.
3. Use smaller puffs of breath because the lungs are smaller.

(FIGURE 28-2) **Procedure for opening the airway and giving rescue breathing. Note the differences in the procedure for young children and babies.**

When calling for help:

- Speak slowly and clearly.
- Tell exactly where the victim is, including town, address, description of the location, and any landmarks.
- Describe the accident, number of people injured, and nature of the injuries.
- Ask what you should do while waiting for medical help to arrive, and listen carefully to the instructions.
- Let the other person hang up first, to be sure they have no more questions or advice for you.

Initial Assessment Priorities

When giving first aid, treat life-threatening conditions first by following the procedure described below.

Determine Whether the Victim Is Conscious

Tap the person on the shoulder, and ask loudly, ''Are you all right?'' Even though Masahiko answered ''No,'' his answer told Sonya that he was conscious.

Check ABCs

If the person is unconscious, call 911, then check the ABCs: *A*irway, *B*reathing, and *C*irculation of blood. Check in this order, because a person whose airway is closed will stop breathing, and when breathing stops, the heart will soon stop circulating blood. Sonya checked all ABCs at once by asking if Masahiko was all right. Anyone who can talk, however poorly, has an open airway, can breathe, and has a beating heart.

Airway

To open the airway, turn the person gently onto his or her back after checking for head, neck, and spinal injuries. If the person has these injuries, *do not move him or her until the head and neck have been stabilized.* With one hand under the chin and one on the forehead, lift the chin and tip the head back. See Figure 28-2.

Breathing

Check for breathing by putting your cheek next to the person's nose and mouth and listening and feeling for breath. Also watch the chest to see if it is rising and falling. If the victim is not breathing, start rescue breathing at once, using the procedure shown in Figure 28-2. If the person's airway is open, your breath should easily enter his or her lungs and the chest will rise. The person should exhale automatically when you remove your mouth. If your breath will not enter the victim's lungs, repeat the procedure for opening the airway. If it still doesn't work, follow the procedures on page 629 for an unconscious choking victim.

Circulation of Blood

Look for a pulse to determine whether the heart is working. The easiest pulse to find is usually at the carotid artery in the neck. You can find it in the groove on either side of the windpipe, beside the Adam's apple. See Figure 28-3.

(FIGURE 28-3) **Check circulation by feeling for a pulse at the carotid artery on the side of the neck.**

CPR for Adults:

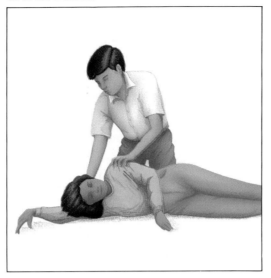

1. Lay the person on his or her back.

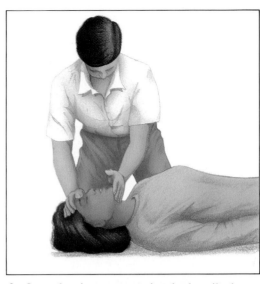

2. Open the airway as previously described, and give two slow breaths.

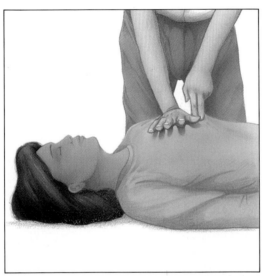

3. Place the heel of your hand nearest the victim's head on the victim's breastbone, starting two finger-widths up from the bottom of the breastbone. Then place your other hand on top of your first hand.

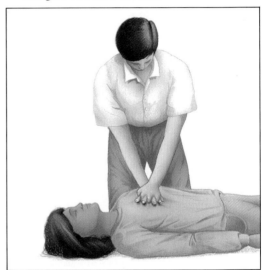

4. With your arms straight, put your weight on your hands and press down on the sternum, and then release the pressure so the chest can expand. Give compressions at a rate of 80–100 thrusts per minute. After 15 compressions, give two rescue breaths. After 4 sets of 15 compressions and two breaths, stop and check for a pulse. If the victim has a pulse, stop giving compressions. If not, repeat this step.

CPR for Young Children and Babies:
Follow the same basic procedure as above, with the following exceptions.
1. An infant should be held, with one hand supporting the head.
2. Use two or three fingers instead of your hands.
3. Depress the sternum only 1/2 to 1 inch.
4. Give compressions at a rate of 2 per second, about as fast as you can do it.
5. After 5 compressions, give one slow breath.

(FIGURE 28-4) **Procedure for performing CPR. Note the differences for young children and babies.**

CPR Procedures *Do not attempt cardio-pulmonary resuscitation (CPR) with the instructions from this or any other book unless you've had CPR training. Instead, study these directions for an understanding of CPR, or use them for review if you are trained.*

If you cannot find the victim's pulse and you are trained in the procedure, you may be able to save his or her life with CPR. Figure 28-4 describes CPR. When administered improperly, CPR can cause further injury.

CPR is hard work. It's all right not to start CPR if you don't feel up to it or aren't sure you know how. If you do start CPR, be prepared to keep on without pause until you are relieved by another trained CPR provider or you are simply too exhausted to continue. If, after CPR, the victim's heart starts beating on its own, check for breathing and continue rescue breathing if needed.

CPR is given *only* when a person is not breathing and has no pulse (heartbeat). If CPR is successful in reviving the person, he or she will most likely require additional medical treatment to remain alive. For this reason, you should always call 911 for emergency medical assistance, or send someone to call for you, before beginning CPR.

Control Bleeding If an injured person's breathing and circulation are adequate, the next priority is to stop severe bleeding that is life threatening. Use direct pressure, as described in Figure 28-5.

If you do not have sterile gauze, you will have to make do with whatever clean materials you have. Sanitary napkins make ideal dressings, and sometimes they are available when other materials are not. They are sold in restroom vending machines, and female bystanders may be carrying them in their purses.

cardiopulmonary resuscitation (CPR):

a lifesaving procedure designed to revive a person who is not breathing and has no heartbeat.

Procedure to Stop Bleeding

1. Wash your hands with soap and water. Cover your hands with something that blood will not soak through.

2. If possible, cover the wound with a sterile dressing, such as gauze.

3. If possible, raise the bleeding wound above the heart.

4. Use your palm to apply pressure directly over the dressing on the bleeding wound. Keep applying pressure for at least 10–12 minutes to give blood clots time to form.

5. If bleeding starts again, resume pressure until it stops.

6. Wrap a pressure bandage tightly over the dressing. If blood soaks through, place another dressing on top.

7. Monitor ABCs.

(FIGURE 28-5) **Follow these steps to stop or control severe bleeding. If it is not stopped, the victim might bleed to death before medical help arrives. Take steps to avoid direct contact with someone else's blood.**

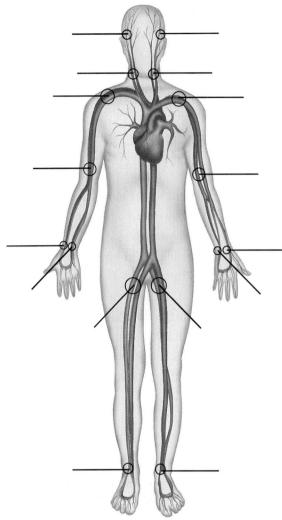

(FIGURE 28-6) **The body's pressure points are the locations of main arteries and veins. To stop bleeding, apply pressure with your fingers or the heel of your hand to the pressure point *nearest* the bleeding wound that is *between* the heart and the wound. Except for the head, this point would be just above the wound.**

If direct pressure and elevation do not stop bleeding on the head or a limb, apply pressure to the main artery supplying blood to the affected part. The places on the body where these arteries are located are called pressure points. Figure 28-6 shows the body's pressure points.

Try to avoid direct contact with someone else's blood, because it can carry an organism or a virus that causes a very serious disease such as hepatitis or AIDS. If your first-aid kit has rubber gloves, wear them. Otherwise, put something between your hand and the wound. You can, for example, place the victim's hand between yours and the wound. After providing first aid to a bleeding victim, wash your hands immediately. Meanwhile, do not eat or drink, and keep your hands away from your eyes, nose, and mouth.

Treat Poisoning As soon as the victim's ABCs are in order and bleeding is stopped, you must treat poisoning if it has occurred. (You'll learn how to treat poisoning later in the chapter.)

Assess Other Injuries The next step in handling an emergency is to look carefully for other injuries. If the person is conscious, ask him or her what hurts. Very gently, inspect the person's body for anything that looks broken or not quite right.

Look for Signs of Shock You must watch for signs of shock when helping an injured person or a victim of a serious accident. Shock is a condition in which the body's vital processes are severely depressed—circulation and breathing slow way down. If the shock process is not stopped, the person will die. Shock can result from major injuries, loss of blood, burns, poisoning, electric shock, allergic reactions, and sudden temperature changes. Even when the victim of a serious accident appears uninjured, he or she can have hidden injuries that could cause shock. Shock can kill a person even when the injury that triggered it is not life threatening.

The signs of shock include rapid, shallow breathing; rapid heartbeat; a weak pulse; pale, clammy skin; blue color around lips and fingernails; nausea; apathy; agitation; and weakness. Any time you start to see signs of shock, call immediately for an ambulance equipped with oxygen.

Treatment for Shock To treat shock, keep the victim calm, lying face up with feet elevated 10 to 12 in. This helps supply more blood to the brain. Victims who are unconscious or who may vomit should have their head turned to the side so they will not choke on their vomit. Do not elevate the feet if you suspect a head injury.

A shock victim's normal body temperature needs to be maintained. In some cases, you may need to cool an overheated shock victim, but usually you need to keep the victim warm. Cover or wrap the victim just enough to maintain body temperature.

Sonya treated Masahiko for shock immediately after checking his ABCs and determining that he was not bleeding severely. She knew that treatment is much more likely to be successful, and to save a life, if it is begun *before* signs of shock have started to appear. This means that any time you are treating an injury that might cause shock, you should begin treating for shock right away.

Because it was a chilly afternoon and getting colder, Sonya sent the motorist who had stopped to help to get blankets from a nearby home. She covered Masahiko with them and watched him closely. Knowing that a shock victim's breathing or heartbeat can fail, Sonya was ready to provide rescue breathing and, because she was trained, start CPR if necessary.

Attitude

It is important to approach an emergency situation with a calm and reassuring attitude. If you are upset or panicky, the victim will sense it and possibly become more panicked. That's why Sonya took control of herself after Masahiko's accident. Try to reassure injured persons that you will help them and that they will be all right. Since fear can bring on shock, calm reassurance can help save a victim's life. The power of fear is so great that people have died after being bitten by nonpoisonous snakes!

Good Samaritan Laws

Most states have a Good Samaritan law that will protect you from legal liability if you help someone in an emergency. As long as you do your best, use common sense, and are careful not to cause additional harm to the injured person, the law should shield you from any legal problems. However, do not attempt procedures in which you have had no training.

• • • • •
Review

1. *What are the first three steps that should be taken in an emergency?*

2. ▪▪ *LIFE SKILLS: Intervention Strategies Explain how to provide rescue breathing.*

3. ▪▪ *LIFE SKILLS: Intervention Strategies How would you stop severe bleeding?*

4. *When and how would you treat a person for shock?*

5. ▪▪ *LIFE SKILLS: Using Community Resources Find out where you can get CPR and first-aid training in your community. Write or call two of these places and obtain a schedule of their classes.*

6. *Critical Thinking You are the first to arrive on the scene of an auto accident where there are two victims. What should you do?*

• • • • •
Objectives

■ *Differentiate among five types of wounds and their treatment.*

■ *Describe the first-aid steps for a fracture.*

■ *Describe the first-aid procedures for suspected injuries of the head and spine.*

Injuries that may require first aid occur frequently in daily life. For instance, during athletic events, outdoor activities, or even common activities in the home, you or someone nearby may require first aid for an injury. The following are the recommended first-aid treatments for some common types of injuries.

Wounds

Wounds are among the most common injuries. Figure 28-7 shows the different kinds of wounds and their treatment.

Infections With any type of wound, there is danger that an infection will later develop as invading bacteria begin to multiply. Signs of infection include fever, pus, pain, swelling, and redness. Immunization helps prevent tetanus, which is a very serious, life-threatening infection. Anyone with a serious wound should have a tetanus shot if they are not up-to-date with their immunizations. Anyone who has not had a tetanus shot for more than 10 years should get one whether they have a wound or not.

Scalp Wounds The head has a large supply of blood, and much of it runs near the surface. Consequently, a relatively minor wound of the scalp or face can cause profuse bleeding that must be stopped by applying pressure.

Embedded Foreign Body When a foreign body, such as a piece of glass or even a knife, is embedded in a body part, it should be left in place. If you attempt to take it out, you could easily do more damage than good. Bandage the wound with the foreign body held in place, and get medical help for the victim.

Avoid Contact With Blood Remember that blood and some other body fluids can carry organisms and viruses that cause serious diseases. It is extremely important to avoid all contact with blood or other body fluids when you are treating another person's bleeding wounds.

Blisters

Pressure or friction may cause blisters. Treat blisters as follows:

- Protect an unbroken blister and avoid further pressure or friction.
- Wash a broken blister with soap and water and cover it with a sterile dressing.
- If a blister is likely to break,
  1. wash the area with soap and water,
  2. *do not* attempt to pierce and drain the blister,
  3. cover the blister with a bandage or sterile dressing,
  4. watch for signs of infection, and seek medical attention as needed.

Laceration

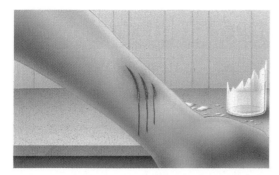

In a laceration the skin is torn. Lacerations usually bleed freely, and risk of infection is small·if the wound is kept clean. First-aid steps:
1. Stop severe bleeding.
2. Make sure the cut is clean.
3. Cover with a clean sterile dressing.
4. Take victims with serious wounds to a doctor. Even if you doubt that seeing a doctor is necessary, go anyway. It's best not to take chances.

Incision

An incision is a clean cut, as made by a knife or a sharp piece of glass. Incisions usually bleed freely, and risk of infection is small if the wound is kept clean. First-aid steps:
1. Stop severe bleeding.
2. Make sure the cut is clean.
3. Cover with a clean sterile dressing.
4. Take victims with serious wounds to a doctor. Even if you doubt that seeing a doctor is necessary, go anyway. It's best not to take chances.

Abrasion

Skin is scraped away or worn away in an abrasion. A skinned knee from falling off a bicycle is a typical abrasion. Many abrasions do not bleed very freely and will need to be washed clean to avoid infection. First-aid steps:
1. Rinse carefully under running water.
2. If dirt or other matter is stuck in the abrasion, try to remove larger pieces by wiping very gently with a clean, damp cloth or tissue. Small bits can be left in place, if necessary, and will work their way out as the wound heals.
3. Cover with a bandage.

Puncture

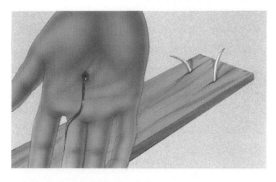

A puncture wound is a hole through the skin and into deeper tissue. Stepping on a nail causes a puncture wound. Puncture wounds are difficult to clean, because they are deep and narrow. They seldom bleed much, and risk of infection is greater than with other kinds of wounds. First-aid steps:
1. Encourage the wound to bleed, to help clean it.
2. Wash the area around the wound to help prevent infection.
3. Because tetanus germs can thrive in a puncture wound, any victim of such a wound should be up-to-date on tetanus shots or make arrangements for a booster immediately.

Avulsion

In an avulsion, skin or another part of the body is torn off, or nearly torn off and attached by a flap of skin. First-aid steps:
1. Use direct pressure on the wound to stop the bleeding.
2. If a flap of skin is cut off or hanging loose, gently lay it back in place before bandaging the wound.
3. If a body part has been removed, send it to the hospital with the victim. If possible, wrap the body part in sterile gauze, place it in a plastic bag, and put the bag on ice, but don't delay getting the victim to a hospital.
4. Treat for shock.

(FIGURE 28-7) **Types of wounds and their treatment.**

First Aid for Fractures

1. Avoid moving fracture victims unless you need to move them out of danger or transport them to a medical facility. If medical help is on the way, keep the injured person still.

2. Treat fracture victims for shock.

3. Build a splint to hold the broken bone in whatever position you find it. Trying to straighten out a fractured bone could cause further damage.

4. Place the splint so it immobilizes both the broken bone and the joints immediately above and below the fracture.

5. Provide padding between the splint and the skin. For example, for a broken forearm, you can splint the break so the wrist is supported as well as the bone, and then support the forearm in a sling so the elbow doesn't move.

6. Don't make the splint too tight. Fractures often cause swelling. Check to make sure the victim has a pulse on the side of the splint away from the heart; that tells you that the splint is not too tight.

(FIGURE 28-8) **A splint prevents further injury by immobilizing a bone. Splints can be made from pieces of wood; from rolled-up magazines, newspapers, or pillows; or from pieces of stiff cardboard.**

Fractures

fracture:

a broken bone.

A broken bone is called a **fracture**. Fractures can be either open or closed. With a closed fracture, also called a simple fracture, the skin is unbroken. If the skin is broken at the site of the fracture, it is called an open fracture, or a compound fracture. Open fractures are more serious because germs and contamination that cause infection can reach the bone, making the fracture more difficult to treat.

Sometimes a fracture is obvious, because the bone is exposed or a limb is lying at a strange angle that would be possible only with a broken bone. Sometimes the victim cannot move toes or fingers without pain. You may even hear a snap as the bone breaks. Swelling, discoloration, or loss of movement are often present with fractures.

A fracture must be immobilized so that the bone can't move and further injure the victim. To immobilize a bone, use a splint as described in Figure 28-8. A splint is a rigid strip of wood, metal, or some other material that will not easily bend. Other parts of the body can also be used as a splint. For example, a broken leg may be bound to the other leg to immobilize the broken bone. If the fracture is open, cover the wound with a clean dressing before applying a splint. You may need to stop bleeding as well.

You won't always know whether an injury is a fracture or something else. Sometimes all you know is that the victim is in pain. To administer first aid, you need not be certain that the injury is a fracture. If you suspect a fracture, treat it as such and splint it.

Dislocations

In a **dislocation**, the end of a bone comes out of its joint. The dislocated joint will be swollen and deformed, and the person will feel severe pain. Dislocations should be splinted in the same way as fractures. For a dislocated shoulder, splint the upper arm with the elbow supported in a sling and the upper arm strapped to the side of the chest. This gives the dislocated joint the greatest possible support. Treat the victim for shock.

Neck and Spine

An accident victim who complains of pain in the neck or back may have a fractured neck or spine. Moving someone with a broken spinal column could paralyze or kill the person. If the slightest chance of a broken neck or back exists, do not move the person. Treat for shock, send for medical help, and stay until help arrives. Place your hands or a rolled-up blanket or coat on either side of the person's head to keep it from moving.

Head Injury

Any bump on the head that causes a victim to lose consciousness, even if only for a second or two, is potentially serious. Blood vessels sometimes break inside the skull, and then pressure may build and squeeze the brain. This can happen quickly or take place slowly over hours or days. Nausea, slurred speech, slowed breathing, convulsions, and loss of memory can be signs of a head injury, as can blood or body fluid leaking from the ears or nose.

You can sometimes find clues to internal head injuries by examining the pupils of the victim's eyes. Pupils are normally the same size on both sides, or nearly so, and they react to light, becoming smaller in bright light and bigger in dim light. If one pupil is significantly bigger than the other, or if the pupils do not react to light and dark, assume the individual has a serious head injury. You can check for reaction to light by shining a flashlight into one eye then the other, or by shading first one eye then the other from a strong light.

When you suspect a head injury, do the following:

- Treat for shock, but *do not* elevate the victim's feet.
- Stay with the victim, watching carefully for signs of deterioration.
- Monitor breathing. Be ready to give rescue breathing if needed, or CPR if you are trained. If you do so, however, do not tilt the head back. Keeping the head and neck still, pull the jaw forward. Use this procedure also when you suspect an injury to the neck or spine.

dislocation:

an injury in which the end of a bone comes out of its joint.

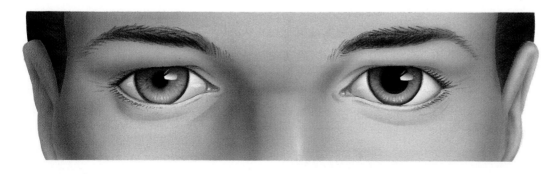

(FIGURE 28-9) **Examine the eyes if you suspect a head injury. If the pupils are not the same size or do not react to light, it may indicate a serious head injury.**

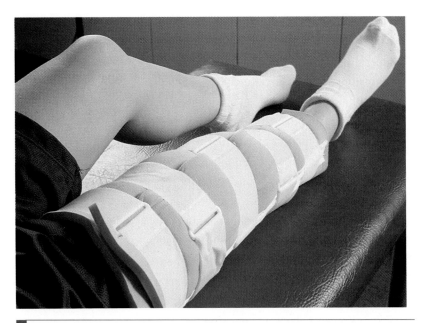

(FIGURE 28-10) **A splint can be used to immobilize a limb that has suffered a sprain or a strain, as well as to immobilize a fracture.**

With either a sprain or a strain, the victim will experience pain and swelling.

It can be difficult to tell a sprain or strain from a fracture. If you think the injury might be a fracture, you should treat it as a fracture instead of as a sprain. Leave off the elastic bandage and apply a splint instead. It never does any harm to treat a sprain or a strain as a fracture. Otherwise, use the procedure shown in Figure 28-11.

Internal Injuries

Following any accident, a victim may have injuries inside the body that you can't easily detect. Internal bleeding is especially dangerous. Pain in the chest or abdomen is cause for concern. When an accident victim seems to deteriorate without obvious reason, suspect internal injuries. The victim may turn pale, or the person's breathing and pulse may be unusually rapid. If you suspect internal injuries, treat for shock and get the victim to a doctor right away.

sprain:

a torn or stretched ligament.

strain:

a stretched or torn muscle or tendon.

Sprains and Strains

When a ligament is torn or stretched, the resulting injury is called a **sprain**. In a **strain**, the muscle itself is torn or stretched. Sharply twisting a joint, for example, may cause a sprain, while strains often occur when a person is lifting a heavy weight.

RICE–First Aid for Sprains and Strains

Rest: Do not use the injured part.

Ice: Use ice packs to prevent swelling.

Compression: Wrap the injured part in an elastic bandage.

Elevation: Elevate the injured part above the level of the heart.

(FIGURE 28-11) **Remember the steps for treating a sprain or a strain as RICE—Rest, Ice, Compression, Elevation.**

Review

1. *List and describe five types of wounds.*

2. *What steps should be taken for a fracture until the victim can see a doctor?*

3. *What is the most important thing to remember when giving first aid to a victim with a possible neck or spine injury?*

4. *Critical Thinking Assuming both wounds were minor, would it be more important to have a doctor examine a puncture wound or an incision? Explain.*

• • • • •
Objectives

- *Describe the first aid for a heart-attack victim.*

- *Explain what to do if you find a person unconscious from an unknown cause.*

- *Know how and when to perform the Heimlich maneuver.*

■■ **LIFE SKILLS: Intervention Strategies**

The most serious emergencies are those in which the victims would die or suffer permanent damage without intervention. For example, a classmate sitting next to you in the cafeteria could start choking. It is also possible that an individual could collapse in your presence from a heart attack or a stroke. Knowing what to do and acting quickly could save a life. The information in this section will help prepare you to give aid, should a life-threatening emergency occur.

Choking

A person chokes when something, such as a piece of food, gets stuck in his or her airway and prevents breathing. To save a choking person's life, you must act immediately. You don't have time even for a telephone call. Brain cells die when they are deprived of oxygen for even a few minutes. Unless the obstruction is removed immediately, a choking victim will die or suffer permanent brain damage.

Signs of Choking A choking victim will usually grab his or her neck. The victim may be breathing very shallowly, or not at all, and he or she may be trying to cough but be unable to do so. If you think someone is choking, do the following:

- Ask the person if he or she is choking and needs help. Because people need air to talk, a person who can talk is not choking.
- If the choking person is able to cough at all, encourage him or her to continue coughing as hard as possible.
- If other people are nearby, send someone to call for medical help.
- If the victim is unable or barely able to cough, take immediate action to dislodge the object blocking the airway.

The Heimlich Maneuver You can often dislodge an object from a person's airway by using the **Heimlich maneuver,** which is a series of sharp thrusts to the abdomen. These thrusts compress the lungs, forcing the air out. The air, in turn, sometimes pushes the obstruction out of the airway. The procedure to use when performing the Heimlich maneuver for a conscious person is shown in Figure 28-12.

If a person becomes unconscious, lay the person on his or her back. Using your finger, dislodge any obstruction from the person's throat. Alternate a rescue breath with 8 to 10 abdominal thrusts and a finger sweep until the obstruction is dislodged or help arrives. Don't give up hope. As the victim's body becomes starved for oxygen, the muscles in the throat will start to relax. You may suddenly be successful even after you have started to think it is too late.

Heimlich maneuver:

a series of sharp thrusts to the abdomen, used to dislodge an object from a choking person's airway.

The Heimlich Maneuver

1. Have the choking person stand up, positioning yourself behind him or her.

If a baby is choking, lay the baby face down on your lap with its head slightly lowered. With one hand supporting the baby's head, slap the baby's back forcefully five times. Then turn the baby on its back and give five *chest* thrusts to its breast bone, using only two fingers instead of your fist. Alternate back blows with chest thrusts until the baby's airway is clear. If the baby becomes unconscious, stop after each set of chest thrusts to check the airway and attempt to give two slow breaths.

If *you* are choking, you can perform the Heimlich maneuver on yourself. To do this, lean over the back of a chair, fence, or similar object, and thrust your abdomen into the object, hard, as shown in Figure 28-13.

2. Reach around the victim with both hands, placing one fist with its thumb side against the abdomen, a little above the navel and below the rib cage. Grasp the fist in your other hand.

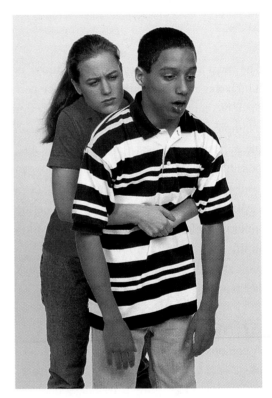

3. Make a sharp, hard thrust with your fist into the abdomen and up toward the rib cage. Continue making hard, vigorous thrusts until you dislodge the obstruction, or until the victim collapses and becomes unconscious.

(FIGURE 28-12) **The Heimlich maneuver. This lifesaving first-aid measure can dislodge an object that is causing someone to choke.**

(FIGURE 28-13) **If you begin to choke on an object while you are alone, you can use the Heimlich maneuver on yourself. One technique for doing so is being demonstrated here.**

In a choking emergency, you need to act immediately. Therefore, you may wish to practice the Heimlich maneuver in advance with a friend. However, you should fake the thrusts. You can cause damage by thrusting too hard when it is not needed.

Heart Attack

During a heart attack, part of the heart is not receiving enough blood, and the heart is not pumping well. The signs and symptoms of a heart attack include:

- sudden pain in the chest under the breastbone, possibly radiating into the arms, shoulders, side of the neck, or jaw
- weakness, nausea, or sickness
- rapid, weak, or irregular pulse
- pale or blue skin
- perspiration, anxiety, or fear

To treat a heart attack, follow the steps in Figure 28-14. **Cardiac arrest** may follow a heart attack, meaning that the heart will stop working altogether. In case of cardiac arrest, perform CPR if you are trained.

cardiac arrest:

condition in which the heart stops working.

Steps in Treating a Heart Attack

1. Sit or lay the victim down, propping up the head.

2. Help administer any heart medication the person may have, unless the person is unconscious.

3. Immediately send for an ambulance equipped with oxygen, and contact the victim's own doctor if possible.

4. Stand by in case rescue breathing becomes necessary.

5. In case of cardiac arrest, perform CPR if you have been trained.

6. Treat for shock.

(FIGURE 28-14) **In the event a person suffers a heart attack, you could save his or her life by acting quickly and following these steps.**

Unconsciousness

If a person becomes unconscious and you don't know why, check ABCs and send for help immediately. Check for medical alert identification that could tell you about any special medical condition. The information might appear on a bracelet, necklace, or anklet such as those shown in Figure 28-15. Some people carry medical alert information on a card, so check the victim's pockets and wallet.

While waiting for help to arrive, treat the individual for shock and stand by in case rescue breathing is needed. If the person vomits, turn his or her head sharply to the side to prevent choking. Use your finger, covered with a cloth if possible, to wipe out the mouth.

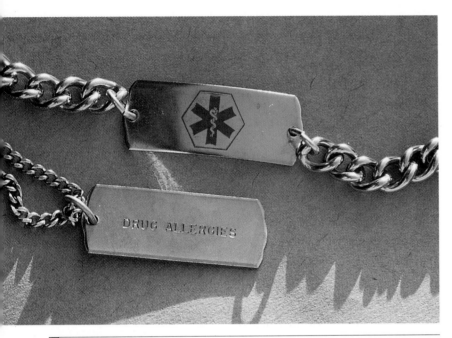

■ (FIGURE 28-15) **A medical alert identification tag warns of conditions such as diabetes, heart conditions, allergies, or even contact lenses.**

Convulsions

Convulsions may result from epilepsy, poisoning, high fever, or other conditions. During convulsions, every muscle suddenly becomes rigid, then the body starts jerking violently. The victim may also lose control of bowels and bladder. Convulsions can be frightening and upsetting to an observer. It is important to keep yourself calm while attempting to give aid.

Individuals who are convulsing should be prevented from causing themselves injury—for example, from rolling off a

Treatment for Stroke

1. Send for an ambulance equipped with oxygen, immediately.

2. Keep the stroke victim quiet and lying on the side in case of vomiting. If the victim vomits, make sure the head is turned sharply to the side, to reduce the chance of choking.

3. Treat for shock by keeping the victim warm, but do not raise the legs.

4. Be ready to give rescue breathing if necessary or CPR if you have been trained.

■ (FIGURE 28-16) **Some of the symptoms of a stroke are similar to other, less life-threatening conditions. If there is any doubt in your mind, follow these first-aid steps for treating a stroke.**

sidewalk into traffic. Loosen tight clothing, and remove any objects from the immediate area. Otherwise, there is nothing you can do except wait for the convulsions to stop.

Do not try to put anything into a person's mouth while he or she is convulsing or if he or she is unconscious. If the victim is unconscious, turn his or her head to the side. Observe the victim's breathing, in case you need to provide rescue breathing. The convulsions will go away in a minute or two. If the victim has medicine for convulsions, you may help administer it *after* the convulsions have stopped and *only* if the person is conscious. Victims who are unconscious after convulsions should be laid on their sides. Send for medical help, or take the individual to a doctor.

Stroke

In a **stroke**, also called a cerebral vascular accident, blood supply to part of the brain is obstructed because a blood vessel in the brain has burst or become plugged with a clot. Stroke victims may show some or all of the following signs and symptoms:

- dizziness or loss of consciousness
- difficulty in breathing or talking
- mental confusion or slurred speech
- partial paralysis on one side of the body
- mouth pulled sideways
- pupils of unequal size
- bright red face
- bulging neck veins

Figure 28-16 lists the treatment for stroke.

Something Wrong— Cause Unknown

If a person appears to be ill or in pain but you can't tell what the problem is, treat for shock and send for help. Watch the person in case rescue breathing becomes necessary.

What Would You Do

Making Responsible Decisions

Your Best Friend's Mother Collapses

You have just finished studying Section 28.3 of the First Aid and CPR chapter of this book. You are at your best friend's house, and as you close the book, your best friend's mother collapses and gasps that she is having chest pains. Her breathing is rapid and shallow. Her skin is pale and tinged with blue. What would you do?

Remember to use the decision-making steps:

1. State the Problem.
2. List the Options.
3. Imagine the Benefits and Consequences.
4. Consider Your Values.
5. Weigh the Options and Decide.
6. Act.
7. Evaluate the Results.

Review

1. Explain what to do for someone who is having a heart attack.

2. What is the first-aid procedure for a victim who is unconscious from an unknown cause?

3. **LIFE SKILLS: Intervention Strategies** Describe the steps and purpose of the Heimlich maneuver.

4. **Critical Thinking** Is it always possible to determine whether a victim is suffering from shock or a stroke? Explain.

stroke: *the rupture or blockage of an artery in the brain, leading to oxygen deprivation and damage to brain cells.*

● ● ● ● ●
Objectives

- *Contrast two health emergencies caused by heat, and compare their treatments.*

- *Know how to identify and protect your body from cold-related health emergencies.*
  ### ▪▪ LIFE SKILLS: Practicing Self-Care

- *Describe three types of burns and their treatment.*

- *List the steps to be taken when poison is swallowed.*

This section covers emergencies you could encounter—indoors or outdoors—at school, home, work, or sporting events.

Heat-Related Emergencies

Overexertion in too much heat can lead to emergencies that require first aid.

Heat Exhaustion   With heat exhaustion, a person collapses from heat, exertion, and loss of water and salt through perspiration. The victim starts to go into shock, and the body's cooling mechanisms may begin working too hard, actually over-cooling.

(FIGURE 28-17) **Vigorous exercise or hard work, especially during warm months, can result in heat exhaustion or heatstroke due to overheating and the loss of body fluids and salts. Knowing the difference between these two common conditions could help you save a friend's life.**

The person's skin will feel clammy (cool and moist). Other signs and symptoms include weakness, dizziness, headache, nausea, rapid and shallow breathing, and dilated pupils.

A victim of heat exhaustion should lie down in the shade and cool off. If the victim is conscious and not nauseated, replace body fluids by giving the victim plenty of drinking water. Suggest that the victim avoid heat and strenuous exercise for a few days, even when feeling better.

Heatstroke (Sunstroke) After working or exercising strenuously in a hot environment, a person can suffer from heatstroke. The skin becomes red and very hot and dry. With heat exhaustion, the body is still trying to cool off by perspiring freely. With heatstroke, the hot, dry skin tells you the body's mechanism for cooling itself is not working anymore. It has been overwhelmed by too much heat and exercise. The internal body temperature becomes very high—106° F or even higher. Heatstroke is life threatening. If the following steps are not taken to cool the body, the victim will die.

- Call EMS
- Move the victim out of the heat.
- Put the victim in cool (not cold) water, or apply wet cloths all over the body.
- If conscious, the person should drink water in small quantities.
- Take the victim to a hospital emergency room as quickly as possible.

Heat Cramps A cramp is a sudden, very painful knot in a muscle, often a leg muscle. Heat cramps are caused by exercising in conditions where too much body salt and water are being lost through perspiration. Generally, a cramp will go away if you stretch out the affected muscle. You can also give drinking water to a person with heat cramps to replace body fluids.

Treatment for Frostbite

1. *Cover the affected area, and provide extra blankets or clothing. Take the victim indoors if possible.*

2. *Gently thaw the frozen part by soaking in warm—not hot—water, wrapping in warm blankets, or treating with a warm object. Any water or object that feels hot on your own hand is too hot for thawing frostbite.*

3. *Stop applying heat as soon as the skin is flushed.*

4. *Avoid damaging tissue. Do not rub the affected area, since this may cause gangrene.*

5. *Keep the victim away from hot fires or stoves.*

6. *Do not allow the blisters to break.*

(FIGURE 28-18) **Frostbite may occur during exposure to extreme cold. If you must give first aid for frostbite, follow these steps, but wait until you are sure the frozen parts will remain thawed.**

Cold-Related Emergencies

Overexposure to cold or the loss of too much body heat can also lead to emergencies that require first aid.

Frostbite With frostbite, ice crystals form in the fluids of soft tissues of the body. Typically, whitish or yellowish spots appear on the nose, fingers, toes, ears, or cheeks. Blisters may develop later. To treat frostbite, follow the steps in Figure 28-18.

Frostbitten tissue has been injured and may take time to heal. Have the person gently exercise any affected parts except the feet. It is better not to thaw frostbitten tissue until you can keep the tissue thawed. Frostbitten tissue can be severely damaged if it thaws out and refreezes before it has a chance to heal. In most cases, a frostbite victim should consult a doctor.

hypothermia:

below-normal body temperature.

Hypothermia The prefix "hypo" means low, or under. **Hypothermia,** therefore, is a condition in which a person's body temperature is too low. This condition results not just from being exposed to cold but also from losing heat from the body faster than the body can rewarm itself.

As the body loses heat and its internal temperature begins to drop, the body takes steps to protect itself. First, some of the blood flow to the extremities (arms, legs, and head) is cut off. Shivering begins, to rewarm the body, and may become violent.

Eventually, the heart rate and breathing rate slow, the victim loses muscle strength and coordination, and other signs and symptoms such as slurred speech, fatigue, confusion, hallucinations, and irrational behavior may appear. Finally, the victim stops shivering. This means that the victim's body has lost the ability to rewarm itself.

Like heatstroke, hypothermia is a life-threatening condition. The treatment for hypothermia is described in Figure 28-19. To find out how to avoid hypothermia, complete the Life Skills activity on page 637.

Treatment for Hypothermia

If the victim is shivering:

1. A shivering person will recover if you eliminate further loss of heat. Move the victim to a warm place, wrapping him or her in coats, blankets, or sleeping bags to help the body rewarm itself.

2. Give warm drinks to rewarm the body from the inside, if the person can hold the glass alone. Never give alcoholic drinks to a cold person. Alcohol may make people feel warmer, but it actually increases heat loss.

If the victim has stopped shivering:

1. A person who has ceased shivering will die unless you rewarm his or her body. Get the person to a hospital if you can do it quickly.

2. Warm the central part of the body first, without warming the extremities. Soak the person in a warm—not hot—bath with arms and legs hanging out, or use warm objects such as water bottles or electric heating pads next to the trunk.

3. Giving warm drinks will help, if the person is conscious and sufficiently coordinated to hold the glass alone. A person without enough coordination to hold a glass is in danger of choking or breathing liquid into the lungs.

(FIGURE 28-19) **Follow these steps if you must give first aid for hypothermia.**

*Life*SKILLS:

Preventing Hypothermia . . . .

Preventing hypothermia is much easier than treating this life-threatening condition. Remember, it is easier to stay warm than it is to rewarm your body after it has lost heat.

As you get cold, 50 percent of your body's heat loss can be through your head and neck. This is because a large portion of the blood in your body flows through your head and neck, much of it near the surface. Air currents carry away heat as it radiates from your blood.

Water is a better conductor of heat than air is, and if it is cooler than your body temperature, it will conduct heat from your body faster than air. This is why you may feel cold in water that is 70°F , when air at 70°F is comfortable. Even though the water is not very cold, you can develop hypothermia if you stay in it for too long. Solids conduct heat even faster than liquids do, so you can also lose body heat quickly by lying or sitting on something cold.

Answer the following questions to see if you know how to prevent hypothermia.

1. If you are wearing a warm jacket and start to feel cold, what items of clothing might you add to prevent heat loss?

2. Why do you suppose people wore nightcaps before houses were heated efficiently?

3. Assume you are in water at 70°F, and the air temperature is 70°F. If you start shivering or feeling chilled, what should you do? Why?

4. Why should you put down a blanket before laying an injured person on the ground?

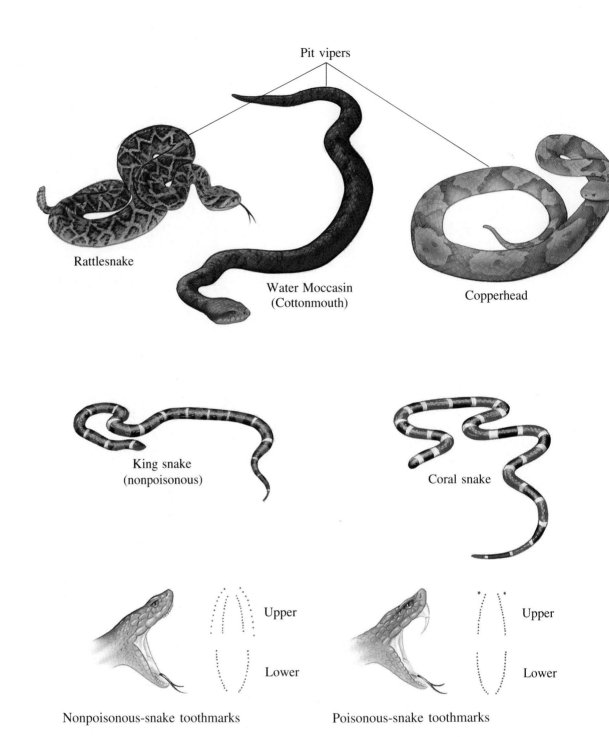

Pit vipers

Rattlesnake

Water Moccasin
(Cottonmouth)

Copperhead

King snake
(nonpoisonous)

Coral snake

Upper

Lower

Upper

Lower

Nonpoisonous-snake toothmarks

Poisonous-snake toothmarks

(FIGURE 28-20) **Any snake with a triangular head is dangerous. The coral snake, for which the harmless king snake is often mistaken, is the only poisonous snake in North America that does not have a triangular head. You can distinguish the coral snake from the king snake by remembering this rhyme: red on yellow kill a fellow, red on black, venom lack. Notice the difference between the toothmarks of a nonpoisonous snake, such as the king snake, and those of a poisonous snake, such as the pit vipers and the coral snake.**

Drowning

Drowning may occur in deep water some distance from shore, in a swimming pool a few feet from the side, or even in a bathtub. In a drowning emergency, *do not* attempt to swim to the victim unless you have received the proper training in water-safety and life-saving techniques. Instead, toss a flotation device or rescue line to the victim and then call for help.

Once retrieved, potential drowning victims who have stopped breathing must be given rescue breathing immediately and continually until they begin to breathe. If the victim was in deep water, you should begin rescue breathing as soon as the victim reaches shallow water. If it is necessary, provide CPR if you are trained to do so. Send for medical help immediately.

Snakebite

Only four of the hundreds of kinds of snakes in the United States are poisonous. They are pictured in Figure 28-20. The coral snake, which is related to the deadly cobra, is rarely seen. The others belong to a family of snakes called pit vipers, which includes rattlesnakes, copperheads, and water moccasins (also called cottonmouths). All pit vipers have a triangular-shaped head and two large fangs in the upper jaw.

A pit viper's bite usually leaves two prominent holes where the fangs went in. The poison is in the fangs, so if you are ever bitten by a pit viper that doesn't leave fang marks, don't worry. Even with a bite that does leave fang marks, a victim may not have been poisoned.

Snakebites are rarely fatal, but they often cause permanent damage that can sometimes make it necessary to amputate a limb. Therefore, a poisonous snakebite should be treated as a serious emergency. Take the following steps to treat a snakebite:

Procedure for Applying a Constricting Band

1. Tie the band 2 to 4 inches above any swelling from the bite, but not around a joint. The ideal band would be 1 to $1\frac{1}{2}$ inches wide, but a shoelace would serve if nothing else is available.

2. Check snugness. The band should be snug enough to dimple the skin all the way around, but still loose enough for you to slide a finger under it.

3. Check for a pulse below the band. If there is none, loosen the band until there is.

(FIGURE 28-21) **CAUTION: The purpose of a constricting band is to slow circulation just under the skin, where most poison travels, NOT to cut off circulation altogether.**

- Wash the wound with soap and water to reduce the chance of infection.
- To slow the spread of poison through the body, keep the person quiet and calm, preferably lying down.
- If the bite is on an arm or leg, keep the affected part below the level of the heart and follow the steps in Figure 28-21 to help slow the spread of poison.
- Monitor ABCs and watch for shock.
- Do not apply tourniquet, attempt to remove venom, or apply ice.

A snakebite victim needs medical treatment within four hours. Whenever possible, the victim should be carried to the doctor, rather than being allowed to walk. Fear and panic can aggravate snakebite symptoms, so you should try to be soothing and reassuring. If you are bitten when you are alone and you must walk for help, you should apply a constricting band and then walk at a slow pace, resting frequently, in order to keep your blood circulating as slowly as possible.

Stings

If you have been stung by a bee, hornet, wasp, or scorpion, you know it can cause intense pain, burning, and itching at the sting site. First aid for insect and scorpion stings includes the following steps:

- Examine the sting site carefully. If part of the stinger is still embedded in the wound, *do not* try to pull it out. It may have the poison sac still attached, and by grasping it, you can squeeze more poison into the wound. Instead, scrape it out with a fingernail, broken stick, or the edge of a credit card.

- Use a paste of baking soda, a towel soaked in ammonia, or ice to help reduce the pain and swelling.

- Observe the victim for a while. A small percentage of people are allergic to bee stings and can experience a severe, life-threatening reaction. Victims who are in obvious distress, feeling nauseated, dizzy, faint, or who are having trouble breathing should be treated for shock and be examined by a doctor right away.

- Stand by to perform rescue breathing, if necessary, or CPR if you are trained to give it.

Spider Bites

Of the thousands of species of spiders in the United States, only two are poisonous—the black widow and the brown recluse. The black widow's bite is painful and will make a victim extremely ill, but it is rarely fatal except to the seriously ill, the very young, or the very old. Only the female black widow is poisonous. The brown recluse spider's

(FIGURE 28-22) **The brown recluse (above) and the black widow (right). Both black widow and brown recluse spider bites require medical treatment. On rare occasions, they can be fatal.**

bite can form a bad sore in a few hours, but it is not likely to be fatal.

If you must give first aid for a spider bite, follow the steps below.

- Wash the bite with soap and water to reduce the chance of infection.
- Use a paste of baking soda and water, a towel soaked in ammonia, or ice to reduce the pain and swelling.
- Treat for shock and be prepared to give rescue breathing if necessary.
- Seek medical attention immediately.

Human and Animal Bites

The mouths of humans and other mammals are full of bacteria, so their bites carry danger of serious infection. To prevent infection, human and other animal bites should be washed with soap and water, then rinsed thoroughly under running water. Dress a bite as you would any other wound. For severe or infected bites, the victim should see a doctor. Because bites can cause tetanus, bite victims should receive tetanus shots if they are not up to date on immunizations.

The most serious risk from animal bites is rabies. This viral infection of the nervous system is always fatal without preventive treatment. After a bite, observe the animal for unusual behavior or signs of illness. Rabid animals may drool or be unusually calm or excited. If you can do it safely, confine the animal so that it can be examined by a veterinarian or health department official. *Do not* get near the animal in order to capture it, and *do not* handle it. Only a professional should do so. Rabies can always be prevented if treatment is started soon enough. However, the series of treatments is long and painful. Victims can avoid suffering through it if a doctor can be sure that the animal did not have rabies.

Hyperventilation

Hyperventilation is rapid breathing that may be accompanied by chest pains, tingling of the fingertips and around the mouth, dizziness, or fainting. Emotional distress or poor circulation to the brain can precipitate it. Hyperventilation lowers the level of carbon dioxide in the blood. The following treatment is designed to raise the blood level of carbon dioxide to normal.

- Try to calm the victim. Have the person sit and lower his or her head.
- Have the person breathe into a paper bag or cupped hands. Breathing exhaled air helps restore the normal level of carbon dioxide in the blood.
- Seek medical attention if the symptoms persist.

(FIGURE 28-23) **Your breath contains more carbon dioxide than the surrounding air. By breathing into a paper sack for a few minutes, you can raise the level of carbon dioxide in your blood and get rid of the symptoms of hyperventilation.**

Nosebleeds

A nosebleed is spontaneous bleeding from a nostril that usually results from drying and cracking of the membranes lining the inside of the nose. Most nosebleeds will stop on their own fairly easily. If the bleeding does not stop soon on its own, use the following procedure.

- Use latex gloves if it is necessary to come in contact with the victim's blood.
- Have the victim sit upright, lean slightly forward, and firmly pinch both nostrils closed for 10 to 15 minutes.
- Apply cold cloths firmly against the bleeding nostril.

- If the bleeding continues, try putting a plug of rolled-up gauze into the bleeding nostril. Do not use cotton for this purpose, because it could be hard to remove later.
- If the bleeding continues and nothing seems to help, take the victim to a doctor. Something else might be wrong.

Electric Shock

Electric shock occurs when an electric current passes through a person's body. The current may cause cardiac arrest (the heart stops beating) and respiratory failure (the person stops breathing). In case of electric shock, follow the steps in Figure 28-24.

Steps to Take in Case of Electric Shock

1. Do not touch an electric shock victim who is still touching a live wire or other source of electricity.

2. Turn off the current if you can do so quickly and safely. Otherwise, use an object made of a substance that does not conduct electricity (such as wood or plastic) to pull any wires away from the victim. Do not use metal! Stand on insulating material such as paper, wood, or rubber. Be sure your hands and the materials you use are dry.

3. Check the victim's ABCs—airway, breathing, and circulation (heartbeat).

4. If the airway is open and the victim isn't breathing, begin rescue breathing at once. If there is no pulse, begin CPR as well, if you are trained. If the victim doesn't regain consciousness right away, do not give up hope. Victims who have been struck by lightning, or who have suffered other serious electrical shock, may need rescue breathing for an hour or more before they begin breathing on their own again.

5. Send for medical help.

6. Treat the victim for shock.

(FIGURE 28-24) **In addition to these lifesaving measures, an electric shock victim may also need treatment for burns.**

Poisoning

Poisons can cause intense pain, permanent injury, impaired health, and even death. The steps you take immediately after a poisoning can save a life and prevent permanent injury.

A victim of poisoning needs medical attention immediately. Until medical help is available, monitor the victim's pulse and breathing. Be ready to give rescue breathing, or if you are trained, CPR.

Poisoning by Ingestion If victims are conscious and able to talk, you can usually ask what they drank or ate. Sometimes eyewitness accounts can be useful. If a person is unconscious or unable to talk, you should suspect poison if you detect the symptoms in Figure 28-25. For the benefit of the medical personnel who will assist, save the container or label of the suspected poison. If the person vomits, save a sample of the material for examination.

If you must give first aid to a person who drank or ate a poison, do not give anything by mouth or try to induce vomiting until you have determined what the poison is and checked with the nearest poison control center for instructions. They may tell you to dilute the poison by having the victim drink a glass of water or milk immediately. Often they will tell you to induce vomiting. Syrup containing *ipecac* is often recommended for this purpose. However, some poisons that can be swallowed contain strong acids or alkalis that damage tissue on contact. Because they cause as much damage coming up as going down, you will be told not to induce vomiting in those cases.

You can reach the poison control center in an emergency by dialing 911, or O for operator, and asking to be connected. Find out the number of the nearest poison control center in advance and keep it posted by your telephone.

Signs and Symptoms of Poisoning

Presence of a poisonous substance or its container

Sudden, unexplained illness or pain, especially in the abdomen

Nausea or vomiting

Burns near the lips or mouth

Odor of chemicals or fuel on the breath

Changes in the pupils (dilation or constriction)

(FIGURE 28-25) **These symptoms may indicate poisoning. Your first step should be to call 911 or contact the nearest poison control center.**

Drug Overdose Drugs are a common cause of poisoning. Even nonprescription drugs can be poisonous if taken in large doses or in bad combinations. Outdated drugs may be poisonous as well. Follow the same steps for a drug overdose as for poisoning by ingestion. In addition, try to keep the person awake and calm.

Poisoning by Inhalation Many substances can be poisonous if they are inhaled, including a number of chemicals, fuels, and gases. Carbon monoxide is a frequent cause of inhalation poisoning. Produced by incompletely burned fuels, carbon monoxide accumulates in poorly ventilated areas where fuels are being burned or where fuel-burning engines are running. Because it is odorless, it can overcome victims before they are even aware of the danger.

If you attempt to rescue a victim of inhalation poisoning, *exercise extreme caution.* Take several deep breaths before entering a closed space where someone has collapsed, and hold your breath while you

(FIGURE 28-26) **Defective or improperly maintained space heaters and automobile exhaust systems are common sources of poisonous fumes, such as carbon monoxide. Sudden or unexplained drowsiness is a symptom of inhalation poisoning by carbon monoxide.**

immediately move the victim to fresh air. If the person is not breathing, perform rescue breathing. Send for an ambulance equipped with oxygen, and treat for shock.

Contact Poisoning Several types of poisonous substances can burn the skin or be absorbed through it on contact. Treatment for contact poisoning is the same as that for chemical burns: remove clothing and flush the area thoroughly with water for at least five minutes. If the poison is a pesticide, send for an ambulance. Chapter 6 tells you how to treat for contact with poisonous plants such as poison ivy.

Muscle Cramps

A cramp is a sudden knotting of a muscle, usually in the foot, leg, or abdomen. Cramps can be very painful, and they may last anywhere from a few minutes to a few hours. You can help the cramp go away sooner by massaging or stretching the muscle. If a muscle cramps when you are swimming, tread water while you massage the muscle. Call for help if you need it.

Burns and Scalds

Skin can be burned by fire, sun, hot liquids, heated objects, chemicals, and electricity. Burns are classified by the depth and degree of tissue damage. Figure 28-27 describes the classes of burns and their treatment.

Chemical burns can also be first-, second-, or third-degree, depending on how many layers of skin have been damaged. Take the following steps to treat chemical burns:

- Remove any clothing that covers the affected area or has the chemical on it.
- Hold the burned part under running water for as long as 10 to 15 minutes to wash away all traces of the chemical. If burns are extensive, you may use a hose or shower.
- Once the burn is free of the chemical, you may be able to treat it as you would any other burns. Call a poison control center or doctor to be sure of proper treatment.

If the chemical is in the victim's eye, the eye must be washed out under running water for a full 15 minutes. Hold the person's head under a water fountain or faucet so that the flow of water is away from the nose and toward the ear. Bandage *both* eyes with a soft material to rest the injured eye. If the good eye can see, it will move and the injured eye will move too. Take the victim to a doctor as soon as possible.

1st-Degree Burns

A first-degree burn affects only the epidermis, the top layer of skin. The skin turns red and may hurt but does not blister. Sunburn is the most common first-degree burn. Even without treatment, a first-degree burn will heal in a few days.

▶ Treatment

Cold water and ice can help lower the skin temperature, stop the burning, and relieve the pain. So can pain-relieving preparations you can buy in the drugstore.

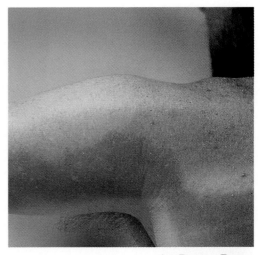

1st-Degree Burns

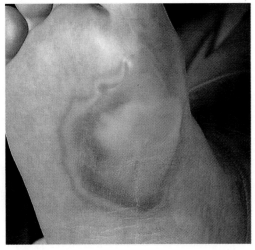

2nd-Degree Burns

2nd-Degree Burns

A second-degree burn forms blisters and affects both layers of skin—the epidermis and dermis. Unless they affect more than 15 percent of the body, second-degree burns are not serious.

▶ Treatment

1. Place the burned area into cool water right away. Cooling it will stop further burning and help relieve the pain.
2. Cover the burn with a clean dressing to prevent infection.
3. Do not pop blisters. The intact skin protects the burned part from infection. Blisters heal on their own in a few days.

3rd-Degree Burns

In a third-degree burn, the dermis and epidermis are destroyed. The tissue underneath is injured and may be partly destroyed as well. Third-degree burns are easily infected. They are typically whitish in color, though they may be charred brown or black. The burns may not hurt at all at first, if the nerve endings have been destroyed.

▶ Treatment

1. Rinse the burned area with cool water only. Very cold water can bring on or intensify shock.
2. Do not apply ointments or creams.
3. Do not remove pieces of clothing stuck to the burns.
4. Cover the burns lightly with sterile dressings or clean cloth.
5. Keep burned limbs elevated, above the heart if possible.
6. Unless victims are unconscious or vomiting, have them drink water to replace fluids lost through the burn.
7. Treat for shock.
8. Monitor breathing.
9. Send for medical help immediately, or take the victim to a hospital or doctor. Third-degree burns will not heal on their own.

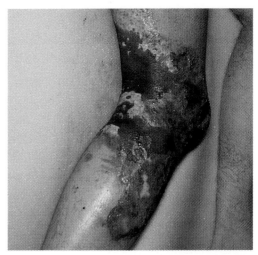

3rd-Degree Burns

(FIGURE 28-27) **First-, second-, and third-degree burns are easily distinguished. Note that the treatment is different for each of these three types of burns.**

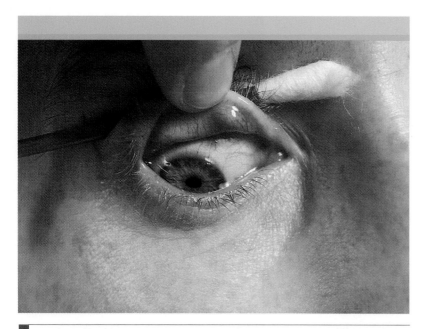

(FIGURE 28-28) **To inspect the upper eyelid, push down gently on the lid with a small stick, such as a matchstick or cotton swab, placed across the lid. Grasping the eyelashes, pull the eyelid upward against the stick and have the person look down while you inspect the lid.**

Foreign Body in the Eye

To remove a foreign body from the eye, first have the victim try blinking several times. Often, blinking and tears will wash the foreign body away. Pulling on the eyelashes of the upper lid may help as well. Gently pulling the upper lid down over the lower lid can permit tears and the lower eyelashes to dislodge the object.

If blinking and tearing don't work, move the person to good light so you can see the eye clearly. To inspect the inside of the lower lid, pull the lid down by pressing on the eyelashes. Use the procedure shown in Figure 28-28 to inspect the inside of the upper lid. If the object is on the inner surface of an eyelid, gently remove it with the corner of a moist, clean cloth or tissue twisted to a point.

If you find an object of any sort embedded in the surface of the eyeball, gently bandage both eyes to restrict their movement. Then take the victim to a doctor.

Fainting

Temporary loss of consciousness is called fainting. Usually, the cause is a shortage of blood flow to the brain. Sometimes a person will be pale and dizzy before fainting. Usually, the victim regains consciousness in a few minutes.

If a person faints near you, keep the person lying down. Elevate his or her feet to increase circulation to the brain. If *you* feel faint, lie down with your head lowered and your feet elevated to increase the blood flow to your brain. If this is not possible, sit down or kneel and bend over so that your head is lower than your heart.

Review

1. Contrast the treatments for heat exhaustion and heatstroke. Which condition is more serious?

2. **LIFE SKILLS: Practicing Self-Care** The temperature is below freezing. You have come in after getting the newspaper and are shivering. You must now walk to school. How can you prevent hypothermia?

3. Explain how the treatments for second- and third-degree burns differ.

4. What steps would you take if you discovered someone who had swallowed poison?

5. *Critical Thinking* A burn victim has two burns. One is blistered and painful, and the other is deep and whitish colored but does not hurt. Which is the more serious burn? Explain.

Highlights

Summary

- Appropriate first aid can mean the difference between life and death or between recovery and permanent injury.

- The steps to take in an emergency are: survey the scene; rescue the victim; send for medical help; treat the life-threatening conditions; identify injuries and provide first aid; remain with the victim, monitoring breathing and pulse until medical help arrives.

- Check the airway, breathing, and circulation (ABCs) of unconscious persons, in that order, before beginning first aid.

- CPR can revive people whose breathing and heartbeat have stopped. It should be attempted only by trained individuals.

- To stop bleeding, apply direct pressure and elevate the wound above the heart.

- All victims of serious injury or illness should be treated for shock. Shock can kill a person even when the injury that triggered it is not life-threatening.

- People with fractures or neck and spinal injuries should not be moved except to be rescued from immediate danger.

- Being calm and reassuring while giving first aid helps prevent panic, which can kill someone even if an injury or illness is not life-threatening.

- Call 911 or the nearest poison control center for advice before giving first aid for poisoning.

Vocabulary

first aid emergency care given to an ill or injured person before medical attention is available.

cardiopulmonary resuscitation (CPR) a lifesaving procedure designed to revive a person who is not breathing and has no heartbeat.

fracture a broken bone.

dislocation an injury in which the end of a bone comes out of its joint.

sprain a torn or stretched ligament.

strain a stretched or torn muscle or tendon.

Heimlich maneuver a series of sharp thrusts to the abdomen, used to dislodge an object from a choking person's airway.

cardiac arrest condition in which the heart stops working.

stroke the rupture or blockage of an artery in the brain, leading to oxygen deprivation and damage to brain cells.

hypothermia below-normal body temperature.

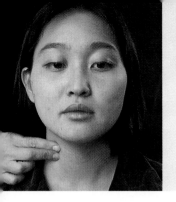

Concept Review

1. What information should you remember to give when making an emergency telephone call?

2. What are the ABCs of emergency treatment?

3. What is the first-aid treatment for shock and why is this treatment so important?

4. It is important to approach an emergency with the right attitude. How should you behave and why?

5. What are some danger signs to watch for around a wound? What do these signs indicate?

6. What are some symptoms of a head injury? What clues should you look for if you suspect a head injury?

7. What are four symptoms of a heart attack?

8. What is the first-aid treatment for a victim of convulsions?

9. What parts of the body most often suffer from frostbite? What is the most important thing to remember when giving first aid for frostbite?

10. What are the four poisonous snakes in the United States? How soon after being bitten does a snakebite victim need medical treatment?

11. How should the stinger of an insect be removed from its victim? Why? What is the main danger from an insect sting?

12. Why should a person who has swallowed a strong acid be advised not to vomit?

13. Describe the appearance of a first-degree burn.

Expressing Your Views

1. You have started baby-sitting to make some extra money. You are afraid an emergency might arise while the children are in your care. Which first-aid procedures would be important for a baby sitter to know?

2. Do you think the good samaritan laws are fair? Why or why not?

3. Suppose you were bitten by a strange dog while walking near your home. What would you do?

4. You and your friends are planning a camping trip. What do you think should be included in a first-aid kit?

Life Skills Check

1. Intervention Strategies
Rescue breathing is a technique that can save lives in a number of different kinds of medical emergencies. If a family member or friend were to stop breathing, what steps would you take to give rescue breathing?

2. Practicing Self-Care
If you suffer from diabetes or epilepsy, what can you do to ensure that others are aware of your condition?

3. Practicing Self-Care
Suppose you want to be an ambulance driver. Knowing that you will have to treat bleeding victims, what steps should you take to protect yourself from a serious disease such as hepatitis or AIDS?

Projects

1. Inventory the first-aid supplies at home, and make suggestions to a parent or guardian about what items are needed. You might also put together a first-aid kit for your car.

2. Working with a group, present a short skit in which a group member experiences one of the emergencies discussed in the chapter. Others in the group should portray people arriving at the scene—police officers, medics, friends, and family members.

Without performing the actual techniques, show the audience correct emergency first-aid procedures.

3. Interview an EMT, paramedic, or emergency-room nurse. Ask about the type of training required and the personal qualities they feel are necessary for the job. Also ask the person to relate a particularly rewarding experience he or she has had on the job. Share what you learn with the class.

Plan for Action

First aid and CPR are very important lifesaving skills. Make a list of your activities, and identify the ways you could save lives during an emergency by knowing and using first aid or CPR.

Ethical Issues in Health

Guns have become a factor that seriously affects teenage health and safety. In a recent survey at an inner-city high school, more than half the students interviewed said they knew someone who had brought a gun to school, and most said they knew someone who had been shot. Sadly, this is not a surprising statistic. Accidents, homicides, and suicides are the leading causes of death among American teenagers. Many of the accidents and a majority of the homicides and suicides of teens involve guns. Statistics from the National Center for Health show that guns were used in more than 70 percent of teenage homicides and in more than 60 percent of the suicides by teenage males. As a result, gunshot wounds are the second leading cause of death among 15- to 19-year-olds in the United States.

To try to stop students and other people from bringing guns to school, schools across the nation are beginning to use metal detectors. In the same way that these devices are used in airports, metal detectors can be installed in a school's doorways so that all students must pass through one of the devices before entering the school. Hand-held metal detectors can also be used to search individuals suspected of carrying a gun or knife. Nearly half of the students surveyed in one inner-city school agreed that metal detectors should be installed in schools to prevent the entry of guns and other weapons. Many school board members and administrators also believe that as long as guns continue to be a serious problem in schools, metal detectors will be necessary to protect students and school employees.

One reason why guns play such a major role in the deaths of American teenagers may be the large number of guns that are available. Studies show that half of all homes in the United States have firearms (rifles, shotguns, and handguns). It is estimated that 70 million Americans own about 200 million firearms, many of them handguns. Although many people feel that having guns in their homes provides safety, those most likely to be injured by gunshots are the family members of people who have guns. Other high-risk groups include male teens, those who abuse alcohol, and people who frequently get into physical fights to settle arguments.

In an attempt to reduce the impact of guns on the health of all Americans, several laws have been proposed that would control the sale of firearms (handguns, rifles, and shotguns). Some of these laws would require people to obtain a license to own guns. Others would require a waiting period for the purchase of a gun.

Advocates of gun-control laws point out that most people are shot and killed as the result of arguments and fights with family members. They argue that requiring a waiting period before the purchase of a gun would reduce the number of homicides and suicides, because an enraged or depressed person would not have immediate access to a gun. They also argue that licensing would help reduce gunshot injuries, because people with criminal records or histories of mental illness would be denied licenses to own and carry guns.

Those who oppose gun control point out that by itself, a gun cannot kill or injure people—it must be fired by someone. Since most people who own guns use them responsibly, opponents of gun control believe that only those who use guns unlawfully should be punished. Opponents of gun-control laws are also concerned that such laws will not be obeyed by criminals, leaving law-abiding citizens defenseless. The National Rifle Association (NRA) is the most powerful group in the United States that opposes gun-control laws. Citing the United States Constitution, the NRA's philosophy is that all citizens have the right to own and use guns for self-defense, hunting, and recreational purposes.

Situation for Discussion

Mark and George attend the same high school. Last Saturday night, Mark saw George and Wendy dancing and kissing at a friend's party. Mark had been dating Wendy, but they had recently split up. As the party broke up, a loud confrontation between Mark and George began on the front lawn. Several blows were exchanged, but the fight was stopped by other party-goers. As George was leaving, Mark yelled, "I'll see you later, George! You're a dead man!"

a. What is the potential outcome of this situation?

b. Could a gun-control law prevent an injury or homicide in this case? Explain.

c. What other ways are there to protect George, Mark, their families and friends, and other students at their school from injury or death?

d. How could the disagreement be settled without physical harm to either person?

The Nervous System and Its Organs

▶ Your nervous system regulates and coordinates your body activities in response to
▶ changes in the internal and external environment. The changes, called stimuli, initiate
▶ impulses in millions of **sensory receptors** spread throughout your body. The most familiar
▶ are the **sense organs:** the eyes, ears, nose, skin, and tongue. In addition to these organs,
▶ there are other sensory receptors within the body and close to the surface of the skin.

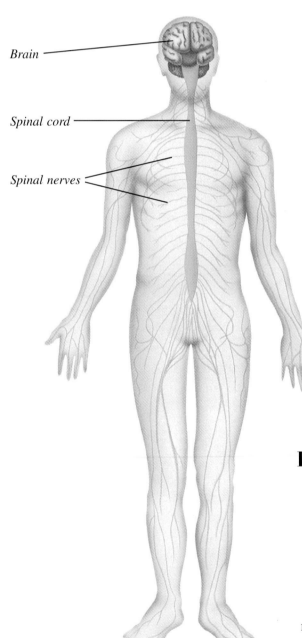

Brain

Spinal cord

Spinal nerves

CENTRAL NERVOUS SYSTEM ◆

The **brain** and **spinal cord** make up the central nervous
system. The brain is the organ responsible for thought,
memory, consciousness, creativity, and emotion. It also
receives sensory impulses, controls and coordinates
muscular movements, and regulates vital body
processes. The spinal cord is the pathway for
sensory and motor nerve impulses traveling to and
from the brain. It also processes some information
without the aid of the brain, as demonstrated
by reflexes such as the withdrawal reflex.

Cerebrospinal fluid fills the open spaces in the brain
and surrounds the spinal cord. This fluid acts as a
shock absorber, protecting the brain and spinal
cord from damage. It transports metabolic wastes
out of the central nervous system. Nutrients,
hormones, and other vital substances are
transported throughout the central nervous
system by the cerebrospinal fluid.

PERIPHERAL NERVOUS SYSTEM ◆

The 31 pairs of **spinal nerves** as well as all the other
nerves and nerve cells outside of the central nervous
system make up the peripheral nervous system. This
system carries nerve impulses to and from the body's
sensory cells and the central nervous system. The central
nervous system analyzes the information it receives from
the peripheral nervous system and responds to it. The
motor neurons of the peripheral nervous system carry out
the instructions received from the central nervous system.

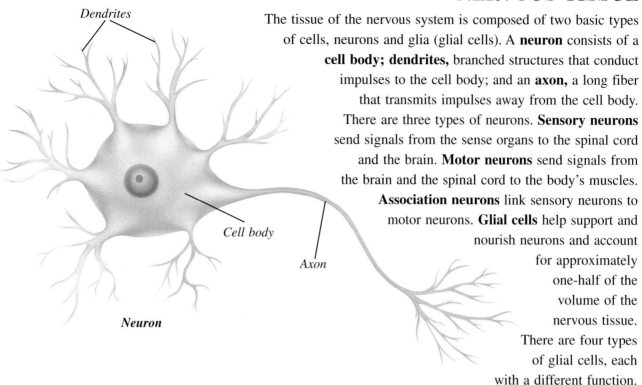

Dendrites

Cell body

Axon

Neuron

NERVOUS TISSUE ◆

The tissue of the nervous system is composed of two basic types of cells, neurons and glia (glial cells). A **neuron** consists of a **cell body; dendrites,** branched structures that conduct impulses to the cell body; and an **axon,** a long fiber that transmits impulses away from the cell body. There are three types of neurons. **Sensory neurons** send signals from the sense organs to the spinal cord and the brain. **Motor neurons** send signals from the brain and the spinal cord to the body's muscles. **Association neurons** link sensory neurons to motor neurons. **Glial cells** help support and nourish neurons and account for approximately one-half of the volume of the nervous tissue. There are four types of glial cells, each with a different function.

◆ # NEUROTRANSMITTERS

Neurons are separated from each other and from other body cells by a tiny gap called a **synapse.** When a nerve impulse reaches a synapse, the axon releases a chemical called a **neurotransmitter.** The neurotransmitter transfers the impulse across the synapse to the target cell. Then, the synapse is cleared so that another impulse can cross. Over 60 different chemicals have been identified either as neurotransmitters or as substances that modify the activity of neurotransmitters.

Axon

Target cell

Synapse

Neurotransmitter molecules

Neurotransmitters and Drugs

The use of **psychoactive drugs** alters the transmission of nerve impulses. For example, caffeine stimulates the nervous system by facilitating synaptic transmission. Cocaine, amphetamines, and some antidepressant drugs cause substances to remain in the synapse longer. The result is prolonged stimulation of the nervous system. Some psychoactive drugs are addictive. The body adjusts to the changes these drugs cause. If the drug is withdrawn, the body will be unable to function as it had previously. The addicted drug user will then experience withdrawal symptoms.

BRAIN

The brain contains about 1 trillion cells, and it consists of three basic parts: the cerebrum, the cerebellum, and the brain stem. The **cerebrum,** which is the largest part of the brain, initiates all the body's voluntary actions. The **cerebellum** controls balance and muscle movement. The **brain stem,** which connects the cerebrum to the spinal cord, has nerve centers that regulate swallowing, the digestive process, circulation and respiration.

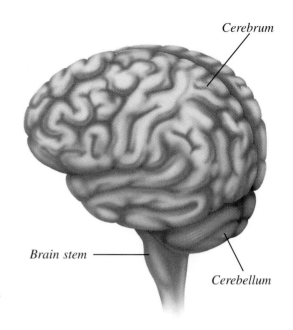

Cerebrum

Brain stem

Cerebellum

CEREBRAL HEMISPHERES

The cerebrum is made up of a right hemisphere and a left hemisphere, each divided into four lobes. Each hemisphere controls the actions of the opposite side of the body. In most people, the left hemisphere is dominant. In general, the left hemisphere is responsible for speech, writing, and reading. It also plays a major role in verbal, analytical, and computational skills. The right hemisphere is more involved with nonverbal functions, such as emotion, intuition, awareness and interpretation of space, and creativity. The cerebrum's hemispheres are connected by a structure called the corpus callosum, and there is constant communication between the two sides.

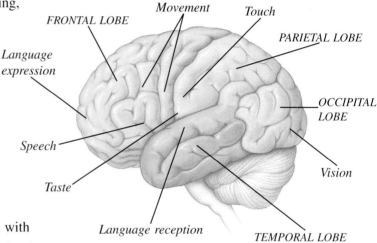

FRONTAL LOBE

Movement

Touch

PARIETAL LOBE

Language expression

OCCIPITAL LOBE

Speech

Vision

Taste

Language reception

TEMPORAL LOBE

Blood-Brain Barrier

Some substances taken into the body can interfere with the proper functioning of the brain. Fortunately, a structure called the **blood-brain barrier** prevents most harmful substances from passing from the capillaries of the brain into the cerebrospinal fluid. The cells lining the brain's blood vessels are tightly joined together and play the primary role in forming the blood-brain barrier. In addition, projections from one type of glial cell cover the outside of the brain's blood vessels, making passage into the brain even more difficult. A special carrier system allows water, oxygen, carbon-dioxide, glucose, and nutrients to pass through the blood-brain barrier.

BRAIN INJURY

Accidents and illnesses can damage or destroy brain cells. When permanent damage is done to enough cells, disability results. The degree and type of disability depend on how many brain cells are injured and on where the damage occurs. Severe trauma to the head as well as repeated minor trauma to the head, such as that incurred by boxers, can cause permanent brain damage.

SPINAL CORD

The **spinal cord** is a cable of nerve tissue that extends from the base of the brain to just below the level of the ribs. In adults, it is about the thickness of the little finger. The spinal cord is surrounded by the spinal column (backbone), which protects it. Thirty-one pairs of spinal nerves connect the spinal cord with the rest of the body. The spinal nerves are composed of both sensory neurons and motor neurons. These neurons transfer millions of messages between the body and the brain.

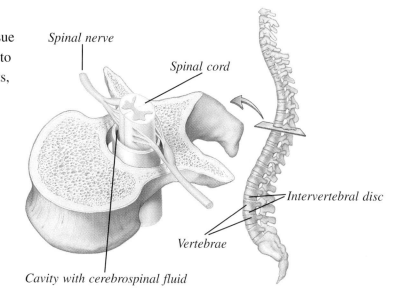

Spinal nerve

Spinal cord

Intervertebral disc

Vertebrae

Cavity with cerebrospinal fluid

SPINAL-CORD INJURIES

Spinal-cord injuries are relatively common. About 45 percent of all spinal-cord injuries are incurred in motor-vehicle accidents. Injuries to the spinal cord can alter or prevent communication between the brain and the body. If the injury is serious enough paralysis can occur. In general, the higher up on the spinal cord the injury is, the more severe the damage will be. Damage to the spinal cord in the neck can result in paralysis from the neck down, while injures lower on the spinal cord may produce paralysis only in the legs.

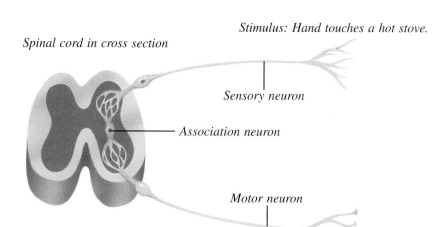

Spinal cord in cross section

Stimulus: Hand touches a hot stove.

Sensory neuron

Association neuron

Motor neuron

Reflex: Muscle moves hand away from stove.

REFLEXES

Reflexes are involuntary responses to stimuli and are not controlled by the brain. Reflex movements take only a split second to occur. For example, when a person touches a hot stove, a nerve impulse travels through a sensory neuron in the person's hand to the spinal cord. There, it is transferred first to an association neuron and then to a motor neuron traveling quickly back to the hand. In a split second, the withdrawal reflex pulls the hand away from the stove. If this message had to go through the brain, the response time would be longer increasing the possibility of injury.

Sensory Receptors and Sense Organs

Your senses are the window through which you view the world around you. They allow you to interpret changes in your internal and external environment. One day you may feel well; the next day you may have a headache. Your senses are what provides this information to the brain, which in turn, interprets it. Not everyone interprets information in the same way. That's why some people love hot chili peppers, while others prefer more subtle flavorings.

◆ INTERNAL SENSORY RECEPTORS

Sense receptors located deep within the body enable a person to feel internal pain, hunger, thirst, tiredness, and nausea. Other receptors located in skeletal muscles, tendons, and the connective tissue surrounding joints are sensitive to changes in stretch and tension. They continuously relay information about body position, equilibrium, and movement to the central nervous system, and together they make up what is called the **kinesthetic** sense. Many internal sensations are not recognized at a conscious level. For example, some sensors monitor blood pressure; the information they send to the brain is not processed by the cerebrum, so an individual is not aware of this sensation.

SENSATION AND THE SKIN ◆

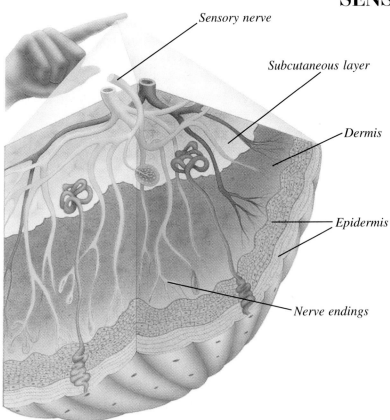

Sensory nerve

Subcutaneous layer

Dermis

Epidermis

Nerve endings

Touch is the sensation produced by pressure on the surface of the body and is sometimes called the **tactile** sense. Pressure receptors are located all over the skin. On sensitive parts of the body, such as the tongue, lips, and finger pads, their concentration is very high. Touch messages are transmitted by bundles of **sensory nerve fibers** that come through the **subcutaneous layer** to the **dermis,** or inner layer of skin. The bundles split into fibers, some of which reach into the **epidermis,** or outer layer of the skin. These **nerve endings** in the epidermis are sensitive to pressure. Other sensory nerve fibers end in specialized receptors in the dermis, which sense temperature or pain.

Smell and Taste

Your sense of taste and your sense of smell are both stimulated by chemicals. Their main purposes are to help you detect harmful substances and to stimulate your appetite and digestion. Even though taste and smell messages travel separately to different regions of the brain, they create a combined feeling of either pleasure or displeasure when you are eating. For example, think of how the aroma of a delicious meal can make your mouth water.

SMELL

Olfactory (smell) receptors are located in a dime-sized area in the roof of the nasal passages. They are able to sense minute amounts of chemicals in the air. These receptors are actually specialized neurons whose dendrites are modified into hairlike projections called cilia. Their axons transmit nerve impulses through an opening in the skull directly to the olfactory bulb in the forebrain. When a person has a stopped-up nose, little air passes over the olfactory receptor cells, resulting in a diminished sense of smell. Compared to some other mammals, humans have a poor sense of smell. For example, humans have anywhere from 5 million to 20 million olfactory receptors, while dogs have 40 million or more.

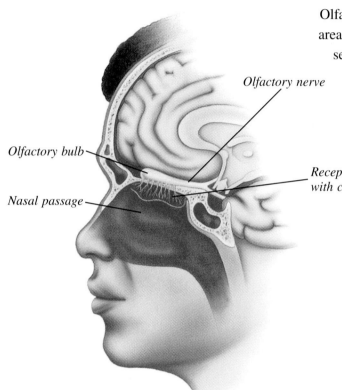

Olfactory nerve

Olfactory bulb

Receptor cells with cilia

Nasal passage

TASTE

The tongue is covered with small, rough bumps called papillae. Each papilla is covered with **taste buds**, clusters of taste sensors. Taste receptors sense chemicals—classified as sweet, sour, salty, or bitter—in foods and beverages. When chewed-up food mixed with saliva washes across the papillae, the chemicals in the food stimulate the taste receptors. The receptors transmit nerve impulses to the brain through the gustatory nerve, and the brain interprets the taste. Babies have about 10,000 taste buds, but this number decreases as a person gets older. There are other reasons why the ability to taste can diminish. For example, there is good evidence that long-term cigarette smoking damages taste receptors, adding to the loss that normally comes with age.

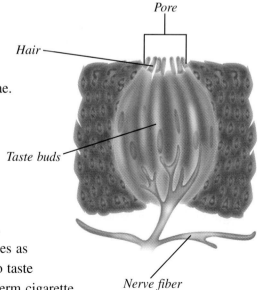

Pore

Hair

Taste buds

Nerve fiber

▸Vision

Human beings have excellent eyesight. In fact, only birds can see better than humans can, although squids and octopuses can see just as well. Your vision is a response to light falling on the retina of the eye. Light rays enter your eye through the pupil and are focused onto the retina, which is actually an extension of your brain. Nerve fibers of the retina join to form the optic nerve, which transmits nerve impulses to the occipital lobe of your brain. Your brain then interprets these impulses as an image, and you "see" it.

◆ EYE

The outer surface of the eye is covered by the **cornea,** a transparent membrane that protects the eye but allows light to enter. Behind the cornea is the **iris,** a thin, colored, circular membrane. In the center of the iris is an opening called the **pupil.** Muscles in the iris control the amount of light that is let in by altering the diameter of the pupil. The pupil dilates, or enlarges, to let more light in and contracts to let in less light. Behind the pupil is the **lens,** a thick, curved structure that focuses the light rays so that they will fall on the **retina,** the thin lining on the back of the eye. Notice that the image on the retina is inverted.

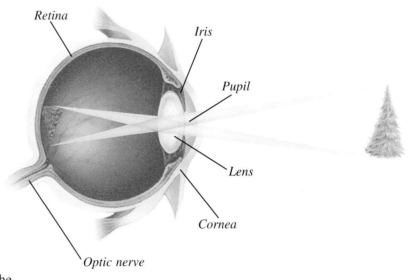

Retina

Iris

Pupil

Lens

Cornea

Optic nerve

◆ RECEPTOR CELLS

There are approximately 1 billion receptor cells in the retina. **Rods** are cells that are extremely sensitive to light; however, they cannot detect color, and they produce poorly defined images. **Cones** are cells that detect color and produce sharp images. At the center of the retina is a concentration of about 3 million cone cells. People usually move their eyes so that the light rays from an object they want to see fall on this area. There are no cones or rods at the point where the optic nerve enters the retina. Light that falls on this area does not stimulate any sight receptors, resulting in a "blind spot" in the field of vision.

EYE DISORDERS

Some people are nearsighted or farsighted; others have an astigmatism. Why is this? For an image to appear clear, the lens must focus light rays directly onto the retina. The lens does this by using tiny muscles and ligaments to adjust its thickness. If the shape of the eyeball is too elongated or too short, the lens will be unable to change sufficiently to focus the image properly. In nearsighted people, the focal point is in front of the retina, resulting in poor distance vision. In farsighted people, the focal point is behind the retina, resulting in poor close vision. Astigmatism is caused by an irregularly shaped cornea. This causes the light rays to be focused erratically and to mostly miss the retina. Corrective lenses adjust the light ray's focal point so that it is on the retina.

Color blindness, a condition that is almost always genetic in origin, is the inability to distinguish colors. It is caused by an abnormality of one or more of the three types of light-sensitive pigments in the cone cells. The inability to distinguish red light from green light is the most common type of color blindness. About 10 percent of all males have some degree of color blindness while less than 1 percent of females are affected. Total color blindness is extremely rare.

When a person has cataracts, the lens of the eye is no longer transparent. Light cannot pass through the lens easily, so vision is diminished. Although aging is the most common cause of cataracts, they can also result from a reaction to a drug, from radiation including solar exposure, and from disease. In the past, people with cataracts became blind; however, today the condition can be corrected surgically. The faulty lens is removed and replaced with an artificial one. Glasses or contact lenses are then prescribed to adjust the vision.

Some diseases cause scarring of the cornea. When this occurs, blindness may result because light cannot pass through the damaged cornea. This condition can be corrected by a corneal transplant. The central portion of the scarred cornea is removed and replaced with a cornea from an organ donor.

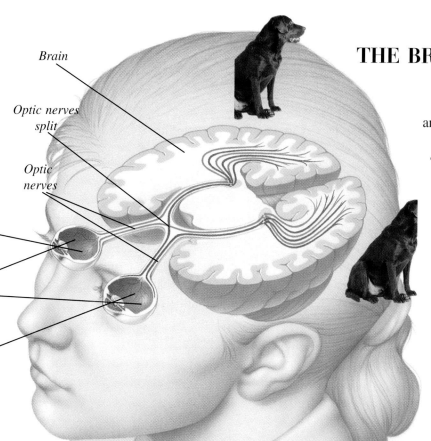

Brain

Optic nerves split

Optic nerves

THE BRAIN FORMS AN IMAGE ◆

When the eyes view an image, each eye sees the image from a slightly different angle. About one-third of the visual fields overlap, but the other two-thirds differ. This overlap produces **binocular vision,** which enables people to perceive depth. Also, the optic nerves do not connect to only one hemisphere. About one-half of each optic nerve crosses over into the opposite side of the brain; because of this, each hemisphere receives visual information from both eyes. The brain combines all the information it receives to produce one image.

659

Hearing and Equilibrium

When you think of your ears, you may only consider your external ear, the part that sticks out on each side of your head. But you also have a middle ear and an inner ear, the portions responsible for sensing sound.

◆ HEARING

The **external ear** funnels sounds through the **ear canal** to the **eardrum.** On the other side of the eardrum is an air-filled cavity called the **middle ear.** This part of the ear opens to the back of the throat through a tube called the eustachian tube. As sound waves apply pressure to the eardrum, the eardrum vibrates. Three bones located in the middle ear—the **hammer,** the **anvil,** and the **stirrup**—transfer this vibration to a fluid-filled chamber, the **cochlea.** Inside are tiny hair cells that serve as sound receptors. They respond to the vibrations and send impulses to the brain, which interprets the vibrations as sound.

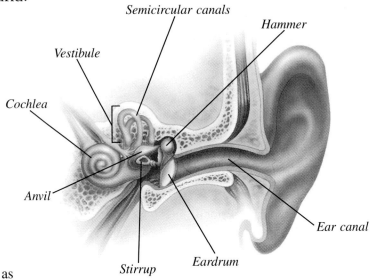

Semicircular canals

Hammer

Vestibule

Cochlea

Anvil

Stirrup

Eardrum

Ear canal

Equilibrium

The two other portions of the inner ear, the **semicircular canals** and the **vestibule,** are involved with the sense of equilibrium. The semicircular canals detect movement of the head. The vestibule contains sensory cells that respond to changes in head position with respect to gravity. It is the inner ear that contains the sense cells, which enable you to hear, and that produces your sense of equilibrium, or balance and stability in space.

HEARING LOSS

Certain conditions, diseases, and types of trauma can result in hearing loss. For example, a buildup of wax in the ear or an ear infection can create a barrier to sound waves entering the ear, preventing vibration of the ear drum and the inner-ear bones. Repeated inner-ear infections can result in scarring of the eardrum and damage to the bones of the inner ear. If this occurred, sound waves would not be conducted as well and hearing would be diminished. This type of hearing loss is referred to as conductive deafness.

Repeated exposure to excessively loud sounds will destroy the tiny hair cells in the cochlea, resulting in hearing loss. Once destroyed, these hair cells can never be replaced. Rock concerts and exposure to other loud noises, such as power saws, cause this type of hearing loss. Wearing ear plugs protects the ears from this type of damage. There is now evidence that prolonged exposure to even moderately loud sounds, such as head phones, has a cumulative effect and can cause hearing loss classified as nerve deafness.

Q and A ◆◆◆◆◆◆◆◆

Q: I've heard that exercise leads to a "runner's high." What is that?

A: The body produces neurotransmitters that travel to other parts of the body and affect them in various ways. Endorphins are one type of neurotransmitter. One endorphin, enkephalin, is produced by the brain and spinal cord in response to stress. Enkephalin binds to the same receptors in the brain as the narcotic morphine does. Enkephalin secretion results in lessened pain and a sense of well-being. Another endorphin, betaedorphin, is produced by the pituitary gland. These two endorphins are secreted during exercise and are responsible for what is called a "runner's high."

Q: What is a concussion?

A: When the head receives a violent blow—such as from a fall—the brain is jarred. The force of the brain hitting the skull interferes with normal brain function and is called a concussion. If the force is mild, loss of consciousness may occur but will usually last only a few seconds. However, if the force is intense, loss of consciousness may be prolonged and damage may be extensive. It is common for a person to experience confusion or even amnesia following a concussion. Although the damage may not be obvious from the outside, concussions can be very dangerous.

Q: Where does earwax come from?

A: Sebaceous glands and ceruminous glands, specialized sweat glands, located in the ear canal produce this waxlike secretion. Earwax, called cerumen, protects the ear from infection and traps debris or small insects that enter the ear. It also helps prevent the ear drum from drying out. Usually the wax moves outward, moving anything it trapped along with it.

Q: Why can certain smells trigger emotions or vivid memories?

A: Scientists are not completely certain; they do know that the olfactory system is so sensitive that as few as four molecules of a substance can stimulate an olfactory receptor, even though there may be no conscious recognition of a smell. They also know that the olfactory nerve fibers link directly to areas of the brain where memories and emotions are held. The perfume industry is aware of these connections and makes full use of it when developing new scents.

Q: Is it safe to wear contact lenses overnight?

A: Wearing contact lenses, even soft lenses, overnight prevents the cornea from receiving adequate oxygen, and low-oxygen conditions increase the growth of some bacteria. People who wear their lenses overnight increase their risk for bacterial infection 10 to 15 times. Since bacterial infection of the eye can cause permanent damage to a person's vision, it is not worth the risk.

Q: Where do tears come from, and what is their purpose?

A: Tears are produced by a gland found above and to the outside of each eyeball. Each gland produces a watery secretion that mixes with a slightly oily secretion from accessory glands. The tear glands have between 10 and 12 ducts, and every time the eyes blink, tears are spread across the surface of the eye. Tears protect the eyes by lubricating them and washing away debris. Also, they contain an enzyme that helps prevent eye infection. Tears drain into two ducts in the inner corners of the eye. These ducts drain into the back of the nose.

The Skeletal System

Your skeletal system supports and protects the soft tissues and vital organs of your body. Your heart and lungs are shielded by your ribs, your spinal cord is protected by your vertebrae, and your brain is protected by your skull. Without rigid bones and flexible joints, you would not be able to stand, sit, bend, walk, or run. By themselves, bones cannot move. Your skeletal system moves because muscles attached to your bones contract or relax in response to messages sent from the nervous system. Some of the skeletal bones are held together by strong fibers called **ligaments.**

HUNDREDS OF BONES

The skeleton contains about 206 bones, depending on how they are counted. The pelvis, for instance, can be counted as a single bone or as six bones fused together. Children have 33 vertebrae in their spine, but in adults the bottom five become fused to form the sacrum. There are 24 ribs in 12 pairs, and there are 56 phalanxes (finger and toe bones). The hard shell of the skull consists of 28 bones and provides protection for the brain and the delicate sense organs.

The bones of the body vary greatly in size. The thigh bone, or femur, is the largest single bone in the body.

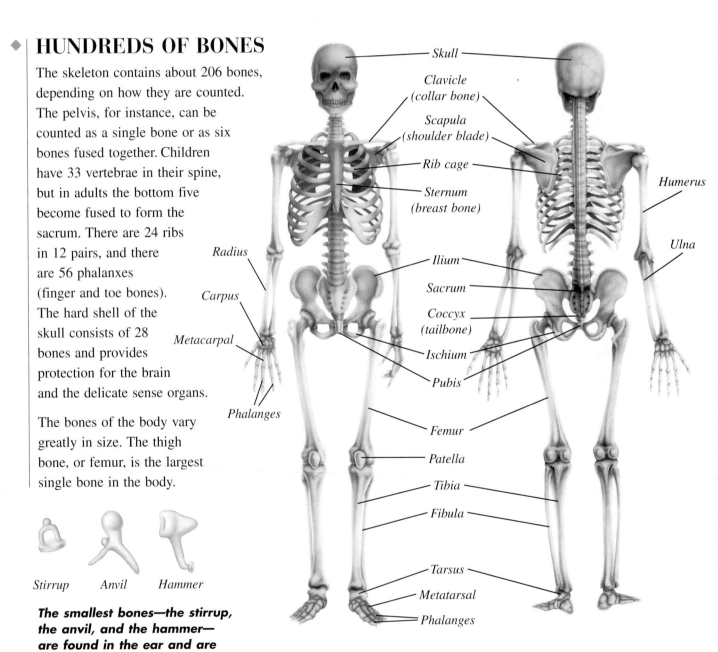

Skull

Clavicle (collar bone)

Scapula (shoulder blade)

Rib cage

Sternum (breast bone)

Humerus

Radius

Ulna

Carpus

Ilium

Sacrum

Metacarpal

Coccyx (tailbone)

Phalanges

Ischium

Pubis

Femur

Patella

Tibia

Fibula

Tarsus

Metatarsal

Phalanges

Stirrup   Anvil   Hammer

The smallest bones—the stirrup, the anvil, and the hammer— are found in the ear and are less than one-half inch long.

VIEW OF A BONE ◆

They may seem hard and lifeless, but bones are made of living tissue. The outer membrane of the bone, called the **periosteum,** contains many nerves, as well as blood vessels that transport food and oxygen to the bone's many cells. Inside the periosteum is the **bony layer,** which contains more blood vessels, bone cells (osteoblasts), and nerves. At the center of some bones is the **marrow,** which makes blood cells and stores fat.

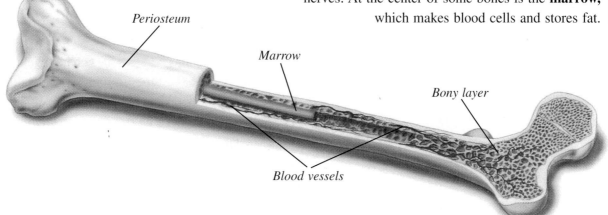

Periosteum

Marrow

Bony layer

Blood vessels

◆ BONE GROWTH

The long bones of the body, such as the femur, continue to grow until a person is about 20 years old. In the end of long bones is a band of cartilage called the **epiphysis,** or growth plate. Here, cartilage forms that will later be replaced by bone. As a young person matures, this cartilage formation slows down and finally stops. The growth plate becomes completely hardened, and growth in the length of the bone is no longer possible.

At birth, the bones of an infant's skull are incompletely developed and are separated by areas of soft tissue called **fontanels,** or soft spots. Fontanels allow for movement of the skull bones as the baby passes through the birth canal. There are no growth plates in these bones. The skull bones simply grow until they meet, closing up the soft spots. Some fontanels close up as early as two months after birth, but the one at the top of the head does not close up until about one year after birth.

There are several factors that can interfere with bone growth. If the epiphysis is injured, growth in the bone may stop. Deficiencies in the diet— especially of the vitamins A, C, and D—can interfere with bone growth. Steroid use by young people can cause premature closure of the epiphysis.

CARTILAGE ◆

Cartilage is a tough connective tissue found in various regions of the body. In the skeletal system, cartilage connects the ribs to the sternum, helps form the movable joints, and is found between the bones of the pelvis. The tip of the nose and the outer ears are made of cartilage, as are the **intervertebral disks.** These disks, which are shown on page 655, serve as cushions that prevent the vertebrae from rubbing and scraping against each other. Sometimes a disk becomes compressed and presses against a spinal nerve, which can be very painful. As people age, a disk's outer layer may develop cracks. If the inside of the disk protrudes through a crack, a condition called a herniated disk results. Disk damage can also result from misuse of the spine, such as the repeated improper lifting of heavy objects.

◆ PELVIS

Although the bones of males and females are essentially alike except for size, the pelvis is an exception. To accommodate pregnancy and childbirth, the female's pelvis has a slightly different shape than that of the male. It is usually wider so there is enough room for a developing fetus. The opening at the bottom of the pelvis is larger so that a baby's head can pass through during childbirth. The female pelvic bones are usually lighter and have less muscle attachment. This lighter structure causes females to be more susceptible to pelvic fractures than males.

JOINTS ◆

Joints are the locations where bones come together. There are three basic types of joints. **Immovable joints** provide little or no movement. For example, the bones that make up the skull's cranium are joined by immovable joints called **sutures. Slightly movable joints** allow limited movement. This type of joint is found between the vertebrae of the spine.

The names of the **freely movable joints** suggest the kind of motion each allows—hinge, pivot, ball-and-socket, and gliding. **Hinge joints,** found in the knees and elbows, allow back-and-forth movement—like a hinge in a door. **Pivot joints,** such as those in the neck, allow either back-and-forth movement or up-and-down movement. The shoulder and hip joints are **ball-and-socket joints,** which allow the greatest range of movement. **Gliding joints,** found in the wrist and ankles, allow for flexibility.

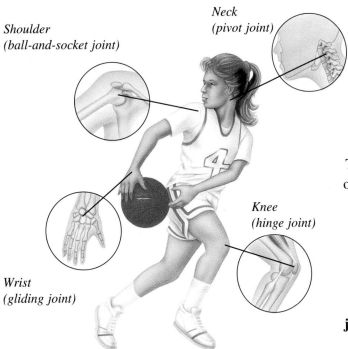

Shoulder
(ball-and-socket joint)

Neck
(pivot joint)

Knee
(hinge joint)

Wrist
(gliding joint)

Q and A ◆◆◆◆◆◆◆◆◆

Q: What is scoliosis? Do many teenagers have it?

A: Scoliosis, a sideways curve in the spine, is fairly common among young people. While most people have a small degree of curvature of the spine, it is usually not severe enough to require medical treatment. With scoliosis, the curvature is more pronounced and can result in pain and lack of mobility. Surgery may be required to straighten the vertebrae, but early detection eliminates the need in most cases. Other symptoms of scoliosis include unlevel shoulders or hips, a hump on the back, or a prominent shoulder blade.

Q: What does it mean when someone says an athlete has been "scoped"?

A: The severity of a joint injury can be assessed by inserting a thin, tubular instrument called an arthroscope through the skin and into the joint. In many cases, another tube that contains other instruments can be used to repair the damage. This procedure is called an arthroscopy, commonly called "scoping."

The Muscular System

Your muscular system enables your body to move. Each muscle consists of muscle cells that can contract or relax. Because muscle cells are usually long and slender, they are called fibers. Skeletal muscles move your bones and help protect your inner organs. Smooth muscles deep within your body help move food, air, and body fluids. Cardiac muscle is a special type of muscle found only in your heart. Your body has more than 600 muscles, which make up about 30 percent of the female body and about 40 percent of the male body.

◆ SKELETAL MUSCLES

Muscles attached to bones are called skeletal muscles. They are also called "voluntary" muscles because a person can choose whether to move them. In addition to muscle fibers, skeletal muscles contain connective tissue, nerves, and blood vessels. Each muscle is surrounded by a fibrous membrane. At one end of the muscle, the fibers of this membrane connect with a tough band of elastic tissue called a **tendon.** Tendons connect most skeletal muscles to bones.

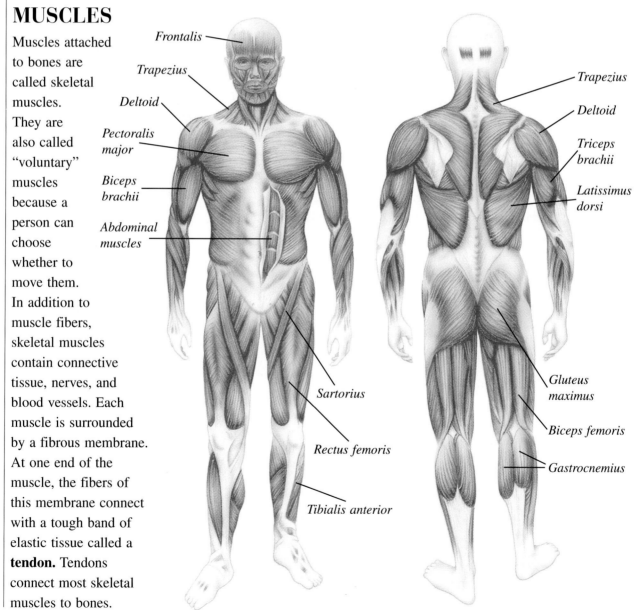

Frontalis

Trapezius

Deltoid

Pectoralis major

Biceps brachii

Abdominal muscles

Sartorius

Rectus femoris

Tibialis anterior

Trapezius

Deltoid

Triceps brachii

Latissimus dorsi

Gluteus maximus

Biceps femoris

Gastrocnemius

Body Systems Handbook

The Achilles' tendon joins the calf muscles to the heel bone; it can be felt by touching the back of the ankle while wiggling the foot.

Achilles tendon

Smooth muscles are found in internal organs, such as the stomach, intestines, urinary bladder, uterus, and blood vessels. Unlike skeletal muscles, which can be contracted voluntarily, smooth muscles are involuntary. Smooth muscles are responsible for the contractions of the esophagus and the intestines called **peristalsis.** Smooth muscles are also responsible for the contractions of labor during childbirth.

Cardiac muscle fibers are strong like skeletal muscles, but the heart is an involuntary muscle. The contraction and relaxation of cardiac muscle fibers pumps blood through the body automatically and rhythmically.

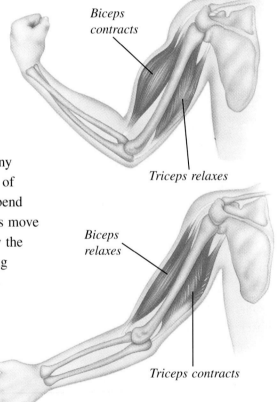

Biceps contracts

Triceps relaxes

Biceps relaxes

Triceps contracts

◆ # MUSCLE ACTION

Muscle fibers respond to nerve impulses by contracting. When enough nerve impulses are received, the entire muscle contracts and pulls any attached tissue along with it, resulting in movement of that tissue. Skeletal muscles often work in pairs to bend and straighten joints. The biceps and triceps muscles move the arms at the elbow. In the illustration, notice how the biceps is attached to two different bones. Contracting the biceps muscle pulls upward on one of the bones of the lower arm, causing the arm to bend. When the biceps relaxes and the triceps contracts, the arm is pulled in the opposite direction.

Even the simplest body movements involve the coordination of many muscles. For example, it takes 13 muscles to smile and 34 muscles to frown.

COMMON MUSCLE PROBLEMS

Considering that muscles are used every time you move, it is not surprising that muscle injuries are common. Although regular exercise preceded by a proper warm-up reduces the risk of muscle injury, it can still occur—especially when a person ignores his or her limitations. Charley horses and pulled hamstrings are common jogging-related injuries. A **charley horse** is a painful contusion, or bruising, of the muscle and is frequently accompanied by a tear in muscle fibers. A **pulled hamstring** is an overextension or strain of one of the muscles in the back of the thigh. Inflammation of the flexor muscles of the front portion of the lower leg causes another common condition, known as **shin splints. A muscular cramp** is a prolonged and painful involuntary muscular contraction. A **spasm** is a brief, involuntary contraction. The exact cause of muscle cramps and spasms is unknown. Experts suggest that they may result from several causes: insufficient oxygen, calcium, or magnesium; fatigue; or various drugs. **Tendinitis** is the inflammation of the connective tissue surrounding a tendon.

Q and A

Q: Why does muscular fatigue develop?

A: The causes of muscular fatigue are not well understood. One explanation is that when muscles contract they produce lactic acid. Lactic acid creates an environment in which muscles are not able to respond to stimulation. However, new research indicates that there are other contributing factors, such as depletion of stored energy and muscle glycogen, inadequate blood flow to the muscles, and low oxygen levels. Well-conditioned athletes experience less muscle fatigue. It is known that they accumulate less lactic acid in their muscles and that conditioning actually increases the capillary density of the skeletal muscles, increasing blood flow.

Q: Why does weight training make a person look muscular?

A: Muscles develop differently depending on the type of exercise they receive. For example, when a muscle is contracted moderately but repeatedly, as in swimming, it develops new capillaries and some increased strength. When a muscle is contracted in short, forceful actions, as in weightlifting, the muscle fibers increase in diameter and the entire muscle enlarges more than in repeated, moderate activity. This form of exercise increases the strength of the muscle, but a weight lifter will not have the endurance of a swimmer.

Q: What does it mean if a person has TMJ?

A: Stress or a poor bite (malocclusion of the teeth) can cause some people to clench their jaw, especially in their sleep. Contracting the jaw muscles in this way causes pressure on the temporomandibular joint located in the jaw just below the ear. This can result in headaches, earaches, or pain in the jaw, neck, or shoulder. This condition is called temporomandibular joint syndrome, or TMJ. Stress management and dental splints are often prescribed for sufferers of TMJ.

The Circulatory System

Your circulatory system includes the cardiovascular system and the lymphatic system. The cardiovascular system, which consists of the heart (cardio-), blood, and blood vessels (-vascular), transports oxygen, nutrients, antibodies, and infection-fighting cells to each cell in your body. It also helps rid the body of wastes. In addition to blood, your body has another fluid, lymph, that circulates throughout it. The lymphatic system is a drainage subsystem for the larger circulatory system and is active in fighting disease.

BLOOD

Blood consists of various specialized cells and a fluid called **plasma.** The yellowish plasma contains water, nutrients, wastes, and other materials. The cells found in blood include **red blood cells,** which carry oxygen; **white blood cells,** which protect the body against disease; and **platelets,** which initiate the process of blood clotting.

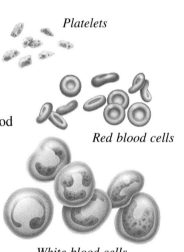

Platelets

Red blood cells

White blood cells

Heart

Arteries

Veins

BLOOD VESSELS

The blood vessels of the circulatory system form a continuous system. There are three types of blood vessels. **Arteries** are the thick-walled vessels that carry blood from the heart to all parts of the body. **Veins,** which have thinner walls, carry blood back to the heart from all parts of the body. Veins also contain tiny valves that prevent blood from flowing downward from the pull of gravity. **Capillaries,** which are the smallest of the blood vessels, link the arteries to the veins. Because of their small diameter, blood cells must pass through capillaries in single file. No cell in the body is more than a few cells away from a capillary.

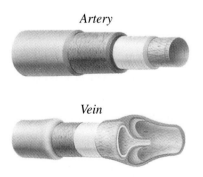

Artery

Vein

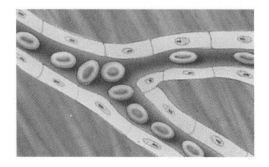

The wall of a capillary is only one cell thick, which allows oxygen and nutrients to leave the bloodstream easily and be taken up by the body's cells.

◆ HEART

The heart is the circulatory system's pump. Actually, the heart is two pumps placed side-by-side. The right side of the heart pumps blood to the lungs, and the left side pumps blood to the rest of the body. The atria receive blood and pump it into the ventricles. The ventricles push the blood out of the heart. The ventricles' job requires a greater force, so the ventricles are larger and more muscular. Valves in the heart allow blood to move through it in one direction only.

Blood enters the **right atrium** of the heart and is pumped into the **right ventricle.** When the right ventricle contracts, blood is pumped through the **pulmonary arteries** to the lungs, where the blood gives off carbon dioxide and picks up oxygen.

Oxygen-rich blood returns to the heart through the **pulmonary veins** and enters the **left atrium.** It is then pumped to the **left ventricle.** The left ventricle contracts, pumping blood into the **aorta** and out to various parts of the body.

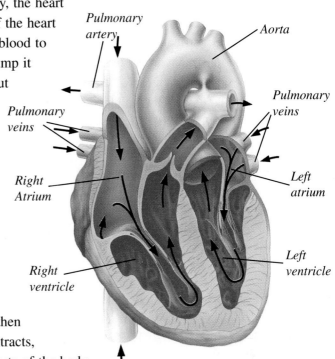

Pulmonary artery

Aorta

Pulmonary veins

Pulmonary veins

Right Atrium

Left atrium

Right ventricle

Left ventricle

CARDIAC OUTPUT ◆

During exercise, the muscles and the body organs need more oxygen and nutrients. The heart accommodates this need in two ways. First, it pumps blood out faster, increasing the **heart rate.** Second, the heart increases its **stroke volume,** the amount of blood pumped out of the heart with each heartbeat. The amount of blood pumped with each beat multiplied by the number of beats per minute is called **cardiac output.** As a person exercises regularly and becomes more conditioned, the heart begins to work more efficiently and stroke volume increases. In very well-conditioned athletes, the heart itself enlarges in response to the increased demand. This type of enlargement is not harmful and disappears rapidly if the exercise level diminishes.

HEART ARRHYTHMIA

The heart beats in a regular rhythm as the walls of the atria and ventricles alternately contract and relax. This is called the **cardiac cycle.** If the cardiac cycle is disrupted and the heart gets out of rhythm, a condition called **arrhythmia** results. Arrhythmia can lead to serious consequences, including death. When a person begins to exercise, the heart adjusts to the greater demand for oxygen by increasing its rate. If the person exercising has a heart problem or is in a weakened condition, there is a chance that as the heart rate increases, the heart will get out of rhythm. When the heart's atria get out of synch, a person can survive because blood is still able to move through the heart. However, if the ventricles are affected, sudden death may occur because blood does not get pumped to the vital organs. To help avoid exercise-related heart-rhythm problems, always warm up first so the heart can adjust slowly. There are other causes for arrhythmia. For example, the drug cocaine can cause arrhythmia by disabling the nerves that regulate the contractions of the heart.

THE ROLE OF THE LYMPHATIC SYSTEM

The cells of the body are bathed in a clear watery fluid called **lymph.** This fluid helps move materials between the capillaries and the body's cells. Lymph is formed from water, proteins, and other nutrients that move out of the blood into the spaces between the body's cells. This fluid must be returned to the circulatory system. A system of **lymphatic vessels** similar to the veins and capillaries collect the fluid and return it to the circulatory system. The lymph capillaries parallel the blood capillary system and are connected to larger lymph vessels that eventually connect to one of two ducts. These two ducts, the thoracic and the right lymphatic, open into two veins just above the heart.

The lymphatic system is also a part of the body's immune system. In addition to the lymph fluid and vessels, this system includes the lymph glands, the thymus gland, the spleen, and the tonsils. For information about the role of the lymphatic system in fighting disease, refer to the section in this handbook on the immune system.

Q: What does the doctor actually listen for with a stethoscope?

A: A stethoscope amplifies heart sounds so they can easily be heard. Heart sounds are produced by the contracting and relaxing of the heart and the opening and closing of its valves. These heart sounds can provide information about the health of the heart. One thing the doctor listens for is a heart murmur. A murmur is a sound that occurs when the heart's valves do not function properly. For example, a valve may not close completely, thereby allowing blood to leak back into the chamber it just left. Often heart murmurs are not serious. However, when they do create a problem, open heart surgery can be performed to repair or replace a damaged valve.

Q: What's a pacemaker?

A: Two small groups of cells in the wall of the heart set the pace for cardiac contraction. They are the heart's natural pacemaker. Sometimes disease causes these cells to become slow in their initiation of the contraction. If medication does not help, doctors can insert an electronic, artificial pacemaker near the heart. This pacemaker is battery-operated, and wires from it send a small electric impulse to the heart at regular intervals. Over 50,000 people in the United States have either external or internal pacemakers.

Q: Why have some young athletes died suddenly from heart failure?

A: Young athletes who have healthy hearts and who do not abuse drugs seldom die of heart failure. However, athletes with underlying, undiagnosed heart conditions are at risk. The most common cause of sudden death from heart disease is hypertrophic cardiomyopathy (HCM). HCM is a genetic disease that causes an abnormal thickening of the left ventricle. This condition can kill with no prior symptoms of disease, and it accounts for roughly half of the heart-related fatalities in young athletes. In some other cases of sudden death, the suspected cause is the use of an illegal drug, which can cause a fatal heart arrhythmia.

The Respiratory System

Every breath you take provides your body's cells with essential oxygen. As they perform their various tasks, the cells produce the waste product carbon dioxide. Your respiratory system provides a way to remove carbon dioxide from your body and to obtain oxygen from the atmosphere. The respiratory system includes the pharynx, the larynx, the trachea, the bronchi, and the lungs.

◆ RESPIRATORY TRACT

Normally, air enters the body through the **nostrils.** Hairs in the nose help filter out dust and other small particles. The cells of the nasal cavity warm and moisten the air before it enters the lungs. Some cells lining the **nasal cavity** secrete mucus, which also traps debris. If a person breathes through his or her mouth, the air passes through the **oral cavity.** The nasal and oral cavities meet at the throat, or **pharynx.** Air from the nose or mouth passes through the pharynx to the voice box, or **larynx,** where the vocal cords are located. The larynx is attached to the windpipe, or **trachea.** This long passageway leads to the **lungs.** In the illustration, notice that the pharynx leads to both the esophagus (food passageway) and the trachea. When a person swallows, the **epiglottis** covers the opening to the trachea, preventing foods or liquids from entering the lungs.

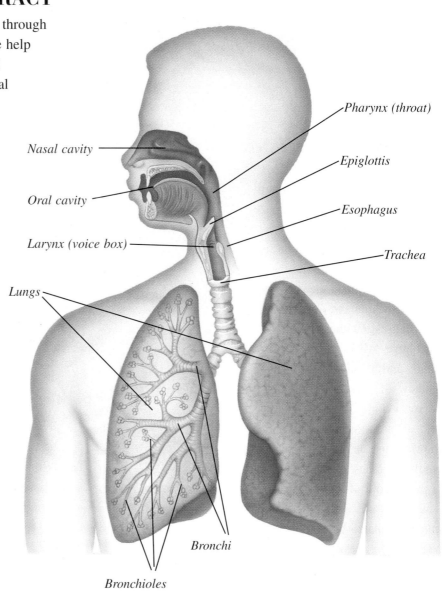

Nasal cavity

Oral cavity

Larynx (voice box)

Lungs

Pharynx (throat)

Epiglottis

Esophagus

Trachea

Bronchi

Bronchioles

The lungs are located in the chest cavity. Below the lungs is a sheet of muscle tissue, the **diaphragm,** which separates the chest cavity from the abdominal cavity. Two tubes known as **bronchi** connect the trachea to the **lungs.** The bronchi are subdivided many times, forming smaller and smaller passages, the smallest of which are known as **bronchioles.** At the end of each bronchiole is a cluster of tiny air sacs called **alveoli.** Each lung contains about 150 million alveoli, each of which is surrounded by **capillaries.** Oxygen passes from the alveoli into these capillaries for delivery to the body's cells. Simultaneously, carbon dioxide in the bloodstream moves from the capillaries into the alveoli, where it is exhaled from the lungs. This simultaneous exchange of gases is called **respiration.**

Bronchiole

Capillaries

Alveoli

Oxygen

Carbon dioxide

◆ BREATHING

Air moves into and out of the lungs with every breath. Why is this? The movement of the diaphragm and rib muscles changes the size of the chest cavity. When a person **inhales,** the diaphragm contracts and moves downward and the rib muscles expand the chest cavity upwards and outwards. This causes the chest cavity to enlarge. Air rushes into the lungs, and the alveoli expand as they fill with air. When a person **exhales,** the diaphragm relaxes and moves upward and the rib muscles relax. The chest cavity becomes smaller, and air is pushed out of the lungs. This process is automatic and is regulated by the respiratory control center in the brain stem.

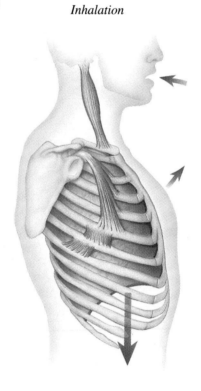

Inhalation

Diaphragm contracts

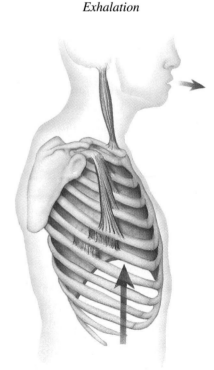

Exhalation

Diaphragm relaxes

LUNG DYSFUNCTION

Efficient breathing depends on two factors: an adequate amount of oxygen must reach the alveoli, and there must be adequate surface area available for gas exchange in the alveoli. There are numerous reasons why the first condition might not be met. If the diaphragm and rib muscles do not function correctly, air will not flow into the lungs. An inhaled object or an abnormal growth can block the air passage. (Chapter 28 describes how the Heimlich maneuver is used to remove objects from the air passages.) In a disease such as asthma, the air passages can become constricted, restricting the flow of air to the lungs. Many conditions that block air passages can be treated successfully.

Anything that impairs the function of the alveoli reduces the total surface area available for gas exchange. For example, if the alveoli are filled with fluid, as with pneumonia, or covered with the debris found in cigarette smoke, respiration is diminished. The disease emphysema causes the alveoli to be less elastic. Because they are unable to expand sufficiently, less oxygen fills the alveoli and gas exchange is diminished. If the alveoli are punctured, as sometimes happens with a broken rib, they lose air pressure and collapse. The alveoli can also be damaged by noxious fumes. For example, the dangerous practice of inhaling chemical substances for nonmedical reasons damages the alveoli as well as the brain. Diseases that cause oxygen deficiency are extremely debilitating. Abstaining from smoking is the most important thing a person can do to prevent respiratory problems. Keep in mind that there is no way to replace damaged or destroyed alveoli.

Q _and_ A

Q: Why do people yawn?

A: Even when people breathe normally, not all of the alveoli are filled with oxygen. That means that some blood may pass through the lungs without getting enough oxygen. It is thought that this low blood-oxygen concentration triggers the yawn reflex. Yawning causes a person to take a deep breath, which makes more oxygen available to the alveoli and increases the blood-oxygen concentration.

Q: What's wrong when a person has laryngitis?

A: Sometimes an infection or an irritation from inhaling noxious vapors can cause the cells lining the larynx to become inflamed. When this occurs, the vocal cords may not vibrate as easily as usual and the voice may sound hoarse. This condition is known as laryngitis. Laryngitis is usually mild and goes away by itself. However, if the tissue becomes so swollen that it obstructs the airway, a tracheotomy may have to be performed. In this procedure, a hole is made in the trachea below the larynx, allowing air to reach the lungs.

Q: What is diaphragmatic breathing?

A: Usually when people breathe, they do not fully utilize the lower third of their lungs. In diaphragmatic breathing, the diaphragm is lowered, allowing air to fill the abdominal area, which appears to blow up like a balloon. Diaphragmatic breathing is a very effective way to relax. To practice diaphragmatic breathing, place your hands on your abdomen and breathe in, trying to fill your abdomen with air. If done correctly, the abdomen should raise and lower as air goes in and out of the lungs.

The Digestive System

The digestive system allows your body to take in and process food to nourish its cells. Digestion begins in the mouth and continues in the stomach and the small intestine. Other digestive organs, such as the pancreas, liver, and gallbladder, contribute to the process of digestion.

MOUTH

Digestion begins in the mouth with three pairs of **salivary glands.** The smell, and even the thought, of food causes these glands to increase their production of saliva. **Saliva** contains enzymes that break down starches and other complex carbohydrates in food. As a person chews, food is broken into small pieces and mixed with the saliva, which moistens it, making it easier to swallow. Once the food is chewed sufficiently, swallowing forces it into the esophagus.

ESOPHAGUS AND STOMACH

After food is swallowed, it passes through a muscular tube called the **esophagus** and enters the **stomach.** Glands in the stomach lining secrete a variety of enzymes and other chemical compounds. These secretions aid in digesting the food and are collectively called **gastric juices.** Most of the protein and carbohydrates in food are broken down in the stomach. The churning action of the stomach muscles furthers the digestion process by mixing the food and enzymes. After about four hours, the food has become a liquid called **chyme.** The chyme then passes into the small intestine.

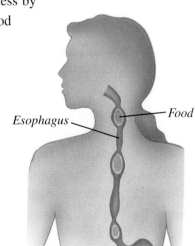

A wavelike motion called peristalsis pushes food through the esophagus and into the stomach.

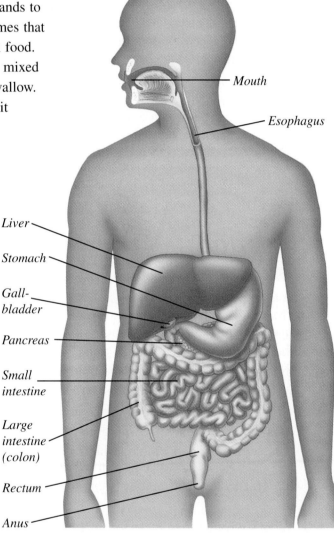

Mouth

Esophagus

Liver

Stomach

Gall-bladder

Pancreas

Small intestine

Large intestine (colon)

Rectum

Anus

SMALL INTESTINE

Digestion is completed in the **small intestine.** Enzymes secreted by the liver and pancreas enter the portion of the small intestine close to the stomach. The digestion of carbohydrates and proteins continues, and the digestion of fats occurs. The remainder of the small intestine has the critical function of absorbing the digested food.

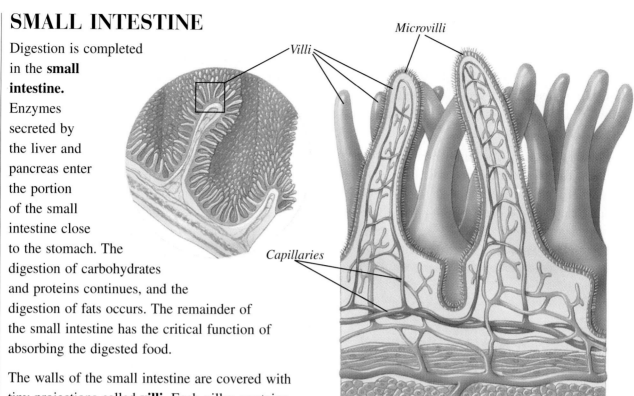

Villi

Microvilli

Capillaries

The walls of the small intestine are covered with tiny projections called **villi.** Each villus contains capillaries and lymph vessels and is covered with hairlike projections called **microvilli.** Nutrients move from the small intestine into the capillaries, where they are transported to the cells of the body. The presence of the villi and microvilli increases the total surface area available for nutrient absorption. In fact, for the average person, the total surface area available for nutrient absorption is larger than a tennis court! The middle section of the small intestine contains the greatest concentration of villi, and most absorption takes place there.

PANCREAS, LIVER, AND GALLBLADDER

The small intestine produces only a few digestive enzymes. Others are supplied by the pancreas and the liver. These organs communicate with each other through hormonal messages that coordinate their enzyme secretions. The **pancreas** secretes enzymes that are active in the digestion of carbohydrates, proteins, and fats. The **liver** secretes a greenish fluid called **bile.** Bile enables large molecules of fat to be broken down. The **gallbladder,** a small, muscular, green sac attached to the liver, stores excess bile until it is needed. The pancreas and the liver have other functions as well. The liver is vital in regulating metabolism. Toxins, such as drugs and alcohol, are broken down by the liver. It also filters damaged red blood cells, debris, and pathogens from the bloodstream. The pancreas produces insulin, which is vital in regulating blood-sugar levels.

LARGE INTESTINE

Undigested food moves into the **large intestine,** or colon, where water is absorbed from the waste and returned to the bloodstream. No food absorption takes place here. Peristalsis moves the solid waste, called feces, through the colon to the **rectum.** Here, it is stored briefly and then eliminated from the body through an opening called the **anus.**

DISORDERS OF THE DIGESTIVE SYSTEM

The two most common disorders of the digestive system, constipation and diarrhea, are discussed in Chapter 5, page 118. Another common problem is a **gastric ulcer,** an open sore that develops in the stomach. If the sore creates damage to blood vessels in the stomach wall, a **bleeding ulcer** can develop. Left untreated, bleeding ulcers can cause death. It is now known that most, but not all, ulcers are caused by the bacteria *H. pylori* and can be treated successfully with antibiotics.

The gallbladder removes water from bile and stores it in a concentrated form. Sometimes bile becomes too concentrated, and hard concentrations of minerals and salts, called **gallstones,** form. If the gallstones are large enough to block the flow of bile out of the gallbladder, they cause a great deal of pain and must be removed surgically. Smaller gallstones can be removed or destroyed by less invasive techniques. One technique involves using directed sound waves to shatter the gallstones.

Q: How long does it take food to pass through the digestive system?

A: Some foods take longer to digest than others. Studies have been conducted in which people volunteered to eat small beads with a meal. About 70 percent of the beads appeared in the feces within 72 hours. However, it took a full week to recover all of the beads.

Q: Is the appendix a part of the digestive system?

A: The vermiform (worm-shaped) appendix is located off the large intestine close to where it meets the small intestine. This rounded saclike structure is about 3.5 inches long. The appendix serves no function in digestion, and its purpose is unknown. The appendix can become inflamed, and if it ruptures, it is a life-threatening situation. However, an inflamed appendix is not caused by contaminated food.

Q: What causes a person to vomit?

A: One way the digestive system responds to irritations is by eliminating the irritant. The vomiting reflex is an efficient method of eliminating the contents of the upper digestive system. First, a person salivates heavily and feels nauseated. Then the muscle separating the stomach and small intestine relaxes, and strong peristaltic waves travel upward. Regurgitation of the contents of the stomach and upper small intestine results. This reflex is controlled by the vomiting center in the medulla of the brain and can also be stimulated by strong emotional experiences.

Q: What causes indigestion?

A: Indigestion is a broad term that covers a variety of conditions. Most causes are not serious and are related to food. Some people have difficulty digesting highly-seasoned foods or carbonated beverages. Other people experience indigestion if they eat too fast or too much. Your emotional and physical state greatly influence your ability to digest food. Emotions can cause the stomach muscles to contract forcefully, causing it to churn. It is not a good idea to eat when you are overly tired or upset.

The Endocrine System

Your endocrine system is composed of specialized tissues called **endocrine glands.** Unlike other glands, your endocrine glands do not have ducts (tubes) that deliver their secretions to a particular point. Instead, they secrete chemical substances called hormones directly into the bloodstream. The main endocrine glands are the thyroid, the pituitary, the adrenals, the endocrine cells in the pancreas, and the reproductive organs. Hormones are also produced by the hypothalamus of the brain, the pineal gland, the parathyroid glands, the thymus, and the walls of the stomach and the intestine.

HORMONES AND THE CENTRAL NERVOUS SYSTEM

Hormones act as chemical messengers and regulate many body functions. Each hormone carries a particular message to specific cells of the body. The central nervous system regulates the secretion of these hormones. In fact, the central nervous system and the endocrine system are so closely linked that they are sometimes called the **neuroendocrine system.**

Coordinating centers in the **hypothalamus** of the brain regulate the activities of these two systems. The hypothalamus is sometimes called the master switch of the endocrine system because most endocrine glands are either directly or indirectly under its control. The hypothalamus constantly monitors the internal state of the body and sends out messages that keep body functions stable. Sometimes the messages are in the form of nerve impulses; at other times, they are hormonal. Nerve impulses produce rapid changes, while the release of hormones causes slower but longer-lasting effects.

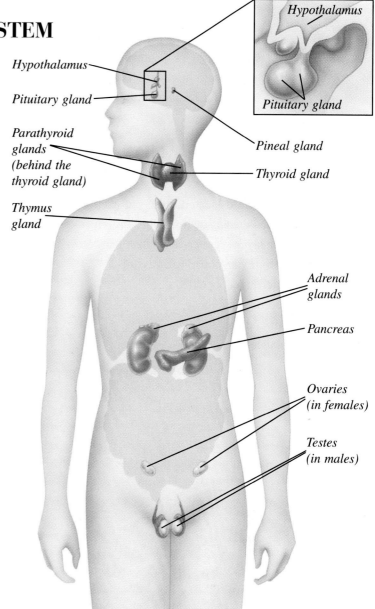

Hypothalamus

Pituitary gland

Hypothalamus

Pituitary gland

Pineal gland

Thyroid gland

Parathyroid glands (behind the thyroid gland)

Thymus gland

Adrenal glands

Pancreas

Ovaries (in females)

Testes (in males)

PITUITARY GLAND

The pea-sized **pituitary gland** lies at the base of the brain and is connected to the hypothalamus by a slender stalk. Hormones produced by the hypothalamus move through the pituitary gland. In response to these hormones, the pituitary gland produces at least six hormones of its own. These hormones regulate growth and direct the reproductive organs, the adrenal glands, and the thyroid gland. In women, pituitary hormones stimulate uterine contractions during childbirthand the release of breast milk during nursing. Because the pituitary gland controls so many different functions—and even controls other glands—it is often called the master gland.

Thyroid gland

THYROID GLAND

The butterfly-shaped **thyroid gland** is located at the base of the front of the neck. It secretes hormones that play a crucial role in determining the speed at which the body transforms food into energy (metabolic rate) and the speed at which the body uses that energy. One thyroid hormone is responsible for normal growth of the brain, bones, and muscles during childhood. The thyroid gland also helps maintain a normal heart rate, has a roll in maintaining the body's calcium level, and affects reproductive functions.

ADRENAL GLANDS AND "FIGHT OR FLIGHT"

There is an **adrenal gland** located on top of each kidney. These glands produce dozens of different hormones. The adrenal's inner layer secretes hormones that cause a "fight-or-flight" response to stressful situations. The outer layer secretes hormones that help regulate the body's metabolism and its salt-and-water balance.

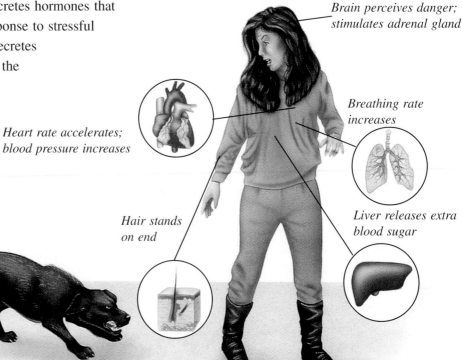

Brain perceives danger; stimulates adrenal gland

Heart rate accelerates; blood pressure increases

Breathing rate increases

Liver releases extra blood sugar

Hair stands on end

When the brain senses danger, the hypothalamus stimulates the release of adrenal hormones. These hormones stimulate other body responses.

678

◆ OTHER ENDOCRINE GLANDS

Several other endocrine glands aid in maintaining normal body functions. The **pancreas** secretes two hormones that help regulate how much glucose is in the bloodstream. The **pineal gland** is thought to control the body's internal time clock. The **parathyroid glands** control the calcium level in the blood. The reproductive organs—**testes** in males and **ovaries** in females—produce hormones that regulate the development of sex characteristics and initiate the production of reproductive cells. The **thymus** plays an important role in immune response and is discussed in the section on the immune system.

HORMONE DISORDERS

Many hormonal disorders are well recognized and are fairly easily treated. Others can be difficult to diagnose, and their treatment may cause side effects that will also need treatment. Some disorders are characterized by the under-production of a particular hormone. For example, if a child's pituitary gland produces inadequate amounts of growth hormone, the growth that precedes puberty will not occur, and the child will remain short. (Not everyone who is short has this condition; many people just inherit a short stature.) Supplying the missing hormone can correct the condition. A number of hormone deficiencies can be treated by simply supplying the missing hormone.

Q: Is it safe to take hormones?

A: The use of hormones to replace a missing hormone is called hormone replacement therapy. When prescribed by a physician to treat a specific condition and when used exactly as directed, hormone replacement therapy is usually safe. For example, the hormone insulin is commonly used to treat diabetes. When closely monitored, this has proved safe and effective. The safety of some types of hormone replacement therapy is not well established. For example, after menopause a woman's estrogen level drops dramatically. Often, hormone replacement therapy is used to replace the missing estrogen. Research indicates that this will help prevent osteoporosis and reduce a woman's risk of developing heart disease. However, the effects of long-term estrogen use are unknown, and some studies indicate that it may increase the risk of developing breast cancer.

Estrogen belongs to a group of hormones called steroid hormones. These hormones are secreted by the cortex of the adrenal glands, the ovaries, the placenta, and the testes. Steroid hormones have the ability to pass into the nucleus of a cell, where they can trigger changes in the chromosomes. There are legitimate medical uses for these hormones; however, the abuse of steroid hormones is quite dangerous. Anabolic steroids are powerful synthetic chemicals that resemble one of the hormones produced in the testes. They increase muscle size, but because they can alter the chromosomes, they have serious and potentially deadly side effects.

The Immune System

You constantly come in contact with bacteria and viruses that have the potential to make you ill, but your body's defense system manages to control these organisms. Chapter 21 of your textbook discusses this defense system. When the body's nonspecific defenses are unable to overcome an invading organism, your immune system goes to work. Rather than being an organ system, your immune system is a functional system; it works by using components of the lymphatic and circulatory systems.

◆ WHITE BLOOD CELLS

The white blood cells, or **leukocytes,** defend the body against infection. They begin their lives as immature cells in the bone marrow. As they mature, leukocytes become specialized for specific functions. The leukocytes that are important in the immune response are the **macrophages** and several types of **lymphocytes.** As shown in the photograph, the macrophages can

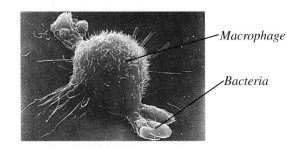
Macrophage
Bacteria

surround and digest bacteria and other invaders. Some can move from the bloodstream through the fluid that surrounds the body cells to reach the site of an infection. The lymphocytes are involved in the production of antibodies, in recognizing and destroying specific types of cells, and in remembering a specific pathogen in case it is encountered again.

◆ THYMUS GLAND

Some of the immature lymphocytes leave the bone marrow and go to the **thymus gland.** There they undergo a change and become one of the different types of **T-cells** (for thymus) of immune system. This change takes place just before birth and during the first months of life. The thymus also functions as an endocrine gland. Its hormone, thymosin, is important to the maturation of T-cells and is thought to influence them after they leave the thyroid. At about 12 years of age, the thymus begins to shrink. In adults, the thymus is very small, and its function is not clearly understood.

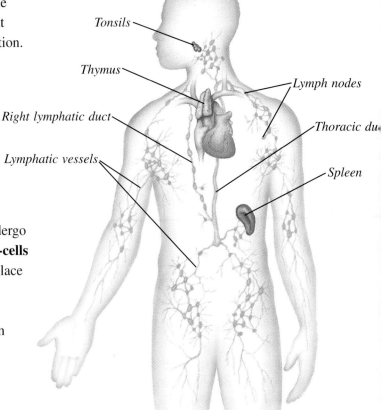
Tonsils
Thymus
Right lymphatic duct
Lymphatic vessels
Lymph nodes
Thoracic du
Spleen

LYMPH NODES AND GLANDS

Once the macrophages and the lymphocytes mature, they circulate in the bloodstream until they reach one of the secondary lymphatic organs, such as the lymph nodes, the spleen, or the tonsils. The lymphatic vessels and the **lymph nodes** are described in the section on the circulatory system. As lymph circulates through these nodes, macrophages along the walls engulf any pathogens, damaged cells, or cell debris present in the lymph fluid. Large lymph nodes are called **lymph glands** and are located in the armpits, in the groin, and at the base of the neck. The "swollen" glands that accompany some infections are actually enlarged lymph glands.

SPLEEN AND TONSILS

The **spleen** performs the same function for the blood that the lymph nodes do for the lymph. Here, white blood cells rid the blood of foreign matter. The spleen contains more lymphatic tissue than any other part of the body. The **tonsils** are large lymph nodes found in the walls of the pharynx. At birth, the tonsils are quite small. They increase in size until about age six or seven, when they begin to shrink. The lymph nodes in the tonsils are not always able to disable invading organisms, and the tonsils frequently become infected. At one time it was standard practice to remove the tonsils if repeated infections occurred. Now they are viewed as a line of defense against invading bacteria, and if possible, they are left in place.

STRESS AND THE IMMUNE SYSTEM

Researchers now know that the central nervous system can communicate chemically with the immune system and that the immune system produces chemicals that can reply to the nervous system. A new field of medicine called **psychoneuroimmunology** investigates what influence these two systems have on each other. One area of particular interest is the effect that stress has on the immune system and on subsequent illnesses or diseases. Researchers have found that stressful events can actually suppress the immune system, causing the person under stress to be more susceptible to illness. As knowledge about the relationship between the central nervous system and the immune system increases, new ways of preventing and treating disease will emerge.

Q: What is pus?

A: Pus is a mixture of white blood cells, dead pathogens, debris from broken-down body cells, and blood plasma. It is a sign that the body's defense system is at work. When pus collects in an infected region of the body, an abscess occurs. No abscess, no matter how small, should ever be squeezed. This can cause bacteria to enter to bloodstream and spread to another part of the body.

Q: What are antihistamines?

A: During an allergic response, the body produces histamines. Histamines cause an inflammatory reaction and increase mucus production. They are responsible for the teary eyes, the runny nose, and the itchy throat that are associated with allergies. Certain medications—appropriately called antihistamines—block the histamines' effects and alleviate allergy symptoms.

The Excretory System

Your excretory system removes the waste products of metabolism from your body. It also removes excess water and minerals. Your kidneys are the main organ of excretion, but your respiratory and digestive systems also play a role. In addition, a small amount of waste products are excreted by the sweat glands.

◆ KIDNEYS AND URINARY TRACT

In addition to its role in digestion, the liver converts the toxic waste products of metabolism into less toxic ones: urea and uric acid. These and other toxic substances in the bloodstream must be removed. The renal arteries carry blood containing toxic substances to the kidneys. The **kidneys** remove urea and uric acid from the bloodstream and turn them into a liquid called **urine.** Peristaltic contractions move urine from the kidneys through the **ureters** to the **bladder.** Urine collects in the bladder until it leaves the body through the **urethra.**

In addition to forming urine, the kidneys maintain the body's internal chemical balance by first removing water and minerals from the bloodstream and then reabsorbing the amount of water and minerals needed by the body. The clean blood with its adjusted chemical composition then leaves the kidneys through the renal veins. The kidneys are amazingly efficient; one healthy kidney can easily meet the body's needs.

Another waste product, perspiration, is excreted by the skin. Perspiring is also the body's way of keeping itself cool.

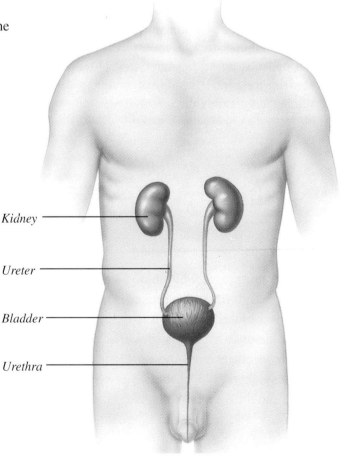

Artery

Vein

Ureter

Kidney

Ureter

Bladder

Urethra

◆ URINE FORMATION

Each kidney contains a little over 1 million blood-filtering units called **nephrons.** Nephrons consist of a tiny tube, or tubule, with a cup-shaped structure at one end, and they produce urine in a two-phase process. First, **filtration** occurs. Blood coming from the renal artery flows into the capillary network in the cup. Pressure forces water and small molecules, such as urea, out of the capillaries and into the long tubule connected to the cup. Second, **reabsorption** takes place. About 99 percent of the water and some of the other substances that were filtered out of the blood move into capillaries that surround the tubule. The fluid that remains in the tubule is urine. The tubules join to form larger tubes, which connect with the ureter where it joins the kidney. **Urine** is a concentrated mixture of water, urea, and various mineral salts. Complex mechanisms regulate urine formation, and the contents of the urine can vary depending on the state of the body. This is why an analysis of the urine, called a urinalysis, is so useful in diagnosing some diseases.

DISORDERS OF THE URINARY SYSTEM

Urinary-tract infections are fairly common, especially in females. This is because the female's urethra is much shorter than that of the male. This allows bacteria easier access to the bladder and ureters. It is important to treat urinary-tract infections early. Once an infection is well established, it can travel up the urinary tract to the kidneys and cause a kidney infection. Acute or repeated kidney infections can cause permanent damage to the nephrons.

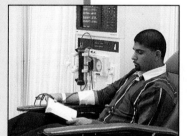

Kidney stones are more common in males than in females. They consist of hardened calcium salts, uric acid, and other by-products that collect inside the kidneys. Approximately 60 percent of kidney stones pass through the urethra and leave the body. If a stone becomes lodged in the ureter, it must be removed. Surgical removal was once the only option, but less invasive methods are now available. For example, fiber-optic laser surgery is used to break the stones into pieces that are small enough to pass through the urethra.

If the kidneys do not function properly, **hemodialysis** equipment can be used to filter waste products from the blood. As shown in the photograph on the right, blood is pumped from an artery in the wrist to the machine, where it is cleansed; it is then pumped back to the body. There are undesirable side effects to dialysis, and for many people, a kidney transplant is a better long-term solution.

Q _and_ A ◆◆◆◆◆◆◆◆◆◆

Q: How do people control when they urinate?

A: Two circular muscles at the base of the bladder control the flow of urine from the body. Adults have voluntary control of the outermost muscle, but young children do not. The bladder can hold up to 600 mL of urine, a little over half a liter. Stretch receptors in the wall of the bladder sense how full it is, and when it contains about 200 mL, a person usually feels the need to urinate. When the volume approaches 300 mL, the need to urinate becomes urgent.

Medical and Dental Careers

Many health-care workers provide direct care to help improve a person's health. These highly trained professionals diagnose limitations, illnesses, and injuries; provide necessary treatment; and operate highly specialized medical equipment.

♦ PHYSICIAN

Physicians examine, diagnose, and treat medical conditions. Many physicians treat patients for a variety of illnesses and conditions. Such physicians are called general practitioners, or family doctors. Many other physicians specialize in treating certain types of conditions. For example, cardiologists diagnose and treat people with heart ailments, obstetricians care for pregnant women and deliver babies, and orthopedists specialize in treating disorders of the bones, joints, tendons, and muscles.

To become a physician, a person usually completes a four-year college program in science. Four years of medical school follow. After graduating from medical school, physicians must complete an internship and, if he or she has chosen a specialty, a residency at a hospital, during which he or she receives another three to four years of intense training in both general medicine and the specialty.

A general practitioner, or family practice physician, performs physical exams and diagnoses and treats a variety of common ailments.

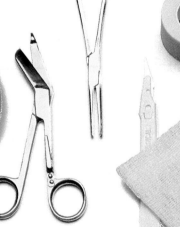

X-RAY TECHNOLOGIST

X-ray technologists operate X-ray equipment. They are often called on to prepare and administer special formulas that make certain body parts more visible on the X ray. If, for example, an X ray is to be taken of the stomach, the technologist gives the patient a drink that highlights the contents of the patient's stomach. An X-ray technologist may also operate medical imaging equipment, such as a CAT scan or an MRI.

A person who wants to become an X-ray technologist can receive training in college or at a hospital or technical school.

Using high-tech equipment, X-ray technologists work with people of all ages, helping physicians determine the cause of a patient's symptoms.

PHYSICAL THERAPIST

A **physical therapist** helps people with physical disabilities regain the strength to function as independently as possible. People who have amputations, broken bones, nerve or spinal injuries, severe back pain, or diseases such as cerebral palsy or multiple sclerosis can be helped by physical therapy. Therapists use ice packs, hot baths, electrodes, deep massage, exercise, and traction in their treatments.

Physical therapists work in nursing homes, hospitals, and rehabilitation centers. They must have patience, good coordination and physical strength, and good communication skills. Training programs and certification requirements vary from state to state.

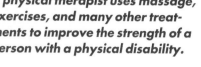

A physical therapist uses massage, exercises, and many other treatments to improve the strength of a person with a physical disability.

Emergency medical technicians, or EMTs, must react quickly to administer medical care in emergency situations.

EMERGENCY MEDICAL TECHNICIAN

An **emergency medical technician** (EMT) provides quick medical attention in emergency situations, such as automobile accidents. EMTs are trained to assess the seriousness of an injury or illness and to provide care for victims of heart attacks, near drownings, motor-vehicle accidents, accidental poisoning, and serious wounds. EMTs treat victims at the scene of the accident and often transport them to hospitals for additional medical care.

An emergency medical technician must be at least 18 years old, hold a high-school diploma, and have a valid driver's license. After completing an extensive training program, those certified as EMTs find jobs at hospitals, police or fire departments, or with private companies. With advanced training, a person can earn an EMT paramedic rating, which enables him or her to perform more advanced medical procedures.

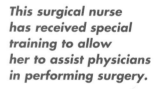

NURSE

A **nurse** works to care for those in need of medical attention. Depending on their level of training and their specialty, nurses perform a variety of duties, such as performing physical exams, observing and assessing patient symptoms, administering medication and treatments, and helping patients with proper nutrition, personal hygiene, and general health care.

Registered nurses (RNs) are licensed to practice by a state board. States have different education requirements that may include a diploma, an associate degree, or a bachelor's degree from an accredited college or university. With additional specialized training, an RN may become a nurse practitioner (NP). Licensed practical nurses (LPNs) usually complete a two-year college program or a technical-school program. In addition to many hours of clinical experience during their schooling, nurses must pass a state-board examination before they can be hired.

This surgical nurse has received special training to allow her to assist physicians in performing surgery.

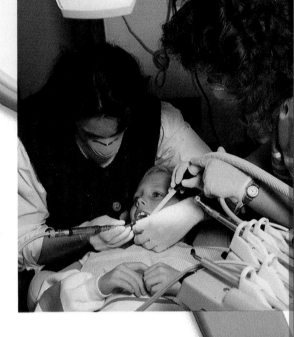

A dentist treats patients for diseases of the teeth and gums and repairs mechanical damage to the teeth to improve their appearance or function.

DENTAL LABORATORY TECHNICIAN

A **dental laboratory technician** makes retainers, dentures, braces, bridges, and crowns according to a dentist's exact specifications. He or she must have excellent manual dexterity, because precision and accuracy are crucial to the perfect fit of dental devices.

Most dental laboratory technicians acquire their skills in commercial laboratories. On-the-job training also is provided by hospitals and federal agencies. Schooling without the actual hands-on training takes about two years. Training with no formal schooling can last as long as five years.

The procedures followed by a dental laboratory technician require manual dexterity and artistic ability.

DENTIST

A **dentist** examines and treats patients for diseases and conditions of the teeth and gums. A general dentist checks teeth for abscesses, fills decayed teeth, determines whether orthodontic devices are needed, and instructs his or her patients on home dental care. He or she also does the preliminary work for fitting a patient with dentures, crowns, or bridges. As with physicians, there are many dental specialties as well.

After successfully completing college and four years of dental school, every aspiring dentist must pass many practical and written examinations as well as a state board exam. Specialists must complete two to three years of additional study and pass exams in their field of specialization.

Careers in Health-Care Administration

Hospitals and other health-care facilities must employ administrators to coordinate the activities of all employees—medical and nonmedical—so that patients receive the best possible care. Health-care administrators range from housekeepers to computer specialists to hospital directors.

MEDICAL RECORDS TECHNICIAN

A **medical records technician** is responsible for what happens to the information recorded by the nurse and doctor on your medical record or chart. They collect the information, classify it, use it to compute statistics, and finally transcribe the data into hospital files.

A medical records technician often holds an associate's degree in this field. However, a person who has earned a bachelor's degree in biology needs only to finish a one-year program for certification. Those who hold bachelor's degrees in medical records administration often supervise medical records technicians.

A medical records technician must organize information about many patients and monitor its accuracy and completeness.

An executive housekeeper in a hospital must see to it that the facility is always clean and sanitary, and in some cases, sterile.

EXECUTIVE HOUSEKEEPER

An **executive housekeeper** trains and manages a hospital's housekeeping staff, which can include custodians, kitchen workers, and laundry attendants. He or she is responsible for assuring that the proper precautions are taken to maintain the sanitary or even sterile environment required in certain areas of a hospital.

A hospital's executive housekeeper must be certified by the National Executive Housekeepers' Association. In addition to several college-level courses, he or she must complete a vocational or technical training program and possibly a management training program.

MEDICAL CLAIMS EXAMINER

A **medical claims examiner** evaluates the charges listed on an insurance claim form to determine whether they are proper and covered by the patient's insurance policy. If the examiner suspects errors have been made, he or she helps work out any problems before making payment to either party. Medical claims examiners work for insurance companies.

Most medical claims examiners hold a college degree. In addition, everyone entering this field should possess a general understanding of medical terms and procedures in order to evaluate each claim properly.

A medical claims examiner spends a great deal of time on the telephone, evaluating the validity of insurance claims and determining whether certain procedures are covered by a policy.

A systems analyst for a health care facility must help meet the changing computer needs of the facility.

SYSTEMS ANALYST

A **systems analyst** evaluates how information should be processed by a computer system. In a health-care institution, he or she is responsible for determining what type of computer system is needed by the facility. The analyst also chooses the printers, terminals, and software that will best meet the facility's current and future needs.

The educational background of a health-care systems analyst can range from a two-year degree with work-related experience to a master's degree in business or computer science. A general knowledge of health-care facilities and the functions they perform is quite useful in this field.

Community Service Careers in Health

Many people assist in the field of health care by providing a multitude of services and products to hospital personnel and patients, and to the general public. Some service careers require extensive training, while others can be started after a few courses beyond high school or with on-the-job training.

◆ PHARMACIST

A **pharmacist** dispenses drugs according to strict specifications provided by physicians and dentists. He or she also discusses possible side effects and drug interactions and advises customers on the proper usage of many nonprescription medications. Most pharmacists work in pharmacies or hospitals.

To become a pharmacist, a person must graduate from a five-year pharmacy program at an accredited college or university. Successful completion of an internship under the direct supervision of a registered pharmacist is also required. Finally, a pharmacy student must pass a state examination to become a registered pharmacist.

A pharmacist fills prescriptions and advises customers about the use of prescription and nonprescription drugs.

One of the tasks of an environmental health inspector is to check the temperatures of certain foods to ensure that they are safe to eat.

◆ ENVIRONMENTAL HEALTH INSPECTOR

An **environmental health inspector** works for a local, state, or federal government agency, monitoring facilities such as restaurants, dairies, and food-processing plants. Inspectors routinely test the air and the food and water used in these establishments for harmful pathogens and pollutants to determine whether the facilities are complying with government regulations regarding hygiene.

Environmental health inspectors generally have earned a four-year college degree. Some agencies also require several years of job-related experience.

COUNSELOR

A **counselor** works with individuals and families who are having difficulties in their social, economic, and personal lives. He or she helps people overcome the problems associated with drug and alcohol dependency, illness, and relationship, marriage, and family issues. A counselor begins by talking to his or her clients about their problems; he or she then assesses the situation and makes recommendations for how the problems could be resolved. The counselor also refers clients to other professionals and organizations if more-specialized help is needed.

Most counselors have at least a bachelor's degree in psychology or social work, but a master's degree in one of these fields is usually necessary for employment. In most parts of the country, a state examination is required to obtain a license.

This counselor is telling a young woman how long it will be until her HIV antibody test results are available. She will also answer questions about AIDS and HIV infection.

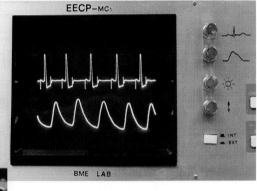

Dr. Kevin Cheng has helped save many lives by designing an artificial heart, which he is demonstrating here.

BIOMEDICAL ENGINEER

A **biomedical engineer** designs new medical equipment and does research to improve existing devices. Biomedical engineers are often assisted by biomedical equipment technicians, who install and service complicated pieces of machinery, such as lasers, electrocardiographs (EKGs), and electroencephalographs (EEGs).

A biomedical engineer usually works for a research facility such as a university, a health-care company, or a large hospital. He or she must have at least a bachelor's degree in engineering with specialization in biomedical training. Research positions require a master's degree or even a doctorate of philosophy in biomedical engineering.

Careers in Health Education

Education is part of any health-care worker's job. However, there are many types of health-care professionals who specialize in educating people about how to improve their overall physical and mental health.

◆ HEALTH TEACHER

A **health teacher** conducts courses on health in public or private schools. He or she helps students understand the material by starting class discussions, delivering lectures on health topics, and giving exams. Often, a health teacher discusses health concerns with individual students who feel uncomfortable talking about their concerns in class.

A health teacher should hold at least a bachelor's degree in health education. A strong background in human anatomy and physiology, biology, psychology, sociology, or other health-related topics is also quite useful. Teaching at the college level usually requires a graduate degree.

A health teacher gives lectures and answers questions about health-related topics.

◆ SCHOOL PSYCHOLOGIST

A **school psychologist** works closely with students, teachers, and parents to help students overcome social and emotional problems and neurological disorders that might interfere with learning. He or she often administers tests to assess mental health but spends most of his or her time talking to students and listening to what they have to say about their situations. School psychologists also advise a school's administrative body and suggest how policies might be changed to enhance learning.

Nearly all psychologists have at least a master's degree in psychology. Some hold doctorate degrees in psychology, which usually require eight years of schooling at a college or university. Most psychologists obtain clinical experience during their formal education by assisting and observing other psychologists interacting with patients.

A school psychologist assists students with various problems that might interfere with their ability to learn.

◆ SPECIAL-EDUCATION INSTRUCTOR

A **special-education instructor** uses knowledge of sign language and Braille to help people who are deaf or hard of hearing and people who are visually impaired develop better communication skills. Such instructors work in clinics, rehabilitation centers, and schools.

A special-education instructor must complete a bachelor's degree in special education. A master's degree with specialization in either the visually or hearing impaired is usually necessary as well. Some clinical work with visually- and hearing-impaired people is required before graduating with either degree.

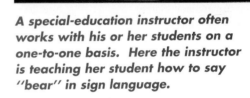

A special-education instructor often works with his or her students on a one-to-one basis. Here the instructor is teaching her student how to say "bear" in sign language.

◆ REGISTERED DIETICIAN

A **dietician** manages the food-service program in restaurants and cafeterias, hospitals, nursing homes, health-care clinics, private companies, and the military. He or she works closely with the kitchen staff to make sure that nutritious meals are served. Some dieticians are self-employed and work with individuals to help them improve their eating habits or control certain illnesses through proper nutrition.

A registered dietician must have a bachelor's degree in dietetics and must become certified with the American Dietetic Association.

Dieticians plan meals and manage the food-service program of many health-care facilities.

GlossaryIndex

*Page numbers in **boldface** type indicate the introduction of vocabulary terms.*

Depression, 40, 42, 62, 68, 115, 156–157, 166–167, 172, 246, 369, 412, 592
stress and, 157, 196
suicide and, 227, 229–230
in terminally ill person, 215
Dermatitis, 77
Dermatologist, 128
Dermis *the second layer of skin; contains the most important structures of the skin,* **127**
Designer drugs *synthetic drugs that are similar in chemistry to certain illegal drugs,* **305**
Diabetes, 13, 22, 41, 69, 108, 508–509, 529
type I, 513, 519
type II, 512–513
Diabetic coma, 519
Diaphragm, as contraceptive, 396
Diarrhea *loose bowel movements that occur when food moves too quickly through the digestive system,* **118**
Diastolic blood pressure, 523
Diet, 91, 111–112. *See also* Food selection; Nutrition
cancer and, 530
vegetarian, 96–97
Dietary fiber *a subclass of complex carbohydrates with a high ratio of plant material that is not absorbed by the body,* **71,** 83, 90
Dietary Guidelines for Americans, 82
Digestive disorders, 118–120
Digestive system, 674–676
Disaster *an event that affects the lives and health of people in one or more communities,* **602,** 603–604
Disease, 445
infectious. *See* Infectious disease noninfectious, 509–530
signs and symptoms of, 445–446
Dislocation *an injury in which the end of a bone comes out of its joint,* **627**
Displacement, as defense mechanism, 160
Dissociative disorder *a condition in which someone's personality changes to the point that the person believes he or she is someone else,* **165,** 166–167
Diuretic, 116, 251

Diving safety, 608–609
Divorce *the legal end to a marriage,* **395,** 406–407, 411–413
emotional impact on children, 412–413
DNA, 510
Dose *the exact amount of a drug,* **252,** 253
Douching, 337
Down's syndrome, 515–516
Drinking water, 444, 545–546
Drowning, 608–610, 639
Drown proofing *a technique to stay afloat that can be used even by those who cannot swim,* **609**
Drug *a substance that causes a physical or emotional change in a person,* **246**
absorption of, 254–255
accidental poisoning with, 601–602
dose of, 252–253
effects on the body, 253–256
healthier options, 245–246
illegal, 247–248, 261
over-the-counter. *See* Over-the-counter drugs
passage from mother's blood to fetus, 341
prescription. *See* Prescription drugs
psychoactive, 249, 299–316
from rain forest plants, 246–247
side effects and allergies, 256
unrecognized, 248
Drug abuse *intentional improper use of a drug,* 228, **248,** 252, 299–316. *See also* Intravenous drug use
depression and, 157
first aid in drug overdose, 643
HIV transmission from, 501
needle exchange programs, 534–535
during pregnancy, 310–311
sexual activity and, 477
vehicle accidents and, 593–594
violent behavior and, 429
Drug addiction, 299–301. *See also* Addiction
Drug allergy *an unwanted effect that accompanies the desired effect of a drug,* **256**
Drug dependence, 300–301
treatment for, 313–316
Drug interactions, 254–256, 602

Drug misuse *improper use of a drug,* **248**
Drug-oriented society, 245–249
Drug tolerance, 300–301
Drug-treatment programs, 313–316
Drug use *taking a medicine properly and in its correct dosage,* **248**
during pregnancy, 341
Drunken driving, 261, 267–268, 271, 593–594
Dying, 213–218
needs of terminally ill person, 216
suicide and terminal illness, 240–241
Dysfunctional family *a family that does not fulfill the basic functions of a healthy family,* **413,** 414

E

Ear-piercing equipment, 455, 494
Earthquake, 604
Eastern Indian foods, 93
Eating disorders *compulsive eating behaviors caused by emotional problems or an obsession with body weight,* 104–105, 113–117, 163, 166, 336
Ecosystem *a system made up of living things and their physical surroundings,* **539,** 540–541, 544
Ecstasy, 305, 308–309
Ectopic pregnancy, 345
Egg *female reproductive cell, also called an ovum; contains one-half of the instructions needed for the development of a new human being,* **325,** 332
Ejaculation, 327–328
Elder abuse *abuse of an elderly person,* **422**
Electric shock, steps to help in emergency, 642
Electrocution *death resulting from the flow of electrical current through the body,* **600**
Electrolysis, as hair removal, 135
Electrolyte balance, 78, 116, 118
Embryo *a fertilized egg after it has attached itself to the wall of the uterus,* **340,** 341
Emergency. *See also* Accident; Injury
choking, heart attack, and others,

these defects include low birth weight, mental retardation, facial deformities, and behavioral problems, **276,** 277, 516

Fetus *a developing individual from the ninth week of pregnancy until birth,* **341,** 342

Fever, 450

Fiber. *See* Dietary fiber

Fingernails, 135

Firearms, 429, 610
    gun-control laws, 650–651

Fire safety, 599–600
    campfires, 610

First aid *emergency care given to an ill or injured person before medical attention is available,* **615,** 616
    training in, 617–618

Fitness. *See* Physical fitness

Flashback *unexpected return to an unpleasant LSD experience, often months after the original experience ended,* **305**

Flexibility *the ability to move muscles and joints through their full range of motion,* 42, **45**
    exercise goals and how to achieve them, 55, 58–59
    measurement of, 45

Flossing, 139–140

Flu. *See* Influenza

Fluorine, 78

Folacin, 77

Food, nutritional components of, 70–82

Food additives, 119–120

Food and Drug Administration, 563

Food chain *a sequence of organisms that begins with a food producer and continues with one or more organisms, each of which eats the one before it,* **542**

Food intolerance *a negative reaction to food which is not brought about by the immune system,* **119,** 120

Food label. *See* Nutritional labeling

Food poisoning, 442, 444

Food pyramid, 84–88
    checking your diet against, 94

Food safety, 98–100, 444

Food selection
    checking your diet against the food pyramid, 94

checking your knowledge of, 84
cultural diversity in, 92–93
guidelines for improving, 91
influences on, 67–69
in restaurants, 96
safe food buying, 98–100

Food storage, 98–100

Fracture *a broken bone,* **626,** 628
    first aid for, 626

Freud, Sigmund, 171

Friendship, 364–367
    how to keep a friend, 365–366
    how to make a friend, 364–365
    peer groups, 366–367

Frostbite, 635

Fructose, 89

Fruit(s), as snacks, 95

Fruit group, 87

Funeral, 216, 221–222

Fungal disease, 458

G

Gamma globulin, 455

Gangs, 430–432

Gene *a short segment of a DNA molecule that serves as a code for a particular bit of hereditary information,* **510**

Genetic factors, in alcoholism, 275–276

Genetic screening, 516

Genital herpes *an STD caused by a virus that often causes painful blisters or ulcers; it cannot be cured,* **467,** 468–470, 472, 475

Genital warts *an STD caused by the human papilloma virus, or HPV, that causes warts on the genital and anal areas and has been linked to cervical cancer and penile cancer,* 468–469, **472**

Germ(s), 442

German measles. *See* Rubella

Global warming *long-term change in temperature that is related to air pollution and the greenhouse effect,* 544, 547, **548**

Goal setting, 207

Gonorrhea *an STD, caused by bacteria that can infect the mucous membranes of the penis, vagina, throat, or rectum,* **464,** 465–466,

468–469, 472, 475

Good Samaritan laws, 623

Goodwill Industries of America, 566

Grains, as snacks, 95

Grand mal epilepsy, 517

Graves' disease, 520

Greenhouse effect *the trapping of heat from the sun by certain gases in the atmosphere called greenhouse gases,* 544, 547, **548**

Grieving process, 219–222

Group therapy, 171–172, 279, 314

Guidance counselor, 314–315

Gum disease, 137–138

Guns, 429, 610
    gun-control laws, 650–651

Gynecologist, 338

H

Hair, 126, 133–135

Hallucination *imaginary sights and sounds, often induced by the use of hallucinogens,* **305**

Hallucinogen *a drug that distorts a person's senses,* 304, **305**

Handwashing, 444, 455–456, 558

Hangover *uncomfortable physical effects brought on by alcohol use; symptoms of a hangover include headache, nausea, upset stomach, and dizziness,* **264**

Harmony, 7, 578

Hashish, 305–306

Hazardous wastes *wastes that are dangerous to the health of living things or that are harmful to the environment,* **550,** 555–556

Hazing, 423

HCG (human chorionic gonadotropin), 342

HDL (high-density lipoproteins) *compounds that remove cholesterol from the blood and transport it back to the liver,* **73**

Headache, tension, 196, 204

Head injury, 597, 627

Head lice, 134

Health *state of well-being that comes from a good balance of the five aspects of health,* 5–10, **8**
    assessing your own health, 14–16

viral, 452–455

Infertility, 329, 336, 463, 465–467

Influenza, 13, 196, 441, 443, 446, 450–454, 558

Inhalants *chemicals that produce strong psychoactive effects when they are inhaled,* 248, **306,** 308–309

Inhalation poisoning, 643–644

Injury. *See also* Accident; Safety
avoiding injuries during exercise, 50–52, 58
exercise-related injuries, 52
unintentional, 22
work-related, 605–606

Insomnia *temporary or continuing loss of sleep,* **61,** 62

Insulin, 512–513, 519

Insurance. *See* Health insurance

Interferon, 455

Intoxicated *being affected by alcohol; effects of intoxication can range from mild lightheadedness to severe and complete loss of judgment and reflexes,* **262**

Intrauterine device (IUD), 396

Intravenous drug use, 307, 455, 493–494, 501, 534–535

Iodine, 78–79

Iron, 78–79, 83, 96

IUD. *See* Intrauterine device

J

Jealousy, 157

Jock itch, 129, 458

Journal writing, 12–13

Juvenile diabetes. *See* Diabetes, type I

K

Kaposi's sarcoma, 491

Killer T-cells, 448–449

"Kosher" items, 92

L

Labor, 343–344

Laceration, 625

Lactose intolerance, 119

Landfill, 549

Land pollution, 548–550

Latex condom *a covering for the penis that helps protect both partners from sexually transmitted diseases and also helps prevent pregnancy,* 395–396, **477,** 501

LDL (low-density lipoproteins) *compounds that carry cholesterol to cells for cell processes,* **73**

Lean mass *total body weight minus the weight due to fat,* 106, **107**

Lifestyle, 11
underlying causes of death, 13

Life-support machines, 214, 240

Lipids, 72

Living will *a document expressing a person's wish to be allowed to die in case of terminal illness or incurable injury rather than be kept alive by artificial means,* **217,** 218, 240

Love, 152
in marriage, 393
nonsexual ways of expressing, 377–378, 476, 498–499

Low-density lipoproteins. *See* LDL

LSD, 304–305, 308–309

Lung cancer, 23, 287–288, 291, 530

M

Magnesium, 78–79, 83

Mainstream smoke *smoke that is inhaled directly into the mouth through a cigarette, pipe, or cigar,* **291**

Makeup, 128

Malaria, 442, 458

Male reproductive system, 325–330
care of, 330
disorders of, 329–330

Mammogram, 336

Marijuana, 248, 299, 305–306, 308–309

Marriage, 393–394

Maslow's hierarchy of needs, 162

Maturity, 386

Measles, 443, 452, 454, 559

Meat, poultry, fish, dry beans, eggs, and nuts group, 87–88

Media messages
about body image, 178–179
about body weight, 146–147
definition of, 34–35
drug advertisements, 245
influence on your sexuality, 372

romanticism of suicide, 229
SMCR model to evaluate, 320–321
about tobacco, 292, 320–321
about violence, 429, 436–437

Medicaid, 579

Medical alert identification, 632

Medical checkup, 529

Medical costs, 574–580

Medicare, 579

Medicine *a substance used to treat an illness or ailment,* **250,** 251
guidelines for appropriate use of, 253

Melanin, 125, 127, 133

Memorial service, 216, 221–222

Memory loss, 266, 388

Menopause, 387

Menstrual cramps, 334–335

Menstrual cycle, 333–334

Mental disorders, 163–167
stress and, 195–196
suicide and, 230
treatment for, 168–172

Mental health *the ability to recognize reality and cope with the demands of daily life,* 6, **8,** 151–159
assessment of your health, 153
exercise and, 42
strategies to promote, 159–162

Mercury, 120

Mescaline, 308–309

Metabolism, body weight and, 105–112

Metal detector, 650

Metastasis, 524

Methadone maintenance programs, 313–314

Methamphetamine, 308–309

Methane, 548

Mexican foods, 92–93

Microorganism *a tiny living thing that can be seen only with a microscope,* **442**
helpful, 447

Middle adulthood *the period of adulthood between the ages of 41 and 65,* **386,** 387

Middle Eastern foods, 93

Midwife, 344

Milk, yogurt, and cheese group, 87

Minerals *inorganic substances that are generally absorbed to form structural components of the body,*

396–398

    teen, 374–376, 394, 398

Parents Anonymous, 423

Parkinson's disease *an incurable disease characterized by a gradual loss of control of muscle function; Parkinson's disease most commonly affects the elderly,* **389**, 584

Passive immunity, 451

Passive-smoker *a nonsmoker who is exposed to the sidestream smoke of a cigarette, cigar, or pipe,* 290, **291**

Pathogen *any agent that causes disease,* **442**, 445

Patient's Bill of Rights, 572–573

PCP, 304–305, 308–309

Peace Corps, 564

Peer group, 366–367

Peer pressure

    to abuse drugs, 299–300

    reasserting your resistance, 361–362

    resisting, 186

    resisting nonverbally, 361

    resisting sexual pressure, 378–380

    resisting verbally, 360–361, 379

    risk taking and, 592

Pellagra, 77

Pelvic inflammatory disease (PID) *an infection of the uterus and fallopian tubes often caused by STDs; if untreated, may result in infertility,* **465**, 466–467

Penicillin, 251

Penis *male reproductive structure that deposits sperm inside the female body,* 325, **327**, 328–329, 354

Personality disorder *an emotional condition in which a person's patterns of behavior negatively affect that person's ability to get along with others,* 166, **167**

Pesticide, 601

Petit mal epilepsy, 517

Phobia, 165–166

Physical abuse *bodily harm inflicted on another person,* 208, 419, **420**, 421

Physical dependence *a condition in which the body becomes so used to the presence of a drug that it needs it in order to function,* **301**

Physical fitness *a state in which your body can meet daily life demands; the ability to perform daily tasks vigorously and to perform physical activities, while avoiding diseases related to a lack of activity,* 7, **10**, 38, **42**, 44

    measurement of, 44–45

    physical disabilities and, 43

Physical health *your physical characteristics and the way your body functions,* 6, **7**

Physical maturity, 385

Physician aid in dying, 241

Pica *an eating disorder in which the person eats nonfood substances like starch, clay, or soil,* **117**

PID. *See* Pelvic inflammatory disease

Placenta, 340–341, 343–344

Plaque, arterial, 40, 73, 521–522

Plaque, dental *a film of food particles, saliva, and bacteria on teeth,* **138**, 140

Pneumonia, 13, 491

Poison Control Center, 602, 643

Poisoning, 589

    drug overdose, 643

    first aid in, 643–644

    treatment of, 622

    ways to avoid, 601–602

Poison ivy, 130–131

Polio, 450, 452, 559

Pollution, 544–555

    reducing personal contribution, 555–556

Positive self-talk *talking to yourself in a positive way about your chracteristics and abilities,* **183**

Potassium, 78–79, 83, 118

PPO (preferred provider organization) *organizations that offer subscribers discounted medical care when they use preselected health-care providers,* **576**, 577

Pregnancy, 334, 339–346

    alcohol use during, 276–277, 516

    complications of, 345, 374

    drug use during, 310–311, 341

    ectopic, 345

    nutrition during, 83, 96

    smoking during, 289

    teen, 373–376

    transmission of HIV to fetus, 495

Pregnancy test, 342

Premature birth, 345–346, 374

Premenstrual syndrome (PMS), 335

Premium *payment a person makes to an insurance company in exchange for coverage,* **574**, 575

Prenatal care, 374

Prescription *a doctor's written order for a specific medicine,* **247**

Prescription drugs, 247, 251–253, 301

    reading label of, 254, 256

Primary care physician *a family medicine physician, pediatrician, or general internal medicine physician,* **571**

    selection of, 572–573

Private health organizations, 566

Progesterone, 355

Prostate gland, 326

    enlarged, 329

Proteins *class of nutrients consisting of long chains of amino acids, which are the basic components of body tissue and provide energy,* 70, **75**

    dietary, 75, 82–83, 96–97

Protist disease, 458

Psilocin, 308–309

Psilocybin, 308–309

Psoriasis, 131, 134

Psychoactive drug *a drug that affects a person's mood and behavior,* 249, **299**, 300–316

Psychoactive effect *an effect on a person's mood or behavior,* **248**, 252

Psychoactive substance *a substance that causes a change in a person's mood and behavior,* **286**

Psychoanalysis, 171

Psychological dependence *a constant desire to take a psychoactive drug,* **301**, 314

Psychologist, 169, 235

Psychotherapist, 169

Puberty *the period of physical development during which people become able to produce children,* **354**

    female, 332, 354–355

    male, 326, 354–355

Pubic hair, 326, 332, 354–355

Pubic lice, 468–469, 473–475

Public health *the health of a community as a whole; the organized efforts of a community to promote the health*

self-examination of, 330
undescended, 329
Testicular cancer, 330
Testicular torsion, 329
Testosterone, 312, 326, 354–355
Tetanus, 451, 624, 641
Tetracycline, 251
THC, 305–306, 308–309
Therapist, 169–172, 208, 220, 235, 423
selection of, 170
Thiamine. *See* Vitamin B$_1$
Third-degree burn, 645
Thyroid gland, 520
Thyroid hormone, 79
Thyroiditis, Hashimoto's, 520
Time management, 207
TMJ syndrome, 196
Tobacco. *See also* Smoking
chemicals of, 285–287
as drug, 247
effect of nicotine, 287–288
effect on body, 285–291
media messages about, 320–321
reasons to avoid, 292–293
tobacco-free life, 292–294
Toddler, 348
Toenails, 135
Toilet tank, displacement device in,
555–556
Tolerance, 300–301
Tooth. *See* Teeth
Topical medication, 255
Toxemia of pregnancy, 345, 374
Toxic shock syndrome, 336, 338
Trace minerals, 78–79
Traditional healer, 578–579
Tranquilizer, 248, 251, 308–310
Transdermal patch, 255
Trans fats, 73
Treatment center, 169
Trichinosis, 458
Trichomoniasis, 472–473, 475
Tropical rain forest, medicines from,
246–247
Trustworthiness, 26, 365
Tuberculosis (TB), 457–458, 491
Tumor, 524

U

Ulcer, stomach, 287
Ultraviolet radiation, 131–132, 547

Umbilical cord, 340–341, 343–344
Unconsciousness, 632
Underarm hair, 326, 354
Underweight, 41
Undescended testes, 329
Unintentional injury *injuries that are
not the result of purposeful acts,* **22**
United Nations, in international public
health, 563–564
Unrecognized drugs, 248
Unsaturated fats *fats that contain one
or more double bonds between
carbon atoms and have less than the
maximum number of hydrogen atoms
bonded to carbon,* 72, **73**
Urethra, 326–327, 332
Urethritis, nongonococcal, 468–469, 472
Urinary tract infection, 442
Uterine contractions, 343–344
Uterus *the hollow muscular organ that
provides a place for the baby to
grow before birth; also called the
womb,* 332, **333,** 340–342, 355
menstrual cycle, 333–334

V

Vaccination. *See* Immunization
Vaccine, 251
Vagina *female reproductive structure
that receives the sperm,* **332,** 355
Vaginal intercourse, 494
Vaginal suppository, 396
Vaginitis, 335, 468–469, 472–473
Values *a person's strong beliefs and
ideals,* **26,** 28, 30, 299, 437
conflicts between personal and
parental values, 373–374
universal, 26
Vas deferens, 325–327
Vasodilator, 251
Vegetable(s), as snacks, 95
Vegetable group, 86–87
Vegetarian diet, 83, 96–97
Vehicle safety, 593–597
Venereal disease. *See* Sexually
transmitted disease
Violence, 276, 418, 420, 604–605,
650–651
alcohol or drug abuse and, 429
gang-related, 430–432
media messages about, 429, 436–437

preventing violent conflict, 429–432
Viral disease, 452–455
prevention of, 452–453
treatment of, 453
Virus *a microscopic disease-causing
particle consisting of genetic
material and a protein coat,* 442,
443, 448
Vitamin(s) *organic substances that
assist in the chemical reactions that
occur in the body,* 70, **76**
in diet, 76–78
fat-soluble, 76
Reference Daily Intakes of, 83
water-soluble, 76–78
Vitamin A, 76, 83, 86–87, 96
Vitamin B$_1$, 77
Vitamin B$_2$, 77
Vitamin B$_3$, 77
Vitamin B$_6$, 77
Vitamin B$_{12}$, 77, 97
Vitamin C, 77–78, 83, 86–87, 96, 453
Vitamin D, 76, 83, 87, 126
Vitamin E, 76, 83
Vitamin K, 76
Voice, changes at puberty, 354–355
Vulva, 332

W

Walking, 46–47, 56
Warming up, 50, 607–608
Warts, 129, 452
Wasp sting, 640
Water
composition of body, 78–80
functions in body, 80–81
intake of, 81
requirement for, 70, 97, 456,
541–542
use in human activities, 541–542
Water pollution, 444, 539, 545–548, 555
Water purification, 444
Water safety, 608–610
Water-soluble vitamins, 76–78
Waxing (hair removal), 135
Weedkiller, 601
Weekend exerciser, 51–52
Weight. *See* Body weight
Weight training, 48, 50
Wellness *optimal health in each of the
five aspects of health,* **8,** 9–10

Acknowledgments

*For permission to reprint copyrighted
material, grateful acknowledgment is
made to the following sources:*

Allyn & Bacon: From "Stretching
exercises for flexibility" from *Exploring
Health: Expanding the Boundaries of
Wellness* by Jerrold S. Greenberg and
George B. Dintiman. Copyright © 1992
by Prentice-Hall, Inc. All rights reserved.
From "Why Do Men Rape Women?"
from *Sex on Your Terms* by Elizabeth
Powell. Copyright © 1991 by Elizabeth
Powell.

American College Health Association:
From "A Case of Acquaintance Rape"
from a brochure by the American
College Health Association.
Copyright © 1997 by American
College Health Association.

Joseph Bauer: From "Letters to You
from Teenagers in Jail" by Joseph Bauer
from *Seventeen,* August 1991.
Copyright © 1991 by Joseph Bauer.

Mercel Dekker, Inc.: Adapted from
"Anabolic steroids, a review of the
clinical toxicology and diagnostic
screening" from *Clinical Toxicology,*
vol. 28, no. 3, 1990, pp. 287-310.
Copyright © 1990 by Marcel
Dekker, Inc.

Amy Dolph: Quote by Amy Dolph from
"Teenagers and Aids" by Barbara
Kantrowitz from *Newsweek,* August 3,
1992. Copyright © 1992 by Amy Dolph.

*Elsevier Science Inc., 655 Avenue of the
Americas, New York, NY 10010-5107:*
Table "Ranking of Stressors by High
School Students" from "What's Bad
About Stress?" from *Journal of
Psychosomatic Research,* vol. 16, 1972.
Copyright © 1972 by Pergamon Press.

ETR Associates, Santa Cruz, CA:
Excerpted and adapted from "Sexuality
Myth Activity Answer Sheet" (Retitled:
"Myths and Facts About Sexual
Intimacy") from *Entering Adulthood:
Coping with Sexual Pressures* by Nancy
Abbey and Elizabeth Raptis Picco.
Copyright © 1989 by Network
Publications, a division of ETR
Associates. All Rights Reserved. For
information about this and other related
materials, call 1-800-321-4407.

The Alan Guttmacher Institute: Adapted
from graph "Teenage Pregnancy in the
United States" (Retitled: "Adolescent
Pregnancy Rates of Western Nations")
by James Trussell from *Family Planning
Perspectives,* vol. 20, no. 6, November/
December 1988. Copyright © 1988
by The Alan Guttmacher Institute.

Prentice Hall, Needham, MA: Adapted
from graph "Factors Associated with the
Occurrence of Homicide" by Deborah
Prothrow-Stith From *Health: Skills for
Wellness* by B.D. Pruitt, Kathy Teer
Crumpler, and Deborah Prothrow-Stith.
Copyright © 1997 by Prentice Hall.

Scholastic Inc.: From "Who Am I
not to Fight?" by Lauren Tarshis from
Scholastic Update. Copyright © 1991
by Scholastic Inc.

Sports Illustrated: From "Senseless:
'You See a Red Rag, Shoot'" by Rick
Telander from *Sports Illustrated,* vol. 72,
no. 20, May 14, 1990. Copyright © 1990
by Time Inc. All rights reserved.

*Texas Commission on Alcohol and
Drug Abuse:* From Alcohol . . . Is a
Drug, from Crack . . . Shattered
Dreams!" by Texas Commission on
Alcohol and Drug Abuse.

Weekly Reader Corporation: Adapted
from graph "Teens Know, Ignore Risks"
from *Current Science®,* vol. 78, no. 2,
September 18, 1992. Copyright © 1992
by Weekly Reader Corporation.

PHOTO CREDITS

Abbreviations used: (bkgd) background, (t) top, (c) center, (b) bottom, (l) left, (r) right.

FRONT COVER: (tl), Comstock; (bl), Schieren/StockFood America; (br-bkgd), Ben Simmons/Stock Market; (br) John Langford/HRW Photo.

BACK COVER: (bkgd), Comstock; (br) Lori Adamski Peek/Tony Stone Images.

TITLE PAGE: Comstock.

TABLE OF CONTENTS: Page iv (t), Anthony Edgeworth/The Stock Market; iv (b), David Young-Wolff/PhotoEdit; v (tl), Bruce Ayers/Tony Stone Images; v (tr), Tony Stone Images; v (cl), Michelle Bridwell/HRW Photo; v (bl), Roy Morsch/The Stock Market; vi (t), Allen Russell/ProFiles West; vi (b), Robert J. Bennett; vii (tl), Rick Williams/HRW Photo; vii (cl), American Cancer Society; vii (cr), Thomas Braise/Tony Stone Images; viii (t), Jim Whitmer; viii (b), Rhoda Sidney/PhotoEdit; ix (tl), Robert Brenner/PhotoEdit; ix (tr), Francesco Reginato/Image Bank; ix (b), Jon Riley/Tony Stone Images; x (t), David R. Frazier Photolibrary; x (b), Norbet Stiatsky/FPG International; xi (c), David Young-Wolff/PhotoEdit; xi (t), Julie Bidwell; xi (b), Lisa Davis/HRW Photo.

UNIT ONE: Page 2 (tl), Jerry Howard/Positive Images; 2 (tr), David R. Frazier Photolibrary; 2 (c), David Lissy/FPG International; 2 (bl), Bob Daemmrich/Tony Stone Images; 2 (br), Mark Harmel/FPG International; 2-3 (bkgd), Spencer Grant/FPG International. **Chapter One:** Page 4, David R. Frazier Photolibrary; 5, Lawrence Migdale/HRW Photo; 7, Steve Vidler/Nawrocki Stock Photo; 9, Roy Morsch/The Stock Market; 10, Anthony Edgeworth/The Stock Market; 18, Steve Vidler/Nawrocki Stock Photo; 19, Roy Morsch/The Stock Market. **Chapter Two:** Page 20, Michelle Bridwell/Frontera Fotos; 21, Sam Dudgeon/HRW Photo; 23, Norma Morrison; 24, M. Wallace/PhotoEdit; 28, Sam Dudgeon/HRW Photo; 30, David R. Frazier/HRW Photo; 31, Norma Morrison; 32, Sam Dudgeon/HRW Photo; 33, David R. Frazier/HRW Photo; 34, Eric Sander/Gamma Liaison; 35 (t), John Langford/HRW Photo; 35 (b), Mitchell Layton/Duomo Photography.

UNIT TWO: Page 36 (tl), Ron Rovtar/FPG International; 36 (cl), Zao Productions/Image Bank; 36 (cr), Arthur Tilley/Tony Stone Images; 36 (bl), Dan McCoy/Rainbow; 36 (br), Jerry Howard/Positive Images; 36-37 (bkgd), Bruno Joachim Studio. **Chapter Three:** Page 38, Larry Lawfer/Black Star; 39, Myrleen Ferguson/PhotoEdit; 43 (tc), Jim Dunn/Allsport USA; 43 (t), Bob Martin/Allsport USA; 45 (tr), Lisa Davis/HRW Photo; 45 (tl), 46, David R. Frazier/HRW Photo; 47, David Young-Wolff/PhotoEdit; 48, Sports Chrome East/West; 49, David R. Frazier/HRW Photo; 51, Gerry Schnieders/Unicorn Stock Photos; 52, Lisa Davis/HRW Photo; 53, Focus on Sports; 59, John Terence Turner/Tony Stone Images; 60, Chris Harvey/Tony Stone Images; 62, Myrleen Ferguson/PhotoEdit; 63, John Terence Turner/Tony Stone Images; 64, Bob Martin/Allsport USA; 65, Chris Harvey/Tony Stone Images; 64. **Chapter Four:** Page 66, David Young-Wolff/PhotoEdit; 67, John Langford/HRW Photo; 68, Robert E. Daemmrich/Tony Stone Images; 71, Sandy Roessler/FPG International; 73 (bl), 73 (br), Frederick C. Skvara, M.D., All rights reserved; 81, Bruce Ayers/Tony Stone Images; 86 (t), Charles D. Winters; 86 (b), Tony Stone Images; 87, Michelle Bridwell/HRW Photo; 88, Ken Giese; 89, Sergio Purtell/HRW Photo; 90, Karen Leeds/The Stock Market; 92, P. Markow/FPG International; 95, (tl), 95 (cr), Roy Morsch/The Stock Market; 95 (cl), 101, Richard Embery/FPG International; 102, John Langford/HRW Photo; 103, J. Brenner/FPG International. **Chapter Five:** Page 104, Michelle Bridwell/HRW Photo; 105, David Young-Wolff/PhotoEdit; 107 (all), Michelle Bridwell/HRW Photo, Courtesy of University of Texas Adult Fitness Program; 108, 110 (all), 112, Michelle Bridwell/HRW Photo; 113, 114, Tony Freeman/PhotoEdit; 117, Michelle Bridwell/HRW Photo, Courtesy of Anderson High School; 119 (t), A.G.E. Fotostock/Westlight; 119 (b), Charles D. Winters; 121, Michelle Bridwell/HRW Photo; 122, Tony Freeman/PhotoEdit; 123, Michelle Bridwell/HRW Photo, Courtesy of Anderson High School. **Chapter Six:** Page 124, Myrleen Ferguson/PhotoEdit; 125 (all), John Langford/HRW Photo; 126, George Ancona/International Stock; 128, Rick Williams/HRW Photo; 129 (t), Science Photo Library/Photo Researchers; 129 (b), NMSB/Custom Medical Stock Photo; 130 (tl), Bill Quest/The Stock Shop/Medichrome; 130 (bl), Jim Strawser/Grant Heilman Photography; 130 (bc), Tony Freeman/PhotoEdit; 130 (br), Gilbert S. Grant/Photo Researchers; 132, Robert Alexander/Photo Researchers; 134, J.L. Carson/Custom Medical Stock Photo; 135, Science Photo Library/Photo Researchers; 136, Richard Hutchings/PhotoEdit; 138, E. H. Gill/Custom Medical Stock Photo; 141, Tony Freeman/PhotoEdit; 142, Jeffrey Sylvester/FPG International; 144. George Ancona/International Stock; 145, Robert Alexander/Photo Researchers; 146 (l), Clint Clemens/International Stock; 146 (r), Michael Keller/The Stock Market; 147, Welzenbach/The Stock Market.

UNIT THREE: Page 148 (tl), Mary Kate Denny/PhotoEdit; 148 (tr), Allen Russell/ProFiles West; 148 (cl), Mieke Maas/Image Bank; 148 (bc), C. Orrico/Superstock; 148 (cr), Lori Adamski Peek/Tony Stone Images; 148-149 (bkgd), Ivan Massar/Positive Images. **Chapter Seven:** Page 150, Bob Daemmrich/Stock Boston; 151, Michelle Bridwell/HRW Photo, Courtesy of Westlake High School; 152, Bob Winsett/ProFiles West; 154 (l), 154 (r), Michelle Bridwell/HRW Photo, Courtesy of Westlake High School; 158, Michelle Bridwell/HRW Photo, Courtesy of McCallum High School; 161, Lawrence Migdale/HRW Photo; 165, David Young-Wolf/PhotoEdit; 168, Ogust/The Image Works; 169 (t), Zigy Kaluzny/Tony Stone Images; 169 (b), Lisa Davis/HRW Photo; 170, Roy Morsch/The Stock Market; 171, Elizabeth Crews/The Image Works; 174, Michelle Bridwell/HRW Photo, Courtesy of Westlake High School; 175, Lawrence Migdale/HRW Photo. **Chapter Eight:** Page 176, Richard Hutchings/PhotoEdit; 177, Dan Porges/Peter Arnold; 178, Peggy/Yoram Kahana/Peter Arnold; 179 (all), FPG International; 180, Tony Freeman/PhotoEdit; 182, Lisa Davis/HRW Photo; 185, Alan Oddie/PhotoEdit; 186, John Langford/HRW Photo; 187, Alan Oddie/PhotoEdit; 188, Dan Porges/Peter Arnold; 189, Peggy/Yoram Kahana/Peter Arnold. **Chapter Nine:** Page 190, Richard Hutchings/PhotoEdit; 191, John Langford/HRW Photo; 192 (t), The Image Works; 192 (t), Richard Hutchings/InfoEdit; 192 (b), David Young-Wolff/PhotoEdit; 194, Tony Freeman/PhotoEdit; 195 (r), Walter Chandoha; 195 (l), 196, John Langford/HRW Photo; 198, Michael Newman/PhotoEdit; 201, John Langford/HRW Photo; 203 (tl), Robert W. Ginn/Unicorn Stock Photos; 203 (br), Neal Graham/Omni Photo; 203 (cl), 204, Lawrence Migdale; 205, Robert W. Ginn/Unicorn Stock Photos; 206, Jim Pickerell/Tony Stone Images; 207,

David R. Frazier/HRW Photo; 209, 210, Robert W. Ginn/Unicorn Stock Photos; 211, David R. Frazier/HRW Photo. **Chapter Ten:** Page 212, Michelle Bridwell/HRW Photo; 213, Julie Bidwell; 216, Michelle Bridwell/HRW Photo, Austin Hospice; 221, Julie Bidwell; 222, Michelle Bridwell/HRW Photo; 223, Julie Bidwell; 224, Michelle Bridwell/HRW Photo; 225, Julie Bidwell. **Chapter Eleven:** Page 226, Sam Dudgeon/HRW Photo; 227, Lisa Davis/HRW Photo; 228, Tony Freeman/PhotoEdit; 229, "People" Weekly is a registered trademark of Time, Inc., used with permission. Cover photograph by Frank Micelotta/Outline. Inset by Gary Bernstein; 231, Michael Grecco/Stock Boston; 232, Lisa Davis/HRW Photo; 233, Sam Dudgeon/HRW Photo; 234, Skjold/PhotoEdit; 236, Robert Brenner/PhotoEdit; 237, Skjold/PhotoEdit; 238, 239, Lisa David/HRW Photo; 240, Custom Medical Stock Photo.

UNIT FOUR: Page 242 (tl), The Telegraph Colour Library/FPG International; 242 (tr), Michael Newman/PhotoEdit; 242 (cl), 242 (br), Tony Freeman/PhotoEdit; 242 (bl), Robert J. Bennett; 242-243 (bkgd), Jim Morris/Zephyr Pictures. **Chapter Twelve:** Page 244, John Langford/HRW Photo; 245, David de Lossy/Image Bank; 248, David R. Frazier/HRW Photo; 249, Robert J. Bennett; 254, 256 (all), 257, John Langford/HRW Photo; 258, David de Lossy/Image Bank; 259, David R. Frazier/HRW Photo. **Chapter Thirteen:** Page 260, Lisa Davis/HRW Photo; 261, David R. Frazier/HRW Photo; 262, Rick Williams/HRW Photo; 266 (all), Martin M. Rotker/Photo Researchers; 271, Alan Pitcairn/Grant Heilman Photography; 272, Michelle Bridwell/HRW Photo; 273, John Langford/HRW Photo; 276, John Terence Turner/FPG International; 277, George Steinmetz; 278, Michelle Bridwell/HRW Photo; 280, Hank Morgan/Rainbow; 281, Rick Williams/HRW Photo; 282, 283, Michelle Bridwell/HRW Photo. **Chapter Fourteen:** Page 284, Lisa Davis/HRW Photo; 285, Michelle Bridwell/HRW Photo, Courtesy of McCallum High School; 288 (l), Harry J. Przekop/The Stock Shop/Medichrome; 288 (r), Biophoto Assoc./Photo Researchers; 290, Michelle Bridwell/HRW Photo, Courtesy of Milto's Restaurant; 291, Joe Tye/STAT (Stop Teenage Addiction To Tobacco); 292, American Cancer Society; 294, Michelle Bridwell/HRW Photo, Courtesy of University of Texas Rec Sports Program; 296, Michelle Bridwell/HRW Photo, Courtesy of McCallum High School; 297, American Cancer Society. **Chapter Fifteen:** Page 298, Sam Dudgeon/HRW Photo, Courtesy of Elisabet Ney Sculpture Conservatory; 299 (all), Michelle Bridwell/HRW Photo, Courtesy of McCallum High School; 300, Superstock; 301, Joe Bator/The Stock Market; 303, Michelle Bridwell/HRW Photo; 306, Sam Dudgeon/HRW Photo; 307 (t), Steve Raymer/National Geographic Society; 307 (b), Bruce Byers/FPG International; 311, Bob Daemmrich/Stock Boston; 313, Leonard Kamsler/The Stock Shop/MediChrome; 314, Bob Daemmrich/Stock Boston; 315 (t), Michelle Bridwell/HRW Photo, Courtesy of Austin Community College and Dr. Maria Cisneros-Solis; 315 (b), Park Street Photography; 316, Jonathan Meyers/FPG International; 317, Joe Bator/The Stock Market; 318, Michelle Bridwell/HRW Photo, Courtesy of McCallum High School; 319, Michelle Bridwell/HRW Photo, Courtesy of Austin Community College and Dr. Maria Cisneros-Solis; 320 (t), P. Langone/International Stock; 320 (b), Mitchell Layton/Duomo Photography; 321, Marka/International Stock.

UNIT FIVE: Page 322 (tl), Lewis Harrington/FPG International; 322 (bl), E. Lettau/FPG International; 322 (bc), Michelle Bridwell/HRW Photo, courtesy of Austin Community College and Dr. Maria Cisneros-Solis; 322 (br), Janeart Ltd./Image Bank; 322 (cr), Thomas Braise/Tony Stone Images; 322-323 (bkgd), Maria Taglienta/Image Bank. **Chapter Sixteen:** Page 324, Jeffrey Reed/The Stock Shop/Medichrome; 325, Michelle Bridwell/Frontera Fotos; 328 (bl), Francis Leroy, Biocosmos/Science Photo Library/Photo Researchers; 328 (cr), L.V. Bergman & Associates; 335, Richard Hutchings/PhotoEdit; 339, David Young-Wolff/PhotoEdit; 342 (tl), 342 (tc), 342 (tr), 342 (cr), Bonnier Fakta Bokforlag AB, Lennart Nilsson, A CHILD IS BORN; 342 (cl), CNRI/Phototake NYC; 344, Penny Gentieu/Black Star; 346 (t), Simon Fraser/Science Photo Library/Photo Researchers, Princess Mary Hospital, Newcastle; 346 (b), James McLoughlin/FPG International; 347, David Young-Wolff/PhotoEdit; 348, Guy Marche/FPG International; 349 (tr), Francis Leroy, Biocosmos/Science Photo Library/Photo Researchers; 349 (cr), L.V. Bergman & Associates; 350, CNRI/Phototake; 351, Guy Marche/FPG International. **Chapter Seventeen:** Page 352, 353 (t), John Langford/HRW Photo; 353 (b), Bob Daemmrich/The Image Works; 356, David R. Frazier/HRW Photo; 358, Peter W. Gonzalez; 361, David R. Frazier/HRW Photo; 365, Michelle Bridwell/Frontera Fotos; 366, Richard Hutchings/PhotoEdit; 367, John Langford/HRW Photo; 372, 373, Jim Whitmer; 374, Frank Siteman/Stock Boston; 375, Jim Whitmer; 378, Peter W. Gonzalez; 380, 381, Jim Whitmer; 382, John Langford/HRW Photo; 383, Jim Whitmer. **Chapter Eighteen:** Page 384, Mug Shots/The Stock Market; 385, Ken Lax; 386, Tomas del Amo/ProFiles West; 387 (t), Superstock; 387 (b), Lori Adamski Peek/Tony Stone Images; 388, ZEFA (UK)/The Stock Market; 390, Jeffrey Arronson/Network Aspen; 391, S. Vidler/Superstock; 395, Catherine Karnow/Woodfin Camp; 398, Tony Stone Images; 399, Catherine Karnow/Woodfin Camp; 400, Ken Lax; 401, ZEFA (UK)/The Stock Market. **Chapter Nineteen:** Page 402, 403, John Langford/HRW Photo; 404, 405, Bob daemmrich Photography; 406, Rosanne Olson/Tony Stone Images; 407, The Stockhouse; 408, Jose Carrillo/PhotoEdit; 409, Ron Chapple/FPG International; 410, Mitch Kezar/Black Star; 411, 414, John Langford/HRW Photo; 415, Roseanne Olson/Tony Stone Images; 416, John Langford/HRW Photo; 417, Mitch Kezar/Black Star. **Chapter Twenty:** Page 418, 419, John Langford/HRW Photo; 421 (l), Jim Whitmer; 421 (r), Robert Brenner/PhotoEdit; 428, Rhoda Sidney/PhotoEdit; 431, 432, 433, John Langford/HRW Photo; 434, Robert Brenner/PhotoEdit; 435, John Langford/HRW Photo; 436 (l), Henry Gris/FPG International; 436 (r), New Line Cinema/Shooting Star; 437, Larry Schwartzwald/Sygma.

UNIT SIX: Page 438 (tl), U.N./FPG International; 438 (tr), Stephen Derr/Image Bank; 438 (cl), Robert Brenner/PhotoEdit; 438 (bl), Ken Lax; 438 (br), Francesco Reginato/Image Bank; 438-439 (bkgd), Alan Goldsmith/The Stock Market. **Chapter Twenty-One:** Page 440, Elizabeth Zuckerman/PhotoEdit; 441, Lisa Davis/HRW Photo; 443, Grapes/Michaud/Photo Researchers; 444, Sergio Purtell/HRW Photo; 445, Richard Hutchings/PhotoEdit; 446, Michelle Bridwell/HRW Photo; 447, Ellen Dirksen/Visuals Unlimited; 451, SPL/Custom Medical Stock Photo; 452, UPI/Bettmann Archive; 453, Martin/Custom Medical Stock Photo; 455, Lisa Davis/HRW Photo; 456, Michelle Bridwell/HRW Photo, Courtesy of Dr. Robia Poonwala; 458, NMSB/Custom Medical Stock Photo; 460, Richard Hutchings/Photo Researchers; 461, Sergio Purtell/HRW Photo. **Chapter Twenty-Two:** Page 462, Michelle Bridwell/HRW Photo; 463,

Michelle Bridwell/HRW Photo, Courtesy of Del Valle High School; 466 (tl), 466 (r), Frederick C. Skvara, M.D.; 466 (cl), SIU/Peter Arnold; 467, SPL/Custom Medical Stock Photo; 471 (l), Nussenblatt/Custom Medical Stock Photo; 471 (r), Lee Moskowitz/The Stock Shop/Medichrome; 473, D. Nicolinni/Medical Images; 474 (all), Carroll H. Weiss/Camera M.D. Studios; 475, Bob Winsett/ProFiles West; 476, Ginger Chih/Peter Arnold; 478, Michelle Bridwell/HRW Photo, City of Austin, STD Clinic; 479, 481, Rick Williams/HRW Photo; 482, SIU/Peter Arnold; 483, Bob Winsett/ProFiles West. **Chapter Twenty-Three:** Page 484, 485, John Langford/HRW Photo; 491, Lisa Davis/HRW Photo; 492, Michelle Bridwell/HRW Photo, Courtesy of McCallum High School; 494, John Langford/HRW Photo; 495, Lisa Davis/HRW Photo; 496, Robert E. Daemmrich/Tony Stone Images; 498, David Pollack/The Stock Market; 499, Mug Shots/The Stock Market; 500, Tony Freeman/PhotoEdit; 502, Allan Tannenbaum/Sygma; 503, Wil Phinney; 504 (l), AP LaserPhoto/Craig Fuji/Wide World Photos; 504 (r), J. Stettenheim/SABA Press Photos; 506, John Langford/HRW Photo; 507, Lisa Davis/HRW Photo. **Chapter Twenty-Four:** Page 508, Michelle Bridwell/HRW Photo, Courtesy of American Diabetes Association; 509, Jeff Isaac Greenberg/Photo Researchers; 511 (all), Science Source/Photo Researchers; 512, Photo Researchers, Simon Fraser/RVI, Newcastle-Upon-Tyne/Science Photo Library; 513 (l), Michelle Bridwell/HRW Photo; 513 (r), SIU Biomed Com/Custom Medical Stock Photo; 514, Mike Tamborrino/The Stock Shop/Medichrome; 515, Richard Hutchings/Science Source/Photo Researchers; 519, Michelle Bridwell/HRW Photo; 520, AP/Wide World Photos; 523 (l), M. Abbey/Photo Researchers; 523 (r), Science Photo Library/Photo Researchers; 524, Bill Longcore/Science Source/Photo Researchers; 525, Richard Hirmeisen/The Stock Shop/Medichrome; 527, Michelle Bridwell/HRW Photo; 528, Michelle Bridwell/HRW Photo, Courtesy of University of Texas Adult Fitness Program; 530, Lisa Davis/HRW Photo; 531, Photo Researchers, Simon Fraser/RVI, Newcastle-Upon-Tyne/Science Photo Library; 532, Jeff Isaac Greenberg/Photo Researchers; 533, Lisa Davis/HRW Photo; 534, Michael Tamborrino/FPG International.

UNIT SEVEN: Page 536 (tl), Sandy Roessler Clark/FPG International; 536 (tc), Phil Jason/Tony Stone Images; 536 (tr), Nigel Dickinson/Tony Stone Images; 536 (bl), 536 (bc), Russel Dian/HRW Photo; 536-537 (bkgd), Superstock. **Chapter Twenty-Five:** Page 538, Keith Gunnar/FPG International; 539, 541, John Langford/HRW Photo; 543, J. Van Eps/Superstock; 544, L. Linkhart/Superstock; 550, David R. Frazier Photolibrary; 553, Scott Berner/The Stock Shop/Medichrome; 554, John Langford/HRW Photo; 555, Jon Riley/Tony Stone Images; 556, John Langford/HRW Photo; 557, Robert Landau/Westlight; 559, Ken Karp/Omni Photo; 564, Tor Eigeland/SIPA Press; 565, Michael Newman/PhotoEdit; 567, John Langford/HRW Photo; 568, Jon Riley/Tony Stone Images; 569, Michael Newman/PhotoEdit. **Chapter Twenty-Six:** Page 570, 571 (b), Ken Lax; 571 (t), David Young-Wolff/PhotoEdit; 573, John Langford/HRW Photo; 577, David R. Frazier Photolibrary; 579, Michael Heron/Woodfin Camp; 581, David R. Frazier Photolibrary; 582, David Young-Wolff/PhotoEdit; 583, Ken Lax; 584, Superstock.

UNIT EIGHT: Page 586 (tl), George Gibbons/FPG International; 586 (tr), Denise DeLuise/Zephyr Pictures; 586 (cl), Norbert Stiatsky/FPG International; 586 (bl), Grafton M. Smith/Image Bank; 586 (cr), Patricia J. Bruno/Positive Images; 586-587 (bkgd), Weinberg-Clark/Image Bank. **Chapter Twenty-Seven:** Page 588, Spencer Swanger/Tom Stack & Associates; 589, Paul Barton/The Stock Market; 591, 592, Lisa Davis/HRW Photo; 593, Kenneth Murray/Photo Researchers; 596, Barbara L. Moore/New England Stock Photos; 599 (cl), T. Rosenthal/Superstock; 599 (br) Tony Freeman/PhotoEdit; 599 (tr), 600 (all), Ken Lax; 601, Clark Linehan/New England Stock Photos; 603, Warren Faidley/WeatherStock; 604, Peter Menzel/Tony Stone Images; 605, Gabe Palmer/The Stock Market; 607, Tony Freeman/PhotoEdit; 608, Michelle Bridwell/HRW Photo; 609, Paul E. Clark/New England Stock Photos; 610, Rodney Jones/HRW Photo; 611, Barbara L. Moore/New England Stock Photos; 612, Paul Barton/The Stock Market; 613, Lisa Davis/HRW Photo. **Chapter Twenty-Eight:** Page 614, Robert Copeland/Westlight; 615, Michelle Bridwell/HRW Photo; 617, Michelle Bridwell/HRW Photo, Courtesy of Austin EMS; 618 (all), Park Street Photography; 619, 628, Lisa Davis/HRW Photo; 630 (all), Sam Dudgeon/HRW Photo; 631, Ken Lax; 632, Michael Newman/PhotoEdit; 634, Robert E. Daemmrich/Tony Stone Images; 637, Lisa Davis/HRW Photo; 640 (l), Ann Moreton/Tom Stack & Associates; 640 (r), Buddy Mays/FPG International; 641, Lisa Davis/HRW Photo; 644, Dan McCoy/Rainbow; 645 (tr), SPL/Custom Medical Stock Photo; 645 (cl), Mike English, M.D./The Stock Shop/Medichrome; 645 (br), John Radcliffe/Science Photo Library/Photo Researchers; 646, Lisa Davis/HRW Photo; 647, Michelle Bridwell/HRW Photo; 648, Lisa Davis/HRW Photo; 649, Michelle Bridwell/HRW Photo; 650, Ken Korsh/FPG International.

BODY SYSTEM HANDBOOK: Page 653, Michelle Bridwell/HRW Photo; 666 (l), Tim Haske/ProFiles West; 666 (r), Tony Freeman/PhotoEdit; 680, David M. Phillip/Visuals Unlimited; 682, Michael Gadomski/Bruce Coleman; 683, Tim Fuller/HRW Photo.

HEALTH CAREERS HANDBOOK: Page 684 (tr), Rosanne Olson/Tony Stone Images; 684 (stethoscope), Tom McCarthy/ProFiles West; 684 (b), M.E. Sparks/ProFiles West; 685 (tr), Steve Gottlieb/FPG International; 685 (cl), Linda K. Moore/Rainbow; 685 (c), Alfred Pasieka/Bruce Coleman; 685 (b), Dan McCoy/Rainbow; 686 (t), Melanie Carr/Zephyr Pictures; 686 (br), Tom Tracy/FPG International; 686 (bkgd), Sam Dudgeon/HRW Photo; 687 (t), Ken Lax; 687 (tr), Kent Vinyard/ProFiles West; 687 (bl), David R. Frazier Photolibrary; 688 (t), Jeff Kaufman/FPG International; 688 (b), 689 (r), 689 (bkgd), Lisa Davis/HRW Photo; 689 (l), P. Barry Levy/ProFiles West; 690 (tr), Bob Daemmrich/Stock Boston; 690 (bl), Michelle Bridwell/HRW Photo, Courtesy of Souper Salads, Austin, Texas; 690 (br), Robert Burch/Bruce Coleman; 691 (tr), Louis Bencze/Tony Stone Images; 691 (c), Hank Morgan/Rainbow; 691 (bl), Jack W. Dykinga/Bruce Coleman; 692 (t), Grant LeDuc/Stock Boston; 692 (b), Melanie Carr/Zephyr Pictures; 693 (tl), Michelle Bridwell/HRW Photo, Courtesy of Kocurek Elementary; 693 (bc), Michelle Bridwell/HRW Photo, Courtesy of Anderson High School; 693 (cr), Pat Lanza/Brude Coleman.

ART CREDITS: Boston Graphics: Page 11, 13, 22, 61, 106, 131, 132, 262, 429, 487, 488, 574, 590, 606. Christy Krames: Page 343, 654, 655, 671, 672, 680. Dick Truxaw: Page 57. All other illustrated charts by Precision Graphics. All other anatomical art by Network Graphics. Tables by Paradigm Design.